Microsoft®
Word 2013:
Comprehensive

Microsoft® Word 2013: Comprehensive

JILL MURPHY
Custom Performance Solutions

LABYRINTH
LEARNING™

Berkeley, CA

Microsoft Word 2013: Comprehensive

Copyright © 2014 by Labyrinth Learning

Labyrinth Learning
2560 9th Street, Suite 320
Berkeley, California 94710
800.522.9746
On the web at lablearning.com

President:
Brian Favro

Product Development Manager:
Jason Favro

Managing Editor:
Laura Popelka

Production Editor:
Margaret Young

Production Manager:
Rad Proctor

eLearning Production Manager:
Arl S. Nadel

eLearning Development:
Judy Mardar and Andrew Vaughnley

Developmental Editors:
Trisha Conlon and Sandra Rittman

Indexing:
Joanne Sprott

Cover Design:
Mick Koller, SuperLab Design

Interior Design:
Mark Ong, Side-by-Side Studio

ITEM: 1-59136-482-5
ISBN-13: 978-1-59136-482-5

Manufactured in the United States of America.

10 9 8 7 6 5 4

Contents in Brief

Table of Contents

WORD 2013 LESSON 12:
SHARING AND SECURING CONTENT IN BACKSTAGE VIEW

WORD 2013 LESSON 13:
PERSONALIZING WORD

WORD 2013 LESSON 14:
INTEGRATING WORD WITH EXCEL, POWERPOINT, AND THE WEB

Quick Reference Tables

Preface

In today's digital world, knowing how to use the most popular suite of desktop software applications is critical. Our goal is to teach new users how to take advantage of this technology and to help experienced users understand how the applications have changed from previous versions. We begin with fundamental concepts and take learners through a systematic progression of exercises, resulting in skill mastery.

An online student resource center accompanies this book. It contains Concepts Review quizzes, student exercise files, and other learning tools. The URL for the student resource center is printed on the inside front cover of this textbook.

Supplemental Options

Video Tutorials: Our easy-to-follow instructional design is complemented with hundreds of videos that demonstrate the concepts and skills covered in this textbook. All videos can be accessed online with a single license key. Videos are an option for all learners. Keys can be purchased at http://lablearning.com/Store/Shop-Videos.

eLab Course Management System: eLab is a web-based learning systems that integrates seamlessly with this textbook. eLab is an option for students enrolled in instructor-led courses that have adopted eLab as part of their course curriculum.

Visual Conventions

This book uses visual and typographic cues to guide students through the lessons. Some of these cues are described below.

Type this text	Text you type at the keyboard is printed in this typeface.
Action words	The important action words in exercise steps are presented in boldface.
Ribbon	Glossary terms are presented in black text with a blue background.
TIP	Tips, notes, and warnings are called out with special icons.
Command→ Command→ Command→ Command	Commands to execute from the Ribbon are presented like this: Ribbon Tab→Command Group→Command→Subcommand.
FROM THE KEYBOARD Ctrl+S to save	These margin notes present shortcut keys for executing certain tasks.
FROM THE RIBBON File→Save	These margin notes show Ribbon paths for executing certain tasks.

It is recommended that students set their screen resolutions to 1024 x 768. This will help ensure that their screens most closely match the printed illustrations. Multiple factors, including screen resolution, DPI setting, monitor size, and window size, can affect the appearance of the Microsoft Ribbon. In this book, screen captures were taken with a screen resolution of 1024 x 768.

Acknowledgements

This textbook has benefited greatly from the reviews and suggestions of the following instructors.

Kim Anderson, *Elgin Community College*

Ann Blackman, *Parkland College*

Kristen Bogue, *Bridgerland Applied Technology College*

Jeanann Boyce, *Montgomery College, Takoma Park Campus, MD*

Margie Brunson, *Central Carolina Technical College*

Lori Collins, *Pike-Lincoln Technical Center*

Julie Davis, *Mt. Diablo Adult Ed (Loma Vista Adult School)*

Evangelina Galelgos-Garner, *South Texas Vocational Technical Institute*

Teresita Galvizo, *South East High School*

Rebecca Haney, *Isothermal Community College*

Holly Heggestad, *Madison Area Technical College*

Kathleen Holliman, *Wallace Community College Selma*

Terri Holly, *Indian River State College*

Joan Johnson, *Lake Sumter Community College*

Ronald Kaufer, *Lonestar College – Tomball*

Robin Landry, *RPCC/TEC*

Gayle Larson, *Highline Community College*

Teresa Loftis, *San Bernardino Adult School*

Tina Mazuch, *Northeast Community College*

John Mims, *Central New Mexico Community College Workforce Training Center*

Sue Mookram, *Plaza College and Queens College*

Kay Nelson, *The Lifelong Learning Center, Missoula County Public Schools*

Youcef Oubraham, *HCCC*

Monika Olsen, *Acalanes Adult Education*

Kari Phillips, *DATC*

Kate Prussing, *SERRC – The Learning Connection*

Teresa Roberts, *Wilson Community College*

Maryla Scarpa, *Vincennes University Jasper*

Rosemarie Shamieh, *Glendale Community College*

Lal Shimpi, *Saint Augustine's University*

Mary Jo Slater, *Community College of Beaver County*

Francine Smith, *Wayne Community College*

Michelle Vlaich-Lee, *Greenville Technical College*

Cynthia Wade, *CierraTEC*

Deanna Wallace, *TTC Nashville*

Ali Ware, *Humboldt County Office of Education*

Microsoft® Word 2013:
Comprehensive

WORD 2013

Introducing Word Basics

LEARNING OBJECTIVES

After studying this lesson, you will be able to:

- Use the Word Start screen and window
- Work with the Ribbon and Quick Access toolbar
- Open, close, and navigate in documents
- Type a new document
- Use Word Help

Microsoft Word 2013 is a dynamic word-processing program that lets you easily create and modify a variety of documents. In this lesson, you will start Word, and then you'll work with the Word interface. You will open and navigate through a multipage document, and create and save a document. Finally, you will work with Word Help, and then exit Word.

Using My Virtual Campus

My Virtual Campus is a social networking technology company.
They sell their web application to colleges and universities,
allowing students, alumni, faculty, and staff to use this social networking website that is closed to the public and branded for their institution. The marketing manager has asked you to create a brief summary to describe their best-selling website and how it is used. This will provide you a good opportunity to see just how easy Word 2013 is to use. And if you run into any problems along the way, you will appreciate how much help is at your fingertips.

My Virtual Campus

Our best-selling website, a social networking Intranet established specifically for college communities worldwide, has been gaining popularity at an extraordinary rate.

The website is useful for all types of networking opportunities; for example, social events and career prospects can be publicized, prospective students can check out the campus, and professors and students can participate in extended training occasions and collaborate on special projects. It also proves useful when looking for a roommate or offering items for sale. Alumni can post job opportunities for current students and other noteworthy news, and so forth.

In general, here's how it works. You join and create a profile about yourself, choosing how much personal information to enter. Then, you can invite other people to join also. You can chat in real-time with other members, post photos to share, and most importantly, you control what information others can see about you.

Security is taken very seriously by My Virtual Campus and every step has been taken to ensure your privacy and protect your confidential information.

Presenting Word 2013

Video Library   http://labyrinthelab.com/videos   Video Number: WD13-V0101

Word provides tools to assist you in virtually every aspect of document creation. From desktop to web publishing, Word has the right tool. For these and many other reasons, Word is the most widely used word-processing program in homes and businesses.

Starting Word

The method you use to start Word and other Office 2013 applications depends on whether you are using the Windows 7 or Windows 8 operating system.

- **Windows 7:** Click Start ⊞, choose Microsoft Office from the All Programs menu, and then choose Microsoft Word 2013.
- **Windows 8:** Locate the Word 2013 tile on the Windows Start screen; click the tile to start Word.

Viewing the Word Start Screen

The Word Start screen is the first screen you see. It offers several ways to begin working. Don't be concerned if your Start screen is arranged differently from this example. You can rearrange the templates on the right, and the appearance also depends on your screen's resolution.

You can begin by working on a recent document or by opening another document you saved earlier.

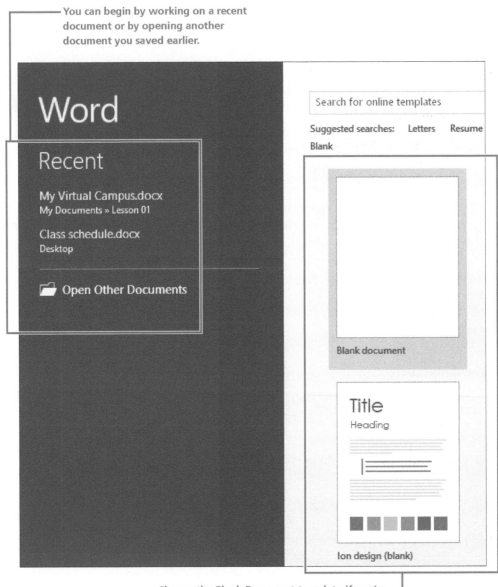

Choose the Blank Document template if you're creating a document from scratch. Or, use one of Word's other built-in templates.

DEVELOP YOUR SKILLS WD01-D01A
Start Word (Windows 8)

Windows 7 Users: Skip to the next exercise.

In this exercise, you will start the Word program.

1. If necessary, start your computer.
   The Windows Start screen appears.

2. Locate the **Word 2013 tile**.

3. Click the tile to start Word.
   The Word program loads and the Word Start screen appears.

4. Make sure the Word window is **maximized** ▫ .

5. Click the **Blank Document** template to open the Word window.

DEVELOP YOUR SKILLS WD01-D01B
Start Word (Windows 7)

Windows 8 Users: Skip this exercise.

In this exercise, you will start the Word program.

1. If necessary, start your computer.
   The Windows Desktop appears.

2. Click **Start** at the left edge of the taskbar and choose **All Programs**.

3. Choose **Microsoft Office**, and then choose **Microsoft Word 2013** from the menu.
   The Word program loads and the Word Start screen appears.

4. Make sure the Word window is **maximized** ▫ .

5. Click the **Blank Document template** to open the Word window.

Viewing the Word 2013 Window

http://labyrinthelab.com/videos   Video Number: WD13-V0102

The following illustration describes the main elements of the Word window. Don't be concerned if your document window looks somewhat different from this example. The Word screen is customizable.

File tab—leads to **Backstage view**, where you can open, print, and save your work.

Quick Access toolbar— frequently-used commands appear here.

Title bar—your document name and the application name appear here.

The **Ribbon**—where you find tools you need to build your documents.

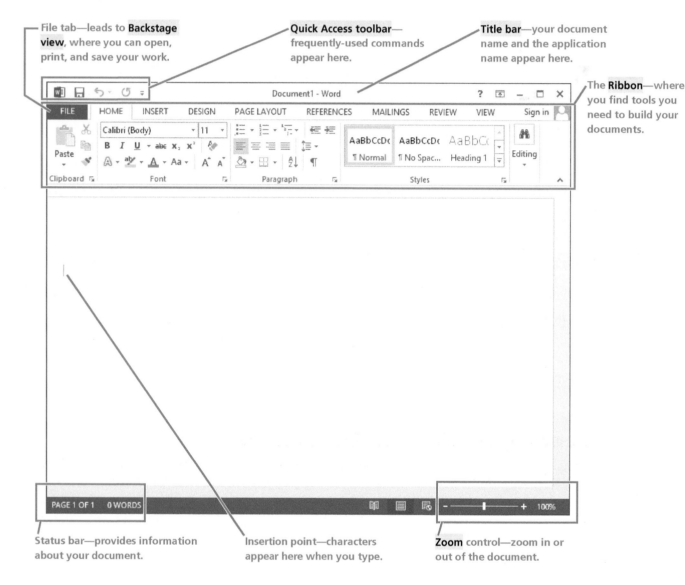

Status bar—provides information about your document.

Insertion point—characters appear here when you type.

Zoom control—zoom in or out of the document.

Opening Documents

Video Library   http://labyrinthelab.com/videos   Video Number: WD13-V0103

FROM THE RIBBON
File→Open

In Word and other Office 2013 applications, the Open screen is where you navigate to a storage place and open previously saved documents. Once a document is open, you can edit or print it.

FROM THE KEYBOARD
Ctrl+O to open a document

The Open command on the File tab.

The document storage pane.

When a storage place is chosen, the associated items appear in this pane.

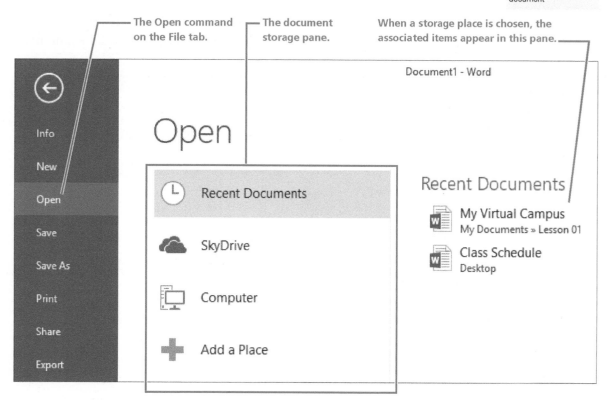

Opening Older Word Documents

If you open a document created in a previous version of an Office 2013 application (2010 and earlier), it opens in Compatibility Mode. The term appears in the Title bar. Older documents do not understand the new features in Office 2013 applications, so those features are limited or disabled.

When an older document is open, a Convert command is available in Backstage view. Use it to upgrade the file and make the new features of Office 2013 applications available. The convert process overwrites the original file.

Open a Document

In this exercise, you will open an existing document through the Open screen in Backstage view.

Before You Begin: Navigate to the student resource center to download the student exercise files for this book.

1. Choose **File→Open** to display the Open screen in Backstage view.

2. Double-click the **Computer** ⊡ icon.

3. When the Open dialog box appears, follow these steps to open a document:

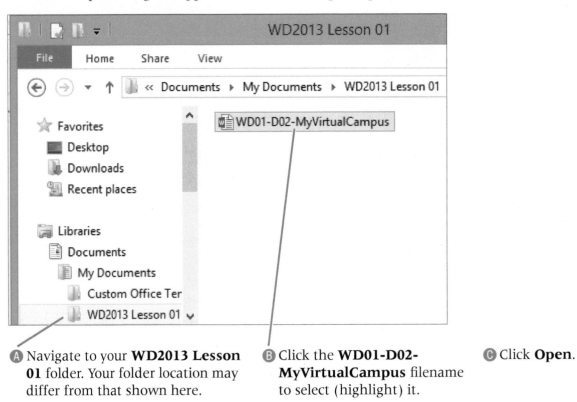

Ⓐ Navigate to your **WD2013 Lesson 01** folder. Your folder location may differ from that shown here.

Ⓑ Click the **WD01-D02-MyVirtualCampus** filename to select (highlight) it.

Ⓒ Click **Open**.

 You can also double-click a filename to open the file.

4. Make sure the Word window is **maximized** ▫.

Working with the Word 2013 Interface

Video Library   http://labyrinthelab.com/videos   Video Number: WD13-V0104

The band running across the top of the screen is the Ribbon. This is where you find the tools for building, formatting, and editing your documents. It consists of three primary areas: tabs, groups, and commands. The tabs include Home, Insert, Design, and so on. A group houses related commands. Groups on the Home tab, for instance, include Clipboard, Font, and Paragraph.

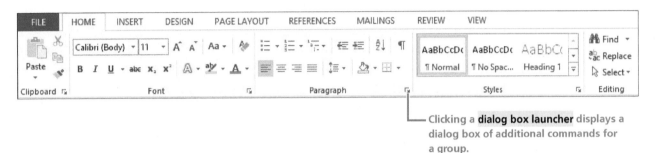

Clicking a **dialog box launcher** displays a dialog box of additional commands for a group.

The arrangement of buttons on the Ribbon can vary, depending on your screen resolution and how the Word window is sized.

FROM THE RIBBON

Right-click a tab→Collapse the Ribbon

Double-click the active tab to display the Ribbon again

FROM THE KEYBOARD

Ctrl + F1 to collapse/ display the Ribbon

Collapsing the Ribbon

If you want more room to work, you can collapse the Ribbon so only the tabs are visible. Clicking a tab expands the Ribbon temporarily, and then it collapses again when you work in the document.

DEVELOP YOUR SKILLS WD01-D03
Work with the Ribbon

In this exercise, you will explore various aspects of the Ribbon, including tabs, the dialog box launcher, and collapsing and expanding the Ribbon.

1. Click the **Insert** tab on the Ribbon to display the available commands.

2. Take a moment to investigate some other tabs; return to the **Home** tab.

3. Choose **Home→Font→dialog box launcher** 🔲 to open the Font dialog box.
   This dialog box provides additional tools for formatting text.

4. Click **Cancel** to close the dialog box.

Collapse and Expand the Ribbon

5. Follow these steps to collapse and expand the Ribbon:

A Right-click a tab.　　**B** Choose **Collapse the Ribbon**.　　**C** To display the Ribbon, right-click a tab and choose **Collapse the Ribbon** to turn the feature off.

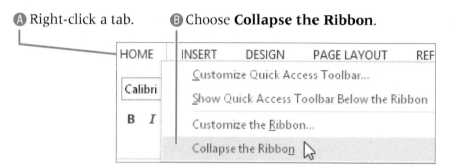

Customizing the Quick Access Toolbar

Video Library　http://labyrinthelab.com/videos　Video Number: WD13-V0105

The Quick Access toolbar in the upper-left corner of the Word window contains frequently used commands. You can add or remove buttons to suit your needs, and you can move the toolbar below the Ribbon if you like. If you're using a touch-mode screen, you can add a touch-mode button, which spaces buttons wider apart, making them easier to tap.

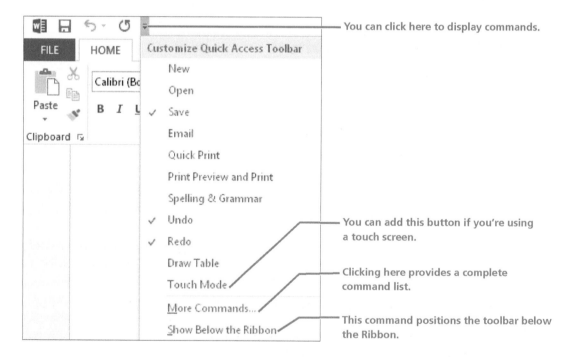

QUICK REFERENCE · WORKING WITH THE QUICK ACCESS TOOLBAR

Task	Procedure
Add a button	▪ Click the Customize Quick Access toolbar button, and then choose a command or choose More Commands. Or, right-click a button on the Ribbon and choose Add to Quick Access Toolbar.
Remove a button	▪ Right-click the button on the Quick Access toolbar you want to remove. ▪ Choose Remove from Quick Access Toolbar.
Change the toolbar location	▪ Click the Customize Quick Access Toolbar button. ▪ Choose Show Below (or Above) the Ribbon.

DEVELOP YOUR SKILLS WD01-D04
Work with the Quick Access Toolbar

In this exercise, you will reposition the Quick Access toolbar, and then you will customize it by adding a button, and then you'll remove the button.

1. Follow these steps to move the Quick Access toolbar below the Ribbon:

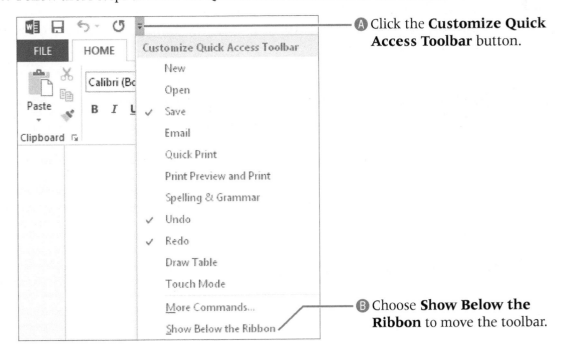

Ⓐ Click the **Customize Quick Access Toolbar** button.

Ⓑ Choose **Show Below the Ribbon** to move the toolbar.

The toolbar appears below the Ribbon. Now you will return it to its original position.

2. Click **Customize Quick Access Toolbar** again, and this time choose **Show Above the Ribbon**.

3. Make sure the **Home** tab is active.

4. Follow these steps to add the Bullets button to the toolbar:

Ⓐ Right-click **Bullets** in the Paragraph group to display the menu.

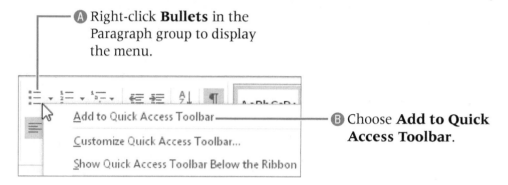

Ⓑ Choose **Add to Quick Access Toolbar**.

5. Follow these steps to remove the Bullets button:

Ⓐ Right-click **Bullets** on the Quick Access toolbar.

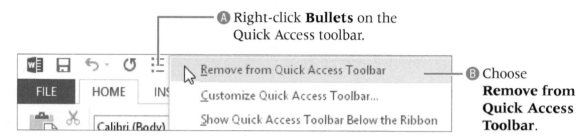

Ⓑ Choose **Remove from Quick Access Toolbar**.

Navigating in a Word Document

Video Library   http://labyrinthelab.com/videos   Video Number: WD13-V0106

If you are working in a multipage document, it is helpful to know about various techniques for moving through a document. You can navigate using the scroll bar located at the right side of the screen, or you can use keystrokes.

Navigating with the Scroll Bar

The scroll bar lets you browse through documents; however, it does not move the insertion point. After scrolling, you must click in the document where you want to reposition the insertion point.

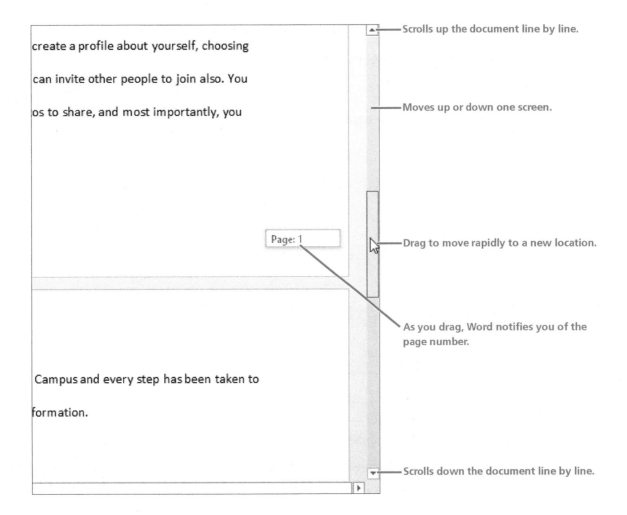

create a profile about yourself, choosing

can invite other people to join also. You

os to share, and most importantly, you

Page: 1

Campus and every step has been taken to

formation.

Scrolls up the document line by line.

Moves up or down one screen.

Drag to move rapidly to a new location.

As you drag, Word notifies you of the page number.

Scrolls down the document line by line.

Positioning the Insertion Point

When the mouse pointer is in a text area, it resembles an uppercase "I" and is referred to as an I-beam. The insertion point is positioned at the location where you click the I-beam and it begins flashing. Wherever the insertion point is flashing is where the action begins.

Scroll and Position the Insertion Point

In this exercise, you will use the scroll bar to move through a document. You will also position the insertion point.

1. Follow these steps to scroll in the document:

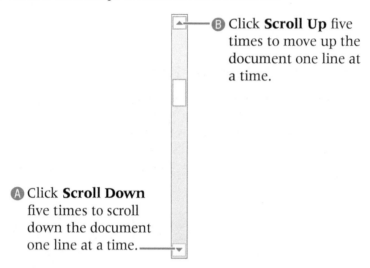

Ⓑ Click **Scroll Up** five times to move up the document one line at a time.

Ⓐ Click **Scroll Down** five times to scroll down the document one line at a time.

2. Place the **I-beam** I mouse pointer in the body of the document.
   Notice that the mouse pointer looks like an I-beam when it's inside the document.

3. Click the **I-beam** I anywhere in the document to position the blinking insertion point.
   The insertion point appears where you clicked. If the background is highlighted, you accidentally selected the text. Deselect by clicking the mouse pointer in the document background.

4. Move the mouse pointer into the left margin area.
   The white ⤧ selection arrow is now visible. You'll learn more about the selection arrow later in the course.

5. Follow these steps to use the scroll bar:

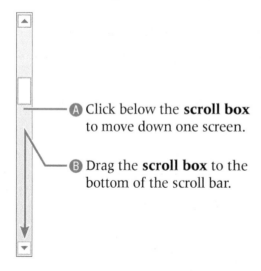

Ⓐ Click below the **scroll box** to move down one screen.

Ⓑ Drag the **scroll box** to the bottom of the scroll bar.

Notice that the insertion point is not blinking anywhere on the screen because all you have done is scroll through the document. You have not repositioned the insertion point yet.

6. Click the **scroll bar** above the scroll box, and then click the **I-beam** I at the end of the text to position the insertion point on the last page.

7. Drag the **scroll box** to the top of the scroll bar and click the **I-beam** I in front of the first word of the first paragraph.

Navigating with the Keyboard

Video Library   http://labyrinthelab.com/videos   Video Number: WD13-V0107

Whether you use the mouse or the keyboard to navigate through a document is up to you. Navigating with the keyboard always moves the insertion point, so it will be with you when you arrive at your destination. The following table provides keystrokes for moving quickly through a document.

KEYBOARD NAVIGATION			
Press	**To Move**	**Press**	**To Move**
→	One character to the right	Page Down	Down one screen
←	One character to the left	Page Up	Up one screen
Ctrl + →	One word to the right	Ctrl + End	To the end of the document
Ctrl + ←	One word to the left	Ctrl + Home	To the beginning of the document
↓	Down one line	End	To the end of the line
↑	Up one line	Home	To the beginning of the line

DEVELOP YOUR SKILLS WD01-D06
Use the Keyboard to Navigate

In this exercise, you will use the keyboard to move through a document.

1. Click the **I-beam** I in the middle of the first line of the first paragraph.

2. Tap the right arrow → and left arrow ← three times each to move to the right and left, one character at a time.

3. Tap the down arrow ↓ and up arrow ↑ three times each to move down, and then up, one line at a time.

Use Additional Keys

4. Press Ctrl + Home to move the insertion point to the beginning of the document.

5. Use the arrow keys to position the insertion point in the middle of the first line of the first paragraph.

6. Press Ctrl + ← three times to move to the left, one word at a time.

7. Press Ctrl + → three times to move to the right, one word at a time.

8. Tap ⌊Home⌋ to move to the beginning of the line.

9. Tap ⌊End⌋ to move to the end of the line.

10. Spend a few moments navigating with the keyboard.

11. Press ⌊Ctrl⌋ + ⌊End⌋ to move the insertion point to the end of the document.

12. Move the insertion point back to the beginning of the document.

Closing Documents

Video Library   http://labyrinthelab.com/videos   Video Number: WD13-V0108

FROM THE RIBBON
File→Close

FROM THE KEYBOARD
⌊Ctrl⌋+⌊F4⌋ to close

Word and other Office 2013 applications offer keyboard and Ribbon options for closing a document. If you haven't saved your document, Word will prompt you to do so.

You can also use Close ⌊×⌋ in the upper-right corner of the Word window to close a document.

DEVELOP YOUR SKILLS WD01-D07
Close the Document

In this exercise, you will close a file.

1. Choose **File→Close**.

2. If Word asks you if you want to save the changes, click **Don't Save**.

3. If a blank document is open on the screen, use the same technique to close it.

Starting a New Document

Video Library   http://labyrinthelab.com/videos   Video Number: WD13-V0109

FROM THE RIBBON
File→New

FROM THE KEYBOARD
⌊Ctrl⌋+⌊N⌋ to open a new document

In Word and other Office 2013 applications, you can start a new document using a keyboard shortcut or the Ribbon. With the keyboard shortcut, the new document is based on the Blank Document template. Using the Ribbon command offers a choice of templates in Backstage view.

DEVELOP YOUR SKILLS WD01-D08
Start a New Document

In this exercise, you will open a new, blank document. There should not be any documents in the Word window at this time.

1. Press ⌐Ctrl⌐ + ⌐N⌐ to open a new document based on the Blank Document template.
   Now you will close the document and use the Ribbon command to start a new document.

2. Choose **File→Close**.

3. Choose **File→New**.
   Notice that when you use the File→New command, Word gives you choices other than the Blank Document template.

4. Click the **Blank Document template** to open a new document.

Typing and Editing in Word

Video Library   http://labyrinthelab.com/videos   Video Number: WD13-V0110

When you insert text in an existing document, you must position the insertion point before you begin typing. When you insert text in Word, existing text moves to the right as you type. When you type paragraphs, you should not tap ⌐Enter⌐ at the end of each line. Word will automatically wrap your text to the next line when you reach the right-hand margin. You use ⌐Enter⌐ when you want short lines to remain short, such as in an inside address.

Use ⌐Backspace⌐ and ⌐Delete⌐ to remove text. The ⌐Backspace⌐ key deletes characters to the left of the insertion point. The ⌐Delete⌐ key removes characters to the right of the insertion point.

Saving Your Work

It's important to save your documents! Power outages and accidents can result in lost data, so save frequently.

You can also use Save 🖫 on the Quick Access toolbar.

FROM THE RIBBON
File→Save As
File→Save

FROM THE KEYBOARD
⌐Ctrl⌐+⌐S⌐ to save

Comparing Save and Save As

If the document was never saved, Word displays the Save As screen. If the document was previously saved, the Save command replaces the prior version with the edited one without displaying the Save As screen.

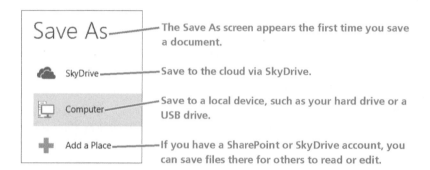

The Save As screen appears the first time you save a document.

Save to the cloud via SkyDrive.

Save to a local device, such as your hard drive or a USB drive.

If you have a SharePoint or SkyDrive account, you can save files there for others to read or edit.

Storing documents in SkyDrive is beyond the scope of this course. You will save your files on a local device.

After choosing a place in the Save As screen, the Save As dialog box opens where you will navigate to your storage location and name and save the file.

Word's DOCX File Format

Word 2003 and earlier versions saved documents in the *doc* file format. Word 2007 introduced the *docx* file format. Users of Word 2003 and prior versions may not be able to read Word files in the *docx* format. However, you can choose to save your document in the older *doc* format to maintain backward compatibility. Also, when you open a document created in earlier Word versions, the title bar displays *Compatibility Mode* next to the title. This means certain Word 2013 features not compatible with older versions are turned off while working in the document.

DEVELOP YOUR SKILLS WD01-D09
Create and Save a Document

In this exercise, you will begin by saving your document (in this case a blank document). This technique is used throughout this course so you can start each exercise with a fresh file.

1. Click **Save** 🖫 on the Quick Access toolbar.

   Since this is the first time you are saving this document, Word displays the Save As screen in Backstage view. Once you have saved the file, this button saves the current version of the file over the old version without displaying the Save As screen.

2. Double-click the **Computer** 🖳 icon to open the Save As dialog box.

3. Follow these steps to save your document:

Keep in mind that your dialog box may contain different files and folders than shown here.

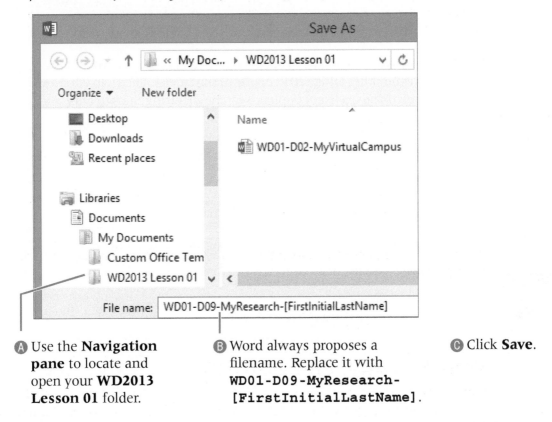

Ⓐ Use the **Navigation pane** to locate and open your **WD2013 Lesson 01** folder.

Ⓑ Word always proposes a filename. Replace it with `WD01-D09-MyResearch-[FirstInitialLastName]`.

Ⓒ Click **Save**.

In step B, replace the bracketed text with your first initial and last name. For example, if your name is Bethany Smith, your filename would look like this: WD01-D09-MyResearch-BSmith.

4. Type the following text and let Word Wrap do its thing.

If you make a typo, use Backspace *or* Delete *to remove it. Remember to position the insertion point next to the typo.*

> In general, here's how it works. You join and create a profile about yourself, choosing how much personal information to enter. Then you can invite other people to join also. You can chat in real-time with other members, post photos to share, and most importantly, you control what information others can see about you.

5. **Save** 🔲 the file and leave it open.

Getting Help in Word 2013

Video Library   http://labyrinthelab.com/videos   Video Number: WD13-V0111

The Microsoft Word Help button appears in the upper-right corner of the Word screen and other Office 2013 application screens. The Help window contains a search box, a list of popular searches, Getting Started aids, and online training options.

FROM THE KEYBOARD
F1 to open Help

DEVELOP YOUR SKILLS WD01-D10
Use Word Help

In this exercise, you will work with several Help techniques.

1. Click **Help** ? in the upper-right corner of the Word window.

2. Follow these steps for an overview of Word Help:

Ⓐ Hover the mouse pointer over these buttons to display **ToolTips**.

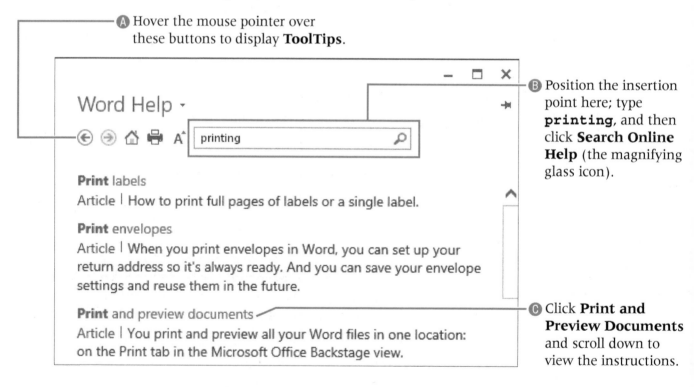

Ⓑ Position the insertion point here; type **printing**, and then click **Search Online Help** (the magnifying glass icon).

Ⓒ Click **Print and Preview Documents** and scroll down to view the instructions.

3. Take a few moments to experiment with Help. Try searching for **save** and **compatibility mode**. Feel free to explore any topics that interest you.

4. Click **Close** ⊠ in the upper-right corner of the Help window.

Exiting from Word

Video Library   http://labyrinthelab.com/videos   Video Number: WD13-V0112

You exit Word and other Office 2013 applications by clicking the Close button in the upper-right corner of the window. If you have more than one document open, you need to close each document. It's important to exit your application in an orderly fashion. Turning off your computer before exiting could cause you to lose data.

DEVELOP YOUR SKILLS WD01-D11
Exit from Word

In this exercise, you will exit from Word. Since you haven't made any changes to your document, you won't bother saving it again.

1. Click **Close** ⊠ in the upper-right corner of the Word window.

2. If you are prompted to save your changes, click **Don't Save**.

3. If you have more than one document open, close any remaining documents without saving.
   Word closes and the Windows Desktop appears.

Concepts Review

To check your knowledge of the key concepts introduced in this lesson, complete the Concepts Review quiz by choosing the appropriate access option below.

If you are...	Then access the quiz by...
Using the Labyrinth Video Library	Going to http://labyrinthelab.com/videos
Using eLab	Logging in, choosing Content, and navigating to the Concepts Review quiz for this lesson
Not using the Labyrinth Video Library or eLab	Going to the student resource center for this book

Reinforce Your Skills

Work with the Word Interface

In this exercise, you will start Word and examine the Start screen and Word window. You will use correct terminology for the Word window, and you will collapse and expand the Ribbon. Finally, you will customize the Quick Access toolbar.

Start Word and Examine the Word Start Screen

1. Start **Word** and note how the Start screen helps you begin your work.

2. Open **WD01-R01-Worksheet** from your **WD2013 Lesson 01** folder and save it as
   `WD01-R01-Worksheet-[FirstInitialLastName]`.

3. Refer to your worksheet and list three ways the Start screen helps you begin your work.

Word Terminology

It's important to use the correct terms when talking about Word. If you need to discuss an issue with your IT department, the staff can help you more efficiently if they are clear on what you are referring to.

4. In your worksheet, enter the correct terms for items A–F in the following illustration.

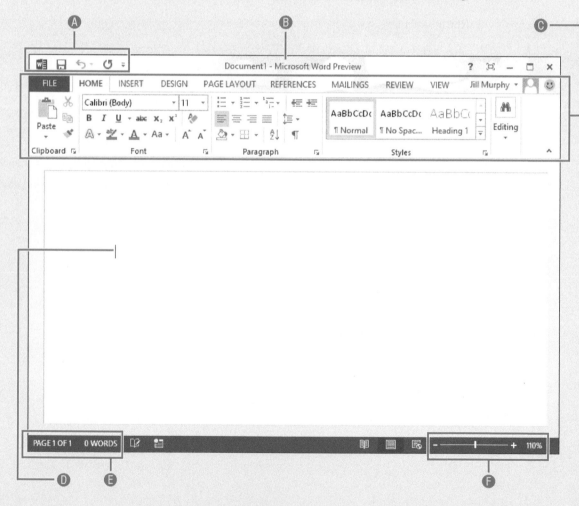

Open a Document

5. Refer to your worksheet and enter the phrase that appears in **Word's title bar** when you open a file that was created in an earlier version of Word.

6. Navigate to your **WD2013 Lesson 01** folder and open **WD01-R01-FarmersMarket**.

7. Refer to your worksheet and enter the name of the group that organized the field trip to the farmers' market.

Collapse the Ribbon

8. Collapse the **Ribbon**.

9. In your worksheet, list the steps you took to complete step 8.

10. Expand the **Ribbon**.

The Quick Access Toolbar

11. Move the **Quick Access toolbar** below the Ribbon.

12. In your worksheet, list the steps you took to complete step 11.

13. Choose **Page Layout→Page Setup** and add **Margins** ▯ to the Quick Access toolbar.

14. In your worksheet, list the steps you took to complete step 13.

15. Move the **Quick Access** toolbar back above the Ribbon.

16. Remove **Margins** ▯ from the toolbar.

17. Save your worksheet, close all files, and exit from **Word**. Submit your final file based on the guidelines provided by your instructor.

    To view examples of how your file or files should look at the end of this exercise, go to the student resource center.

Navigate in Word, Type a Document, and Use Help

In this exercise, you will use mouse and keyboard techniques to navigate in a multipage document. Then you will close the document, open and type in a new document, and then save your work. Finally, you will use Word's Help feature, and then exit from Word.

Navigate with the Scroll Bar and Keyboard

1. Start **Word**. Open **WD01-R02-Worksheet** from your **WD2013 Lesson 01** folder and save it as `WD01-R02-Worksheet-[FirstInitialLastName]`.

2. Open **WD01-R02-KidsNewsletter** from your **WD2013 Lesson 01** folder.

3. Follow these steps to scroll in the document:

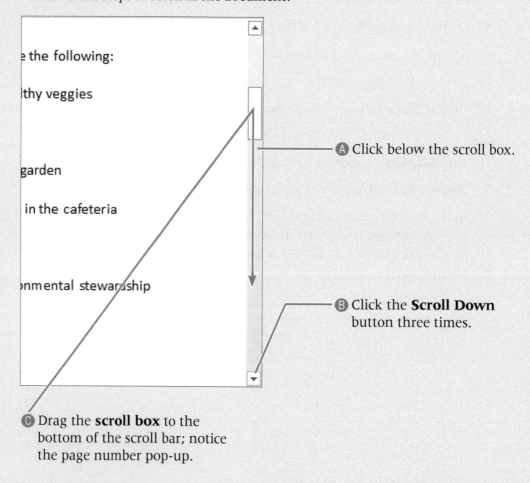

the following:

lthy veggies

garden

in the cafeteria

onmental stewardship

Ⓐ Click below the scroll box.

Ⓑ Click the **Scroll Down** button three times.

Ⓒ Drag the **scroll box** to the bottom of the scroll bar; notice the page number pop-up.

4. Hover the mouse pointer over the body of the document and notice the pointer shape, and then hover the mouse pointer in the left margin and notice its shape.

5. Press ⌈Ctrl⌉+⌈Home⌉ and notice the position of the insertion point.

6. Position the insertion point in the middle of the first line of the first paragraph and press ⌈Ctrl⌉+⌈→⌉ three times.

7. Tap ⌈Home⌉ and notice the position of the insertion point.

8. Press ⌈Ctrl⌉+⌈End⌉ and notice the position of the insertion point.

9. Refer to your worksheet and answer the questions for steps 4–8.

Close the Document and Start a New Document

10. Choose **File→Close** to close **WD01-R02-KidsNewsletter**. If you are prompted to save changes, click **Don't Save**.

11. Choose **File→New** and open a new document using the **Blank Document template**.

12. Choose **File→Close** to close the new document, and then press ⌈Ctrl⌉+⌈N⌉ to start a new document.

    The new document is based on the Blank Document template.

13. Type the following text using ⌈Backspace⌉ or ⌈Delete⌉ to correct typos.

    The Kids for Change "Think Globally, Act Locally" program is designed to help young people develop their understanding of an increasingly interrelated world. We have an exciting guest speaker for our next monthly meeting.

14. Refer to your worksheet and answer the questions for steps 11–13.

Save Your Document

15. Choose **File→Save As** from the Ribbon and navigate to your **WD2013 Lesson 01** folder.

16. Save your document as **WD01-R02-GuestSpeaker-[FirstInitialLastName]**.

> The Kids for Change "Think Globally, Act Locally" program is designed to help young people develop their understanding of an increasingly interrelated world. We have an exciting guest speaker for our next monthly meeting.

17. Choose File→Close to close the document.

18. Refer to your worksheet and answer the question for step 16.

19. Choose **File→Open**, navigate to your **WD2013 Lesson 01** folder, and open **WD01-R02-FarmVisitLtr**.

    This document was created in Word 2003, which means it is a doc file rather than a Word 2013 docx file. Notice the phrase to the right of the file name in the title bar.

Explore Help and Exit from Word

20. Click **Help** [?] in the upper-right corner of the Word window.

21. Use the **Search Box** to search for **Undo**, and then click the **Undo, Redo, or Repeat an Action** link.

    Make a note of the shortcut keystrokes for Undo.

22. Use the Help **Search Box** to search for **Clipboard** and click the **Use the Office Clipboard** link. Read the first paragraph of the Help text, and make a note of what is stored in the Clipboard.

23. **Close** [×] the **Help** window. Then, choose **File→Close** to close **WD01-R02-FarmVisitLtr**.

24. Refer to your worksheet and answer the questions for steps 20–22.

25. Save your worksheet, and exit from **Word**. Submit your final files based on the guidelines provided by your instructor.

    To view examples of how your file or files should look at the end of this exercise, go to the student resource center.

REINFORCE YOUR SKILLS WD01-R03

Use the Word Interface and Work with Documents

In this exercise, you will work with the Word interface, open and navigate in an existing document, and create and save a new document. Finally, you will work with Word Help, and then exit from Word.

Start Word and Examine the Word Start Screen

1. Start **Word**. Open **WD01-R03-Worksheet** from your **WD2013 Lesson 01** folder and save it as **WD01-R03-Worksheet-[FirstInitialLastName]**.

2. Refer to your worksheet and answer the step 2 question.

Word Window Terminology

3. Refer to your worksheet and answer the step 3 questions.

Open a Document and Collapse the Ribbon

4. Choose **File→Open** from the Ribbon and open **WD01-R03-OrgsPrtctEarth**.

5. Refer to your worksheet and answer the step 5 question.

The Quick Access Toolbar

6. In your worksheet, list the steps for removing a button from the Quick Access toolbar.

Navigate with the Scroll Bar and Keyboard

7. Refer to your worksheet and answer the step 7 questions.

Close a Document and Start a New Document

8. Choose **File→Close** to close WD01-R03-OrgsPrtctEarth.

9. Choose **File→New** and start a new document using the **Blank Document template**.

10. Type the following text:

    `Organizations that are founded to protect our earth work in concert with nature through activities such as planting and caring for trees, protecting groundwater, and restoring wetlands. They work at the local, state, national, and international levels to improve policy for short- and long-term solutions. Their goal is to achieve a healthy planet. Kids for Change helps to connect kids to organizations such as these.`

11. Refer to your worksheet and answer the step 11 questions.

Save Your Document in the Word DOCX File Format

12. Choose **File→Save**, navigate to your **WD2013 Lesson 01** folder, and save your document as `WD01-R03-HealthyPlanet-[FirstInitialLastName]`.

13. Refer to your worksheet and answer the step 13 question.

Get Help and Exit from Word

14. Click **Help** ? in the upper-right corner of the Word window.

15. Refer to step 15 in your worksheet, and use **ToolTips** to identify the buttons in the upper-left corner of the Help window.

16. **Close** × the **Help** window.

17. Click **Close** × in the upper-right corner of the Word window to close the document. Close any other open documents.

18. Save your worksheet, and exit from **Word**. Submit your final files based on the guidelines provided by your instructor.

Apply Your Skills

Open a Document and Work with the Word Interface

In this exercise, you will open a document and scroll through it to determine its length. You will examine the Ribbon in some detail, modify the Quick Access toolbar, and collapse the Ribbon. Finally you will return the Ribbon and the Quick Access toolbar to their default states.

Start Word and Open a Document

1. Start **Word**. Click the **Open Other Documents** link on the left side of the Word Start screen below the Recent list.

2. Navigate to your **WD213 Lesson 01** folder, open **WD01-A01-Worksheet**, and save it as `WD01-A01-Worksheet-[FirstInitialLastName]`.

3. Open **WD01-A01-CorpEvents** from your **WD2013 Lesson 01** folder.

4. Refer to your worksheet and answer the question for step 4.

Work with the Word 2013 Interface

5. Refer to your worksheet, and respond to step 5.

6. Choose **Insert→Illustrations** and add the **SmartArt** button to the **Quick Access** toolbar.

7. Position the **Quick Access toolbar** below the Ribbon; then collapse the **Ribbon**.

8. Tap `Prt Screen` on your keyboard to capture a picture of your screen.

9. Start a blank document and paste the screen capture into the document.

10. Save the file as `WD01-A01-ScreenShot-[FirstInitialLastName]` in your **WD2013 Lesson 01** folder.

11. Remove the **SmartArt** button from the **Quick Access** toolbar, expand the **Ribbon**, and move the **Quick Access** toolbar above the Ribbon.

12. Choose File→Close to close **WD01-A01-CorpEvents** and **WD01-A01-ScreenShot-[FirstInitialLastName]**.

13. Save your worksheet, and exit from **Word**. Submit your final files based on the guidelines provided by your instructor.

    To view examples of how your file or files should look at the end of this exercise, go to the student resource center.

APPLY YOUR SKILLS WD01-A02

Navigate in Word, Create a Document, and Use Help

In this exercise, you will open a document and scroll through it, and then you will create and save a document. Finally, you will use Help to learn about saving a Word file as a PDF file.

Navigate in Word

1. Start **Word**. Open **WD01-A02-Worksheet** from your **WD2013 Lesson 01** folder and save it as `WD01-A02-Worksheet-[FirstInitialLastName]`.

2. Open **WD01-A02-UniversalEvents** from your **WD2013 Lesson 01** folder.

3. Scroll to the bottom of the document, click the **scroll box**, and then, referring to your worksheet, respond to the question for step 3.

4. Choose File→Close to close **WD01-A02-UniversalEvents** and start a new blank document based on the **Blank Document template**.

Type and Save a New Document

5. Type the following:

   `Universal Corporate Events will manage every phase of your corporate travel needs. We work directly with travelers to provide the flights that meet their needs, and we arrange ground transportation to and from all events. We have staff available 24x7 to assist travelers if any unforeseen situations arise.`

6. Save the file as `WD01-A02-Travel-[FirstInitialLastName]` in your **WD2013 Lesson 01** folder, and then close it.

Use Help

7. Open **Help** ?, search for **Save**, and click the **Save as PDF** link.

8. Press Alt + Prt Screen to capture a picture of the Help screen.

9. Paste the screenshot in your worksheet where indicated, and save the worksheet.

10. Close **Help**, close any open documents, and then exit from **Word**.

11. Submit your final files based on the guidelines provided by your instructor.
    To view examples of how your file or files should look at the end of this exercise, go to the student resource center.

Use the Ribbon and Use Help to Research Word Features

In this exercise, you will use the dialog box launcher on the Ribbon to open dialog boxes, and you will research terms in Word Help. Finally, you will type a document showing the results of your research.

Start a New Document and Use a Dialog Box Launcher

1. Start **Word**. Start a new document based on the **Blank Document template**.

2. Choose **Home→Paragraph→dialog box launcher**.

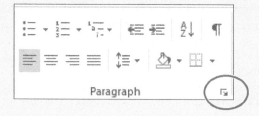

3. Click the **Line and Page Breaks** tab and notice the term Widow/Orphan Control under the Pagination heading; close the dialog box.

4. Type **HELP RESEARCH** at the top of your document and tap Enter.

Use Help

5. Open **Help** and search for **Widow/Orphan Control**.

6. Click the **Add a Page Break** link.

7. Scroll down and note what the **Widow/Orphan Control** feature accomplishes.

8. Minimize the **Help** window, and type a description of **Widow/Orphan Control** in your document.

   Minimize and restore the Help window as needed.

9. Click the **dialog box launcher** in the Font group, notice the term **Superscript** in the Effects section, and then close the dialog box.

10. Search for **Superscript** in Help and click the **"Superscript" is under "Home/Font"** link. Note the description of Superscript.

11. Type a description of superscript in your document, and then search in Help for **Save**.

12. Click the **Save Documents Online** link, and type a short description of how you save a document to the SkyDrive.

13. Save your file as **WD01-A03-HelpResearch-[FirstInitialLastName]** in the **WD2013 Lesson 01** folder.

14. Submit your final file based on the guidelines provided by your instructor.

Extend Your Skills

In the course of working through the Extend Your Skills exercises, you will think critically as you use the skills taught in the lesson to complete the assigned projects. To evaluate your mastery and completion of the exercises, your instructor may use a rubric, with which more points are allotted according to performance characteristics. (The more you do, the more you earn!) Ask your instructor how your work will be evaluated.

WD01-E01 That's the Way I See It

As an IT professional, you realize that many people need help adapting to Office 2013. You decide to start your own consulting business to fill this need. Your first client would like assistance with customizing the Quick Access toolbar in order to work more effectively. So, you will create a handout in Word that lists the steps for customizing the Quick Access toolbar.

Because your client uses a laptop, she would like to learn to collapse the Ribbon to free up space on the screen. Include instructions for collapsing the Ribbon in your handout. Finally, the client is interested in learning more about saving files "in the cloud." In the handout, include instructions for how to search Help for information on saving files in SkyDrive.

Save your handout as **WD01-E01-WordHandout-[FirstInitialLastName]** in your **WD2013 Lesson 01** folder. You will be evaluated based on the inclusion of all elements specified, your ability to follow directions, your ability to apply newly learned skills to a real-world situation, your creativity, and the relevance of your topic and/or data choice(s). Submit your final file based on the guidelines provided by your instructor.

WD01-E02 Be Your Own Boss

You are the owner of Blue Jean Landscaping and are also a bit of a "techie." You have decided to upgrade the company from Word 2010 to Word 2013. You want to provide online tutorials and reference materials to aid employees in the conversion. Start Word and use Help or online resources to locate three aids for this purpose (for example, opening older Word documents in Word 2013, Touch Mode, or how the Ribbon look has changed). Create a document named **WD01-E02-WordResources-[FirstInitialLastName]** and save it in the **WD2013 Lesson 01** folder. In the document, include the resource information and explain how each will help the employees (write three to five sentences per topic). Don't list resources without including an explanation.

You will be evaluated based on the inclusion of all elements specified, your ability to follow directions, your ability to apply newly learned skills to a real-world situation, your creativity, and your demonstration of an entrepreneurial spirit. Submit your final file based on the guidelines provided by your instructor.

Transfer Your Skills

In the course of working through the Transfer Your Skills exercises, you will use critical-thinking and creativity skills to complete the assigned projects using skills taught in the lesson. To evaluate your mastery and completion of the exercises, your instructor may use a rubric, with which more points are allotted according to performance characteristics. (The more you do, the more you earn!) Ask your instructor how your work will be evaluated.

WD01-T01 Use the Web as a Learning Tool

Throughout this book, you will be provided with an opportunity to use the Internet as a learning tool by completing WebQuests. According to the original creators of WebQuests, as described on their website (WebQuest.org), a WebQuest is "an inquiry-oriented activity in which most or all of the information used by learners is drawn from the web." To complete the WebQuest projects in this book, navigate to the student resource center and choose the WebQuest for the lesson on which you are currently working. The subject of each WebQuest will be relevant to the material found in the lesson.

WebQuest Subject: How Microsoft Word is used in business.

Submit your final file(s) based on the guidelines provided by your instructor.

WD01-T02 Demonstrate Proficiency

As the owner of Stormy BBQ, you have decided to customize the Word interface to help you work more effectively. In particular, you want to add buttons to the Quick Access toolbar that will help you in creating a brochure advertising your fresh, locally-grown vegetables and local, farm-raised pork and beef ribs.

Start Word and open a new, blank document. Examine the buttons on the Ribbon to determine which will be most useful for you. You may wish to use ToolTips or Help to determine the purpose of some of the buttons. Add five buttons to the Quick Access toolbar, and then list specific reasons for choosing each. Indicate if you prefer to have the Quick Access toolbar above or below the Ribbon and state the reason for your preference. Take a screen shot of your customized toolbar and paste it into your Word document. Reset the Quick Access toolbar to its default state when you are finished.

Save your file as **WD01-T02-CustomizeWord-[FirstInitialLastName]** in your **WD2013 Lesson 01** folder. Submit your final file based on the guidelines provided by your instructor.

WORD 2013

Creating and Editing Business Letters

In this lesson, you will create business letters while learning proper business letter formatting. You will learn techniques for entering and editing text, copying and moving text, and printing documents. In addition, you will learn to use Word's AutoComplete and AutoCorrect tools to insert frequently used text and to control automatic formatting that Word applies as you type.

LESSON OUTLINE

LEARNING OBJECTIVES

After studying this lesson, you will be able to:

- Select and edit text and use AutoCorrect
- Set AutoFormat As You Type options
- Copy and move text
- Set page layout options
- Preview and print a document

Taking Care with Business Letters

You are a sales assistant at My Virtual Campus. A new prospect, Richmond University, has expressed interest in the networking website that My Virtual Campus sells. The sales manager has asked you to prepare a standard letter for potential new clients, thanking them for their interest and providing information about the website.

You start by referring to your business writing class textbook to ensure that you format the letter correctly for a good first impression and a professional appearance.

November 24, 2013

Ms. Paige Daniels
Richmond University
15751 Meadow Lane
Chester Allen, VA 23333

Dear Ms. Daniels:

Travis Mayfield referred you to us after he spoke with you about our extraordinary product. I want to take this opportunity to personally thank you for considering My Virtual Campus' social-networking website for your institution. As Travis may have mentioned, we pride ourselves in providing the latest in technology as well as excellent customer service with satisfaction guaranteed.

Enclosed you will find information to review regarding the features of the website. After reading the material, please contact our sales manager, Bruce Carter, at your earliest convenience to discuss your options. Thank you again for considering our amazing website.

Sincerely,

<your name>
Customer Service Representative
Sales Department

<typist's initials if other than sender>
Enclosures (2)
cc: Bruce Carter

Defining Typical Business Letter Styles

Video Library   http://labyrinthelab.com/videos   Video Number: WD13-V0201

There are several acceptable styles of business letters. The styles discussed in this text include block and modified block. All business letters contain similar elements but with varied formatting.

Block Style

The block style is the most common business-letter style. All elements are single spaced and left aligned, except for double spacing between paragraphs.

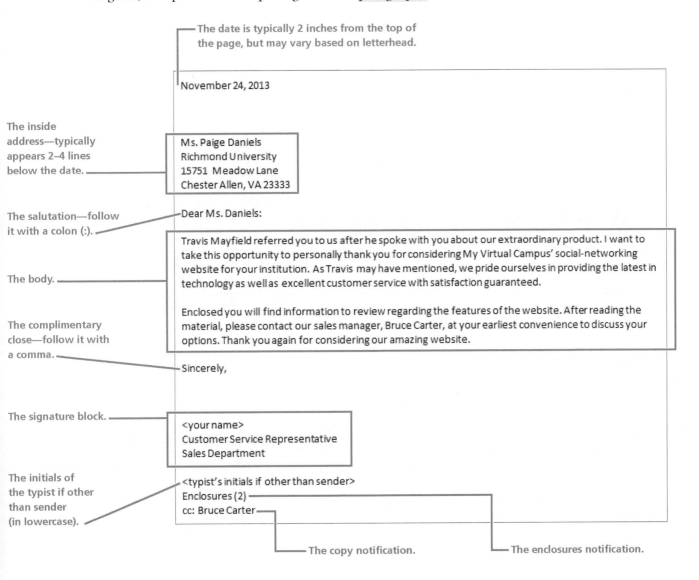

The date is typically 2 inches from the top of the page, but may vary based on letterhead.

November 24, 2013

The inside address—typically appears 2–4 lines below the date.

Ms. Paige Daniels
Richmond University
15751 Meadow Lane
Chester Allen, VA 23333

The salutation—follow it with a colon (:).

Dear Ms. Daniels:

The body.

Travis Mayfield referred you to us after he spoke with you about our extraordinary product. I want to take this opportunity to personally thank you for considering My Virtual Campus' social-networking website for your institution. As Travis may have mentioned, we pride ourselves in providing the latest in technology as well as excellent customer service with satisfaction guaranteed.

Enclosed you will find information to review regarding the features of the website. After reading the material, please contact our sales manager, Bruce Carter, at your earliest convenience to discuss your options. Thank you again for considering our amazing website.

The complimentary close—follow it with a comma.

Sincerely,

The signature block.

<your name>
Customer Service Representative
Sales Department

The initials of the typist if other than sender (in lowercase).

<typist's initials if other than sender>
Enclosures (2)
cc: Bruce Carter

The copy notification.

The enclosures notification.

Modified Block Style

Modified block is another commonly use letter format. The following illustration points out the differences in the modified block-style business letter compared to the block-style business letter.

The date line, complimentary close, and signature block begin at the center of the page. All other lines are left aligned.

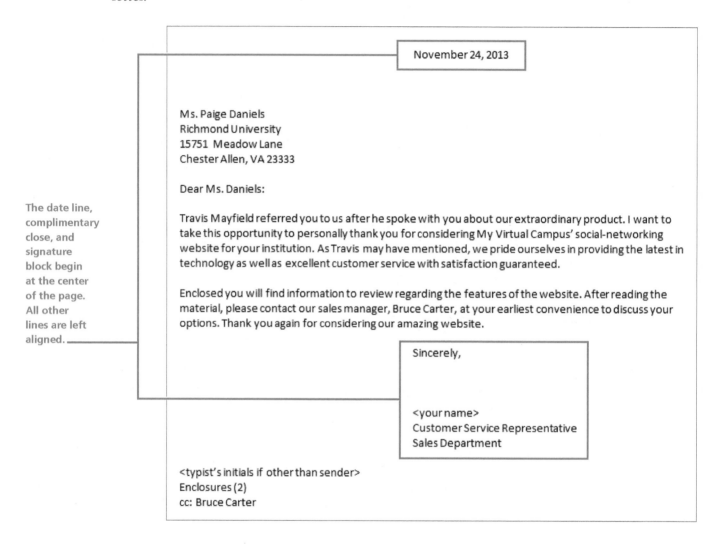

November 24, 2013

Ms. Paige Daniels
Richmond University
15751 Meadow Lane
Chester Allen, VA 23333

Dear Ms. Daniels:

Travis Mayfield referred you to us after he spoke with you about our extraordinary product. I want to take this opportunity to personally thank you for considering My Virtual Campus' social-networking website for your institution. As Travis may have mentioned, we pride ourselves in providing the latest in technology as well as excellent customer service with satisfaction guaranteed.

Enclosed you will find information to review regarding the features of the website. After reading the material, please contact our sales manager, Bruce Carter, at your earliest convenience to discuss your options. Thank you again for considering our amazing website.

Sincerely,

<your name>
Customer Service Representative
Sales Department

<typist's initials if other than sender>
Enclosures (2)
cc: Bruce Carter

Inserting Text

Video Library   http://labyrinthelab.com/videos   Video Number: WD13-V0202

You always insert text at the flashing insertion point. Therefore, you must position the insertion point at the desired location before typing.

Using AutoComplete

Word's AutoComplete feature does some of your typing for you. It recognizes certain words and phrases, such as names of months and days, and offers to complete them for you.

November (Press ENTER to Insert)
Nove

AutoComplete proposing the word
November when *Nove* is typed.

You accept AutoComplete suggestions by tapping ⌐Enter⌐. If you choose to ignore the suggestion, just keep typing; the suggestion disappears.

AutoComplete does not offer to complete the months March through July, because the names are short.

Using the Enter Key

You use ⌐Enter⌐ to begin a new paragraph or to insert blank lines in a document. Word considers anything that ends by tapping ⌐Enter⌐ to be a paragraph. Thus, short lines such as a date line, an inside address, or even blank lines themselves are considered paragraphs.

Tapping ⌐Enter⌐ inserts a paragraph symbol in a document. These symbols are visible when you display formatting marks.

Showing Formatting Marks

Although formatting marks appear on the screen, you will not see them in the printed document. Viewing these characters can be important when editing a document. For example, you may need to see the formatting marks to determine whether the space between two words was created with the ⌐Spacebar⌐ or ⌐Tab⌐.

FROM THE RIBBON
Home→Paragraph→
Show/Hide ¶

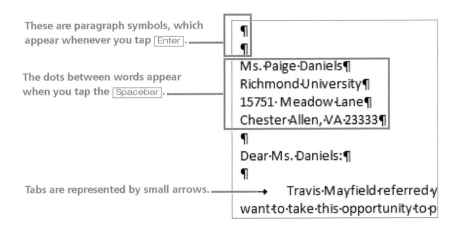

These are paragraph symbols, which appear whenever you tap ⌐Enter⌐.

The dots between words appear when you tap the ⌐Spacebar⌐.

Tabs are represented by small arrows.

Ms.·Paige·Daniels¶
Richmond·University¶
15751·Meadow·Lane¶
Chester·Allen,·VA·23333¶
¶
Dear·Ms.·Daniels:¶
¶
→   Travis·Mayfield·referred·y
want·to·take·this·opportunity·to·p

Spacing in Letters

The default spacing in Word 2013 is 1.08 rather than the traditional single spacing. It adds an extra 8 points (a little less than an eighth of an inch) at the end of paragraphs. Therefore, rather that tapping ⌐Enter⌐ twice at the end of a paragraph, you just tap ⌐Enter⌐ once, and Word adds the extra spacing.

FROM THE RIBBON
Home→Paragraph→
Line and Paragraph
Spacing

When you choose the Blank Document template on the Word Start screen or on the New screen, you are using the default 1.08 spacing. Some documents, however, typically require single spacing, such as business letters, reports, and proposals. Word offers these methods for applying single spacing:

- Single Spaced (Blank) template
- Line and Paragraph Spacing button

Applying Traditional Spacing Using the Single Spaced Template

Choosing the Single Spaced (Blank) template from the Word Start screen or from the New screen opens a single-spaced document. This is a good choice if the majority of your document will be single spaced. If you will use single spacing only in part of your document, the Line and Paragraph Spacing button is a good choice.

Single spaced (blank)

Changing Spacing Using the Line and Paragraph Spacing Button

If you start a new document using 1.08 spacing and then decide to apply single spacing to a portion of the document, you can choose the options indicated in the following figure. You must select (highlight) the text to be single spaced, or at a minimum, select the paragraph symbol at the end of the text before changing the spacing. Paragraph symbols carry formatting in them.

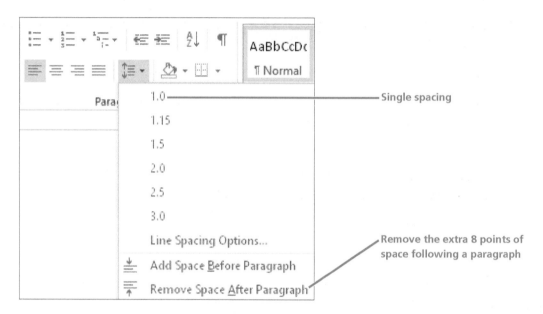

If you wish to use other spacing such as double- or triple-spacing, the Line and Paragraph Spacing button is the place to go.

QUICK REFERENCE	WORKING WITH LINE SPACING
Task	**Procedure**
Word Default Spacing	▪ Choose the Blank Document template on the Word Start screen; choose File→New and choose Blank Document; or, press ⎡Ctrl⎤+⎡N⎤
Single Spacing	▪ Choose the Single Spaced (Blank) template on the Word Start screen; or, choose File→New and choose Single Spaced (Blank).
	▪ Click Create.
Other Line Spacing Options	▪ Choose Home→Paragraph→Line and Paragraph Spacing.

Type a Business Letter

In this exercise, you will use the Single Spaced (Blank) template to create a business letter. You will also use AutoComplete and work with the ⎡Enter⎤ *key.*

1. Start **Word** and make sure the Word window is **maximized** ▢.

2. Click the **Single Spaced (Blank)** template to start a new single-spaced letter.

   A window appears describing the template.

3. Click **Create** ▢.

4. Choose **File→Save** and save the document in your **WD2013 Lesson 02** folder as **WD02-D01-DanielsLetter-[FirstInitialLastName]**.

   Replace the bracketed text with your first initial and last name. For example, if your name is Bethany Smith, your filename would look like this: WD02-D01-DanielsLetter-BSmith.

 Throughout this book, you will usually save your working document with a new name in step 1 so you can start each exercise with a fresh document.

Begin the Letter and Use AutoComplete

5. Choose **Home→Paragraph→Show/Hide** ¶ to display formatting marks.

   New documents contain a paragraph symbol; you won't see it if you don't turn on the Show/Hide feature. Paragraph symbols carry formatting in them. In this example, the document formatting includes single spacing.

6. Choose **View→Show→Ruler** to display the ruler.

7. Tap ⎡Enter⎤ five times to place the insertion point 2 inches from the top of the page.

8. Type **Nove** but stop typing when AutoComplete displays a pop-up tip.

9. Tap ⎡Enter⎤ to automatically insert *November* in the letter.

10. Finish typing the date as **November 24, 2013**.

11. Continue typing the letter as shown, tapping ⌐Enter⌐ wherever you see a paragraph symbol.

If you catch a typo, you can tap ⌐Backspace⌐ *enough times to remove the error, and then continue typing.*

```
¶
¶
¶
¶
¶
November·24,·2013¶
¶
¶
¶
Ms.·Paige·Daniels¶
Richmond·University¶
15751·Meadow·Lane¶
Chester·Allen,·VA·23333¶
¶
Dear·Ms.·Daniels:¶
¶
¶
```

12. Type the body paragraph as shown. Let Word Wrap do its thing and tap ⌐Enter⌐ twice at the end of the paragraph.

```
Travis·Mayfield·referred·you·to·us·after·he·spoke·with·you·yesterday·about·our·extraordinary·product.·I·
want·to·take·this·opportunity·to·thank·you·for·considering·My·Virtual·Campus'·social·networking·website·
for·your·institution.·As·Travis·may·have·mentioned,·we·pride·ourselves·in·providing·the·latest·in·
technology·as·well·as·excellent·customer·service.¶
¶
¶
```

 If you see a wavy red line, Word thinks the word *might* be misspelled. Wavy blue lines indicate possible grammatical errors. Ignore red and blue wavy lines for now.

13. Continue typing the letter as shown, tapping ⌷Enter⌷ where you see a paragraph symbol. Type your name where indicated.

I·have·enclosed·information·for·your·review·regarding·the·various·features·of·the·website.·After·reading·
the·material,·please·contact·our·sales·manager,·ASAP,·to·discuss·your·options.·Thank·you·again·for·
considering·our·amazing·website.¶
¶
Yours·truly,¶
¶
¶
¶
<your·name>¶
Customer·Service·Representative¶
Sales·Department¶
¶
¶

14. Choose **Home→Paragraph→Show/Hide ¶** to turn off formatting marks.

15. Choose **View→Show→Ruler** to turn off the ruler.

Feel free to turn Show/Hide and the ruler on or off as you see fit throughout this course.

16. Click **Save 💾** on the Quick Access toolbar.

Always leave the file open at the end of an exercise unless instructed to close it.

Creating an Envelope

Video Library   http://labyrinthelab.com/videos   Video Number: WD13-V0203

Microsoft Word is smart and versatile when it comes to creating envelopes. When you type a business letter with the recipient's name and address at the top, Word recognizes this as the delivery address. Word gives you two options: print the address directly on the envelope or insert the envelope at the top of the document.

FROM THE RIBBON
Mailings→Create→ Envelopes

The address from the letter is automatically inserted on the envelope.

You can type a return address or place a checkmark in the Omit box if a return address already exists.

You can print the envelope now or add it to your document.

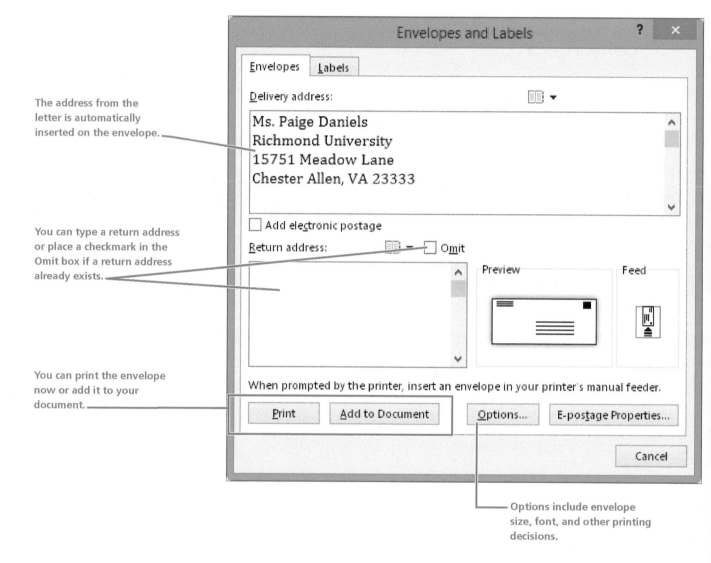

Options include envelope size, font, and other printing decisions.

When you enter a return address, you will be prompted to save it as the default so you don't have to type it each time.

Create an Envelope

Word 2013

In this exercise, you will create an envelope and add it to your letter.

1. Press Ctrl + Home, and then choose **Mailings→Create→Envelopes** 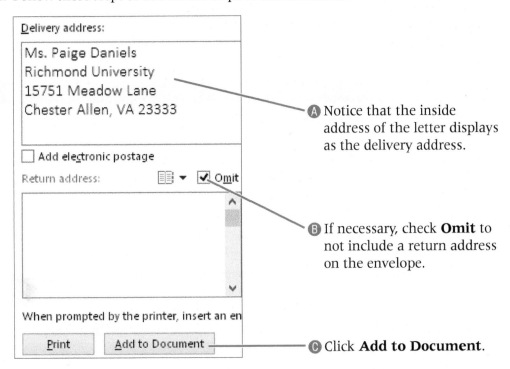.

2. Follow these steps to add an envelope to the document:

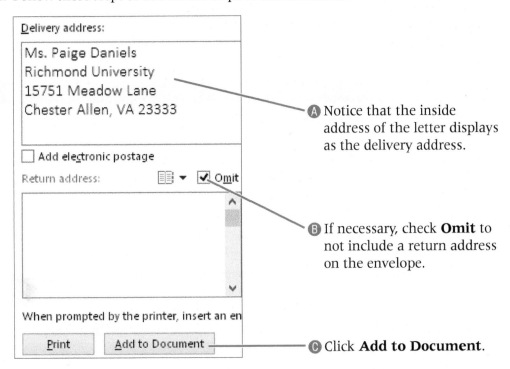

A Notice that the inside address of the letter displays as the delivery address.

B If necessary, check **Omit** to not include a return address on the envelope.

C Click **Add to Document**.

3. Observe the envelope, and then click **Undo** ↶ on the Quick Access toolbar to remove the envelope; you don't need it for this exercise.

   You'll learn more about Undo later.

Selecting Text

Video Library   http://labyrinthelab.com/videos   Video Number: WD13-V0204

You must select (highlight) text if you wish to perform an action on it. Suppose you want to delete a line. You select the line first, and then tap Delete.

Word provides many mouse and keyboard selection techniques. Deselect text by clicking in the text area of the document or by tapping an arrow key. The following Quick Reference table illustrates various selection techniques.

SELECTION TECHNIQUES

Item to Be Selected	Mouse Technique
One word	Double-click the word.
Continuous block of text	Hold down the left mouse button while dragging over the desired text.
A line	Place the mouse pointer selection arrow in the left margin, and click to select the line.
A sentence	Press Ctrl and click anywhere in the sentence.
One paragraph	Place the selection arrow in the left margin and double-click; or, triple-click the I-beam anywhere *within* the paragraph.
Multiple paragraphs	Place the selection arrow in the left margin and drag up or down; or, drag the I-beam over the desired paragraphs.
Entire document	Triple-click in the left margin; or, hold Ctrl and click in the left margin.
Nonadjacent areas	Select the first text block, and then hold Ctrl while dragging over additional blocks of text.
Item to Be Selected	**Keyboard Technique**
One word	Click at the beginning of the word, and then hold Shift+Ctrl while tapping →.
Continuous block of text	Click at the beginning of the text, and then hold Shift while tapping an arrow key. Or, click at the beginning of the text block, hold Shift, and then click at the end of the text block.
A line	Press Shift+End to select from the insertion point to the end of the line. Press Shift+Home to select from the insertion point to the beginning of the line.
Entire document	Press Ctrl+A, or press Ctrl and click in the left margin.

The Mini toolbar appears when you select text. It contains frequently used commands. You can choose a command or ignore the toolbar and it will fade away.

Select Text

In this exercise, you will practice various selection techniques using the letter you just created. Selecting text causes the Mini toolbar to fade in. You can ignore it for now.

1. Follow these steps to select text using the left margin:

A Place the selection arrow in the margin to the left of the first line of the inside address; click to select the line.

B Use the selection arrow to select this line. (Notice that the previously selected line is no longer selected.)

> Ms. Paige Daniels
> Richmond University
> 15751 Meadow Lane
> Chester Allen, VA 23333
>
> Dear Ms. Daniels:
>
> Travis Mayfield referred you to us after he spoke with you yesterday about our extraordinary product. I want to take this opportunity to thank you for considering My Virtual Campus' social-networking website for your institution. As Travis may have mentioned, we pride ourselves in providing the latest in technology as well as excellent customer service.

C Select this paragraph by double-clicking with the selection arrow.

2. Using the selection arrow, drag down the left margin to select text.

3. Click once anywhere in the body of the document to deselect.

4. Triple-click with the selection arrow anywhere in the left margin to select the entire document.

5. Click once anywhere in the body of the document to deselect.

Select Words

6. Double-click any word to select it.

7. Double-click a different word, and notice that the previous word is deselected.

Select Nonadjacent Selections
You can select multiple locations simultaneously.

8. Double-click to select one word.

9. Press and hold Ctrl as you double-click another word; release Ctrl .
   Both selections are active. You can select as many nonadjacent areas of a document as desired using the Ctrl key.

10. Follow these steps to drag and select a block of text:

Ⓐ Position the **I-beam** (not the selection arrow) here.　　　　　Ⓑ Drag to the right to select this phrase.

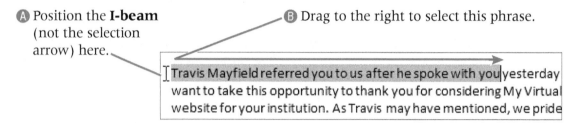

I Travis Mayfield referred you to us after he spoke with you|yesterday
want to take this opportunity to thank you for considering My Virtual
website for your institution. As Travis may have mentioned, we pride

11. Click in the document to deselect.

Editing Text

Video Library   http://labyrinthelab.com/videos   Video Number: WD13-V0205

Word offers many tools for editing documents, allowing you to insert and delete text. You'll find Word's undo and redo features are very helpful.

Inserting and Deleting Text

Remember, you must position the insertion point before you begin typing. You can use Backspace and Delete to remove one character at a time. If you select a block of text, Backspace or Delete removes the entire block.

Using Undo and Redo

Word's Undo button on the Quick Access toolbar lets you reverse your last editing or formatting change(s). You can reverse simple actions such as accidental text deletions, or you can reverse more complex actions, such as margin changes.

FROM THE KEYBOARD
Ctrl+Z to undo the last action

Ctrl+Y to redo the last action

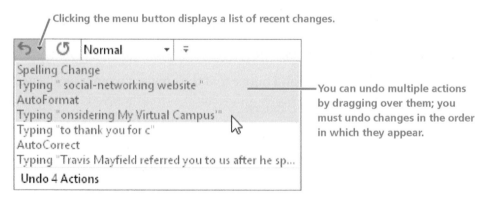

Clicking the menu button displays a list of recent changes.

You can undo multiple actions by dragging over them; you must undo changes in the order in which they appear.

The Redo button reverses Undo. Use Redo when you undo an action and then change your mind.

Insert and Delete Text and Use Undo and Redo

In this exercise, you will insert and delete text. You will delete characters using both ⎡Backspace⎤ and ⎡Delete⎤, and you will select and delete blocks of text. You will also use the Undo and Redo buttons on the Quick Access toolbar. You will begin by saving your document. This technique is used throughout this course so you can start your exercise with a fresh file.

1. Save your file in the **WD2013 Lesson 02** folder as **WD02-D04-DanielsLetter-[FirstInitialLastName]**.

2. In the first line of the first paragraph, double-click the word *yesterday* and tap ⎡Delete⎤ to remove it.

   > spoke with you yesterday about
   > for considering My Virtual Camp

3. Click with the **I-beam** I at the beginning of the word *thank* in the second line of the first paragraph, type **personally**, and tap ⎡Spacebar⎤.

4. Position the insertion point at the end of the first paragraph between the word *service* and the final period.

5. Tap ⎡Spacebar⎤ and type **with satisfaction guaranteed**.

6. Drag to select the first three words of the second paragraph, and then type **Enclosed you will find** to replace the selected text.

7. In the same line, position the insertion point after the word *your* and tap ⎡Backspace⎤ until the words *for your* are deleted; then type **to**.

8. Double-click the word *various* in the same line and tap ⎡Delete⎤.

9. In the next line, double-click *ASAP* and type **Bruce Carter, at your earliest convenience** in its place.

10. Delete the comma following *convenience*.

11. Place the selection arrow in the margin to the left of *Yours truly*.

12. Click once to select the line and type **Sincerely,** in its place.

Use Undo and Redo

13. You've decided that you prefer *Yours truly,* so click **Undo** ⟲ on the Quick Access toolbar enough times to remove *Sincerely.*

14. Well, maybe *Sincerely* is better after all. Click **Redo** ⟳ on the Quick Access toolbar enough times to insert *Sincerely.*

15. Save the document.

Working with AutoCorrect

Video Library   http://labyrinthelab.com/videos   Video Number: WD13-V0206

AutoCorrect is predefined text used for automatically correcting common spelling and capitalization errors. You may have noticed AutoCorrect changing the spelling of certain words while working through previous exercises.

The AutoCorrect feature corrects more than spelling errors. For example, you can set up an AutoCorrect entry to insert the phrase *as soon as possible* when you type *asap* and tap Spacebar or other characters, such as a Tab, Comma, or Period.

DEVELOP YOUR SKILLS WD02-D05
Use AutoCorrect

In this exercise, you will practice typing some terms that AutoCorrect will fix for you.

1. Press Ctrl + End to move the insertion point to the end of the document.

2. If necessary, tap Enter a few times to provide some space to practice.

3. Type **teh** and tap Tab.
   AutoCorrect capitalizes the word because AutoCorrect thinks it is the first word of a sentence.

4. Type **adn** and tap Spacebar; AutoCorrect fixes the error.

5. Now select and Delete the words you were just practicing with.

Using the AutoCorrect Options Smart Tag

Video Library   http://labyrinthelab.com/videos   Video Number: WD13-V0207

Word uses smart tags, small buttons that pop up automatically, to provide menus of options that are in context with what you are doing. One of those smart tags is AutoCorrect Options.

If Word automatically corrects something that you don't want corrected, a smart tag option allows you to undo the change. For example, when Word automatically capitalizes the first C in the cc: line, you can quickly undo the capitalization.

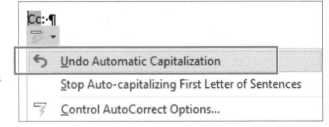

 You will see many smart tags as you work. If you do not want to use a smart tag, you can ignore it and it will disappear on its own.

Use the AutoCorrect Smart Tag

In this exercise, you will add typist initials to the letter and use the smart tag to undo capitalization when AutoCorrect incorrectly capitalizes the first initial.

1. Save your file as **WD02-D06-DanielsLetter-[FirstInitialLastName]**.

2. Choose **Home→Paragraph→Show/Hide ¶** to display formatting marks.

   The typist initials should appear on the second blank line following the signature block.

3. If necessary, tap Enter so there are at least two paragraph symbols.

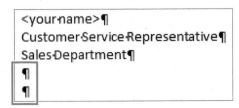

4. Follow these steps to add initials to the letter:

Ⓐ Type **ss** as the typist's initials (lowercase) and tap Enter. Notice that AutoCorrect incorrectly capitalized the first initial.

Ⓑ Position the mouse pointer over the first initial until you see a small blue rectangle. Slide the mouse pointer down to display the AutoCorrect smart tag.

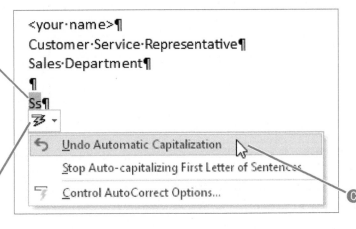

Ⓒ Click the tag and choose **Undo Automatic Capitalization**.

Word marks the initials with a wavy red line, indicating that it's a possible spelling error. You can ignore it.

5. Make sure the insertion point is on the blank line below the initials.

6. Type **Enclosures (2)** and tap Enter.

7. Choose **Home→Paragraph→Show/Hide ¶** to turn off formatting marks.

8. Save the document.

Customizing AutoCorrect

Video Library   http://labyrinthelab.com/videos   Video Number: WD13-V0208

In addition to correcting errors, AutoCorrect lets you automatically insert customized text and special characters. It's also useful for replacing abbreviations with full phrases. For example, you could set up AutoCorrect to insert the name of your company whenever you type an abbreviation for it. And you can customize AutoCorrect by deleting entries that are installed with Word; however, please do not delete any in this classroom.

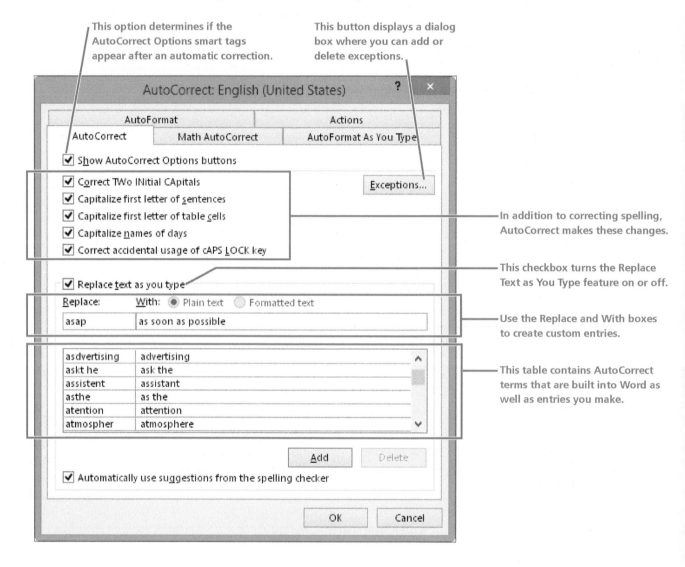

This option determines if the AutoCorrect Options smart tags appear after an automatic correction.

This button displays a dialog box where you can add or delete exceptions.

In addition to correcting spelling, AutoCorrect makes these changes.

This checkbox turns the Replace Text as You Type feature on or off.

Use the Replace and With boxes to create custom entries.

This table contains AutoCorrect terms that are built into Word as well as entries you make.

Using AutoCorrect Exceptions

You can designate exceptions to AutoCorrect when you don't want it to replace text that it normally would. For example, there is an option to capitalize the first letter of sentences. When word sees a period, it assumes that's the end of a sentence and it will capitalize the next word. However, you may not always want the capitalization to occur.

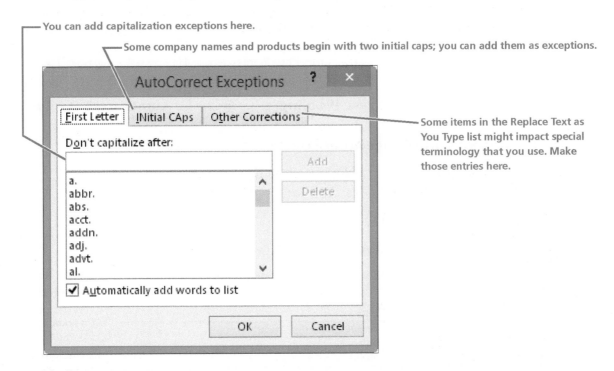

You can add capitalization exceptions here.

Some company names and products begin with two initial caps; you can add them as exceptions.

Some items in the Replace Text as You Type list might impact special terminology that you use. Make those entries here.

QUICK REFERENCE	USING AUTOCORRECT
Task	**Procedure**
Create a custom AutoCorrect entry	▪ Choose File→Options.
	▪ Choose Proofing and click AutoCorrect Options.
	▪ Enter shortcut text in the Replace box and replacement text in the With box.
Create an AutoCorrect exception	▪ Click Exceptions in the AutoCorrect dialog box.
	▪ Choose the appropriate tab and enter the exception.

DEVELOP YOUR SKILLS WD02-D07

Create a Custom AutoCorrect Entry

In this exercise, you will copy Bruce Carter on your memo. You need a courtesy copy notification. Since you work for him, you know you'll need to type his name frequently; therefore, it's a perfect candidate for a custom AutoCorrect entry.

1. Save your file as **WD02-D07-DanielsLetter-[FirstInitialLastName]**.

2. Choose **File→Options**.

Word 2013

3. Follow these steps to display the AutoCorrect dialog box:

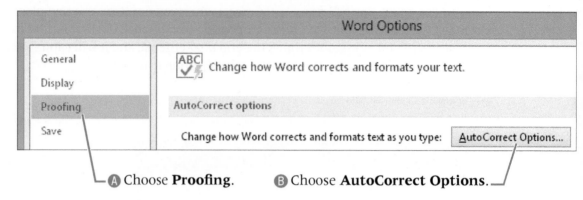

Ⓐ Choose **Proofing**. Ⓑ Choose **AutoCorrect Options**.

4. If necessary, click the **AutoCorrect** tab.

5. Follow these steps to add a custom AutoCorrect entry:

Ⓐ Type **bmc** in the Replace box.

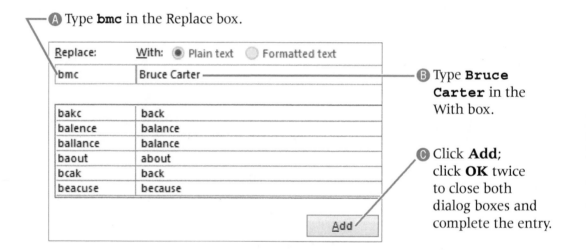

Ⓑ Type **Bruce Carter** in the With box.

Ⓒ Click **Add**; click **OK** twice to close both dialog boxes and complete the entry.

6. Make sure the insertion point is on the blank line following the Enclosures line. Add a blank line if necessary.

7. Follow these steps to add a courtesy copy notation:

Ⓐ Type **cc:** and tap Spacebar. Use the **AutoCorrect Options** smart tag to undo the automatic capitalization.

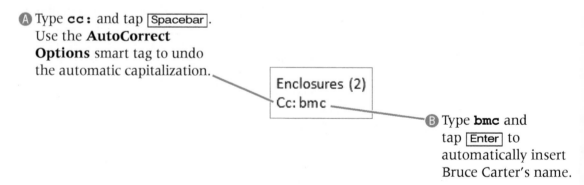

Ⓑ Type **bmc** and tap Enter to automatically insert Bruce Carter's name.

Delete the Custom AutoCorrect Entry

8. Choose **File→Options**.

9. Choose **Proofing** in the left panel, and then click **AutoCorrect Options**.

10. Follow these steps to remove the Bruce Carter entry:

Ⓐ Type **bmc** here and see that the list scrolls to Bruce Carter.

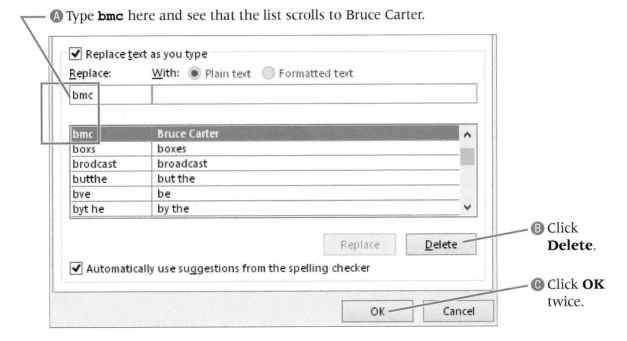

Ⓑ Click **Delete**.

Ⓒ Click **OK** twice.

11. Save the document.

Setting AutoFormat As You Type Options

Video Library   http://labyrinthelab.com/videos   Video Number: WD13-V0209

One of the tabs in the AutoCorrect dialog box is AutoFormat As You Type. You may have noticed certain formatting taking place automatically; this is happening because certain options are already set for you. For example, AutoFormat will replace two typed hyphens (--) with a dash (—), an ordinal (1st) with superscript (1st), or a fraction (1/2) with a fraction character (½).

AutoFormat can also be set to create an automatic bulleted list when you start a line with an asterisk (*), a hyphen (-), or a greater than symbol (>) followed by a space or tab. Likewise, it can be set to create a numbered list when you start a line with a number followed by a period or tab.

Task	Procedure
Customize AutoCorrect	■ Choose File→Options, then choose Proofing in the left panel.
	■ Click AutoCorrect Options, then click the AutoCorrect tab.
	■ Type the misspelled word or an abbreviation in the Replace box and type the correct term in the With box.
	■ Click OK twice.
Customize AutoFormat As You Type	■ Choose File→Options, then choose Proofing in the left panel.
	■ Click the AutoFormat As You Type tab and add a checkmark where you want Word to AutoFormat.
	■ Remove a checkmark for an item you don't want Word to AutoFormat.
	■ Click OK twice.

DEVELOP YOUR SKILLS WD02-D08
Turn On Automatic Numbering

In this exercise, you will turn on the option that automatically creates a numbered list when you begin a sentence with a number.

1. Choose **File→Options**.

2. Click **Proofing** in the left panel, and then click **AutoCorrect Options**.

3. Follow these steps to turn on automatic numbering:

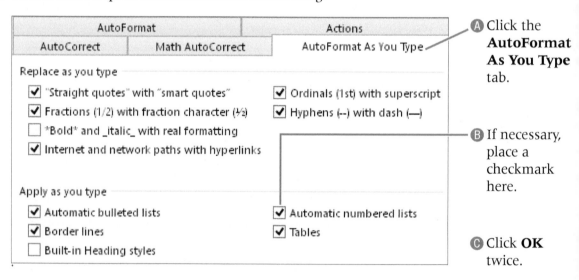

Ⓐ Click the **AutoFormat As You Type** tab.

Ⓑ If necessary, place a checkmark here.

Ⓒ Click **OK** twice.

4. Position the insertion point at the end of the document, tap [Enter], and then type **1.** (with a period) and tap [Spacebar].

5. Type **Item one** and tap [Enter].
   Word automatically generates the next number.

6. Select the numbered entries and tap [Delete].

Copying and Moving Text

Word 2013

Video Library   http://labyrinthelab.com/videos   Video Number: WD13-V0210

Cut, Copy, and Paste allow you to copy and move text within a document or between documents. The Cut, Copy, and Paste commands are located on the Home tab in the Clipboard group.

FROM THE KEYBOARD

Ctrl + X to cut

Ctrl + C to copy

Ctrl + V to paste

Working with the Clipboard

The Clipboard lets you collect multiple items and paste them in another location in the current document or in a different document. The Clipboard task pane must be visible on the screen to collect the items; otherwise, only one item at a time is saved for pasting.

FROM THE RIBBON

Home→Clipboard→ dialog box launcher to display the Clipboard

The Clipboard holds up to 24 items. When the items you cut or copy exceed 24, the Clipboard automatically deletes the oldest item(s). By default, a pop-up appears near the right edge of the taskbar when you copy an item, notifying you of the number of items in the Clipboard.

5 of 24 – Clipboard Item collected.

The *dialog box launcher* opens the Clipboard.

Paste all items at once.

Clear all items from the Clipboard.

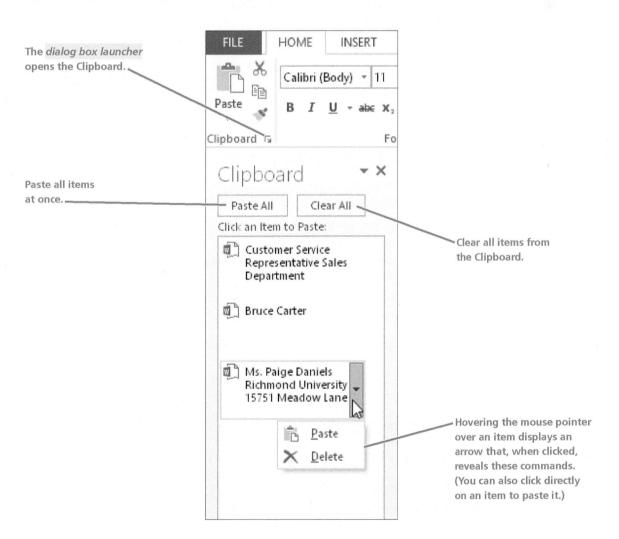

Hovering the mouse pointer over an item displays an arrow that, when clicked, reveals these commands. (You can also click directly on an item to paste it.)

CUT, COPY, AND PASTE COMMANDS	
Command	**Description**
Cut	Removes text and places it on the Clipboard
Copy	Leaves text where it is and places a copy on the Clipboard
Paste	Inserts cut or copied text at the insertion point

Use Cut, Copy, and Paste

In this exercise, you will move and copy information and work with the Clipboard.

1. Save your file as **WD02-D09-DanielsLetter-[FirstInitialLastName]**.

2. If necessary, choose **Home→Paragraph→Show/Hide** ¶ to display the formatting marks.

3. Follow these steps to place the date on the Clipboard:

Ⓐ Click here to open the Clipboard.

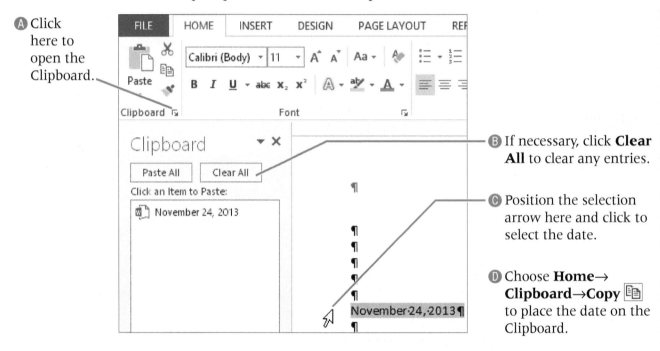

Ⓑ If necessary, click **Clear All** to clear any entries.

Ⓒ Position the selection arrow here and click to select the date.

Ⓓ Choose **Home→ Clipboard→Copy** 🗒 to place the date on the Clipboard.

4. Press ⌈Ctrl⌉ + ⌈End⌉ to move the insertion point to the bottom of the document.

5. Follow these steps to paste the date at the bottom of the document:

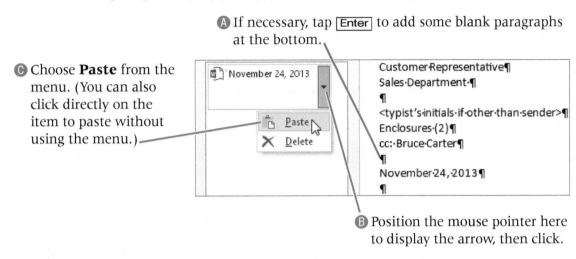

Ⓐ If necessary, tap Enter to add some blank paragraphs at the bottom.

Ⓒ Choose **Paste** from the menu. (You can also click directly on the item to paste without using the menu.)

November 24, 2013

Paste
Delete

Customer·Representative¶
Sales·Department·¶
¶
<typist's·initials·if·other·than·sender>¶
Enclosures·(2)¶
cc:·Bruce·Carter¶
¶
November·24,·2013¶
¶

Ⓑ Position the mouse pointer here to display the arrow, then click.

Notice the Paste Options smart tag that appears when you paste the text.

6. Click the **smart tag** to view its menu, and then click in the document to close it.

7. Tap Esc to dismiss the smart tag.

If you don't tap Esc, the button will disappear on its own.

8. Click **Undo** ↶ to undo the paste.

Move the Inside Address

9. Scroll to the top of the letter, and use the selection arrow to drag and select all four lines of the inside address.

10. Press Ctrl + X to cut the text and place it on the Clipboard.

11. Press Ctrl + End to move to the bottom of the document.

12. Click the inside address on the **Clipboard** to paste it at the insertion point.

13. Click **Close** ✕ on the **Clipboard** task pane.
    In the next exercise, you will return the inside address to its original position in the letter.

14. Save the document.

Editing with Drag and Drop

Video Library   http://labyrinthelab.com/videos   Video Number: WD13-V0211

The drag and drop feature produces the same result as cut, copy, and paste. It is efficient for moving or copying text a short distance within the same page. You select the text you wish to move, then drag it to the desired destination. If you press and hold ⟨Ctrl⟩ while dragging, the text is copied to the destination.

Drag and drop does not place the selection on the Clipboard task pane.

DEVELOP YOUR SKILLS WD02-D10
Use Drag and Drop

In this exercise, you will use drag and drop to move the inside address back to the top of the document.

1. If necessary, scroll so you can see both the inside address and the blank line above the salutation.

2. Save your file as **WD02-D10-DanielsLetter-[FirstInitialLastName]**.

3. Click and drag to select the inside address.

4. Position the mouse pointer over the highlighted text.
   The pointer now looks like a white arrow.

5. Follow these steps to move the selected text:

   Ⓐ Press the mouse button, and drag the mouse pointer to the blank line above the salutation. A thick insertion point travels with the arrow. The rectangle on the arrow indicates you are in drag-and-drop mode.

   Ⓑ Release the mouse button to complete the move; click to deselect.

6. Save the document.

Switching Between Documents

Video Library   http://labyrinthelab.com/videos   Video Number: WD13-V0212

There are several techniques for switching between documents. In the next exercise, you will use the taskbar at the bottom of the screen to do it. When several documents are open at the same time, they may share one taskbar button.

A small image of each open document displays when you hover the mouse pointer over the taskbar button. Below, the Daniels letter is the active document, and you can tell because it's lighter than the others. Clicking the image opens the document on the screen.

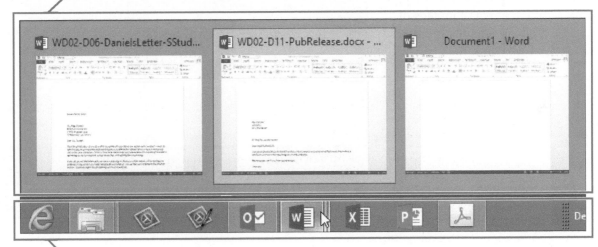

Open Word documents

Taskbar buttons for open programs (Notice the Word button has three documents stacked on it.)

Your buttons may be different from the ones shown here, depending on which program buttons are displayed on your computer's taskbar.

Switch and Copy Between Documents

In this exercise, you will copy and paste between two documents using the taskbar buttons to switch from one document to another.

1. Open **WD02-D11-PubRelease** from the **WD2013 Lesson 02** folder and save it as `WD02-D11-PubRelease-[FirstInitialLastName]`.

2. Follow these steps to switch to your WD02-D10-DanielsLetter-[FirstInitialLastName] file:

Ⓐ Hover the mouse pointer over the **Word taskbar button** to display small images of the documents.

Ⓑ Click **WD02-D10-DanielsLetter-[FirstInitialLastName]**.

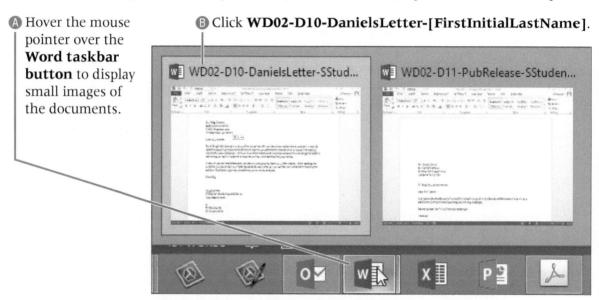

3. Select *Bruce Carter* in the second line of the second paragraph.

4. Press `Ctrl` + `C` to copy the name.

Switch Documents

5. Using the taskbar, switch to **WD02-D11-PubRelease-[FirstInitialLastName]**.

6. Select the *YOUR NAME* line in the inside address.

7. Press `Ctrl` + `V` to paste *Bruce Carter* over the selected text, and then, if necessary, tap `Enter` to move *ADDRESS* back to the second line.

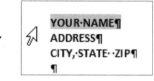

8. Click the insertion point in front of *Bruce Carter*, type **Mr.**, and tap `Spacebar`.

9. Select the last two lines of the inside address and type the following:

```
My Virtual Campus
123 Cherry Blossom Lane
Salisbury, MD 21801
```

10. There should be two blank lines between the inside address and the RE: line. Add or delete blank lines as needed.

11. Select *SALES MANAGER* in the salutation and press [Ctrl]+[V] to paste *Bruce Carter* again.

12. Select *Bruce* and type **Mr.** in its place.

13. Select *SALES MANAGER* in the body paragraph and paste the name again.

14. Using the **taskbar**, switch back to the Daniels letter.

15. Select *Paige Daniels* in the inside address and press [Ctrl]+[C] to copy her name.

16. Switch back to the publicity release and paste her name over *YOUR NAME* at the bottom.

17. Save the changes you made in **WD02-D11-PubRelease-[FirstInitialLastName]**, and then close it.

Using Page Layout Options

Video Library   http://labyrinthelab.com/videos   Video Number: WD13-V0213

The three most commonly used page layout options are margins, page orientation, and paper size. All of these are located in the Page Setup group on the Page Layout tab.

Setting Margins

Margins determine the amount of white space between the text and the edge of the paper. You can set margins for the entire document, a section, or selected text. The Margins gallery displays preset top, bottom, left, and right margins. The Custom Margins option at the bottom of the gallery opens a dialog box where you can set custom margins.

Margins Orientation Size Columns Breaks Line N a-bc Hypher	
Last Custom Setting ———————	——Most recent custom margin settings.
Top: 1" Bottom: 1"	
Left: 1.5" Right: 1.5"	
Normal ———————————	——Word's default 1-inch margins.
Top: 1" Bottom: 1"	
Left: 1" Right: 1"	
Narrow	
Top: 0.5" Bottom: 0.5"	
Left: 0.5" Right: 0.5"	——These options represent some typical margin settings.
Moderate	
Top: 1" Bottom: 1"	
Left: 0.75" Right: 0.75"	
Wide	
Top: 1" Bottom: 1"	
Left: 2" Right: 2"	
Mirrored ———————————	——Mirrored margins are for facing pages, as in a book or a magazine.
Top: 1" Bottom: 1"	
Inside: 1.25" Outside: 1"	
Custom Margins... ———————	——Customize the document margins here.

QUICK REFERENCE	SETTING MARGINS
Task	**Procedure**
Change margins from the Margins gallery	▪ Choose Page Layout→Page Setup→Margins and choose a predefined margin setting.
Set custom margins	▪ Choose Page Layout→Page Setup→Margins and choose Custom Margins.
	▪ Enter settings for top, bottom, left, and right margins.

Set Margins

In this exercise, you will use the Margins gallery and the Page Setup dialog box to change the document's margins.

1. Choose **Page Layout→Page Setup→Margins** ⬜.
2. Choose **Narrow** from the gallery and observe the impact on your document.
3. Click **Margins** ⬜ again and choose **Wide** to see how that affects the document.
4. Open the gallery again and change the margins back to **Normal**.

Set Custom Margins

5. Display the gallery and choose **Custom Margins** from the bottom of the menu to open the Page Setup dialog box.

Clicking the dialog box launcher ⬛ at the bottom-right corner of the Page Setup group also opens the Page Setup dialog box.

Notice the options for changing the top, bottom, left, and right margins.

6. Set the left and right margins to **1.5 inches**.
7. Click **OK** and notice the change in your document's margins.
8. Click **Margins** ⬜ and choose **Normal**.

Setting Page Orientation and Paper Size

Video Library   http://labyrinthelab.com/videos   Video Number: WD13-V0214

You can set page orientation and paper size using the Page Layout tab. The page orientation determines how the text is laid out on the paper. The options are Portrait (vertical) or Landscape (horizontal). The default orientation is Portrait. Some common uses for landscape orientation include brochures, flyers, wide tables, and so forth.

Most documents use the standard letter-size paper. However, Word supports the use of many other paper sizes, including legal, and also allows you to create custom sizes.

Working with Print and Print Preview

The Print command and Print Preview feature are available in Backstage view. The left pane includes printer and page layout options; the right pane is a preview of your document showing how it will look when printed. You can experiment with different options and see the results immediately.

Set number of copies to print, choose a different printer, and view printer properties.

Preview the document before printing.

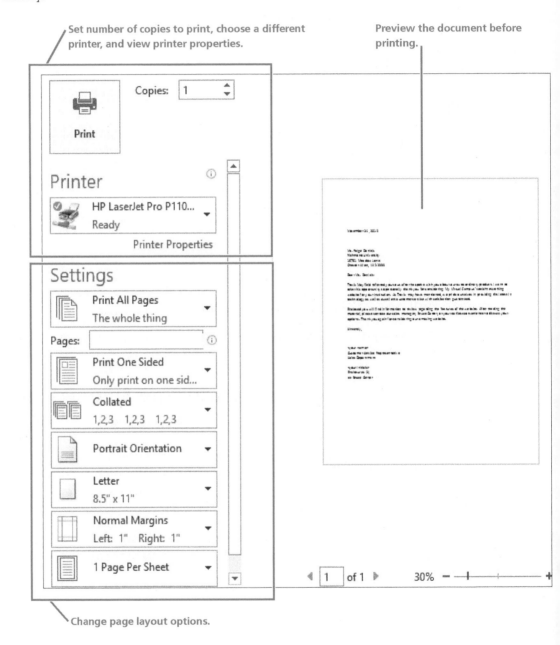

Change page layout options.

QUICK REFERENCE	SETTING PAGE ORIENTATION AND PAPER SIZE AND WORKING WITH PRINT
Task	**Procedure**
Change the page orientation	■ Choose Page Layout→Page Setup→Orientation. ■ Choose the desired orientation.
Change the paper size	■ Choose Page Layout→Page Setup→Size. ■ Choose the desired size; or, choose More Paper Sizes to create a custom paper size.
Print and Print Preview	■ Choose File→Print.

DEVELOP YOUR SKILLS WD02-D13

Change Page Layout and Print Options

In this exercise, you will experiment with the page orientation and paper size options. You will preview page orientation, and you will work with printing options.

Work with Page Orientation

1. Choose **File→Print**.

   The page is currently in the default Portrait orientation. Previewing the entire page allows you to see this clearly.

2. Click **Back** ⬅ in the upper-left corner to close Backstage view.

3. Choose **Page Layout→Page Setup→Orientation** ⬚ →**Landscape**.

4. Choose **File→Print** to preview landscape orientation.

5. Click **Back** ⬅.

6. Choose **Page Layout→Page Setup→Orientation** ⬚ again, and then choose **Portrait** to change the page back to a vertical layout.

View Paper Size Options

7. Choose **Page Layout→Page Setup→Size** ⬚ →**Legal**.

8. Scroll down to observe the legal paper.

9. Choose **Size** ⬚ again and choose **Letter**.

Explore Print Options

10. Choose **File→Print**.

11. Set the Copies box to **2**.

12. Click below the Settings heading and choose **Print Current Page**.

Observe Page Settings Options

13. Follow these steps to view other settings in the Print screen:

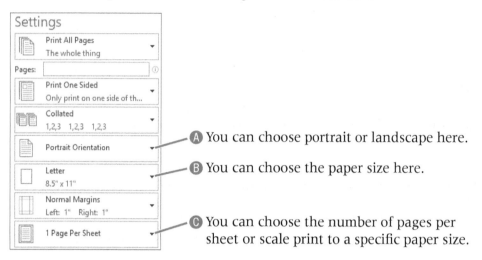

Ⓐ You can choose portrait or landscape here.

Ⓑ You can choose the paper size here.

Ⓒ You can choose the number of pages per sheet or scale print to a specific paper size.

14. You won't print at this time, so click **Back** [←].

15. Choose **Home→Paragraph→Show/Hide** ¶ to turn off formatting marks.

16. Save and close the document, then exit from **Word**.

Concepts Review

To check your knowledge of the key concepts introduced in this lesson, complete the Concepts Review quiz by choosing the appropriate access option below.

If you are...	Then access the quiz by...
Using the Labyrinth Video Library	Going to http://labyrinthelab.com/videos
Using eLab	Logging in, choosing Content, and navigating to the Concepts Review quiz for this lesson
Not using the Labyrinth Video Library or eLab	Going to the student resource center for this book

Reinforce Your Skills

Create a Block-Style Letter with an Envelope

In this exercise, you will use traditional spacing in a block-style business letter and let Word Wrap and AutoComplete take effect. Then you will create an envelope for the letter.

Create a New Document and Insert Text

1. Start **Word** and create a new document based on the **Single Spaced (Blank)** template.

2. When the template description window appears, click **Create** .

3. Choose **Home→Paragraph→Show/Hide** ¶ to display formatting marks.

4. Tap Enter five times to position the insertion point approximately **2 inches** from the top of the page.

5. Type **Nove** to begin the date, tap Enter when the AutoComplete prompt appears, and then finish typing the date as **November 19, 2013**.

6. Tap Enter four times.

7. Complete the block style letter as shown on the next page, tapping Enter wherever a paragraph symbol appears.

¶

¶
¶
¶
¶
¶
November·19,·2013¶
¶
¶
¶
Current·Resident·¶
123·Peach·Blossom·Lane¶
Atlanta,·GA·30313¶
¶
Dear·Neighbor:¶
¶
I·am·the·recycling·representative·for·Kids·for·Change,·and·our·motto·is·Think·Globally,·Act·Locally.·We·
know·that·recycling·large·objects·takes·extra·effort·since·they·do·not·fit·in·your·city-provided·recycle·
cans.·We·would·like·to·give·you·a·hand.·¶
¶
On·Tuesday,·November·26th,·we·will·collect·oversized·recyclable·objects·in·your·neighborhood.·Please·
place·your·collectables··at·the·curb·in·front·of·your·house·before·9:00·a.m.·Please·visit·
http://recycleatlanta.org/·to·ensure·you·are·following·the·city's·recycling·guidelines.··¶
¶
Thank·you·for·caring·about·our·planet.¶
¶
Yours·truly,¶
¶
¶
¶
Tania·Tulip¶
Recycling·Representative¶
Kids·for·Change¶
¶

Create an Envelope

8. Press Ctrl + Home .

9. Choose **Mailings→Create→Envelopes** 🖃 .

10. In the **Envelopes and Labels** dialog box, if necessary, check the **Omit** box to prevent a return address from being added to the envelope.

11. Click **Add to Document**.

12. Save the letter in your **WD2013 Lesson 02** folder as `WD02-R01-Recycle-[FirstInitialLastName]`. Close the file and exit **Word**.

13. Submit your final file based on the guidelines provided by your instructor.

    To view examples of how your file or files should look at the end of this exercise, go to the student resource center.

Edit a Document

In this exercise, you will edit a letter, create an AutoCorrect shortcut, and move a paragraph. You will then copy the letter into a new document, change margins and page orientation, and preview the letter.

Select and Edit Text

1. Start **Word**. Open **WD02-R02-CuyahogaCamp** from your **WD2013 Lesson 02** folder and save it as `WD02-R02-CuyahogaCamp-[FirstInitialLastName]`.

2. Make the following edits to the letter:

   - At the end of the first paragraph, replace the period with a comma and complete the sentence with the following, adding and deleting spaces as needed: `including hiking, bird watching, tree planting, and bug hunting.`

   - Double-click the word *sing* at the end of the third paragraph and tap `Delete`.

   - Position the insertion point at the end of the fourth paragraph, and tap `Delete` twice to combine the fourth and fifth paragraphs.

   - In the last paragraph, select the *8* in *28th* and replace it with **7**.

   - The date of the 28th was correct after all; click **Undo** `↺` on the Quick Access toolbar, and then click in the letter to deselect the text affected by the Undo command.

Work with AutoCorrect

Cuyahoga Camp is a term you will use frequently, so you will create an AutoCorrect shortcut.

3. Choose **File→Options** and choose **Proofing** from the left panel; then click **AutoCorrect Options**.

4. Type **cc** in the **Replace** box, tap `Tab`, and type **Camp Cuyahoga** in the **With** box. Click the **Add** button, and the click **OK** twice.

5. Position the insertion point to the right of *spend* in the first line of the first paragraph and tap `Spacebar`.

6. Type this text after the space: **a day with us at cc for**

   Word automatically corrects cc *to* Camp Cuyahoga.

7. At the end of the sentence, select *with us* and tap `Delete`.

8. Position the insertion point on the blank line following Olivia Pledger at the end of the letter, type **cc**, and tap `Enter`.

   AutoCorrect corrects cc *to be* Camp Cuyahoga. *Now you will delete your AutoCorrect shortcut.*

   > Olivia Pledger
   > Camp Cuyahoga

9. Choose **File→Options**, and then choose **Proofing** from the left panel.

10. Click **AutoCorrect Options**, and type **cc** in the **Replace** box.

    Your shortcut is now highlighted in the list.

11. Click **Delete**, and then click **OK** twice.

Move a Paragraph

12. Position the mouse pointer in the margin to the left of the second paragraph and drag down to select the paragraph and the blank line following it.

    The selected paragraph and blank line below it are highlighted.

    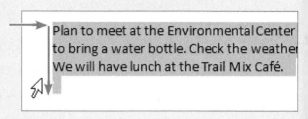

13. Press Ctrl + X to cut the paragraph.

    When you issued the Cut command, everything that was selected (paragraph and following blank line) was deleted and placed on the Clipboard, ready for you to paste it elsewhere.

14. Position the insertion point to the left of *We* in the last paragraph, and press Ctrl + V to paste the text.

Copy Text and Switch Between Documents

Since you will send this letter to other attendees, you will practice copying and pasting it into a blank document.

15. Choose **File→New**. Start a new document using the **Single Spaced (Blank)** template.

16. Click **Create** to open the blank document.

17. Use the **Word** taskbar button to switch back to **WD02-R02-CuyahogaCamp-[FirstInitialLastName]**.

18. Position the mouse pointer to the left of the word *Kids* in the first paragraph and drag down to the end of the letter.

19. Tap Ctrl + C and use the **Word** taskbar button to switch back to your new document.

20. Click in the document and press Ctrl + V.

    That was just a test; you won't save the letter now.

21. Choose **File→Close**. Click **Don't Save** when the message appears.

Use Page Layout Options and Print Preview

22. Click in the **Cuyahoga Camp** document to deselect.

23. Choose **Page Layout→Page Setup→Margins** and choose **Narrow**.

24. Choose **Page Layout→Page Setup→Orientation** and choose **Landscape**.

25. Choose **File→Print** to preview the document.

    The document looked better to begin with.

26. Click **Back**.

27. Click **Undo** twice to return the letter to its original margins and orientation.

28. Save and close the document and exit from **Word**.

29. Submit your final file based on the guidelines provided by your instructor.

    To view examples of how your file or files should look at the end of this exercise, go to the student resource center.

Create, Edit, and Print Preview a Letter

In this exercise, you will type a fundraising letter and an envelope and make some editing changes. You will create an AutoCorrect shortcut, and then add some text to the letter that you will copy from another document. Finally, you will preview the letter and modify the margins.

Insert Text and Use AutoComplete

You have been asked to draft a letter to send to Kids for Change members regarding the car wash fundraiser, which will be discussed at the next monthly meeting.

1. Start **Word**. Create a new document using the **Single Spaced (Blank)** template.

2. When the window appears describing the template, click **Create** 📄.

3. Save the letter as **WD02-R03-CarWash-[FirstInitialLastName]** in your **WD2013 Lesson 02** folder.

4. If necessary, choose **Home→Paragraph→Show/Hide** ¶ to display formatting marks.

5. Type this letter, tapping Enter wherever you see a paragraph symbol. Use **AutoComplete** to help with the dates.

¶
¶
¶
¶
¶
August·6,·2013¶
¶
¶
¶
MEMBER·NAME¶
STREET·ADDRESS¶
CITY,·STATE·ZIP¶
¶
Dear·MEMBER,·¶
¶
Our·local·chapter·of·Kids·for·Change·is·planning·to·hold·a·car·wash·fundraiser·to·collect·$300·in·order·to·adopt·a·seal·at·the·Center·for·Seals.··We're·aiming·for·August·31st·as·the·car·wash·date.·The·next·monthly·meeting·will·be·a·planning·session·for·the·car·wash.·Here·are·some·things·to·think·about·before·the·meeting:¶
¶

Create an Envelope

6. Position the insertion point at the top of the document.

7. Choose **Mailings→Create→Envelopes** 🔲.

8. In the dialog box, if necessary, check the **Omit** box to prevent a return address, and then click **Add to Document**.

Select and Edit Text

Looking back over what you have typed, you see some changes you would like to make.

9. In the first line of the first paragraph, select *is planning* and replace it with **plans**.

10. Toward the end of the same line, select *in order* and tap ⎡Delete⎤.

11. In the next line, select *August 31ˢᵗ as the car wash date* and replace it with **Saturday, September 7th.**

12. Tap ⎡Spacebar⎤ and the suffix following 7 changes to a superscript.

13. Tap ⎡Backspace⎤ to remove the extra space. Save your changes.

Work with AutoCorrect

Next you will check to see if an AutoFormat as You Type option caused th *to change to a superscript.*

14. Choose **File→Options**, and then choose **Proofing** from the left panel.

15. Click **AutoCorrect Options**. When the dialog box opens, click the **AutoFormat As You Type** tab.

   The checkmark in the box next to Ordinals (1st) with Superscript is causing the superscripts. The checkmark in the box next to Automatic Numbered Lists will help you with the next part of the letter.

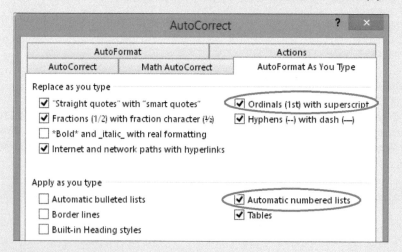

16. Click **OK** twice.

17. Hover the mouse pointer over the superscript in the September date, and drag down to display the **AutoCorrect Options smart tag**.

18. Click the tag and observe, but don't click, the Undo Superscript option.

19. Click away from the tag to close it.

20. Position the insertion point next to the paragraph symbol in the blank line following the main paragraph and tap Enter.

21. Type **1.** and tap Spacebar to begin automatic numbering.

    The AutoCorrect Options smart tag appears.

22. Click the **smart tag** to see the menu options; click away from the tag to close it.

23. Type the rest of the letter as shown, tapping Enter where you see a paragraph symbol.

    Hint: When you finish item 5, tap Enter three times: twice to turn off numbering and once to generate a blank line after the list.

    > meeting·will·be·a·planning·session·for·the·car·wash.·Here·are·some·things·to·think·about·before·the·meeting:¶
    > ¶
    >   1.→Choose·a·location.·Our·options·are·the·parking·lots·at·Jake's·Gas·Station,·Beulah's·Diner,·or·Dick's·Grocery·Store.¶
    >   2.→What·hours·can·you·volunteer·on·September·7th?¶
    >   3.→Can·you·supply·a·hose,·vacuum,·soap,·brushes,·sponges,·or·rags?¶
    >   4.→Should·we·set·a·price·or·request·a·donation?¶
    >   5.→Can·you·design·a·flyer·to·let·people·know·that·this·is·for·a·good·cause?¶
    > ¶
    > We·look·forward·to·a·great·planning·session.·See·you·at·the·meeting!¶
    > ¶
    > Sincerely,¶
    > ¶
    > ¶
    > ¶
    > Robert·Chan¶
    > Kids·for·Change¶

Copy Text and Switch Between Documents

The supervisor wants to include information about the Center for Seals so the members will know the good work this organization does. You will copy the information from a document the supervisor provided.

24. Open **WD02-R03-Seals** from your **WD2013 Lesson 02** folder.

25. Press Ctrl + A to select all and then press Ctrl + C to copy all.

26. Close the **WD02-R03-Seals** document.

    Your car wash letter will be in the foreground.

27. Position the insertion point after the space following the first sentence in the first paragraph and tap Enter.

    > Our·local·chapter·of·Kids·for·Change·plans·to·hold·a·car·wash·fundraiser·to·collect·$300·to·adopt·a·seal·at·the·Center·for·Seals.·¶
    > We·are·aiming·for·Saturday,·September·7th·for·the·car·wash.·The·next·monthly·meeting·will·be·a·planning·session·for·the·car·wash.·Here·are·some·things·to·think·about·before·the·meeting:¶

28. Position the insertion point at the end of the first paragraph and press Ctrl + V.

    The Seals information is now part of the first paragraph.

Use Page Layout Options and Print Preview

Next you will preview the letter to see if it is well balanced on the page.

29. Choose **File→Print**, and preview the letter.

    You decide to widen the margins.

30. Click **Back** .

31. Choose **Page Layout→Page Setup→Margins** and choose **Custom Margins** at the bottom of the gallery.

32. Use the spin boxes to change the Left and Right margins to 1.5", then click **OK**.

33. Choose **File→Print** to preview the letter.

    That looks better.

34. Click **Back** .

35. Save and close your letter, then exit from **Word**.

36. Submit your final file based on the guidelines provided by your instructor.

Apply Your Skills

Create a Letter and an Envelope

In this exercise, you will create a modified block-style letter, and you'll turn on the ruler to ensure the correct spacing for the date, complimentary close, and signature block. You will use AutoComplete to help you with the dates, and you will add an envelope to the letter.

Create a Block-Style Letter and Enter Text

1. Start **Word**. Create a new document using the **Single Spaced (Blank)** template.

2. Save the file in your **WD2013 Lesson 02** folder as `WD02-A01-BellLetter-[FirstInitialLastName]`.

3. Choose **View→Show→Ruler**.

4. Create the **modified block-style letter** shown in the following illustration.

Today's Date

Mrs. Suzanne Lee
8445 South Princeton Street
Chicago, IL 60628

Dear Mrs. Lee:

Congratulations on your outstanding sales achievement! Universal Corporate Events is organizing your Paris tour, which departs Saturday, October 6th and returns Wednesday, October 16th.

Please plan to attend the orientation meeting on Wednesday, September 18th in the Lake View conference room at 10:00 a.m.

We look forward to making your trip a memorable event!

Best regards,

Jack Bell
Universal Corporate Events

---

5. Follow these guidelines as you type your letter:
   - Space down the proper distance from the top of the page.
   - Use **AutoComplete** to help you with the dates.
   - Use ⎯Tab⎯ to align the date, closing, and signature block at **3 inches** on the ruler. (You'll need to tap ⎯Tab⎯ six times.)
   - Use correct spacing.

Create an Envelope

6. Create an envelope with no return address, and add it to the top of your letter.

7. Save and close the document; exit from **Word**.

8. Submit your final file based on the guidelines provided by your instructor.

   To view examples of how your file or files should look at the end of this exercise, go to the student resource center.

Edit a Document

In this exercise, you will make changes to a letter and copy text from another document into it. Then you will create an AutoCorrect entry, change margins, and preview your letter.

Edit Text and Work with AutoCorrect

1. Start **Word**. Open **WD02-A02-SFTours** from your **WD2013 Lesson 02** folder and save it as `WD02-A02-SFTours-[FirstInitialLastName]`.

2. Make the following editing changes, adjusting spacing as needed:

   - In the first line of the first paragraph, select *needs regarding planning your* and replace it with **annual**.
   - In the second line of the same paragraph, insert **San Francisco** to the left of *meeting*, and at the end of that sentence, Delete *in San Francisco*.
   - In the first line of the Sausalito paragraph, type **San Francisco** to the left of *skyline* and Delete *San Francisco* later in that sentence.
   - In the same sentence, type **the** to the left of *Bay*.
   - In the second sentence, type **waterfront** before *restaurant* and Delete *built over the water*. In the same sentence, Delete *the waterfront* and the comma that follows it.
   - In the second line of the Muir Woods paragraph, replace *wonderful* with **majestic**.

Switch Between Documents and Copy Text

Now you will copy some tour ideas from another document.

3. Open **WD02-A02-SiliconValley** from your **WD2013 Lesson 02** folder.

4. Select the entire document and copy it.

5. Switch back to the original letter, and position the insertion point on the second blank line following the Muir Woods paragraph.

6. Paste the copied text in the document; switch back to **WD02-A02-SiliconValley** and close it.

7. Type the current date at the top of the letter, positioning it approximately one inch from the top of the page.

8. Add the appropriate space after the date and type the following inside address:

   ```
   Ms. Addison Alexander
   Reukert Technology
   123 Apple Blossom Lane
   Detroit, MI 48217
   ```

9. If necessary, adjust the space between the address and the salutation.

Work with AutoCorrect, Margins, and Print Preview

10. Create an **AutoCorrect shortcut** for *Universal Corporate Events* using **uce** as the shortcut characters, but don't close the dialog box.

11. Press ⎇Alt + Prt Screen to take a screenshot of the dialog box showing your new entry; click **OK** twice to close the dialog boxes.

12. Paste the screenshot into a new, blank Word document and save it as **WD02-A02-ScnCap-[FirstInitialLastName]** in your **WD2013 Lesson 02** folder.

13. Close the file.

14. Change the margins in your letter to the **Narrow** setting in the Margins gallery.

15. Add the following complimentary close and signature block using your AutoCorrect shortcut for the company name, and ensure correct spacing.

    ```
    Sincerely,
    Geoff Simons
    Universal Corporate Events
    ```

16. Open the **Word Options** window, and delete the **AutoCorrect entry** you just created.

17. Save and close your file; exit from **Word**.

18. Submit your final files based on the guidelines provided by your instructor.
    To view examples of how your file or files should look at the end of this exercise, go to the student resource center.

APPLY YOUR SKILLS WD02-A03

Type and Edit a Letter, Use AutoCorrect, and Copy Text

In this exercise, you will prepare a block-style letter and an envelope to send to a Universal Corporate Events employee, and you will make editing changes to the letter and work with AutoCorrect. You will copy text from another document, and you will preview the letter.

Insert Text and Add an Envelope

1. Start **Word**. Create a new document based on the **Single Spaced (Blank)** template.

2. Save your letter as **WD02-A03-WilliamsLtr-[FirstInitialLastName]** in your **WD2013 Lesson 02** folder.

3. Type this letter.

¶
¶
¶
¶
¶
Current·Date¶
¶
¶
¶
Mr.·Bill·Williams¶
Universal·Corporate·Events¶
14·University·Avenue¶
San·Rafael,·CA·94901¶
¶
Dear·Bill:¶
¶
You·have·been·selected·to·be·our·on-site·ambassador·at·Vaughn·Storage·Devices'·Hawaiian·event,·
scheduled·for·September·1,·2013·through·September·7,·2013.·Martin·McCann·is·the·other·
representative·who·will·be·working·this·event.¶
¶
You·will·be·responsible·for·helping·clients·with·airline·reservations,·hotel·arrangements,·and·side·tour·
transportation.·You·will·also·coordinate·between·the·hotel·and·event·speakers·and·entertainment.··¶
¶
¶

4. Create an envelope with no return address; add it to the top of your letter.

Edit Text

5. Make the following edits to the letter:
   - In the first line of the first paragraph, change *ambassador* to **representative**.
   - In the same line, change *Hawaiian* to **Kauai**.
   - In the second line of the first paragraph, change the September dates to **8** through **14**.
   - At the beginning of the second paragraph, position the insertion point after *You*, tap [Spacebar], and type **and Martin**.
   - Change *entertainment* at the end of the second paragraph to **entertainers**.

Work with AutoFormat

Next you will type ordinals (numbers that indicate order). Word's AutoFormat feature automatically changes the ordinal suffixes to superscripts. You will turn that feature off.

6. Open the **Word Options window**, choose **Proofing** from the left panel, and click **AutoCorrect Options**.

7. Click the **AutoFormat as You Type** tab, click in the box next to **Ordinals (1st) with Superscript** to remove the checkmark, and click **OK** twice.

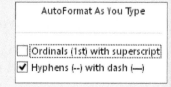

8. Position the insertion point on the second blank line at the end of the document and type the following: **The side tours will take place on September 9th, 10th, 11th, and 12th.**

9. Reset the **Ordinals** checkbox back to its original state.

Switch Between Documents and Copy Text

10. Open **WD02-A03-SideTours** from the **WD2013 Lesson 02** folder.

11. Select and copy the text.

12. Switch back to the original letter and paste the text at the end of the sentence you just typed.

13. Switch back to **WD02-A03-SideTours** and close it.

14. Add the following closing and signature block to the end of the letter; be sure to use the correct spacing.

Sincerely,

Jose Ramirez
Universal Corporate Events

Use Page Layout Options

15. Choose **Page Layout→Page Setup→Size**, and choose **Executive** from the gallery.

16. Preview the document. You may need to adjust the zoom control in the bottom-right corner of the window to see the letter and the envelope at the same time.
    You realize that executive size paper doesn't work well with a standard business envelope.

17. Change the paper size back to **Letter**.

18. Save your letter and close it; exit from **Word**.

19. Submit your final file based on the guidelines provided by your instructor.

Extend Your Skills

In the course of working through the Extend Your Skills exercises, you will think critically as you use the skills taught in the lesson to complete the assigned projects. To evaluate your mastery and completion of the exercises, your instructor may use a rubric, with which more points are allotted according to performance characteristics. (The more you do, the more you earn!) Ask your instructor how your work will be evaluated.

WD02-E01 That's the Way I See It

You have decided to start your own landscaping business, and you are going to conduct some online research to see what's involved. Your friend is studying for his MBA, and you will send him a letter containing the results of your research and ask him what he thinks of your idea.

Create a block-style letter, including a list of five landscaping tools that your research shows you will need to purchase. Then research what is involved in becoming certified as a landscape professional, and explain to your friend how you plan to earn your certification. Finally, list three tips for running a successful landscaping business. The letter should include at least three paragraphs (one to give an overview of the business, one or more to discuss certification, and one for the conclusion) and a list of three tips. The spacing in the inside address and signature block should be 1.0. Proof your work and, as necessary, use Copy and Paste or drag and drop to make changes.

Set the orientation to Landscape, and then view your letter in Print Preview. Exit Backstage view and return the orientation to Portrait. Save the file in your **WD2013 Lesson 02** folder as **WD02-E01-NewBusiness-[FirstInitialLastName]**. You will be evaluated based on the inclusion of all elements specified, your ability to follow directions, your ability to apply newly learned skills to a real-world situation, your creativity, and the relevance of your topic and/or data choice(s). Submit your final file based on the guidelines provided by your instructor.

WD02-E02 Be Your Own Boss

Blue Jean Landscaping has a new client from outside of your region who learned about your services on the Internet. She would like you to landscape her front yard. Use your imagination to decide on the client's location and climate. Conduct online research to determine what shrubs and other plants work well for the climate you chose (for example, a home in Chicago would take different plants compared to a home in San Francisco). Send the client a modified block-style letter with indented paragraphs and traditional letter line spacing to propose four plant options that would work well for her. The letter should contain both an introductory and concluding paragraph, as well as a list of four plant options, and each option should be associated with two to three sentences that explain why it is a good choice for the client's front yard. Since you will, no doubt, type "Blue Jean Landscaping" multiple times, set up an AutoCorrect entry associated with BJL.

Save the letter as **WD02-E02-NewClient-[FirstInitialLastName]** in your **WD2013 Lesson 02** folder. Proof your work and, as necessary, use Copy and Paste and drag and drop to make edits. Remove the AutoCorrect entry. Then save and close the letter. You will be evaluated based on the inclusion of all elements specified, your ability to follow directions, your ability to apply newly learned skills to a real-world situation, your creativity, and your demonstration of an entrepreneurial spirit. Submit your final file based on the guidelines provided by your instructor.

Transfer Your Skills

In the course of working through the Transfer Your Skills exercises, you will use critical-thinking and creativity skills to complete the assigned projects using skills taught in the lesson. To evaluate your mastery and completion of the exercises, your instructor may use a rubric, with which more points are allotted according to performance characteristics. (The more you do, the more you earn!) Ask your instructor how your work will be evaluated.

WD02-T01 Use the Web as a Learning Tool

Throughout this book, you will be provided with an opportunity to use the Internet as a learning tool by completing WebQuests. According to the original creators of WebQuests, as described on their website (WebQuest.org), a WebQuest is "an inquiry-oriented activity in which most or all of the information used by learners is drawn from the web." To complete the WebQuest projects in this book, navigate to the student resource center and choose the WebQuest for the lesson on which you are currently working. The subject of each WebQuest will be relevant to the material found in the lesson.

WebQuest Subject: Proper business correspondence etiquette.

Submit your final file(s) based on the guidelines provided by your instructor.

WD02-T02 Demonstrate Proficiency

As the owner of Stormy BBQ, you've decided to hold a chili cook-off to attract new clients. Use online research to learn how to have a successful cook-off, and also research rules for the chefs to ensure that they are competing on a level playing field.

Create a letter using the style of your choice (making sure to properly format it) to send out to prospective chili chefs listing three important guidelines for a successful cook-off and three competition rules for your chefs. The letter should include both an introductory and a concluding paragraph, as well as the rules that have been established. Make up the name of the first chef you wish to invite and include the information in the inside address. Create an envelope addressed to the chef with no return address.

Proof your work and, as necessary, use Copy and Paste or drag and drop to make edits. Change all margins to 0.5" and view the effect in Print Preview.

Save your letter in the **WD2013 Lesson 02** folder as `WD02-T02-ChiliChef-[FirstInitialLastName]`. Submit your final file based on the guidelines provided by your instructor.

Creating a Memorandum and a Press Release

In this lesson, you will expand your basic Word skills. You will create a memo, apply character formatting, and use spelling and grammar checking. You will refine your word choice with the thesaurus, and you'll learn some efficient ways to navigate in documents. Finally, you will transform PDF files into fully editable Word documents.

LEARNING OBJECTIVES

After studying this lesson, you will be able to:

- Use Word's default tabs
- Insert dates, symbols, and page breaks
- Work with proofreading tools and the thesaurus
- Work with character formatting features
- Edit PDF files in Word

Preparing a Memorandum

My Virtual Campus continues to grow and add the latest advances in technology. The public relations representative has asked you to create a memorandum and attach a press release announcing the launch of MyResume, which is being integrated into the website. You understand the importance of protecting proprietary information, so you use the appropriate trademark designations in your documents.

When the marketing department decides to change the product name, the Find and Replace feature makes changing the name throughout the document a snap.

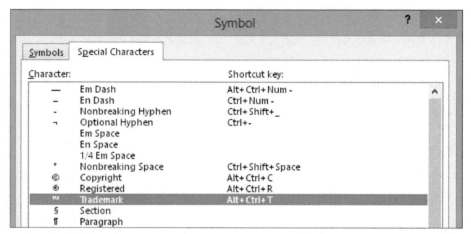

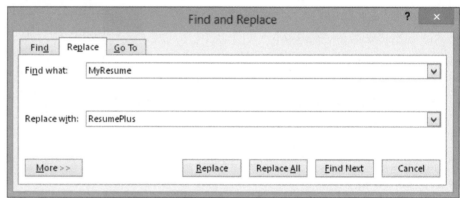

Typing a Memorandum

Word 2013

Video Library http://labyrinthelab.com/videos   Video Number: WD13-V0301

There are a variety of acceptable memorandum styles in use today. They all contain the same elements, but with varied formatting. The style shown here is a traditional style with minimal formatting.

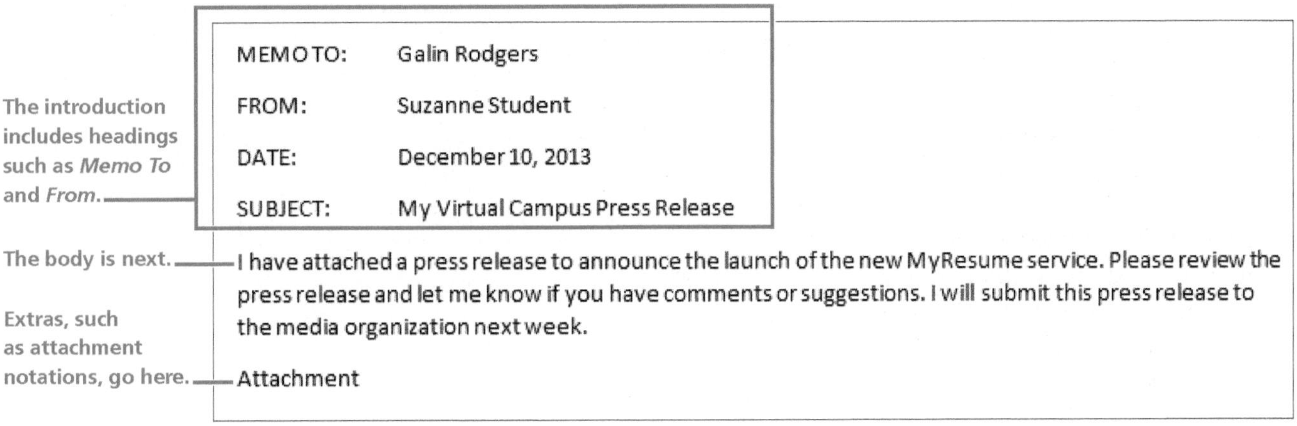

The introduction includes headings such as *Memo To* and *From*.

MEMO TO:	Galin Rodgers
FROM:	Suzanne Student
DATE:	December 10, 2013
SUBJECT:	My Virtual Campus Press Release

The body is next.

I have attached a press release to announce the launch of the new MyResume service. Please review the press release and let me know if you have comments or suggestions. I will submit this press release to the media organization next week.

Extras, such as attachment notations, go here.

Attachment

Introducing Default Tabs

The Tab key moves the insertion point to the nearest tab stop on the ruler. In Word, the default tab stops are set every one-half inch, thus the insertion point moves one-half inch when you tap Tab. In this lesson, you will use Word's default tab settings.

FROM THE RIBBON
View→Show→Ruler

Inserting and Formatting the Date

Word lets you insert the current date in a variety of formats. For example, the date could be inserted as 12/10/13, December 10, 2013, or 10 December 2013.

FROM THE RIBBON
Insert→Text→Insert Date and Time

FROM THE KEYBOARD
Alt + Shift + D to insert the date

Updating the Date Automatically

You can insert the date as text or as a field. Inserting the date as text has the same effect as manually typing the date. Fields, on the other hand, are updated whenever a document is saved or printed.

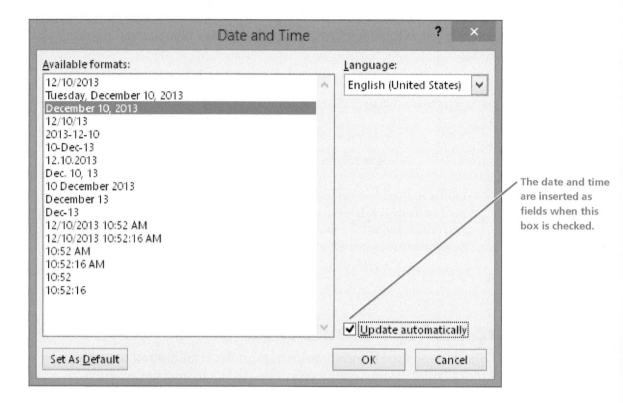

The date and time are inserted as fields when this box is checked.

Set Up a Memo and Insert the Date

In this exercise, you will create a memo using Word's default tab settings and automatically insert the date. You'll also use Word's Blank Document template, which applies 1.08 line spacing with extra space following paragraphs.

1. Start a new document using the **Blank Document template**. Make sure the Word window is **maximized** ▢.

2. Save the file in your **WD2013 Lesson 03** folder as **WD03-D01-MartinMemo-[FirstInitialLastName]**.

   Replace the bracketed text with your first initial and last name. For example, if your name is Bethany Smith, your filename would look like this: WD03-D01-MartinMemo-BSmith.

3. If necessary, choose **Home→Paragraph→Show/Hide** ¶ to display formatting marks.

   Next you will turn on the ruler so you can observe that Word's default tabs are set at every one-half inch.

4. If necessary, choose **View→Show→Ruler**.

   The ruler opens below the Ribbon and on the left side of the screen.

5. Follow these steps to begin the memo:

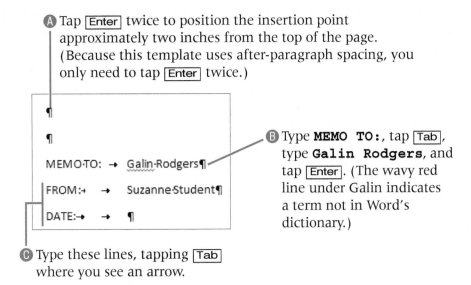

Ⓐ Tap ⌈Enter⌉ twice to position the insertion point approximately two inches from the top of the page. (Because this template uses after-paragraph spacing, you only need to tap ⌈Enter⌉ twice.)

Ⓑ Type **MEMO TO:**, tap ⌈Tab⌉, type **Galin Rodgers**, and tap ⌈Enter⌉. (The wavy red line under Galin indicates a term not in Word's dictionary.)

Ⓒ Type these lines, tapping ⌈Tab⌉ where you see an arrow.

6. Choose **Insert→Text→Insert Date and Time** 📅.

7. Follow these steps to insert the date:

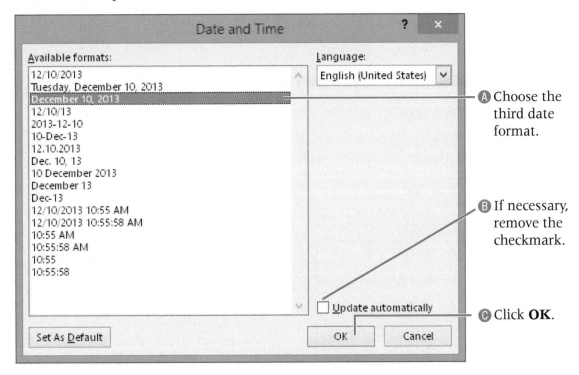

Ⓐ Choose the third date format.

Ⓑ If necessary, remove the checkmark.

Ⓒ Click **OK**.

Leaving Update Automatically checked instructs Word to insert the date as a field, which means the original date would be lost if you opened and saved the document at a later date. In this instance, you do not want the date to change.

The date shown here may differ from the current date that you use.

Word 2013

8. Choose **Home**→**Paragraph**→**Show/Hide** ¶ to turn off formatting marks.

9. Complete the rest of the memorandum as shown, using $\boxed{\text{Tab}}$ to align the text in the Subject line. Bear in mind that you only need to tap $\boxed{\text{Enter}}$ once between paragraphs due to this template's after-paragraph spacing.

MEMO TO: Galin Rodgers

FROM: Suzanne Student

DATE: December 10, 2013

SUBJECT: My Virtual Campus Press Release

I have attached a press release to announce the launch of the new MyResume service. Please review the press release and let me know if you have comments or suggestions. I will submit this press release to the media organization next week.

Attachment

---

10. Choose **View**→**Show**→**Ruler** to turn off the ruler.

11. Save the document and leave it open; you will modify it throughout this lesson.

Inserting Symbols

Video Library   http://labyrinthelab.com/videos   Video Number: WD13-V0302

Word lets you insert a variety of symbols and other characters not found on the keyboard. The following illustration shows the Symbol menu.

FROM THE RIBBON

Insert→Symbols
→Symbol

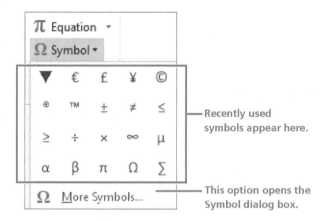

Recently used symbols appear here.

This option opens the Symbol dialog box.

The following figure points out the main features of the Symbol dialog box.

This tab displays commonly used special characters, such as copyright © and registered trademark ®.

You can choose characters from a variety of fonts.

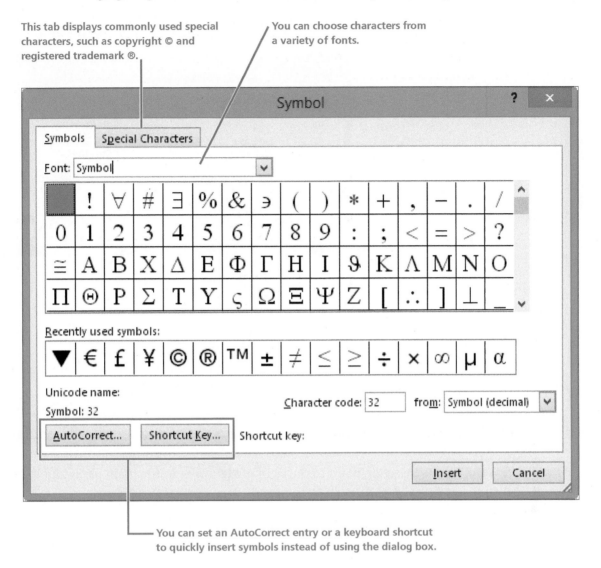

You can set an AutoCorrect entry or a keyboard shortcut to quickly insert symbols instead of using the dialog box.

Insert Symbols

In this exercise, you will add a trademark symbol and a registered trademark symbol to your document.

1. Save your file as **WD03-D02-MartinMemo-[FirstInitialLastName]**.

2. Position the insertion point to the right of My Virtual Campus in the **Subject** line.

3. Choose **Insert→Symbols→Symbol** Ω, and then choose **More Symbols** at the bottom of the menu.

4. Follow these steps to insert the registered trademark symbol:

Ⓐ Click the **Special Characters** tab.

Ⓑ Choose **Registered**.

Ⓒ Click **Insert**. (The dialog box remains open so you can insert additional symbols.)

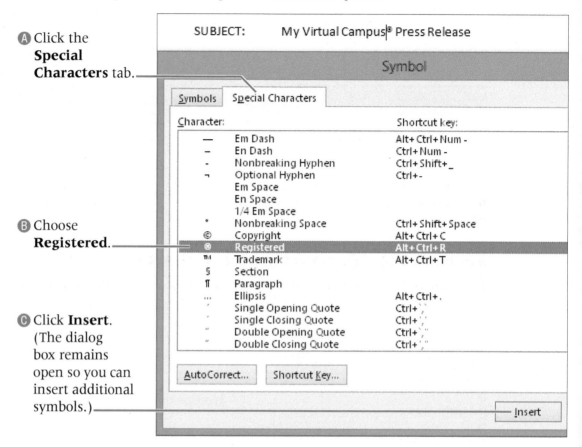

SUBJECT: My Virtual Campus® Press Release

Symbol

Symbols	Special Characters

Character: Shortcut key:

—	Em Dash	Alt+Ctrl+Num -
–	En Dash	Ctrl+Num -
-	Nonbreaking Hyphen	Ctrl+Shift+_
¬	Optional Hyphen	Ctrl+-
	Em Space	
	En Space	
	1/4 Em Space	
°	Nonbreaking Space	Ctrl+Shift+Space
©	Copyright	Alt+Ctrl+C
®	Registered	Alt+Ctrl+R
™	Trademark	Alt+Ctrl+T
§	Section	
¶	Paragraph	
...	Ellipsis	Alt+Ctrl+.
‘	Single Opening Quote	Ctrl+`,`
’	Single Closing Quote	Ctrl+`,`
"	Double Opening Quote	Ctrl+`,"`
"	Double Closing Quote	Ctrl+`,"`

AutoCorrect...	Shortcut Key...

Insert

5. Position the insertion point to the right of *MyResume* in the main paragraph.
You may need to drag the dialog box out of the way.

6. Click the **Trademark** (™) symbol, and then click **Insert**.

7. Click the **Symbols** tab and choose different fonts from the **Font** list to see other sets of symbols.

8. When you finish experimenting, click **Close**.

9. Save the memo.

Working with Page Breaks

Video Library   http://labyrinthelab.com/videos   Video Number: WD13-V0303

If you are typing text and the insertion point reaches the bottom of a page, Word inserts an *automatic* page break. Automatic page breaks are convenient when working with long documents. For example, imagine you are writing a report and you decide to insert a new paragraph in the middle. Word automatically repaginates the report.

A manual page break remains in place unless you remove it. You insert manual page breaks whenever you want to control the starting point of a new page.

FROM THE RIBBON

Page Layout→Page
Setup→Breaks→Page

FROM THE KEYBOARD

Ctrl + Enter to insert
a manual page break

Removing Manual Page Breaks

If you turn on the Show/Hide feature, you can see the page break in Print Layout view. You delete a page break the same way you delete other content in a document.

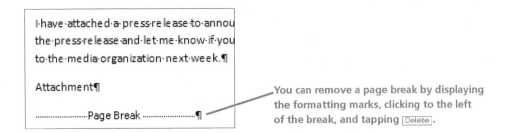

You can remove a page break by displaying the formatting marks, clicking to the left of the break, and tapping Delete.

DEVELOP YOUR SKILLS WD03-D03
Work with Page Breaks

In this exercise, you will insert a page break, thereby creating a new page, so you can copy and paste a press release into the new page.

1. Save your file as **WD03-D03-MartinMemo-[FirstInitialLastName]**.

   Next you will ensure you are in Print Layout view so you can see the page break. You can see a page break in other views, but you will use Print Layout view.

2. Choose **View→Views→Print Layout** .

3. Press Ctrl + End to position the insertion point at the end of the document. If necessary, tap Enter to generate a blank line below the *Attachment* line.

4. Choose **Insert→Pages→Page Break** .

5. If necessary, scroll to the bottom of page 1 to see the new page 2.

6. Scroll up until the *Attachment* line is visible.

7. If necessary, choose **Home→Paragraph→Show/Hide** ¶ to display formatting marks.

8. Position the insertion point to the left of the page break and tap Delete.

9. Try scrolling down to the second page and you will see that it is gone.

10. Check to see that the insertion point is just below the *Attachment* line, and press ⌈Ctrl⌉ + ⌈Enter⌉ to reinsert the page break.

11. Choose **Home→Paragraph→Show/Hide** ¶ to hide the formatting marks.

Copy and Paste from Another Document

12. Open **WD03-D03-PressRelease** from your **WD2013 Lesson 03** folder.

    Notice that a number of terms are flagged by the spelling checker (red wavy underlines) and grammar checker (blue wavy underline). Ignore these notations for now.

13. In the press release document, press ⌈Ctrl⌉ + ⌈A⌉ to select the entire document.

14. Press ⌈Ctrl⌉ + ⌈C⌉ to copy the document.

    Now you will switch to your memo.

15. Follow these steps to switch to the memo:

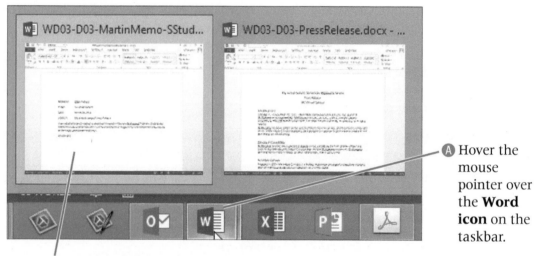

Ⓐ Hover the mouse pointer over the **Word icon** on the taskbar.

Ⓑ Click **WD03-D03-MartinMemo-[FirstInitialLastName]** to display it in the foreground.

16. Make sure the insertion point is at the top of **page 2**.

17. Choose **Home→Clipboard→Paste** 📋.

    Now you will switch back to the press release and close it.

18. Use the taskbar button to switch to the press release document.

19. Choose **File→Close**.

    The memo document should now be in the foreground.

20. Save the file.

Working with Proofreading Tools

Video Library   http://labyrinthelab.com/videos   Video Number: WD13-V0304

Word's spelling and grammar tools help you avoid errors. You can choose to use the default *on-the-fly* checking, where Word marks possible errors as you type, or you can save proofing until you've completed your document. Word provides many choices allowing you to set the level of grammar and style checking from strict to casual.

Proofing tools can help polish your writing; however, they are proofreading *aids*, not the final word. You still need human judgment in a final round of proofing.

FROM THE RIBBON
Review→Proofing
→Spelling & Grammar

FROM THE KEYBOARD
F7 for proofreading tools

Word 2013

Options can be turned on and off, including checking spelling and grammar as you type, which is the default.

You can have Word check your writing style by choosing this option and clicking the Settings button.

When correcting spelling and grammar in Word

- ☑ Check spelling as you type
- ☑ Mark grammar errors as you type
- ☑ Frequently confused words
- ☑ Check grammar with spelling
- ☐ Show readability statistics

Writing Style: Grammar Only ▼   Settings...

Recheck Doc...

Grammar & Style
Grammar Only

Grammar Settings

Writing style:
Grammar & Style

Grammar and style options:
- ☑ Punctuation
- ☑ Questions
- ☑ Relative clauses
- ☐ Subject-verb agreement
- ☑ Verb phrases

Style:
- ☑ Clichés, Colloquialisms, and Jargon
- ☑ Contractions
- ☐ Fragment - stylistic suggestions
- ☑ Gender-specific words
- ☑ Hyphenated and compound words
- ☑ Misused words - stylistic suggestions
- ☑ Numbers
- ☑ Passive sentences

Choose options to suit your writing style.

Using the Spelling Checker

Word can automatically check your spelling as you type. It flags spelling errors with wavy red lines. You can address a flagged error by right-clicking it and choosing a suggested replacement word or other option from the pop-up menu.

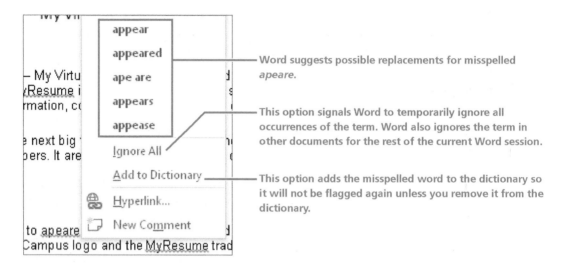

Word suggests possible replacements for misspelled *apeare*.

This option signals Word to temporarily ignore all occurrences of the term. Word also ignores the term in other documents for the rest of the current Word session.

This option adds the misspelled word to the dictionary so it will not be flagged again unless you remove it from the dictionary.

Working with Word's Dictionaries

The main Word dictionary contains thousands of common words, though it does not include all proper names, technical terms, and so forth. Word marks a term not found in the main dictionary as a possible error. If you use that term frequently, you can add it to a custom dictionary so it will not be marked as an error.

Using Dictionary Options

When Suggest from Main Dictionary Only is checked, Word only searches the main dictionary; if that option is unchecked, Word searches in custom dictionaries as well. Adding a word to the dictionary during spell checking adds it to a custom dictionary.

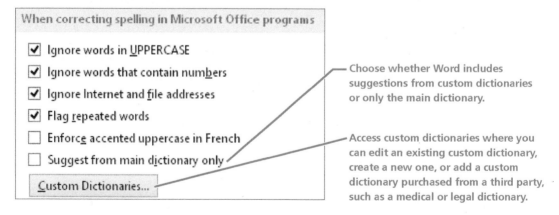

Choose whether Word includes suggestions from custom dictionaries or only the main dictionary.

Access custom dictionaries where you can edit an existing custom dictionary, create a new one, or add a custom dictionary purchased from a third party, such as a medical or legal dictionary.

The options you set for custom dictionaries in Word apply to all Office programs.

Adding or Deleting Words in a Custom Dictionary

In addition to adding words through the spelling checker, you can add words using the Custom Dictionaries dialog box. If you add a word to the dictionary by mistake, you can remove it.

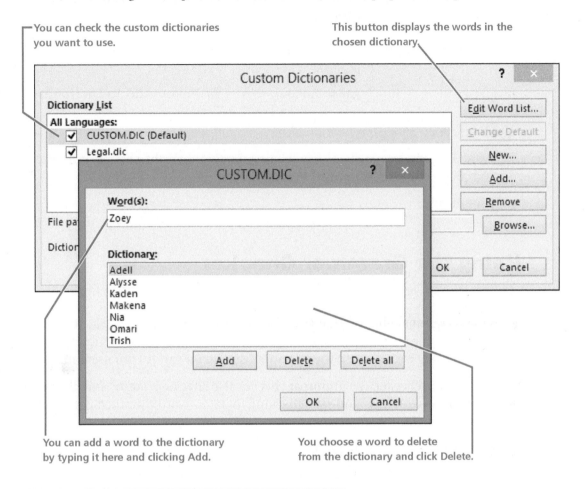

You can check the custom dictionaries you want to use.

This button displays the words in the chosen dictionary.

You can add a word to the dictionary by typing it here and clicking Add.

You choose a word to delete from the dictionary and click Delete.

DEVELOP YOUR SKILLS WD03-D04

Use the Automatic Spelling Checker

In this exercise, you will add a term to Word's dictionary. You will also delete a repeated word.

1. Save your file as **WD03-D04-MartinMemo-[FirstInitialLastName]**.

   Notice that the term MyResume in the first line of page 2 has a wavy red underline. MyResume is spelled correctly, but it does not appear in Word's dictionary. Thus, Word flags it as a possible spelling error.

2. Follow these steps to add *MyResume* to the dictionary:

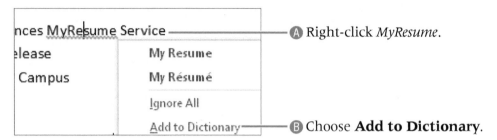

(A) Right-click *MyResume*.

(B) Choose **Add to Dictionary**.

You will delete MyResume from the dictionary a little later.

3. Word flagged a repeated word in the first paragraph; right-click *our* with the wavy red line and choose **Delete Repeated Word**.

4. Save the file.

Using the Grammar Checker

Video Library   http://labyrinthelab.com/videos   Video Number: WD13-V0305

Word has a grammar checker that flags errors with wavy blue lines. Like the spelling checker, you right-click the error and choose a replacement phrase or other option from the menu. The grammar checker isn't perfect; there is no substitute for careful proofreading.

Like the spelling checker, the grammar checker also checks *on the fly*, and like the spelling checker, you can turn it off and save checking for later. Word uses the Spelling and Grammar task panes for making suggestions.

Add the flagged term to the dictionary, or...   ...choose a replacement term.

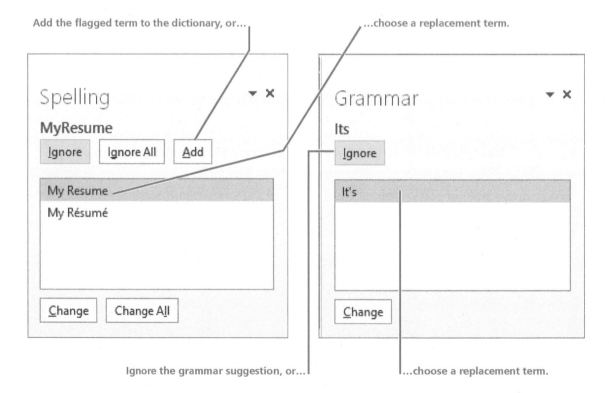

Ignore the grammar suggestion, or...   ...choose a replacement term.

QUICK REFERENCE	USING SPELLING AND GRAMMAR OPTIONS
Task	**Procedure**
Set level of grammar and style checking	■ Choose File→Options and choose the Proofing category. ■ Choose the Writing Style and click Settings.
Work with custom dictionaries	■ Choose File→Options and choose the Proofing category. ■ Click the Custom Dictionaries button.
Turn off spelling and grammar checking as you type	■ Choose File→Options and choose the Proofing category. ■ Uncheck the options for checking spelling and marking grammar as you type.

DEVELOP YOUR SKILLS WD03-D05

Use the Spelling and Grammar Checkers

In this exercise, you will make spelling and grammar corrections to the Martin Memo using the Spelling and Grammar task panes.

1. Save the file as **WD03-D05-MartinMemo-[FirstInitialLastName]**.

2. Position the insertion point at the beginning of the first line on **page 2**.

3. Choose **Review→Proofing→Spelling & Grammar** ✓.

   The Spelling task pane opens, and wiht *is noted as a possible spelling error.*

4. The error is a typo, and the suggestion *with* is correct, so click **Change**.

   Now Word points out Its *as a possible grammatical error.*

5. Click **Change** to accept the grammar suggestion.

6. The next error is a spelling error, and the suggestion *Delivery* is correct, so click **Change**.

7. Finish checking the rest of the document using your good judgment regarding what changes to make. When *Galin* is flagged, click **Ignore All**.

8. When the message appears indicating that the spelling and grammar check is complete, click **OK**.

Remove a Word from the Custom Dictionary

9. Choose **File→Options** and choose the **Proofing** category.

10. Follow these steps to delete MyResume:

Ⓐ Click **Custom Dictionaries**.   Ⓑ Click **Edit Word List**.

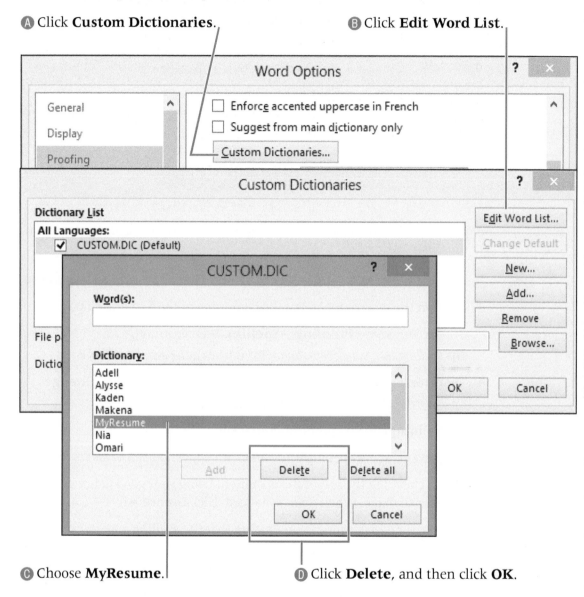

Ⓒ Choose **MyResume**.   Ⓓ Click **Delete**, and then click **OK**.

11. Click **OK** two more times.

    MyResume is flagged again, because you removed it from the dictionary.

12. Right-click *MyResume* and choose **Ignore All**.

13. Save the file.

Using the Thesaurus to Find a Synonym

Video Library   http://labyrinthelab.com/videos   Video Number: WD13-V0306

You can view a list of synonyms by right-clicking a word and choosing Synonyms from the menu. For a more extensive list, choose Thesaurus from the bottom of the submenu to open the Thesaurus task pane.

The Thesaurus task pane goes beyond displaying a list of alternate words. As you know, a word can have different meanings depending upon the context in which it is used. For example, the word *launch* can be used to mean *presentation*, *takeoff*, *hurl*, or *open*. Using the task pane, you can look up those additional synonyms by clicking any word displayed in the results list.

FROM THE RIBBON
Review→Proofing
→Thesaurus

FROM THE KEYBOARD
Shift + F7 to open the Thesaurus

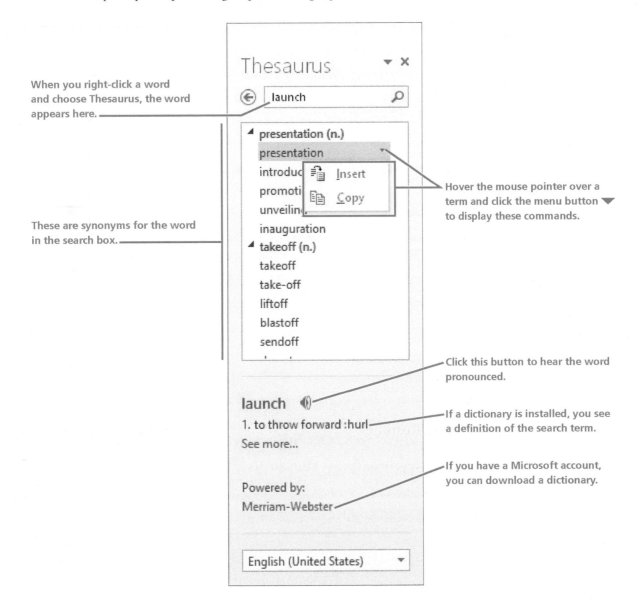

When you right-click a word and choose Thesaurus, the word appears here.

These are synonyms for the word in the search box.

Hover the mouse pointer over a term and click the menu button ▼ to display these commands.

Click this button to hear the word pronounced.

If a dictionary is installed, you see a definition of the search term.

If you have a Microsoft account, you can download a dictionary.

Use the Thesaurus

In this exercise, you will use the pop-up menu to locate a synonym. You will also use the Thesaurus task pane.

1. Save your file as **WD03-D06-MartinMemo-[FirstInitialLastName]**.

2. Scroll down to view the press release page.

3. Right-click the word *launch* in the first sentence of the *Announcement* paragraph.

4. Follow these steps to replace the word with a synonym:

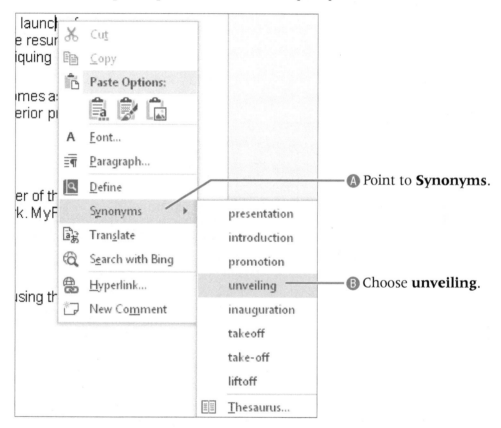

Ⓐ Point to **Synonyms**.

Ⓑ Choose **unveiling**.

Now you'll look up synonyms in the Thesaurus task pane.

5. Choose **Review→Proofing→Thesaurus** 📖.

6. Follow these steps to re-insert *launch* in place of *unveiling*.

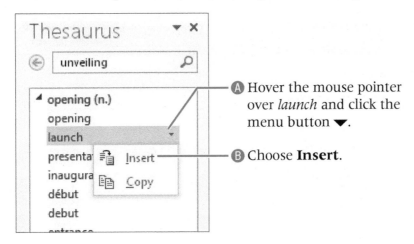

Ⓐ Hover the mouse pointer over *launch* and click the menu button ▼.

Ⓑ Choose **Insert**.

7. While the Thesaurus task pane is still open, click any word in the list to view synonyms for that word.

8. Click **Close** ✕ in the upper-right corner of the Thesaurus task pane.

9. Save the file.

Formatting Text

Video Library   http://labyrinthelab.com/videos   Video Number: WD13-V0307

You can format text using the Font group on the Home tab. Options include changing the font, size, and color and applying various enhancements, including bold, italics, and underline. You can also clear all added formatting from text, returning it to its default formats. You can change the text formatting before you start typing, or you can select existing text and then make the changes.

FROM THE KEYBOARD
Ctrl+B for bold
Ctrl+I for italics
Ctrl+U for underline

Additional options are available through the Font dialog box. The dialog box launcher in the bottom-right corner of the Font group opens the dialog box.

Clear All Formatting

Dialog box launcher

The following illustration describes the Font dialog box.

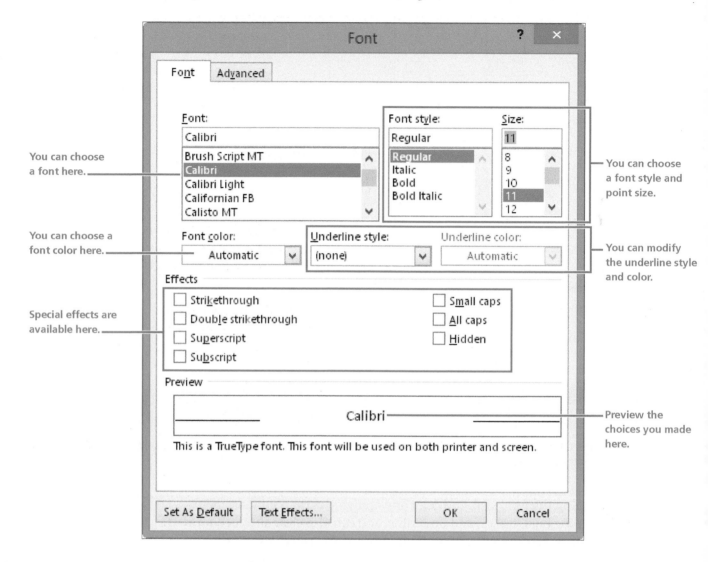

You can choose a font here.

You can choose a font color here.

Special effects are available here.

You can choose a font style and point size.

You can modify the underline style and color.

Preview the choices you made here.

Using Live Preview

Live Preview shows what a formatting change looks like without actually applying the format. Many formatting features provide a Live Preview. In the following example, selecting a block of text and then hovering the mouse pointer over a font name previews how the text would look.

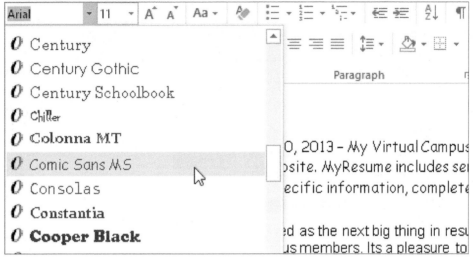

Live Preview of the Comic Sans MS font

Format Text

In this exercise, you will explore fonts using Live Preview. You will use both the Ribbon and the Font dialog box to format text.

1. Save your file as **WD03-D07-MartinMemo-[FirstInitialLastName]**.

2. Scroll to the top of the second page and select the three heading lines.

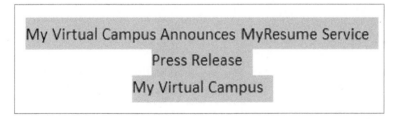

3. Choose **Home→Font** and click the drop-down arrow ▾ to the right of **Calibri (Body)**.

4. Slide the mouse pointer down the font list to see the effect of different fonts with Live Preview.

5. Click in the document to close the font list, and then make sure the first three lines on page 2 are still selected.

   Now you'll use the Font dialog box to change the font and font size.

6. Follow these steps to make the changes:

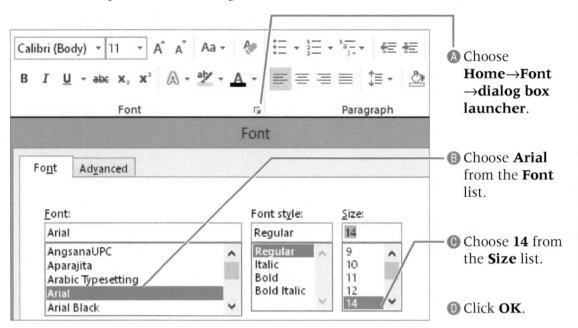

Ⓐ Choose **Home→Font →dialog box launcher**.

Ⓑ Choose **Arial** from the **Font** list.

Ⓒ Choose **14** from the **Size** list.

Ⓓ Click **OK**.

7. With the three lines still selected, press [Ctrl]+[B] and then [Ctrl]+[U] to apply bold and underline to the headings.

8. Choose **Home→Font→Underline** [U] to remove the underline.

9. Follow these steps to apply bold formatting to multiple selections at the same time:

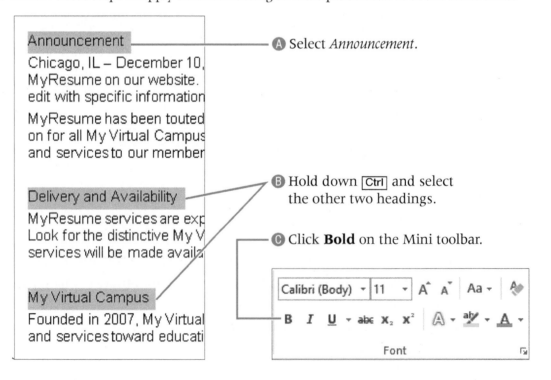

Ⓐ Select *Announcement*.

Ⓑ Hold down [Ctrl] and select the other two headings.

Ⓒ Click **Bold** on the Mini toolbar.

10. Save the file.

Working with the Format Painter

Video Library   http://labyrinthelab.com/videos   Video Number: WD13-V0308

The Format Painter lets you copy text formats, including font, font size, and color, from one location to another. This saves time and helps create consistent formatting throughout a document. The Format Painter command is on both the Ribbon and the Mini toolbar.

FROM THE RIBBON
Home→Clipboard
→Format Painter

FROM THE KEYBOARD
Ctrl+Shift+C to copy a format

Ctrl+Shift+V to paste a format

Word 2013

QUICK REFERENCE	COPYING TEXT FORMATS WITH THE FORMAT PAINTER
Task	**Procedure**
Copy text formats with the Format Painter	■ Select the text with the format(s) to copy.
	■ Choose Home→Clipboard→Format Painter once to copy formats to one location (double-click to copy to multiple locations).
	■ Select the text location(s) to format.
	■ If you double-clicked initially, click the Format Painter again to turn it off.

DEVELOP YOUR SKILLS WD03-D08
Use the Format Painter

In this exercise, you will use both the Mini toolbar and the Format Painter to apply and copy formats. You will also copy a format and apply it to multiple blocks of text.

1. Save your file as **WD03-D08-MartinMemo-[FirstInitialLastName]**.

2. Scroll to page 2, if necessary, and select the *Announcement* heading line.

3. When the Mini toolbar appears, follow these steps to apply color to the heading line. (If the toolbar fades away, right-click the selected term to redisplay it.)

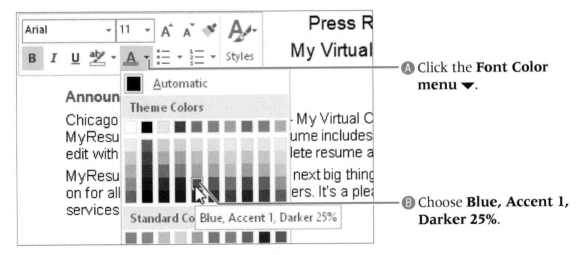

Ⓐ Click the **Font Color menu** ▼.

Ⓑ Choose **Blue, Accent 1, Darker 25%**.

4. Keep the text selected and the Mini toolbar active, and follow these steps to apply additional formats to the text:

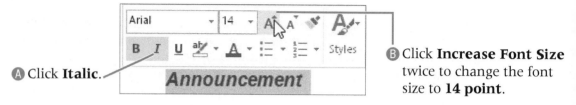

Ⓐ Click **Italic**.

Ⓑ Click **Increase Font Size** twice to change the font size to **14 point**.

Copy Formats to One Location

5. Make sure the *Announcement* heading line is selected.

6. Click the **Format Painter** on the Mini toolbar.

   A paintbrush icon is added to the mouse pointer once it is positioned over the document.

7. Drag the mouse pointer across the *Delivery and Availability* heading; release the mouse button.

   The 14 point italic blue formats should be copied to the heading.

8. Make sure the *Delivery and Availability* heading line is still selected.

9. Choose **Home→Clipboard→Format Painter** , and then select the last heading, *My Virtual Campus*, to copy the format again.

Copy Formats to More Than One Location

10. Scroll to the top of page 1 and select the heading *MEMO TO:* (include the colon).

11. Choose **Home→Font→Bold** B.

12. Double-click the **Format Painter** and drag over *FROM:* to apply the formatting from *MEMO TO:*.

13. Drag over *DATE:* and *SUBJECT:* to format those headings.

14. Choose **Home→Clipboard→Format Painter** to turn it off.

15. Save the file.

Using Find and Replace

Video Library   http://labyrinthelab.com/videos   Video Number: WD13-V0309

The Find command lets you search a document for a word or phrase. You can also search for text formats, page breaks, and a variety of other items. Find is often the quickest way to locate a phrase, format, or other item. You can use Find and Replace to search for text and replace it with something else.

FROM THE RIBBON
Home→Editing→Find
Home→Editing
→Replace

FROM THE KEYBOARD
Ctrl+F for Find
Ctrl+H for Replace

Word 2013

Searching with the Navigation Pane

Clicking Find opens the Navigation task pane. When you search for an item, the results display in the task pane, giving you a quick view of everywhere the item appears.

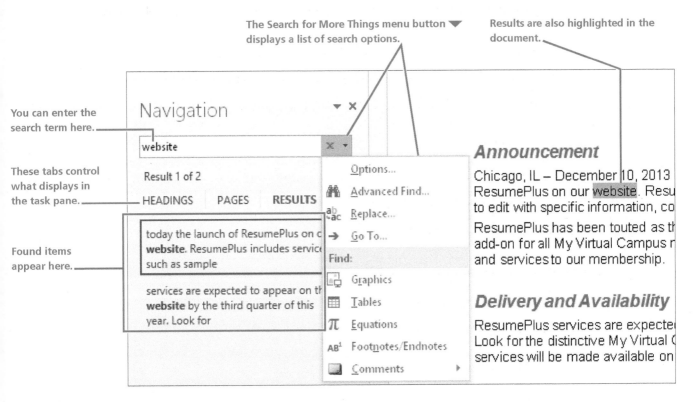

The Search for More Things menu button ▼ displays a list of search options.

Results are also highlighted in the document.

You can enter the search term here.

These tabs control what displays in the task pane.

Found items appear here.

Using the Find and Replace Dialog Box

The Find and Replace dialog box includes the Find, Replace, and Go To tabs. The Find tab allows you to perform a more detailed search than the Navigation pane. The Replace tab allows you to enter a *Replace With* item to replace the *Find What* item. The Go To tab allows you to jump to a specific place in the document.

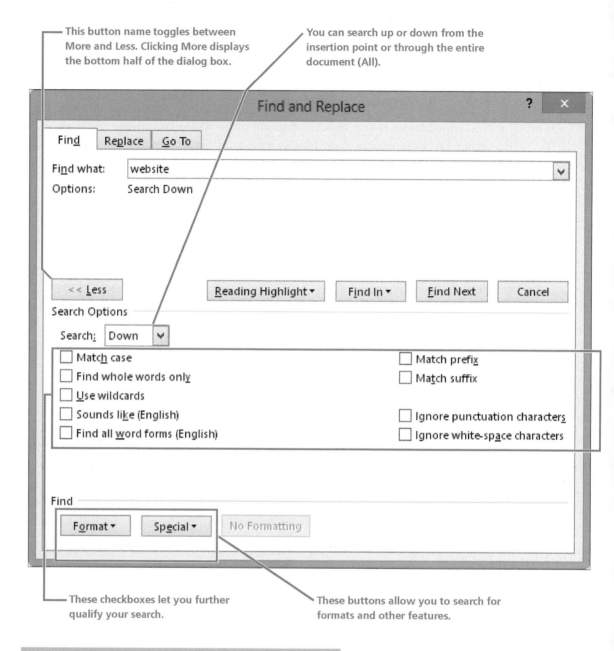

This button name toggles between More and Less. Clicking More displays the bottom half of the dialog box.

You can search up or down from the insertion point or through the entire document (All).

These checkboxes let you further qualify your search.

These buttons allow you to search for formats and other features.

Use Find

In this exercise, you will search with the Navigation pane and explore search options in the Find and Replace dialog box.

1. Save your file as **WD03-D09-MartinMemo-[FirstInitialLastName]**.

2. Position the insertion point at the top of page 2, and make sure no text is selected.

3. Choose **Home→Editing→Find** 🔍 to open the Navigation pane.

4. Type **website** in the search box to find all occurrences of the term.

   Notice that the search results appear in the Navigation pane, and they are highlighted in the document as well.

TIP If you don't see the search results, click the Results tab toward the top of the task pane.

5. Scroll to the top of the document and position the insertion point anywhere in the first line of the memo.

6. Click in the **Navigation pane** search box, delete *website*, and type **Announce** (with a capital A) in its place.

   Word located announce *in the first paragraph of the memo with a lowercase* a, *even though you typed it in uppercase.*

7. Click the second instance in the Navigation pane results list and notice that *Announces* is highlighted in the first line of the press release.

   Word found Announce, *even though it is part of* Announces. *By default, the search feature is not case sensitive and doesn't recognize the difference between a whole word and part of a word. You will change this, however, in the next few steps.*

Use the Match Case Option

Now you will use the Search for More Things menu to display the Find and Replace dialog box, and then you will use the Match Case option.

8. Place the insertion point in the first line of the first page.

9. Follow these steps to display the Find and Replace dialog box and activate Match Case:

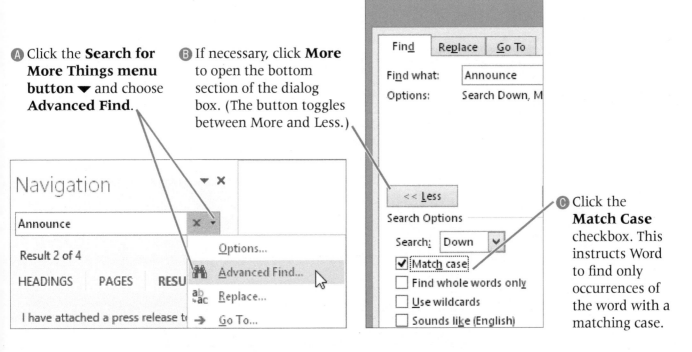

Ⓐ Click the **Search for More Things menu button** ▼ and choose **Advanced Find**.

Ⓑ If necessary, click **More** to open the bottom section of the dialog box. (The button toggles between More and Less.)

Ⓒ Click the **Match Case** checkbox. This instructs Word to find only occurrences of the word with a matching case.

10. Click **Find Next** and Word locates the capitalized *Announces*.

11. Click **Find Next** again and Word locates the capitalized *Announcement*.

12. Click **Find Next** again and Word indicates that the entire document has been searched.

    Word skipped over the lowercase forms of announce.

13. Click **OK** in the message box; then close the Find and Replace dialog box and the Navigation task pane.

14. Save the file.

Using Replace

Video Library   http://labyrinthelab.com/videos   Video Number: WD13-V0310

The Replace feature allows you to replace words, formats, and other elements in a document. As an example, you could search for a particular font and replace it with another.

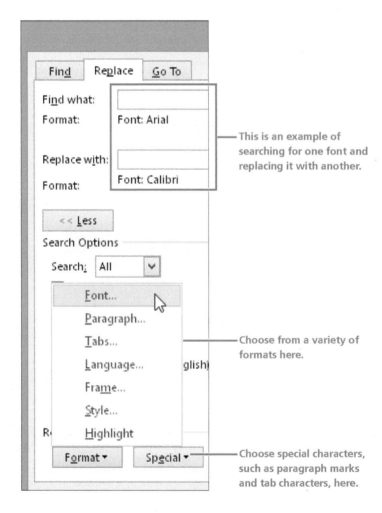

This is an example of searching for one font and replacing it with another.

Choose from a variety of formats here.

Choose special characters, such as paragraph marks and tab characters, here.

Use Replace

In this exercise, you will use the Replace feature. The Marketing Department decided to change the name MyResume to ResumePlus, so having Word automatically make the replacements for you is a real time saver.

1. Save your file as **WD03-D10-MartinMemo-[FirstInitialLastName]**.

2. Position the insertion point at the top of the document, and make sure no text is selected.

3. Press `Ctrl`+`H` to display the Find and Replace dialog box.
   Notice that the Replace tab is active in the dialog box.

4. If necessary, click **More** to expand the dialog box. (The button toggles between More and Less.)
   Match Case is still active from the previous exercise.

5. Uncheck **Match Case** to turn it off.

6. Click **Less** to collapse the More options section of the dialog box.

7. Follow these steps to replace MyResume with ResumePlus:

Ⓐ Replace the current text with **MyResume**.   Ⓑ Type **ResumePlus** here.   Ⓒ Click **Find Next**.

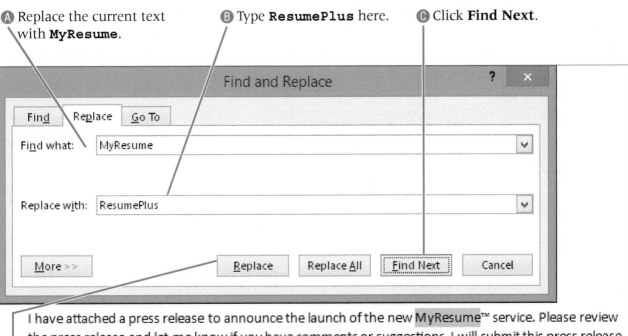

Ⓓ Click **Replace** to make the change, and Word moves to the next occurrence of MyResume.

8. Click **Replace All** to make all remaining changes at once.
   The message box informs you that Word made seven replacements.

Use Replace All with caution. You should be confident about the replacements Word will make before you use this feature. Using *Replace* allows you to monitor each replacement.

9. Click **OK** to dismiss the message, and then close the **Find and Replace** dialog box and observe the *ResumePlus* replacements. You can ignore the wavy red lines.

10. Save the file.

Navigating in Documents

Video Library   http://labyrinthelab.com/videos   Video Number: WD13-V0311

Two highly efficient navigation methods are bookmarks and hyperlinks. You can create bookmarks to move to specific locations in a document, and you can insert hyperlinks that function just like hyperlinks in web pages. A hyperlink in Word uses bookmarks or heading styles to jump to places that are within the same document.

Using Bookmarks

You can assign a bookmark name to text or other objects in a document. Once a bookmark is set up, you can easily navigate to it by choosing the desired bookmark name from the Bookmark dialog box or the Go To tab in the Find and Replace dialog box.

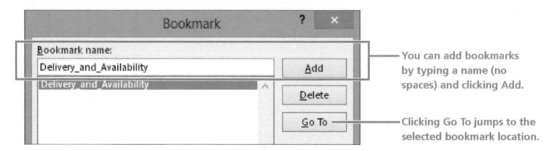

You can add bookmarks by typing a name (no spaces) and clicking Add.

Clicking Go To jumps to the selected bookmark location.

QUICK REFERENCE	USING BOOKMARKS
Task	**Procedure**
Create a bookmark	▪ Select the text/object to use as a bookmark and choose Insert→Links→Bookmark.
	▪ Type the bookmark name (without spaces) and click Add.
Jump to a bookmark using the Bookmark dialog box	▪ Choose Insert→Links→Bookmark, choose a bookmark name, and click Go To.
Jump to a bookmark using the Find and Replace dialog box	▪ Choose Home→Editing→Find.
	▪ In the Navigation pane, click the Search for More Things menu ▼ button and choose Go To.
	▪ Choose Bookmark in the Go To What box, type or select the Bookmark name, and click Go To.

DEVELOP YOUR SKILLS WD03-D11

Create and Use Bookmarks

In this exercise, you will create bookmarks and use them to jump to different areas of the document. Then you will delete the bookmarks.

1. Save your file as **WD03-D11-MartinMemo-[FirstInitialLastName]**.

2. With page 2 displayed, select the word *Delivery* in the second heading.

3. Choose **Insert→Links→Bookmark** 🔖.

4. Follow these steps to create a Bookmark:

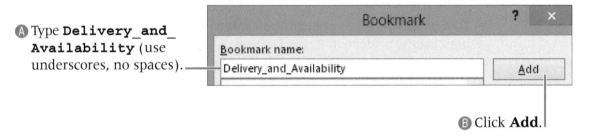

Ⓐ Type **Delivery_and_Availability** (use underscores, no spaces).

Ⓑ Click **Add**.

5. Scroll, if necessary, and select the *Announcement* heading.

6. Choose **Insert→Links→Bookmark** 🔖.

7. In the **Bookmark Name** box, replace the current text with **Announcement** and click **Add**.

8. Press Ctrl + Home to move to the beginning of the document.

9. Choose **Insert→Links→Bookmark** 🔖.

10. Choose **Delivery_and_Availability** and click **Go To**.

11. Close the Bookmark dialog box, then choose **Insert→Links→Bookmark.**

12. Choose **Announcement** and click **Go To**.

Delete Bookmarks

13. With *Announcement* selected in the dialog box, click **Delete**.

14. Select **Delivery_and_Availability** and click **Delete**.

15. Close the dialog box and save the file.

Using Hyperlinks

Video Library   http://labyrinthelab.com/videos   Video Number: WD13-V0312

A hyperlink is text or a graphic that jumps you to another place when clicked. To use a hyperlink *within* a document, the location you link to must first be set up as a bookmark or be formatted with a heading style.

There are four primary types of hyperlinks.

- **Hyperlinks to other documents or files:** A hyperlink can open another Word document or even another program, such as Excel or PowerPoint.
- **Hyperlinks to web pages:** You can create a link to jump to a web page by entering a URL address for the hyperlink.
- **Hyperlinks to areas within the current document:** This works much like a Bookmark, jumping the reader to another location in the document.
- **Hyperlinks to email addresses:** You can create a hyperlink to an email address. When the hyperlink is clicked, a new message window opens with the email address already in the To: box.

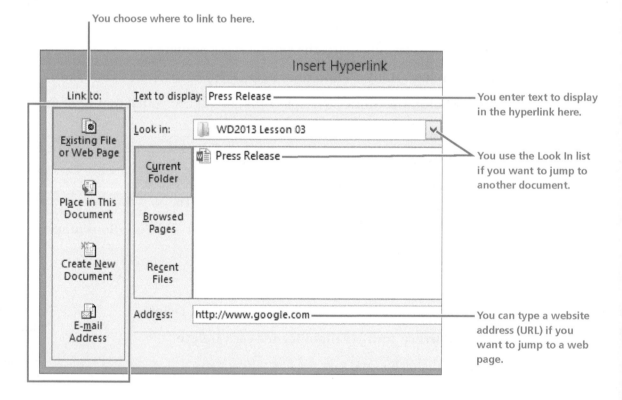

You choose where to link to here.

You enter text to display in the hyperlink here.

You use the Look In list if you want to jump to another document.

You can type a website address (URL) if you want to jump to a web page.

QUICK REFERENCE	CREATING HYPERLINKS
Task	**Procedure**
Create a hyperlink	■ Select the text/graphic to use as a hyperlink and choose Insert→Links→Hyperlink.
	■ Choose the item to link to in the left pane.
	■ In the center pane:
	◆ Choose the filename if linking to a file.
	◆ Type the URL in the Address box if linking to a web page.
	◆ Choose a heading or bookmark name if you chose Place in This Document in the Link To list.
	■ Click OK.
Remove a hyperlink	■ Click in the hyperlink, then choose Insert→Links→Hyperlink and click Remove Link; or, right-click the hyperlink and choose Remove Hyperlink.

DEVELOP YOUR SKILLS WD03-D12
Work with Hyperlinks

In this exercise, you will create a hyperlink and use it to jump to another document. Then, you will remove the hyperlink.

1. Save your file as **WD03-D12-MartinMemo-[FirstInitialLastName]**.

2. Move the insertion point to the beginning of the document.

3. Select the words *Press Release* in the **Subject** line.

4. Choose **Insert→Links→Hyperlink** 🌐.

5. Follow these steps to create a hyperlink to another document:

    Ⓐ Choose **Existing File or Web Page**.

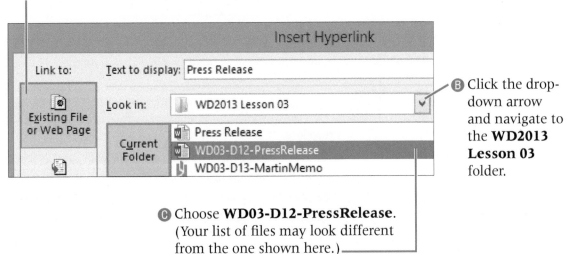

    Ⓑ Click the drop-down arrow and navigate to the **WD2013 Lesson 03** folder.

    Ⓒ Choose **WD03-D12-PressRelease**. (Your list of files may look different from the one shown here.)

6. Click **OK** to create the hyperlink.

   The text formatting changes once this hyperlink is created.

Use and Remove the Hyperlink

7. Press ⌈Ctrl⌉ and click the link to open Press Release.

8. Close **Press Release** but leave the Martin Memo open.
   Notice that the hyperlink changes color once it is used.

9. Click anywhere in the hyperlink.

10. Choose **Insert→Links→Hyperlink** 🌐.

11. Click **Remove Link** in the bottom-right corner of the dialog box.

12. Save the memo document, then choose **File→Close** to close the document.

Opening, Editing, and Saving a PDF File

Video Library   http://labyrinthelab.com/videos   Video Number: WD13-V0313

You can open, edit, and save a PDF file in Word 2013 without purchasing and learning separate, and often expensive, editing software. After editing the file, you can save it as a Word or PDF file. The file you open is considered a read-only file, so you must save it under a different name.

You can optimize a PDF file based on how your audience will likely read the file. And there are additional options, such as the range of pages you want to save and the ability to create bookmarks in the PDF file.

If your audience will be printing the PDF, leave the option at Standard. If the file will only be viewed online, you can choose the Minimize Size option.

Choose additional publishing options here.

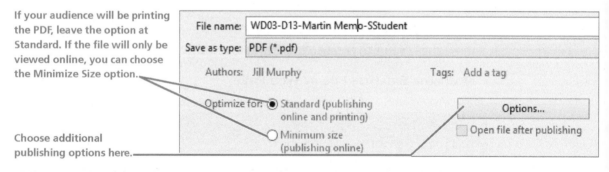

QUICK REFERENCE	OPENING PDF FILES AND SAVING AS PDF FILES
Task	**Procedure**
Open a PDF file in Word	■ Choose File→Open, navigate to the file location, and double-click the file.
	■ When the message appears, click OK.
Saving a Word document as a PDF file	■ Choose File→Save As and navigate to your file storage location.
	■ Choose PDF (*.pdf) from the Save as Type list and, if desired, choose optimization and publishing options.

DEVELOP YOUR SKILLS WD03-D13

Open and Edit a PDF File

In this exercise, you will open a PDF file in Word and make editing changes. You will then resave the file as a PDF.

1. Choose **File→Open**.

2. Navigate to your **WD2013 Lesson 03** folder and open **WD03-D13-MartinMemo.pdf**.

3. When the message box appears, click **OK**.

   The PDF file opens with all the Word editing and formatting tools available.

When you open a PDF in Word, there may be formatting issues. Don't worry about that now. Concentrate on opening so in the future, you know how to open and edit a PDF for which you don't have the original Word file.

4. Scroll to the top of page 2 and select the three lines at the top of the page.

5. In the Mini toolbar, click the **Font Color** **A** menu ▼ and choose **Blue, Accent 1, Darker 25%**.

   If the toolbar fades away, right-click the selected text to redisplay it.

6. Still using the Mini toolbar, change the Font Size to **16 point**.

7. Choose **File→Save As** and navigate to your **WD2013 Lesson 03** folder.

8. Append your first initial and last name to the filename: `WD03-D13-MartinMemo-[FirstInitialLastName]`.

9. Choose **PDF (*.pdf)** from the Save as Type list.

10. Click **Save** at the bottom of the dialog box. (If the PDF file opens in a PDF reader, close the PDF window.)

    Remember, the original file is read-only, so saving it under a different name saved the changes in a new file. Now you'll close the original file without saving.

11. The original file is still open in Word, so choose **File→Close**.

12. When prompted to save the file, click **Don't Save**. Exit **Word**.

Concepts Review

To check your knowledge of the key concepts introduced in this lesson, complete the Concepts Review quiz by choosing the appropriate access option below.

If you are...	Then access the quiz by...
Using the Labyrinth Video Library	Going to http://labyrinthelab.com/videos
Using eLab	Logging in, choosing Content, and navigating to the Concepts Review quiz for this lesson
Not using the Labyrinth Video Library or eLab	Going to the student resource center for this book

Reinforce Your Skills

Type a Memorandum

In this exercise, you will type a memorandum announcing a meeting, aligning the memo heading using the default tab grid. You will insert a page break and copy a document into page 2. Then you will use the proofreading tools to help ensure the accuracy of your memo.

Create a Memorandum Using Default Tabs

1. Start **Word** and create new a document using the **Blank Document template**.

2. Save the file as **WD03-R01-FoodDrive-[FirstInitialLastName]** in your **WD2013 Lesson 03** folder.

3. If necessary, choose **Home→Paragraph→Show/Hide ¶** to display formatting marks.

4. Type the following memo, tapping [Enter] where you see paragraph symbols and [Tab] where you see arrows.

   Because you are using the default template, which has additional spacing, you only need to tap [Enter] once between paragraphs.

¶

¶

MEMO·TO: → Kids·for·Change¶

FROM:→ → Suzanne·Frost¶

DATE:→ → October·1,·2013¶

SUBJECT: → Combat·Hunger·Food·Drive¶

Think·globally,·act·locally!¶

Kids·for·Change·is·sponsoring·a·holiday·season·food·drive·in·coordination·with·our·local·community·food·bank.·The·drive·will·begin·on·November·1st,·and·we·have·lots·of·organizing·to·do·before·then.·¶

We·are·looking·for·volunteers·to·help·us·in·this·effort.·There·is·a·To·Do·list·on·the·next·page.·Look·it·over·and·see·what·you·would·like·to·volunteer·for.·We·will·discuss·the·list·and·assign·teams·during·our·October·meeting.·¶

We're·looking·forward·to·a·successful·drive·for·2013!¶

¶

¶

Work with Page Breaks and Insert a Symbol

5. Position the insertion point at the end of the memo.

6. Choose **Insert→Pages→Page Break** ⊟.
   Now you will copy a To Do list from another document into page 2.

7. Open **WD03-R01-ToDo** from the **WD2013 Lesson 03** folder.

8. Select the entire document and press Ctrl + C to copy it; close the file.

9. Make sure your insertion point is at the **top of page 2** and press Ctrl + V to paste the text.
   Now you will insert a symbol on the second page.

10. Position the insertion point after *heart* in the second line and tap Spacebar.

11. Choose **Insert→Symbols→Symbol** Ω and choose **More Symbols**.

12. Choose the **Webdings** font and the **heart-shaped symbol**; if necessary, use Character Code 89 to locate the symbol.

13. Click **Insert**, and then close the dialog box.

Use Proofreading Tools
There are some spelling errors in the To Do list; you will correct those now.

14. Right-click the red underlined word in the first bullet point and choose *create* from the menu.

15. Right-click the red underlined word in the third bullet point and choose *collect*.

16. Use your good judgment in making the next two spelling corrections.
    Now you will use the Thesaurus to find a synonym.

17. Select *goal* at the end of the second-to-last bullet point.

18. Choose **Review→Proofing→Thesaurus** 📖 to open the task pane.

19. Hover the mouse pointer over *objective* (the second one in the list), and then click the drop-down arrow to open the menu.

20. Click **Insert** to replace *goal* with *objective*.

21. Close the **Thesaurus task pane**.

22. Save and close your file, and exit from **Word**.

23. Submit your final file based on the guidelines provided by your instructor.
    To view examples of how your file or files should look at the end of this exercise, go to the student resource center.

Format a Document and Save It in PDF

In this exercise, you will format the headings in a document, use Find and Replace, and add bookmarks and hyperlinks. Finally, you will save it as a PDF file.

1. Start **Word**. Open **WD03-R02-Energy** from the **WD2013 Lesson 03** folder and save it as `WD03-R02-Energy-[FirstInitialLastName]`.

Format Text and Use the Format Painter

2. Select *Home Energy Inspector* at the top of the document.

3. Choose **Home→Font→dialog box launcher** 🔲.

4. Choose **Century Gothic**, **Bold, 14 point**, and then choose **Small Caps** in the Effects area.

5. Click **OK** to apply the formats.
   You've decided you'd like to try some more options, so you'll clear your formats.

6. Make sure the heading is still selected.

7. Choose **Home→Font→Clear All Formatting** 🔣.

8. With the heading still selected, choose **Home→Font**. Then click the **menu button** ▼ next to Calibri (Body) and choose **Comic Sans MS**.

9. Choose **Home→Font→Font Size menu button** ▼ and choose **16 point**.

10. Choose **Home→Font→Bold** 🅱.

11. Choose **Home→Font→Font Color** 🅰 **menu button** ▼ and choose a **blue** color.
    Now you're ready to format the other headings.

12. Select the *What About Energy Leaks?* heading.

13. Choose **Home→Font→Font menu button** ▼ and choose **Euphemia**.

14. Choose **Home→Font→Bold** 🅱.
    Next you'll use the Format Painter to copy the format to the other headings.

15. Make sure the heading is still selected.

16. Choose **Home→Clipboard** and double-click the **Format Painter** 🖌.
    Remember, double-clicking the Format Painter keeps it turned on.

17. Use the **Format Painter** 🖌 to format the rest of the headings:
    - What About Appliances?
    - What Are the Best Light Bulbs?
    - What are the Worst Offenders?
    - Who Is Responsible?

18. Choose **Home→Clipboard→Format Painter** 🖌 to turn off the feature.

Find and Replace

You've noticed some words you would like to change, so you will use Find and Replace to make the changes.

19. Position the insertion point at the top of the document.

20. Choose **Home→Editing→Replace** ᵃᵇ to open the Find and Replace dialog box.

21. Type **program** in the Find What box and **project** in the Replace With box.

22. Click **Find Next**, and then click **Replace**.

23. When the message appears, click **OK**.

24. Use the **Find and Replace** feature to change *offenders* to *wasters*.
    Hint: There are two occurrences of offenders.

25. When the message appears, click **OK**; close the dialog box.

Navigate with Bookmarks and Hyperlinks

Next you will create a bookmark for the last topic in the document and a hyperlink to another document.

26. Press ⎡Ctrl⎤+⎡End⎤ to move to the end of the document.

27. Select the last heading, *Who Is Responsible?*

28. Choose **Insert→Links→Bookmark** 🔖.

29. Type **WhoIsResponsible** (no spaces) in the **Bookmark Name** box; click **Add**.

30. Select the first heading at the top of the document.

31. Choose **Insert→Links→Hyperlink** 🌐 to open the Insert Hyperlink dialog box.

32. Make sure **Existing File or Web Page** is chosen in the Link To area.

33. In the Look In area, navigate to your **WD2013 Lesson 03** folder, choose **WD03-R02-EnergyHelp** from the file list, and click **OK**.

34. Click **OK** again to create the hyperlink.
    The formatting changes when the hyperlink is applied. Now you'll test your hyperlink and bookmark.

35. Press ⎡Ctrl⎤ and click the hyperlink to open the Energy Help document, and then close it.
    The appearance of the hyperlink changes after it is used.

36. Choose **Insert→Links→Bookmark** 🔖 from the menu.

37. Choose the bookmark and click **Go To**; close the dialog box.

Save the Document as a PDF

38. Choose **File→Save As** and navigate to your **WD2013 Lesson 03** folder.

39. Use the same file name and choose **PDF (*.pdf)** from the Save As Type menu.

40. Leave the optimization at **Standard**, and then click **Save**. (If the PDF file opens in a PDF reader, close the PDF window.)

41. Save and close the original document, and then exit from **Word**.

42. Submit your final file based on the guidelines provided by your instructor.
    To view examples of how your file or files should look at the end of this exercise, go to the student resource center.

Type and Format a Memorandum

In this exercise, you will create a memorandum, insert a page break, copy text, and use proofing tools. You will create a hyperlink to an external document and save your memo as a PDF file.

Type a Memo and Insert a Page Break

1. Start **Word**. Create new a document using the **Blank Document template** that is saved to the **WD2013 Lesson 03** folder as `WD03-R03-Green-[FirstInitialLastName]`.

2. If necessary, choose **Home→Paragraph→Show/Hide ¶** to turn on formatting marks.

3. Type the following memo using these guidelines:
   - Use formatting marks as a guide for spacing.
   - Use the Insert Date and Time feature on the Insert tab to insert and format the current date, and choose not to update automatically.

¶

¶

MEMO·TO: →   Kids·for·Change·Members¶

FROM:→   →   Harvey·Rodrick¶

DATE:→   →   Today's·Date¶

SUBJECT: →   Green·Construction¶

An·extension·is·being·added·to·the·building·where·we·hold·our·meetings.·We·would·like·to·ensure·that· the·owner,·Mr.·Evans,·hires·a·company·that·specializes·in·green·construction.·See·page·2·to·learn·what's· involved·in·this·type·of·construction.¶

Mr.·Evans·has·agreed·to·meet·with·us·to·consider·our·ideas.·Please·take·time·before·our·next·monthly· meeting·to·research·this·topic·so·we·can·prepare·a·winning·presentation.·¶

¶

¶

---

4. Make sure the insertion point is at the end of the document, and then press Ctrl + Enter to insert a page break.

5. Open **WD03-R03-Construction** from the **WD2013 Lesson 03** folder.

6. Select all of contents of the document, and then press Ctrl + C to copy it.

7. Close the **Construction** document, and then paste the copied material at the top of page 2 of the **Green** document.

Use Proofing Tools

8. Tap F7 to start proofing.

> **NOTE**
>
> If F7 does not work as expected, you may need to tap F-Lock at the top of your keyboard so F7 behaves as a function key.

Fluoorescent is highlighted in the Spelling task pane.

9. Click **Change** to correct the spelling.

10. Click **Change** to correct *sustainable*.
Daniel's last name is spelled correctly.

11. Click **Add** to add his name to the dictionary.
The Grammar checker caught the incorrect use of a pronoun.

12. Click **Change** to make the correction, and then when the message appears, click **OK**.
Now you will remove the name you added to the dictionary so the next student using your computer will have the same experience.

13. Choose **File→Options**, and then choose **Proofing** from the left panel.

14. Click **Custom Dictionaries**, and then in the Custom Dictionaries dialog box, click **Edit Word List**.

15. If necessary, scroll to locate *Datar* and click **Delete**, and then click **OK**.

16. Click **OK** two more times.
Datar is flagged again because you removed it from the dictionary.

Format Text

17. Select the *Green Construction* heading at the top of page 2, format it with **Century Gothic**, **14 point**, **Bold**; deselect the heading.

18. Scroll to the bottom of page 2, and then apply **Bold** and **Italics** to *Daniel Datar*.

19. Scroll to the top of page 1, and then apply **Bold** to the memo heading elements: *MEMO TO:*, *FROM:*, *DATE:*, and *SUBJECT:*.

20. Select *Green Construction* in the subject line, format it with a shade of green of your choice, and then apply **Bold**.

21. In the last sentence of the first paragraph on page 1, italicize *See page 2*.

22. Underline the last two words on page 1, *winning presentation*.

Use Find and Replace

23. Position the insertion point at the top of the document.

24. Choose **Home→Editing→Replace** to open the Find and Replace dialog box.

25. Type **concepts** in the **Find What** box and **ideas** in the **Replace With** box.

26. Click **Find Next**, and then when *concepts* is highlighted, click **Replace**.

27. Click **OK** when the message appears, and then close the dialog box.

    You've located some additional information on solar heating, so you will create a hyperlink to that information.

Create and Test a Hyperlink to Use for Navigation

28. Select *Solar heating* on page 2.

29. Choose **Insert→Links→Hyperlink** 🌐.

30. Make sure **Existing File or Web Page** is chosen.

31. In the Look In area, navigate to your **WD2013 Lesson 03** folder, and then choose **WD03-R03-Solar** from the list.

32. Click **OK** twice to create the hyperlink.

33. Press Ctrl and click the hyperlink to open the **Solar** document, and then close it.

Save the Document as a PDF

34. Choose **File→Save As**, and then navigate to your **WD2013 Lesson 03** folder.

35. Use the same filename, and then choose **PDF (*.pdf)** from the Save As Type menu.

36. Leave the optimization at **Standard**, and then click **Save**. (If the PDF file opens in a PDF reader, close the PDF window.)

    Next you will open and edit a PDF file. This is so you can understand the mechanics of how to do it.

When you open a PDF file in Word, there will be formatting issues. Don't worry about making the file look perfect. Concentrate more on how to open and edit, so you will be able to accomplish this task in the future when you need to edit a PDF file for which you don't have an original Word file.

Open and Edit the PDF

37. Open the **PDF** file you just saved.

38. When the message appears, click **OK**.

    The conversion to PDF misaligned the data in the FROM: and DATE: lines of the memo heading.

39. Add tabs to the *FROM:* and *DATE:* lines to realign them.

40. Change **Harvey Rodrick** in the FROM: line to `Miles Chung`.

41. Resave the file as a **PDF** in the **WD2013 Lesson 03** folder, named `WD03-R03-Green2-[FirstInitialLastName]`. (If the PDF file opens in in a PDF reader, close the PDF window.)

42. Close the original **PDF** without saving.

43. Save and close all documents; exit from **Word**.

44. Submit your final file based on the guidelines provided by your instructor.

Apply Your Skills

Create a Memorandum and a Press Release

In this exercise, you will type a memorandum, insert a page break, and copy text into page 2 of the memo. You will then insert a trademark symbol, correct spelling errors, and use the Thesaurus to find a synonym.

Type a Memorandum and Insert a Page Break

1. Start **Word**. Use the **Blank Document template** and save the file in your **WD2013 Lesson 03** folder as `WD03-A01-NewOffice-[FirstInitialLastName]`.

2. Type the following memo using proper spacing and tabs for aligning the memo head.

MEMO TO:	Malcolm Wesley
FROM:	Melissa Jones
DATE:	August 8, 2013
SUBJECT:	Bangalore Press Release

Malcolm, I've attached the press release for our Bangalore announcement. Would you please look it over and let me know if you have any changes or suggestions? Thanks!

3. Insert a **page break** at the end of the memo.

4. Open **WD03-A01-BangalorePR** from your **WD2013 Lesson 03** folder and copy everything from the document and paste it into the second page of the memo. Close the Bangalore file.

Insert a Symbol and Use Proofing Tools

5. Insert the **trademark symbol** after *Universal Corporate Events* in the first line of the first body paragraph in the press release.

6. Correct the spelling errors, and then use the **Thesaurus** to replace *aspects*, in the second line of the second paragraph, with a synonym of your choice.

7. Save and close the file; exit from **Word**.

8. Submit your final file based on the guidelines provided by your instructor.

   To view examples of how your file or files should look at the end of this exercise, go to the student resource center.

Use Formatting, Find and Replace, and a Bookmark

In this exercise, you will format headings in a document, use Find and Replace to make some editing changes, and create a bookmark to use for navigation. Finally, you will save the file as a PDF file.

Make Formatting Changes and Use Find and Replace

1. Start **Word**. Open **WD03-A02-IndiaTips** from your **WD2013 Lesson 03** folder and save it as `WD03-A02-IndiaTips-[FirstInitialLastName]`.

2. Select the first two heading lines.

3. Choose **Home→Font→Font menu button ▼**, and then use **Live Preview** to test several different fonts, and then test the **Tahoma** font.

4. Choose **Tahoma** and also apply **14 point, Bold**.

5. Select the *What Not to Do* heading, and then apply **Tahoma**, **Bold**, and **Italic**.

6. Use the **Format Painter** to copy the formatting to the other headings.

7. Use the Replace feature to make the following changes:
   - Replace *conversing* with *talking*
   - Replace *irritation* with *frustration*
   - Replace *another's* with *another person's*
   - Replace *appropriate* with *proper* (3 occurrences)

Navigate with a Bookmark and Save the File as a PDF

8. Select the *Dining* heading at the end of the document, and then create a **bookmark** named **Dining**.

9. Scroll to the top of the document and test your bookmark.

10. Save your file as a **PDF** using the same filename.

11. Save your original Word file and close it; exit from **Word**.

12. Submit your final file based on the guidelines provided by your instructor.
    To view examples of how your file or files should look at the end of this exercise, go to the student resource center.

Create, Format, and Navigate in a Memo

In this exercise, you will type a memo, insert a page break, and copy text into the new page. You will use the proofing tools, and then format the headings. You will use Find and Replace, insert a hyperlink, and finally, you will save the memo as a PDF file.

Create a Memorandum

1. Start **Word**. Create a new document using the **Blank Document template** and save to your **WD2013 Lesson 03** folder as **WD03-A03-HenslowMemo-[FirstInitialLastName]**.

2. Type the following memo using the appropriate spacing, automatically insert the date using the third date format, and don't check the Update Automatically feature.

MEMO TO:	Dennis Henslow
FROM:	Jordan Miller
DATE:	Today's Date
SUBJECT:	Additions to the London Trip

Dennis, since you're a Londoner, would you please take a look at the additional tours we're thinking of making available to our clients. Let me know if you agree or if you have any suggestions.

Insert a Page Break and Use Proofing Tools

3. Insert a **page break** at the end of the memo, and then open **WD03-A03-LondonTours** from your **WD2013 Lesson 03** folder.

4. Copy the content of the document, and then close it.

5. Paste the content into page 2 of your memo, and then correct the spelling and grammar. *Hint:* Cotswolds *is spelled correctly. The grammar error is in the second line of the first paragraph.*

Format Text

6. Format the heading at the top of page 2 with **Verdana**, **14 point**, **Bold**.

7. Format the *Local Excursions* heading with **Verdana**, **Bold**, and **Underline**.

8. Use the **Format Painter** 🖌 to copy the formatting to the *Day Trips* heading, and then deselect the heading.

Use Find and Replace and Insert a Hyperlink

9. Use the **Replace** feature to find *St. Paul's Cathedral* and replace it with *Westminster Abbey*.

10. Select *Stonehenge*, and then insert a hyperlink to **WD03-A03-Stonehenge** in your **WD2013 Lesson 03** folder.

11. Test the hyperlink, and then close the **Stonehenge** file.

Save the File in PDF

12. Save your memo as a PDF file using the same filename.

    Next you will open and edit a PDF file. This is so you can understand the mechanics of how to do it.

When you open a PDF file in Word, there will be formatting issues. Don't worry about making the file look perfect; instead, concentrate more on how to open and edit so you will be able to accomplish this task in the future.

Open and Edit the PDF

13. Open your **WD03-A03-HenslowMemo.pdf** file. When the message appears, click **OK**.

    The conversion to PDF misaligned the FROM: and DATE: lines in the memo heading.

14. Add tabs to the *FROM:* and *DATE*: lines to realign them.

15. Scroll to page 2 and remove the **underlines** from the *Local Excursions* and *Day Trip* headings.

16. Resave the file in **PDF** to the **WD2013 Lesson 03** folder. Name the file **WD03-A03-HenslowMemo2-[FirstInitialLastName]**. (If the PDF file opens in a PDF reader, close the PDF window.)

17. Save and close your Word version of the Henslow memo; exit from **Word**.

18. Submit your final file based on the guidelines provided by your instructor.

Extend Your Skills

In the course of working through the Extend Your Skills exercises, you will think critically as you use the skills taught in the lesson to complete the assigned projects. To evaluate your mastery and completion of the exercises, your instructor may use a rubric, with which more points are allotted according to performance characteristics. (The more you do, the more you earn!) Ask your instructor how your work will be evaluated.

WD03-E01 That's the Way I See It

Your friend has hired you to do marketing for her local small business. You need to research what is involved in producing a press release, because her company is planning to announce a new service soon. Conduct online research to determine:

- The purpose of a press release
- The main elements that typically appear in a press release
- How to create effective content for a press release
- Three suggestions for distributing a press release

Create a new Word document named **WD03-E01-PressRel-[FirstInitialLastName]** and saved to your **WD2013 Lesson 03** folder. Then, type the information you find into the document.

Create a page break, and then type a press release for the new service (make up the service you will be promoting) using the guidelines you have discovered and documented. Make sure to format the document so it is easy to read, using the Format Painter tool as needed. Preview how the file will appear when printed, and then save it as a PDF file named **WD03-E01-PressRelPDF-[FirstInitialLastName]** in your **WD2013 Lesson 03** folder.

You will be evaluated based on the inclusion of all elements specified, your ability to follow directions, your ability to apply newly learned skills to a real-world situation, your creativity, and the relevance of your topic and/or data choice(s). Submit your final files based on the guidelines provided by your instructor.

WD03-E02 Be Your Own Boss

You are the owner of Blue Jean Landscaping. Use your imagination to determine a new service that your company plans to offer and write a press release to announce the service. Be sure to include the primary elements of a press release and explain your service in an interesting way so a reporter reading your press release will be motivated to write a good story. Indicate how you will distribute your press release.

Use the formatting skills you have learned in this lesson to make the press release visually appealing. Save your finished press release as a PDF file as **WD03-E02-BJLPressRel-[FirstInitialLastName]** in your **WD2013 Lesson 03** folder.

You will be evaluated based on the inclusion of all elements specified, your ability to follow directions, your ability to apply newly learned skills to a real-world situation, your creativity, and your demonstration of an entrepreneurial spirit. Submit your final file based on the guidelines provided by your instructor.

Transfer Your Skills

In the course of working through the Transfer Your Skills exercises, you will use critical-thinking and creativity skills to complete the assigned projects using skills taught in the lesson. To evaluate your mastery and completion of the exercises, your instructor may use a rubric, with which more points are allotted according to performance characteristics. (The more you do, the more you earn!) Ask your instructor how your work will be evaluated.

WD03-T01 Use the Web as a Learning Tool

Throughout this book, you will be provided with an opportunity to use the Internet as a learning tool by completing WebQuests. According to the original creators of WebQuests, as described on their website (WebQuest.org), a WebQuest is "an inquiry-oriented activity in which most or all of the information used by learners is drawn from the web." To complete the WebQuest projects in this book, navigate to the student resource center and choose the WebQuest for the lesson on which you are currently working. The subject of each WebQuest will be relevant to the material found in the lesson.

WebQuest Subject: Why does a company need a press kit?

Submit your final file based on the guidelines provided by your instructor.

WD03-T02 Demonstrate Proficiency

As the owner of Stormy BBQ, create a memo to your employees about a new product you will be offering. (Use your imagination to come up with a new product.) In the memo, ask your employees to review the press release and offer any changes or suggestions they have. Create the press release on page 2 of the memo, advertising the new product. Conduct online research to determine the elements required for an effective press release, if necessary. Use Spell Check to make sure all words are spelled correctly, and then format the memo and press release using the tools you have learned in this lesson to make your document visually appealing.

Save your completed work as a PDF file named **WD03-T02-NewProdPDF-[FirstInitialLastName]** in your **WD2013 Lesson 03** folder. Submit your final file based on the guidelines provided by your instructor.

Creating a Simple Report

LEARNING OBJECTIVES

After studying this lesson, you will be able to:

- Use paragraph alignment settings
- Set custom tab stops
- Format lists
- Apply borders, shading, and styles
- Insert page numbers

In this lesson, you will create a simple report. Reports are important documents often used in business and education. You will format your report using various paragraph formatting techniques, including paragraph alignment, custom tab stops, and Word's indent feature. You will work with bulleted and numbered lists, and you will add interest to the report by applying borders, shading, and styles. You will be introduced to headers and footers, and you will use the Navigation pane to navigate by heading styles and to quickly reorganize your document.

Formatting a Research Report

A business analyst at My Virtual Campus has asked you to assist in researching the use of social media at universities. The report will be a useful tool for management to have as background information. It is important to understand how the "always connected" generation is using technology to pursue their education, to study, and to perform classroom activities. You will use paragraph formatting techniques such as indents, styles, and bullets and numbering to prepare an easy-to-read, properly formatted, and professional-looking document.

My Virtual Campus

SOCIAL MEDIA IN UNIVERSITIES

Universities today are engaging constantly-connected Millennials through social media. Use of Facebook, YouTube, Twitter, blogging, and podcasting have all experienced double-digit increases on campus in the last year. Students are checking out universities through student-run blogs, and recruiters are checking out students on Facebook and LinkedIn.

The Net Generation

In her article appearing in The Teaching Professor, August/September 2009, Dalton State College psychology professor Christy Price makes the following observations:

"...the ideal learning environment was Millennials' preference for a variety of teaching methods, as opposed to a "lecture only" format."

"Respondents thought professors who involved them in class with a variety of methods (not just lecture) as more connected to millennial culture."

Formatting Reports

Video Library http://labyrinthelab.com/videos   Video Number: WD13-V0401

There is a variety of acceptable report formats. Different formats can be used for marketing publications and other types of business and educational documents. The following example shows a traditional business report in unbound format.

The title is positioned at approximately 2 inches from the top of the page and centered.

The title is in uppercase and bold; you can also apply a distinctive font to the title.

SOCIAL MEDIA IN UNIVERSITIES

Universities today are engaging constantly-connected Millennials through social media. Use of Facebook, YouTube, Twitter, blogging, and podcasting have all experienced double-digit increases on campus in the last year. Students are checking out universities through student-run blogs, and recruiters are checking out students on Facebook and LinkedIn.

The Net Generation

In her article appearing in The Teaching Professor, August/September 2009, Dalton State College psychology professor Christy Price makes the following observations:

> "...the ideal learning environment was Millennials' preference for a variety of teaching methods, as opposed to a "lecture only" format."
>
> "Respondents thought professors who involved them in class with a variety of methods (not just lecture) as more connected to millennial culture."

The body is double-spaced with paragraphs indented to ½ inch.

Quotations and other text you want to emphasize are indented on the left and right.

Formatting Paragraphs

Paragraph formatting includes paragraph alignment, line spacing, and bullets and numbering, to mention a few. In Word, a paragraph is created anytime you tap [Enter]. In other words, a paragraph could consist of several lines that end with [Enter] or just one line, such as a heading, that ends with [Enter]. Tapping [Enter] to generate a blank line creates a paragraph, even though there is no text in it. What's more, Word stores formats in the paragraph symbol.

Each of these is a paragraph because each ends with a paragraph symbol (heading, blank lines, text paragraph).

Social·Media·Benefits·for·Students¶
¶
        Technology·can·be·used·to·reach·the·Net°Generation·in·an·effective·way.·They·consider· technology·a·natural·way·to·pursue·their·education,·to·study,·and·to·perform·classroom·activities.·¶
¶
    ♦ → Search·for·classes·online¶
            o → Locate·desired·subjects,·dates,·and·times¶
            o → Review·syllabi¶

Each of these lines is a paragraph.

Comparing Paragraph Formatting to Character Formatting

Selecting paragraphs for formatting purposes is a little different from selecting characters. With character formatting, you typically select the entire block of text you want to format, which is necessary in the majority of cases. With paragraph formatting, you need only click in the paragraph to *select* it. On the other hand, if you want to apply formatting to more than one paragraph, you must select at least part of each paragraph.

Using Paragraph Alignment

Paragraph alignment determines how text aligns between the margins. Left alignment gives paragraphs a straight left margin and ragged right margin. Center alignment is usually applied to headings. Right alignment generates a straight right and ragged left margin. Justify provides straight left and right margins.

FROM THE RIBBON
Home→Paragraph→ Alignment Option

FROM THE KEYBOARD
[Ctrl]+[L] align left
[Ctrl]+[E] center
[Ctrl]+[R] align right
[Ctrl]+[J] justify

Here's how the different paragraph alignment settings look in Word.

Left-aligned ——— | Centered ——— | Right-aligned ———

SOCIAL MEDIA IN UNIVERSITIES

SOCIAL MEDIA IN UNIVERSITIES

SOCIAL MEDIA IN UNIVERSITIES

Justified ——— Universities today are engaging constantly-connected Millennials through social media. Use of Facebook, YouTube, Twitter, blogging, and podcasting have all experienced double-digit increases on campus in the last year. Students are checking out universities through student-run blogs, and recruiters are checking out students on Facebook and LinkedIn.

DEVELOP YOUR SKILLS WD04-D01
Align Text

In this exercise, you will use the alignment buttons in the Paragraph group of the Home tab to align your report heading.

1. Start **Word**. Create a new, blank document using the **Blank Document template** and make sure the Word window is **maximized**.

2. Save the file as **WD04-D01-SocMediaRprt-[FirstInitialLastName]** in your **WD2013 Lesson 04** folder.

   Replace the bracketed text with your first initial and last name. For example, if your name is Bethany Smith, your filename would look like this: WD04-D01-SocMediaRprt-BSmith.

3. Tap Enter twice to position the insertion point approximately **2 inches** from the top of the page.

4. Turn on Caps Lock, and then choose **Home→Font→Bold** B.

5. Type the report title, **SOCIAL MEDIA IN UNIVERSITIES**.

6. Choose **Home→Font→Bold** B and then tap Caps Lock to turn both off.

7. Tap Enter twice to provide blank lines before the body of the report, which you will add shortly.

8. Position the insertion point in the report heading.

Align the Heading

9. Choose **Home→Paragraph→Align Right** ≣.

10. Choose **Home→Paragraph→Align Left** ≣.

11. Choose **Home→Paragraph→Center** ≣.

12. Save the file and leave it open; you will modify it throughout the lesson.

Adding Hyphenation

Video Library   http://labyrinthelab.com/videos   Video Number: WD13-V0402

Typically, when you create a document, you let Word Wrap do its thing; that is, it adds all of the text it can on a line until it comes to a word that won't fit, and then it wraps down to the next line. Sometimes this can cause your right margin to appear too ragged. You can use hyphenation to create a more even margin.

FROM THE RIBBON
Page Layout→Page Setup→Hyphenation

- **Automatic:** The entire document is hyphenated automatically, and as you edit or revise the document hyphenation continues.

- **Manual:** Manual hyphenation searches for words you might want to hyphenate and provides a prompt where you can accept, modify, or reject the hyphenation.

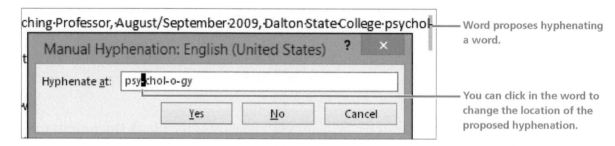

Word proposes hyphenating a word.

You can click in the word to change the location of the proposed hyphenation.

DEVELOP YOUR SKILLS WD04-D02
Use Manual Hyphenation

In this exercise, you will copy the content for your report from another document, and then you will use manual hyphenation to smooth out the right-hand margin.

1. Save your file as **WD04-D02-SocMediaRprt-[FirstInitialLastName]**.

2. If necessary, choose **Home→Paragraph→Show/Hide** ¶ to turn on formatting marks.

3. Open **WD04-D02-RprtContent** from your **WD2013 Lesson 04** folder.

4. Press ⌨Ctrl+⌨A to select all content, and then press ⌨Ctrl+⌨C to copy it.

5. Close **WD04-D02-RprtContent**.

    You will now paste the copied document in the Social Media Report document.

6. Follow these steps to paste the document into the report:

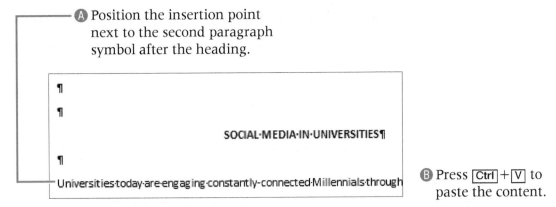

A Position the insertion point next to the second paragraph symbol after the heading.

¶

¶

SOCIAL·MEDIA·IN·UNIVERSITIES¶

¶

Universities·today·are·engaging·constantly·connected·Millennials·through

B Press ⌈Ctrl⌉+⌈V⌉ to paste the content.

7. Choose **Home→Paragraph→Show/Hide** ¶ to turn off formatting marks.

8. Press ⌈Ctrl⌉+⌈Home⌉.

Hyphenate Words

9. Choose **Page Layout→Page Setup→Hyphenation** ᵇᶜᵃ and choose **Manual** from the menu.

10. When Word proposes hyphenating *Facebook*, click **No**.
    In this example, we prefer to keep Facebook as one word even though it could be hyphenated.

11. When Word proposes hyphenating *psychology*, click **Yes** to accept the suggestion.

12. When Word proposes hyphenating *opposed*, click **Yes** to accept the suggestion.

13. When Word suggests hyphenating *increases*, click **Cancel** to end Manual hyphenation.

14. Save the report.

Inserting a Nonbreaking Hyphen or Space

Video Library   http://labyrinthelab.com/videos   Video Number: WD13-V0403

Word allows you to keep terms together that should remain together on one line, such as dates or hyphenated names. You use nonbreaking hyphens and nonbreaking spaces to accomplish this.

FROM THE KEYBOARD

⌈Ctrl⌉+⌈Shift⌉+⌈Hyphen⌉ to add a nonbreaking hyphen

⌈Ctrl⌉+⌈Shift⌉+⌈Spacebar⌉ to add a nonbreaking space

QUICK REFERENCE	USING NONBREAKING HYPHENS AND SPACES
Task	**Procedure**
Insert Nonbreaking Hyphens	▪ Choose Insert→Symbols→Symbol, and then choose More Symbols. ▪ Click the Special Characters tab, choose Nonbreaking Hyphen, and click Insert.
Insert Nonbreaking Spaces	▪ Choose Insert→Symbols→Symbol, and then choose More Symbols. ▪ Click the Special Characters tab, choose Nonbreaking Space, and click Insert.

Insert Nonbreaking Hyphens and Spaces

In this exercise, you will insert nonbreaking hyphens and spaces in your document. Then you will test to see if the words stay together as one term.

1. Save your file as **WD04-D03-SocMediaRprt-[FirstInitialLastName]**.

2. Scroll to the top of the document.

3. Follow these steps to insert a nonbreaking hyphen in double-digit:

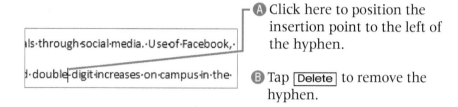

Ⓐ Click here to position the insertion point to the left of the hyphen.

Ⓑ Tap ⌷Delete⌷ to remove the hyphen.

4. Choose **Insert→Symbols→Symbol** Ω.

5. Choose **More Symbols** from the menu, and when the Symbol dialog box opens, click the **Special Characters** tab.

6. Choose **Nonbreaking Hyphen**, click **Insert**, and close the dialog box.

7. Position the insertion point to the left of *double-digit*.

8. Tap ⌷Spacebar⌷ several times to move double-digit to the right until it wraps to the next line as a single term.

   Notice the nonbreaking hyphen you inserted kept the hyphenated word together.

9. Click **Undo** ↺ on the Quick Access toolbar to undo the spaces you inserted.

Insert and Test a Nonbreaking Space

10. Scroll to the end of the document.

11. Follow these steps to insert a nonbreaking space:

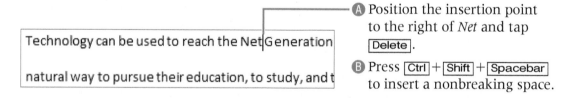

Ⓐ Position the insertion point to the right of *Net* and tap ⌷Delete⌷.

Ⓑ Press ⌷Ctrl⌷+⌷Shift⌷+⌷Spacebar⌷ to insert a nonbreaking space.

12. Position the insertion point to the left of *Net* and tap ⌷Spacebar⌷ until *Net Generation* wraps to the next line as one term.

   The nonbreaking space kept the words together as one term.

13. Click **Undo** ↺ on the Quick Access toolbar.

14. Save the report.

Indenting Text

Video Library   http://labyrinthelab.com/videos   Video Number: WD13-V0404

Indents offset text from the margins. You can set indents by using the buttons on the Ribbon or by dragging the indent markers on the ruler.

Adjusting Indents with the Ribbon

The Increase Indent and Decrease Indent buttons adjust the indent of an entire paragraph (or one or more selected paragraphs) and they affect the left indent only. They adjust the indent based on the default tab stops, which are set at every half inch.

FROM THE RIBBON
Home→Paragraph→ Decrease/Increase Indent

FROM THE KEYBOARD
Ctrl + Shift + M to decrease the indent

Ctrl + M to increase the indent

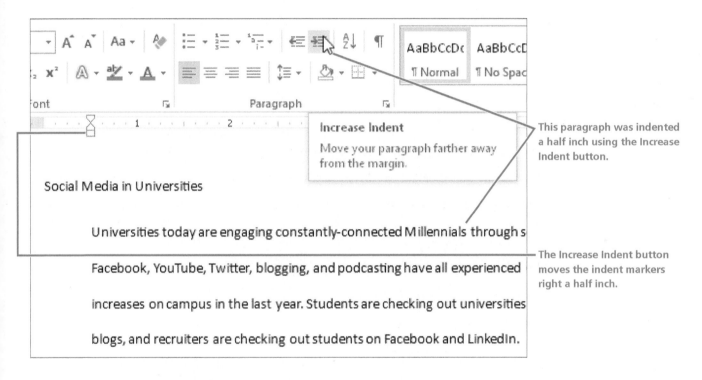

Increase Indent

Move your paragraph farther away from the margin.

This paragraph was indented a half inch using the Increase Indent button.

The Increase Indent button moves the indent markers right a half inch.

Experiment with Left Indents

In this exercise, you will use the Increase Indent button to indent quotations to one inch. Then you will use the Decrease Indent button to return the quotations to the left margin.

1. Save your file as **WD04-D04-SocMediaRprt-[FirstInitialLastName]**.

2. If necessary, choose **View→Show→Ruler** to turn on the ruler.

3. Follow these steps to indent multiple paragraphs:

A Select these two paragraphs.

B Click **Increase Indent** twice to indent the paragraphs one inch.

C Notice the indent markers moved to the 1-inch mark.

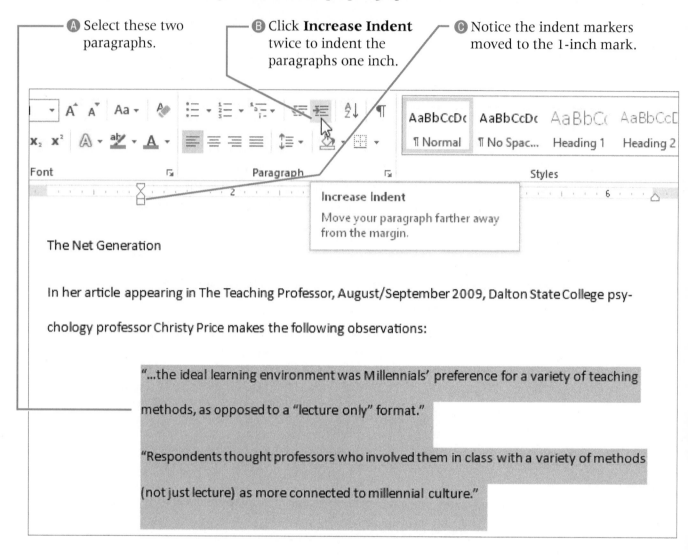

4. Make sure the paragraphs are still selected.

5. Choose **Home→Paragraph→Decrease Indent** twice to return the paragraphs to the left margin.

6. Save the report.

Setting Custom Indents on the Ruler

Video Library   http://labyrinthelab.com/videos   Video Number: WD13-V0405

You can set indents by dragging the indent markers on the horizontal ruler. The following illustration shows the ruler and the indent markers.

INDENT MARKERS	
Item	**Description**
First Line Indent	Indents the first line of the paragraph.
Hanging Indent	This triangle is *attached* to the Left Indent rectangle. Place the mouse pointer in the triangle and drag right to indent everything except the first line.
Left Indent	This rectangle is *attached* to the Hanging Indent triangle. Place the mouse pointer in the rectangle and drag left/right to position all lines simultaneously. Whether the triangles are aligned with each other or separated, dragging the rectangle positions both triangles simultaneously.
Right Indent	Drag to indent the entire paragraph from the right.

Using Hanging Indents

Hanging indents are not often used, thus many people are not familiar with the term. The following illustration shows an example of a hanging indent, where the first line is *outdented* and the remaining lines of the paragraph are *indented*.

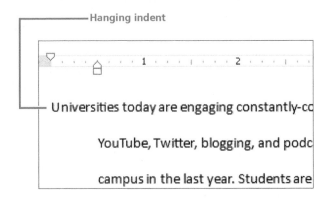

Use the Indent Markers to Indent Paragraphs

In this exercise, you will use the indent markers on the horizontal ruler to indent the quotations from both the left and right. You will also use the First Line Indent marker to indent the first line of the other paragraphs.

1. Save your file as **WD04-D05-SocMediaRprt-[FirstInitialLastName]**.

2. Follow these steps to adjust the left and right indents:

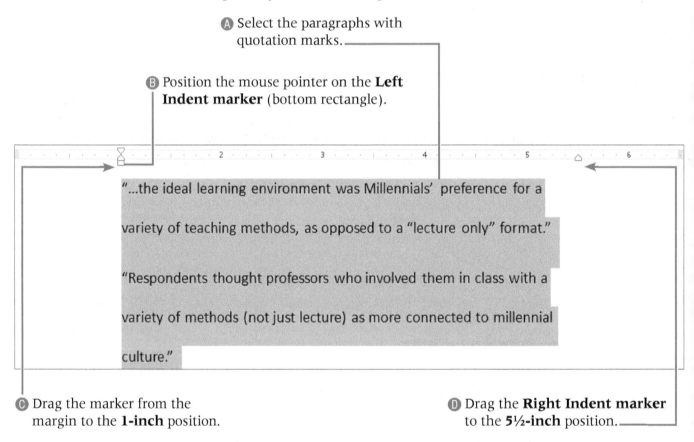

Ⓐ Select the paragraphs with quotation marks.

Ⓑ Position the mouse pointer on the **Left Indent marker** (bottom rectangle).

"...the ideal learning environment was Millennials' preference for a variety of teaching methods, as opposed to a "lecture only" format."

"Respondents thought professors who involved them in class with a variety of methods (not just lecture) as more connected to millennial culture."

Ⓒ Drag the marker from the margin to the **1-inch** position.

Ⓓ Drag the **Right Indent marker** to the **5½-inch** position.

3. Follow these steps to indent the first line of paragraphs:

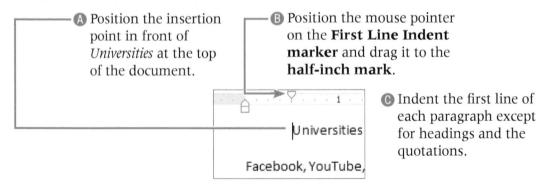

Ⓐ Position the insertion point in front of *Universities* at the top of the document.

Ⓑ Position the mouse pointer on the **First Line Indent marker** and drag it to the **half-inch mark**.

Universities

Facebook, YouTube,

Ⓒ Indent the first line of each paragraph except for headings and the quotations.

4. Save the report.

Using Custom Tab Stops

Video Library http://labyrinthelab.com/videos Video Number: WD13-V0406

Default tab stops are set every one-half inch, so the insertion point moves one-half inch whenever you tap Tab. You can customize tab stops if you want other settings, or if you want to use a special tab, such as one that center aligns.

Never use the spacebar to line up columns of text. Even if it looks right on the screen, it most likely will not print correctly.

Setting Custom Tab Stops with the Ruler

Word has four types of custom tab stops: left, right, center, and decimal. You can set all four types using the horizontal ruler. It is critical that you position the insertion point on the line where you plan to set tabs. Tab settings are carried inside the paragraph symbol to the next paragraph when you tap Enter.

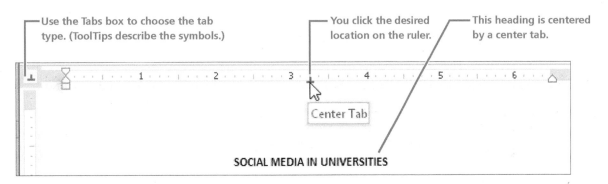

— Use the Tabs box to choose the tab type. (ToolTips describe the symbols.)

— You click the desired location on the ruler.

— This heading is centered by a center tab.

Center Tab

SOCIAL MEDIA IN UNIVERSITIES

DEVELOP YOUR SKILLS WD04-D06
Set Tabs Using the Ruler

In this exercise, you will use custom tabs to set up text in a columnar format.

1. Save your file as **WD04-D06-SocMediaRprt-[FirstInitialLastName]**.

2. If necessary, choose **Home→Paragraph→Show/Hide ¶** to display formatting marks.

3. If necessary, choose **View→Show→Ruler** to turn on the ruler.

4. Follow these steps to set tabs for the heading line of your table:

Ⓐ Position the insertion point on the blank line after the paragraph, at the top of the next page.

Ⓑ Make sure the **Left Tab** is visible here. Click in the box as necessary to rotate to Left Tab.

Ⓒ Click at the **2-inch mark**. (Click toward the bottom of the ruler.)

Ⓓ Click at the **4-inch mark**.

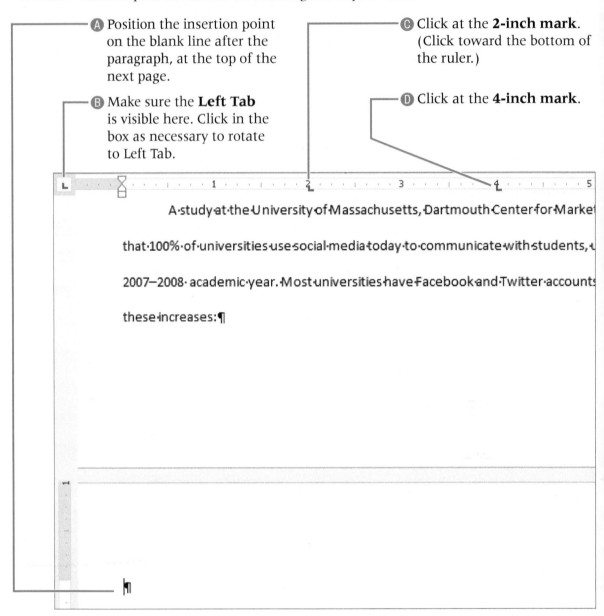

A·study·at·the·University·of·Massachusetts,·Dartmouth·Center·for·Marke

that·100%·of·universities·use·social·media·today·to·communicate·with·students,·

2007–2008· academic·year.·Most·universities·have·Facebook·and·Twitter·account

these·increases:¶

5. Type the following heading line, tapping ⟦Tab⟧ where you see small arrows.

Media	→	2009–2010	→	2010–2011¶

6. Tap ⟦Enter⟧ at the end of the line, and notice that the ruler still reflects the tabs you set in the previous line.

7. Save the report.

Working with the Tabs Dialog Box

Video Library   http://labyrinthelab.com/videos   Video Number: WD13-V0407

You can set custom tab stops in the Tabs dialog box. You can specify precise positions for custom tabs, choose the type of tab (alignment), clear custom tab stops, and set leader tabs.

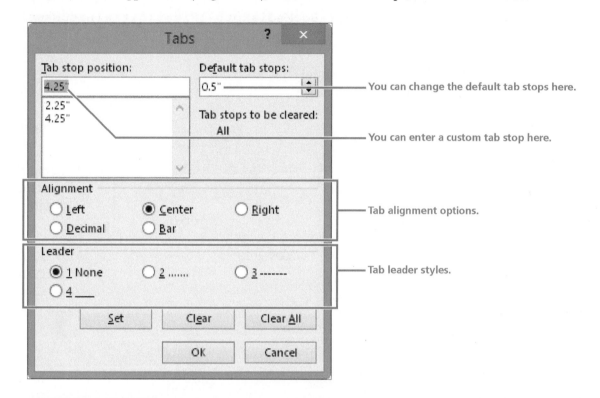

You can change the default tab stops here.

You can enter a custom tab stop here.

Tab alignment options.

Tab leader styles.

QUICK REFERENCE	USING THE INDENT MARKERS
Task	**Procedure**
Set tabs	■ Choose the desired tab in the Tabs box and click the desired location on the ruler; or, choose Home→Paragraph→dialog box launcher and click Tabs.
	■ Enter the settings in the Tab Stop Position field, choose the Alignment, and click Set.
Modify tab settings	■ Drag the tab(s) to a new location on the ruler; or, in the Tabs dialog box, clear the tab(s) you want to change, enter new settings in the Tab Stop Position field, and click Set.
Clear tabs	■ Drag the tab(s) off the ruler; or, use the Clear or Clear All button in the Tabs dialog box.

Word 2013

Use the Tabs Dialog Box

In this exercise, you will use the Tabs dialog box to clear tabs that were set for the table's heading line and to set custom tabs for the body of the table.

1. Save your file as **WD04-D07-SocMediaRprt-[FirstInitialLastName]**.

2. Follow these steps to clear all tabs:

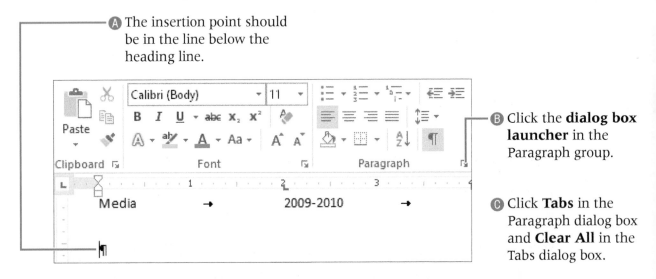

Ⓐ The insertion point should be in the line below the heading line.

Ⓑ Click the **dialog box launcher** in the Paragraph group.

Ⓒ Click **Tabs** in the Paragraph dialog box and **Clear All** in the Tabs dialog box.

3. Follow these steps to set new tabs for the rest of the table:

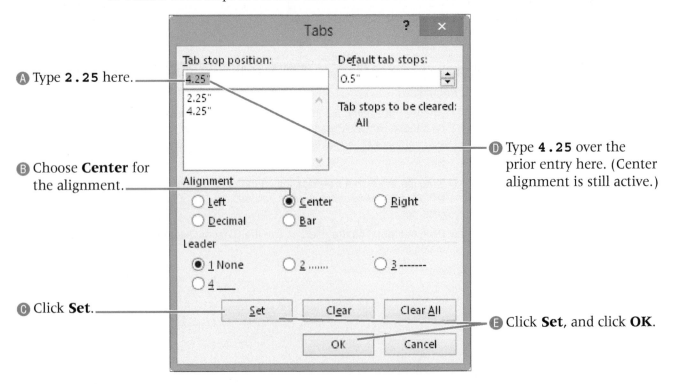

Ⓐ Type **2.25** here.

Ⓑ Choose **Center** for the alignment.

Ⓒ Click **Set**.

Ⓓ Type **4.25** over the prior entry here. (Center alignment is still active.)

Ⓔ Click **Set**, and click **OK**.

4. Type the rest of the table, tapping ⌨Tab wherever an arrow appears, and tapping ⌨Enter at the end of each line.

Media	→	2009–2010	→	2010–2011¶
Facebook	→	87%	→	98%¶
Twitter	→	59%	→	84%¶
Blogs	→	51%	→	66%¶
Podcasts	→	22%	→	41%¶

5. Select the first line in the table and choose **Home→Font→Bold** B.

6. Save the file.

Modifying Tab Stops with the Ruler

Video Library   http://labyrinthelab.com/videos   Video Number: WD13-V0408

To adjust a tab setting on the ruler, you select the paragraphs containing the tab stops you want to change, and then drag the tab to the new location. Delete a tab by dragging it off the Ruler.

If you accidentally drag a tab stop off the ruler while trying to move it, just click Undo.

DEVELOP YOUR SKILLS WD04-D08

Modify and Delete Tab Stops from the Ruler

In this exercise, you decided the percentages could be better centered below the headings. You will use the ruler to modify the tab stops for the body of the table but not the heading line. Then you will delete a tab stop.

1. Save your file as **`WD04-D08-SocMediaRprt-[FirstInitialLastName]`**.
2. Follow these steps to adjust the tabs:

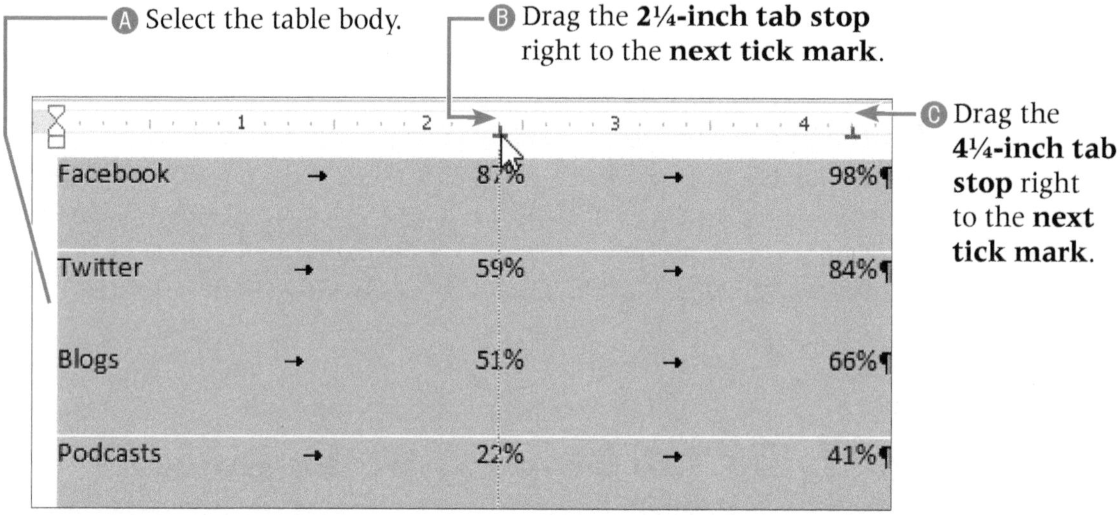

A Select the table body.
B Drag the 2¼-inch tab stop right to the next tick mark.
C Drag the 4¼-inch tab stop right to the next tick mark.
Facebook
87%
98%
Twitter
59%
84%
Blogs
51%
66%
Podcasts
22%
41%

Now you will delete a tab stop.

3. Place the mouse pointer on the **4 3/8 inch tab** and drag it straight down off the ruler to remove the tab.
4. Click **Undo** on the Quick Access toolbar to replace the tab stop.
5. Save the report.

Using Numbered and Bulleted Lists

Video Library   http://labyrinthelab.com/videos   Video Number: WD13-V0409

Numbered and bulleted lists are effective in drawing your reader's attention to items of interest. You can turn them on before you begin typing or apply them after you type the list. Numbered lists are automatically renumbered if you insert or delete an item. A good example of when to use a numbered list is when sequence is important, as in a series of steps. Items in a bulleted list have no sequence.

FROM THE RIBBON
Home→Paragraph→
Bullets

Home→Paragraph→
Numbering

Promoting and Demoting List Items

Demoting an item increases the indent level by shifting it to the right. To promote an item decreases the indent level by moving it back to the left. When you demote items in a list, it creates an outline effect, indicating the level of importance of the items in the list.

FROM THE KEYBOARD
Shift+Tab to promote a list item

Tab to demote a list item

- Search for classes online
  - Locate desired subjects, dates, and times
  - Review syllabi
- Use course homepages

These two items were demoted by increasing the indent level.

QUICK REFERENCE	WORKING WITH LISTS
Task	**Procedure**
Convert text to a bulleted or numbered list	■ Select the text to be formatted, and choose Home→Paragraph→Bullets or Numbering.
Turn off bullets and numbering	■ Tap Enter twice at the end of the list; or, click the Bullets or the Numbering button.
Demote an item in a list	■ Select the item and choose Home→Paragraph→Increase Indent; or, tap Tab.
Promote an item in a list	■ Select the item and choose Home→Paragraph→Decrease Indent; or, press Shift+Tab.
Customize Bullets and Numbering	■ Choose Home→Paragraph→Bullets or Numbering menu button ▼ and choose Define New Bullet or Define New Number Format.
Remove a custom bullet or numbering from the gallery	■ Right-click the image and choose Remove.

Work with Bullets and Numbering

In this exercise, you will convert text to a numbered list, and then you'll create a bulleted list, promoting and demoting levels within the list.

1. Save your file as **WD04-D09-SocMediaRprt-[FirstInitialLastName]**.

2. Follow these steps to create a list:

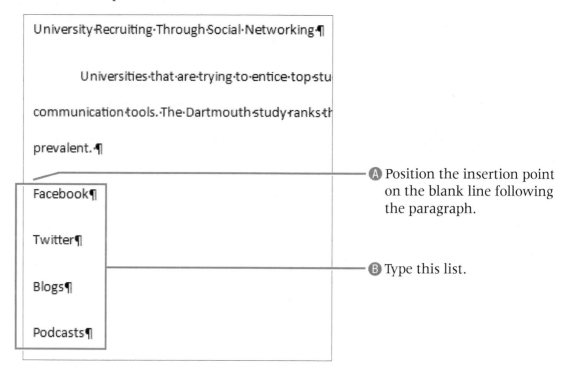

Ⓐ Position the insertion point on the blank line following the paragraph.

Ⓑ Type this list.

3. Select the list and choose **Home→Paragraph→Numbering** ▤.

4. Position the insertion point on the first blank line following the last paragraph.
   You will switch to single spacing before typing the bulleted list.

5. Choose **Home→Paragraph→Line and Paragraph Spacing menu button** ▼, and then choose **1.0** from the menu.

6. Follow these steps to create a bulleted list:

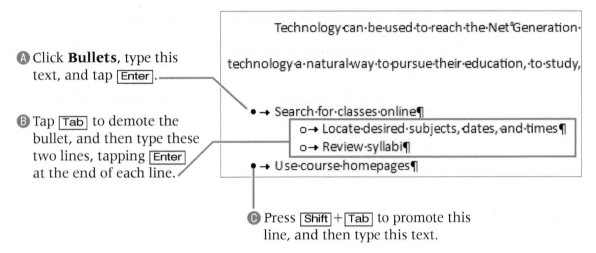

A Click **Bullets**, type this text, and tap [Enter].

B Tap [Tab] to demote the bullet, and then type these two lines, tapping [Enter] at the end of each line.

C Press [Shift]+[Tab] to promote this line, and then type this text.

7. Type the rest of the list as shown, demoting and promoting the bullet levels as needed.

```
• →  Use·course·homepages¶
        o→ Read·announcements¶
        o→ Get·student·handouts¶
        o→ Conduct·threaded·conversations·on·message·boards¶
        o→ Communicate·with·instructors·in·chat·rooms¶
• →  View·faculty·office·hours·online¶
• →  Review·academic·history·online¶
```

8. Save the report.

Using the Bullets and Numbering Libraries

FROM THE RIBBON

Home→Paragraph→
Bullets menu button ▾

Home→Paragraph→
Numbering menu
button ▾

Video Library   http://labyrinthelab.com/videos   Video Number: WD13-V0410

The Bullets and Numbering libraries enable you to choose a style for your bulleted or numbered list. You can also define your own custom formats.

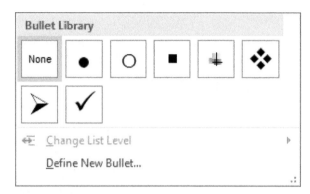

Bullet Library

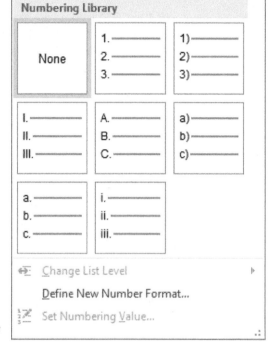

Numbering Library

Change the Bullet Style

In this exercise, you will choose a different bullet style for the first-level bullets from the Bullet Library.

1. Save your file as **WD04-D10-SocMediaRprt-[FirstInitialLastName]**.

2. Follow these steps to apply a different bullet:

Ⓐ Click in this **first-level bullet** line.   Ⓑ Click the **menu button ▼** on the Bullet button.

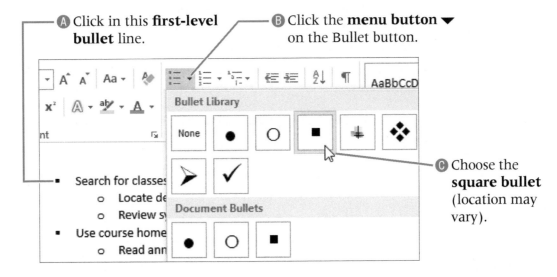

Ⓒ Choose the **square bullet** (location may vary).

Notice that the bullet shape changed for all first-level bullets.

3. Save the report.

Customizing Bullet and Number Styles

Video Library   http://labyrinthelab.com/videos   Video Number: WD13-V0411

You can customize bullet styles by defining a symbol, picture, font, or alignment. You can customize the numbering style, font, format, and alignment.

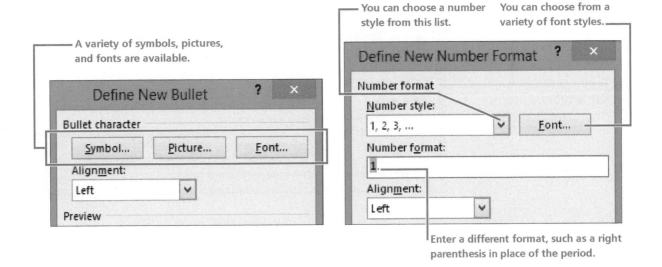

A variety of symbols, pictures, and fonts are available.

You can choose a number style from this list.   You can choose from a variety of font styles.

Enter a different format, such as a right parenthesis in place of the period.

Restarting or Continuing Numbering

Many documents have more than one numbered list. You may want the numbering to continue sequentially from one list to the next. For example, if one list ends with the number 4 you may want the next list to begin with 5. If you type text after the first list, when you begin the next list, Word assumes you want to restart numbering at 1. If you want to continue numbering, Word provides an AutoCorrect smart tag where you can choose Continue Numbering.

DEVELOP YOUR SKILLS WD04-D11
Experiment with Custom Bullets

In this exercise, you will use the Define New Bullet dialog box to create a custom bullet. You will use a symbol as the new bullet style.

1. Save your file as **WD04-D11-SocMediaRprt-[FirstInitialLastName]**.

2. Click anywhere in a **first-level bulleted line** (such as *Search for classes online*).

3. Choose **Home→Paragraph→Bullets** ▤ **menu button** ▼ and choose **Define New Bullet**.

4. Follow these steps to define a symbol as a new bullet:

Ⓐ Click the **Symbol** button to open the Symbol dialog box.

Ⓑ Choose the **Wingdings** font.

Ⓒ Choose this symbol. (If you cannot locate it, see the next instruction.)

Ⓓ If you cannot locate the symbol, enter its Character Code: **119**.

Ⓔ Click **OK** twice.

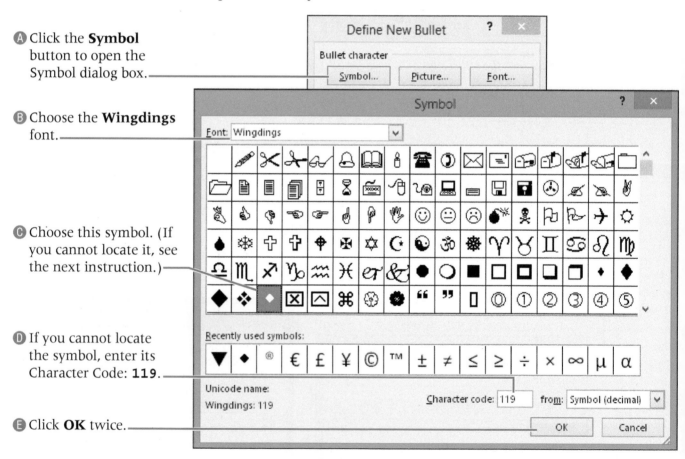

Notice that all the first-level bullets have changed to the custom bullet.

5. Choose **Home→Paragraph→Bullets** ▦ **menu button** ▼ to display the Bullet Library.

The new bullet was added to the library. Now you'll remove the bullet so the next student who uses your computer will have the same experience.

6. Right-click the new bullet in the Bullet Library area, and choose **Remove**.

7. Display the **Bullet Library** again and notice that the new bullet was removed; close the menu.

8. Save the report.

Setting Line Breaks

Video Library   http://labyrinthelab.com/videos   Video Number: WD13-V0412

FROM THE KEYBOARD
Shift + Enter to create
a line break

When working with bullets and numbering, tapping Enter generates a new bullet or number. What if you want to type something relative to a bulleted or numbered item on the next line(s) without generating a new bullet or number? A manual line break starts a new line (without inserting a paragraph mark) and continues the text on the new line. Line breaks are inserted with the Shift + Enter keystroke combination.

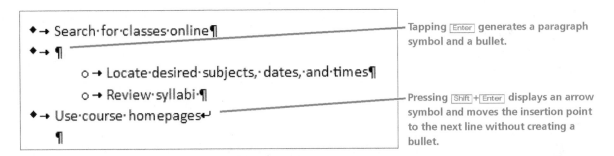

Tapping Enter generates a paragraph symbol and a bullet.

Pressing Shift + Enter displays an arrow symbol and moves the insertion point to the next line without creating a bullet.

DEVELOP YOUR SKILLS WD04-D12
Insert Line Breaks in a List

In this exercise, you will use line breaks to add descriptive information about Facebook and Twitter. The line breaks will allow you to type additional information without generating a new number.

1. Save your file as **WD04-D12-SocMediaRprt-[FirstInitialLastName]**.

2. If necessary, choose **Home→Paragraph→Show/Hide** ¶ to display formatting marks.

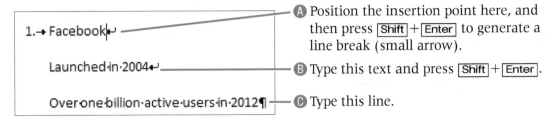

Ⓐ Position the insertion point here, and then press Shift + Enter to generate a line break (small arrow).

Ⓑ Type this text and press Shift + Enter.

Ⓒ Type this line.

3. Position the insertion point to the right of *Twitter* in your numbered list.

4. Press ⎡Shift⎤+⎡Enter⎤ to generate a line break.

5. Type **Launched in 2006** and press ⎡Shift⎤+⎡Enter⎤.

6. Type the following: **Over 500 million active users in 2012.**

7. Save the report.

Using Paragraph Space Settings

Video Library   http://labyrinthelab.com/videos   Video Number: WD13-V0413

The default spacing in Word 2013 is 1.08 rather than the traditional single spacing (1.0). Word adds 8 points (a little less than an eighth of an inch) of after-paragraph spacing when you use the Blank Document template. You can modify the amount of space that comes before or after a paragraph.

FROM THE RIBBON

Page Layout→
Paragraph→Before

Page Layout→
Paragraph→After

Indent		Spacing	
≣ Left:	0"	↑≣ Before:	0 pt
≣ Right:	0"	↓≣ After:	8 pt
	Paragraph		

Before and After paragraph spacing

72 points = 1 inch

DEVELOP YOUR SKILLS WD04-D13
Set Paragraph Spacing

In this exercise, you will change the paragraph spacing between the headings and their following paragraphs.

1. Save your file as **WD04-D13-SocMediaRprt-[FirstInitialLastName]**.

2. Click in the heading *The Net Generation* on page 1.

3. Choose **Page Layout→Paragraph**, click the **After** box, type **2**, and tap ⎡Enter⎤.
   Notice there is a little less space following the heading.

The spin box controls in the Spacing section use 6-point increments. If you want to use a different measurement, you must enter it manually.

4. Repeat the process for the remaining three headings.

5. Save the report.

Formatting with Borders and Shading

Video Library   http://labyrinthelab.com/videos   Video Number: WD13-V0414

You can apply borders and shading to selected text, paragraphs, and objects, such as tables. Page borders are also available to outline an entire page. In this lesson, you will apply borders to paragraphs. You can choose the style, color, and thickness of borders, and you can also select various shading colors and patterns.

Using Borders and Shading Buttons and the Dialog Box

The Borders and Shading buttons have memory. The button face displays the last choice you made. That way you can apply the same type of border or shading several times in a row without opening the menu.

FROM THE RIBBON

Home→Paragraph→
Borders menu button ▾

Home→Paragraph→
Shading menu button ▾

Default bottom border ⎯⎯⎯⎯⎯⎯   ⎯⎯⎯⎯ Button face where the last
                                            choice was Outside Borders

Choosing Borders and Shading from the Borders button menu displays the dialog box. The following illustrations show the features available in the Borders tab and Shading tab.

Remove borders
or specify a
border type.

Choose the style,
color, and width.

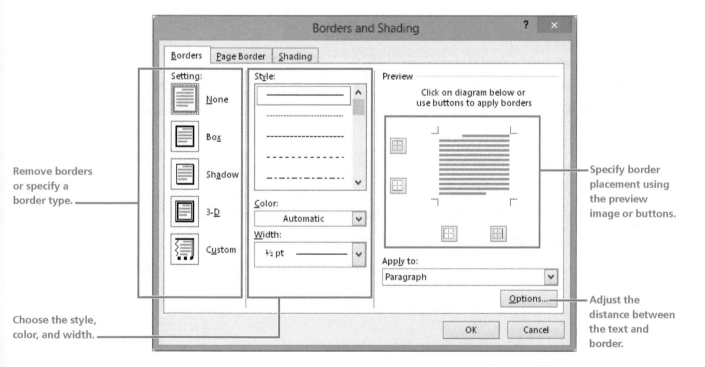

Specify border
placement using
the preview
image or buttons.

Adjust the
distance between
the text and
border.

Word 2013

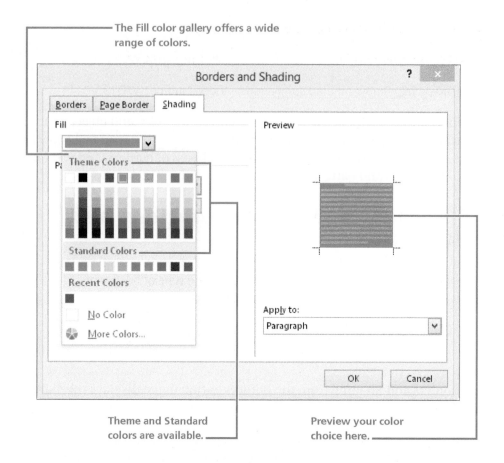

The Fill color gallery offers a wide range of colors.

Theme and Standard colors are available.

Preview your color choice here.

Apply Borders and Shading to Headings

In this exercise, you will apply borders and shading to the headings using the Borders and Shading dialog box.

1. Save your file as **WD04-D14-SocMediaRprt-[FirstInitialLastName]**.
2. Click anywhere in the heading **The Net Generation**.
3. Choose **Home→Paragraph→Borders ▦ menu button ▼**.
4. Choose **Borders and Shading** at the bottom of the menu to open the dialog box.
5. If necessary, click the Borders tab to bring it to the front of the dialog box.

6. Follow these steps to apply a border to the heading:

Ⓐ Choose **Box** as the border setting.

Ⓑ Scroll down and choose the **double line** style.

Ⓒ Choose **¾ pt** as the border width.

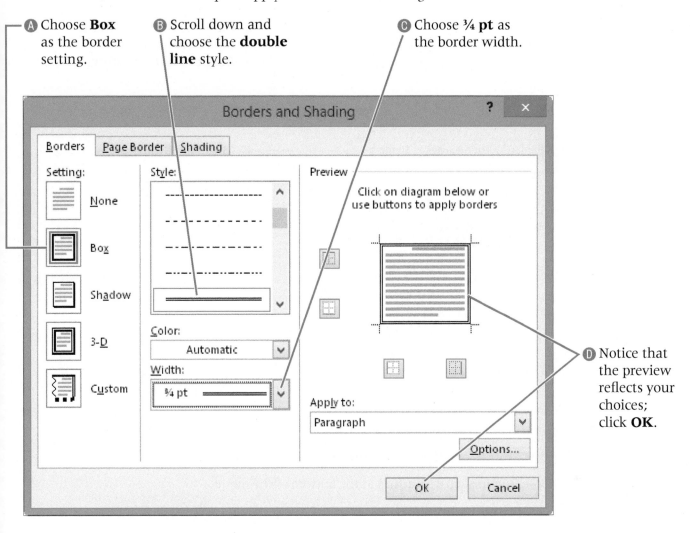

Ⓓ Notice that the preview reflects your choices; click **OK**.

The border extends between the margins. Paragraph borders fill the space between the margins, unless the paragraph(s) is indented or a specific amount of text is selected.

7. Follow these steps to apply shading:

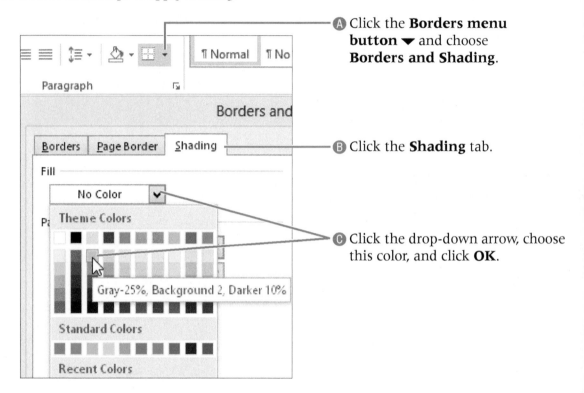

Ⓐ Click the **Borders menu button** ▾ and choose **Borders and Shading**.

Ⓑ Click the **Shading** tab.

Ⓒ Click the drop-down arrow, choose this color, and click **OK**.

The text appears too close to the top border. Next you will adjust the spacing between the text and the top border.

8. Choose **Home→Paragraph→Borders** ⊞ **menu button** ▾.

9. Choose **Borders and Shading** at the bottom of the menu.

10. Click **Options** in the Borders tab.

11. Enter **8** in the **Top** box, and then click **OK** twice.
    Eight points of space were added between the text and the border.

Use the Format Painter to Copy the Heading Formats

12. Make sure your insertion point is still positioned in *The Net Generation* heading.

13. Double-click the **Format Painter** 🖌 in the Clipboard group of the Home tab.
    Remember, double-clicking keeps the Format Painter turned on.

14. Select the following headings to format them:
    - Rapid Increase in the Use of Social Media
    - University Recruiting Through Social Networking
    - Social Media Benefits for Students

15. Click the **Format Painter** 🖌 to turn it off.

16. Save the report.

Formatting Text with Styles

Video Library   http://labyrinthelab.com/videos   Video Number: WD13-V0415

A style is one of the most powerful formatting tools in Word. It is a *group of formats* enabling you to apply multiple formats to a block of text all at once. Styles are based on the current template's theme, which is a set of colors, fonts, and graphic effects. Word contains styles for document elements, such as headings, titles, and special character formats, providing consistent formatting throughout a document.

Understanding Types of Styles

Word has many built-in styles, and you are always working within a style in Word. There are two basic types of styles: character and paragraph.

- Character styles: Character styles are applied to the word the insertion point is in or a selected group of words. Character styles only contain character formats, not paragraph formats. You can apply character styles to text *within* a paragraph that is formatted with a paragraph style.

- Paragraph styles: Paragraph styles are applied to all text in selected paragraphs or to the paragraph containing the insertion point. You can use any character or paragraph formats in a paragraph style. For example, you may want to format a heading with a large, bold font (character formatting) and apply paragraph spacing before and after the heading (paragraph formatting).

Using the Styles Gallery and the Styles Task Pane

Styles are located in the Styles gallery on the Ribbon and in the Styles task pane. Live Preview makes it easy to test a variety of styles in the gallery, while the Styles task pane provides style descriptions in ToolTips.

The gallery is limited to frequently used styles and is always at hand on the Ribbon. The Styles task pane is where you go if you need a more in-depth approach to styles.

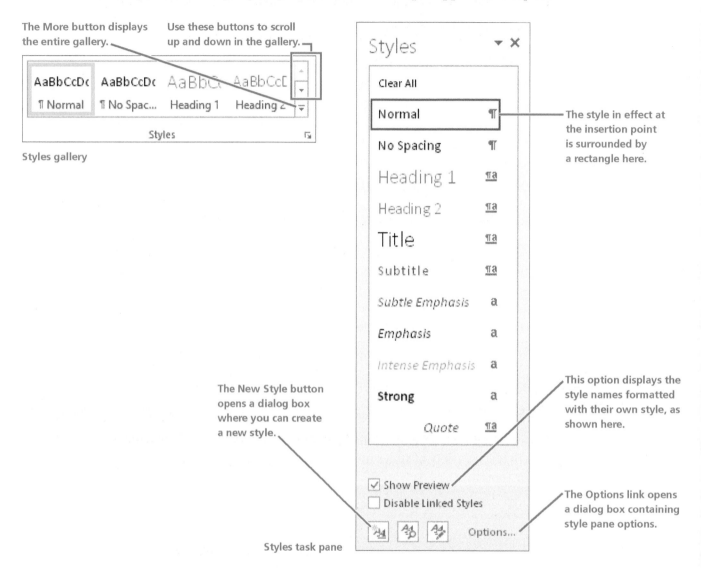

The More button displays the entire gallery.

Use these buttons to scroll up and down in the gallery.

Styles gallery

The New Style button opens a dialog box where you can create a new style.

Styles task pane

The style in effect at the insertion point is surrounded by a rectangle here.

This option displays the style names formatted with their own style, as shown here.

The Options link opens a dialog box containing style pane options.

Collapsing Heading Topics

When you apply a heading style and then hover the mouse pointer over the heading, a small triangle marker appears at the left. You can click the marker to collapse and expand the text below it. This allows you to focus on certain portions of the document.

In this example, clicking the triangle marker collapsed the text below the heading.

▷ The Net Generation

Rapid Increase in the Use of Social Media
    A study at the University of Massachusetts, Dartmouth Center

that 100% of universities use social media today to communicate with

Apply Styles

In this exercise, you will use Live Preview in the Styles gallery to find styles that will give your report a professional, polished look. You will apply the Title style to the report's main heading and you will apply the Heading 1 style to the other headings.

1. Save your file as **WD04-D15-SocMediaRprt-[FirstInitialLastName]**.

2. Click anywhere in the report's main heading, **Social Media in Universities**.

3. Follow these steps to view and apply the Title style to the main heading.

Ⓐ Click the **More** button to display the Styles gallery on the Home tab.

Ⓑ Hover the mouse pointer over **Title** to see its effect, and then click to apply the style.

4. Follow these steps to apply the Heading 1 style to the next heading:

Ⓐ Click to place the insertion point here.　　　Ⓑ Click **More** ⊟ in the bottom-right corner of the Styles gallery.

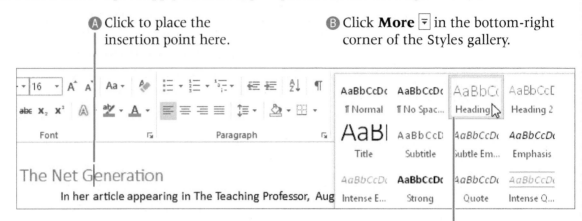

Ⓒ Click **Heading 1** to apply the style.

The Styles task pane includes all the styles that are in the Styles gallery. Now you will use the task pane to apply the Heading 1 style to the next heading.

5. Follow these steps to apply the Heading 1 style from the Styles task pane:

Ⓐ Click the Styles group **dialog box launcher.**

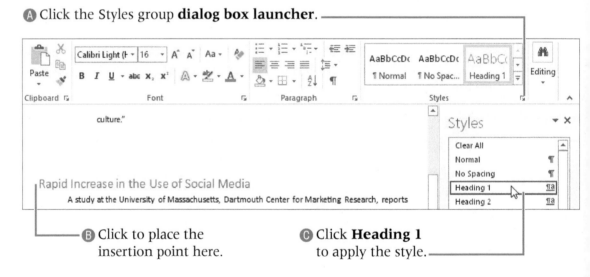

Ⓑ Click to place the insertion point here.　　　Ⓒ Click **Heading 1** to apply the style.

6. Using the method of your choice, apply the **Heading 1** style to the remaining two headings: *University Recruiting Through Social Networking* and *Social Media Benefits for Students.*

Collapse and Expand Text

7. Scroll up to *The Net Generation* heading.

8. Hover the mouse pointer over the heading to display the **triangle marker** to the left of the heading.

9. Click the marker to collapse the text below the heading.

10. Click the marker again to expand the text.

11. Save the report.

Creating a New Custom Style

Video Library   http://labyrinthelab.com/videos   Video Number: WD13-V0416

Thus far, you have applied built-in styles. However, there may be situations where the built-in styles do not meet your needs. For example, you may have corporate formatting standards set for different types of documents. You can create custom styles to meet those standards.

There are two approaches you can take to create custom styles. The method you choose is a matter of personal preference; both are equally effective.

- **Style by definition:** Choose all formats in the Create New Style from Formatting dialog box.
- **Style by example:** Format a block of text with the formats you wish to include in your style. The Create New Style from Formatting dialog box is able to copy the formats in your formatted text.

The following illustration points out the important elements in the Create New Style from Formatting dialog box.

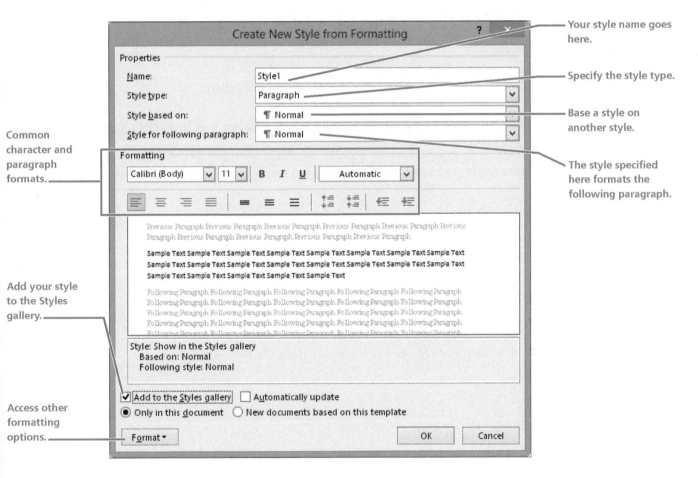

Create a New Style

In this exercise, you will create a new "style by example." It will be a character style, and you will apply the style to selected blocks of text.

1. Save your file as **WD04-D16-SocMediaRprt-[FirstInitialLastName]**.

2. Follow these steps to format the "style by example" text:

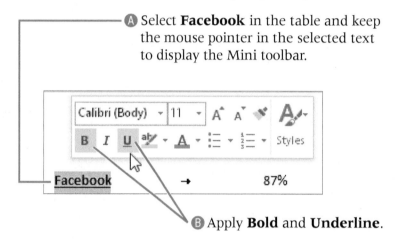

Ⓐ Select **Facebook** in the table and keep the mouse pointer in the selected text to display the Mini toolbar.

Ⓑ Apply **Bold** and **Underline**.

3. If necessary, choose **Home→Styles** and click the **dialog box launcher** ⌐ to open the Styles task pane.

4. Click **New Style** in the bottom of the task pane. (Use ToolTips if necessary.)

5. Follow these steps to complete the new style:

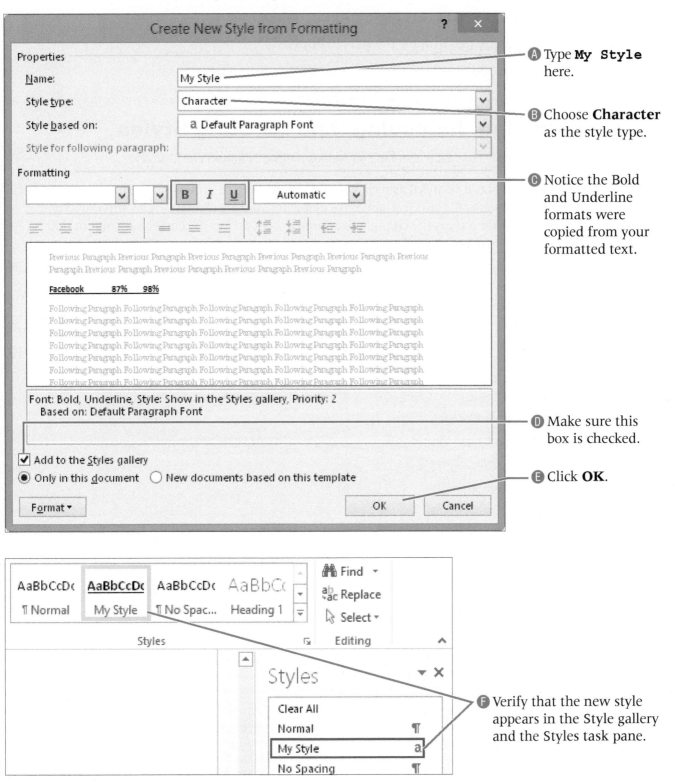

Ⓐ Type **My Style** here.

Ⓑ Choose **Character** as the style type.

Ⓒ Notice the Bold and Underline formats were copied from your formatted text.

Ⓓ Make sure this box is checked.

Ⓔ Click **OK**.

Ⓕ Verify that the new style appears in the Style gallery and the Styles task pane.

Now you will apply the style to the rest of the row headings.

6. Select **Twitter** and choose **Home→Styles→My Style**.

7. Select **Blogs** and click **My Style** in the Styles task pane.

8. Use either method to apply the style to **Podcasts**.

9. Save the report.

Modifying, Removing, and Deleting Styles

Video Library   http://labyrinthelab.com/videos   Video Number: WD13-V0417

You can modify built-in styles as well as styles that you create. The ability to modify styles is one of the great powers of Word. You can make global formatting changes by modifying a style. When you change a style, the changes are applied to all text in the current document that is formatted with the style.

You can remove a style from the Styles gallery without removing it from the Styles task pane. You can leave it in the task pane for future use, or if you prefer, you can delete it from the task pane. Completely deleting a style removes its formatting in the document.

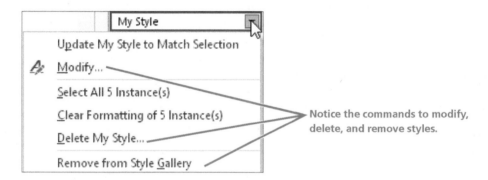

Notice the commands to modify, delete, and remove styles.

QUICK REFERENCE	USING WORD STYLES
Task	**Procedure**
Apply a style	■ **Character Style:** Select the text and choose a style from the Styles gallery or the Styles task pane.
	■ **Paragraph Style:** Click in the paragraph and choose a style from the Styles gallery or the Styles task pane. To apply a style to more than one paragraph, select at least part of each paragraph.
Create a new style by definition	■ Click the New Style button, choose all desired formats from within the dialog box, and then click OK.
Create a new style by example	■ Format a block of text and click the New Styles button.
	■ Name the style and click OK.
Modify a style	■ Choose Modify from the style's menu, make the desired changes, and then click OK.
Add a style to the Styles gallery	■ Choose Add to Style Gallery from the style's menu.
Remove a style from the Styles gallery	■ Choose Remove from Style Gallery from the style's menu, or right-click the style in the gallery and choose Remove from Style Gallery.
Delete a custom style	■ Choose Delete [style name] from the style's menu.

DEVELOP YOUR SKILLS WD04-D17
Modify and Remove a Style

In this exercise, you will modify a style to see how it impacts all text formatted with that style. Then you will remove the style from the Styles gallery and the Styles task pane.

1. Save your file as **WD04-D17-SocMediaRprt-[FirstInitialLastName]**.

2. Hover the mouse pointer over **My Style** in the Styles task pane and click the **menu button▼**.

3. Choose **Modify** from the menu to open the Modify Style dialog box.

   This dialog box contains the same elements as the Create New Style from Formatting dialog box.

4. Click **Italic** $\boxed{I}$ to add that format, and click **OK**.

   The row headings are italicized. Now you will remove the style from the Styles gallery and the Styles task pane.

5. Hover the mouse pointer over **My Style** in the Styles task pane and click the **menu button ▼**.

6. Choose **Remove from Style Gallery**.

   My Style no longer appears in the gallery.

7. Open the menu for **My Style** in the task pane, and choose **Delete My Style**.

8. When the message appears verifying the deletion, click **Yes**.

   The style is removed from the task pane and the style formatting is removed from the row headings in the document.

9. **Close** ⊠ the Styles task pane, and save your report.

Navigating with the Navigation Pane

Video Library   http://labyrinthelab.com/videos   Video Number: WD13-V0418

The Navigation pane provides a great way to navigate through your document using heading styles. This gives you a bird's-eye view of your document so you can easily see the overall flow of topics.

FROM THE RIBBON

View→Show→
Navigation Pane

FROM THE KEYBOARD

Ctrl + F to open the
Navigation pane

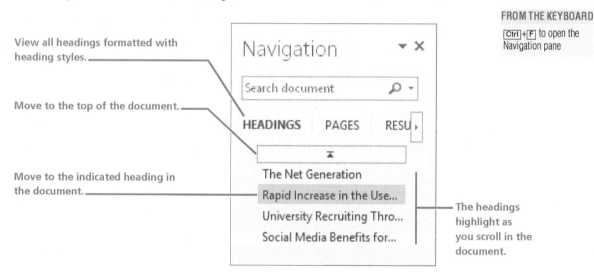

View all headings formatted with heading styles.

Move to the top of the document.

Move to the indicated heading in the document.

The headings highlight as you scroll in the document.

Rearranging Topics

Rearranging parts of your document is one of the most powerful uses of the Navigation pane. When you drag a heading to a new location, all of its lower-level headings and associated text move with it.

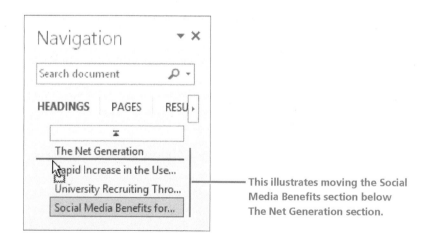

This illustrates moving the Social Media Benefits section below The Net Generation section.

QUICK REFERENCE	REARRANGING A DOCUMENT USING THE NAVIGATION PANE
Task	**Procedure**
Display headings in the Navigation pane	■ Choose View→Show→Navigation Pane and click the Headings button at the top of the pane.
Rearrange a section	■ Click and drag a heading up or down to a new location.

DEVELOP YOUR SKILLS WD04-D18
Navigating and Rearranging Topics

In this exercise, you will use the Navigation pane to move through the report using heading styles. Then, you will use the Navigation pane to move a topic.

1. Save your file as **WD04-D18-SocMediaRprt-[FirstInitialLastName]**.

2. Choose **View→Show→Navigation Pane**, and click **Headings** at the top of the pane.

3. Click the **Social Media Benefits for Students** link in the pane to jump to that topic.

4. Scroll to the top of the report and notice that the highlighting in the pane changes as you scroll to show you where you are in the document.

5. In the Navigation pane, drag the **Social Media Benefits** topic below **The Net Generation** topic.

6. Scroll in the document to see how the topics were rearranged.

7. Delete the extra blank line below The Net Generation topic and, if necessary, below Social Media Benefits for Students topic to tighten up the text.

8. Close ⊠ the **Navigation pane** and save the document.

Introducing Headers and Footers

Video Library   http://labyrinthelab.com/videos   Video Number: WD13-V0419

Headers and footers appear at the top and bottom of every page in a document, respectively, above and below the margins. You can place text, page numbers, dates, and other items in the header and footer areas. When you enter information in these areas, it is repeated on every page of the document.

Word offers a variety of header and footer formatting styles, or you can create your own.

FROM THE RIBBON
Insert→Header & Footer→Header/Footer

Insert→Header & Footer→Page Number

Rapid Increase in the Use of Social Media

A study at the University of Massachusetts, Dartmouth Center for Marketing Research, reports that 100% of universities use social media today to communicate with students, up from 61% in the 2007–2008 academic year. Most universities have Facebook and Twitter accounts. The study reports these increases:

1

One of Word's built-in page number designs.

QUICK REFERENCE	WORKING WITH HEADERS, FOOTERS, AND PAGE NUMBERS
Task	**Procedure**
Insert a built-in header/footer/page number	■ Choose Insert→Header & Footer→Header/Footer/Page Number and choose a built-in style.
Create or modify header/footer	■ Choose Insert→Header & Footer→Header/Footer and choose Edit Header/Footer.
Format page numbers	■ Choose Insert→Header & Footer→Page Number and choose Format Page Numbers.
Delete a header/footer/page number	■ Choose Insert→Header & Footer→Header/Footer/Page Number and choose Remove Header/Footer/Page Numbers.
Open/close header/footer	■ Double-click the header/footer areas to open them. ■ Double-click the main document to close the header/footer.

DEVELOP YOUR SKILLS WD04-D19
Add a Header and Page Numbers to the Report

In this exercise, you will add headers and page numbers to the report. You will use Word's built-in formats.

1. Save your file as **WD04-D19-SocMediaRprt-[FirstInitialLastName]**.

2. Choose **Insert→Header & Footer→Header** □ and choose the **Sideline** format from the gallery.

3. Click **Document Title** and type **My Virtual Campus** in its place.

4. Double-click in the document to close the header.

5. Choose **Insert→Header & Footer→Page Number** 📄 and slide the mouse pointer down the menu to **Bottom of Page**.

6. Scroll down in the gallery and choose **Large Color 3**.

7. Double-click in the document to close the page-number footer.
   You can open the header/footer area by double-clicking anywhere in the header/footer area.

8. Double-click in the footer area to open it, and then double-click in the document again to close the footer area.

9. Scroll through the report and observe the headers and page numbers.

10. Save the report.

Using the Resume Reading Bookmark

Video Library   http://labyrinthelab.com/videos   Video Number: WD13-V0420

When you close a document and then reopen it, Word remembers your last editing point and presents a pop-up bookmark offering to let you pick up where you left off. This Resume Reading feature provides a fast startup if you don't recall exactly where you were when you last worked in the document.

Welcome back!
Pick up where you left off:

Social Media Benefits for Students
A few seconds ago

Use the Resume Reading Bookmark

In this exercise, you will make an editing change to your report, and then save and close it. When you reopen the report, the Resume Reading Bookmark will let you quickly jump to where you left off.

1. Save your file as **WD04-D20-SocMediaRprt-[FirstInitialLastName]**.

2. Scroll to the **University Recruiting Through Social Networking** heading.

3. In the first line below the heading, change *top* to **the best**.

4. Save and close the report.

5. Follow these steps to display the Resume Reading Bookmark:

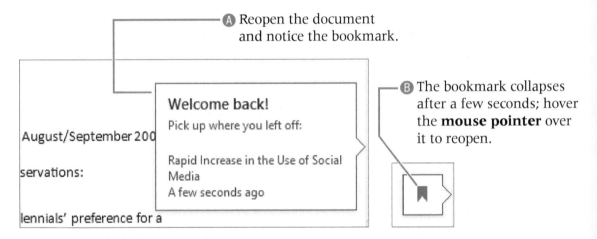

Ⓐ Reopen the document and notice the bookmark.

Ⓑ The bookmark collapses after a few seconds; hover the **mouse pointer** over it to reopen.

Welcome back!
Pick up where you left off:

Rapid Increase in the Use of Social Media
A few seconds ago

6. Click the **bookmark** to jump to your last editing location.

7. Save and close the report. Exit **Word**.

Concepts Review

To check your knowledge of the key concepts introduced in this lesson, complete the Concepts Review quiz by choosing the appropriate access option below.

If you are...	Then access the quiz by...
Using the Labyrinth Video Library	Going to http://labyrinthelab.com/videos
Using eLab	Logging in, choosing Content, and navigating to the Concepts Review quiz for this lesson
Not using the Labyrinth Video Library or eLab	Going to the student resource center for this book

Reinforce Your Skills

Format a Recycling Report

In this exercise, you will polish a report that Kids for Change members researched. You will use paragraph alignment, hyphenation, and indents. You will set custom tabs on the ruler to use in a tabular table, and finally, you will add after-paragraph spacing to several paragraphs.

Format Reports and Paragraphs

1. Start **Word**. Open **WD04-R01-ElecRecyc** from your **WD2013 Lesson 04** folder and save it as `WD04-R01-ElecRecyc-[FirstInitialLastName]`.

2. Position the insertion point in the heading at the top of the document.

3. Choose **Home→Paragraph→Center** ≡.

4. Keep the insertion point at the top of the document.

5. **Choose Page Layout→Page Setup→Hyphenation** ᵇₑ⁻, and choose **Manual** from the menu.

6. When the message appears to hyphenate *following*, click **Yes**.

7. Click **Yes** to hyphenate *replaced*.

8. When the Hyphenation Is Complete message appears, click **OK**.
   Now you will insert a nonbreaking hyphen and nonbreaking space so terms will stay together if future editing repositions them.

9. Position the insertion point after *earth* in the first paragraph and tap `Delete` to remove the hyphen.

> Kids for Change realize that society today is drowning in electronic de
> ing reasons to recycle and guidance to help you when electronic equi
> placed by newer models. Disposing of electronics in an earth-healthy

10. Choose **Insert→Symbols→Symbol** Ω and choose **More Symbols**.

11. Click the **Special Characters** tab and choose **Nonbreaking Hyphen**.

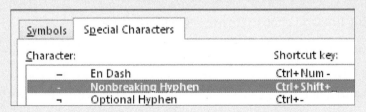

12. Click **Insert**, then **Close**.

13. Position the insertion point after *Agency* in the second paragraph and tap Delete .

> The United States Environmental Protection Agency (EPA) points out the following recycling benefits on their website:

14. Choose **Insert→Symbols→Symbol** Ω and choose **More Symbols**.

15. When the Symbol dialog box opens, click the **Special Characters tab** and choose **Nonbreaking Space**.

16. Click **Insert**, then **Close**.

Indent Text

17. If necessary, choose **View→Show→Ruler** to turn on the ruler.

18. Position the insertion point in the third paragraph.

19. Place the mouse pointer on the **Left Indent marker** (the rectangle) and drag it to the **half-inch mark**, and then place the mouse pointer on the **Right Indent marker** and drag it to the **6-inch mark**.

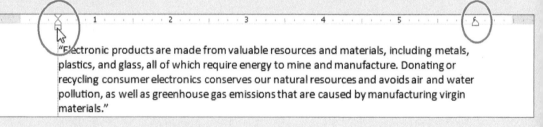

> "Electronic products are made from valuable resources and materials, including metals, plastics, and glass, all of which require energy to mine and manufacture. Donating or recycling consumer electronics conserves our natural resources and avoids air and water pollution, as well as greenhouse gas emissions that are caused by manufacturing virgin materials."

Notice where the indent markers are now positioned.

Work with Tab Stops

20. Position the insertion point at the bottom of the document.

21. Type the following heading line using the default tab grid, tapping Tab where you see small arrows, and then tap Enter at the end of the line.

> Ellsworth·Electronics →　　→　　　→　　Arlington·Electronics →　　→　　　→　　Wilson·Appliances¶
> ¶

22. Select the heading line and choose **Home→Font→Bold** B .

23. Position the insertion point in the blank line below the heading line where you will set custom tabs.

24. Click the tabs box to display the **Center Tab**. (It looks like an upside down T.)

25. Perform these actions to set the following tab stops:
- Click the ruler one tick mark to the right of a ½-inch.
- Click one tick mark to the right of the 3-inch mark.
- Click at the 5½-inch mark.

Ellsworth·Electronics → → → Arlington·Electronics → → → Wilson·Appliances¶
¶

26. Type the following table, tapping Tab where you see a small arrow.

Ellsworth·Electronics→	→	→	Arlington·Electronics→	→	→	Wilson·Appliances¶
→ Audio	→		Mobile·phones	→		Stoves¶
→ Car·&·GPS	→		Computers	→		Refrigerators¶
→ Mobile·phones	→		Digital·cameras	→		Freezers¶
→ Video·games	→		MP3·players	→		Washing·machines¶

Now you will adjust the last tab stop so it is better centered.

27. Select all lines to which the tab stop applies and drag the tab one tick mark to the right of 5½ inches.

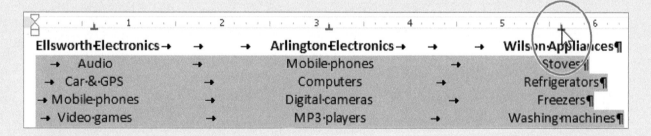

Ellsworth·Electronics→	→	→	Arlington·Electronics→	→	→	Wils·on·Appliar·ces¶
→ Audio	→		Mobile·phones	→		Stoves·¶
→ Car·&·GPS	→		Computers	→		Refrigerators¶
→ Mobile·phones	→		Digital·cameras	→		Freezers¶
→ Video·games	→		MP3·players	→		Washing·machines¶

Apply Bullets and Numbers

28. Select the lines highlighted below and choose **Home→Paragraph→Bullets** ☰.

The EPA provides the following examples of energy saved and metals retrieved:
- Recycling one million laptops saves the energy equivalent to the electricity used by more than 3,500 US homes in a year.
- For every million cell phones we recycle, 35 thousand pounds of copper, 772 pounds of silver, 75 pounds of gold, and 33 pounds of palladium can be recovered.

29. Make sure the text is still selected; choose **Home→Paragraph→Bullets menu button** ▼, then **Define New Bullet**.

30. Click **Symbol** in the Define New Bullet dialog box.

31. Choose **Webdings** in the Font list, and then choose the symbol shown here. (If you cannot locate it, type **52** in the Code field at the bottom of the dialog box.)

32. Click **OK** twice to set the new bullet symbol.

33. Select the lines shown below in the fifth paragraph.

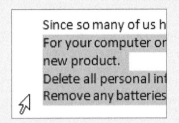

34. Choose **Home→Paragraph→Numbering** 📋.

Apply Paragraph Space Settings

35. Position the insertion point in the second paragraph.

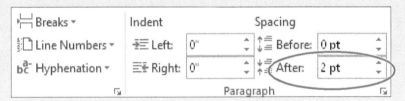

36. Choose **Page Layout→Paragraph**, type **2** in the Spacing After field, and tap ⌾Enter⌾.

Breaks ▾	Indent		Spacing	
Line Numbers ▾	Left:	0"	Before:	0 pt
Hyphenation ▾	Right:	0"	After:	2 pt
			Paragraph	

37. Use the same process to apply additional space to both the paragraph starting with *The EPA provides* and the paragraph starting with *Since so many*.

38. Save and close the file; exit from **Word**.

39. Submit your final file based on the guidelines provided by your instructor.

    To view examples of how your file or files should look at the end of this exercise, go to the student resource center.

Format a Composting Report

In this exercise, you will format a composting research document, transforming it into a professional-looking report.

Format with Borders and Shading

1. Start **Word**. Open **WD04-R02-ActLocally** from your **WD2013 Lesson 04** folder and save it as **WD04-R02-ActLocally-[FirstInitialLastName]**.

2. Position the insertion point in the heading at the top of the document.

3. Choose **Home→Paragraph→Borders menu ▾**, and then choose **Borders and Shading**.

4. Choose **Shadow** as the border Setting, choose the sixth color in the last column (a dark green), and then set the Width to **2 ¼ pt**.

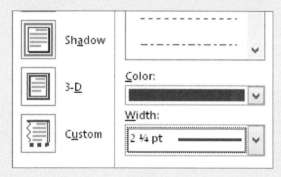

You will now apply shading to the area within the border.

5. Click the **Shading tab**.

6. Click the **Fill drop-down arrow**, choose the **second color** in the **last column**, and click **OK**.

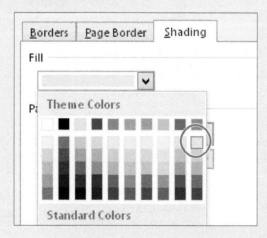

Use and Modify a Style and Collapse Headings

7. Select the *Obtain a Composting Bin* heading and choose **Home→Styles→Heading 2**.

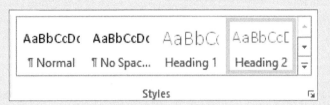

8. Apply the **Heading 2** style to the rest of the headings in the document.
   Now you will modify the style so it will blend with the heading at the top of the document.

9. Click in one of the headings formatted with the **Heading 2** style.

10. Right-click the **Heading 2** style in the Styles group and choose **Modify** from the menu.

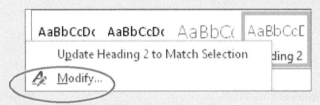

11. Click the **Bold** button, and then click the drop-down arrow and choose the darkest green theme color.

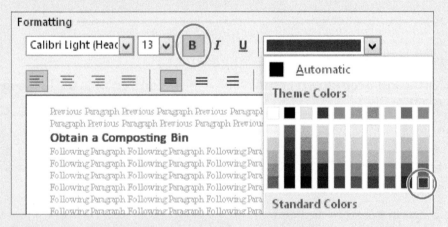

12. Click **OK** to save the changes to the heading style.
    Notice that all headings formatted with Heading 2 are now green and bold. Now you will collapse some of the headings.

13. Hover the mouse pointer over the *What Materials Can You Compost?* heading and notice the little triangle to the left of the heading.

14. Click the triangle to collapse the text below the heading, and then click it again to expand the text.

15. Try expanding and collapsing some other headings, and then expand all headings.

Use the Navigation Pane to Rearrange Topics

16. Choose **View→Show→Navigation Pane**.

17. If necessary, click the **Headings tab** toward the top of the task pane.

18. Select the *Become a Composting…* topic, drag it to just above *Summary*, and drop it.

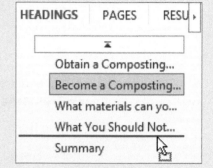

19. Close the **Navigation pane**.

Insert a Page Number Footer

20. Choose **Insert→Header & Footer→Page Number menu ▼**.

21. Choose **Bottom of Page→Plain Number 1**.

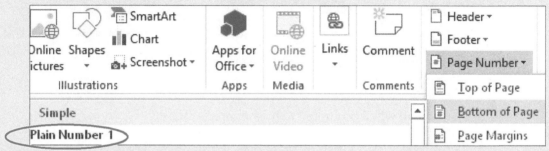

The chosen page number style appears in the footer of the document.

22. Double-click the body of the document to close the footer area.

Use the Resume Reading Bookmark

Now you'll save and close the file so when you open it again, the bookmark will appear. First, however, you will make an editing change so you can see how the bookmark guides you to your last location.

23. Go to page 2 and position the insertion point to the right of *ratio* in the *Carbon-nitrogen ratio* bullet point.

24. Tap Enter to generate another bullet and type **Inocula**.

25. Save and close the document; reopen it.

26. Click the **bookmark** and notice how it jumps you to the area where you were last working. (If the bookmark collapses, hover the mouse pointer over it to open it.)

27. Close the file and exit from **Word**.

28. Submit your file based on guidelines provided by your instructor.

    To view examples of how your file or files should look at the end of this exercise, go to the student resource center.

Format a Groundwater Report

In this exercise, you will work with paragraph formats, indents, and custom tab stops. You will create a numbered list and add after-paragraph spacing to headings. You'll work with borders and styles, and add a header, and then you'll use the Resume Reading bookmark.

Align Paragraphs and Hyphenate Text

1. Start **Word**. Open **WD04-R03-Groundwater** from your **WD2013 Lesson 04** folder and save it as **WD04-R03-Groundwater-[FirstInitialLastName]**.

2. Position the insertion point in the heading at the top of the document.

3. Choose **Home→Paragraph→Center** 🖹.
   Next you will hyphenate the document.

4. Choose **Page Layout→Page Setup→Hyphenation**, and then choose **Manual**.

5. Click **Yes** when Word prompts you to hyphenate *atmosphere*.

6. Click **Yes** to hyphenate *below*.

7. Click **No** when prompted to hyphenate *hazardous*.

8. Click **OK** when the Hyphenation Is Complete message appears.

Indent Text

9. Select the lines at the bottom of the document starting with *Reduce Household chemical* through the last line of text.

10. Choose **Home→Paragraph→Increase Indent** 🖹.

Work with Tab Stops

The kids have decided to conduct further research into groundwater contamination. You will create a table listing the kids and the topics each is assigned to.

11. If necessary, choose **Home→Paragraph→Show/Hide** ¶ to turn on formatting marks.

12. Position the insertion point on the last paragraph symbol at the bottom of the document.

13. Type the following heading line, tapping ⌧Tab wherever you see a small arrow, and tap ⌧Enter at the end of the line.

14. Select the heading line and choose **Home→Font→Bold** B.

15. Position the insertion point on the line below the heading line.

16. Choose **Home→Paragraph→dialog box launcher** 🖻.

17. Click **Tabs** in the bottom-left corner of the dialog box.

18. Type **2** in the **Tab Stop Position** box, click the **Center** option in the Alignment area, and then click **Set**.

19. Type **4.5** in the **Tab Stop Position** box, click **Set**, and then click **OK** to accept both of the new tabs.

20. If necessary, choose **View→Show→Ruler** to turn on the ruler, and then observe your custom tabs.

21. Type the following table, tapping ⎡Tab⎤ wherever you see a small arrow. Tap ⎡Enter⎤ at the end of the table.

Next you will remove the tabs from the ruler. It's good practice to confine custom tabs to the area where they are used.

22. Position the mouse pointer on the **tab at the 2**" mark and drag it down off the ruler.

23. Use the same process to remove the **tab at the 4.5**" mark.

Create a Numbered List

24. Select the lines that you indented earlier, starting with *Reduce household* and continuing through *water education*.

25. Choose **Home→Paragraph→Numbering** ⬚.

The first item might look better if it didn't extend so far to the right. If you use ⎡Enter⎤ to shorten it, you will create a new number. So instead, you'll use a line break, which will shorten the line without generating a number.

26. Scroll up, position the insertion point to the left of *chemicals* in item 1, and press ⎡Shift⎤+⎡Enter⎤.

Use Paragraph Space Settings

27. Position the insertion point in the *What is Groundwater?* heading.

28. Choose the **Page Layout** tab, type **2** in the Spacing After field, and then tap ⎡Enter⎤.

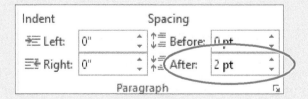

29. Repeat the process in steps 27 and 28 to add **2** points below the *How Can We Help?* heading.

Apply Borders and Styles

30. Position the insertion point in the heading at the top of the page and choose the **Home→Styles→dialog box launcher** 🔲.

31. In the Styles task pane, click the **Title** style to apply it to the heading.

32. Keep the insertion point in the heading, and choose **Home→Paragraph→Borders menu button ▼**.

33. Choose **Bottom Border**.

34. Position the insertion point in the *What is Groundwater?* heading.

35. Click **Heading 2** in the Styles task pane.

36. Choose **Page Layout→Paragraph**.

    Notice that the 2 points after-paragraph spacing is back to 0. The Heading 2 style overrode your formatting. Leave the spacing as it is.

37. Click in the *How Can We Help?* heading and apply the **Heading 2** style.

38. Keep the insertion point in the heading, hover the mouse pointer over **Heading 2** in the task pane, click the **drop-down arrow**, and choose **Modify**.

    You will now change the font color for the Heading 2 style.

39. Click the **drop-down arrow** to open the color gallery, choose the **Black, text 1** theme color, and then click **OK**.

    The color changes for both Heading 2 items.

40. Close the **Styles** task pane, and choose **View→Show→Ruler** to turn off the ruler.

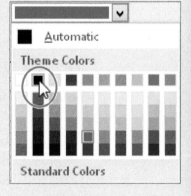

Use the Navigation Pane

41. Position the insertion point at the top of the document.

42. Choose **View→Show→Navigation Pane**.

43. Click **Headings** to display the document's heading list, if necessary.

44. Click *How Can We Help?* in the Headings list.

    Word jumps down to the heading selected.

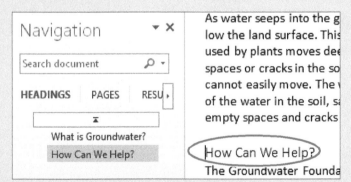

45. Close the **Navigation pane**.

Add a Header

46. Choose **Insert→Header & Footer→Header** and choose **Blank** at the top of the list.

47. Type **Groundwater** and double–click in the document to close the header area.

    Next you will make an editing change, and then close and reopen the document. Then you will use the Resume Reading bookmark to go to the last location where you were working in the document.

48. Click to the left of the left-most tab symbol in the first line of your table.

49. Press Ctrl + Enter to insert a page break and move the entire table to the next page.

Use the Resume Reading Bookmark

50. Save and close the document, and then reopen it to display the Resume Reading bookmark.

51. Click the **bookmark** and Word jumps to the area where you last worked in the document.

52. Choose **Home→Paragraph→Show/Hide** ¶ to turn off formatting marks.

53. Save and close the document; exit from **Word**.

54. Submit your final file based on guidelines provided by your instructor.

Apply Your Skills

Format a Trip Report

In this exercise, you will create a report using paragraph alignment, hyphenation, and indents. You will then set custom tabs, apply bullets, and add after-paragraph spacing.

Format Paragraphs

1. Start **Word**. Open **WD04-A01-Belize** from your **WD2013 Lesson 04** folder and save it as `WD04-A01-Belize-[FirstInitialLastName]`.

2. Center-align the heading at the top of the document.

3. Choose **Page Layout→Page Setup→Hyphenation**, and then choose **Manual**.

4. When prompted to hyphenate *ambergriscaye* in the URL, click **No**.

5. Click **No** when prompted to hyphenate *Caribbean*.

6. Click **Yes** for all of the remaining hyphenation prompts.

7. Click **OK** when the Hyphenation Is Complete message appears.

8. Insert a **nonbreaking space** in all occurrences of *San Pedro*.
   Hint: There are four occurrences; you might want to use the Find feature to locate all of them.

Indent Text and Set Custom Tabs

9. Turn on the ruler, if necessary.

10. Click in the paragraph below the *Overview* heading.

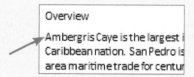

11. Use the **indent markers** on the ruler to indent the paragraph ¼ **inch**.

12. Use the same process to indent the *Diving and Snorkeling* paragraph, the *Ruins* paragraphs, and the *Artists* paragraph.

13. If necessary, turn on the **Show/Hide** ¶ feature.

14. Position the insertion point at the second paragraph symbol at the end of the document.

15. Type the following heading row, using the formatting marks as a guide. Be sure to tap Enter at the end of the heading line.

16. Apply **Bold** ⒝ to the heading line.

17. Position the insertion point in the line below the heading and set custom **Center tabs** at **1.75"** and **3.75"**.

18. Type the rest of the table as shown, using the formatting marks as a guide.

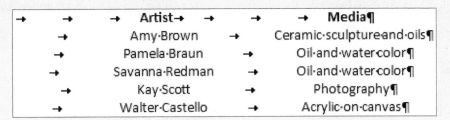

Use Bullets and Paragraph Spacing

19. Scroll to the top of the document and select the four lines shown here.

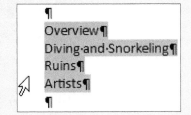

20. Apply bullets to the selected lines and customize the bullets using a symbol of your choice.

21. Apply **6 points of after-paragraph** spacing to the headings *Overview, Diving and Snorkeling, Ruins,* and *Artists*.

22. Save and close the file; exit from **Word**.

23. Submit your final file based on guidelines provided by your instructor.

    To view examples of how your file or files should look at the end of this exercise, go to the student resource center.

APPLY YOUR SKILLS WD04-A02

Format an Itinerary

In this exercise, you will create a document using borders and styles. You will use the Navigation pane to rearrange topics, and you will add headers and footers to the document. Finally, you will use the Resume Reading bookmark.

Use Borders and Styles

1. Start **Word**. Open **WD04-A02-Tahiti** from your **WD2013 Lesson 04** folder and save it as `WD04-A02-Tahiti-[FirstInitialLastName]`.

2. Open the **Styles task pane** and format the heading at the top of the document with the **Title** style.

3. Apply a **Bottom Border** from the **Borders** ⊞ **menu button** ▼.

4. Format the headings for each day (Day One – Tahiti, Day Two – Tahiti, and so on) with the **Heading 2** style.

    Now you will use the small gray triangle to the left of a Heading 2 style to collapse and expand the text under it.

5. Hover the mouse pointer over the *Day One – Tahiti* heading and click the **triangle** to collapse the text below it.

6. Click the **triangle** again to expand the text.

   Now you will create a "style by example" to use on the subheadings for each day's schedule.

7. Select the subheading *Discover the Real Papeete* and format it with **10 point Verdana** font.

8. Apply the font color shown.

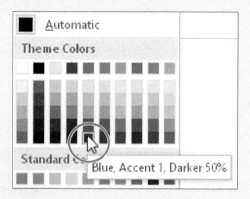

9. Click **New Style** at the bottom of the Styles task pane.

10. Name the style **My Style** and click **OK**.

11. Apply the style to all the subheadings in the itinerary.

    Next you will modify the style and all of the subheadings will automatically update.

12. In the Styles task pane, click the **My Style drop-down arrow** and choose **Modify**.

13. Click **Italic** *I* in the dialog box, and then click **OK**.

    All of the subheadings are italicized.

14. Close the **Styles task pane**.

Use the Navigation Pane and Add a Header and Footer

15. Choose **View→Show→Navigation Pane** to open it, and if necessary, click **Headings** at the top of the pane.

16. Drag and drop the **Day Two** heading above **Day One**; close the **Navigation pane**.

17. Rename the first heading **Day One – Tahiti** and rename the second heading **Day Two – Tahiti**.

18. Choose **Insert→Header & Footer→Header**, and then scroll down the gallery and choose **Sideline**.

19. Click in **Document Title**, type **Universal Corporate Events**, and close the header area.

20. Choose **Insert→Header & Footer→Footer**, scroll down the gallery, choose **Sideline**, and then close the footer area.

Use the Resume Reading Bookmark

Now you'll make an editing change so when you reopen the document, Word will provide a bookmark to return you to the area where you were last working in the document.

21. Scroll down to **Day Seven**. In the subtitle, replace *a Perfect* with **an Ideal**.

22. Save and close the document; reopen it.

23. Click the **bookmark** to jump to the location where you were last working in the document.

24. Close the file and exit **Word**.

25. Submit your final file based on guidelines provided by your instructor.

    To view examples of how your file or files should look at the end of this exercise, go to the student resource center.

APPLY YOUR SKILLS WD04-A03

Format a Sales Report

In this exercise, you will align text, use indents, and type a table using custom tab stops. You will customize bullets, insert a line break, and add after-paragraph spacing. After using the Navigation pane to reorganize text, you will add header text, and then you will use the Resume Reading bookmark.

Format Paragraphs and Indent Text

1. Start Word. Open **WD04-A03-SalesRpt** from the **WD2013 Lesson 04** folder and save it as **WD04-A03-SalesRpt-[FirstInitialLastName]**.

2. Center the *Sales Report* heading.

3. Use **Increase Indent** 📇 to indent the paragraph that begins with *The following table*.

4. Use manual hyphenation and accept any proposed hyphenations.

5. Click at the end of the paragraph you just indented and tap Enter twice.

6. Click **Decrease Indent** 📇 to position the insertion point at the left margin.

Apply Bullets and Set Custom Tab Stops

7. Type **Pending Deals** and tap Enter.

   Next you will set tabs for your Pending Deals table.

8. Use the Tabs dialog box to set **Left tabs** at **2.5"** and **4.5"**.

9. Type this table.

Pending·Deals¶		
Company	Destination	Dates¶
Rogers·Electronics	Hawaii	Sept·2·through·7¶
Wilson·Construction	Miami	Sept·11·through·17¶
Milltown·Mortgage	New·York·City	October·11·through·17¶

10. **Bold** 𝐁 the heading row.

11. Select the entire table, and use the ruler to move the 2½" tab to **2¾"** and the 4½" tab to **4¾"**.

12. Select the six lines below *Mega Storage Devices* and apply **bullets**.

13. Add bullets to the lines below the other companies: **Springer Business College, Martin Medical Supplies,** and **Citizens Bank**.

14. Customize all of the bullets using a symbol of your choice. (Use the same symbol for all bullets.)

15. Click at the end of the *Accommodations* line below *Springer Business College* and insert a line break.

16. Type this text: **The owner's cousin works for a hotel chain.**

17. Select the heading line in your table and add **4 points of after-paragraph spacing**.

Apply Borders and Styles

18. Format the *Sales Report* heading with the **Heading 1** style.

19. The style overrode your centering, so center the heading again.

20. Choose **Home→Paragraph→Borders** ⊞ and apply a **Bottom Border**.

21. Format the *Pending Deals* and *Bookings* headings with the **Heading 2** style.

22. Modify the **Heading 2** style by adding **Bold**.
    Notice that both headings update.

23. Format the company names (such as Mega Storage Devices) in the Bookings section with the **Heading 3** style.

Use the Navigation Pane and Insert a Header

24. Use the Navigation pane to move *Martin Medical Supplies* above *Springer Business College.*
    You may need to click the triangle to the left of Bookings to expand the text below it.

25. Insert a header using the **Blank style**, and type **Universal Corporate Events** as the header.

Make Use of the Resume Reading Bookmark

26. Position the insertion point at the end of the last bullet point below the Citizens Bank heading.

27. Tap Enter and type **Fuentes Imports** and apply the **Heading 3** style to that line.

28. Save and close the document, and then reopen it and use the **Resume Reading bookmark** to navigate to the area where you were last working in the document.

29. Close the file and exit **Word**.

30. Submit your final file based on guidelines provided by your instructor.

Extend Your Skills

In the course of working through the Extend Your Skills exercises, you will think critically as you use the skills taught in the lesson to complete the assigned projects. To evaluate your mastery and completion of the exercises, your instructor may use a rubric, with which more points are allotted according to performance characteristics. (The more you do, the more you earn!) Ask your instructor how your work will be evaluated.

WD04-E01 That's the Way I See It

As the owner of a small business in your community, you want to improve your business acumen so you can grow your business further. Therefore, you are taking night classes at your local community college. Your professor assigned the following research project.

- List three types of business reports. Format the names of the reports with a built-in heading style. Customize the style with borders and shading.
- Type a brief paragraph describing each type of report below each of the headings; use the indent feature to indent the paragraphs below the headings.
- List three elements included in each type of report, making them bulleted items. Then customize the bullets using a symbol or picture of your choice. Add after-paragraph spacing to the bulleted items.

Save your findings in a Word document named **WD04-E01-BizReports-[FirstInitialLastName]** and saved to your **WD2013 Lesson 04** folder. You will be evaluated based on the inclusion of all elements specified, your ability to follow directions, your ability to apply newly learned skills to a real-world situation, your creativity, and the relevance of your topic and/or data choice(s). Submit your final file based on the guidelines provided by your instructor.

WD04-E02 Be Your Own Boss

You belong to a small business breakfast club that meets monthly. Members support each other by sharing knowledge and experiences. Your business, Blue Jean Landscaping, has been very successful, and you've been asked to present a report detailing your success.

Provide a heading for the report and format it with a built-in heading style. Customize the heading style with formatting of your preference. Write a brief introductory paragraph, and then use the First Line Indent marker to indent the first line of the paragraph. Use a numbered list to point out the top five elements that are most responsible for your success. Add several points of after-paragraph spacing to the numbered items.

As a result of your success, you are planning to expand your business to three new locations. Create a tabular table using custom tab stops to list the names of the locations, the number of employees for each location, and the opening dates. Provide a heading above the table using a built-in heading style. Include a page-number footer for the report.

Compose a report in Word and save it as **WD04-E02-BizSuccess-[FirstInitialLastName]** in your **WD2013 Lesson 04** folder.

You will be evaluated based on the inclusion of all elements specified, your ability to follow directions, your ability to apply newly learned skills to a real-world situation, your creativity, and your demonstration of an entrepreneurial spirit. Submit your final file based on the guidelines provided by your instructor.

Transfer Your Skills

In the course of working through the Transfer Your Skills exercises, you will use critical-thinking and creativity skills to complete the assigned projects using skills taught in the lesson. To evaluate your mastery and completion of the exercises, your instructor may use a rubric, with which more points are allotted according to performance characteristics. (The more you do, the more you earn!) Ask your instructor how your work will be evaluated.

WD04-T01 Use the Web as a Learning Tool

Throughout this book, you will be provided with an opportunity to use the Internet as a learning tool by completing WebQuests. According to the original creators of WebQuests, as described on their website (WebQuest.org), a WebQuest is "an inquiry-oriented activity in which most or all of the information used by learners is drawn from the web." To complete the WebQuest projects in this book, navigate to the student resource center and choose the WebQuest for the lesson on which you are currently working. The subject of each WebQuest will be relevant to the material found in the lesson.

WebQuest Subject: Design elements of a well-formatted report.

Submit your file(s) based on the guidelines provided by your instructor.

WD04-T02 Demonstrate Proficiency

Stormy BBQ has been losing business lately. There is a new restaurant in town, and you suspect your customers are migrating to the competition. Create a report, which you will share with your employees, researching the competition.

Provide a heading for the report and format it with a border and shading. Add after-paragraph spacing to the heading.

Include three reasons you believe the competition is attracting your customers. Each of the reasons should be a heading formatted with a built-in heading style, customized with the heading formatting style of your choice. Write a short paragraph below each of the headings describing your reasons in more detail. Use the indent markers on the ruler to indent the paragraphs ¼".

Using the Numbering feature, list three steps you intend to take to win back your customers. Add your company name as a header and provide a page number in the footer area.

Save the report as **WD04-T02-Competition-[FirstInitialLastName]** in your **WD2013 Lesson 04** folder. Submit your file based on the guidelines provided by your instructor.

Working with Tables

LESSON OUTLINE

LEARNING OBJECTIVES

After studying this lesson, you will be able to:

- Insert a table in a document
- Modify, sort, and format tables
- Apply built-in table styles
- Perform calculations in tables
- Insert and size columns and rows

A table is one of Word's most useful tools for organizing and formatting text and numbers. Tables are flexible and easy to use. Word provides a variety of features that let you set up, modify, and format tables. In this lesson, you will merge and split table cells, sort rows, quickly apply table styles, and perform calculations within tables.

Creating Tables for My Virtual Campus

You are an administrative assistant for the product development team at My Virtual Campus. The team is always looking for new ideas to enhance the websites. You have a few ideas of your own that may be useful for students: a list of typical expenses with totals, and a simple layout for viewing class schedules. You decide to create tables to present your ideas at the next product development meeting.

Personal Expenses	Estimate	Actual	Difference
Food	425	435	$ 10.00
Entertainment	100	150	$ 50.00
Transportation/Gas	50	55	$ 5.00
Cell Phone	75	85	$ 10.00
Totals	650	725	$ 75.00

You can insert formulas in tables.

The Table Styles gallery makes it easy to format a table.

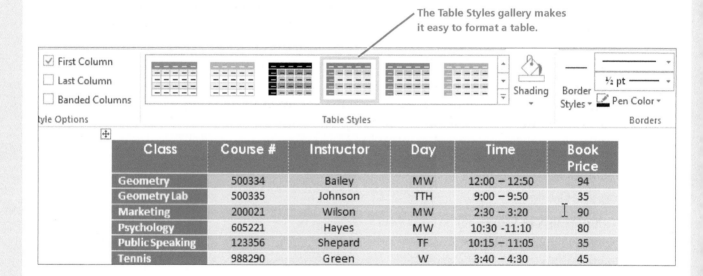

Class	Course #	Instructor	Day	Time	Book Price
Geometry	500334	Bailey	MW	12:00 – 12:50	94
Geometry Lab	500335	Johnson	TTH	9:00 – 9:50	35
Marketing	200021	Wilson	MW	2:30 – 3:20	90
Psychology	605221	Hayes	MW	10:30 -11:10	80
Public Speaking	123356	Shepard	TF	10:15 – 11:05	35
Tennis	988290	Green	W	3:40 – 4:30	45

Introducing Tables

Video Library   http://labyrinthelab.com/videos   Video Number: WD13-V0501

Tables provide a convenient method of organizing and aligning data in an easy-to-read format, and they are a nice way to break up a text-heavy document. Using Word's table styles adds flair to your documents, and tables draw your reader's attention to key items.

Tables are organized in columns and rows. Where columns and rows intersect, they form a rectangle known as a cell. You can type text or numbers in cells, and you can even perform simple calculations.

	Column		Cell		
Row	Personal Expenses		Estimate	Actual	Difference
	Food		425	435	$ 10.00
	Entertainment		100	150	$ 50.00
	Transportation/Gas		50	55	$ 5.00
	Cell Phone		75	85	$ 10.00
	Totals		650	725	$ 75.00

Contextual Tabs

Contextual tabs appear in context with the task you are performing. The Tables feature, as well as other Word features, uses contextual tabs. They appear on the Ribbon when the insertion point is in a table. The following illustration shows the Table Tools' Design and Layout tabs, where you can format tables.

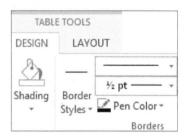

Navigating in a Table

You can move the insertion point by clicking in a cell, or you can use a variety of keystrokes for navigating.

TABLE NAVIGATION KEYSTROKES	
Move To	**Keystroke**
Next cell	Tab
Previous cell	Shift + Tab
Next row	↓
Previous row	↑
Beginning of row	Alt + Home
End of row	Alt + End
Top of column	Alt + Page Up
End of column	Alt + Page Down

Navigate and Enter Data

In this exercise, you will navigate in a table and enter data.

1. Open **WD05-D01-StdntTables** from your **WD2013 Lesson 05** folder and save it as **WD05-D01-StdntTables-[FirstInitialLastName]**.

   Replace the bracketed text with your first initial and last name. For example, if your name is Bethany Smith, your filename would look like this: WD05-D01-StdntTables-BSmith.

2. Position the insertion point in the first cell of the **Expense Table** on the first page.

3. Tap Tab twice to move to the end of the first row.

4. Tap Tab again to move the beginning of the second row.

5. Press Shift + Tab three times to move back one cell at a time.

6. Press Alt + End to move to the end of the row.

7. Press Alt + Home to move to the beginning of the row.

8. Test some other keystrokes.

   Refer to the preceding table as necessary for navigation keystrokes.

9. Enter the following data in your table.

Personal Expenses	Estimate	Actual
Food	425	435
Entertainment	100	150
Transportation/Gas	50	55
Cell Phone	75	85

10. Save the file and leave it open; you will modify it throughout the lesson.

Inserting Tables

Video Library   http://labyrinthelab.com/videos   Video Number: WD13-V0502

You can insert a table using the Table button, the Insert Table dialog box, and the Quick Tables gallery. You can even draw a table with the mouse pointer.

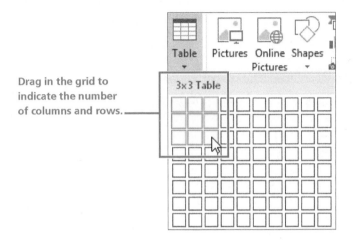

Drag in the grid to indicate the number of columns and rows.

Using the Insert Table dialog box, you can choose various options for the table.

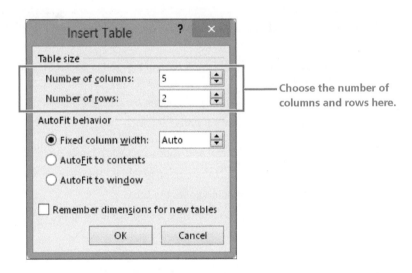

Choose the number of columns and rows here.

The Quick Table gallery lets you choose predesigned tables, such as calendars and various table layouts.

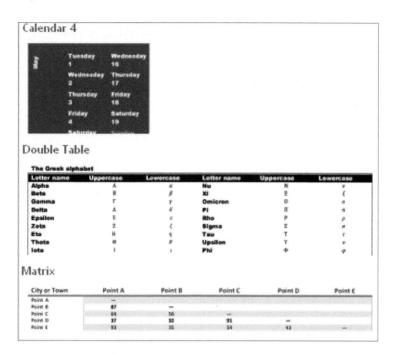

QUICK REFERENCE	INSERTING A TABLE
Task	**Procedure**
Insert a table	▪ Choose Insert→Tables→Table and drag in the grid to select the number of columns and rows.
Insert a table using the Insert Table dialog box	▪ Choose Insert→Tables→Table and choose Insert Table. ▪ Set the number of rows and columns.
Insert a Quick Table	▪ Choose Insert→Tables→Table and choose a Quick Tables style.
Draw a table	▪ Choose Insert→Tables→Table and choose Draw Table. ▪ Click and drag to draw a rectangle for the table. ▪ Drag to draw the row and column lines inside the rectangle.

You can add a row to the bottom of a table by tapping ⎢Tab⎥ when the insertion point is in the last table cell.

Insert Tables

In this exercise, you will create a 3x3 table and enter data. You will also add rows to the bottom of the table. Then you will insert a Quick Table.

1. Save your file as **WD05-D02-StdntTables-[FirstInitialLastName]**.

2. If necessary, choose **Home→Paragraph→Show/Hide ¶** to display formatting marks.

3. Position the insertion point on the blank row below the *Schedule Planning* heading on page 2.

4. Follow these steps to insert a table:

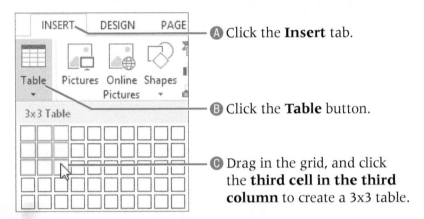

Ⓐ Click the **Insert** tab.

Ⓑ Click the **Table** button.

Ⓒ Drag in the grid, and click the **third cell in the third column** to create a 3x3 table.

5. Enter the text shown, tapping ⎍Tab⎍ when you need to add a new row.

Course	Days	Units
Math	MWF	3
Science	MWF	3
International Tourism	TTH	2
Biology	TH	3
Biology Lab	W	1

Insert a Quick Table

Because you are hoping to join a fraternity/sorority, you will insert the Greek Alphabet table to help you learn the characters. You can use this table for any purpose by deleting the text and replacing it with your own data.

6. Navigate to the top of page 4, and choose **Insert→Tables→Table** 🖩.

7. Follow these steps to insert the table:

Ⓐ Drag the mouse pointer down to **Quick Tables**.

Ⓑ Scroll down the gallery and click this table.

The Quick Table is added to your document.

8. Save your file.

Converting Tables

Video Library   http://labyrinthelab.com/videos   Video Number: WD13-V0503

Sometimes data is best set in tabular columns and sometimes it's best in a table. When you first begin laying out your data, you may not know which options to choose. Word's ability to convert from one to the other prevents you from having to start over.

Converting Text to a Table

Tabs are commonly used as separators in columnar tables. Note that there must only be one tab between columns for the conversion to work properly. When you convert, you are telling Word to replace each tab with a new table column.

This illustration shows a tabular table with one tab between columns.

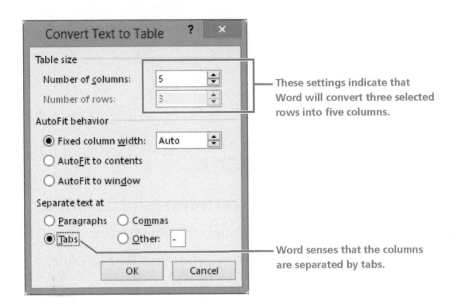

Second·Semester·Schedule	→		→		→		¶
Class	→	Instructor	→	Day	→	Time	→	Book·Price¶
Psychology	→	Hayes	→	MW	→	10:30–11:10	→	80¶

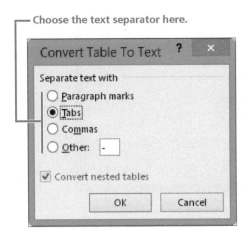

Convert Text to Table   ? ×

Table size

Number of <u>c</u>olumns: 5

Number of rows: 3

These settings indicate that Word will convert three selected rows into five columns.

AutoFit behavior

● Fixed column <u>w</u>idth: Auto

○ Auto<u>F</u>it to contents

○ AutoFit to win<u>d</u>ow

Separate text at

○ <u>P</u>aragraphs   ○ <u>C</u>ommas

● <u>T</u>abs   ○ <u>O</u>ther: -

Word senses that the columns are separated by tabs.

OK   Cancel

Converting a Table to Text

You can specify whether the converted text should be separated by paragraph marks, tabs, commas, or another character that you specify.

Choose the text separator here.

Convert Table To Text   ? ×

Separate text with

○ <u>P</u>aragraph marks

● <u>T</u>abs

○ Co<u>m</u>mas

○ <u>O</u>ther: -

☑ Convert nested tables

OK   Cancel

Task	Procedure
Convert text to a table	■ Turn on formatting marks and ensure there is only one tab separating the columns.
	■ Select all lines to be converted, and choose Insert→Tables→Table→Convert Text to Table.
	■ Choose the text separator and the number of columns.
Convert a table to text	■ Click in any table cell and choose Table Tools→Layout→Data→Convert to Text.
	■ Choose the desired text separator.

DEVELOP YOUR SKILLS WD05-D03

Convert Text to a Table

In this exercise, you will convert text currently in tabular columns into a table. Then you will convert the table back to regular text.

1. Save your file as **WD05-D03-StdntTables-[FirstInitialLastName]**.

2. Scroll to page 3 and select all the rows, including the *Second Semester Schedule* heading.

3. Choose **Insert→Tables→Table** ⊞, and choose **Convert Text to Table**.

4. Follow these steps to create a table from the selected text:

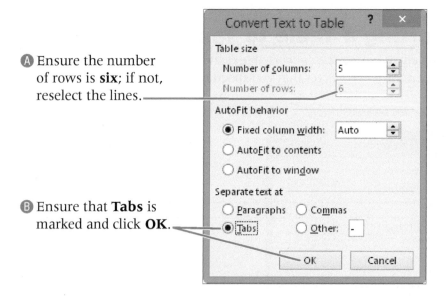

Ⓐ Ensure the number of rows is **six**; if not, reselect the lines.

Ⓑ Ensure that **Tabs** is marked and click **OK**.

The text is now in a five-column table. Don't worry about the heading being in one cell. You'll fix that a little later.

Convert a Table to Text

5. Click in any table **cell**.

Notice the two new Table Tools tabs, Design and Layout, have been added to the Ribbon. These are contextual tabs, meaning they appear in context with what you are working on, in this case, when the insertion point is in a table.

6. Choose **Table Tools→Layout→Data→Convert to Text** 📄. When the dialog box appears, verify that **Tabs** is chosen and click **OK**.

   The table is converted back to a tabular table.

7. Click **Undo** ↺ to return the text to table format.

8. Save the file.

Selecting Data in a Table

Video Library   http://labyrinthelab.com/videos   Video Number: WD13-V0504

The mouse pointer changes shape depending on whether you're selecting a cell, row, column, or the entire table. The following illustrations display the various pointer shapes when selecting in a table.

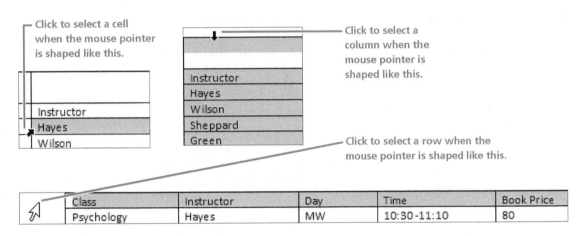

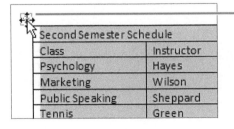

Customizing Alignment, Direction, and Cell Margins

Data can be aligned horizontally or vertically, and you can change the direction of text. You can also modify the cell margins. These commands are found in the Alignment group on the contextual Layout tab that appears when the insertion point is positioned in a table.

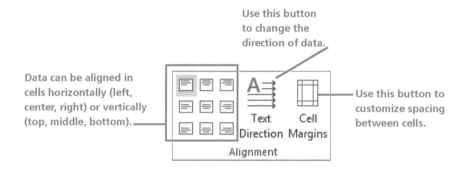

Use this button to change the direction of data.

Data can be aligned in cells horizontally (left, center, right) or vertically (top, middle, bottom).

Use this button to customize spacing between cells.

DEVELOP YOUR SKILLS WD05-D04

Select and Align Data, and Modify Cell Margins

In this exercise, you will center-align data, change text direction, and increase cell margins.

1. Save your file as **WD05-D04-StdntTables-[FirstInitialLastName]**.

2. Follow these steps to center the heading row data:

   Ⓐ Position the mouse pointer in the margin left of the second row and click when the mouse pointer looks like this.

   Ⓑ Choose the **Layout tab**.

   Ⓒ Click **Align Center**.

3. Follow these steps to center the data in a range of cells:

   Ⓐ Click and drag to select these cells.

Hayes	MW	10:30-11:10	80
Wilson	MW	2:30-3:20	90
Sheppard	TF	10:15-11:05	35
Green	W	3:40-4:30	45

   Ⓑ Choose **Table Tools→Layout→ Alignment→ Align Center**.

Change Text Direction

4. Select the **second row**.

5. Choose **Table Tools→Layout→Alignment→Text Direction** 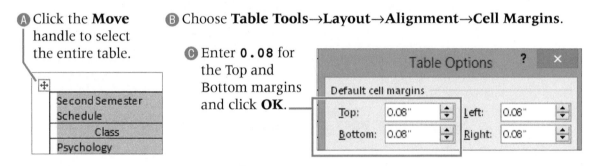 twice to change to vertical with the text facing to the right.

6. Click **Undo** twice to change back to horizontal alignment.

Change Cell Margins

7. Follow these steps to increase the distance between the text and cell borders:

ⓐ Click the **Move** handle to select the entire table.

ⓑ Choose **Table Tools→Layout→Alignment→Cell Margins**.

ⓒ Enter **0.08** for the Top and Bottom margins and click **OK**.

8. Save your file.

Merging and Splitting Cells

Video Library http://labyrinthelab.com/videos Video Number: WD13-V0505

You can merge two or more adjacent cells in the same row or column into a single cell. The merge option is often used to center a heading across the top of a table. You can also split a single cell into multiple cells.

A dialog box, shown in the following illustration, appears when you click the Split Cells button so you can determine the specifics of your split.

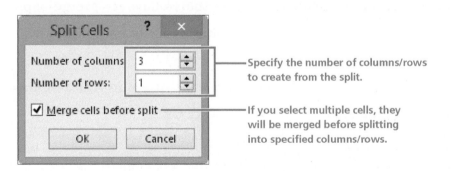

Specify the number of columns/rows to create from the split.

If you select multiple cells, they will be merged before splitting into specified columns/rows.

The contextual Layout tab containing the Merge Cells and Split Cells commands appears when the insertion point is in a table.

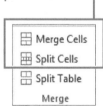

Task	Procedure
Merge cells	▪ Select the cells to merge, and choose Table Tools→Layout→Merge→Merge Cells.
Split cells	▪ Select the cell to split, and choose Table Tools→Layout→Merge→Split Cells.
	▪ Choose the number of rows and/or columns.

DEVELOP YOUR SKILLS WD05-D05
Merge and Split Cells in a Table

In this exercise, you will merge the cells in the first row to create one cell, where you will center the title across the width of the table. You will practice splitting cells, and then you will convert the title to regular text.

1. Save your file as **WD05-D05-StdntTables-[FirstInitialLastName]**.

2. Follow these steps to merge the table row and center the title:

Ⓐ Select the first row. Ⓑ Click the **Layout** tab and click **Merge Cells**. Ⓒ Click **Align Center**.

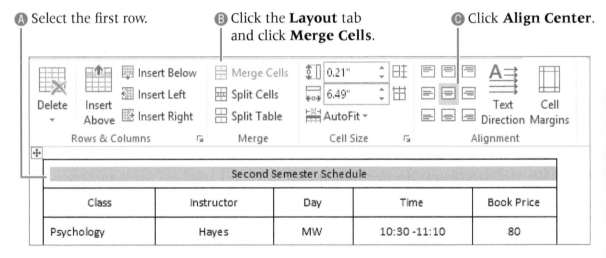

3. With the first row still selected, choose **Table Tools→Layout→Merge→Split Cells** ▦.

4. When the dialog box opens, choose **three columns** and **one row**; click **OK**.

5. Click **Undo** ↺ to merge the cells again.

6. With the first row still selected, choose **Table Tools→Layout→Data→Convert to Text**.

7. Verify that **Paragraph Marks** is chosen and click **OK**.

8. Save the file.

Formatting with Borders, Shading, and Styles

Video Library   http://labyrinthelab.com/videos   Video Number: WD13-V0506

Borders, shading, and styles can enhance the readability of a table, and they add pizzazz. These tools are conveniently located on the contextual Design tab that appears when the insertion point is in a table. The Borders and Shading buttons have memory, meaning they reflect the last option chosen in the current session. This is convenient if you want to apply the same effect multiple times. Newly created tables have borders by default.

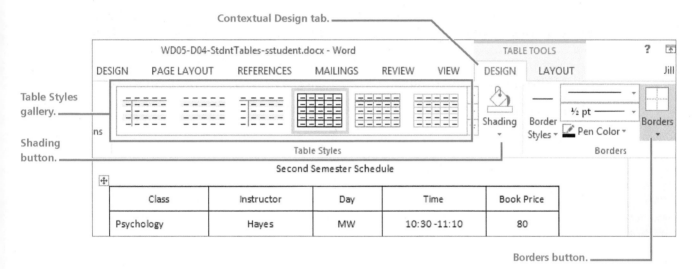

Modifying Formats

Just like regular text, you can easily modify table formats using the formatting tools on the Home tab. Or use the *Mini toolbar*, which provides convenient formatting tools right at your mouse pointer when you select data.

DEVELOP YOUR SKILLS WD05-D06
Use Borders, Shading, and Styles

In this exercise, you will remove all borders from your table, and then apply borders and shading to the first row. Then you will choose a table style to format your table.

1. Save your file as **WD05-D06-StdntTables-[FirstInitialLastName]**.

2. Click the **move handle** in the upper-left corner of the Second Semester Schedule table to select it.

   Remember, the insertion point has to be in the table or you have to hover the mouse pointer over the table for the move handle to appear.

3. Choose **Table Tools→Design→Borders→Borders** ⊞ **menu button** ▼ and choose **No Border**.

You may see gridlines within the table, but they won't print; they are just there to guide you. The Borders button menu on the Design tab provides the option to turn gridlines on or off.

4. Select the **first table row**, choose **Table Tools→Design→Borders→Borders** ⊞ **menu button** ▼, and choose **Outside Borders**.

5. Keep the first row selected and choose **Table Tools→Design→Table Styles→Shading** ⬛ **menu button** ▼.

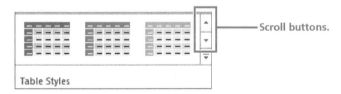

6. Choose the third color in the third column, **Tan, Background 2, Darker 25%**.

Use Table Styles

7. Make sure the insertion point is in the table, and choose **Table Tools→Design→Table Styles**.

8. Click the **scroll buttons** to look through the gallery, and then hover the **mouse pointer** over several styles to see a **Live Preview** of the styles.

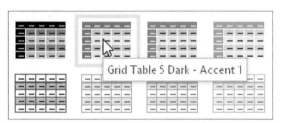

————Scroll buttons.

Table Styles

9. Click the **More** 🔽 button below the scroll buttons to open the gallery and choose **Grid Table 5 Dark – Accent 1** (toward the bottom of the gallery).

Grid Table 5 Dark - Accent 1

The style overrides your cell margin spacing and borders and shading. In turn, you can override Table Styles formatting.

10. Select the first row of the table; choose **Home→Font→Font menu button** ▼ and choose **Century Gothic**.

11. With the first row still selected, choose **Home→Font→Font Size menu button** ▼ and choose **12 points**.

12. Save the file.

Sorting Data in a Table

Word 2013

Video Library http://labyrinthelab.com/videos Video Number: WD13-V0507

The Sort button in the Data group on the contextual Layout tab opens the Sort dialog box, which provides options to sort one or more columns in ascending or descending order, and choose whether the first row of the table contains column headings.

You can choose to sort a table by up to three levels. For example, say you have a table containing column headings for city, state, and zip. You can have Word sort the table first by state, then by city within state, and then by zip code within city for a three-level sort.

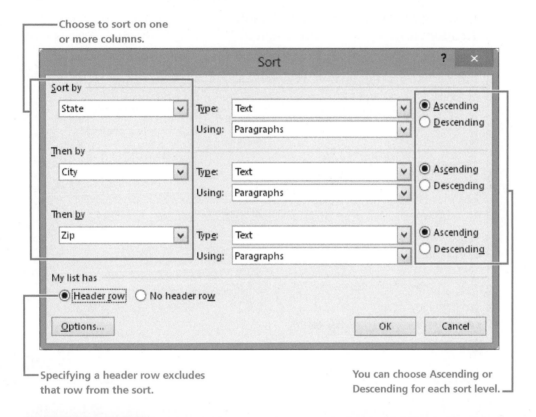

Choose to sort on one or more columns.

Specifying a header row excludes that row from the sort.

You can choose Ascending or Descending for each sort level.

QUICK REFERENCE	SORTING TABLES
Task	**Procedure**
Sort a table	■ Click in the table and choose Table Tools→Layout→Data→Sort.
	■ Choose Header Row or No Header Row, and select the columns to sort by.
	■ Choose the Type of data and choose Ascending or Descending for each sort level.

Sort Table Rows

In this exercise, you will practice sorting the Second Semester Schedule table.

1. Save your file as **WD05-D07-StdntTables-[FirstInitialLastName]**.

2. Position the insertion point in any cell in the **Second Semester Schedule** table.

3. Choose **Table Tools→Layout→Data→Sort** .
   Word displays the Sort dialog box.

4. Follow these steps to sort the table:

   Ⓐ If necessary, choose   Ⓑ Choose **Book**   Ⓒ Word automatically sensed
     Header Row.   **Price** here.   the data Type as **Number**.

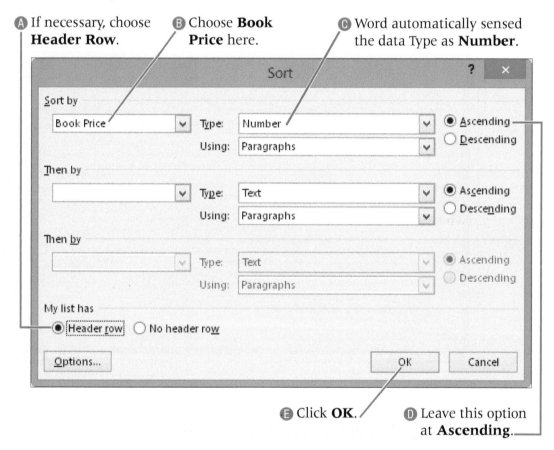

   Ⓔ Click **OK**.   Ⓓ Leave this option
                            at **Ascending**.

   Word sorts the table numerically by book price.

5. Choose **Table Tools→Layout→Data→Sort** again.

6. In the Sort dialog box, make sure **Header Row** is chosen, choose **Class** from the Sort By list, and click **OK**.
   The table is now sorted in ascending order by Class.

7. Save your file.

Inserting Rows and Columns

Video Library   http://labyrinthelab.com/videos   Video Number: WD13-V0508

You can insert columns and rows in an existing table. If you wish to insert multiple columns or rows, you must first select the same number of existing columns or rows as you wish to insert. For example, to insert two new rows, select two existing rows.

You can use the buttons in the Rows & Columns group on the Layout tab to insert columns and rows, or you can use the drop-down menu that appears when you right-click a selected column or row.

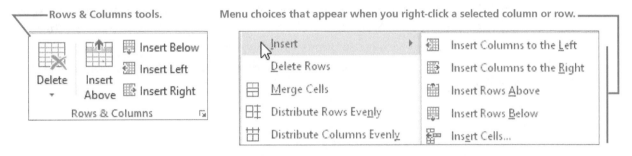

A quick and easy way to insert a column or row is with the Insert Control that appears when the insertion point is in the table and you move the mouse pointer between two columns or rows, as shown here.

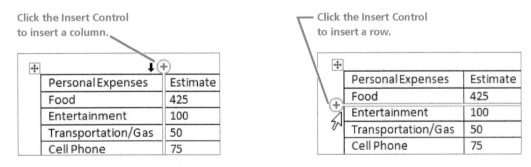

Moving Rows and Columns

You can move a row or column by using the Cut and Paste commands or by using the mouse to drag and drop. When you select the entire row or column and move it to another location, Word automatically makes room for the selection by moving the other rows down or the other columns to the right.

If you select an individual cell within a row or column, when you paste, Word replaces any existing data in the cell. You can prevent data loss by inserting a blank row or column prior to moving.

Task	Procedure
Insert rows or columns	■ Click in the desired row/column or select the same number of rows/columns you wish to insert.
	■ Choose Table Tools→Layout→Rows & Columns, and then choose Insert Above/Below or Insert Left/Right. Or, position the mouse pointer between two rows/columns and click the Insert Control.
Delete table elements	■ Select the desired row(s), column(s), or cell(s).
	■ Choose Table Tools→Layout→Rows & Columns→Delete and choose the item to delete.
Move a row or column using Cut and Paste	■ Select the entire row(s) or column(s) and choose Home→Clipboard→Cut.
	■ Select the row to paste the data above or the column to paste the data to the left of.
	■ Choose Home→Clipboard→Paste.
Move a row or column using drag and drop	■ Select the entire row(s) or column(s) and drag to the first cell in the desired row or column.

DEVELOP YOUR SKILLS WD05-D08

Insert Rows and a Column

In this exercise, you will insert multiple rows and a new column in the table.

1. Save your file as **WD05-D08-StdntTables-[FirstInitialLastName]**.

2. Position the mouse pointer to the left of the **Marketing** row until it becomes the white arrow.

3. Click and drag down to select the **Marketing and Psychology** rows.

4. Choose **Table Tools→Layout→Rows & Columns→Insert Above** 🔲 to insert two new rows above the Marketing row.

5. Add the following data to the new blank rows:

Geometry	Bailey	MW	12:00 – 12:50	94
Geometry Lab	Johnson	TTH	9:00 – 9:50	35

6. Follow these steps to insert a new column:

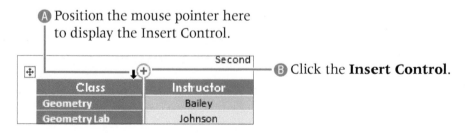

Ⓐ Position the mouse pointer here to display the Insert Control.

Ⓑ Click the **Insert Control**.

A new column is inserted to the right of the Class column.

7. Type **Course #** as the new column heading.

8. Enter the following data in the column.

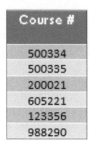

Course #
500334
500335
200021
605221
123356
988290

9. Scroll back up to the *Expense Table* on page 1 and position the insertion point in the **Actual** column.

10. Choose **Table Tools→Layout→Rows & Columns→Insert Right** .

11. Type **Difference** as the new column heading; save the file.

Performing Calculations in Tables

Video Library   http://labyrinthelab.com/videos   Video Number: WD13-V0509

When the Formula dialog box opens, it displays the Sum function. The Sum function recognizes whether there are numbers in the cells above or to the left of the formula cell and indicates that in the formula automatically. However, sometimes you may need a formula for something other than addition. In that case, you use cell addresses in the formula. Although the columns and rows are not lettered or numbered as they are in Excel, which is the Microsoft application designed to "crunch numbers," you must use cell addresses for certain calculations in a table. The first cell in a table is considered to be cell A1 (first column, first row).

Word's formulas are not nearly as sophisticated as Excel's; however, they are adequate for simple calculations.

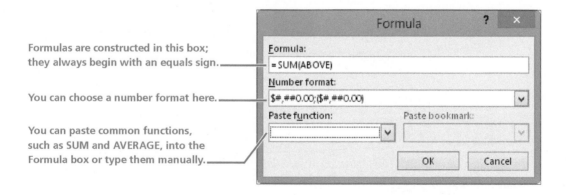

Formulas are constructed in this box; they always begin with an equals sign.

You can choose a number format here.

You can paste common functions, such as SUM and AVERAGE, into the Formula box or type them manually.

Constructing Formulas

You construct formulas by typing directly into the Formula dialog box. In Word, formulas can contain a combination of the following elements.

- **Arithmetic operators:** The most common arithmetic operators are + (addition), − (subtraction), / (division), and * (multiplication). For more complex formulas, use Microsoft Excel and copy and paste into Word.

- **Cell addresses:** In Word tables, columns are labeled A, B, C, etc., and rows are numbered 1, 2, 3, etc. Each cell has an address formed by the column letter and row number. For example, cell A1 refers to the cell in column A and row 1. You can use cell references in formulas. For example, the formula =D2–C2 subtracts the number in cell C2 from the number in cell D2.

- **Functions:** Functions are predefined formulas that perform calculations on cells. The most common functions are SUM, AVERAGE, MIN, and MAX.

  A function is followed by a set of parentheses in which you enter arguments. Arguments include numbers, cell addresses, a range of cells, or direction references (see next bullet).

  A range of cells is separated by a colon. For example, to include cells C2, C3, and C4 only in a formula, you would type C2:C4.

- **Direction references:** In Word, functions can use direction references to indicate cell ranges. The direction references are ABOVE, BELOW, LEFT, and RIGHT. As an example, the formula =SUM(ABOVE) would sum all numbers above the cell containing the formula.

If a number relating to a formula changes, right-click the cell containing the formula and choose Update Field to recalculate the formula.

QUICK REFERENCE	CONSTRUCTING FORMULAS
Task	**Procedure**
Create a formula	■ Choose Table Tools→Layout→Data→Formula and delete the formula in the formula box.
	■ Type an equals (=) sign and construct the formula using cell addresses.
	■ Use the appropriate operator: + (add), − (subtract), * (multiply), / (divide).
Calculate with a function	■ Choose Table Tools→Layout→Data→Formula and delete the formula in the formula box.
	■ Type an equals (=) sign and choose a function from the Paste Function list.
	■ Enter the arguments within the parentheses.

DEVELOP YOUR SKILLS WD05-D09
Construct Formulas

In this exercise, you will use formulas to calculate the difference for each expense item and calculate the totals for the Estimate, Actual, and Difference columns.

1. Save your file as **WD05-D09-StdntTables-[FirstInitialLastName]**.

2. Click in the **second row** of the *Difference* column.

   This cell is named D2 because it is the fourth column (D) in the second row (2).

3. Choose **Table Tools→Layout→Data→Formula** fx.

4. Follow these steps to create a formula to subtract the *Estimate* from the *Actual* expense:

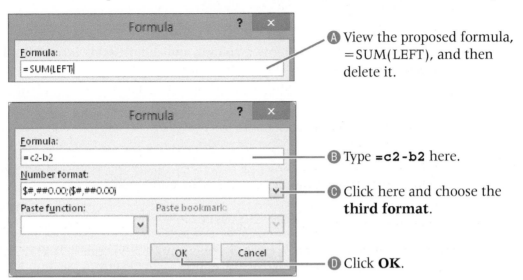

Ⓐ View the proposed formula, =SUM(LEFT), and then delete it.

Ⓑ Type **=c2-b2** here.

Ⓒ Click here and choose the **third format**.

Ⓓ Click **OK**.

This formula subtracts the estimated food expense (column b, row 2) from the actual food expense (column c, row 2). Notice that the result, $10.00, displays with a dollar sign and two decimal places because of the dollar format chosen.

If you wish to display the dollar format without the two decimal places, you must delete them manually from each cell.

5. Click in the cell beneath the formula.

6. Choose **Table Tools→Layout→Data→Formula** fx.

7. Remove the proposed formula and type **=c3-b3**.

8. Click the **Number Format** menu arrow, choose the **third format**, and click **OK**.

9. Enter formulas in the remaining rows in the *Difference* column choosing the same format as before.

Create a Formula to Total the Columns

10. Position the insertion point in the last table cell and tap ⎁Tab⎁ to create a new row.

Personal Expenses	Estimate	Actual	Difference
Food	425	435	$ 10.00
Entertainment	100	150	$ 50.00
Transportation/Gas	50	55	$ 5.00
Cell Phone	75	85	$ 10.00

11. Type **Totals** in the first cell and tap ⎁Tab⎁ to move to the next cell.

12. Choose **Table Tools→Layout→Data→Formula** fx.

Word assumes you want to add the numbers above the formula cell.

13. Click **OK**.

The result should be 650. Notice that the total does not have the dollar sign or decimals, since you did not specify any special formatting.

14. Calculate the total for *Actual* column with no formatting.

15. Calculate the total for the *Difference* column and add the same formatting as the other numbers in the column.

16. Save the file.

Sizing Rows and Columns

Video Library   http://labyrinthelab.com/videos   Video Number: WD13-V0510

You can easily resize columns and rows in a table. Word offers a variety of techniques for this. The adjust pointer, a double-headed arrow, appears whenever you position the mouse pointer on a row or column gridline. You can adjust the column width and row height by dragging the gridline.

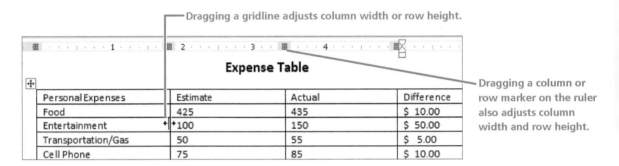

Dragging a gridline adjusts column width or row height.

Dragging a column or row marker on the ruler also adjusts column width and row height.

The Cell Size group in the contextual Layout tab provides handy tools for working with column and row sizes.

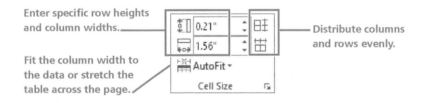

Enter specific row heights and column widths.

Distribute columns and rows evenly.

Fit the column width to the data or stretch the table across the page.

DEVELOP YOUR SKILLS WD05-D10
Adjust Column Widths

In this exercise, you will adjust column widths using the adjust pointer and the tools in the Cell Size group on the Layout tab.

1. Save your file as **WD05-D10-StdntTables-[FirstInitialLastName]**.

2. Follow these steps to change the width of the first column:

Ⓐ Position the mouse pointer here, and it changes to the adjust pointer (a double-headed arrow).

Ⓑ Drag to the right about a half inch and release the mouse button.

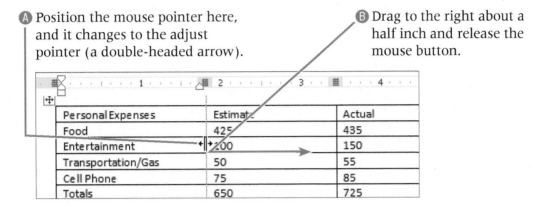

3. Follow these steps to distribute the last three columns evenly:

Ⓑ Drag right to select all three columns.

Ⓐ Position the mouse pointer at the top of this column. (It should appear as a small black arrow.)

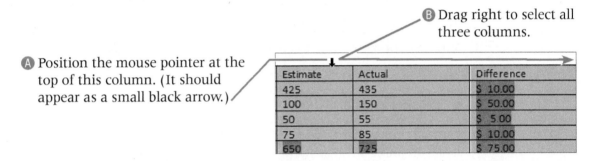

4. Choose **Table Tools→Layout→Cell Size→Distribute Columns** ⊞ to make the selected columns the same size.

AutoFit Columns

5. Scroll to the **Schedule Planning table** on **page 2** and select the **entire table**.

6. Choose **Table Tools→Layout→Cell Size→AutoFit** 🔲, and choose **AutoFit Contents**.
   All columns are now as wide as they need to be based on the width of their contents.

7. Save and close the file. Exit **Word**.

Concepts Review

To check your knowledge of the key concepts introduced in this lesson, complete the Concepts Review quiz by choosing the appropriate access option below.

If you are...	Then access the quiz by...
Using the Labyrinth Video Library	Going to http://labyrinthelab.com/videos
Using eLab	Logging in, choosing Content, and navigating to the Concepts Review quiz for this lesson
Not using the Labyrinth Video Library or eLab	Going to the student resource center for this book

Reinforce Your Skills

Insert Tables and Align Data

Kids for Change are partnering with the local Center for Environmental Health to identify products in the home that present a risk to babies. In this exercise, you will create, enter data in, and navigate a table. You will convert a tabular document to a table and format alignment, text direction, and cell margins. Finally, you will merge and split cells.

Navigate in a Table

1. Start **Word**. Open **WD05-R01-RiskTeam** from your **WD2013 Lesson 05** folder and save it as **WD05-R01-RiskTeam-[FirstInitialLastName]**.

2. Position the insertion point in the first table cell and tap [↓].

3. Tap [Tab] to move to the right one cell.

4. Press [Shift]+[Tab] to move to the left one cell.

5. Press [Shift]+[Tab] again to move to the end of the previous row.

6. Press [Alt]+[Home] to move to the beginning of the row.

7. Press [Alt]+[End] to move to the end of the row.

8. Press [Alt]+[Page Down] to move to the bottom of the column.

9. Press [Alt]+[Page Up] to move to the top of the column.

Insert Tables

10. If necessary, choose **Home→Paragraph→Show/Hide** to display formatting marks.

11. Position the insertion point on the second blank line below the table.

12. Insert a **3x6 table** and enter the data shown here.

Remember, you can add rows to the bottom of a table by tapping [Tab] when you reach the last table cell.

Product	Risk factor	Risk
Foam products	Chlorinated Tris	Gene mutations
Drop-side cribs	Side can drop	Suffocate or strangle
Sleep positioners	Face against positioner	Suffocate or strangle
Blankets	Baby becomes entangled	Suffocate
Crib tents	Baby becomes entangled	Strangle
Changing tables	Baby can fall	Injury
Bath seats	Can tip	Drown

Next you will insert a calendar quick table so you can keep track of meetings with the Center for Environmental Health.

13. Position the insertion point at the end of the document and tap Enter .

14. Choose **Insert→Tables→Table** ⊞ and slide the mouse pointer down to **Quick Tables**.

15. Insert **Calendar 2**.

16. Position the insertion point at the end of the document and tap Enter .
Now you will copy a tabular table from another file and paste it into your document.

17. Open **WD05-R01-FoodRisk** from your **WD2013 Lesson 05** folder.

18. Copy the contents of the document and paste it at the end of your **Risk Team** document.

19. Close the **Food Risk** file.

Convert Text to a Table

20. Select the entire tabular table.

21. Choose **Insert→Tables→Table→Convert Text to Table**.

22. Accept the defaults in the dialog box and click **OK**.

Select Table Data

23. Click in the **food risk** table to deselect.

24. Position the mouse pointer at the top of the middle column, and when the mouse pointer appears as a black down-pointing arrow, click to select the column.

25. Position the insertion point just inside the left edge of the **Walker** cell, and when the mouse pointer appears as a black-tilted arrow, click to select the cell.

26. Position the mouse pointer in the margin to the left of the **Parker** row, and when the mouse pointer appears as a white-tilted arrow, click to select the row.

27. Click the insertion point in the table to display the move handle, then position the mouse pointer over the move handle. When the mouse pointer appears, click to select the entire table.

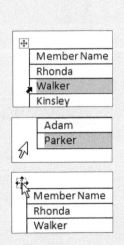

Align Data, Change Text Direction, and Modify Cell Margins

28. Select the **Food and Risk Factor columns**.

29. Choose **Table Tools→Layout→Alignment→Align Center** ▤.

30. Select the first column and choose **Layout→Alignment→Align Center Right** ▤.
    The first column should still be selected.

31. Choose **Table Tools→Layout→Alignment→Align Center Left** ▤.

32. Select the first row and choose **Table Tools→Layout→Alignment→Text Direction** ▤.

33. Click **Text Direction** ▤ again.

34. Click **Undo** ↺ twice to return to horizontal alignment.

35. Select the entire table and choose **Table Tools→Layout→Alignment→Cell Margins** ▦.

36. In the Table Options dialog box, change the **top and bottom margins** to **0.04** and click **OK**.

Merge and Split Cells

37. Click in the first table row.

38. Choose **Table Tools→Layout→Rows & Columns→Insert Above** ▦.
    The new row should be selected.

39. Choose **Table Tools→Layout→Merge→Merge Cells** ▤.

40. Click in the new row and type **Food Risk**.

41. Choose **Table Tools→Layout→Merge→Split Cells** ▦.

42. Accept the default number of columns and rows and click **OK**.

43. Click **Undo** ↺ to merge the cells again.

44. Save and close the file; exit from **Word**.

45. Submit your final file based on the guidelines provided by your instructor.
    To view examples of how your file or files should look at the end of this exercise, go to the student resource center.

REINFORCE YOUR SKILLS WD05-R02

Format, Organize, and Calculate Tables

In this exercise, you will use borders, shading, table styles, and font formatting. You will sort a table, work with columns and rows, and perform calculations. Finally, you will adjust column widths.

Format with Borders, Shading, and Styles

The Kids for Change members are planning a demonstration of safe cleaning products at the Community Center. They need to figure out how much salt, lemon, vinegar, and baking soda they will need.

1. Start **Word**. Open **WD05-R02-SafeClean** from your **WD2013 Lesson 05** folder and save it as **WD05-R02-SafeClean-[FirstInitialLastName]**.

2. Position the insertion point in the table on page 1 and choose **Table Tools→Design→Table Styles**.

3. Open the gallery and choose **Grid Table 4 – Accent 6**.

   Hint: It's a green style.

4. Select the table, choose **Table Tools→Design→Borders→Borders** menu button ▾, and then choose **Outside Borders**.

5. Select the first row, choose **Table Tools→Design→Borders→Borders** menu button ▾, and then choose **Bottom Border**.

6. With the first row still selected, choose **Table Tools→Design→Table Styles→Shading** menu button ▾.

7. Choose the last green color in the right-hand column, **Green, Accent 6, Darker 50%**.

8. Select the entire table, choose **Home→Font→Font menu button** ▾, and then choose **Comic Sans MS**.

9. Select in the first column starting at *Clean coffee pot* through the end of the column.

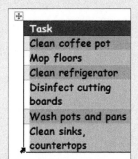

10. Choose **Home→Font→Italic** *I*.

Sort Table Data

Dylan, a Kids for Change member, volunteers at a green cleaning supplies company so he can become familiar with safe cleaning products. He has been asked to complete the Order Tracking Sheet.

11. Go to page 2 of the **Safe Clean** file and select the entire table.

12. Choose **Table Tools→Layout→Data→Sort** and, if necessary, choose the **Header Row** option in the Sort dialog box.

13. Click the **Sort By field drop-down arrow** and choose **Item #**; click **OK**.

    The Item # column is now in ascending numeric order.

14. Use the same process to sort by the **Customer ID column** in ascending order.

Insert a Column and Row

15. Position the insertion point in the **Price column**.

16. Choose **Table Tools→Layout→Rows & Columns→Insert Right**.

17. Position the insertion point in the last cell of the new column and tap Tab to add a row.

18. Type **Total** in the first cell of the new row, and then type **Total** at the top of the new column.

Perform Calculations in a Table

19. Position the insertion point in the second cell of the last column.

20. Choose **Table Tools→Layout→Data→Formula** *fx*.

    You will multiply Quantity by Price to calculate the total price for the first customer.

21. Delete the contents of the **Formula box** and type **=d2*e2** in the box.

    Remember, the asterisk (*) is the multiply sign.

22. Choose the **dollar** format (third format) from the Number Format drop-down list, and then click **OK**.

23. Repeat the process to calculate the total and apply the currency format for the rest of the customers.

    Now you will total the last column.

24. Position the insertion point in the last cell of the Total column.

25. Choose **Table Tools→Layout→Data→Formula** fx

    The formula defaults to =SUM(ABOVE), which is what you want.

26. Choose the **dollar** format, and then click **OK**.

Size Columns

27. Select the entire table.

28. Choose **Table Tools→Layout→Cell Size→AutoFit** and choose **AutoFit Contents**.

    The width of the columns is adjusted based on the widest entry in each column.

29. Save and close the file; exit from **Word**.

30. Submit your final file based on the guidelines provided by your instructor.

    To view examples of how your file or files should look at the end of this exercise, go to the student resource center.

REINFORCE YOUR SKILLS WD05-R03

Insert and Format Tables

This holiday season, Kids for Change members are working with the local fire department to collect toys for needy kids. The members will be assigned to different neighborhoods for collecting. In this exercise, you will format a table that tracks how many toys each member collects.

Navigate in a Table

1. Start **Word**. Open **WD05-R03-Toys** from your **WD2013 Lesson 05** folder and save it as **WD05-R03-Toys-[FirstInitialLastName]**.

2. Position the insertion point in the first table cell (page 1) and press [Alt]+[End] to move to the end of the row.

3. Press [Alt]+[Page Down] to move to the bottom of the column.

4. Press [Alt]+[Home] to move to the beginning of the row.

5. Tap [Tab] twice to move two cells to the right.

6. Press [Shift]+[Tab] to move to the left one cell.

7. Tap [↑] to move up one row.

Insert a Table

Kids for Change members decided to take up a collection from friends and family to purchase additional toys. You will insert a Quick Table to track the donations.

8. Scroll to the end of the document and press Ctrl + Enter to insert a page break.

9. Choose **Insert→Tables→Table** ▦ and slide the mouse pointer down to **Quick Tables**.

10. In the submenu, scroll down and choose **Tabular List**.

11. Select the *ITEM* heading and type **MEMBER** in its place.

12. Select the *NEEDED* heading and type **AMOUNT** in its place.

13. Select the remaining rows and tap Delete.

14. Enter the new data as shown.

MEMBER	AMOUNT
Ella	$20
Tom	$17
Roger	$32
Stella	$15
Jennifer	$22
Max	$29
Jose	$35
Albert	$40

Convert Text to a Table

15. Scroll to page 2 and select the rows in the tabular table from *Exposure* through *Lacerations*.

16. Choose **Insert→Tables→Table** ▦ and choose **Convert Text to Table**.

17. When the Convert Text to Table dialog box appears, click **OK**.

Select Table Data

18. Position the mouse pointer in the margin to the left of the third row and click to select the row.

19. Position the mouse pointer at the top of the Danger column, and when the mouse pointer appears as a black down-pointing arrow, click to select the column.

20. Position the mouse pointer in the bottom-left corner of the Pull toys cell, and when the mouse pointer appears as a tilted black arrow, click to select the cell.

21. Click the move handle in the upper-left corner of the table to select the entire table.

Align Data, Change Text Direction, and Modify Cell Margins

22. Scroll to the table on page 1.

23. Select the second and third columns.

24. Choose **Table Tools→Layout→Alignment→Align Center Right** ▤.

25. Choose **Table Tools→Layout→Alignment→Align Center** ▤.

26. Select the first table row.

27. Choose **Table Tools→Layout→Alignment→Text Direction** ▣.

28. Click **Undo** ↻ to return to horizontal alignment.

29. Select the entire table.

30. Choose **Table Tools→Layout→Alignment→Cell Margins** ▢.

31. Change the **top and bottom margins** to **0.06**, then click **OK**.

Merge Cells

32. Select the four Sycamore cells in the third column.

33. Choose **Table Tools→Layout→Merge→Merge Cells** ▦.

34. Delete three of the Sycamore entries.

35. Use the same technique to merge the Homestead Valley and Middle Ridge cells, and then delete three Homestead Valley and three Middle Ridge entries.

Use Borders, Shading, and Table Styles

36. Select the entire table.

37. Choose **Table Tools→Design→Borders→Borders** ▦ **menu button** ▼, and then choose **No Border**.

38. Choose **Table Tools→Design→Table Styles**, click the More ▣ button on the Styles gallery, and then choose the **Grid Table 4 – Accent 5** style.

    Hint: It's a blue style.

Sort Data

Several Kids for Change regional directors plan to meet following the toy collection to discuss plans for next year's collection. They compiled a mailing list of directors who will be notified of the meeting.

39. Scroll to the table on page 3 and position the insertion point in the table.

40. Choose **Table Tools→Layout→Data→Sort** ▣.

41. If necessary, choose **Header Row** in the Sort dialog box, then choose sort by **State**, then by **City**, then by **Zip**, and then click **OK**.

    The California cities sorted in ascending alphabetic order within State, and the Dallas zip codes sorted in ascending numeric order within City.

Insert Rows and Resize Columns

42. Scroll to the table on page 4.

    Region 5 was accidentally omitted.

43. Position the mouse pointer to the left of the last two rows until the **Insert Control** appears.

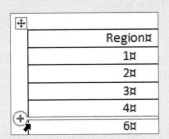

44. Click the control to insert a blank row between the last two rows, and then enter the following data in the new row.

5	1,951	2,543

45. Select the entire table, choose **Table Tools→Layout→Cell Size→AutoFit** ⊞, and choose **AutoFit Contents**.

Perform Calculations

46. Position the insertion point in the last table cell and tap Tab to insert a new row at the bottom of the table.

47. Type **Totals** in the first cell of the new row and tap Tab to move to the next cell.

    Now you will calculate the totals for all regions for both years.

48. Choose **Table Tools→Layout→Data→Formula** *fx*.

49. Accept the default Sum function in the Formula box and click **OK**.

50. Use the same process to calculate this year's total.

51. Save and close the file and exit from **Word**.

52. Submit your final file based on the guidelines provided by your instructor.

Apply Your Skills

Insert Tables, and Align and Merge Cells

In this exercise, you will navigate in a table, insert a new table, and convert a table to tabular text. You will select and align data and use cell margins. Then you will merge cells to create a table heading.

Navigate in and Insert a Table

1. Start **Word**. Open **WD05-A01-CorpEvents** from your **WD2013 Lesson 05** folder and save it as **WD05-A01-CorpEvents-[FirstInitialLastName]**.

2. Navigate in the table on page 1 using the keystrokes shown in the *Navigating in a Table* section of the main lesson.

3. If necessary, choose **Home→Paragraph→Show/Hide ¶** to display formatting marks.

4. Scroll to page 2 and position the insertion point on the first blank line below *Oceanic Cruise Lines*.

5. Insert a **4x5 table** and enter the data shown.

Date	Itinerary	Ship	From
03/18/2013	4-night Bahamas Cruise from Miami	Oceanic Star	$279
03/22/2013	3-night Bahamas Cruise from Miami	Oceanic Jewel	$289
03/24/2013	7-night Bahamas Cruise from New York	Oceanic Star	$1159
03/25/2013	7-night Bahamas Cruise from New York	Oceanic Jewel	$599

Convert a Table to Text, Select Data, and Customize Alignment

6. Scroll to page 3 and select the table.

7. Choose **Table Tools→Layout→Data→Convert to Text** 🔲.

8. Make sure **Tabs** is chosen in the Convert Table to Text dialog box and click **OK**.

9. Scroll to page 1 and select data using the selection techniques described in this lesson.

10. Select the second and third columns and click **Align Center** 🔲 on the Layout tab.

11. Select the second row and click **Text Direction** 🔲 on the Layout tab.

12. Click **Undo** 🔲 to return to horizontal alignment.

Use Cell Margins and Merge Cells

13. Select the page 1 table and use the **Cell Margins** ▯ on the Layout tab to set the top and bottom margins at **0.08"**.

14. Merge the first row and type **Travel Special** as the table heading.

15. Save and close the file; exit from **Word**.

16. Submit your final file based on the guidelines provided by your instructor.

    To view examples of how your file or files should look at the end of this exercise, go to the student resource center.

Format, Organize, and Calculate Tables

In this exercise, you will format with borders, shading, and table styles, and then you will sort data. You will insert columns and rows, and finally, you will perform calculations and size columns.

Apply Borders, Shading, and a Table Style

1. Start **Word**. Open **WD05-A02-Universal** from your **WD2013 Lesson 05** folder and save the file as **WD05-A02-Universal-[FirstInitialLastName]**.

2. Select the table on page 1; choose **Table Tools→Design→Borders→Borders** ▦ menu button ▼ and choose **No Border**.

3. Select the first row, and use **Borders** ▭ to apply a **bottom border**.

4. Apply a bottom border to the last row of the table.

5. Select the first row, then choose **Table Tools→Design→Table Styles→Shading** ▨ menu button ▼ and choose **Gold, Accent 4, Darker 25%**.

6. Select the third row and apply **Gold, Accent 4, Lighter 60%**.

7. Apply the same color you used in the third row to the **fifth row**.

8. Scroll to page 2, position the insertion point in the table, choose **Table Tools→Design→Table Styles**, and open the Table Styles gallery.

9. Choose the **Grid Table 6 Colorful – Accent 4** style; it's a yellow style.

Sort Data and Insert a Row and Column

10. Using the page 2 table, sort by the **Travel Package column** in ascending order, specifying that the table has a header row.

11. Scroll to the page 1 table and sort by the **Group Travel column** in descending order, specifying that the table has a header row.

12. Using the same table, sort by the **Visa/Passport column** in ascending order, specifying that the table has a header row.

13. Using the page 1 table, insert a **blank row at the top** of the table, **merge** the cells in the **first row**, and type **Universal Corporate Events**.

14. Use **Align Center** ▤ to center the heading.

15. Scroll to page 3 and add a **column** at the end of the table and a row at the bottom of the table.

Perform Calculations and Size Columns

16. Type **Totals** in the blank cell at the bottom of the first column.

17. Insert a formula using the **Sum function** and **dollar** format to total columns two through four.

18. Delete the **decimal point and zeros** at the end of each total.

    Hint: Position the insertion point to the left of the decimal point before deleting.

19. Type **Totals** in the first cell of the last column and insert a formula using the **Sum function** and **dollar** format to total the rows for the three plans. Be sure to check that the formula is correct before clicking OK.

20. Delete the **decimal point and zeros** at the end of each total.

21. Scroll to page 2 and use the **AutoFit** feature to autofit the contents of the table.

22. Save and close the file; exit from **Word**.

23. Submit your final file based on the guidelines provided by your instructor.

    To view examples of how your file or files should look at the end of this exercise, go to the student resource center.

APPLY YOUR SKILLS WD05-A03

Create and Format Tables

In this exercise, you will navigate in a table, insert a new table, and convert a table to text. You will change cell margins, merge cells, and apply borders and shading. You will also sort data, delete and add columns/rows, perform calculations, and resize cells.

Navigate in and Insert a Table; Convert a Table to Text

1. Start **Word**. Open **WD05-A03-Travel** from your **WD2013 Lesson 05** folder and save the file as **WD05-A03-Travel-[FirstInitialLastName]**.

2. If necessary, position the insertion point in the first table cell on page 1.

3. Tap ↓ twice to move to the third row.

4. Press Shift + Tab to move to the end of the second row.

5. Press Alt + Home to move to the beginning of the row.

6. Press Alt + Page Down to move to the bottom of the column.

7. Press Alt + Page Up to move to the top of the column.

8. If necessary, choose **Home→Paragraph→Show Hide** ¶ to display formatting marks.

9. Scroll to page 2 and position the insertion point next to the first paragraph symbol at the top of the page.

10. Insert a **4x5 table** and enter the data shown.

Day Tours	From	When	Duration
Versailles	$70	Daily except Mon	4 hrs.
Eiffel Tower	$75	Daily	3 hrs.
Louvre Museum	$65	Daily except Tue	2.5 hrs.
Moulin Rouge Show	$153	Daily	4.5 hrs.

11. Scroll to page 3 and select the table.

12. Convert the table to text; ensure that **Tabs** are chosen to separate text.

Select Data, Customize Alignment, and Modify Cell Margins

13. Scroll to page 1 and use the **move handle** to select the table.

14. Select the **Bangkok** row.

15. Select the **Thailand** and **Vietnam** cells.

16. Select columns two through five and click **Align Center** ☰ on the Layout tab.

17. Select the table and change all cell margins to **0.04**.

18. Select the table and change the top and bottom cell margins to **0.06**.

Merge Cells, and Use Borders and Shading

19. Scroll to page 2 and insert a blank row at the top of the table.

20. Merge all cells in the first row, type **Universal Corporate Events** in the row, and center align the row.

21. Select the table, remove all borders, and select the **first row**.

22. Apply **outside borders** to the row, and apply a **blue shading** color of your choice.

Sort a Table, and Work with Columns and Rows

23. Scroll to page 1, sort by the **price column** in ascending order, and indicate that the table has a Header Row.

24. Sort the **Dates column** in ascending order indicating a Header Row.

25. Delete the **Duration column**.

26. Add a row to the bottom of the table and enter the data shown.

Hong Kong	6/9/2013	2438	10%

27. Add a **column** at the end of the table and type **Discount Amount** as the column header.

Perform Calculations and Size Columns

28. In the **second cell** in that column, enter the formula, **=c2*d2**, choosing the **second format** in the Number Format field.

29. Enter **formulas** to calculate the discount amount for the remaining rows using the second number format.

30. Add a **new row** to the bottom of the table and type **Maximum Price** in the first cell.

31. Position the **insertion point** at the bottom of the **Price column**, enter the formula, **=MAX(c2:c7)**, and do not use any special number formatting.

    The formula determines the highest tour price in the column.

32. Select **columns two through five** and position the **adjust pointer** (double-headed) arrow between two of the selected columns.

33. Double-click to autofit the columns to the width of the longest entry in each column.

34. Save and close the file; exit from **Word**.

35. Submit your final file based on the guidelines provided by your instructor.

Extend Your Skills

In the course of working through the Extend Your Skills exercises, you will think critically as you use the skills taught in the lesson to complete the assigned projects. To evaluate your mastery and completion of the exercises, your instructor may use a rubric, with which more points are allotted according to performance characteristics. (The more you do, the more you earn!) Ask your instructor how your work will be evaluated.

WD05-E01 That's the Way I See It

You are the owner of a small store. You have a few corporate customers who order from you in large quantities and you plan to keep track of their orders in a table. Start a new Word document named **WD05-E01-CorpCustomers-[FirstInitialLastName]** and saved to your **WD2013 Lesson 05** folder. Create a 5x6 table with the following column headings: Order Date, Item, Units, Cost, and Total.

Enter five rows of order data for the first four columns. In the Total column, enter formulas for all five rows to multiply Units by Cost. Add a row at the end of the table and use the Sum function to add the Cost and Total columns to determine total costs and sales to date. Add another row to the bottom of the table and enter formulas at the bottom of the Cost and Total columns to determine the maximum cost and maximum total. Enter labels in the last two rows to appropriately describe the data.

Add a row to the top of the table, merge the cells, and enter your company name. Apply a table style of your choice to the table and, if necessary, center-align your company name and right-align the last three columns. AutoFit the last three columns.

You will be evaluated based on the inclusion of all elements specified, your ability to follow directions, your ability to apply newly learned skills to a real-world situation, your creativity, and the relevance of your topic and/or data choice(s). Submit your final file based on the guidelines provided by your instructor.

WD05-E02 Be Your Own Boss

Your company, Blue Jean Landscaping, is offering a spring flower planting special. Start a new Word document named **WD05-E02-SpringFlowers-[FirstInitialLastName]** and saved to your **WD2013 Lesson 05** folder. Create a 3x8 table with the following column headings: Flower Name, Price, and Discount Percent.

Enter data that you decide on in the rows below the heading row. Add a column at the end of the table and enter formulas to calculate the discount amount for each row. Use the dollar format for the numbers. Supply an appropriate column heading for the new column. Sort the table in ascending, alphabetic order by the Flower Name column. Add a row at the bottom of the table and enter a formula in the Price column that determines the highest priced flower and add a suitable label to the row. Apply borders and shading to the table to enhance its readability and make it attractive.

You will be evaluated based on the inclusion of all elements specified, your ability to follow directions, your ability to apply newly learned skills to a real-world situation, your creativity, and your demonstration of an entrepreneurial spirit. Submit your final file based on the guidelines provided by your instructor.

Transfer Your Skills

In the course of working through the Transfer Your Skills exercises, you will use critical-thinking and creativity skills to complete the assigned projects using skills taught in the lesson. To evaluate your mastery and completion of the exercises, your instructor may use a rubric, with which more points are allotted according to performance characteristics. (The more you do, the more you earn!) Ask your instructor how your work will be evaluated.

WD05-T01 Use the Web as a Learning Tool

Throughout this book, you will be provided with an opportunity to use the Internet as a learning tool by completing WebQuests. According to the original creators of WebQuests, as described on their website (WebQuest.org), a WebQuest is "an inquiry-oriented activity in which most or all of the information used by learners is drawn from the web." To complete the WebQuest projects in this book, navigate to the student resource center and choose the WebQuest for the lesson on which you are currently working. The subject of each WebQuest will be relevant to the material found in the lesson.

WebQuest Subject: How tables are used in business.

Submit your final file(s) based on the guidelines provided by your instructor.

WD05-T02 Demonstrate Proficiency

A new chef has just been hired at Stormy BBQ. He is placing the weekly food order for the first time, and the owner has asked you to work with him to be sure his order makes sense. Start a new Word document named **WD05-T02-ChefOrder-[FirstInitialLastName]** and saved to your **WD2013 Lesson 05** folder. Set up a table for the order that includes elements such as the name of the food item, the price, the quantity, and total costs, and then insert the formulas to calculate the total costs.

Assume that it is summer and order fruits and vegetables that are in season and in quantities that guarantee freshness for the week. Sort the table in an order that you think will make sense for the food seller. Add a row at the top of the table, merge the cells, and enter Stormy BBQ, centered, as the heading. Size the table in a way that ensures that it is easy to read, and apply a table style of your choice that also enhances readability.

Submit your final file based on the guidelines provided by your instructor.

Creating a Research Paper

LESSON OUTLINE

LEARNING OBJECTIVES

After studying this lesson, you will be able to:

- Insert footnotes, endnotes, and citations
- Generate a bibliography
- Insert captions and a table of figures
- Create templates

In this lesson, you will learn about research papers, a requirement for nearly every undergraduate and graduate student, and for many professionally employed individuals. You will use Word to develop a research paper using widely accepted style conventions. Your paper will include footnotes, citations, and a table of figures. Then you will create a research paper template to simplify writing future research papers.

Researching Internet Commerce

Green Clean is a successful environmentally conscious janitorial service company. You are the administrative assistant at Green Clean while continuing with your undergraduate work in marketing. You were assigned the task of writing a research paper. The main topic must be on Internet commerce, and since you are also interested in the environment, you put your own spin on the paper to include what effect ecommerce has had on the environment.

You use Word to set up the research paper. Following Modern Language Association (MLA) guidelines, you use footnotes, citations, and captions. You find that the Bibliography and Table of Figures features make it easy to organize reference information in your paper.

Simpson 2

Brian Simpson

Professor Williams

Marketing 222

May 10, 2013

Internet Commerce and Its Effect on the Environment

The Internet had its origins in the 1960s when the Department of Defense developed a communications network to connect the computers of various military installations. The Department of Defense removed its computers from this network in the 1980s and turned over the control to the National Science Foundation (NSF). In 1992, the U.S. government withdrew funding from the NSF and encouraged private companies to administer and control the "Internet." It was at this point that Internet commerce was born. Companies both large and small suddenly realized the enormous marketing potential of this global computer network. In fact, by 2007 the Internet had no doubt become the largest global marketplace.[1]

The commercial potential of the Internet stems from the fact that it is a global network with inexpensive access.[2] The Internet is also available 24x7. The multimedia capability to the Internet is important for marketing and advertising. Quick product delivery, automated order-taking, and low overhead are several more factors that are driving Internet commerce.[3]

---

[1] This is the opinion of many business leaders and economists.

[2] This is true in the United States, but some nations still have high rates due to limited competition among Internet service providers.

[3] These factors depend upon the capabilities of individual companies.

Using Research Paper Styles

Video Library   http://labyrinthelab.com/videos   Video Number: WD13-V0601

There are several documentation styles, each with their own specific formatting requirements. The MLA style has been the standard for undergraduate and graduate research papers for many years.

Understanding the MLA Documentation Style

The MLA publishes the *Modern Language Association Handbook for Writers of Research Papers*. The MLA style has very specific formatting requirements, *some* of which are already defaults within Microsoft Word. For example, Word's default margins are one inch, which complies with the MLA requirement. However, Word does not comply with *all* MLA guidelines by default.

 This lesson does not presume to be a resource for MLA guidelines. Refer to the MLA handbook or MLA website (http://mla.org) for guidance in complying with MLA requirements.

Following is an overview of *some* of the MLA style guidelines.

Student name and the page
number on every page at one-
half inch from the top.

The student name, professor,
course, and date lines are
positioned here.

Brian Simpson

Professor Williams

Marketing 222

May 10, 2013

The title of the paper follows
the date line.

Internet Commerce and Its Effect on the Environment

The Internet had its origins in the 1960s when the Department of Defense developed a

communications network to connect the computers of various military installations. The Department of

Defense removed its computers from this network in the 1980s and turned over the control to the

National Science Foundation (NSF). In 1992, the U.S. government withdrew funding from the NSF and

encouraged private companies to administer and control the "Internet." It was at this point that Internet

commerce was born. Companies both large and small suddenly realized the enormous marketing

potential of this global computer network. In fact, by 2007 the Internet had no doubt become the

The document is double-spaced
and paragraphs are indented
one-half inch.

largest global marketplace.[1]

The commercial potential of the Internet stems from the fact that it is a global network with

inexpensive access.[2] The Internet is also available 24x7. The multimedia capability to the Internet is

important for marketing and advertising. Quick product delivery, automated order-taking, and low

A superscript number indicates
a footnote or endnote.

overhead are several more factors that are driving Internet commerce.[3]

Note that the seventh edition
of the MLA handbook does not
use superscript numbers in the
footnote area.

[1] This is the opinion of many business leaders and economists.

[2] This is true in the United States, but some nations still have high rates due to limited

competition among Internet service providers.

[3] These factors depend upon the capabilities of individual companies.

You can select the superscripted number in the footnote area and remove the checkmark
from the superscript checkbox in the Font dialog box, if necessary.

Working with Footnotes, Endnotes, and Citations

Video Library   http://labyrinthelab.com/videos   Video Number: WD13-V0602

Footnotes, endnotes, and citations are important parts of most research papers. You use them to comment on, or cite a reference to, a designated part of the text. Footnotes appear at the bottom of pages; endnotes, as the name implies, appear at the end of a document or section; and citations appear on a separate Works Cited page at the end of the document. The Works Cited page is another name for a bibliography.

TIP For simplicity, the following topics use the term *footnote* only. All details described for footnotes apply equally to endnotes.

Inserting Footnotes

When you insert a footnote, Word inserts a footnote reference mark in the document and a corresponding mark at the bottom of the page. Word automatically numbers footnotes and renumbers them if you add or delete one. The Footnote and Endnote dialog box offers features for formatting and controlling various aspects of notes.

FROM THE RIBBON
References→Footnotes →Insert Footnote

FROM THE KEYBOARD
[Alt]+[Ctrl]+[F] to insert a footnote

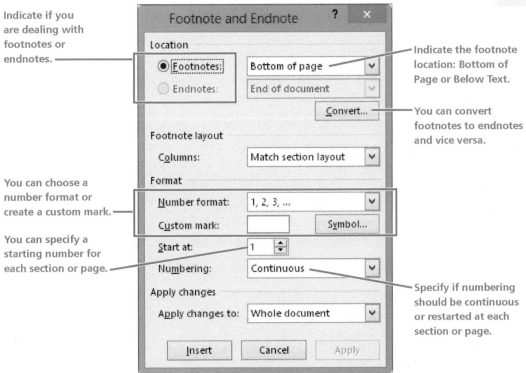

Inserting Citations

You use a citation to refer to material you obtained from an outside source that you are using in the paper. You can enter the source information when you create the citation or insert a placeholder and add the source data later. The citation appears inside parentheses at the end of the cited material; this notation takes the place of the superscript number that is placed for a footnote.

FROM THE RIBBON

References→
Citations &
Bibliography→Insert
Citation

There are a number of citation systems in addition to the MLA documentation style. Examples include the American Psychological Association (APA) style and the *Chicago Manual of Style* (CMS). The source information relating to the citation appears in a bibliography (or Works Cited page, depending on the citation system), usually at the end of the document. You choose the documentation style when you create the citation. The Create Source dialog box contains different fields depending on the documentation style you select.

Choose the type of source (book, website, etc.).

The source information goes here.

Create Source ? ✕

Type of Source | Web site ▾

Bibliography Fields for MLA

Author	[ ] Edit
	☐ Corporate Author [ ]
Name of Web Page	[ ]
Year	[ ]
Month	[ ]
Day	[ ]
Year Accessed	[ ]
Month Accessed	[ ]
Day Accessed	[ ]
Medium	[ ]

☐ Show All Bibliography Fields

Tag name

Placeholder1

OK | Cancel

If you need additional fields, check this box.

Word uses tags internally to reference bibliography entries.

Insert Footnotes and Citations

In this exercise, you will create a research paper and insert footnotes and citations, and you will convert footnotes to endnotes.

1. Start **Word**. Open **WD06-D01-Internet** from your **WD2013 Lesson 06** folder and save it as **WD06-D01-Internet-[FirstInitialLastName]**.

   Replace the bracketed text with your first initial and last name. For example, if your name is Bethany Smith, your filename would look like this: WD06-D01-Internet-BSmith.

2. If necessary, choose **View→Views→Print Layout** 🗐.

   Footnotes may differ in appearance depending on the view you are using.

3. Position the insertion point at the top of the document and type the four lines of text above the title, tapping Enter once after each line, except the last line.

Simpson·1¶

¶

Brian·Simpson¶

Professor·Williams¶

Marketing·222¶

May·10,·2013¶

Internet·Commerce·and·Its·Effect·on·the·Environment¶

The·Internet·had·its·origins·in·the·1960s·when·the·Department·of·Defense·developed·a·

communications·network·to·connect·the·computers·of·various·military·installations.·The·Department·of·

Notice that the paragraph text is double-spaced and the extra space after the paragraphs has been removed per MLA requirements.

Insert Footnotes

4. Position the insertion point to the right of the period at the end of the first paragraph.

5. Choose **References→Footnotes→Insert Footnote** AB¹.

   Word places the footnote reference mark at the insertion point location, and a corresponding footnote appears at the bottom of the page.

6. Follow these steps to complete the footnote:

Ⓐ Note that Word inserts both a separator line and the correct number.

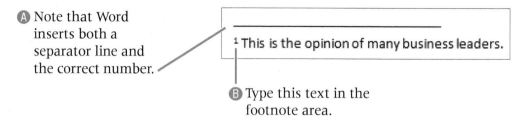

¹ This is the opinion of many business leaders.

Ⓑ Type this text in the footnote area.

7. Use the same process to insert the footnote reference marks and associated footnotes shown here.

The commercial potential of the Internet stems from the fact that it is a global network with inexpensive access.² The Internet is also available 24x7. The multimedia capability to the Internet is important for marketing and advertising. Quick product delivery, automated order-taking, and low overhead are several more factors that are driving Internet commerce.³

⎯ Internet commerce will be a driving force in the global economy of the twenty-first century. There are still obstacles to overcome, but technology and market forces will propel this new commercial medium forward at a rapid pace.

---

¹ This is the opinion of many business leaders.
² This is true in the United States, but some nations still have high rates due to limited competition among Internet service providers.
³ These factors depend upon the capabilities of individual companies.

The formatting of the footnotes does not adhere to MLA requirements. The text should use the same formatting as the body of the document (double-spaced, first line indented). You will format the footnotes later.

8. Type these paragraphs after the last paragraph.

The environmental outlook is indeed bright: According to the latest study by Carnegie Mellon University, more than half (about 65%) of total emissions was produced by consumers driving to and from retail stores as opposed to buying online.

Geoffrey Fowler, in his March 3, 2009 article on the Wall Street Journal website cited the following environmental benefits to e-commerce shopping:

- Uses about one-third less energy than conventional retail shopping

- Uses a one-third smaller carbon footprint than a standard building

- A truck delivering numerous packages along its way is the largest environmental savings, as it uses less energy per package than if the consumers had driven to the shops themselves.

Convert Footnotes to Endnotes

9. Choose **References→Footnotes→dialog box launcher** ⧉ and click **Convert**.

10. When the Convert Notes box opens, click **OK** and then close the **Footnote and Endnote** dialog box.

11. Scroll through the document and notice that the footnotes are no longer at the bottom of page 1; they now appear as endnotes on the last page.

12. Click **Undo** ↺ to reinstate the footnotes at the bottom of page 1.

Select the MLA Style and Insert a Citation

13. Choose **References→Citations & Bibliography→Style menu ▼→MLA Seventh Edition**.

14. Position the insertion point between the word *online* and the period at the end of the first paragraph on page 2; tap [Spacebar].

15. Choose **References→Citations & Bibliography→Insert Citation** ⧉, and then choose **Add New Source**.

16. Follow these steps to create the new source to insert as the citation:

Ⓐ If necessary, choose **Web Site** here.

Ⓑ Type the author's name as shown. Example text appears at the bottom of the window for each field.

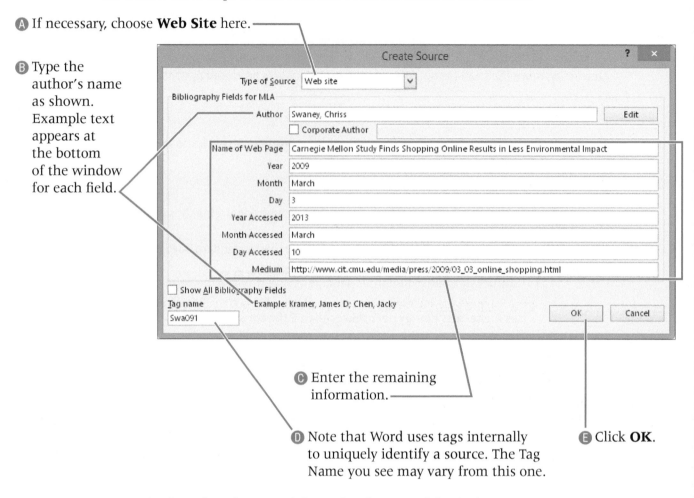

Ⓒ Enter the remaining information.

Ⓓ Note that Word uses tags internally to uniquely identify a source. The Tag Name you see may vary from this one.

Ⓔ Click **OK**.

Notice the author's last name is inserted as the name of the citation.

Remember, Word does not follow all MLA guidelines. Refer to the MLA handbook or website when writing academic papers.

Insert a Citation Placeholder

17. Position the insertion point at the end of the document between *themselves* and the period and tap Spacebar.

18. Choose **Reference→Citations & Bibliography→Insert Citation** 📝, and then choose **Add New Placeholder**.

19. Follow these steps to create a placeholder for a citation named Fowler:

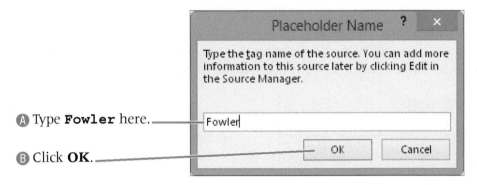

Ⓐ Type **Fowler** here. ——

Ⓑ Click **OK**. ——

20. Save the file.

Editing and Formatting Footnotes

Video Library   http://labyrinthelab.com/videos   Video Number: WD13-V0603

You can edit footnote text directly in the footnote area. In addition to editing the text of a footnote, you can also:

- **Reposition:** You can change the position of a footnote reference mark by dragging it to another location in the document.
- **Format:** You can change various formatting features of footnotes using the Footnote and Endnote dialog box. For example, you can change the numbering scheme, change the starting number, or even replace a footnote number with a special symbol.

In this example, uppercase letters replace the normal numbering for footnotes.

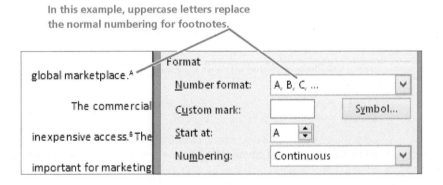

Editing a Footnote

Word's default style for footnote text does not meet MLA documentation style requirements. You must change the formatting if you want to be in compliance with MLA. MLA requirements state the text should be the same formatting as the text in the document; that is, double-spaced with the first line indented. You make those types of formatting changes, as well as editing changes, directly in the footnote area of the document.

Word 2013

Editing a Citation

Once you insert a citation or a citation placeholder you can edit the information in the Edit Source dialog box, which contains the same fields as the Create Source dialog box. The default citation in the body of the document is the author's last name; however, you can choose to suppress it and instead show the name of the web page.

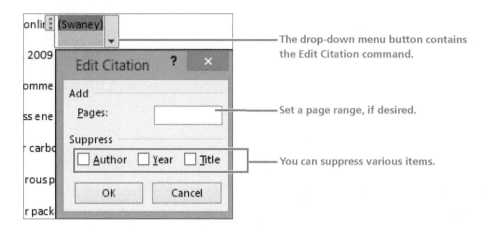

The drop-down menu button contains the Edit Citation command.

Set a page range, if desired.

You can suppress various items.

QUICK REFERENCE	WORKING WITH FOOTNOTES AND CITATIONS
Task	**Procedure**
Insert a footnote	Choose References→Footnotes→Insert Footnote.
Navigate to footnotes	Choose References→Footnotes→Next/Previous Footnote.
Edit/format footnotes in Print Layout view	Edit in the footnote area at the bottom of the page.
Format a footnote	Choose References→Footnotes, click the dialog box launcher, and then make the desired changes.
Delete a footnote	Select the footnote reference mark and tap [Delete] to delete the reference mark and the note.
Insert a citation	Choose References→Citations & Bibliography→Insert Citation, choose Add New Source, and enter data in the dialog box.
Edit a citation source	Click the citation in the document, click the arrow on the right, choose Edit Source, and make the desired changes.
Edit a citation	Click the citation in the document, click the arrow on the right, choose Edit Citation, and make the desired changes.
Delete a citation	Click the citation in the document, click the handle on the left to select the citation, and tap [Delete].

Work with Footnotes and Citations

In this exercise, you will format, edit, and delete footnotes and edit a citation placeholder and source.

1. Save your file as **WD06-D02-Internet-[FirstInitialLastName]**.

2. Position the insertion point at the beginning of the second paragraph on page 1 and scroll, if necessary, to see the three footnote reference marks and the footnotes at the bottom of the page.

3. Choose **References→Footnotes→dialog box launcher** 🔲 to display the Footnote and Endnote dialog box.

4. Follow these steps to change the numbering format:

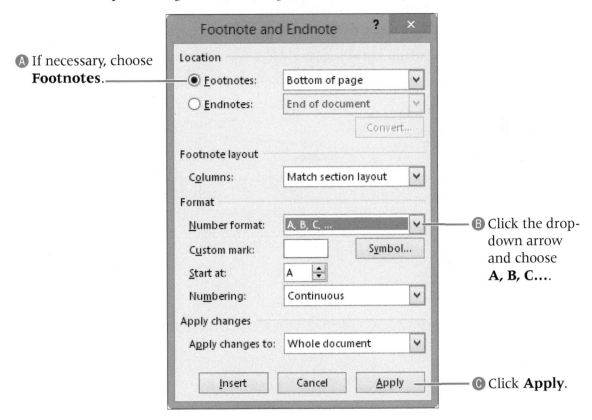

Ⓐ If necessary, choose **Footnotes**.

Ⓑ Click the drop-down arrow and choose **A, B, C....**

Ⓒ Click **Apply**.

The footnote numbers change to alphabetic characters. You use the same technique to change the format of endnotes.

5. Click **Undo** 🔲 to return to number formatting.

6. If necessary, choose **View→Show→Ruler** to display the ruler.

7. Select the three footnotes, and then follow these steps to format the footnotes:

   ▪ Change line spacing to **double-space**.
   ▪ Change the font size to **11 points**.
   ▪ On the ruler, drag the **First Line Indent** marker (top triangle) to the **half-inch** mark.

Delete and Edit Footnotes

8. Follow these steps to delete a footnote:

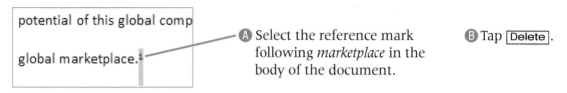

Ⓐ Select the reference mark following *marketplace* in the body of the document.

Ⓑ Tap Delete .

The reference mark and the footnote are removed, and the remaining footnotes renumber.

9. Click **Undo** ↶ to replace the footnote.

10. Position the insertion point between the last word and the period of the first footnote, tap Spacebar , and type **and economists**.

Edit a Citation Placeholder

11. Scroll to the end of page 2 and locate the **Fowler** citation.

12. Follow these steps to open the Edit Source dialog box:

Ⓐ Click the **Fowler** citation placeholder.

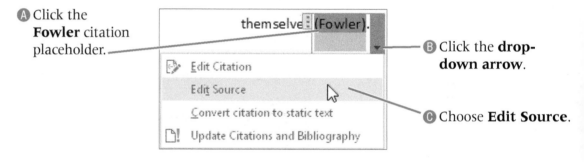

Ⓑ Click the **drop-down arrow**.

Ⓒ Choose **Edit Source**.

13. Follow these steps to add the source information to the Fowler citation:

Ⓐ If necessary, choose **Web Site**.

Ⓑ Enter the author's name as shown.

Ⓒ Enter the remaining data.

Ⓓ Click **OK**.

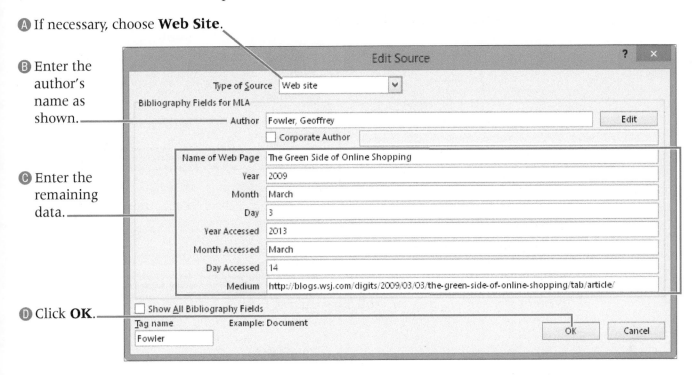

14. Click **Yes** if a message appears asking if you want to update the master list and current document.

The citation may have picked up the name of the web page (title).

15. If necessary, click the drop-down arrow to the right of the Fowler citation and choose **Edit Citation**, check the **Title** box, and click **OK**.

16. Save the file.

Working with Bibliographies

Video Library   http://labyrinthelab.com/videos   Video Number: WD13-V0604

A bibliography is a list of the sources cited in the preparation of the document. Word automatically generates a bibliography based on the source information that you provide in the Create Source dialog box. The bibliography picks up the correct punctuation; however, certain formatting requirements are not Microsoft defaults and must be addressed separately.

The Bibliography button in the Citations & Bibliography group on the References tab contains three built-in options: Bibliography, References, and Works Cited. You can choose any of these; however, the formatting may or may not meet the requirements of the document style you chose. For example, the Works Cited option for the MLA style does not format the title, the paragraph spacing, or the line spacing correctly.

The Bibliography options may not format references as needed. Use the Insert Bibliography command to create citations more precisely.

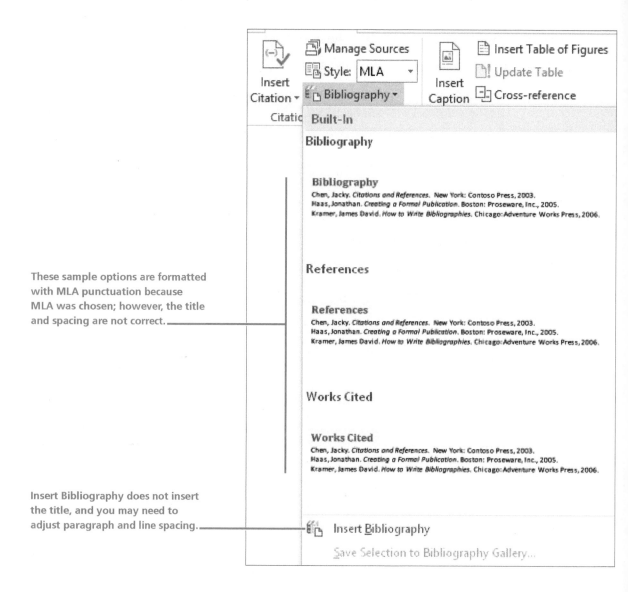

These sample options are formatted with MLA punctuation because MLA was chosen; however, the title and spacing are not correct.

Insert Bibliography does not insert the title, and you may need to adjust paragraph and line spacing.

Updating a Bibliography

When you edit the citation source or add a new one, you can easily update the bibliography list using the Update Field command on the menu when you right-click on the list. The Update Field command reformats the list to single-spacing again; thus, you must remember to change back to double-spacing.

Create a Bibliography

In this exercise, you will create a bibliography for the citations in the document. You will title the page as Works Cited, since the lesson is following the MLA documentation style. Finally, you will edit an existing citation, update the bibliography, and format the paragraphs with double-spacing.

1. Save your file as **WD06-D03-Internet-[FirstInitialLastName]**.

2. Position the insertion point at the end of the document.

3. Tap ⌐Enter⌐ twice; then, press ⌐Ctrl⌐+⌐Enter⌐ to insert a new page for the bibliography.

4. Choose **Home→Paragraph→Center** ≣, and then type **Works Cited** and tap ⌐Enter⌐.

Insert and Update the Bibliography

5. Choose **References→Citations & Bibliography→Bibliography** 🗐.

6. Choose **Insert Bibliography** at the bottom of the menu.

7. Scroll up to the bottom of the second page and click the **Fowler** citation, and then click the arrow on the right.

8. Choose **Edit Source** to open the dialog box.

9. Change the **Day Accessed** to **10** and click **OK**.

10. If the citation picked up the name of the web page, click the drop-down arrow, choose **Edit Citation**, check the **Title** box, and click **OK**.

11. Scroll down the **Works Cited page** and notice nothing has changed yet in the list.

12. Follow these steps to update the bibliography:

🅐 Right-click anywhere in the list.

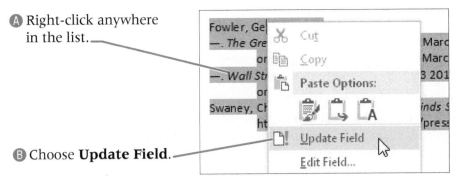

🅑 Choose **Update Field**.

Notice the date accessed for the Fowler citation changed to 10 March 2013.

Format the List

13. Select the bibliography list, but not the Works Cited title.

If you click the list, it highlights in light gray. You must *drag* to select the list, which then highlights in a darker gray.

14. Choose **Home→Paragraph→Line and Paragraph Spacing** 📊, and then choose **2.0**.

15. Save the file.

Inserting Captions and a Table of Figures

Video Library   http://labyrinthelab.com/videos   Video Number: WD13-V0605

You use captions to insert text associated with figures in a paper. Word then uses the captions as entries in the table of figures. Later, if you alter some of the captions, Word updates these when you regenerate the table of figures.

Inserting Captions

Word can automate the creation of captions for certain types of objects. Click AutoCaption and choose the file types you want Word to automatically assign captions to.

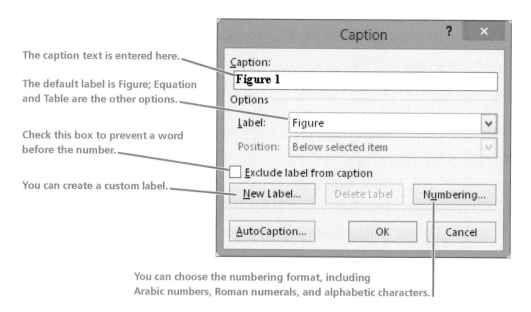

The caption text is entered here.

The default label is Figure; Equation and Table are the other options.

Check this box to prevent a word before the number.

You can create a custom label.

You can choose the numbering format, including Arabic numbers, Roman numerals, and alphabetic characters.

DEVELOP YOUR SKILLS WD06-D04
Add Captions to Figures

In this exercise, you will insert a file between pages 1 and 2 that contains five PowerPoint slides from a presentation. You will add captions to the slides in preparation for creating a table of figures.

1. Save your file as **WD06-D04-Internet-[FirstInitialLastName]**.

2. Position the insertion point after the third footnote reference mark in the body of the document (not the footnote area) at the bottom of the first page.

3. Press Ctrl + Enter to insert a page break.

4. Choose **Insert→Text→Object** ☐ menu ▾→**Text from File**.

5. In the Insert File dialog box, navigate to your **WD2013 Lesson 06** folder, choose **WD06-D04-Slides**, and click **Insert**.

Add and Edit Captions

6. If necessary, choose **Home→Paragraph→Show/Hide ¶** to display formatting marks.

7. Position the insertion point on the first blank line below the first slide.

8. Choose **References→Captions→Insert Caption** 🔲.

9. The Caption dialog box should match the following illustration. If *Figure 1* does not appear in the Caption text box, follow these steps. Otherwise, go to step 10.

Ⓐ Click the **Label menu** button and choose **Figure**.

Ⓑ Click **Numbering** to open the **Caption Numbering** dialog box.

Ⓒ Click the **Format menu** button, and then choose the **1, 2, 3, ...** format.

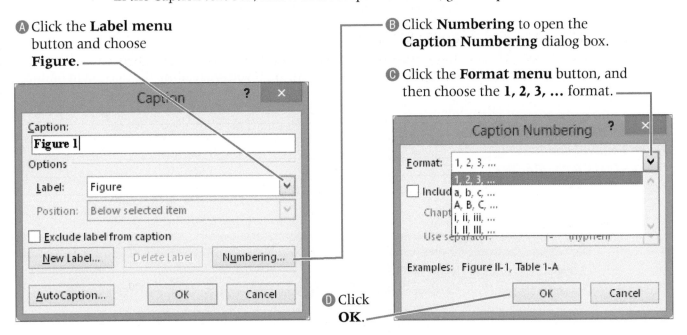

Ⓓ Click **OK**.

10. If necessary, position the insertion point to the right of *Figure 1* in the Caption text box.

11. Tap the [Spacebar], type **DOD and ARPANET**, and click **OK** to insert the caption.
    The caption is placed at the left margin.

12. Choose **Home→Paragraph→Center** 🗏.

13. Position the insertion point in the first blank line below the second slide.

14. Choose **References→Captions→Insert Caption** 🔲.

15. Tap the [Spacebar], type **NSF**, and click **OK**.

16. **Center** 🗏 the caption.

17. Add these captions and center them:

Slide Number	Caption Text
3	MILNET and TCP/IP
4	First Graphical Browser
5	Netscape

Edit a Caption

18. Return to slide 2, select *NSF*, and type **National Science Foundation** in its place.

19. Save the file.

Inserting a Table of Figures

Video Library   http://labyrinthelab.com/videos   Video Number: WD13-V0606

Academic papers often include a table of figures at the front, which guides the reader to illustrations, charts, tables, and other figures. This is particularly helpful in long documents. The table entries conveniently function as hyperlinks if you are reading the document online.

QUICK REFERENCE	CREATING CAPTIONS AND TABLES OF FIGURES
Task	**Procedure**
Insert a caption	▪ Choose References→Captions→Insert Caption, and then type the caption text.
Insert a table of figures	▪ Choose References→Captions→Insert Table of Figures, and then make the formatting choices.
Update a table of figures	▪ Right-click the table and choose Update Field.

DEVELOP YOUR SKILLS WD06-D05
Generate a Table of Figures

In this exercise, you will generate a table of figures from the captions you inserted earlier. You will change the numbering format of your captions, and then you will update the table to reflect the change.

Insert the Table of Figures

1. Save your file as **WWD06-D05-Internet-[FirstInitialLastName]**.

2. Move the insertion point to the top of the document and insert a page break.

3. Press Ctrl + Home to position the insertion point at the top of the new page, and then type **Table of Figures** and tap Enter twice.

4. Format the heading you just typed with **center, bold 16 point**.

5. Place the insertion point in the blank line below the heading.

6. Choose **References→Captions→Insert Table of Figures** 📄.

7. Follow these steps to set up the table:

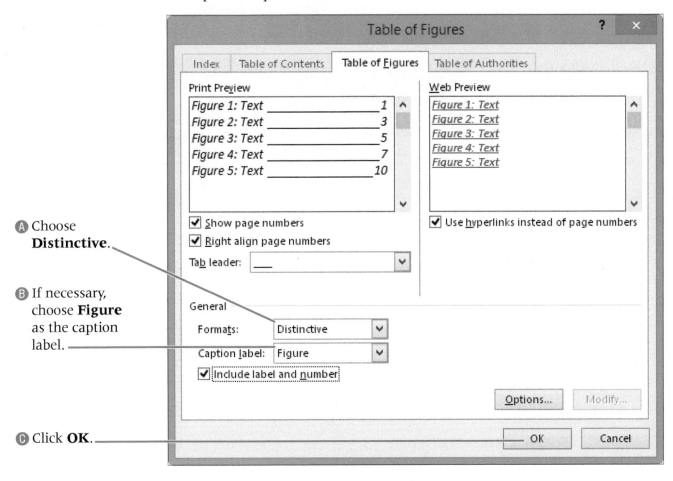

Ⓐ Choose **Distinctive**.

Ⓑ If necessary, choose **Figure** as the caption label.

Ⓒ Click **OK**.

8. Position the insertion point on page 3 so you will be able to see the effect of the next change.

Change the Numbering Format of the Captions

9. Choose **References→Captions→Insert Caption** 📄.

10. Click **Numbering** to display the Caption Numbering dialog box.

11. Choose the **A, B, C, …** format and click **OK**.

12. Click **Close** in the Caption dialog box, and then scroll through the slides.

Notice that the figure numbers changed to alphabetic characters.

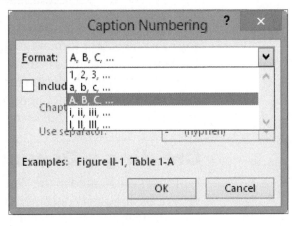

Update the Table of Figures

13. Scroll up to view the **Table of Figures** on page 1.

    Notice that the table is still showing the numeric figure numbers.

14. Follow these steps to update the Table of Figures:

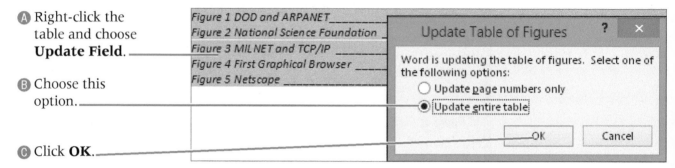

Ⓐ Right-click the table and choose **Update Field**.

Ⓑ Choose this option.

Ⓒ Click **OK**.

The table should match the following illustration.

Table of Figures

Figure A DOD and ARPANET	3
Figure B National Science Foundation	3
Figure C MILNET and TCP/IP	3
Figure D First Graphical Browser	4
Figure E Netscape	4

The text switched from Figures 1–5 to Figures A–E.

15. Save and then close the file.

Working with Templates

Video Library   http://labyrinthelab.com/videos   Video Number: WD13-V0607

All Word documents are based on templates, which can include text, formatting, graphics, and any other objects or formats available in Word. The default Word template is Blank Document. The benefit of templates is that they do not change when documents *based on them* change. When you start a new document, Word opens a *copy* of the template. This lets you use templates repeatedly as the basis for new documents. Word provides a variety of ready-to-use templates, or you can also create your own personal templates.

Creating a Document from a Template

Templates are located in the Word Start screen or in Backstage view when you choose the New screen. Basing a new document on a template can save you a lot of time since much of the formatting is already included in the template for you.

If you don't find a template you want in the Featured templates, you can search online by entering your own search term or by choosing a suggested search.

If you create personal templates, click here to view them.

Clicking a template displays a window that describes the template; double-clicking a template immediately opens it in the Word window.

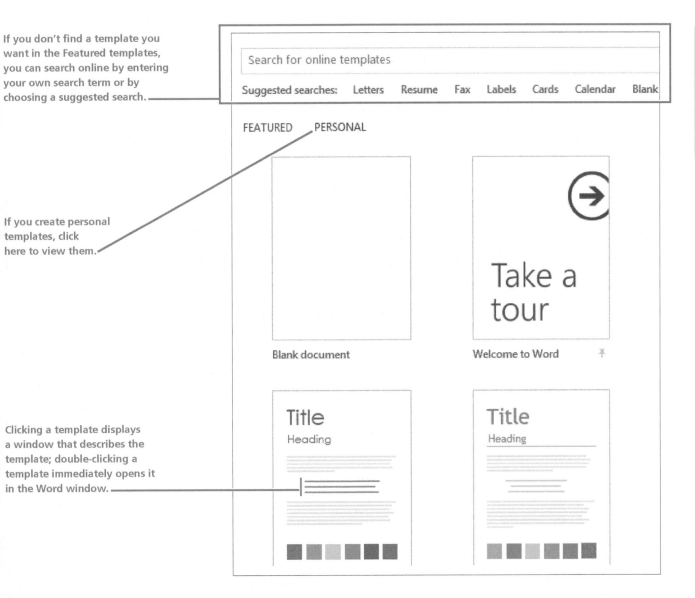

Saving Personal Templates

When you create a document containing specific formatting, you can save it to use later as a template. You should save the template in the Custom Office Templates folder unless instructed to do otherwise. The Custom Office Templates folder is the default in the Save As window when a template is chosen in the Save As Type field. This is what causes your templates to appear when you click the Personal link on the templates screen. You can save a template as a Word Template or as a Word Macro-Enabled Template. A macro-enabled template is one that contains a special series of instructions called a macro.

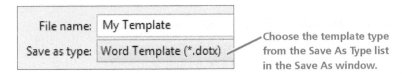

Choose the template type from the Save As Type list in the Save As window.

Create a Template from an Existing Document

In this exercise, you will open a copy of a report and save it as a template. The body text of the report has been removed; however, other elements are still in place, including the cover page, the table of figures, and the double-spacing. You will then save time by starting a new report based on the template.

1. Open **WD06-D06-MyReport** from your **WD2013 Lesson 06** folder.

2. Scroll through the document and notice the elements that are still in place and that will be useful when you create a new report.

3. Choose **File→Save As**, navigate to any file storage location, and choose **Word Template** from the **Save As Type** list at the bottom of the dialog box.

   Notice the file path that appears at the top of the Save As dialog box. Word defaults to the Custom Office Templates folder in the My Documents folder as the file storage location.

4. Save the file as **WD06-D06-MyReport-[FirstInitialLastName]**.

5. Choose **File→Close** to close the template file.

6. Choose **File→New**.

7. Follow these steps to open a copy of your template:

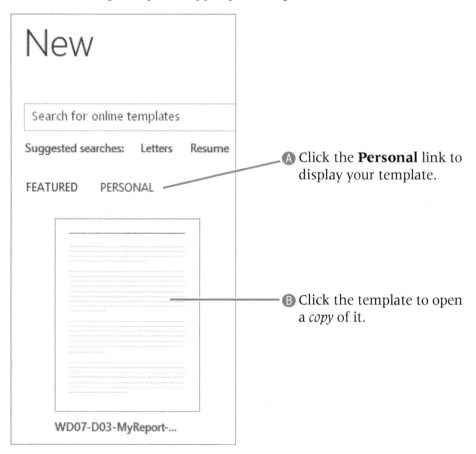

Ⓐ Click the **Personal** link to display your template.

Ⓑ Click the template to open a *copy* of it.

Notice the generic Documentx filename in the title bar at the top of the Word window. This indicates you are working on a copy of the template rather than the template itself.

8. Scroll to page 3 and replace *[DOCUMENT TITLE]* with **Green Life**.

9. Save the document as **WD06-D06-GreenLife-[FirstInitialLastName]** in your **WD2013 Lesson 06** folder.

10. Close the file and exit **Word**.

Deleting a Template

Video Library   http://labyrinthelab.com/videos   Video Number: WD13-V0608

When a template is no longer useful, you may wish to delete it. Templates are easily removed from the Custom Office Templates folder.

QUICK REFERENCE	CREATING AND DELETING TEMPLATES
Task	**Procedure**
Save an existing document as a template	■ Choose File→Save As and navigate to the desired file storage location. ■ Choose Word Template from the Save as Type list, enter the template name, and click Save.
Delete a template	■ Click File Explorer on the taskbar, navigate to the Documents folder, and double-click the Custom Office Templates folder. ■ Choose the desired template and tap Delete.

Delete a Template

In this exercise, you will delete the template you created.

1. Click **File Explorer** 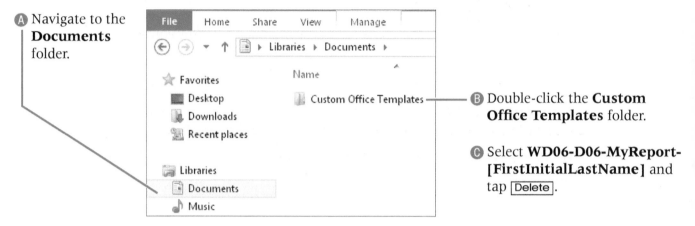 on the taskbar at the bottom of the screen.

2. Follow these steps to delete the My Report template:

Ⓐ Navigate to the **Documents** folder.

Ⓑ Double-click the **Custom Office Templates** folder.

Ⓒ Select **WD06-D06-MyReport-[FirstInitialLastName]** and tap Delete.

3. Close the **File Explorer** window.

Concepts Review

To check your knowledge of the key concepts introduced in this lesson, complete the Concepts Review quiz by choosing the appropriate access option below.

If you are...	Then access the quiz by...
Using the Labyrinth Video Library	Going to http://labyrinthelab.com/videos
Using eLab	Logging in, choosing Content, and navigating to the Concepts Review quiz for this lesson
Not using the Labyrinth Video Library or eLab	Going to the student resource center for this book

Reinforce Your Skills

Create Footnotes, Endnotes, Citations, and a Bibliography

In this exercise, you will work with endnotes, footnotes, and citations. Then you will generate a bibliography. Although you will select the MLA style in the Citations & Bibliography group, because this research paper is not for academic purposes, you will not follow strict MLA formatting guidelines.

Work with Footnotes and Endnotes

1. Start **Word**. Open **WD06-R01-GlobalLocal** from your **WD2013 Lesson 06** folder and save it as **WD06-R01-GlobalLocal-[FirstInitialLastName]**.

2. Position the insertion point after the period following *sales* in the second paragraph.

> Kids for Change is a non-profit organization that helps minors in their
>
> social/community service within the mindset of "Think Globally, Act Locally."
>
> fundraisers, such as car washes, bake sales, and rain barrel sales. The kids are

3. Choose **References→Footnotes→Insert Endnote** .

4. Type this endnote text.

> ---
> i Proceeds go to organizations, such as the local pantry.

5. Position the insertion point after the comma following *construction* in the second to last line of the second paragraph.

> fundraisers, such as car washes, bake sales, and rain barrel sales.
>
> community recycling drives, researching green construction, and
>
> garden program.

6. Choose **References→Footnotes→Insert Endnote** .

7. Type the endnote text as shown in the following illustration.

> ⁱⁱ Kids for Change successfully encouraged a local businessman to use green construction in a building addition.

You noticed a word is missing in the first endnote, so you will make that change now.

8. In the first endnote, position the insertion point to the left of *pantry*, type **food**, and tap `Spacebar`.

You've decided to convert the endnotes to footnotes so they will appear on the same page as the text they refer to.

9. Choose **References→Footnotes→dialog box launcher** ⌐.

10. Click **Convert**.

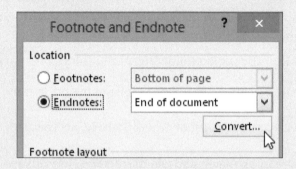

11. When the Convert Notes message appears, click **OK**; close the **Footnote and Endnote** dialog box.

Insert Citations

12. Choose **References→Citations & Bibliography**, and then choose **MLA Seventh Edition** from the Styles drop-down list.

13. Position the insertion point at the end of the fourth bullet point in the **Juniper Russo** citation.

> • Supporting local businesses and agriculture|

14. Tap `Spacebar`.

15. Choose **References→Citations & Bibliography→Insert Citation** ⬇, and then choose **Add New Source**.

16. If necessary, choose **Web Site** in the Type of Source drop-down list.

17. Enter the following information in the Create Source dialog box:
    - Author: **Russo, Juniper**
    - Name of Web Page: **What Does "Think Globally, Act Locally" Mean?**
    - Year: **2011**
    - Month: **August**
    - Day: **3**
    - Year Accesses: **2013**
    - Month Accessed: **December**
    - Day Accessed: **15**
    - Medium: **http://voices.yahoo.com/what-does-think-globally-act-locally-mean-8908513.html?cat=57**

18. Click **OK**.

19. Position the insertion point following *Fluids* at the end of the fourth bullet point in the **Jennifer King** citation.

20. Tap [Spacebar].

21. Choose **References→Citations & Bibliography→Insert Citation** , and then choose **Add New Source**.

22. Make sure **Web Site** is chosen as the Type of Source.

23. Enter the following information in the Create Source dialog box:
    - Author: **King, Jennifer**
    - Name of Web Page: **How Does Car Pollution Affect the Environment & Ozone Layer?**
    - Year Accessed: **2011**
    - Month Accessed: **December**
    - Day Accessed: **15**
    - Medium: **http://greenliving.nationalgeographic.com/car-pollution-affect-environment-ozone-layer-20133.html**

24. Click **OK**.

25. Position the insertion point at the end of the document between the period and *Nations*.

26. Tap [Spacebar].

27. Choose **References→Citations & Bibliography→Insert Citation** , and then choose **Add New Source**.

28. Make sure **Web Site** is chosen as the Type of Source.

29. Enter the following information in the Create Source dialog box:
    - Author: **Trex, Ethan**
    - Name of Web Page: **Whatever Happened to the Hole in the Ozone Layer?**
    - Year: **2012**
    - Month: **May**
    - Day: **23**
    - Year Accessed: **2013**
    - Month Accessed: **December**
    - Day Accessed: **15**
    - Medium: **http://www.mentalfloss.com/blogs/archives/127568**

30. Click **OK**.

Generate and Update a Bibliography

31. Position the insertion point at the end of the document, tap ⟨Enter⟩ twice, and press ⟨Ctrl⟩ + ⟨Enter⟩ to insert a new page for the bibliography.

32. Choose **Home→Paragraph→Center** ☰, type **Works Cited**, and tap ⟨Enter⟩.

33. Choose **References→Citations & Bibliography→Bibliography** 📄.

34. Choose **Insert Bibliography** at the bottom of the menu.
    Now you'll make a change to a citation.

35. Scroll to and click the **King** citation at the bottom of page 1.

36. Click the arrow on the right and choose **Edit Source**.

37. Change the **Year Accessed** to **2013** and click **OK**.

38. If you are prompted to update the master list, click **Yes**.

39. Scroll to the **Works Cited** page, right-click the list, and choose **Update Field**.
    The year accessed changes to 2013.

40. Save and close the file; exit from **Word**.

41. Submit your final file based on the guidelines provided by your instructor.
    To view examples of how your file or files should look at the end of this exercise, go to the student resource center.

Insert Captions and a Table of Figures, and Create a Template

In this exercise, you will add captions to figures and create a table of figures. Then you will create a letter template.

Insert Captions

1. Start **Word**. Open **WD06-R02-Sustainable** from your **WD2013 Lesson 06** folder and save it as **WD06-R02-Sustainable-[FirstInitialLastName]**.

2. If necessary, choose **Home→Paragraph→Show/Hide** ¶ to turn on formatting marks.

3. Position the insertion point on the first blank line following the **Healthy, Safe Home** slide.

4. Choose **References→Captions→Insert Caption** 🖺.

5. If necessary, change the Label field to **Figure**, click the Numbering button, and change the format to **1, 2, 3, …**; click **OK**.

6. Choose **Home→Paragraph→Center** ≡.

7. Tap ⌴Spacebar⌴ and type **Healthy, Safe Home**.

8. Use the same procedure to type the following captions for the remaining slides:
   - **Transportation**
   - **Reduce and Reuse**
   - **Recycle**

Insert a Table of Figures

9. Position the insertion point at the top of the document and press ⌜Ctrl⌝ + ⌜Enter⌝ to insert a page break.

10. Press ⌜Ctrl⌝ + ⌜Home⌝ to position the insertion point at the top of the document.

11. Type **Table of Figures** and tap ⌜Enter⌝ twice.

12. **Center** ≡ the heading you just typed, and then position the insertion point on the blank line below the heading.

13. Choose **References→Captions→Insert Table of Figures** 🖺.

14. If necessary, choose **Formal** as the format and make sure the caption label is **Figure**; click **OK**.

15. Save and then close the file.

Create a Template from an Existing Document

16. Open **WD06-R02-Letter** from your **WD2013 Lesson 06** folder.

    Notice that the letter is already set up with placeholders for the variables.

17. Choose **File→Save As**, navigate to any file storage location, and choose **Word Template** from the Save As Type list.

    The Custom Office Templates folder appears at the top of the Save As dialog box.

18. Save the file as `WD06-R02-Letter-[FirstInitialLastName]`.

19. Choose **File→Close** to close the **Template file**.

20. Choose **File→New**, and then click the **Personal** link toward the top of the New screen.

21. Click your template thumbnail to open a copy of it.

22. Enter the current date, and then replace the inside address and greeting placeholders with information of your choice.

23. Save the file as `WD06-R02-FormLtr-[FirstInitialLastName]` in the **WD2013 Lesson 06** folder; close the file.

Delete a Template

24. Click **File Explorer** ⬜ on the taskbar at the bottom of the screen.

25. Navigate to the **Documents folder** in the left panel.

26. Double-click the **Custom Office Templates** folder on the right.

27. Select **WD06-R02-Letter-[FirstInitialLastName]** and tap Delete.

28. Close **File Explorer**, and then, if necessary, exit from **Word**.

29. Submit your final file based on the guidelines provided by your instructor.

    To view examples of how your file or files should look at the end of this exercise, go to the student resource center.

REINFORCE YOUR SKILLS WD06-R03

Format and Distribute a Research Paper

In this exercise, you will insert a footnote and citations in an organic food research paper. You will choose the MLA style; however, since this is not an academic paper, you will not follow strict MLA formatting guidelines. Then you will insert captions, generate a table of figures, and create a template.

Work with Footnotes and Citations

1. Start **Word**. Open **WD06-R03-OrganicFood** from your **WD2013 Lesson 06** folder, and save it as `WD06-R03-OrganicFood-[FirstInitialLastName]`.

2. If necessary, choose **Home→Paragraph→Show/Hide** ¶ to turn on formatting marks.

3. Position the insertion point to the right of the period at the end of the first paragraph.

4. Choose **References→Footnotes→Insert Footnote** AB¹.

5. Type this text in the footnote area.

---

¹ See Sustainable Animal Agriculture for details on raising animals with care.

Now you will choose the style for citations.

6. Choose **Reference→Citations & Bibliography**, click the **Style menu button ▼**, and choose **MLA Seventh Edition**.

7. Position the insertion point between the period and the word *bay* at the end of the second paragraph below the *Plant Production* heading, and tap [Spacebar].

8. Choose **References→Citations & Bibliography→Insert Citation** 🗒, and then choose **Add New Source**.

9. Make sure **Web Site** is chosen as the Type of Source.

10. Enter the following information:
    ■ Author: **Mayo Clinic, Staff**
    ■ Name of Web Page: **Nutrition and healthy eating**
    ■ Year Accessed: **2013**
    ■ Month Accessed: **December**
    ■ Day Accessed: **15**
    ■ Medium: **http://www.mayoclinic.com/health/organic-food/NU00255**

11. Click **OK**.

    The citation may have picked up the name of the web page (title).

12. If necessary, click the drop-down arrow to the right of the citation and choose **Edit Citation**, check the **Title** box, and click **OK**.

13. Position the insertion point at the end of the fourth bullet point below the *Benefits of Organic Food* heading and tap [Spacebar].

14. Choose **References→Citations & Bibliography→Insert Citation** 🗒, and then choose **Add New Source**.

15. Ensure that **Web Site** is the Type of Source.

16. Enter the following information:
    ■ Author: **Blake, Daniel**
    ■ Name of Web Page: **13 Benefits of Organic Food**
    ■ Year: **2012**
    ■ Month: **December**
    ■ Day: **10**
    ■ Year Accessed: **2013**
    ■ Month Accessed: **December**
    ■ Day Accessed: **13**
    ■ Medium: **http://ecoscraps.com/13-benefits-organic-food/**

17. Click **OK**.

Work with a Bibliography

18. Position the insertion point at the end of the document and press ⌜Ctrl⌝ + ⌜Enter⌝ to insert a page break.

19. Choose **Home→Paragraph→Center** ☰, and then type **Works Cited** and tap ⌜Enter⌝.

20. Choose **References→Citations & Bibliography→Bibliography** 📖, and then choose **Insert Bibliography** at the bottom of the menu.

    Next you will edit the footnote and a citation, and update the bibliography.

21. Click the **Blake** citation on page one, click the arrow, and choose **Edit Source**.

22. Change the Month Accessed to **November** and click **OK**.

23. Click **Yes** if you are prompted to update both lists.

24. Scroll to the bibliography, right-click the list, and choose **Update Field**.

    The month accessed changes to November.

Inserting Captions and a Table of Figures

25. Position the insertion point on the first blank line below the first picture.

26. Choose **References→Captions→Insert Caption** 🖻.

27. If necessary, choose **Figure** in the Label field and make sure the numbering format is **1, 2, 3, …**.

28. If necessary, position the insertion point to the right of **Figure 1** in the Caption text box.

29. Tap ⌜Spacebar⌝, type **Better for the Soil**, and click **OK**.

30. Position the insertion point in the first blank line below the second picture.

31. Choose **References→Captions→Insert Caption** 🖻.

32. Tap ⌜Spacebar⌝, type **Better for the Water**, and click **OK**.

33. Follow the same process to place a caption titled **Increases Consumer Choices** below the third picture and **Fresher, Better Tasting** below the fourth picture.

34. Press ⌜Ctrl⌝ + ⌜Home⌝ to position the insertion point at the top of the document.

35. Press ⌜Ctrl⌝ + ⌜Enter⌝ to insert a page break; position the insertion point at the top of the first page.

36. Type **Table of Figures** and tap ⌜Enter⌝ twice.

37. Select the heading and apply **center, bold 16 points** formatting.

38. Position the insertion point on the blank line below the heading.

39. Choose **References→Captions→Insert Table of Figures** 🖻.

40. In the dialog box, choose **Distinctive** as the format style, ensure that the caption label is **Figure**, and click **OK**.

    Now you'll change the number format style for the captions and update the Table of Figures.

41. Choose **References→Captions→Insert Caption** 🖻**→Numbering**.

42. Choose the **i, ii, iii, …** format and click **OK**.

43. Close the **Caption** dialog box, and then scroll through the pictures and notice the change to lowercase Roman numerals.

44. Scroll to the **Table of Figures** on page 1, right-click the table, and choose **Update Field**.

45. If necessary, choose **Update Entire Table** and click **OK**.

    Notice the figure numbers updated in the table.

46. Save and then close the file.

Create and Delete a Template

Kids for Change will use this document as a handout when giving organic food presentations at community schools. They will send a letter, along with the document, to the school principals for their approval. They will create a template they can use repeatedly for this task.

47. Open the **WD06-R03-PrincipalLtr** from your **WD2013 Lesson 06** folder.

48. Choose **File→Save As**, navigate to any file storage location, and choose **Word Template** from the Save As Type list.

    Notice that Word switches to the Custom Office Templates folder as the file storage location.

49. Save the file as `WD06-R03-PrincipalLtr-[FirstInitialLastName]`, and then choose **File→Close** to close the template file.

    Now you'll open a copy of the template.

50. Choose **File→New**, and then click the **Personal** link to display your template.

51. Click the template thumbnail to open a copy of the template.

52. Save the file as `WD06-R03-PrinLtrFinal-[FirstInitialLastName]` in the **WD2013 Lesson 06** folder.

53. Delete the placeholder text for the date; enter the current date.

54. Replace the placeholder text for the inside address with the following inside address:

    `Ms. Eleanor Roberts`
    `Bascom High School`
    `951 Elm Street`
    `Annapolis, MD 21405`

55. Replace the salutation placeholder name with `Ms. Roberts`.

56. Replace the member name with your name.

57. Save and then close the file.

    Now you will delete the template.

58. Click **File Explorer** on the taskbar at the bottom of the screen.

59. Navigate to the **Documents** folder in the left-hand panel.

60. Double-click the **Custom Office Templates** folder on the right.

61. Select the **WD06-R03-PrincipalLtr-[FirstInitialLastName]** file and tap Delete.

62. Close **File Explorer**; exit from **Word**.

63. Submit your final files based on the guidelines provided by your instructor.

Apply Your Skills

Work with Footnotes, Citations, and a Bibliography

In this exercise, you will create a report detailing some Italian tourist sites and providing tips on train travel in Italy. You will insert footnotes and citations, generate a bibliography, edit a citation, and update the bibliography. Since this is not an academic report, you will not hold to strict MLA guidelines.

Insert Footnotes

1. Start **Word**. Open **WD06-A01-Italy** from your **WD2013 Lesson 06** folder and save it as **WD06-A01-Italy-[FirstInitialLastName]**.

2. Position the insertion point at the end of the first paragraph in the document.

3. Insert this footnote: **Other major attractions are listed on this website.**

4. Position the insertion point after the period following the word *choices* in the paragraph beginning, *In the article, "Italy Train Travel…*.

5. Insert this footnote: **This article also offers advice on train schedules, buying tickets, and boarding your train.**

Enter Citations and Create a Bibliography

6. Choose **MLA Seventh Edition** as the style in the Citations & Bibliography group on the References tab.

7. Position the insertion point after the **Colosseum** bullet point near the top of the document.

8. Tap [Spacebar], ensure that **Web Site** is the Type of Source, and enter the following citation information:
   - Author: **Rome Travel, Guide**
   - Name of Web Page: **Rome travel guide**
   - Year Accessed: **2013**
   - Month Accessed: **May**
   - Day Accessed: **23**
   - Medium: **http://www.rome.info/**

9. Click **OK**.

10. Position the insertion point after *Trastevere* at the end of the third bullet point below the *Off the Beaten Path* heading.

11. Tap [Spacebar], ensure that **Web Site** is the Type of Source, and enter the following information:

- Author: `Casura, Lily`
- Name of Web Page: `Rome off the beaten path`
- Year Accessed: `2013`
- Month Accessed: `May`
- Day Accessed: `23`
- Medium: `http://www.tripadvisor.com/Guide-g187791-1295-Rome_ Lazio.html`

12. Click **OK**.

13. Position the insertion point between *more* and the period at the end of the last paragraph.

14. Tap [Spacebar], ensure that **Web Site** is the Type of Source, and enter the following information:

- Author: `Bakerjian, Martha`
- Name of Web Page: `Italy Train Travel - Tips on Riding Italian Trains`
- Year Accessed: `2013`
- Month Accessed: `May`
- Day Accessed: `23`
- Medium: `http://goitaly.about.com/od/italytransportation/a/ trains.htm`

15. Click **OK**.

16. Position the insertion point at the end of the document, tap [Enter] twice, and insert a page break.

17. Type `Works Cited` as the heading and tap [Enter].

18. **Center** ≡ the heading; position the insertion point on the blank line below the heading.

19. Insert a bibliography on the new page using the **Insert Bibliography** command.
Now you will edit a citation and then update the bibliography.

20. Edit the **Casura** citation source on page 1 by changing the month accessed to `September`. If you are prompted to update the source, click Yes.

21. Update the bibliography and check that the change to the Casura citation is there.

22. Save and then close the file; exit from **Word**.

23. Submit your final file based on the guidelines provided by your instructor.
To view examples of how your file or files should look at the end of this exercise, go to the student resource center.

Insert Captions and a Table of Figures, and Create a Template

One of Universal Corporate Events' clients plans to send their high sales achievers on an African safari as a reward for their hard work. They are preparing a handout to use in conjunction with their presentation. In this exercise, you will add captions to pictures and generate a table of figures. Then you will create a template from an existing letter.

Insert Captions and Create a Table of Figures

1. Start **Word**. Open **WD06-A02-Safari** from your **WD2013 Lesson 06** folder and save it as **WD06-A02-Safari-[FirstInitialLastName]**.

2. Insert and **center** ☰ the following captions for the pictures in your Safari document; use the **1, 2, 3, …** number format and the **Figure** label.
   - Picture 1 caption: **Wildebeest**
   - Picture 2 caption: **Elephants**
   - Picture 3 caption: **Rhinos**
   - Picture 4 caption: **Leopard**
   - Picture 5 caption: **Lion**
   - Picture 6 caption: **Buffalo**

3. Position the insertion point at the top of the document and insert a page break.

4. Position the insertion point at the top of the new page, type **Table of Figures**, and tap Enter twice.

5. Format your heading with **center, bold 16 points**.

6. Position the insertion point on the blank line below the heading and generate the table of figures using the **Distinctive** format and **Figure** as the caption label.
   Next you will edit two captions and then regenerate the table of figures.

7. The Leopard and Lion captions should be plural, so add an **s** to the end of each of the captions.

8. Update the entire table of figures and check to make sure the changes took place.

9. Save and then close the file.

Work with a Template
Universal Corporate Events needs to send travel information to the people going on safari, so they will create a template letter that they can use for all the participants.

10. Open **WD06-A02-SafariLtr** from your **WD2013 Lesson 06** folder.
    Notice the variables in uppercase.

11. Save the file as a **Word Template** in the default **Custom Office Templates** folder; choose **File→Close** to close the template.

12. Choose **File→New** and access your **personal templates**.

13. Open a copy of the template, replace the variable text with the current date, inside address, and salutation of your choice. Enter you own name as the travel agent.

14. Save the file as **WD06-A02-SafariLtrFinal-[FirstInitialLastName]** in your **WD2013 Lesson 06** folder; close the file and exit from **Word**.

   Now you will delete the template.

15. Open **File Explorer** 🗔 from the taskbar, navigate to the **Documents** folder, open the **Custom Office Templates** folder, and delete your template.

16. Close **File Explorer**.

17. Submit your final files based on the guidelines provided by your instructor.

   To view examples of how your file or files should look at the end of this exercise, go to the student resource center.

APPLY YOUR SKILLS WD06-A03

Work with Footnotes, Citations, Captions, and Templates

The intern at Universal Corporate Events has been asked to research travel in Thailand for one of the corporate clients. In this exercise, you will use some of your report-writing skills to help her create her report. Since this is not academic research, you will not conform to strict MLA guidelines.

Work with Footnotes

1. Start **Word**. Open **WD06-A03-Bangkok** from your **WD2013 Lesson 06** folder and save it as **WD06-A03-Bangkok-[FirstInitialLastName]**.

2. Position the insertion point to the right of *markets* in the first line and insert this footnote.

   ---

   [1] Floating markets piled high with tropical fruits and vegetables provide an easy day trip from Bangkok.

3. Position the insertion point to the right of *temples* in the first line and insert this footnote.

   [2] Don't miss Wat Traimit's Golden Buddha or Wat Pho's famous Reclining Buddha.

   Now you will edit the second footnote.

4. Insert the word **renowned** before *Golden*.

Use Citations and Generate a Bibliography

5. Choose the **MLA Seventh Edition** style for citations.

   Now you will insert a citation at the end of the first bullet point.

6. Ensure that **Web Site** is the Type of Source and enter the following information:
   - Author: **Thyberg, David**
   - Name of Web Page: **Bangkok Travel Tips**
   - Year Accessed: **2013**
   - Month Accessed: **September**
   - Day Accessed: **22**
   - Medium: **http://getawaytips.azcentral.com/bangkok-travel-tips-1945.html**

   Now you will insert a citation at the end of the last bullet point on page 1.

7. Ensure that **Web Site** is the Type of Source and enter the following information:
   - Author: **Doman, Gaby**
   - Name of Web Page: **Off the Beaten Track**
   - Year Accessed: **2013**
   - Month Accessed: **September**
   - Day Accessed: **22**
   - Medium: **http://www.tripadvisor.com/Guide-g293916-1104-Bangkok.html**

   Next you will insert a citation at the end of the last bullet point on page 2.

8. Ensure that **Web Site** is the Type of Source and enter the following information:
   - Author: **Rowthorn, Chris**
   - Name of Web Page: **Take the boat out of Bangkok**
   - Year: **2012**
   - Month: **April**
   - Day: **13**
   - Year Accessed: **2013**
   - Month Accessed: **September**
   - Day Accessed: **22**
   - Medium: **http://www.lonelyplanet.com/thailand/bangkok/travel-tips-and-articles/77110**

9. Add a new page at the end of the document for the bibliography, title the page **Works Cited**, and tap ⌈Enter⌉.

10. **Center** ≡ the heading; generate the bibliography on a blank line below the title using the **Insert Bibliography** command.

    Now you'll modify a citation and regenerate the bibliography.

11. Change the date accessed for the **Doman** citation to **August 27**.

12. If a message appears asking if you want to update both lists, click **Yes**.

13. Regenerate the bibliography and check that the change was made.

14. Save and close the **Bangkok** file.

Insert Captions and Create a Table of Figures

The Universal Corporate Events art department has created several logo images for the company to use in its pre-travel seminar announcements. The head of the department is asking for input from the stakeholders.

15. Open **WD06-A03-Logo** from your **WD2013 Lesson 06** folder and save it as **WD06-A03-Logo-[FirstInitialLastName]**.

16. If necessary, display formatting marks.

17. Position the insertion point on the first blank line below the first logo image.

18. Open the **Caption dialog box** and ensure that the label is **Figure** and the numbering choice is **1, 2, 3, ...**.

19. Enter and **Center** ☰ the following captions for all of the logos in the order indicated here.
    - Picture 1 caption: **Option 1**
    - Picture 2 caption: **Option 2**
    - Picture 3 caption: **Option 3**
    - Picture 4 caption: **Option 4**
    - Picture 5 caption: **Option 5**

20. Position the insertion point at the end of the document and insert a **page break**.

21. Type **Table of Figures** at the top of the new page and tap [Enter].

22. If necessary, **center** ☰ the heading; apply **bold** B.

23. Generate the table on the blank line below the heading using the **Formal** format and **Figure** as the caption label.

24. Save and close the file.

Create a Template

Universal Corporate Events wants to standardize the branding for their pre-travel seminar announcements and save it as a template they can use repeatedly.

25. Open **WD06-A03-Seminar** from your **WD2013 Lesson 06** folder.

    Notice the elements of the announcement that will work for any travel seminar.

26. Save the file as a template in the **Custom Office Templates** folder, naming it **WD06-A03-Seminar-[FirstInitialLastName]**.

27. Close the template.

28. Open a copy of the template and replace the *[DESTINATION]* placeholder with **Central America**.

29. Save the file as **WD06-A03-SeminarFinal-[FirstInitialLastName]** in your **WD2013 Lesson 06** folder; close the file.

    Next you will delete the template.

30. Open **File Explorer**; navigate to the **Documents** folder and then to the **Custom Office Template** folder.

31. Delete **WD06-A03-Seminar-[FirstInitialLastName]**.

32. Close **File Explorer**; if necessary, exit from **Word**.

33. Submit your final files based on the guidelines provided by your instructor.

Extend Your Skills

In the course of working through the Extend Your Skills exercises, you will think critically as you use the skills taught in the lesson to complete the assigned projects. To evaluate your mastery and completion of the exercises, your instructor may use a rubric, with which more points are allotted according to performance characteristics. (The more you do, the more you earn!) Ask your instructor how your work will be evaluated.

WD06-E01 That's the Way I See It

You are an intern working for a major grocery store chain. Your manager has asked you to research the pros and cons of reusable shopping bags compared to plastic bags. You have decided to follow MLA conventions in your research paper. Start a new Word document named **WD06-E01-ShopBags-[FirstInitialLastName]** and saved to your **WD2013 Lesson 06** folder.

Type an original introductory paragraph for the paper, and include two footnote comments in the paragraph.

Using the search engine of your choice, find two sources who favor reusable shopping bags and two sources who do not. Pull information from these sources into your research paper, compare the two sides of the issue, and present your opinion. Insert citations at the end of each source and generate a bibliography for the citations.

Open **WD06-E01-ShopBags** from your **WD2013 Lesson 06** folder. Copy and paste the pictures into your research paper, add creative captions to the figures, and create a table of figures.

You will be evaluated based on the inclusion of all elements specified, your ability to follow directions, your ability to apply newly learned skills to a real-world situation, your creativity, and the relevance of your topic and/or data choice(s). Submit your final file based on the guidelines provided by your instructor.

WD06-E02 Be Your Own Boss

As the owner of Blue Jean Landscaping, you plan to hold a rose-pruning seminar for your customers. You will research correct pruning techniques and create a report of your research results to hand out to customers at the event. Write an original introductory paragraph of at least five sentences, and cite three different sources in your report using the MLA Seventh Edition style. Then generate a bibliography of your citations. Because this is not an academic paper, you will not follow strict MLA guidelines. Save your file as **WD06-E02-RoseSeminar-[FirstInitialLastName]** in your **WD2013 Lesson 06** folder.

Create a letter template with variable placeholders that will be used to notify customers of the seminar. Save the template as **WD06-E02-Template-[FirstInitialLastName]**. Use a copy of the template to generate a sample customer letter named **WD06-E02-SampleLetter-[FirstInitialLastName]**. Store the files in your **WD2013 Lesson 06** folder.

You will be evaluated based on the inclusion of all elements specified, your ability to follow directions, your ability to apply newly learned skills to a real-world situation, your creativity, and your demonstration of an entrepreneurial spirit. Submit your final files based on the guidelines provided by your instructor.

Transfer Your Skills

In the course of working through the Transfer Your Skills exercises, you will use critical-thinking and creativity skills to complete the assigned projects using skills taught in the lesson. To evaluate your mastery and completion of the exercises, your instructor may use a rubric, with which more points are allotted according to performance characteristics. (The more you do, the more you earn!) Ask your instructor how your work will be evaluated.

WD06-T01 WebQuest: Use the Web as a Learning Tool

Throughout this book, you will be provided with an opportunity to use the Internet as a learning tool by completing WebQuests. According to the original creators of WebQuests, as described on their website (WebQuest.org), a WebQuest is "an inquiry-oriented activity in which most or all of the information used by learners is drawn from the web." To complete the WebQuest projects in this book, navigate to the student resource center and choose the WebQuest for the lesson on which you are currently working. The subject of each WebQuest will be relevant to the material found in the lesson.

WebQuest Subject: Elements of a research paper based on the MLA Seventh Edition documentation style.

Submit your final file(s) based on the guidelines provided by your instructor.

WD06-T02 Demonstrate Proficiency

The owner of Stormy BBQ is proud to use free-range cattle. He wants his employees to understand the benefits of using natural, grass-fed beef so they can discuss the idea with customers. He has asked you to prepare a report that he can distribute to all employees. Start a new Word document named **WD06-T02-GrassFed-[FirstInitialLastName]** and saved to your **WD2013 Lesson 06** folder. Conduct online research on the benefits of using free-range, natural beef. Write an original introductory paragraph of at least five sentences that includes two commentary footnotes. Cite three sources who favor free-range beef. Generate a bibliography for the citations using the MLA Seventh Edition style, but because this is not an academic paper, you don't need to follow strict MLA guidelines.

Open **WD06-T02-Cattle** from your **WD2013 Lesson 06** folder. Copy and paste the pictures into your report, insert creative captions for the pictures, and generate a table of figures.

Submit your final file based on the guidelines provided by your instructor.

Using Mail Merge

LEARNING OBJECTIVES

After studying this lesson, you will be able to:

- Work with data sources
- Create main documents
- Perform a mail merge
- Work with merge problems
- Generate envelopes and labels

In this lesson, you will manage mail using Word 2013's Mail Merge feature. You will set up data sources where you store name and address information, and you will set up form letters. Then you'll merge your form letters with a data source to produce personalized letters. You'll also generate personalized envelopes and labels. Because you only type the main document once, you only have to proof it once—versus proofing many individually typed letters. When you've validated a data source, you can use it repeatedly without having to check the variable information each time.

Generating a Marketing Mass Mailing

You are the administrative assistant for Green Clean. The company wants to expand their business, and the marketing manager has chosen mass mailings as a good way to generate new prospects. You have been tasked with creating the mailing for the upcoming sales campaign. Mail Merge will save you many hours that would have otherwise been spent addressing each letter individually.

719 Coronado Drive
San Diego, California 92102

Today's Date

Mr. Andre Adams
Mills Insurance
2224 Culver Drive
San Diego, CA 92102

Dear Andre:

Green Clean is a locally owned and operated commercial janitorial service. Our employees are highly trained, and our supervisors check on every job every night to ensure the best quality work.

We follow all EPA guidelines and comply with OSHA standards. We use only environmentally safe cleaning products, providing you with a healthy, nontoxic, clean place of business.

Good customer service is our number one priority. Our proactive account managers stay in touch with our clients and follow through on all requests. We have been in business over twenty years and we have scores of long-term clients.

Andre, one of our account managers will contact you in the near future to discuss you janitorial needs.

Sincerely,

Ahn Tran
President

Variable codes in the form letter merge with the data source to generate personalized letters.

Introducing Mail Merge

http://labyrinthelab.com/videos   Video Number: WD13-V0701

Word's Mail Merge feature is most often used for generating personalized form letters, mailing labels, and envelopes. However, Mail Merge is a versatile tool that can be used with any type of document that combines boilerplate text with variable information, such as standard contracts and legal verbiage. Mail Merge can be a big time-saver and is valuable for managing large mailings.

Components of Mail Merge

Merging creates a merged document by combining information from two files. They are known as the main document and the data source.

- **Main document:** This document controls the merge. It contains the fixed information into which the variable information is merged. A typical form letter, for instance, has a different inside address and greeting line in each letter, while the rest of the text is the same for everyone receiving the letter.
- **Data source:** The data source can be another Word document, a spreadsheet, a database file, or a contacts list in Outlook.
- **Merged document:** This document is the result of the merge. It contains all of the letters addressed to each individual in your data source.

You can merge an existing main document with an existing data source, or you can create the main document and data source while stepping through the merge process.

719 Coronado Drive
San Diego, California 92102

Last N... ▼	First... ▼	Title ▼	Company Name ▼	Address Line 1 ▼	City ▼	State ▼	ZIP Code
Adams	Andre	Mr.	Mills Insurance	2224 Culver Drive	San Diego	CA	92102
Bouras	Talos	Mr.	Conrad Corporation	854 Whitmore Drive	San Diego	CA	92101
Chowdery	Michael	Mr.	Seligman Enterprises	146 Meadow Lane	La Jolla	CA	92103
Novarro	Derek	Mr.	Gourmet Warehouse	3300 Maple Drive	La Jolla	CA	92103
Romero	Nicole	Ms.	Harris Health Services	132 Lake Street	San Diego	CA	92101
Wright	Mary	Ms.	Rogers Electric Company	1240 Potrero Avenue	San Diego	CA	92101

The data source can be a Mail Merge recipient list, a Word table, an Excel database, or an Access table.

Today's Date

«AddressBlock»

«GreetingLine»

Green Clean is a locally owned and operated commercial janitorial service. Our employees are highly trained, and our supervisors check on every job every night to ensure the best quality work.

We follow all EPA guidelines and comply with OSHA standards. We use only environmentally safe cleaning products, providing you with a healthy, nontoxic, clean place of business.

Good customer service is our number one priority. Our proactive account managers stay in touch with our clients and follow through on all requests. We have been in business over twenty years and we have scores of long-term clients.

«First_Name», one of our account managers will contact you in the near future to discuss you janitorial needs.

Sincerely,

Ahn Tran
President

The main document contains standard text and merge codes where variables from the data source will be merged.

green clean

719 Coronado Drive
San Diego, California 92102

Today's Date

Mr. Andre Adams
Mills Insurance
2224 Culver Drive
San Diego, CA 92102

Dear Andre:

Green Clean is a locally owned and operated commercial janitorial service. Our employees are highly trained, and our supervisors check on every job every night to ensure the best quality work.

We follow all EPA guidelines and comply with OSHA standards. We use only environmentally safe cleaning products, providing you with a healthy, nontoxic, clean place of business.

Good customer service is our number one priority. Our proactive account managers stay in touch with our clients and follow through on all requests. We have been in business over twenty years and we have scores of long-term clients.

Andre, one of our account managers will contact you in the near future to discuss you janitorial needs.

Sincerely,

Ahn Tran
President

The completed merge document with variables from the data source.

The Benefits of Using Mail Merge

Mail Merge saves a lot of time. For example, imagine you want to send a letter to 100 customers. Without Mail Merge, you would have to type the same text in all 100 letters (or copy and paste 100 times). However, with Mail Merge, you create one main document with the standard text and one data source containing customer names and addresses.

You will also really appreciate Mail Merge when you later decide you want to make a change. Using Mail Merge, you can edit the main document once and remerge it with the data source to produce a new merged document. Without Mail Merge, you would need to edit each letter individually.

The Mailings Tab

The Mailings tab provides guidance in setting up both the main document and data source, and it helps you conduct the merge. The Start Mail Merge group is the beginning point. Alternatively, you can choose Step-by-Step Mail Merge Wizard from the Start Mail Merge menu to walk you through the process.

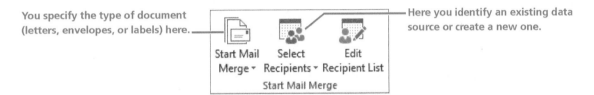

You specify the type of document (letters, envelopes, or labels) here.

Here you identify an existing data source or create a new one.

Working with the Data Source

Data sources typically contain names, addresses, telephone numbers, and other contact information. However, you can include any information in a data source. For example, you could include part numbers and prices to create a parts catalog. You can create a data source in Word, or you can use an external data source, such as an Access or Excel database. Once a data source is created, it can be merged with many different main documents.

Designing Effective Data Sources

It is important to design effective data sources. The most important consideration is the number of fields—the more fields, the more flexibility. You cannot merge a portion of a field. If a field contains both a first and last name, for example, you would not be able to merge the last name without the first name into a greeting line such as *Dear Ms. Alvarez*. In this example, you would need to use one field for the first name and a separate field for the last name. You would also need to use a field for titles (Mr., Ms., and Mrs.). This guideline is not critical if you know you will not use the data source again and the main document does not require this flexibility.

Creating a New Address List

You can use the New Address List dialog box to set up address lists (data sources) for mail merges. This tool stores the addresses in a table in a Microsoft Access database. Each row in the table is referred to as a record. This table, which becomes the data source for the merge, is connected to the mail merge main document.

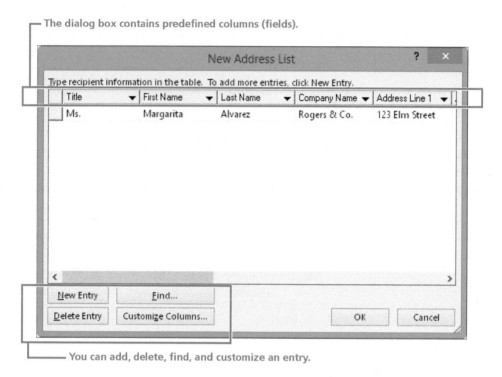

The dialog box contains predefined columns (fields).

You can add, delete, find, and customize an entry.

Customizing an Address List

The Customize Address List dialog box allows you to modify the predefined columns. It's easy to set up the mailing list just as you want it.

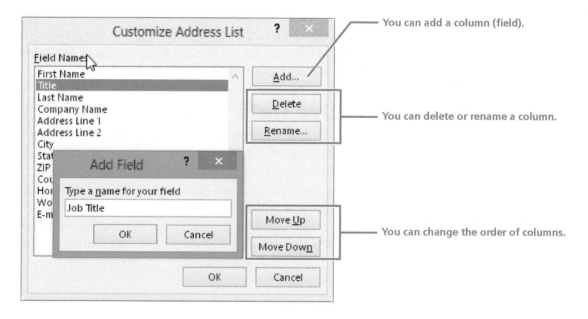

You can add a column (field).

You can delete or rename a column.

You can change the order of columns.

Specify the Main Document and Create a Data Source

In this exercise, you will use the Start Mail Merge group to specify a letter as your main document, to customize the data source, and to enter data.

1. Start **Word**. Open **WD07-D01-SalesLetter** from your **WD2013 Lesson 07** folder and save it as **WD07-D01-SalesLetter-[FirstInitialLastName]**.

   Replace the bracketed text with your first initial and last name. For example, if your name is Bethany Smith, your filename would look like this: WD07-D01-SalesLetter-BSmith.

2. Choose **Mailings→Start Mail Merge→Start Mail Merge 📄 →Letters**.

   You are indicating that the letter you just opened will be the main document. Now you will create your mailing list.

3. Choose **Mailings→Start Mail Merge→Select Recipients 🗒 →Type a New List**.

   The New Address List dialog box opens. Now you will remove unnecessary fields and add a new field.

4. Click **Customize Columns** to open the Customize Address List dialog box.

5. Choose **Address Line 2** and click **Delete**; click **Yes** to verify the deletion.

6. Delete **Country or Region**, **Home Phone**, **Work Phone**, and **E-mail Address**, and then click **Title** at the top of the list.

7. Follow these steps to add a field:

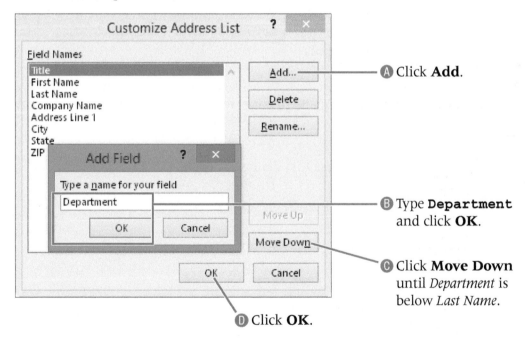

Ⓐ Click **Add**.

Ⓑ Type **Department** and click **OK**.

Ⓒ Click **Move Down** until *Department* is below *Last Name*.

Ⓓ Click **OK**.

Enter Records

The insertion point should be in the Title field.

8. Follow these steps to begin the first record:

Ⓐ Type **Mr.** here.

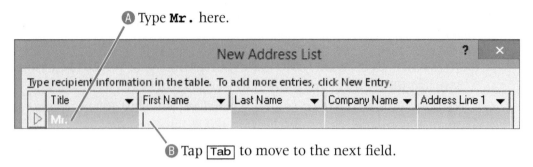

Ⓑ Tap [Tab] to move to the next field.

 TIP Do not type spaces after entering information in a field. Word takes care of adding the necessary spaces. You can click a field and make editing changes if necessary.

9. Type **Talos** and tap [Tab] to move to the next field.

10. Finish entering the Talos Bouras data shown here, tapping [Tab] between fields. The list of fields will scroll as you [Tab] and type.

11. When you complete the first record, click **New Entry** or tap [Tab] to generate a new row for the next record; then, enter the two remaining records shown.

Mr. Talos Bouras	Ms. Nicole Romero	Mr. Michael Chowdrey
Administration	Maintenance	Operations
Conrad Corporation	Harris Health Services	Seligman Enterprises
854 Whitmore Drive	132 Lake Street	900 C Street
San Diego CA 92101	San Diego CA 92101	La Jolla CA 92103

 TIP If you accidentally tap [Tab] after the last record, just click Delete Entry to remove the blank record.

12. Leave the **New Address List** dialog box open.

Reviewing Your Records

Video Library   http://labyrinthelab.com/videos   Video Number: WD13-V0703

It's a good idea to review your records for accuracy before saving the data source. However, if you miss an error, you can always edit it later.

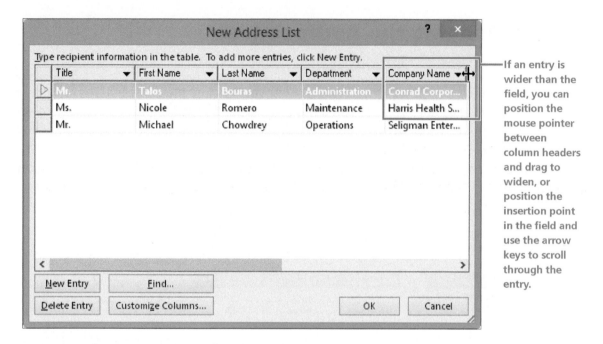

If an entry is wider than the field, you can position the mouse pointer between column headers and drag to widen, or position the insertion point in the field and use the arrow keys to scroll through the entry.

DEVELOP YOUR SKILLS WD07-D02
Review and Save Your Work

In this exercise, you will examine your records for accuracy and save your data source.

1. Position the mouse pointer on the scroll bar at the bottom of the dialog box, and drag left and right to view all the fields.

2. Follow these steps to review your records:

Ⓐ Position the insertion point here and use the arrow keys to move through the entry.

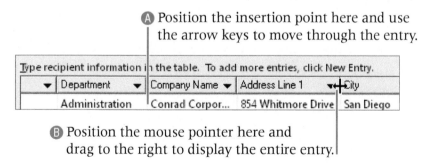

Ⓑ Position the mouse pointer here and drag to the right to display the entire entry.

3. Correct any typos.

4. When you finish reviewing your records, click **OK** to open the Save Address List dialog box.

5. Save the data source file as **WD07-D02-SalesLtrData-[FirstInitialLastName]** in the **WD2013 Lesson 07** folder.

Your data source is now connected to the main document.

Managing the Address List

Video Library   http://labyrinthelab.com/videos   Video Number: WD13-V0704

The Mail Merge Recipients dialog box lets you sort and filter address lists and choose records to include in a mail merge. To edit data, you use the Edit Data Source dialog box to add, delete, and edit entries. If you used a Word table, Excel spreadsheet, or other document for your data source, you can edit directly in that data source document.

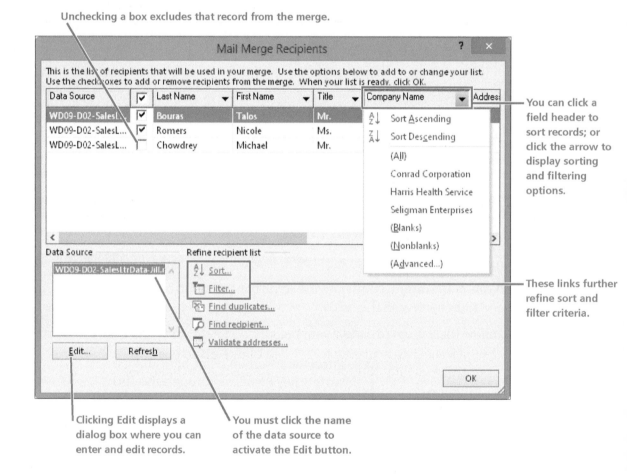

Unchecking a box excludes that record from the merge.

You can click a field header to sort records; or click the arrow to display sorting and filtering options.

These links further refine sort and filter criteria.

Clicking Edit displays a dialog box where you can enter and edit records.

You must click the name of the data source to activate the Edit button.

Use Recipient Options and Edit Records

In this exercise, you will work with the Mail Merge Recipients dialog box, where you can sort, filter, and edit your mailing list.

1. Choose **Mailings→Start Mail Merge→Edit Recipient List** 📇 .

2. Follow these steps to sort and filter the list and open the Edit Data Source dialog box:

Ⓐ Click this field header to sort the list in ascending order by last name.

Ⓑ Click the drop-down arrow and choose **Chowdery** to filter out other entries. Click the arrow again and choose **(All)** to redisplay all records.

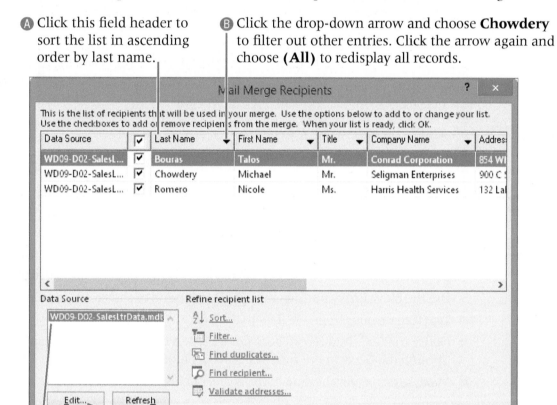

Ⓒ Click the data source to activate the Edit button.

Ⓓ Click **Edit** to open the Edit Data Source dialog box.

Edit a Record

The Edit Data Source dialog box looks and operates like the New Address List dialog box.

3. Follow these steps to edit a record:

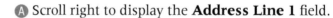 **A** Scroll right to display the **Address Line 1** field.

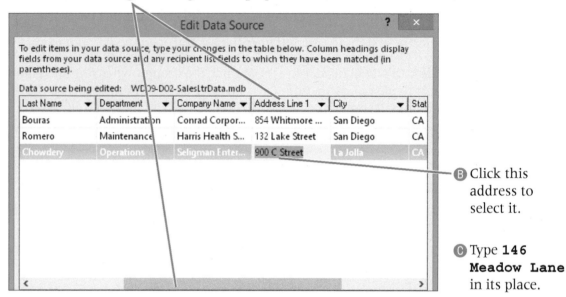

B Click this address to select it.

C Type **146 Meadow Lane** in its place.

4. Follow these guidelines to enter the three records in the following illustration:

   ■ Use the **New Entry** button or tap ⬚Tab at the end of each row for each new record.

   ■ Tap ⬚Tab to move from one field to the next.

   ■ Notice that the third record does not include a department name. Tap ⬚Tab to pass through the Department field and leave it empty.

   ■ Make sure to enter the data in the correct fields.

Ms. Mary Wright	Mr. Derek Navarro	Mr. Andre Adams
Administration	Operations	Mills Insurance
Rogers Electric Company	Gourmet Warehouse	2224 Culver Drive
1240 Potrero Avenue	3300 Maple Drive	San Diego CA 92102
San Diego CA 92101	La Jolla CA 92103	

5. Click **OK** to close the dialog box.

6. Click **Yes** when the message appears verifying your update.
   Notice your changes in the Mail Merge Recipients dialog box.

7. Click **OK** to close the Mail Merge Recipients dialog box.

Working with Main Documents

Video Library   http://labyrinthelab.com/videos   Video Number: WD13-V0705

You accomplish a merge by combining a main document with a data source. A main document is attached to a data source that includes one or more merge fields. Merge fields in a main document correspond to fields in the data source. Some merge codes, such as the Address Block code, are composite fields consisting of a number of grouped fields. For example, Title, First Name, Last Name, Address, City, State, and Zip would be included in the Address Block code.

When you conduct a merge, a customized letter, envelope, or label is created for each record in the data source. The following figure shows the command buttons in the Write & Insert Fields group that you use to insert merge fields into your document.

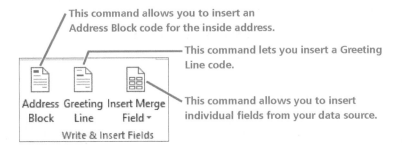

This command allows you to insert an Address Block code for the inside address.

This command lets you insert a Greeting Line code.

This command allows you to insert individual fields from your data source.

---

719 Coronado Drive
San Diego, California 92102

Today's Date

«AddressBlock»

«GreetingLine»

Green Clean is a locally owned and operated commercial janitorial service. Our employees are highly trained, and our supervisors check on every job every night to ensure the best quality work.

We follow all EPA guidelines and comply with OSHA standards. We use only environmentally safe cleaning products, providing you with a healthy, nontoxic, clean place of business.

Good customer service is our number one priority. Our proactive account managers stay in touch with our clients and follow through on all requests. We have been in business over twenty years and we have scores of long-term clients.

«First_Name», one of our account managers will contact you in the near future to discuss you janitorial needs.

Sincerely,

Ahn Tran
President

Here is a form letter with the merge fields inserted. When you execute the merge, the Address Block, Greeting Line, and First Name codes are replaced with information from the data source.

Set Up a Form Letter

In this exercise, you will set up a form letter. The sales letter main document should still be open.

1. If necessary, choose **Home→Paragraph→Show/Hide ¶** to display formatting characters.

2. Select the **Today's Date** line and tap Delete.

3. Choose **Insert→Text→Insert Date and Time** 📅.

4. Choose the third date format, check **Update Automatically**, and click **OK**.

   Checking the Update Automatically option means the date in your letter will always be the current date, which is a convenient option for form letters that you want to use again.

5. Tap Enter four times after inserting the date.

   Now you will insert the Address Block code.

6. Choose **Mailings→Write & Insert Fields→Address Block** 📄.

   The Insert Address Block dialog box allows you to choose a format for the address block.

7. Follow these steps to insert an Address Block code:

Ⓐ Choose different formats and view the preview on the right; then choose **Mr. Joshua Randall Jr.**

Insert Address Block	? ✕
Specify address elements	Preview
☑ Insert recipient's name in this format:	Here is a preview from your recipient list:
Joshua	1 ▷ ▷|
Joshua Randall Jr.	
Joshua Q. Randall Jr.	Mr. Andre Adams
Mr. Josh Randall Jr.	Mills Insurance
Mr. Josh Q. Randall Jr.	2224 Culver Drive
Mr. Joshua Randall Jr.	San Diego, CA 92102
☑ Insert company name	
☑ Insert postal address:	
○ Never include the country/region in the address	
○ Always include the country/region in the address	
◉ Only include the country/region if different than:	Correct Problems
United States	If items in your address block are missing or out of order, use Match Fields to identify the correct address elements from your mailing list.
☑ Format address according to the destination country/region	Match Fields...
	OK Cancel

Ⓑ Leave the remaining options as shown and click **OK**.

The <<AddressBlock>> code appears in the letter. During the merge, Word will insert inside address information from the data source at the Address Block code location.

8. Tap ⌐Enter⌐ twice.

Now you will insert the Greeting Line code.

9. Choose **Mailings→Write & Insert Fields→Greeting Line** 🖹.

10. Follow these steps to modify and insert the Greeting Line code:

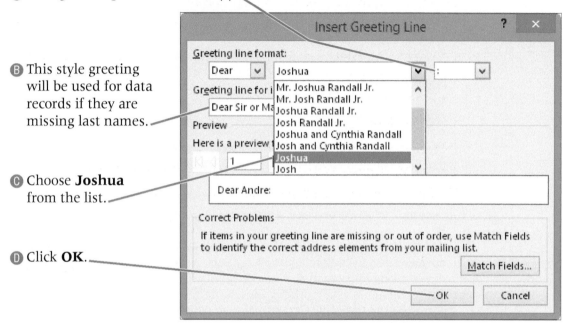

Ⓐ Change this option to a **colon (:)**.

Ⓑ This style greeting will be used for data records if they are missing last names.

Ⓒ Choose **Joshua** from the list.

Ⓓ Click **OK**.

11. Tap ⌐Enter⌐ twice.

12. Follow these steps to insert the First Name code into the letter:

Ⓐ Position the insertion point to the left of One

Ⓑ Click the **Insert Merge Field** menu button ▼.

Ⓒ Choose **First_Name** from the list, then click Insert.

13. Close the Insert Merge Field dialog box.

14. Type a comma and tap ⌐Spacebar⌐; then delete the **uppercase O** and replace it with a **lowercase o**.

15. Take a few moments to review your letter, making sure the merge fields match this example. In particular, make sure you used the proper punctuation and spacing between fields and the text.

The merge fields are highlighted in the following illustration to help you locate them; your merge fields do not need to be highlighted. (The Highlight Merge Fields button is in the Write & Insert Fields group.)

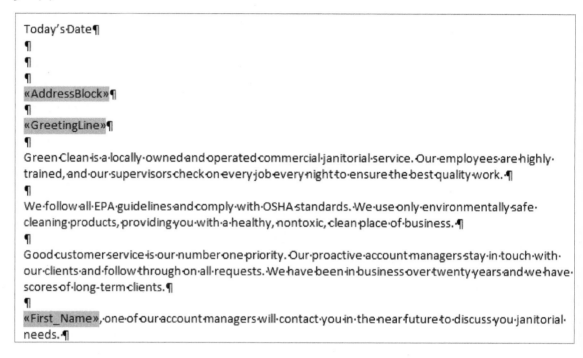

 Any punctuation or spacing errors that occur in your main document will appear in every merged letter.

16. Choose **Home→Paragraph→Show/Hide ¶** to turn off formatting marks.

17. Save your file.

Conducting a Merge

Video Library   http://labyrinthelab.com/videos   Video Number: WD13-V0706

Merging combines a main document with a data source document. If you are merging a form letter with a data source, Word produces a personalized copy of the form letter for each record in the data source.

Previewing the Results

It's always a good idea to preview the merge results before you complete the merge so you can make corrections if needed. If you notice an error that needs to be fixed in the main document, simply click the Preview Results button again to return to the main document.

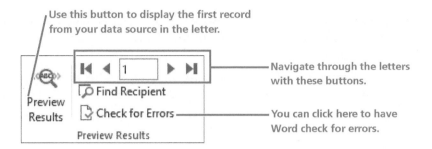

Use this button to display the first record from your data source in the letter.

Navigate through the letters with these buttons.

You can click here to have Word check for errors.

Using "Check for Errors"

When you have many records to preview, rather than previewing each one individually, you can use Check for Errors. Word goes through the document checking for common errors, such as an invalid field code. In the Checking and Reporting Errors dialog box, you have three options for viewing errors.

Finishing the Merge

When you feel confident that your letter and data source are accurate, you use the Finish & Merge command.

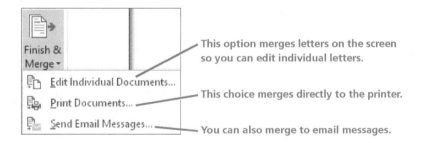

This option merges letters on the screen so you can edit individual letters.

This choice merges directly to the printer.

You can also merge to email messages.

To Save or Not to Save

Merged documents are rarely saved because they can easily be reconstructed by merging the main document with the data source. Instead, merged documents are usually previewed, printed, and closed without saving. But you can certainly save the merged document if you wish to have a record of it. If a merged document contains errors, you can close it without saving, edit the main document or data source, and conduct the merge again.

Conduct a Merge

In this exercise, you will use the Preview Results commands to review your letters. Then you will complete the merge on the screen.

1. Follow these steps to preview the merge:

   Ⓐ Click **Preview Results** to display the first inside address.

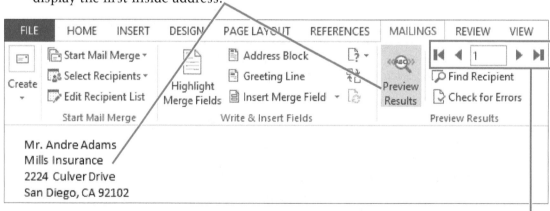

   Ⓑ Use the navigation buttons to scroll through all of your merged documents.

2. Choose **Mailings→Finish→Finish & Merge** 🔲→**Edit Individual Documents** to merge the letters on the screen.

3. Click **OK** to merge all records.

4. Scroll through the letters and scan their contents.

   Notice that there is one letter for each record in the data source.

5. Close the merged document without saving.

6. Choose **Mailings→Preview Results→Preview Results** 🔍 again to display the main document instead of the preview.

Working with Merge Problems

Video Library   http://labyrinthelab.com/videos   Video Number: WD13-V0707

Several common errors can cause a merge to produce incorrect results. The merged document (or preview) will usually provide clues as to why a merge fails to produce the intended results. Once you identify an error in the merged document, such as leaving out a comma or space before or after a merge field, you can make changes to the main document. You can also edit the data source. You can then conduct the merge again to determine if the error was fixed. Repeat this process until the merge works as intended.

Solving Common Merge Problems

Several problems are common in merges. These problems and their solutions are described in the following Quick Reference table.

COMMON MERGE PROBLEMS	
Problem	**Solution**
The same error appears in *every* merge letter.	The problem is in the main document. Correct the error and perform the merge again.
Some letters are missing data.	Some records in the data source are missing data. Add data and perform the merge again.
Some letters have incorrect data.	Some records in the data source are incorrect. Correct the errors, and perform the merge again.

DEVELOP YOUR SKILLS WD07-D06
Fix Merge Problems

In this exercise, you will examine your document for merge problems. This exercise does not address all possible merge problems; it does, however, address one specific error that you will make intentionally. You will insert a colon after the Greeting Line code.

1. Position the insertion point after **<<GreetingLine>>** and type a colon.

2. Choose **Mailings→Finish→Finish & Merge→Edit Individual Documents**.

3. Click **OK** to merge all records.

4. Browse through the merged document and notice that there are two colons following the greeting line in *every* letter.

   Because the error occurs in every letter, you know the error is in the main document.

5. Locate any other errors and notice how often the errors occur (in every merged letter or just one).

   Next you will correct the double colon error and any other errors you discovered that occurred in all letters.

6. Close the merged document without saving; then, edit and save the main document.

7. Follow these guidelines if you find a data error in *just one letter*.
   - ■ Choose **Mailings→Start Mail Merge→Edit Recipient List** 📇 .
   - ■ In the Mail Merge Recipients dialog box, highlight the **Data Source** in the bottom-left corner, and click **Edit**.
   - ■ Fix any errors and click **OK**; click **Yes** to update the data.
   - ■ Click **OK** to close the dialog box.

8. When you have corrected any errors, execute the merge again.

9. Close the merged document without saving it.

10. Save and close the sales letter main document.

Merging Envelopes and Labels

Video Library   http://labyrinthelab.com/videos   Video Number: WD13-V0708

When you begin a mail merge, Word presents you with options for the type of main document you can create. In addition to form letters, you can choose envelopes, labels, and other types of documents. You can use the same data source for various main documents. For example, you can use the same data source for envelopes and mailing labels that you used for the form letter.

Generating Envelopes with Mail Merge

Mail Merge lets you choose the envelope size and formats. The standard business (Size 10) envelope is the default. Check your printer manual for instructions on loading envelopes.

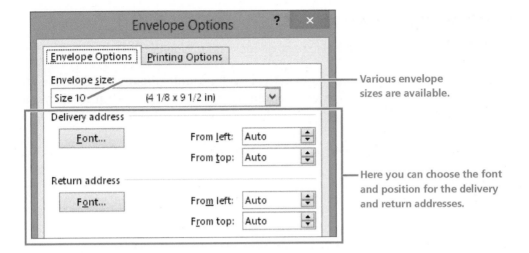

Various envelope sizes are available.

Here you can choose the font and position for the delivery and return addresses.

Choose an Envelope Size and Attach a Data Source

In this exercise, you will choose an envelope as the main document and connect the sales letter data file to the envelope.

1. Start a new blank document.

2. Choose **Mailings→Start Mail Merge→Start Mail Merge** **→Envelopes**.

3. In the Envelope Options dialog box, if necessary, choose **Size 10** as the Envelope Size and click **OK**.

   Now you will attach the data source that you used for your letter.

4. Choose **Mailings→Start Mail Merge→Select Recipients** **→Use an Existing List**.

5. In the Select Data Source dialog box, navigate to your **WD2013 Lesson 07** folder and open **WD07-D02-SalesLtrData-[FirstInitialLastName]**.

Arranging the Envelope

Video Library   http://labyrinthelab.com/videos   Video Number: WD13-V0709

You can insert an Address Block code in the envelope main document. You save an envelope main document like any other main document. The following illustration shows an envelope main document.

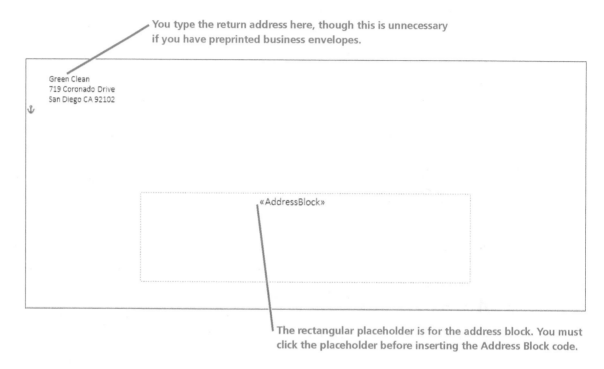

You type the return address here, though this is unnecessary if you have preprinted business envelopes.

Green Clean
719 Coronado Drive
San Diego CA 92102

«AddressBlock»

The rectangular placeholder is for the address block. You must click the placeholder before inserting the Address Block code.

DEVELOP YOUR SKILLS WD07-D08
Merge to Envelopes

In this exercise, you will place the return address and the address block code on the envelope. You will also merge the envelope main document with the data source.

1. If necessary, choose **Home→Paragraph→Show/Hide ¶** to turn on formatting marks.

2. Type the following return address starting at the first paragraph symbol in the upper-left corner of the envelope.

   Green Clean
   719 Coronado Drive
   San Diego CA 92102

3. Position the insertion point next to the paragraph symbol toward the center of the envelope.

4. Choose **Mailings→Write & Insert Fields→Address Block** .

5. Click **OK** to accept the default address block settings.

   Word will merge the address information from the data source into this location when you perform the merge. First, you will preview the merge.

6. Choose **Mailings→Preview Results→Preview Results** to display a record from the data source in the envelope.

7. Use the navigation buttons in the Preview Results group to scroll through all of your merged envelopes.

8. Choose **Mailings→Finish→Finish & Merge** →**Edit Individual Documents** and click **OK** to merge all records.

9. Choose **Home→Paragraph→Show/Hide** to turn off formatting marks.

10. Scroll through the envelopes, and notice that there is one envelope for each record in the data source.

    You could use the envelopes for mailing the letters created in the previous exercises, because they are generated from the same data source.

11. If necessary, fix any problems with the mail merge and merge the envelopes again.

12. When you finish, close the merged document without saving it.

13. Choose **Mailings→Preview Results→Preview Results** to turn off the preview.

14. Save the main document envelope as **WD07-D08-SalesLtrEnv-[FirstInitialLastName]** in your **WD2013 Lesson 07** folder; close the document.

Generating Labels with Mail Merge

Video Library http://labyrinthelab.com/videos Video Number: WD13-V0710

You can use Mail Merge to generate mailing labels for each record in a data source. Mail Merge lets you choose the label format, sheet size, and other specifications. It also lets you insert an Address Block code and other codes in the main document. Like other main documents, a labels main document can be saved for future use. The following illustration shows a portion of the labels main document that you will set up.

«AddressBlock»	«Next Record»«AddressBlock»	«Next Record»«AddressBlock»
«Next Record»«AddressBlock»	«Next Record»«AddressBlock»	«Next Record»«AddressBlock»
«Next Record»«AddressBlock»	«Next Record»«AddressBlock»	«Next Record»«AddressBlock»

Using Label Options

The Label Options dialog box allows you to choose printer options and the type of label you will use. You will find a number on the package of labels you purchase that may correspond to the Product Number in the Label Options dialog box. If you buy a brand name not included in the Label Vendors list, you can match your label size with the label size in the Label Information section.

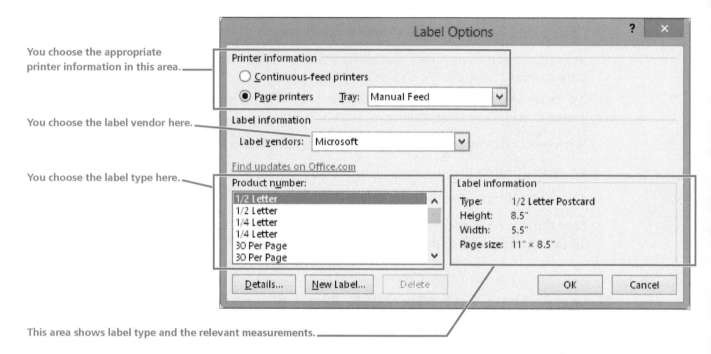

You choose the appropriate printer information in this area.

You choose the label vendor here.

You choose the label type here.

This area shows label type and the relevant measurements.

Use Mail Merge to Generate Mailing Labels

In this exercise, you will set up a labels main document and merge it with the data source used in the previous exercises.

1. Start a new blank document.

2. If necessary, choose **Home→Paragraph→Show/Hide** ¶ to display formatting marks.

3. Choose **Mailings→Start Mail Merge→Start Mail Merge** 📄 **→Labels**.

4. Follow these steps to choose a printer option and a label:

Ⓐ Choose **Default Tray**.　　　　　　　Ⓑ Choose **Avery US Letter**.

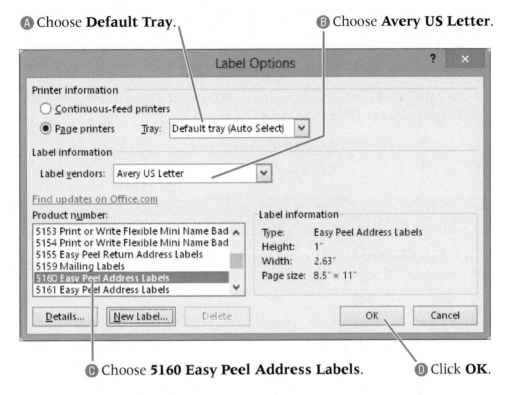

Ⓒ Choose **5160 Easy Peel Address Labels**.　　　Ⓓ Click **OK**.

The labels main document appears in the Word window. Labels are contained in a Word table, but don't worry, you don't have to be a table expert to create labels.

Connect the Data Source

5. Choose **Mailings→Start Mail Merge→Select Recipients** 📇 **→Use an Existing List**.

6. In the Select Data Source dialog box, navigate to your **WD2013 Lesson 07** folder and open **WD07-D02-SalesLtrData-[FirstInitialLastName]**.

7. Make sure the insertion point is next to the paragraph symbol in the first address label.
   Notice that the space for the first label is blank and all the rest have a Next Record code in them. Now you will add the Address Block code.

8. Choose **Mailings→Write & Insert Fields→Address Block** 📄 and click **OK**.

9. Choose **Mailings→Write & Insert Fields→Update Labels** 🔁 to place the Address Block code in all labels.
   Your addresses will fit the labels better if you remove Word's additional spacing.

10. Select the table.

11. Choose **Page Layout→Paragraph**, type **0** in the **Before Spacing** field, and tap Enter.

12. Choose **Mailings→Preview Results→Preview Results** 🔍 to see how the labels will look when you print them. Turn off Preview Results when you are finished.

Conduct the Merge

13. Choose **Mailings→Finish→Finish & Merge** 📄→**Edit Individual Documents**.

14. Click **OK** to merge all the records.

15. Close your merged document without saving it.

16. Save the labels main document in the **WD2013 Lesson 07** folder as `WD07-D09-MergeLabels-[FirstInitialLastName]`.

17. Close the document, then exit from **Word**.

Concepts Review

To check your knowledge of the key concepts introduced in this lesson, complete the Concepts Review quiz by choosing the appropriate access option below.

If you are...	Then access the quiz by...
Using the Labyrinth Video Library	Going to http://labyrinthelab.com/videos
Using eLab	Logging in, choosing Content, and navigating to the Concepts Review quiz for this lesson
Not using the Labyrinth Video Library or eLab	Going to the student resource center for this book

Reinforce Your Skills

Create a Data Source and Main Document

In this exercise, you will create a data source and main document for a Kids for Change mailing. The kids are holding a fundraiser for a micro-lending project that focuses on poor people in India. They will conduct a mailing to announce the upcoming project and canvass their neighborhoods for donations.

Work with a Data Source

1. Start **Word**. Open **WD07-R01-Fundraiser** from your **WD2013 Lesson 07** folder and save it as `WD07-R01-FundRaiser-[FirstInitialLastName]`.

2. Choose **Mailings→Start Mail Merge→Start Mail Merge→Letters** to identify the fund raising letter as the main document.

3. Choose **Mailings→Start Mail Merge→Select Recipients** [icon] **→Type a New List**.
   Now you will customize the list of fields.

4. Click **Customize Columns**.

5. Click **Address Line 2** and click **Delete**.

6. Click **Yes** to confirm the deletion.

7. Also delete the following fields:
   - Country or Region
   - Home Phone
   - Work Phone
   - E-mail Address
   Now you will rename a field.

8. Click **Address Line 1** and click **Rename**.

9. Delete everything except *Address* and click **OK**.

Now you will add two fields.

10. Click **Zip Code** and click **Add**.

11. Type **Member Last Name** in the Add Field dialog box and click **OK**.

12. Also add a field called **Member First Name**.

    Next you will move a field.

13. Click **Member Last Name**, click **Move Down** once, and click **OK** to position Member First Name above Member Last Name.

14. Make sure the insertion point is in the **Title** field, type **Ms.**, and tap Tab.

15. Type **Loretta** in the First Name field and tap Tab.

16. Continue typing and tabbing to complete the first record shown here. Be sure to include the member first name, Eric, and last name, Speck, in the first record.

Ms. Loretta Morales Morales Super Market 311 Ocean Street Miami FL 33130	Mr. Tony D'Agusto Tony's Trattoria 675 Miller Ave. Miami FL 33129	Mr. Allan Morgan 951 4th Street Miami FL 33136	Ms. Margarita Elizondo Elan Fashions 307 Dolphin Way Miami FL 33136
Member: Eric Speck	**Member:** Wendy Chang	**Member:** Stella Hopkins	**Member:** Diego Cantero

17. Tap Tab to begin a new record.

18. Continue typing and tabbing to enter the next three records shown in step 16.

19. Be sure to skip the **Company** field for the third record.

20. Review your records for accuracy; click **OK** when you are satisfied with your work.

21. Save the data source in your **WD2013 Lesson 07** folder as **WD07-R01-FundraiserData-[FirstInitialLastName]**.

    Your fundraiser letter should be on the screen.

Set Up the Main Document

22. If necessary, choose **Home→Paragraph→Show/Hide** ¶ to display formatting marks.

23. In the fundraiser letter, select **[Inside Address]** but not the paragraph symbol at the end of the line and tap Delete.

24. Choose **Mailings→Write & Insert Fields→Address Block** 📄, and then click **OK** to accept the default address block settings.

25. Delete **[Name]** in the greeting line, but not the paragraph symbol at the end of the line.

26. Choose **Mailings→Write & Insert Fields→Greeting Line** 📄.

27. Choose **Joshua** and colon in the Greeting Line Format area as shown and click **OK**.

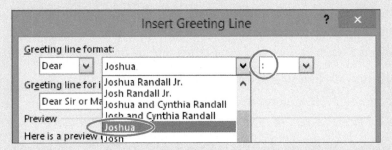

28. In the last sentence of the first paragraph, delete **[Member Name]**.

29. Choose **Mailings→Write & Insert Fields→Insert Merge Field** menu button ▼→**Member_First_Name**.

30. Tap Spacebar and insert the Member_Last_Name field, then close the dialog box.

31. Save and close the letter; exit from **Word**.

32. Submit your final files based on the guidelines provided by your instructor.

    To view examples of how your file or files should look at the end of this exercise, go to the student resource center.

Merge a Letter, Envelopes, and Labels

In this exercise, you will merge a data source with a letter and work with a merge problem. You will also merge the data source with envelopes and labels.

Conduct a Merge and Preview Results

1. Start **Word**. Open **WD07-R02-ParentLtr** from your **WD2013 Lesson 07** folder and save it as **WD07-R02-ParentLtr-[FirstInitialLastName]**.

2. Choose **Mailings→Start Mail Merge→Start Mail Merge→Letters**.

3. Choose **Mailings→Start Mail Merge→Select Recipients** →**Use an Existing List**.

4. Navigate to your **WD2013 Lesson 07** folder and open **WD07-R02-ParentData**.

5. Choose **Mailings→Preview Results→Preview Results** to preview the first record.

   Notice that the greeting line is incorrect.

6. Preview all three records, and notice that the greeting line is incorrect in all.

   This indicates that the error is in the main document.

7. Choose **Mailings→Preview Results→Preview Results** to turn off the preview.

Fix Merge Problems and Complete the Merge

8. In the greeting line, delete *Dear* and the space that follows it; then delete the colon at the end of the greeting line.

   Dear *and the punctuation at the end of the greeting line are included in the Greeting Line code.*

9. Choose **Mailings→Preview Results→Preview Results** 🔍 .

   Notice that the greeting line is now correctly formatted.

   Notice the child's name (Aiden, in the first record) has no spaces around it.

10. Choose **Mailings→Preview Results→Preview Results** 🔍 to return to the main document, and then insert a space before and after the **Child Name** code.

11. Preview the letter again and notice that the **Child Name** variable is correctly spaced.

12. Make sure the spacing between the address block and the greeting line and between the greeting line and the first paragraph are correct.

13. Turn off **Preview Results** 🔍 , and make any changes necessary.

14. Choose **Mailings→Finish→Finish & Merge** 📄 **→Edit Individual Documents**, and then click **OK** to merge all records.

15. Scroll through the merged letters; close the file without saving it.

16. Save and close the parent letter main document.

Generate an Envelope

17. Start a new blank document.

18. Choose **Mailings→Start Mail Merge→Start Mail Merge** 📄 **→Envelopes**.

19. Click **OK** to accept the envelope options defaults.

20. Choose **Mailings→Start Mail Merge→Select Recipients** 📇 **→Use an Existing List**.

21. Navigate to your **WD2013 Lesson 07** folder and open **WD07-R02-ParentData** to attach the data source to the envelope.

22. If necessary, choose **Home→Paragraph→Show/Hide** ¶ to display formatting marks.

23. Type the following return address at the first paragraph symbol in the upper-left corner of the envelope.

    Kids for Change
    726 Throckmorton Ave.
    Sacramento CA 95612

24. Click the insertion point next to the paragraph symbol toward the center of the envelope.

25. Choose **Mailings→Write & Insert Fields→Address Block** 📄 .

26. Click **OK** to accept the address block default formats.

27. Choose **Mailings→Preview Results→Preview Results** 🔍 .

28. Navigate through all three records to ensure they appear correctly on the envelope.

29. Turn off **Preview Results** ⟨ABC⟩ .

30. Save the envelope as **WD07-R02-ParentEnv-[FirstInitialLastName]** in your **WD2013 Lesson 07** folder; close the envelope file.

Generate Mailing Labels

31. Start a new blank document.

32. Choose **Mailings→Start Mail Merge→Start Mail Merge→** ▤ **Labels**.

33. Choose **Avery US Letter** as the Label Vendor, choose **5160 Easy Peel Address Labels** as the Product Number, and click **OK**.

34. If necessary, choose **Home→Paragraph→Show/Hide** ¶ to display formatting marks.

35. Choose **Mailings→Start Mail Merge→Select Recipients** ▤ **→Use an Existing List**.

36. Navigate to your **WD2013 Lesson 07** folder and open **WD07-R02-ParentData**.

37. Make sure the insertion point is next to the paragraph symbol in the first label.

38. Choose **Mailings→Write & Insert Fields→Address Block** ▤ .

39. Click **OK** to accept the address block defaults.

40. Choose **Mailings→Write & Insert Fields→Update Labels** ▤ to insert the Address Block code on all labels.

41. Choose **Mailings→Preview Results→Preview Results** ⟨ABC⟩ to verify that the labels will print correctly.

    Because these addresses are three-line addresses, they fit on the Avery 5160 labels without removing Word's extra spacing.

42. Turn off **Preview Results** ⟨ABC⟩ to return to the labels main document.

43. Save the labels file as **WD07-R02-ParentLabels-[FirstInitialLastName]** in your **WD2013 Lesson 07** folder. Close the file and exit from **Word**.

44. Submit your final files based on the guidelines provided by your instructor.

    To view examples of how your file or files should look at the end of this exercise, go to the student resource center.

REINFORCE YOUR SKILLS WD07-R03

Merge a Letter, Envelopes, and Labels

In this exercise, you will create a data source and a main document. Then you will preview the results and correct any merge problems before conducting the merge. Finally, you will generate envelopes and mailing labels.

Create a Data Source

1. Start **Word**. Open **WD07-R03-Walkers** from your **WD2013 Lesson 07** folder and save it as **WD07-R03-Walkers-[FirstInitialLastName]**.

2. Choose **Mailings→Start Mail Merge→Start Mail Merge** ▤ **→Letters** to designate the Walkers letter as the main document.

3. Choose **Mailings→Start Mail Merge→Select Recipients** 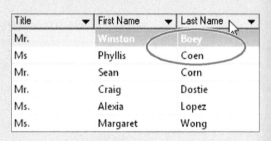→**Type a New List**.
   Now you will customize the data source columns.

4. Click **Customize Columns** to display the Customize Address List dialog box.

5. Click **Company Name** and click **Delete**; click **Yes** to confirm the deletion.

6. Delete the following fields:
   - Address Line 2
   - Country or Region
   - Work Phone
   - E-mail Address

7. Click **Address Line 1** and click **Rename**.

8. Delete everything except the word *Address* and click **OK** twice.

9. Ensure the insertion point is in the **Title** field, type **Mr.**, and tap `Tab` to move to the next field.

10. Type **Sean** in the **First Name** field, tap `Tab`, and type **Corn** in the **Last Name** field.

11. Continue tabbing and typing to complete the Sean Corn record as shown.

Mr. Sean Corn 308 Alhambra Avenue Monterey CA 93940 831-555-1234	Mr. Craig Dostie 31200 Erwin Street Monterey CA 93940 831-555-4567	Ms. Alexia Lopez 2134 Harbor Blvd. Monterey CA 93942 831-555-9632
Ms. Margaret Wong 1308 West Ramona Blvd. Monterey CA 93940 831-555-1598	Ms. Phyllis Coen 4745 Buffin Avenue Monterey CA 93943 831-555-3578	Mr. Winston Boey 263 East Howard Street Monterey CA 93944 831-555-7896

12. Either tap `Tab` or click **New Entry** to begin the next record, and finish entering the remaining records in the table.

13. Review your records for accuracy.
    Now you will sort your list by Last Name.

14. Click the **Last Name** column header to sort the list alphabetically in ascending order.

15. Click **OK**; then, navigate to your **WD2013 Lesson 07** and save the file as **WD07-R03-WalkerData-[FirstInitialLastName]**.

Set Up the Main Document

16. Replace *INSIDE ADDRESS* with the **Address Block** code using the default formats.

17. Replace *GREETING LINE* with the **Greeting Line** code, changing the Greeting Line Format name to **Joshua**.

18. In the last paragraph, replace *HOME PHONE* with the **Home Phone** code.

Conduct the Merge and Preview Results

19. Preview your letters and correct any errors in the main document, paying particular attention to spacing.

   - There should be a blank line between the inside address and the greeting line, and between the greeting line and the body of the letter.
   - There should be a space before the home phone.

Work with Merge Problems

20. Turn off **Preview Results** 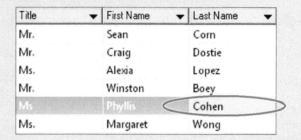 and make any changes necessary to the main document.
   Phyllis Cohen's name is misspelled. You will make that correction now.

21. Choose **Mailings→Start Mail Merge→Edit Recipient List** .

22. Click the data source in the bottom-left corner and click **Edit**.

23. Change the spelling from *Coen* to **Cohen**.

24. Click **OK**; click **Yes** to verify the update and then click **OK** again.

25. Preview the results again to verify the change to the data source and any changes you made to the main document, and then turn off the preview.

Title	First Name	Last Name
Mr.	Sean	Corn
Mr.	Craig	Dostie
Ms.	Alexia	Lopez
Mr.	Winston	Boey
Ms	Phyllis	Cohen
Ms.	Margaret	Wong

26. Choose **Mailings→Finish→Finish & Merge** →**Edit Individual Documents**, and then click **OK** to merge all records.

27. Scroll through your letters, and then close the merged document without saving it.

28. Save and close the main document letter.

Merge Envelopes

29. Start a new blank document.

30. Choose **Mailings→Start Mail Merge→Start Mail Merge** →**Envelopes**.

31. Make sure the envelope is **Size 10** and click **OK**.
   Now you will attach the data source to your envelope.

32. Choose **Mailings→Start Mail Merge→Select Recipients** →**Use an Existing List**.

33. Navigate to your file storage location and open **WD07-R03-WalkerData-[FirstInitialLastName]**.

34. If necessary choose **Home→Paragraph→Show/Hide** ¶ to turn on formatting marks.

35. Type the following return address at the top paragraph symbol in the upper-left corner of the envelope:

```
Kids for Change
456 Bayside Road
Monterey CA 93943
```

36. Position the insertion point next to the paragraph symbol toward the middle of the envelope.

37. Choose **Mailings→Write & Insert Fields→Address Block** 📄 , and then click **OK** to accept the default settings.

38. Choose **Mailings→Preview Results→Preview Results** 🔍 . Use the navigation buttons to view all envelopes then turn off the preview.

39. Choose **Mailings→Finish→Finish & Merge** 📄 **→Edit Individual Documents**, and then click **OK** to merge all records.

40. Scroll through the envelopes then close the file without saving it.

41. Save the envelope main document as `WD07-R03-WalkersEnv-`
    `[FirstInitialLastName]` in your **WD2013 Lesson 07** folder; close the document.
    Now you will merge the labels.

Generate Labels with Mail Merge

42. Start a new blank document.

43. Choose **Mailings→Start Mail Merge→Start Mail Merge→** 📄 **Labels**.

44. Choose **Avery US Letter** as the Label Vendor and **5160 Easy Peel Address Labels** as the Product Number; click **OK**.

45. Choose **Mailings→Start Mail Merge→Select Recipients** 📇 **→Use an Existing List**.

46. Navigate to your **WD2013 Lesson 07** folder and open **WD07-R03-WalkerData-[FirstInitialLastName]**.

47. Ensure the insertion point is in the first label.

48. Choose **Mailings→Write & Insert Fields→Address Block** 📄 and click **OK**.

49. Choose **Mailings→Write & Insert Fields→Update Labels** 🔃 to insert the Address Block code on all labels.

50. Choose **Mailings→Preview Results→Preview Results** 🔍 to see how the labels will look when they print, and then turn off the preview.
    Because the addresses are all three-line addresses, they fit on the label without removing Word's extra spacing.

51. Choose **Mailings→Finish→Finish & Merge** 📄 **→Edit Individual Documents**.

52. Click **OK** to merge all records, and then close the merged document without saving it.

53. Save the labels main document in your **WD2013 Lesson 07** folder as `WD07-R03-`
    `WalkerLabels-[FirstInitialLastName]`. Close the document and exit from **Word**.

54. Submit your final files based on the guidelines provided by your instructor.

Apply Your Skills

Create a Data Source and Main Document

In this exercise, you will create a data source, and then you will review the records and sort the list. Then you will specify a letter as a main document and insert merge fields in the letter.

Work with a Data Source

1. Start **Word**. Open **WD07-A01-SmallBiz** from your **WD2013 Lesson 07** folder and save it as `WD07-A01-SmallBiz-[FirstInitialLastName]`.

2. Specify the **SmallBiz letter** as the main document.
    Next you will customize the columns for your new data source.

3. Delete, add, and rename columns as needed to create the following fields in your data source:
    - Title
    - First Name
    - Last Name
    - Company Name
    - Address
    - City
    - State
    - Zip Code
    - Agent Name

4. Add the following records to your data source:

Mr. Tony Simpson Bigger Time Video Distributors 312 York Lane Richmond CA 94804 **Agent Name:** David Roth	Mr. Jason Jones Move It Distribution 2233 Crystal Street San Mateo CA 94403 **Agent Name:** Tammy Nelson	Ms. Debbie Thomas Barker Books 497 Tennessee Street Richmond CA 94804 **Agent Name:** Jacob Williams

5. Sort the data source in ascending alphabetic order by **Company Name**.

6. Save the data source as `WD07-A01-SmallBizData-[FirstInitialLastName]` in your **WD2013 Lesson 07** folder.

Work with the Main Document

7. In the main document, replace *INSIDE ADDRESS* with the **Address Block** code using the default formats.

8. Replace *GREETING LINE* with the **Greeting Line** code and change the ending punctuation to a colon.

9. In the last paragraph, replace *AGENT NAME* with the **Agent Name** code.

10. Preview the letters and check to be sure the spacing is correct.

11. Turn off the preview, and then make any needed changes to the main document.

12. Save and close the document; exit from **Word**.

13. Submit your final files based on the guidelines provided by your instructor.

    To view examples of how your file or files should look at the end of this exercise, go to the student resource center.

APPLY YOUR SKILLS WD07-A02

Merge Documents and Work with Merge Problems

In this exercise, you will merge letters, envelopes, and labels. You will also correct merge problems.

Conduct a Merge and Work with Merge Problems

1. Start **Word**. Open **WD07-A02-VisaLtr** from your **WD2013 Lesson 07** folder and save it as `WD07-A02-VisaLtr-[FirstInitialLastName]`.

2. Designate the letter as the main document.

3. Specify **WD07-A02-VisaData** in your **WD2013 Lesson 07** folder as the data source for this letter.

4. Preview the merge and notice that there are two errors in the greeting line.

5. Close the preview; edit the main document and preview the letters again, checking that the greeting line is correct.

6. Close the preview; save and close the main document.

Merge Envelopes and Labels

7. Start a new blank document and create a **Size 10** envelope as a main document with the following return address:

   ```
   Suzanne Frost
   Sales Manager
   Universal Corporate Events
   Middlefield CT 06455
   ```

8. Attach **WD07-A02-VisaData** as the data source for the envelope.

9. Insert an address block, using the default formats, in the middle of the envelope.

10. Preview the envelopes then close the preview.

11. Save the envelope main document as **WD07-A02-VisaEnv-[FirstInitialLastName]** in your **WD2013 Lesson 07** folder. Close the document.

12. Start a new blank document and create a labels main document using **Avery US Letter** as the Label Vendor and **5160 Easy Peel Address Labels** as the Product Number.

13. Attach **WD07-A02-VisaData** as the data source.

14. Insert the **Address Block** code in the first label using the default formats.

15. Use the **Update Labels** command to replicate the Address Block code on all labels.

16. Preview the results and notice that the addresses don't fit well on the labels.

17. Close the preview, select the labels table, and remove Word's extra spacing in the Paragraph group on the Page Layout tab. Enter 0 in the Before field.

18. Preview the results again to ensure that the labels fit correctly.

19. Close the preview, and save the labels main document as **WD07-A02-VisaLabels-[FirstInitialLastName]** in your **WD2013 Lesson 07** folder.

20. Close the labels main document; exit from **Word**.

21. Submit your final files based on the guidelines provided by your instructor.

    To view examples of how your file or files should look at the end of this exercise, go to the student resource center.

APPLY YOUR SKILLS WD07-A03

Merge a Data Source and Main Documents, and Work with Merge Problems

In this exercise, you will create a data source using customized columns. You will add merge codes to main documents. You will preview and merge the main documents with the data source, make an editing change to a record, and sort the data source.

Work with a Data Source and Main Document

1. Start **Word**. Open **WD07-A03-TokyoLtr** from your **WD2013 Lesson 07** folder and save it as **WD07-A03-TokyoLtr-[FirstInitialLastName]**.

2. Specify the letter as the main document.

3. Start a new data source list.

4. Customize the columns by deleting and renaming fields. The final columns should be those shown here.

   - Title
   - First Name
   - Last Name
   - Company Name
   - Address
   - City
   - State
   - Zip Code

5. Create the data source shown here and save it as **WD07-A03-TokyoData-[FirstInitialLastName]** in your **WD2013 Lesson 07** folder.

Ms. Jasleen Mahal	Mr. George Iverson	Mr. Anthony Waldek
Superior Storage Devices	Superior Storage Devices	Superior Storage Devices
951 Industrial Way	951 Industrial Way	951 Industrial Way
Trenton NJ 08601	Trenton NJ 08601	Trenton NJ 08601

6. In the main document, replace *INSIDE ADDRESS* with the **Address Block** code using the default formats.

7. Replace *GREETING LINE* with the **Greeting Line** code using the default formats.

8. In the first paragraph, replace *COMPANY NAME* with the **Company Name** code.

9. In the last paragraph, replace *FIRST NAME* with the **First Name** code.

Preview the Results and Fix Merge Problems

10. Preview the merge and make sure the spacing is correct; close the preview.

11. Modify spacing in the main document if necessary.
You've realized that the greeting line should be less formal, so you want to change the format to the recipient's first name.

12. Right-click the **Greeting Line** code, and choose **Edit Greeting Line** from the menu.

13. In the Greeting Line Format, click the drop-down arrow next to Mr. Randall, choose **Joshua** from the list, and click **OK**.

14. Preview the letters again to ensure the change was made.

15. Edit the recipient list, and change *Waldek* to **Waldecker**.

16. Sort the list in ascending alphabetic order by the **Last Name** column.

17. Merge the letter with the data source, choosing **Edit Individual Letters**, and then scroll through the letters.

18. Close the merged document without saving it; save and close the main document.

Merge Envelopes and Labels

19. Start a new blank document, designate it as a mail merge envelope, and use a **Size 10** envelope.

20. Insert the following return address on the envelope:

Ms. Tasha Reynolds
Universal Corporate Events
456 Riverview Road
Trenton NJ 08601

21. Attach the Tokyo data source to the envelope and insert the **Address Block** code.

22. Merge the envelopes and check them for accuracy.

23. If necessary, correct any errors and conduct the merge again.

24. Close the merged document without saving it; make any necessary changes.

25. Save the envelope main document as **WD07-A03-TokyoEnv-[FirstInitialLastName]** in your **WD2013 Lesson 07** folder. Close the document.

26. Start a new blank document and designate it as mail merge labels.

27. Choose **Avery US Letter** as the Label Vendor and **5160** as the Product Number.

28. Attach the Tokyo data source, insert the **Address Block** code in the first label, and update the labels to replicate the Address Block code in all.

29. Preview the labels and notice that the addresses don't fit well due to Word's extra spacing.

30. Close the preview, select the labels table, and remove the extra spacing.

31. Preview the labels again to verify the change in spacing; close the preview.

32. Save the labels main document as **WD07-A03-TokyoLabels-[FirstInitialLastName]** in your **WD2013 Lesson 07** folder. Close the document and exit from **Word**.

33. Submit your final files based on the guidelines provided by your instructor.

Extend Your Skills

In the course of working through the Extend Your Skills exercises, you will think critically as you use the skills taught in the lesson to complete the assigned projects. To evaluate your mastery and completion of the exercises, your instructor may use a rubric, with which more points are allotted according to performance characteristics. (The more you do, the more you earn!) Ask your instructor how your work will be evaluated.

WD07-E01 That's the Way I See It

You are planning a field trip for the fifth-grade class you teach. Create a two- to three-page permission letter informing parents of the trip and how it relates to students' school work (e.g., going to an aquarium after studying about ocean life). Ask parents to sign and then return the letter. Save the letter in your **WD2013 Lesson 07** folder as **WD07-E01-ParentLtr-[FirstInitialLastName]**.

Create a three-record data source of parent names and addresses and any other variables you choose. Customize the data source with only the column headings you need in the letter. Save the data source as **WD07-E01-ParentData-[FirstInitialLastName]**. Insert the merge field codes in the form letter and merge the main document and data source. Save the merged document as **WD07-E01-ParentLtrMerge-[FirstInitialLastName]**. Create an envelope main document with your return address, saved as **WD07-E01-ParentEnv-[FirstInitialLastName]**. Merge it with the data source. Save the merged document as **WD07-E01-ParentEnvMerge-[FirstInitialLastName]**.

You will be evaluated based on the inclusion of all elements specified, your ability to follow directions, your ability to apply newly learned skills to a real-world situation, your creativity, and the relevance of your topic and/or data choice(s). Submit your final files based on the guidelines provided by your instructor.

WD07-E02 Be Your Own Boss

You have created a rewards program for Blue Jean Landscaping customers. Create a form letter of two to three paragraphs describing how customers can accumulate points toward purchases. Mention three other benefits (make them up) for program members. Save the letter in your **WD2013 Lesson 07** folder as **WD07-E02-RewardsLtr-[FirstInitialLastName]**.

Create a data source of three customer's names and addresses and any other needed fields. Customize the data source for only those columns needed for the letter. Save the file as **WD07-E02-RewardsData-[FirstInitialLastName]**. Insert the merge field codes in the letter and conduct the merge, saving the merged document as **WD07-E02-RewardsMerge-[FirstInitialLastName]**.

You will include a brochure in the mailing, so use mailing labels for the oversized envelopes. Create a labels document named **WD07-E02-RewardsLabels-[FirstInitialLastName]** and merge it with your data source. Save the merged labels as **WD07-E02-MergeLabels-[FirstInitialLastName]**.

You will be evaluated based on the inclusion of all elements specified, your ability to follow directions, your ability to apply newly learned skills to a real-world situation, your creativity, and your demonstration of an entrepreneurial spirit. Submit your final files based on the guidelines provided by your instructor.

Transfer Your Skills

In the course of working through the Transfer Your Skills exercises, you will use critical-thinking and creativity skills to complete the assigned projects using skills taught in the lesson. To evaluate your mastery and completion of the exercises, your instructor may use a rubric, with which more points are allotted according to performance characteristics. (The more you do, the more you earn!) Ask your instructor how your work will be evaluated.

WD07-T01 Use the Web as a Learning Tool

Throughout this book, you will be provided with an opportunity to use the Internet as a learning tool by completing WebQuests. According to the original creators of WebQuests, as described on their website (WebQuest.org), a WebQuest is "an inquiry-oriented activity in which most or all of the information used by learners is drawn from the web." To complete the WebQuest projects in this book, navigate to the student resource center and choose the WebQuest for the lesson on which you are currently working. The subject of each WebQuest will be relevant to the material found in the lesson.

WebQuest Subject: How mail merge is used in business.

Submit your final file(s) based on the guidelines provided by your instructor.

WD07-T02 Demonstrate Proficiency

Stormy BBQ has added brisket of beef to its menu! They offered a free brisket of beef meal and a $20 gift certificate to the first five customers who visited their restaurant on New Year's Day. They plan to mail the certificates to the qualifying customers. As a Stormy BBQ employee, you have been asked to compose a congratulatory letter to go with the certificates. Since the letter will go to five people, it makes sense to use Word's Mail Merge feature.

Compose an appropriate letter with two or three paragraphs and save it as **WD07-T02-CertLtr-[FirstInitialLastName]** in your **WD2013 Lesson 07** folder. Create a name and address data source for the five winners. Customize the data source by adding any fields you want to use in your letter; delete any fields you don't intend to use. Save the data source as **WD07-T02-CertData-[FirstInitialLastName]**. Merge the letter and the data source and save the merged document as **WD07-T02-CertLtrMerge-[FirstInitialLastName]**.

Create an envelope main document to go with the mailing and include Stormy BBQ's return address and the Address Block code on a Size 10 envelope. Save the envelope main document as **WD07-T02-CertEnv-[FirstInitialLastName]**. Preview the envelopes and verify that they will print correctly.

Submit your final files based on the guidelines provided by your instructor.

WORD 2013
Creating a Newsletter

LEARNING OBJECTIVES

After studying this lesson, you will be able to:

- Insert section breaks
- Use WordArt and clip art
- Create and manipulate newsletter-style columns
- Use Building Blocks
- Apply Themes and Style Sets

In this lesson, you will use Word's Columns feature to create a newsletter. WordArt and clip art will add eye appeal to the newsletter. Using Building Blocks, design tools, and drop caps make creating professional-looking documents fast and easy. And, you will work with formatting tools to add special touches to your graphics. You will view your document in different modes, and you will change magnification with zoom controls.

Creating a Client Newsletter

Welcome to Green Clean, a janitorial product supplier and cleaning service contractor to small businesses, shopping plazas, and office buildings. Green Clean uses environmentally friendly cleaning products and incorporates sustainability practices wherever possible, including efficient energy and water use, recycling and waste reduction, and reduced petroleum use in vehicles. In addition to providing green cleaning services, the company also sells its eco-friendly products directly to customers.

You are an administrative assistant for Green Clean. It is nearing the beginning of a new quarter, and you are setting up the quarterly newsletter that will go to clients to keep them current on the happenings at your company. You will add pizzazz to the two-column newsletter by inserting WordArt and a picture, and by using the design tools to add color and other visual interest.

The Themes gallery provides a quick way to change overall document formatting.

These are examples of WordArt and a picture.

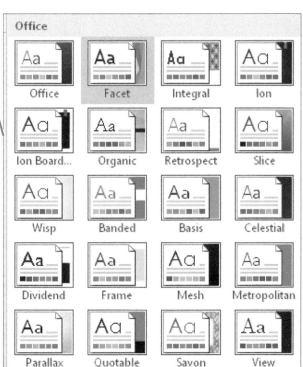

Working with Section Breaks

Video Library   http://labyrinthelab.com/videos   Video Number: WD13-V0801

In Word, whenever you make a document-level formatting change that doesn't apply to the whole document, you need one or more section breaks to define the portion of the document affected by the change. The example in this lesson is a columnar newsletter. The title lines at the top of the document are typed between the margins, which Word considers one column. Then the body of the newsletter is formatted in two columns. You need a section break to separate the one-column titles from the two-column body of the newsletter.

FROM THE RIBBON
Page Layout→Page Setup→Breaks

Inserting Section Breaks

There are four types of section breaks, which are described in the following table.

Type of Section Break	Purpose
Next Page	Inserts a section break and starts the new section on the next page.
Continuous	Inserts a section break and starts the new section on the same page.
Odd Page	Inserts a section break and starts the new section on the next odd-numbered page; Word may insert a blank page to force the odd page section break.
Even Page	Inserts a section break and starts the new section on the next even-numbered page; Word may insert a blank page to force the even page section break.

The following illustration shows the use of continuous section breaks that are sectioning off the two-column portion of a document.

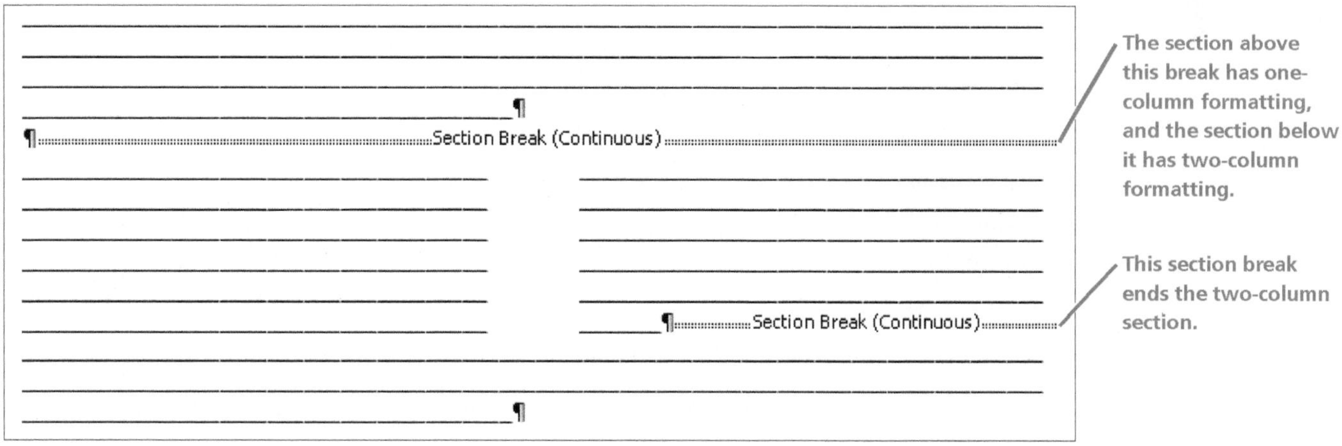

¶ ·····Section Break (Continuous)·····

The section above this break has one-column formatting, and the section below it has two-column formatting.

¶ ·····Section Break (Continuous)·····

This section break ends the two-column section.

Task	**Procedure**
Display the section number in the status bar	Right-click the status bar and choose Section.
Insert a section break	Choose Page Layout→Page Setup→Breaks, and then choose the type of break.
Print document sections	Choose File→Print, and then enter the page and section number range, such as p5s3-p7s4 (page 5, section 3 through page 7, section 4) in the Pages box of the Settings area.
Delete a section break	Display formatting marks, position the insertion point on the section break, and tap Delete . (The section above the break takes on the same formatting as the section below the break.)

DEVELOP YOUR SKILLS WD08-D01

Insert a Section Break

In this exercise, you will begin developing a newsletter by inserting three title lines and a section break.

1. If necessary, start a new document using the **Blank Document** template.

2. Choose **File→Save As** and save the document in your **WD2013 Lesson 08** folder as **WD08-D01-GreenClean-[FirstInitialLastName]**.

   Replace the bracketed text with your first initial and last name. For example, if your name is Bethany Smith, your filename would look like this: WD08-D01-GreenClean-BSmith.

3. If necessary, choose **Home→Paragraph→Show/Hide** ¶ to display formatting marks.

   You need to display formatting marks in order to see a section break.

4. If necessary, right-click the status bar and choose **Section** to display section numbers on the status bar.

5. Type these title lines at the top of the document:

   Quarterly Newsletter
   Green Clean
   Current Quarter

6. Tap Enter three times.

   Now you will insert a continuous section break.

7. Choose **Page Layout→Page Setup→Breaks** ⊟, and then choose **Continuous** from the menu.

   Now you can use document-level formatting above the break that is different from that below the break. Because formatting marks are turned on, you can see the section break.

8. Position the insertion point on the section break and tap Delete .

9. Click **Undo** ↺ to restore the section break.

10. Save the file and leave it open.

Using WordArt

Word 2013

Video Library   http://labyrinthelab.com/videos   Video Number: WD13-V0802

WordArt is great for creating smart-looking text objects. You can use the built-in designs as they are, or you can customize them. The following illustration displays the WordArt gallery.

FROM THE RIBBON
Insert→Text→Insert WordArt

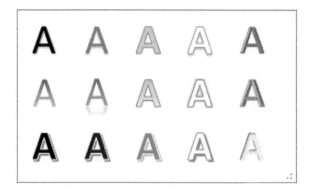

Selecting a WordArt Object

A WordArt object can have either a dotted-line or a solid-line border. When it's a dotted line, you can edit the text. Clicking on the dotted-line border changes it to a solid-line border. This means the entire object is selected, and you can change settings that affect everything within the WordArt object.

A dotted-line border indicates you can edit the text.

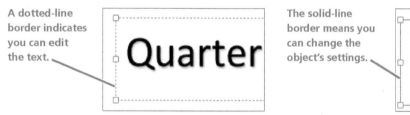

The solid-line border means you can change the object's settings.

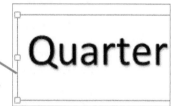

 The terms *object* and *image* are both used when referring to graphical elements such as WordArt, clip art, and pictures.

Formatting WordArt

You edit and format a WordArt object using the tools located on the contextual Drawing Tools Format tab that appears when the object is selected. The small squares that surround a selected object are known as sizing handles. You can drag a handle to increase or decrease the size of the object. Sizing with a corner handle changes the length and width relative to their original proportions.

The rotation handle appears as a small circle with an arrowhead. You can drag the rotation handle left or right to rotate the object.

Mouse pointer as it appears on a WordArt sizing handle

Rotation handle

Layout Options

When an object is selected, a Layout Options smart tag appears to the right of the object. Clicking it displays six text-wrapping options that determine how the surrounding text behaves relative to the object, such as square, top and bottom, and behind text. If text is wrapped around an image and the image is selected, you'll see an anchor icon that indicates the image is attached to text.

FROM THE RIBBON

Picture Tools→
Format→Arrange→
Wrap Text

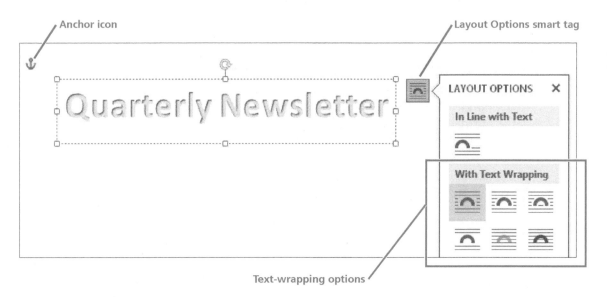

Anchor icon

Layout Options smart tag

Text-wrapping options

DEVELOP YOUR SKILLS WD08-D02

Insert and Format a WordArt Object

In this exercise, you will use the newsletter title as the WordArt object. You will then wrap text around the WordArt object, change the background color, and add a text effect.

1. Save your file as **WD08-D02-GreenClean-[FirstInitialLastName]**.

2. Select *Quarterly Newsletter* in the first line but do not select the paragraph mark at the end of the line.

3. Choose **Insert→Text→Insert WordArt** ◢, and then choose **Fill – Black, Text 1, Shadow** in the upper-left corner of the gallery.

   Notice the text is wrapped around the object. In this case, you don't want the text to wrap; you want it on its own line. You will fix this next.

4. With the WordArt object still selected, follow these steps to place it in line with text.

Ⓐ Click the **Layout Options** smart tag.

Ⓑ Choose **In Line with Text**.

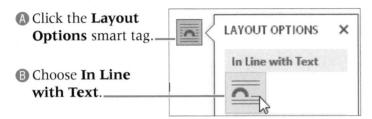

5. Click in the document to close the smart tag, and then click the **WordArt object** to display its border.

The border appears as a dotted line.

6. Click the border to select the entire object.

The border now appears as a solid line. Next, you will change the background color.

7. Choose **Drawing Tools→Format→Shape Styles**.

8. Follow these steps to change the WordArt background color:

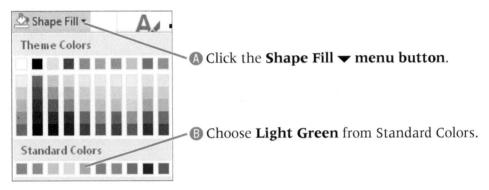

Ⓐ Click the **Shape Fill ▼ menu button**.

Ⓑ Choose **Light Green** from Standard Colors.

9. Choose **Drawing Tools→Format→WordArt Styles**.

10. Follow these steps to change the text color:

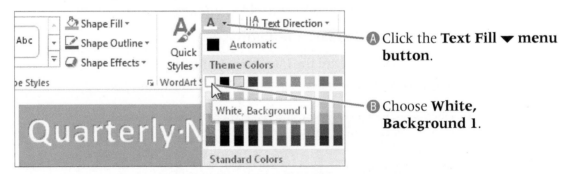

Ⓐ Click the **Text Fill ▼ menu button**.

Ⓑ Choose **White, Background 1**.

11. With the object still selected, choose **Drawing Tools→Format→WordArt Styles**.

12. Follow these steps to change the text effect:

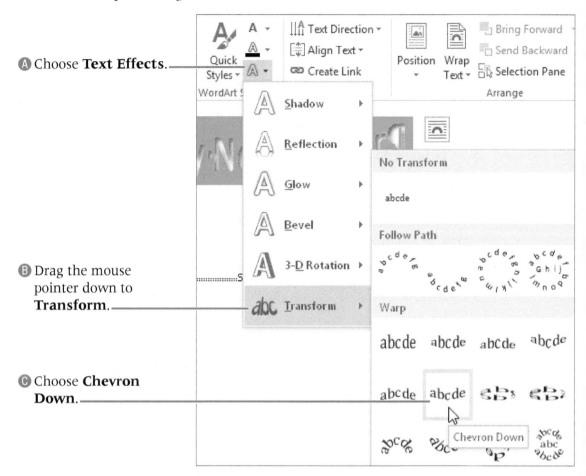

Ⓐ Choose **Text Effects**.

Ⓑ Drag the mouse pointer down to **Transform**.

Ⓒ Choose **Chevron Down**.

Format the Headings

Finally, you will center the headings and format the Green Clean heading.

13. Position the mouse pointer in the left margin area next to the WordArt object, and then click and drag down to select the object and the other two headings.

14. Choose **Home→Paragraph→Center** ☰.

15. Format *Green Clean* with the **Cambria, Bold, 18 pt** font.

Compare your document headings with the following illustration.

16. Save your file.

Inserting Media, Pictures, and Clip Art

Video Library   http://labyrinthelab.com/videos   Video Number: WD13-V0803

Word offers a wide variety of graphic options you can use to liven up your documents, such as videos, pictures, and clip art. Word's graphic objects are easy to work with.

FROM THE RIBBON
Insert→Media→
Online Video

Adding Video to a Document

You can bring your documents to life by inserting online videos, which you can get from websites, blogs, and YouTube, for example. When you search and locate a video you think you might use, you can preview it online before inserting it in your document. Your readers can view the video from inside your document.

You can view the video in the search results screen before inserting it into your document.

Enhancing Your Documents with Pictures and Clip Art

You can browse through your computer or other computers to locate images for your document, or you can search online for images. The Microsoft website offers a variety of royalty-free pictures and clip art.

FROM THE RIBBON
Insert→Illustrations→
Pictures

Insert→Illustrations→
Online Pictures

You can search for pictures saved as files on a computer.

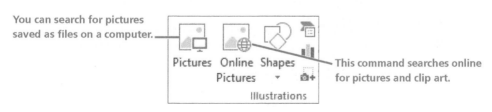

This command searches online for pictures and clip art.

Office.com Clip Art
8 search results for green clean

green clean

Sizing, Rotating, and Moving Images

Once you insert an image, you can change its size and degree of rotation. Like WordArt, clip art images and pictures have sizing handles and a rotation handle. When you hover the mouse pointer over a selected image, the four-headed move arrow appears. You must apply a text-wrapping option in order to freely move an image.

The mouse pointer as it
appears on a sizing handle.

The mouse pointer as it appears
on the rotation handle.

You click and drag the four-
headed arrow to move an
object with a text-wrapping
option applied.

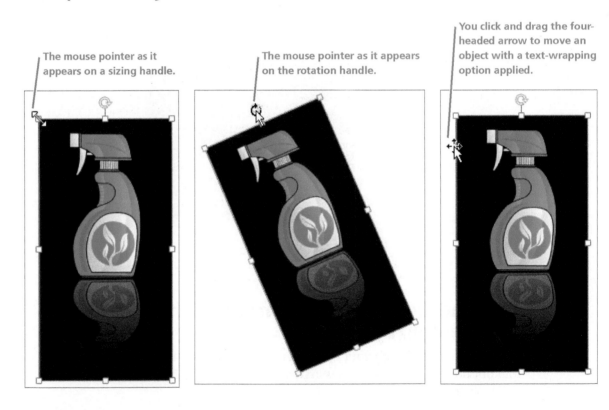

Cropping Images

Cropping allows you to hide parts of an image. You drag a cropping handle to hide the unwanted portion of the image. You can also un-crop an image. Cropping an image in Word does not affect the original image. The area hidden by cropping is not deleted. The mouse pointer appears as a T-shape when it's on a side, top, or bottom cropping handle. It appears as a right angle on a corner cropping handle.

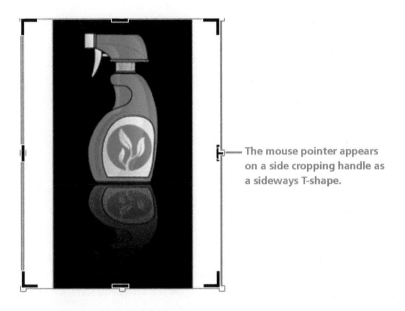

The mouse pointer appears on a side cropping handle as a sideways T-shape.

QUICK REFERENCE	WORKING WITH IMAGES
Task	**Procedure**
Insert an image	■ Choose Insert→Illustrations→Online Pictures; or, choose Insert→Illustrations→Pictures and navigate to the picture's storage location.
Size an image	■ With the image selected, place the mouse pointer on a sizing handle. When it changes to a double-headed arrow, drag to resize the image.
Rotate an image	■ With the image selected, place the mouse pointer on the rotation handle. When it changes to a circular arrow, drag right or left to rotate the image.
Move an image	■ Position the mouse pointer over the image's border. When it changes to a four-headed arrow, drag to move the image. A text wrapping option must be applied.
Crop or un-crop an image	■ Choose Picture Tools→Format→Size→Crop, and then drag a cropping handle on the image. ■ To un-crop, choose the cropping tool and drag a cropping handle across the cropped area.

DEVELOP YOUR SKILLS WD08-D03
Insert, Crop, and Resize Clip Art

In this exercise, you will search for a clip art image online and place it in your document. You will crop the sides off the image as well as resize and move the image.

1. Save the file as **WD08-D03-GreenClean-[FirstInitialLastName]**.

2. Click the insertion point next to the paragraph symbol below the Current Quarter heading.

3. Choose **Insert→Illustrations→Online Pictures** to open the Insert Pictures search window.

4. Follow these steps to search for a piece of clip art:

Ⓐ Click in the search box, type **green clean**, and tap [Enter].

Ⓑ Click this image. (If you can't locate this image, choose an appropriate "green clean" image.)

Ⓒ Click **Insert**.

The image appears at the insertion point. Now you will crop the white margins off the sides of the image. If you are using a different clip art image, practice the cropping steps for the experience.

5. Choose **Picture Tools→Format→Size→Crop** ⌧.

6. Follow these steps to crop the right-hand white margin off the picture:

Ⓐ Position the mouse pointer on the right-side cropping handle so it becomes a sideways T-shape.

Ⓑ Drag to the left until the mouse pointer touches the image's black background. (The cropped area turns gray as you drag.)

7. Repeat **step 6** to remove the white margin on the left side of the image.

8. Click in the document to hide the gray cropped areas, and then select the image again. *Now you will resize the image.*

9. If necessary, choose **View→Show→Ruler** to display the ruler.

10. Follow these steps to resize the image:

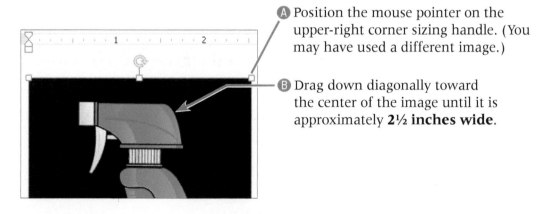

Ⓐ Position the mouse pointer on the upper-right corner sizing handle. (You may have used a different image.)

Ⓑ Drag down diagonally toward the center of the image until it is approximately **2½ inches wide**.

Now you will apply a text-wrapping option so you can drag the image to a new location.

11. With the image still selected, click the **Layout Options smart tag** to the right of the image and choose **Top and Bottom**. (Use ToolTips to locate the correct wrapping option.)

12. Drag the image to center it between the margins.

13. Save the file.

Formatting Images

Video Library http://labyrinthelab.com/videos Video Number: WD13-V0804

There are many tools on the contextual Format tab that allow you to customize images. For example, you can make blocks of color transparent, change the look of your image border, and apply different artistic effects.

FROM THE RIBBON
Picture Tools→
Format→Adjust→
Color

Setting a Transparent Color

Set Transparent Color is an option on the Color button menu. Images are made from tiny pixels of many different colors; that's what causes shade variation. When you click on a color in the object to make it transparent, all pixels of that same color are also made transparent.

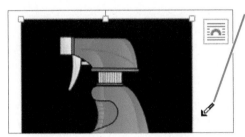

The mouse pointer changes to a pen when you choose Set Transparent Color.

The same image after the background is set to transparent.

Changing the Border Color

You can polish the look of an image with the Picture Border feature. It provides a wide variety of colors, weights, and line styles.

FROM THE RIBBON
Picture Tools→
Format→Picture
Styles→Picture Border

You can choose from theme colors, standard colors, and many additional colors.

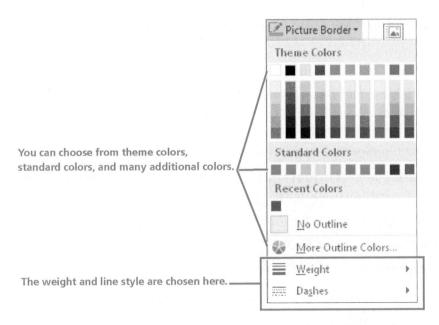

The weight and line style are chosen here.

Applying Artistic Effects

You can take your image styling to the next level using special artistic effects. Some effects include a pencil sketch, line drawing, and painting. The following illustration displays the Pencil Sketch effect.

FROM THE RIBBON

Picture Tools→
Format→Adjust→
Artistic Effects

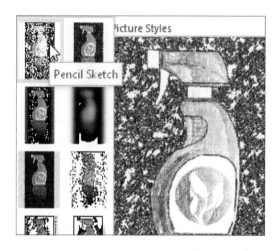

DEVELOP YOUR SKILLS WD08-D04
Format the Clip Art Image

In this exercise, you will remove the black background from the image and change the border. You will also experiment with artistic effects.

If you chose an image other than the one shown in this exercise, experiment with the features indicated but don't be concerned if your image doesn't behave exactly as the instructions indicate.

1. Save the file as **WD08-D04-GreenClean-[FirstInitialLastName]**.

2. If necessary, select the clip art image.

3. Choose **Picture Tools→Format→Adjust→Color** 🖼, and then choose **Set Transparent Color** at the bottom of the gallery.

   Notice when you move the mouse pointer onto the document, it appears as a pen.

4. Click in the black area on the clip art image.

   The background around the image should now be white, and all you see is a green bottle and its shadow. If you are using a different image, remember that Set Transparent makes all pixels of the same color transparent. If there are slight variations in shading, not all pixels will be transparent, which is fine for this exercise. Next you will crop the shadow from the image.

5. Choose **Picture Tools→Format→Size→Crop** 🔲, and then drag the bottom cropping handle up to the bottom of the bottle.

6. Click in the document to hide the gray cropped area, and then select the image again.

   Next you will format the picture border.

7. Choose **Picture Tools→Format→Picture Styles→Picture Border** 🖉.

8. Follow the steps to choose a line weight:

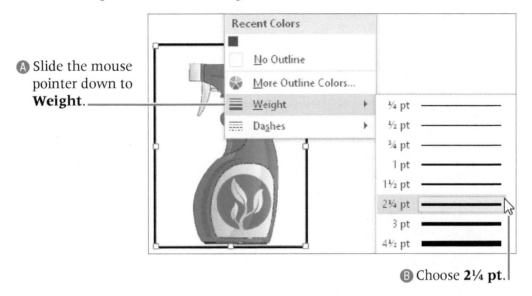

Ⓐ Slide the mouse pointer down to **Weight**.

Ⓑ Choose **2¼ pt**.

9. Choose **Picture Tools→Format→Picture Styles→Picture Border** , and then choose a border color that blends with the image.

   Now you will experiment with artistic effects.

10. Choose **Picture Tools→Format→Adjust→Artistic Effects** .

11. Slide the mouse pointer over several options to preview the effect on your image.

12. You won't apply an artistic effect, so click in the document to close the gallery.

13. Save the file.

Working with the Picture Styles Gallery

Video Library   http://labyrinthelab.com/videos   Video Number: WD13-V0805

Using the Picture Styles gallery is a quick way to enhance your images by adding frames, shadows, and directionality. The gallery uses live preview, allowing you to test various styles before deciding which one you want to apply.

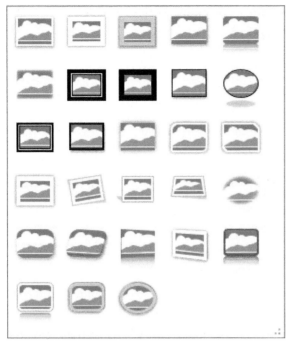

Picture Styles Gallery

Inserting a Picture from a File

In addition to being able to access pictures and clip art online, you can also insert pictures directly from files. For example, you can insert a scanned picture or a picture taken with a digital camera and stored on your computer.

Insert a Picture and Use Picture Styles

In this exercise, you will insert a picture from a file and apply a style from the Picture Styles gallery.

1. Save the file as **WD08-D05-GreenClean-[FirstInitialLastName]**.
2. Select the "green clean" clip art object you placed in the document and tap Delete.
3. If necessary, choose **Home→Paragraph→Show/Hide ¶** to display formatting marks.
4. Position the insertion point on the blank line below the *Current Quarter* heading.
5. Choose **Insert→Illustrations→Pictures**.
6. Navigate to the **WD2013 Lesson 08** folder and double-click the **WD08-D05-GreenClean** picture file to insert it.
7. Crop the words *Green Clean* from the top of the picture, and then click in the document to hide the gray cropped area.

   Next you will right-align the picture to easily see the Picture Styles in Live Preview.
8. Select the picture and choose **Home→Paragraph→Align Right**.
9. Choose **Picture Tools→Format→Picture Styles**, and then click the **More** button to display the entire gallery.
10. Hover the mouse pointer over various options and observe the effect on the picture.

11. Choose the second option in the first row, **Beveled Matte, White**.

12. Choose **Home→Paragraph→Center** ☰.

13. Save the file.

Working with Newsletter-Style Columns

Video Library   http://labyrinthelab.com/videos   Video Number: WD13-V0806

You can use newsletter-style columns to arrange text in multiple columns. In a newsletter layout, text flows down one column and wraps to the top of the next column. Word automatically reformats column layout as you add or delete text.

FROM THE RIBBON
Page Layout→Page
Setup→Columns

Setting Up Columns

You can quickly set your text in columns with the Columns button on the Ribbon, or you can open the Columns dialog box where you can set up more sophisticated column layouts. For example, you can insert a line between columns and customize the width of each column.

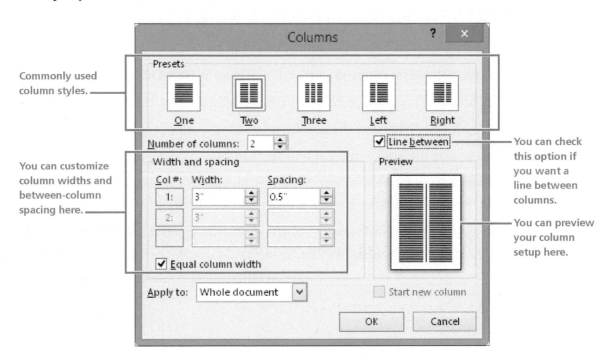

Commonly used column styles.

You can customize column widths and between-column spacing here.

You can check this option if you want a line between columns.

You can preview your column setup here.

Task	Procedure
Set up columns	■ Choose Page Layout→Page Setup→Columns and choose the desired number of columns; or, choose More Columns and enter the desired number of columns.
Insert a line between columns	■ Choose Page Layout→Page Setup→Columns→More Columns and check the Line Between checkbox.
Customize column widths	■ Choose Page Layout→Page Setup→Columns→More Columns and uncheck the Equal Column Width checkbox.
	■ Use the spin box to change the size of column one; column two adjusts automatically.

DEVELOP YOUR SKILLS WD08-D06

Set Up Columns

In this exercise, you will open a document containing the content for your newsletter and copy it into the current document. Then you will format section two of your document with two columns, insert a line between the columns, and customize column widths.

1. Save the file as **WD08-D06-GreenClean-[FirstInitialLastName]**.

2. Open **WD08-D06-NewsltrTxt** from the **WD2013 Lesson 08** folder.

3. Press Ctrl+A to select the entire document.

4. Press Ctrl+C to copy the text, and then close **WD08-D06-NewsltrTxt**.

5. Position the insertion point next to the paragraph mark below the section break.

6. Press Ctrl+V to paste the newsletter text into your document.

7. Make sure the insertion point is in **section 2**.

8. Choose **Page Layout→Page Setup→Columns** ▤, and then choose **Two** from the menu.
   The text of the newsletter is now arranged in two columns.

9. Choose **Page Layout→Page Setup→Columns** ▤, and then choose **More Columns** from the menu to open the Columns dialog box.

Customize Columns

10. Follow these steps to customize the columns:

Ⓐ Remove the checkmark from this checkbox.

Ⓑ Use the spin box to change the width of column 1 to **2"**.

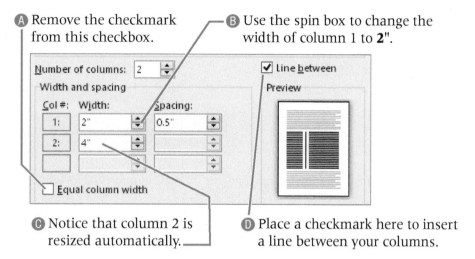

Ⓒ Notice that column 2 is resized automatically.

Ⓓ Place a checkmark here to insert a line between your columns.

11. Click **OK** and then scroll through the document to see the effect.

The columns don't really look good this way. While you could Undo at this point, if you changed your mind at a later time, there is still a quick way to return the columns back to equal size.

12. Choose **Page Layout→Page Setup→Columns** 📋, and then choose **More Columns** to display the Columns dialog box.

13. Click the checkbox next to **Equal Column Width** and click **OK**.

14. Scroll through the document to see how it looks.

It looks like it would be a good idea to balance the columns on the second page. You will do that in the next topic.

15. Save your file.

Working with Column Breaks

Video Library   http://labyrinthelab.com/videos   Video Number: WD13-V0807

You can manually force a column to end by inserting a column break, thus moving text at the break point to the top of the next column. This technique is often used to place headings at the top of columns and to balance columns on the last page of a multicolumn document.

FROM THE RIBBON

Page Layout→Page Setup→Breaks→Column

DEVELOP YOUR SKILLS WD08-D07
Insert a Column Break

In this exercise, you will balance the second page of your newsletter by inserting a manual column break.

1. Save the file as **WD08-D07-GreenClean-[FirstInitialLastName]**.

2. Position the insertion point on **page 2**, at the beginning of the last paragraph in **column 1**. (The paragraph begins with *The Detergent metabolites....*)

3. Choose **Page Layout→Page Setup→Breaks→Column**.

4. If necessary, choose **Home→Paragraph→Show/Hide ¶** to display formatting marks.
   Now you can see the column break.

5. Choose **Home→Paragraph→Show/Hide ¶** to turn off formatting marks.

6. Save your file.

Using Building Blocks

Video Library   http://labyrinthelab.com/videos   Video Number: WD13-V0808

The Building Blocks feature allows you to insert predesigned content into your documents, including cover pages, headers and footers, watermarks, equations, and blocks of text. You can choose from the many built-in Building Blocks, or you can transform your own frequently used content into custom Building Blocks. Some Building Blocks appear in various galleries throughout the Ribbon, such as cover pages and page numbers. You can modify existing Building Blocks, delete custom Building Blocks, and sort the Building Block list in various ways.

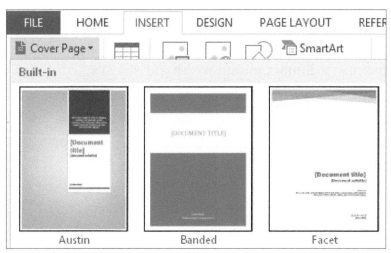

Designs in the Cover Page gallery are examples of Building Blocks.

QUICK REFERENCE	INSERTING BUILDING BLOCKS
Task	**Procedure**
Insert a Building Block	■ Type the Building Block name and tap F3; or, choose Insert→Text→Explore Quick Parts→Building Block Organizer, and then choose the desired entry.

Use a Built-In Building Block

In this exercise, you will add a cover page Building Block to your newsletter.

1. Save the file as **WD08-D08-GreenClean-[FirstInitialLastName]**.

2. Choose **Insert→Pages→Cover Page** 📄, scroll down, and choose **Semaphore**.
   A cover page is attached to the beginning of the document.

3. Click the **Document Title object** and type **Green Clean**.

   Now you will delete the unwanted text objects.

4. Click the **Document Subtitle object** and notice the tab labeled *Subtitle*.

5. Click directly on the **Subtitle tab**.
   This selects the entire object, not just the text.

6. Tap ⟦Delete⟧.
   Other text objects in the bottom-right corner are inside a graphic object frame. Rather than deleting the text objects individually, you can just delete the frame and the objects will be removed with it.

7. Follow these steps to remove unwanted objects:

   Ⓐ Click the insertion point next to the **Author object** to display the graphic object frame.

   Ⓑ Click the frame to select the entire object.

   Ⓒ Tap ⟦Delete⟧.

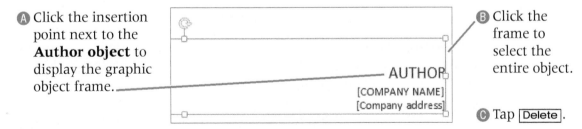

8. Use the same technique to remove the **DATE object** at the top of the cover page. It is in a graphic object frame also.

9. Save your file.

Creating Custom Building Blocks

Video Library   http://labyrinthelab.com/videos   Video Number: WD13-V0809

You can create custom Building Blocks for content you use repeatedly. They can include a wide variety of items such as text, a clip art image, or a WordArt object. You can assign an item to the Quick Part gallery, or you can add it to an existing gallery, such as the Cover Page gallery.

Working with the Quick Part Gallery

The Quick Part gallery is a convenient location for storing custom Building Blocks.

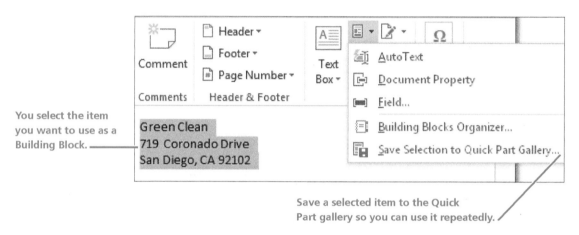

You select the item you want to use as a Building Block.

Save a selected item to the Quick Part gallery so you can use it repeatedly.

After you save a selection to the Quick Part gallery, you can reuse the selection by clicking Explore Quick Parts and choosing the selection from the gallery.

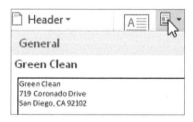

Modifying a Custom Building Block

There are two types of modifications to Building Blocks: changing the properties or modifying the actual content and formatting. If you want to change the name, gallery, where to save it, and so forth, you do so in the Modify Building Block dialog box. However, if you want to modify the actual content, you make the desired changes, select the content, and save the selection with the same name. Word will ask if you want to redefine the existing entry.

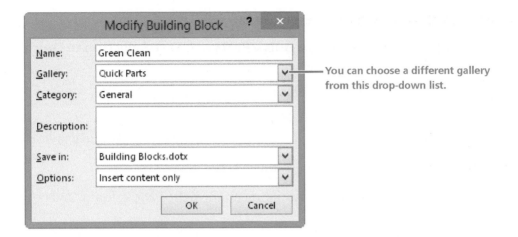

You can choose a different gallery from this drop-down list.

Create a Custom Building Block

In this exercise, you will type the contact information for the Green Clean company. You will then select it and save it to the Quick Part gallery.

1. Save the file as **WD08-D09-GreenClean-[FirstInitialLastName]**.

2. If necessary, choose **Home→Paragraph→Show/Hide ¶** to turn on the formatting marks. Then, press [Ctrl]+[End] to move to the end of the document.

   It turns out that you can use some extra space at the bottom of the right-hand column, so you'll delete the column break.

3. Follow these steps to delete the column break:

   Ⓐ Position the insertion point in front of the column break.

   Ⓑ Tap [Delete].

   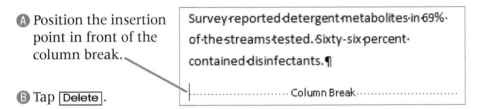

4. Select the first paragraph symbol below the last paragraph in the right-hand column. (If necessary, tap [Enter] to generate a paragraph symbol.)

5. Choose **Home→Paragraph→Line and Paragraph Spacing ⬍≣**, and then choose **1.0** spacing.

6. Display the line spacing menu again, and this time, choose **Remove Space After Paragraph**.

7. Choose **Home→Paragraph→Show/Hide ¶** to turn off formatting marks.

8. Type the following information:

   Green Clean
   719 Coronado Drive
   San Diego, CA 92102

9. Select the three lines that you just typed.

10. Choose **Insert→Text→Explore Quick Parts** ⊞→**Save Selection to Quick Part Gallery**.

11. When the Create New Building Block dialog box appears, click **OK**.

Insert the Custom Building Block

Now you will delete the address from the newsletter so you can test your new Building Block.

12. With the address still selected, tap Delete .

13. If necessary, add a blank line at the bottom of the right-hand column, and position the insertion point on the blank line.

14. Choose **Insert→Text→Explore Quick Parts** ⊞, and then click your new **Building Block** at the top of the menu to insert it in the document.

Modify Building Block Properties

15. Choose **Insert→Text→Explore Quick Parts** ⊞.

16. Right-click the **Green Clean Building Block** at the top of the list and choose **Edit Properties** to open the Modify Building Block dialog box.

17. Follow these steps to change the name of the Building Block:

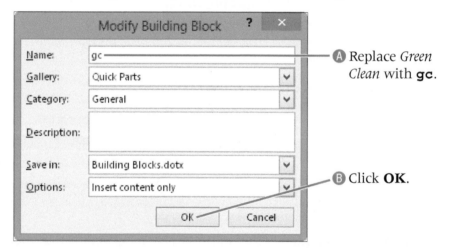

Ⓐ Replace *Green Clean* with **gc**.

Ⓑ Click **OK**.

18. Click **Yes** in the message box to redefine the entry.

Modify Building Block Contents

19. Position the insertion point at the end of the street address, tap Spacebar , and type **Suite 200**.

20. Double-click the zip code and type **92108**.

21. Select the three-line name and address.

22. Choose **Insert→Text→Explore Quick Parts** ⊞, and then choose **Save Selection to Quick Part Gallery**.

23. Type **gc** for the Building Block name, and then click **OK**.

24. Click **Yes** in the message box to redefine the entry.

25. If necessary, select the three-line name and address at the bottom of the column; tap `Delete`.

26. Save your file.

Working with the Building Blocks Organizer

Video Library   http://labyrinthelab.com/videos   Video Number: WD13-V0810

The Building Blocks Organizer contains all Building Blocks, and you can manage them in the organizer. You can sort the list of Building Blocks in ascending order by clicking any of the column headings. You delete a Building Block through the organizer, and you can also insert and modify Building Block properties from within the organizer.

You can click a column heading to sort the list.

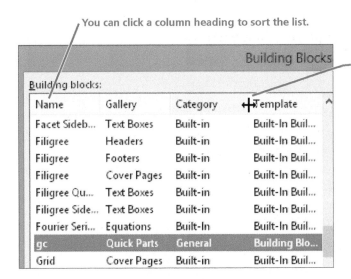

Positioning the mouse pointer between two column headings, then dragging left or right, narrows or widens the column.

QUICK REFERENCE	WORKING WITH CUSTOM BUILDING BLOCKS
Task	**Procedure**
Create a custom Building Block	■ Select the content to convert to a Building Block, choose Insert→Text→Explore Quick Parts, and choose Save Selection to Quick Part Gallery. ■ Make any desired changes in the Create New Building Block dialog box.
Delete a custom Building Block	■ Choose Insert→Text→Explore Quick Parts→Building Blocks Organizer, select the Building Block, and click Delete. ■ Open the gallery containing the Building Block to delete, right-click it, and choose Organize and Delete. ■ With the Building Block highlighted, click Delete.
Sort the Building Block List	■ Choose Insert→Text→Explore Quick Parts→Building Blocks Organizer and click any column header to sort in ascending order.

Delete a Custom Building Block

In this exercise, you will practice sorting the Building Blocks list. You will also delete a Building Block.

1. Save the file as **WD08-D10-GreenClean-[FirstInitialLastName]**.

2. Choose **Insert→Text→Explore Quick Parts** 🖻.

3. Follow these steps to begin the deletion:

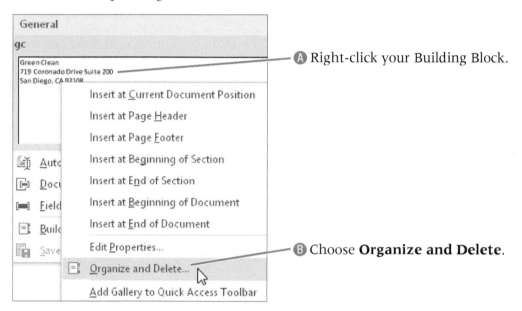

Ⓐ Right-click your Building Block.

Ⓑ Choose **Organize and Delete**.

Your gc Building Block is highlighted in the list.

4. Click **Delete** at the bottom of the dialog box.

5. When the message appears verifying the deletion, click **Yes**.

6. Click a few column headings to see the effect of column sorting, and then click the **Name** column heading to sort by the Name column.

7. Click **Close** at the bottom of the dialog box.

8. Save your file.

Working with Preformatted Text Boxes

Video Library   http://labyrinthelab.com/videos   Video Number: WD13-V0811

A preformatted text box is a box that you can type text in, and it's already formatted for you. Perhaps you have seen a quote in a magazine set in the middle or side of a page with some extra information the author wants to stand out from the rest of the article. These are referred to as pull quotes and sidebars. You can move and resize a text box. When you type in it, the text will wrap automatically. The preformatted text boxes are found in the Building Blocks Organizer.

QUICK REFERENCE	INSERTING A PREFORMATTED TEXT BOX
Task	**Procedure**
Insert a preformatted text box	▪ Choose Insert→Text→Explore Quick Parts→Building Blocks Organizer, select the desired text box, and click Insert.
	▪ Type the text in the box, and then move or resize the box as desired.

DEVELOP YOUR SKILLS WD08-D11

Insert a Preformatted Text Box

In this exercise, you will insert a preformatted text box. You will then resize and move it. Finally, you will type a testimonial from a customer in it.

1. Save the file as **WD08-D11-GreenClean-[FirstInitialLastName]**.

2. If necessary, press `Ctrl`+`End` to move to the end of the document.

3. Choose **Insert→Text→Explore Quick Parts** ▣ **→Building Blocks Organizer**.

4. Follow these steps to insert the Simple Quote text box:

Ⓐ If necessary, click **Name** to sort the list alphabetically.

Ⓑ Scroll down and choose **Simple Quote**.

Ⓒ Notice how the text box is formatted.

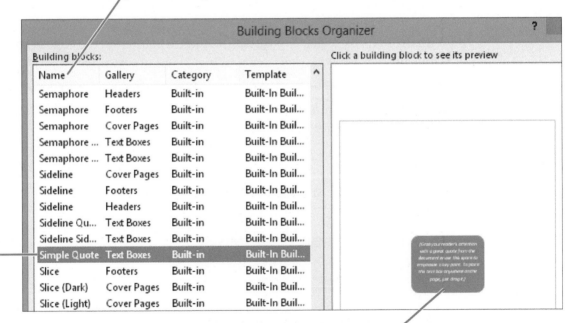

5. Click **Insert**.

Don't worry about the text box location for the moment. You will enter text in the box, resize it, and then move it to a better location.

6. Type this text in the Simple Quote text box:

   We appreciate all you do for us and for our environment! Thank you for such excellent customer service. `Enter` **Daniels & Daniels, Inc.**

7. Drag to select the text. Then, using the Mini toolbar, change the **Font Size** to **10 pt**.

8. If necessary, choose **View→Show→Ruler** to turn it on.

9. Follow these steps to reduce the size of the text box:

   Ⓐ Position the insertion point on this sizing handle.

   Ⓑ Drag down toward the center until the object is about **2½ inches** wide on the ruler.

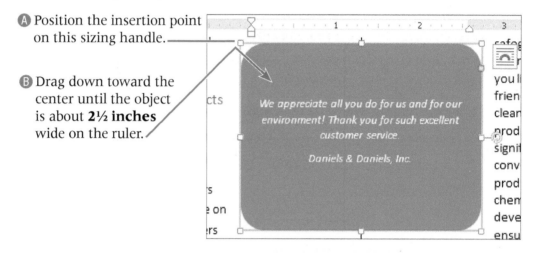

10. With the text box selected, position the mouse pointer on the edge of the box so it becomes a four-headed arrow.

11. Drag the box around in the document and notice the square text wrapping.

    Live Layout lets you see how the text will look as you reposition it. In this example, you will place it at the bottom of the right-hand column on the last page.

12. Drag and drop the box down to the bottom of the column, as shown.

13. Save the file.

Using Themes and Style Sets

Video Library   http://labyrinthelab.com/videos   Video Number: WD13-V0812

Word has document-level formatting features that can instantly add color and visual variety to your entire document all at once. A Theme is a combination of colors, fonts, and graphic elements that you can apply to any document. Style Sets change font and paragraph properties. Style Sets create the biggest impact when you use Word's styles on the Home tab.

Themes and Style Sets appear next to each other on the Design tab, and they interact. That is, applying a Theme provides font and color schemes for the Style Sets. When you hover the mouse pointer over a Theme or Style Set, Live Preview displays the effect before you apply it.

Customizing a Theme

You can customize any Theme to match your creative side. You can change the colors, choose new fonts and paragraph spacing, and add effects to images, such as drawing shapes and SmartArt.

Changing Theme Colors

Built-in color schemes in a Theme are coordinated to work together. Changing a Theme color does not change the built-in Theme; it only modifies the colors in your current document. The colors not only affect the font color, but colors in objects, such as SmartArt and drawing shapes.

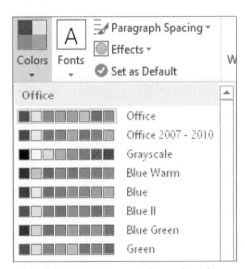

Each of these sets is a complete color scheme affecting text and fill colors.

Changing Theme Fonts

Themes use a set of coordinated fonts. Changing a Theme font changes any text formatted with fonts that have (Headings) or (Body) next to their names. Theme fonts may include the same font of different sizes or two different fonts that blend nicely.

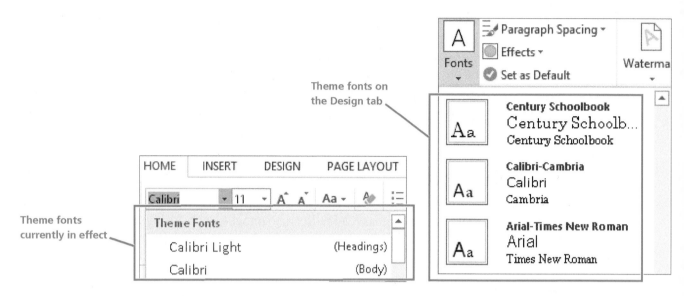

Theme fonts on the Design tab

Theme fonts currently in effect

DEVELOP YOUR SKILLS WD08-D12
Apply a Theme and Style Set to Your Newsletter

In this exercise, you will use Live Preview to examine a variety of Themes and Style Sets. You will also apply a new Theme and Style Set to your newsletter.

1. Save the file as **WD08-D12-GreenClean-[FirstInitialLastName]**.

2. Scroll up to the cover page and make sure the title is visible at the bottom of the page.
   The effect of Themes will be particularly easy to see on this page.

3. Choose **Design→Document Formatting→Themes** to display the Themes gallery.

4. Hover the mouse pointer over several different **Themes** and observe the changes in your document.

5. Choose the **Facet Theme** (the second one in the first row).

6. Scroll through your document and see the impact of the new Theme.
   The headings in the body of the newsletter are formatted with Word's Heading 2 style; therefore, they respond to a change in the Theme. The text box has also taken on a new color from the Theme, and it has changed its position.

7. Drag the text box back to the bottom of the right-hand column.
   Next you will use Live Preview to see some of the color schemes.

8. Scroll to the last page and make sure the text box and a heading are visible.

9. Choose **Design→Document Formatting→Colors**  and slide the mouse pointer through the gallery to see the impact on the text box and titles.

10. Click in the document without choosing a new color.

The green color scheme works well with the company name.

Now you will use Live Preview to examine some of the Theme fonts.

11. Choose **Design→Document Formatting→Fonts** $\boxed{A}$, and then choose the Office font set (Calibri Light and Calibri) at the top of the menu.

Change the Style Set

12. Scroll in the document until one of the headings is positioned toward the bottom of the screen.

13. Choose **Design→Document Formatting**, and then click the **More** button on the Style Set gallery.

14. Follow these steps to apply a new Style Set:

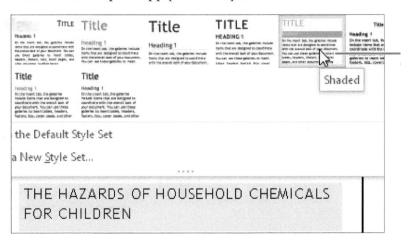

Ⓐ Slide the mouse pointer down and to the right to the **Shaded** style and notice the impact on a title.

Ⓑ Click to apply the style.

15. Save the file.

Inserting Drop Caps

Video Library   http://labyrinthelab.com/videos   Video Number: WD13-V0813

A drop cap is a large uppercase first letter of a paragraph. You have the option of leaving it in the paragraph itself with the text wrapped around it or placing it in the margin next to the paragraph. Other options include changing the font for the drop cap, modifying the number of lines to drop, and setting the distance from the other text.

FROM THE RIBBON
Insert→Text→Add a Drop Cap

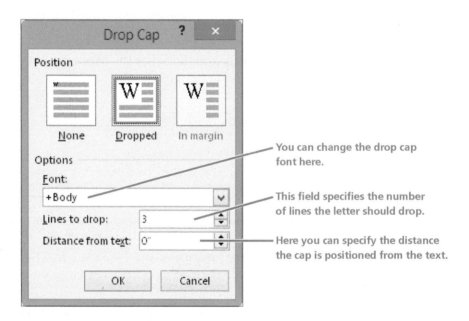

You can change the drop cap font here.

This field specifies the number of lines the letter should drop.

Here you can specify the distance the cap is positioned from the text.

Drop cap in the paragraph with text wrapping.

> **W**e have exciting news to share! After experiencing much success in the Richmond area, Green Clean is expanding into the Charlottesville area. The

Drop cap in the margin.

> **W** e have exciting news to share! After experiencing much success in the Richmond area, Green Clean is expanding into the Charlottesville area. The expansion will include

DEVELOP YOUR SKILLS WD08-D13

Insert a Drop Cap

In this exercise, you will insert a drop cap in the newsletter.

1. Save the file as **WD08-D13-GreenClean-[FirstInitialLastName]**.

2. Scroll to **page 2** and select the *W* in the word *We* in the first column.

3. Choose **Insert→Text→Add a Drop Cap** 🔲→**Dropped**, and then click in the document to deselect the drop cap.

4. Save the file.

WHAT'S NEW?

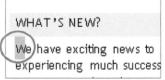

We have exciting news to experiencing much success

Working with Views

Video Library   http://labyrinthelab.com/videos   Video Number: WD13-V0814

Word lets you view your document in several ways. Each view is optimized for specific types of work. The views change the way documents appear on the screen but have no impact on the appearance of printed documents. You can choose views from the View tab or the status bar.

Views on the View tab

Views on the status bar

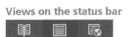

DOCUMENT VIEWS

View	Description
Read Mode	This view provides a book-like reading experience with pages laid out side by side. The Ribbon disappears to display more of your document. You navigate horizontally, as in a book.
Print Layout	With this default view, your documents look similar to the way they will look when printed. You can see graphics, headers and footers, and multi-column layouts.
Web Layout	This view displays your document as it would look as a web page. It appears as one long page without page breaks.
Outline	Outline view is useful for organizing long documents.
Draft	This view simplifies page layout by eliminating elements, such as headers and footers and graphic elements. This view is useful when you want to focus on content.

DEVELOP YOUR SKILLS WD08-D14
Change the View

In this exercise, you will try out various views.

1. Position the insertion point at the top of the document.
2. Locate the **View** buttons at the right end of the status bar.
3. Click the first button, **Read Mode** 📖, and notice how the look of your newsletter has changed.
4. Click the arrow at the right side of the window to scroll through the document.
5. Click the third button, **Web Layout** 📄, and scroll through the document. Notice that it displays as one long page, like a web page.
   Now you'll try a few more views.

6. Choose **View→Views→Outline** 🗐.

   Outline view lets you see your document sections in a hierarchical fashion, which helps you see the overall flow of your document. It is probably not the best view for a document laid out as a newsletter.

7. Choose **View→Views→Draft** 🗐.

   Draft view simplifies the document's layout, so you can focus on content.

8. Finally, choose **View→Views→Print Layout** 🗐.

Using Zoom Controls

The Zoom commands on the View tab let you change the magnification of your document and control the number of pages you can display at one time.

The Zoom button opens the Zoom dialog box. ──

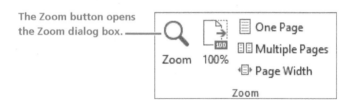

You can customize the percent of magnification here.

Dragging over the Many Pages grid allows you to choose many pages at once. (The grid expands if you click and continue to drag.)

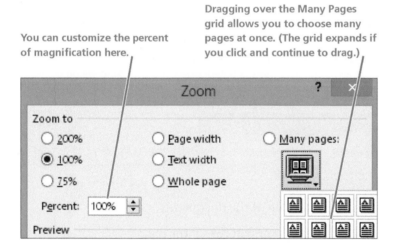

The Zoom bar in the bottom-right corner of the Word window provides a quick way to change magnification.

You can click the Zoom Out and Zoom In buttons to change magnification.

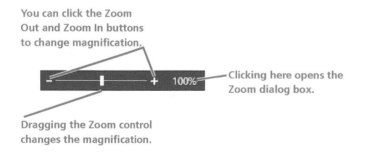

Clicking here opens the Zoom dialog box.

Dragging the Zoom control changes the magnification.

Use the Zoom Controls

In this exercise, you will use your newsletter to practice with the Zoom controls.

1. Position the insertion point at the top of the page following the cover page.

2. Choose **View→Zoom→Zoom** 🔍 to open the Zoom dialog box.

3. Follow these steps to display all pages at once:

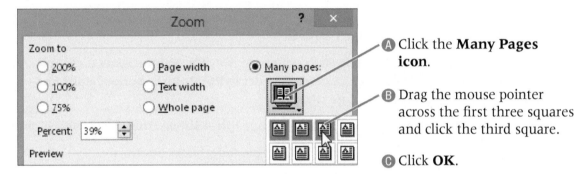

Ⓐ Click the **Many Pages icon**.

Ⓑ Drag the mouse pointer across the first three squares and click the third square.

Ⓒ Click **OK**.

The way the pages are laid out on the screen depends on the size of your screen.

4. Click the **Zoom In** button on the status bar enough times to return to **100%** magnification.

5. Right-click the status bar and choose **Section** to remove the *Section* indicator from the status bar.

6. Save and close the file. Exit **Word**. (If you are prompted to save changes to Building Blocks, click **Don't Save**.)

Concepts Review

To check your knowledge of the key concepts introduced in this lesson, complete the Concepts Review quiz by choosing the appropriate access option below.

If you are...	Then access the quiz by...
Using the Labyrinth Video Library	Going to http://labyrinthelab.com/videos
Using eLab	Logging in, choosing Content, and navigating to the Concepts Review quiz for this lesson
Not using the Labyrinth Video Library or eLab	Going to the student resource center for this book

Reinforce Your Skills

Insert Section Breaks, Graphics, and Newsletter Columns

In this exercise, you will create a newsletter with section breaks and columns, and you will insert and work with graphic images.

Work with Section Breaks

1. Start **Word**. Create a new document using the **Single Spaced (Blank)** template, and save it in your **WD2013 Lesson 08** folder as `WD08-R01-SchoolHabitat-[FirstInitialLastName]`.

2. If necessary, choose **Home→Paragraph→Show/Hide ¶** to display formatting characters.

3. If necessary, right-click the status bar and choose **Section**.

4. Type these lines at the top of the document:

    `Schoolyard Habitat`
    `Kids for Change`

5. Tap Enter three times.

6. Choose **Page Layout→Page Setup→Breaks→ Continuous**.

Insert WordArt

7. Select the *Schoolyard Habitat* heading but not the paragraph mark at the end of the line.

8. Choose **Insert→Text→WordArt**, and then choose **Fill – Blue, Accent 1, Shadow**.
    Next you will use the Layout Options smart tag to position the second line below the WordArt image.

9. With the WordArt object selected, click the smart tag and choose **In Line with Text**.

10. If necessary, click the dotted line border of the image to select the entire image.

11. Choose **Drawing Tools→Format→Word Art Styles→Text Effects**, and then slide the mouse pointer down to **Glow**.

12. In the Glow Variations section, choose **Green, 11 Pt Glow, Accent Color 6**.

13. Choose **Drawing Tools→Format→Word Art Styles→Text Fill ▼ menu button**.

14. Choose the fifth color in the last column, **Green, Accent 6, Darker 25%**.

15. Position the mouse pointer in the margin area to the left of the WordArt image, and drag down to select it and the *Kids for Change* line.

16. Choose **Home→Paragraph→Center**.

17. Format *Kids for Change* with **Comic Sans MS, Bold, 16 pt** font.

18. Position the insertion point on the paragraph symbol below the section break.

19. Choose **Insert→Text→Object ▼ menu button** and choose **Text from File**.

20. Navigate to your **WD2013 Lesson 08** folder and insert **WD08-R01-HabitatContent**.

21. Position the insertion point on the second blank line below the text you just inserted.

22. Choose **Page Layout→Page Setup→Breaks ⊟→Continuous**.

23. Position the insertion point on the second blank line below the second section break.

Insert, Size, and Format a Picture

24. If necessary, choose **View→Show→Ruler** to display the ruler.

25. Choose **Insert→Illustrations→Online Pictures** 🖼.

26. Type **butterfly** in the search box and tap ⎡Enter⎤.

27. Choose the picture shown and click **Insert**. (If you can't locate this picture, choose a similar one.)

28. If necessary, click the picture to select it. Then, position the mouse pointer on the upper-right corner sizing handle.

29. When the mouse pointer appears as a double-headed arrow, drag down toward the middle of the picture until it's approximately **3½ inches wide**.

30. Make sure the picture is still selected.

31. Choose **Picture Tools→Format→Picture Styles**, and then click the **More** ⊽ button at the bottom-right corner of the Picture Styles gallery.

32. Choose the last picture style in the fourth row, **Soft Edge Oval**.

33. Choose **Home→Paragraph→Center** ☰.

Apply Columns

34. Position the insertion point in **section 2**.

35. Choose **Page Layout→Page Setup→Columns ▤→More Columns**.

36. Choose **Two** in the Presets area. Also click to place a checkmark in the **Line Between** checkbox.

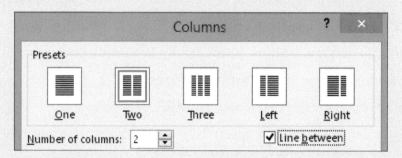

37. Click **OK**.

The Habitat Team *heading should be moved to the top of the second column.*

38. Position the insertion point in front of the heading at the bottom of the first column.

39. Choose **Page Layout→Page Setup→Breaks ▤→Column**.

40. Choose **File→Print** to preview the document.

41. Click the **Back ⊙** button in the upper-left corner of the Print window.

42. Right-click the status bar and choose **Section** to turn off the Section indicator on the status bar, and then click in the document to close the menu.

43. Save and close the file; exit **Word**.

44. Submit your final file based on the guidelines provided by your instructor.

To see examples of how your file or files should look at the end of this exercise, go to the student resource center.

Use Building Blocks, Themes, Style Sets, and Drop Caps

In this exercise, you will insert a built-in Building Block and create a custom Building Block. You will apply a Theme and Style Set to a document, and insert a drop cap. Finally, you will work with views and zoom controls.

Insert a Building Block

Roger Washington, a member of Kids for Change, has written a report on wetlands to present at the next monthly meeting. He has prepared a handout, and now he will add polish to the document.

1. Start **Word**. Open **WD08-R02-Wetlands** from the **WD2013 Lesson 08** folder and save it as `WD08-R02-Wetlands-[FirstInitialLastName]`.

To begin, you will add a cover page Building Block.

2. Choose **Insert→Pages→Cover Page** 📄, and then scroll down and choose **Whisp**.

3. Click the **Document Title** object and type **Wetlands**.

4. Click the **Document Subtitle** object and type **Why They Are Important**.

5. Scroll to the bottom of the cover page, click the **Author Name** object, and type **Roger Washington**.

6. Click the **Company Name** object, click directly on the **Company tab**, and tap Delete.

7. Use the same technique to delete the **Date** text object at the top of the cover page.

8. If necessary, choose **Home→Paragraph→Show/Hide** ¶ to display formatting marks.

9. Scroll to **page 2** and position the insertion point on the second blank line below the last paragraph.

10. Type this text: **If you want to be part of the wetlands project, please contact me.**

Create a Custom Building Block

11. Position the insertion point on the second blank line below the line you just typed.

12. Type this contact information:

    Roger Washington
    415-555-1234
    Roger@Yahoo.com

13. Select the three lines you just typed.

14. Choose **Insert→Text→Explore Quick Parts** 📄**→Save Selection to Quick Part Gallery**.

15. When the Create New Building Block dialog box opens, click **OK**.
    Now you will test your Building Block.

16. With the contact information still selected, tap Delete.

17. Choose **Insert→Text→Explore Quick Parts** 📄, and then click your custom **Building Block** at the top of the menu.

Modify Building Block Properties

18. Choose **Insert→Text→Explore Quick Parts** 📄.

19. Right-click your **Building Block** and choose **Edit Properties**.

20. Change the name of the Building Block to **rw** as shown.

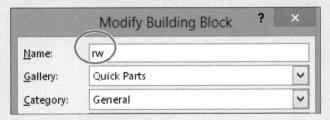

21. Click **OK**. Then, click **Yes** to redefine the entry.

22. Position the insertion point between Roger and the "at sign" (@) in the email address and type **qw**.

23. Select the three lines of contact information.

24. Choose **Insert→Text→Explore Quick Parts** 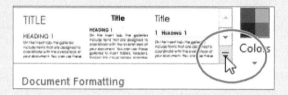→**Save Selection to Quick Part Gallery**.

25. Type **rw** for the name and click **OK**.

26. Click **Yes** to redefine the entry.

Delete a Building Block from the Organizer

27. Choose **Insert→Text→Explore Quick Parts** .

28. Right-click your **Building Block** and choose **Organize and Delete**.
Your Building Block is highlighted in the list.

29. Click **Delete** at the bottom of the dialog box, and then click **Yes** to verify the deletion.

30. Close the **Building Blocks Organizer**.

Use a Theme and a Style Set

31. Choose **Design→Document Formatting→Themes** , and then choose the last Theme in the second row, **Slice**. Scroll through the document to see the impact of the new Theme.

32. Choose **Design→Document Formatting**, and then click the **More** button.

33. Choose the first Style Set in the Built-In category, **Basic (Elegant)**.

Notice that the new Style Set changed the spacing. Next, you will tighten up the spacing in the contact information.

34. Scroll to the bottom of **page 2** and select the three contact lines at the bottom of page 2 and the top of page 3.

35. Choose **Home→Paragraph→Line and Paragraph Spacing** →**Remove Space After Paragraph**.

36. Delete the paragraph symbol above Roger Washington's name.

37. Position the insertion point at the end of Roger's email address and tap ⌈Delete⌋ to remove the blank page at the end of the document.

Insert a Drop Cap

38. Scroll to the top of **page 2** and select the *W* at the beginning of the first paragraph.

39. Choose **Insert→Text→Add a Drop Cap** →**Dropped**.

40. Choose **Home→Paragraph→Show/Hide ¶** to turn off formatting marks.

Work with Views

41. Press Ctrl + Home.

42. Choose **View→Views→Read Mode** .

43. Click the arrow on the right side of the window to see the rest of the document.

44. Click the **Print Layout** button at the right side of the status bar.

45. Choose **View→Views→Draft** . Then, scroll through the document and notice that the graphic elements are suppressed.

46. Choose **View→Views→Print Layout** .

Use Zoom Controls

47. Choose **View→Zoom→Zoom** .

48. In the Zoom dialog box, click the **Many Pages** icon.

49. Drag the mouse pointer across the first two squares, click the second square, and click **OK**. *Notice the setting of the Zoom bar at the right edge of the status bar.*

50. Click the **Zoom In** button enough times to return the magnification to **100%**.

51. Save and close the file. (If you see a message prompting you to save changes to Building Blocks, click **Don't Save**.) Exit **Word**.

52. Submit your final file based on the guidelines provided by your instructor.
To see examples of how your file or files should look at the end of this exercise, go to the student resource center.

REINFORCE YOUR SKILLS WD08-R03

Create a Newsletter

In this exercise, you will create a newsletter using a section break, columns, WordArt, and a picture. You will insert Building Blocks and create a custom Building Block. You will also apply a Theme and a Style Set, and add a drop cap. Finally, you will work with views and zoom controls.

Work with Section Breaks

1. Start **Word**. Open **WD08-R03-WaterPollution** from your **WD2013 Lesson 08** folder and save it as **WD08-R03-WaterPollution-[FirstInitialLastName]**.

2. If necessary, right-click the status bar and choose **Section** to display section numbers on the status bar. Then click in the document to close the menu.

3. If necessary, choose **Home→Paragraph→Show/Hide ¶** to display formatting marks.

4. Position the insertion point on the second paragraph symbol below the heading at the top of the document.

5. Choose **Page Layout→Page Setup→Breaks ⊟→Continuous**.

Use Word Art

6. Select the heading at the top of the document but not the paragraph symbol at the end of the line.

7. Choose **Insert→Text→Insert WordArt** ⧄, and then choose **Fill – Blue, Accent 1, Outline – Background 1, Hard Shadow – Accent 1**.

8. With the WordArt object selected, click the **Layout Options smart tag**.

9. Choose the **Top and Bottom** layout.

10. Choose **Drawing Tools→Format→WordArt Styles→Text Effects** Ⓐ and slide the mouse pointer down to **Transform**.

11. Choose **Square** in the **Warp** category.

12. Position the insertion point on the **WordArt border** and drag to the right to center the object between the margins.

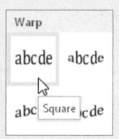

13. Position the insertion point on the second blank line below the last paragraph.

Insert and Format a Picture

14. Choose **Insert→Illustrations→Online Pictures** ▦.

15. Type **fishing** in the search box and tap ⎄Enter⎄.

16. Scroll down the gallery about a third of the way and click the image shown here. (If you can't find this one, choose any other.)

17. Click **Insert**.

18. If necessary, choose **View**→**Show**→**Ruler** to turn on the ruler.

19. Position the mouse pointer on the upper-right sizing handle, and then drag until the picture is about three inches wide.

20. Choose **Picture Tools**→**Format**→**Size**→**Crop** .

21. Position the mouse pointer on the cropping handle on the left side of the picture, and then drag to the right about a half inch. (If you are using a different picture, just crop the picture for the experience.)

22. Click in the document to hide the cropped area, and then select the picture again.

23. Choose **Picture Tools**→**Format**→**Picture Styles**, and then click the **More** button on the bottom-right corner of the Picture Styles gallery.

24. Choose the first style in the second row, **Soft Edge Rectangle**.

Work with Columns

25. Position the insertion point in the body text.

26. Choose **Page Layout**→**Page Setup**→**Columns** →**More Columns**.

27. In the Columns dialog box, choose **Two** in the Presets section and click to add a checkmark in the **Line Between** checkbox.

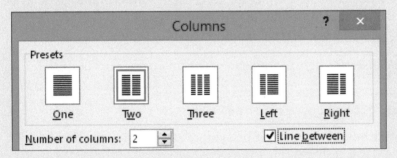

28. Click **OK**.

The tops of the columns are not even, so you'll fix that now.

29. Delete the paragraph symbol above the **Tim Johnson** paragraph.

Now you'll insert a column break so the two lines at the bottom of the left column will float to the top of the second column.

30. Position the insertion point before the first line of the bottom paragraph in the left column.

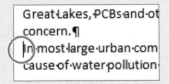

31. Choose **Page Layout**→**Page Setup**→**Breaks** →**Column**.

Use Building Blocks

32. Position the insertion point on the blank line below the picture in the right-hand column.

33. Choose **Insert→Text→Explore Quick Parts→⊞→Building Blocks Organizer**.

34. If necessary, click the **Name** column header to sort the list by name.

35. Choose **Austin Quote** and click **Insert**.

    Don't be concerned about the position of the text box. You'll fix that shortly.

36. Click the dotted line border to make it solid, thus selecting the entire object.

37. Choose **Home→Font** and choose **9 point** as the font size.

38. Click the default text to select it, and then type this text:

    If you can volunteer for the Waterways Tour, please contact me at Timj@Yahoo.com.

    Now you'll resize the text box so it will fit in the right-hand column.

39. Position the mouse pointer on the right-side sizing handle and drag left until the word *Tour* is at the end of the first line.

40. Position the mouse pointer on the border of the text box, and then drag up and to the right until the text box is below the picture in the right-hand column. (It may be necessary to resize the picture to make room for the quote box.)

    Now you'll create a custom Building Block.

41. Position the insertion point at the end of the first paragraph in the left column and tap Enter.

42. Type **Think globally, act locally!**

43. Select the line but not the paragraph symbol at the end of the line.

44. Choose **Insert→Text→Explore Quick Parts ⊞→Save Selection to Quick Part Gallery**.

45. When the Create New Building Block dialog box opens, type **tg** as the name, and click **OK**.

46. Delete the selected text in the document so you can test your Building Block.

47. Choose **Insert→Text→Explore Quick Parts ⊞**, and then click your **Building Block** at the top of the menu.

    Now you'll delete the Building Block so the next student who uses your computer will have the same experience.

48. Choose **Insert→Text→Explore Quick Parts ⊞**, right-click your **Building Block**, and choose **Organize and Delete**.

    Your Building Block is selected in the list.

49. Click **Delete**, and then click **Yes** to verify the deletion.

50. Close the **Building Blocks Organizer**.

Use Themes and Style Sets

51. If necessary, scroll up so you can see the WordArt.

52. Choose **Design→Document Formatting→Themes** [icon], and then choose **Frame**.

    Notice the impact on the WordArt, the headings within the document, and the text box. There has also been a font change.

53. Choose **Design→Document Formatting**, click the **More** button in the Style Set gallery, and choose **Basic (Simple)**.

Insert a Drop Cap

54. Select the *T* at the beginning of the first paragraph.

55. Choose **Insert→Text→Add a Drop Cap** [icon] **→Dropped**.

56. Click in the body of the document to deselect the drop cap.

57. Choose **Home→Paragraph→Show/Hide** [¶] to turn off formatting marks.

Work with Views

58. Click the **Web Layout** [icon] button at the right side of the status bar and notice the change to the document.

59. Choose **View→Views→Outline** [icon] and notice how the view changes.

60. Click the **Print Layout** [icon] button on the status bar.

Use Zoom Controls

61. Drag the **Zoom** button on the Zoom bar to the left and right to see the effect, and then set the zoom at **75%**.

62. Choose **View→Zoom→100%** [icon].

63. Save and close the document; exit **Word**. (If you are prompted to save changes to Building Blocks, click **Don't Save**.)

64. Submit your final file based on the guidelines provided by your instructor.

Apply Your Skills

Use Section Breaks, Graphic Images, and Columns

In this exercise, you will create a newsletter with section breaks, columns, and graphic images.

Work with Section Breaks and Use WordArt

1. Start **Word**. Open **WD08-A01-CorpTravel** from your **WD2013 Lesson 08** folder and save it as `WD08-A01-CorpTravel-[FirstInitialLastName]`.

2. If necessary, choose **Home→Paragraph→Show/Hide** ¶ to display formatting marks.

3. Position the insertion point on the second blank line below the two heading lines at the top of the document and insert a **continuous section break**.

4. Apply **WordArt** to the first line heading using the last style in the second row, **Fill – Gray-50%, Accent 3, Sharp Bevel**.

5. Use the **Layout Options** smart tag to apply **Top and Bottom** text wrapping.

6. Apply the **Can Up** text effect in the Transform category to the WordArt object.

7. Choose **Drawing Tools→Format→Text Fill** 🅰, and then choose **Blue, Accent 5, Lighter 40%**.

8. Format the second heading line, *Meeting and Event Planning Services*, with **Tahoma 14 pt font**.

9. Center both heading lines. (You have to drag the WordArt object to center it.)

10. Position the insertion point at the beginning of the first subheading.

> Dear·Corporate·Travel·Agent,¶
>
> This·month's·newsletter·focuses·or
> focuses·on·Starwood·Hotels·&·Resc
> interview·with·Jet·Blue's·Dennis·Co
>
> ▪ Starwood·Corporate·Rate
> February·07,·2013·–·01:05·PM·ET¶

11. Tap ⌷Enter⌷ and then position the insertion point on the blank line.

Insert and Format Clip Art

12. Choose **Insert→Illustrations→Online Pictures** 🖼️. Search for **hotel**.

13. Insert the image shown. (If you can't locate the image, choose a similar one. The image should be approximately 2″ wide and 1 1/2″ high. If you chose a different image, you may need to resize it.)

14. Add the **White, Background 1, Darker 25%** picture border around the picture.

15. Apply **3 pt line weight** to the border.

16. Use the **Layout Options** smart tag to apply the **Top and Bottom** layout to the clip art.

17. Position the insertion point in front of the second subheading (on page 2).

18. Tap ⎡Enter⎤ and then position the insertion point on the blank line.

19. Use the **Online Pictures** 🖼️ feature and the Office.com Clip Art search box to search for **airplane**.

20. Insert the image shown (or a similar one).

21. Resize the image to approximately **2 inches** wide.

22. Place the same border color around the image as that used for the hotel image, and use a **3-pt line weight**.

23. Position the insertion point on the blank line at the end of the document and type this text:
Thanks to our loyal Universal Corporate Events clients!

24. Tap [Enter].

25. Format the line you just typed with **Bold 14 pt**. Then, position the insertion point on the blank line below that line.

26. Use the **Online Pictures**  feature and the **Office.com Clip Art search box** to search for **travel**.

27. Insert the image shown (or a similar one).

The image should be approximately 2" wide and 2" high. If you chose another image, you may need to resize it.

28. Rotate the image to the left approximately **45 degrees**.

Use Newsletter-Style Columns

29. Scroll to **page 1** and position the insertion point in the text below the section break.

30. Lay out the text in two columns with a line between the columns, and then delete the paragraph symbol at the top of the left column.

31. Scroll to **page 3** and position the insertion point in front of the line shown here.

32. Insert a column break, and then turn off formatting marks.

33. Save and close the file; exit **Word**.

34. Submit your final file based on the guidelines provided by your instructor.

To see examples of how your file or files should look at the end of this exercise, go to the student resource center.

Use Building Blocks, Themes, Style Sets, and Drop Caps

In this exercise, you will use one of Word's built-in Building Blocks and create and modify a custom Building Block. You will change the look of your document with a new Theme and Style Set, and you will add a drop cap. Finally, you will use different views and zoom magnifications.

Use Building Blocks

1. Start **Word**. Open **WD08-A02-Merger** from your **WD2013 Lesson 08** folder and save it as **WD08-A02-Merger-[FirstInitialLastName]**.

2. If necessary, choose **Home→Paragraph→Show/Hide** ¶ to display formatting marks.

3. Position the insertion point on the blank line at the top of the left column on page 1.

4. Insert the **Grid Quote** from the **Building Blocks Organizer**, and then type the two lines of text shown in the Grid Quote text box. (The text you type will be capitalized automatically. That's part of the Grid Quote built-in format.)

   Universal Corporate Events
   January Newsletter

5. If necessary, position the Building Block so it aligns with the text at the top of the right-hand column.

6. Delete the extra paragraph symbol below the Building Block.
   Now you will create a custom Building Block.

7. Position the insertion point on the blank line at the bottom of the right-hand column on **page 2**.

8. Type the following:

   Contact us to help you with your corporate travel needs.
   Universal Corporate Events
   123 Highland Avenue
   Chicago, IL 60657

9. Select the three address lines and remove the after-paragraph spacing.

10. Select the text you typed in **step 8** and save it to the **Quick Part Gallery** as **uce**.

11. Delete the highlighted text in your document, tap Enter to create a blank line, and test your Building Block.

12. Modify your Building Block by adding **Suite 2100** at the end of the street address. Use **uce** as the Building Block name again.

13. Delete the Building Block in the document.

14. Test the Building Block. When you're satisfied that it is working as indicated, delete it from the Building Block Organizer so the next student will have the same experience.

15. Leave the updated Building Block at the bottom of the right-hand column on page 2.

Use Themes and Style Sets and Insert a Drop Cap

16. Use **Live Preview** to preview several different Themes and Style Sets.

17. Apply the **Retrospect** Theme to your document.

18. Apply the **Lines (Distinctive)** Style Set.

19. Select the *G* in the first line of the main article and apply a drop cap in the paragraph, not the margin.

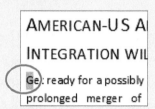

The drop cap is a little too large for the small paragraph, so next you will specify fewer lines for the cap to drop.

20. Make sure the drop cap is selected.

21. Open the **Drop Cap dialog box** using the command shown and change the number of lines to drop to **2**.

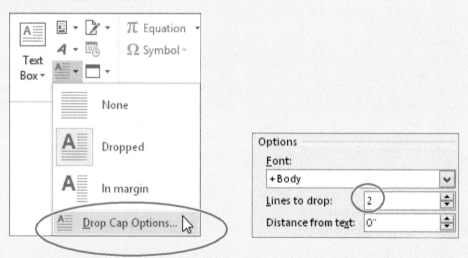

Now that all the formatting is complete, it is a good time to balance the columns on page 2.

22. Position the insertion point at the beginning of the third line of the paragraph shown here (page 2).

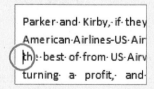

23. Insert a **column break**.

Work with Views and Use Zoom Controls

24. Use the **Read Mode** 📖 button on the status bar to view your document with side-by-side pages.

25. View the entire document by using the arrows on the left and right side of the window.

26. Click the **Web Layout** 📰 button on the status bar and scroll to see how the document appears.

27. Use the **View** tab to switch back to **Print Layout** 📄 view.

28. Drag the **Zoom control** on the Zoom bar to set the magnification at **60%**.

29. Click the **Zoom** 🔍 button on the View tab to open the Zoom dialog box. Use the **Many Pages** option to view two pages.

30. Click the **100%** 🔲 button in the Zoom group of the View tab.

31. Turn off formatting marks. Save and close the file; exit **Word**. (If you are prompted to save changes to Building Blocks, click **Don't Save**.)

32. Submit your final file based on the guidelines provided by your instructor.

    To see examples of how your file or files should look at the end of this exercise, go to the student resource center.

APPLY YOUR SKILLS WD08-A03

Create a Columnar Newsletter

In this exercise, you will create a newsletter using columns, graphic elements, Building Blocks, Themes, and Style Sets. Then you will observe your document using various views and zoom magnifications.

Use Section Breaks and WordArt

1. Start **Word**. Open **WD08-A03-TravelTech** from your **WD2013 Lesson 08** folder and save it as `WD08-A03-TravelTech-[FirstInitialLastName]`.

2. If necessary, choose **Home→Paragraph→Show/Hide** ¶ to display formatting marks.

3. Position the insertion point on the third blank line at the top of the document and insert a **continuous section break**.

4. Position the insertion point on the blank line above the section break and type `Universal Corporate Events`.

5. Select the text, and then open the **WordArt gallery**.

6. Choose **Fill – Black, Text 1, Outline – Background 1, Hard Shadow - Accent 1**.

7. Use the smart tag Layout Options to apply **Top and Bottom wrapping**.

8. With the WordArt selected, apply the **Chevron Up** text effect in the Transform category.

Insert and Format Clip Art

9. Position the insertion point at the end of the first paragraph and tap [Enter].

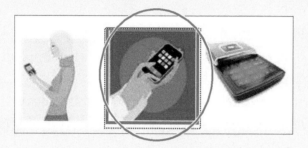

Dear·Corporate·Travel·Agents,¶

Technology·and·mobile·devices·are·more·i
BreakingTravelNews.com·highlights·the·co
Travel·Technology·exhibition·in·Berlin.¶

10. Use **Online Pictures** 🖼️ and **Office.com Clip Art** to search for **mobile device**.

11. Choose the image shown. (If you can't locate this image, choose a similar one.)

12. If necessary, turn on the ruler. Resize the image to approximately **1½ inches wide** and **1½ inches tall**.

13. With the image selected, use **Picture Effects** 🔳 to apply **Offset Left** in the Shadow category.

14. Crop the image from the left to approximately the point shown.

15. Click in the document to turn off the cropping handles.

16. Apply transparent color to the light blue circle in the image. (If you chose a different image, just use the feature for the experience.)
    This did not improve the appearance.

17. Click **Undo** ↩️.

Use Newsletter-Style Columns and Building Blocks

18. Apply a **three-column layout** to the body of the newsletter, using lines between columns.

19. Delete the extra paragraph symbol at the top of the first column on the first page.
    Next, you will balance the columns on the second page.

20. Position the insertion point in the second paragraph of the left column (on page 2) and insert a column break, as shown here.

> The·supporting·programme·
> of·the·eTravel·World·(Hall·
> 7.1.c·from·6·to·9·March)·with·
> more·than·50·papers·and·
> workshops·presented·on·two·
> stages·provides·numerous·
> answers·to·these·questions.·
> Topic·headings·at·the·many·
> forums·include·Social·Travel·

21. Position the insertion point in the second paragraph of the right-hand column (on page 2) and insert a column break, as shown here.

> "To·pivot,·or·not·to·pivot,·that·
> is·the·question"·is·the·title·of·
> the·PhoCusWright@ITB·event·

22. Position the insertion point on the second blank line at the bottom of the third column.

23. Insert the **Semaphore Quote** text box from the Building Block Organizer. (You may need to widen the Name column in the organizer to see the full name.)

24. Type the following in the text box. (The text will be capitalized automatically; this is a characteristic of this particular Building Block.)

    Contact Universal Corporate Events at 415-555-1234 to discuss using mobile devices to meet your travel needs.

25. Center the text in the Building Block.

26. Drag the Building Block below the text and center it between the margins.

Use a Theme and a Style Set

27. Open the **Themes** gallery and choose **Retrospect**.

28. Scroll through the document and observe the impact.

29. Open the **Style Set** gallery and choose **Basic (Stylish)** in the Built-In section.

30. Apply a drop cap (Dropped, not In Margin) to the first letter of the main article (page 1, left column).

31. Make any positioning adjustments of graphic images, and insert/delete any column breaks that you deem necessary.

Use Views and Zoom Controls

32. Turn off formatting marks.

33. Use the **View** tab to observe your document in the following views: **Draft**, **Web Layout**, and **Read Mode**.

34. Use the arrows on the sides of the Read Mode window to scroll through the document.

35. Use the button on the status bar to change to **Print Layout** ▤ view.

36. Click the **Multiple Pages** ▦ button on the View tab and observe the effect.

37. Use the **Zoom controls** on the status bar to return the document to **100%.**

38. Save and close the file; exit **Word**. (If you are prompted to save changes to Building Blocks, click **Don't Save**.)

39. Submit your final file based on the guidelines provided by your instructor.

Extend Your Skills

In the course of working through the Extend Your Skills exercises, you will think critically as you use the skills taught in the lesson to complete the assigned projects. To evaluate your mastery and completion of the exercises, your instructor may use a rubric, with which more points are allotted according to performance characteristics. (The more you do, the more you earn!) Ask your instructor how your work will be evaluated.

WD08-E01 That's the Way I See It

As a small-business owner, you want to keep your customers interested in what you're doing, so you decide to send out monthly newsletters. Determine the type of business you own and then place a WordArt object with your company's name at the top of a new document. The object should span between the margins (one column). Conduct online research related to your type of business to find information you think will be of interest to your customers. Pull the information into your document, remembering to cite your sources. Lay it out in newsletter-style columns. Insert an image that relates to the content, and use a style from the Picture Styles gallery to enhance the image. Create a custom Building Block that contains contact information for your business, and place it at the end of your newsletter. Place headings within the newsletter, and format them with Word heading styles. Apply a Theme and Style Set of your choice, and insert a drop cap at the beginning of the body text. Be sure to delete your custom Building Block when you are finished so the next student to use the computer will have the same experience. Save your newsletter in your **WD2013 Lesson 08** folder as **WD08-E01-BizLtr-[FirstInitialLastName]**.

You will be evaluated based on the inclusion of all elements specified, your ability to follow directions, your ability to apply newly learned skills to a real-world situation, your creativity, and the relevance of your topic and/or data choice(s). Submit your final file based on the guidelines provided by your instructor.

WD08-E02 Be Your Own Boss

As the owner of Blue Jean Landscaping, you decide to keep in touch with customers by distributing a newsletter. Start a new document, and save it to your **WD2013 Lesson 08** folder as **WD08-E02-Landscape-[FirstInitialLastName]**.

Place the company name at the top of the newsletter using a WordArt style. Insert a continuous section break after the WordArt. Search online for decorative plants and shrubs that can be used for landscaping. Pull in the results of your research as the primary content for the newsletter, ensuring you cite your sources. Format the text in newsletter-style columns.

Insert a picture or clip art image that reflects the newsletter content. Place a three-point border on the images, using a color of your choice. Place a Building Block text box containing contact information at the top of the newsletter. Then, insert headings in the document body formatted with Word heading styles. Apply a Theme and Style Set of your choice. Finally, insert a drop cap at the beginning of the main article.

You will be evaluated based on the inclusion of all elements specified, your ability to follow directions, your ability to apply newly learned skills to a real-world situation, your creativity, and your demonstration of an entrepreneurial spirit. Submit your final file based on the guidelines provided by your instructor.

Transfer Your Skills

In the course of working through the Transfer Your Skills exercises, you will use critical-thinking and creativity skills to complete the assigned projects using skills taught in the lesson. To evaluate your mastery and completion of the exercises, your instructor may use a rubric, with which more points are allotted according to performance characteristics. (The more you do, the more you earn!) Ask your instructor how your work will be evaluated.

WD08-T01 Use the Web as a Learning Tool

Throughout this book, you will be provided with an opportunity to use the Internet as a learning tool by completing WebQuests. According to the original creators of WebQuests, as described on their website (WebQuest.org), a WebQuest is "an inquiry-oriented activity in which most or all of the information used by learners is drawn from the web." To complete the WebQuest projects in this book, navigate to the student resource center for this book and choose the WebQuest for the lesson on which you are currently working. The subject of each WebQuest will be relevant to the material found in the lesson.

WebQuest Subject: Exploring newsletter formatting.

Submit your final file(s) based on the guidelines provided by your instructor.

WD08-T02 Demonstrate Proficiency

Stormy BBQ keeps its customer engaged through a monthly newsletter. This month's newsletter will be about how you cook your barbeque dishes and monthly specials. Conduct online research to gather the primary content for your newsletter, ensuring you cite your sources. Place the name of the business at the top of the newsletter, formatting it with WordArt. Insert a section break to separate the WordArt from the main article. Format the newsletter in columns with a line between. Insert pictures or clip art that enhance your message. Place a text box Building Block at the end of the newsletter that contains the winning recipe from last month's barbeque sauce contest. Insert headings within the newsletter that are formatted with Word heading styles, and apply a Theme and Style Set of your choice. Format the first letter of the main content with a drop cap. Practice viewing your newsletter in various views and zoom magnifications. Save your newsletter in your **WD2013 Lesson 08** folder as **WD08-T02-BBQ-[FirstInitialLastName]**.

Submit your final file based on the guidelines provided by your instructor.

Creating a Promotional Brochure and a Form

LEARNING OBJECTIVES

After studying this lesson, you will be able to:

- Use shapes to add graphic interest
- Work with SmartArt graphics
- Add page borders and background page color
- Create online forms using form fields

In this lesson, you will add graphic elements to a brochure, such as shapes, which add visual appeal. SmartArt graphics provide a gallery of predesigned diagrams like lists, processes, cycles, hierarchies, and relationships that communicate ideas clearly and vividly. Borders and page color add zing to your brochure. Live preview galleries allow you to quickly test many choices while deciding what looks best for your brochure. You will also create an online registration form that can conveniently be filled out electronically.

Promoting an Ergonomics Seminar

green clean

As the owner of Ergonomic Office Solutions, you have decided to create a presentation about the benefits of using ergonomic office equipment. Your friend, Tommy Choi, owner of Green Clean, has provided you with his customer database. Knowing Tommy's customers are already interested in the environment, you believe they would be interested in your products. You decide to create a brochure to mail to local businesses promoting a seminar. You will use product pictures as well as Word's shapes and SmartArt to create a brochure that is both informative and visually appealing. You will also create an online registration form that prospective customers can use to enroll in the seminar. You know that Word's powerful form tools will make it easy to create the form.

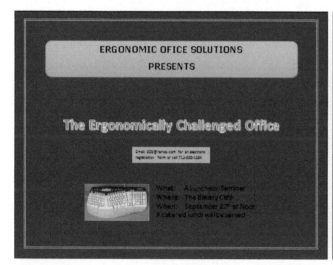 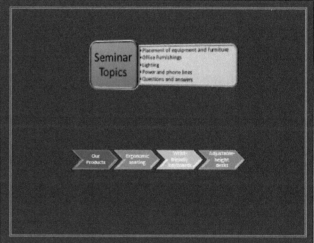

Shapes and pictures add visual interest, and SmartArt graphics engage the reader.

Contact information		2/12/2013
Name	Eugene Washington	
Phone	712-555-4321	
Email	eugene@yahoo.com	

Will you attend the seminar?   Yes ☒ No ☐

What product(s) are you most interested in?
Ergonomic seating

Would you like to receive our newsletter?
Yes ☒ No ☐

Would you like a free equipment consultation?
Yes ☒ No ☐

Word forms make it easy to enroll in the seminar.

Working with Shapes

Video Library http://labyrinthelab.com/videos Video Number: WD13-V0901

Word has a large gallery of graphic shapes, including lines, text boxes, rectangles, ovals, and many others. They can add interest to documents such as flyers and brochures, and you can type text in most shapes. You insert shapes from the Shapes gallery. After you choose a shape, the mouse pointer changes to a crosshair icon resembling a plus sign (+), which you click or drag in the document to create the shape.

FROM THE RIBBON

Insert→Illustrations→
Shapes

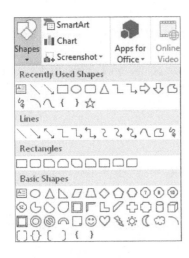

Rotating, Resizing, and Moving Shapes

Clicking a shape displays the handles, which are similar to handles you've seen on other images. You use them to move, resize, or rotate shapes. You can insert a perfect square or circle in one of two ways: by choosing the rectangle or oval tool and clicking in the document, or by holding down Shift while drawing the shape.

The mouse pointer changes shape depending on the action performed or the handle the pointer rests on.

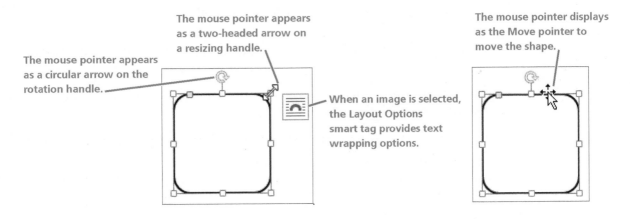

The mouse pointer appears as a circular arrow on the rotation handle.

The mouse pointer appears as a two-headed arrow on a resizing handle.

When an image is selected, the Layout Options smart tag provides text wrapping options.

The mouse pointer displays as the Move pointer to move the shape.

Word 2013

Task	Procedure
Insert a perfect square	Choose the rectangle shape, and then click in the document; or, hold [Shift] while dragging in the document.
Insert a perfect circle	Choose the oval shape, and then click in the document; or, hold [Shift] while dragging in the document.
Maintain an object's proportions	Hold [Shift] while dragging a corner resizing handle.
Add text in a shape	Select the shape, and then begin typing.
Select multiple shapes	Hold [Shift] and click each object.
Align multiple objects	Select objects using [Shift], choose Format→Arrange→Align Objects, and choose the desired alignment.
Move an object	Select the object, position the mouse pointer on a border to display the Move pointer, and drag the object as desired.

DEVELOP YOUR SKILLS WD09-D01

Draw, Size, Rotate, and Move Shapes

In this exercise, you will draw different shapes and size, rotate, delete, and move shapes.

1. Open **WD09-D01-Brochure** from your **WD2013 Lesson 09** folder and save it as **WD09-D01-Brochure-[FirstInitialLastName]**.

   Replace the bracketed text with your first initial and last name. For example, if your name is Bethany Smith, your filename would look like this: WD09-D01-Brochure-BSmith.

2. Choose **Design→Document Formatting→Themes** [Aa], and then choose **Office**.

   The change of Theme won't be apparent until you enter more content. Now you will experiment with and insert a shape.

3. Choose **Insert→Illustrations→Shapes** ⬦ to display the Shapes gallery.

4. Choose the **Rounded Rectangle** from the **Rectangles** section.

5. Click and drag anywhere in the document to draw a rounded rectangle.

   The rectangle has a blue fill color, which is related to the Office theme you chose.

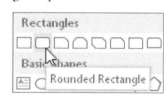

6. Choose **Drawing Tools→Format→Insert Shapes→Shapes** ⬦, and then choose the **Rounded Rectangle** again.

7. Hold the [Shift] key and drag to draw a rounded rectangle that's larger than the last one.

   Notice that this time you drew a perfect square with rounded corners instead of a rectangle, even though you started with the same shape. This happened because you held down the [Shift] key while drawing.

Resize and Rotate Shapes

8. With the square shape selected (displaying handles), follow these steps to resize the shape using the handles:

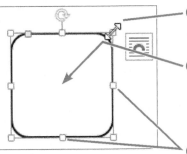

Ⓐ Position the mouse pointer on this sizing handle.

Ⓑ Press Shift and drag diagonally toward the center of the shape to resize while maintaining proportions.

Ⓒ Drag from a side handle to change only the length or width of the object.

Ⓓ Click **Undo** so the shape is a square again.

9. Follow these steps to rotate the square:

Ⓐ Position the mouse pointer on the rotation handle; the pointer appears as a circular arrow.

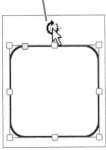

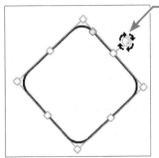

Ⓑ Drag to the right about 45 degrees; the mouse pointer appears as four small arrows when dragging.

10. Experiment with rotation in the opposite direction.

   Next you will delete your practice shapes. You must select a shape before you can delete it.

11. Click one of the shapes to display the handles, and then hold Shift and click the other shape.

Holding Shift allows you to select multiple shapes at once. Then you can delete, move, or format them all at once.

12. Tap Delete to remove both shapes.

Draw a Shape for Your Brochure

13. If necessary, choose **View→Show→Ruler** to display the ruler.

   The Ruler will be helpful in sizing your shape.

14. Choose **Insert→Illustrations→Shapes** 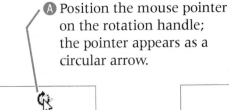.

15. Choose **Rounded Rectangle** from the Shapes gallery. Starting about 1 inch from the top of the page, draw a wide rectangle at the top margin that spans across the page but remains within the margins. It should be about 1¼ inches high.

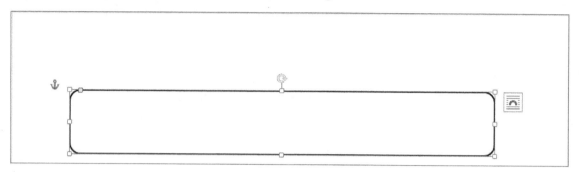

16. Follow these steps to move the shape:

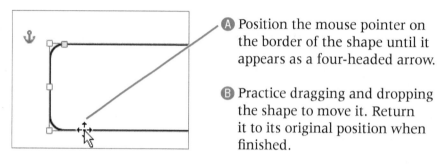

Ⓐ Position the mouse pointer on the border of the shape until it appears as a four-headed arrow.

Ⓑ Practice dragging and dropping the shape to move it. Return it to its original position when finished.

17. Save your file and leave it open.

Adding and Formatting Text in Shapes

Video Library   http://labyrinthelab.com/videos   Video Number: WD13-V0902

You can add text to the shapes you draw. This can be handy if, for example, you want to create a flyer announcing an event. Just select the shape and begin typing. Text is automatically centered, both horizontally and vertically, and it wraps within a shape as you type.

A shape can have either a dotted-line or solid-line border. When the border is a dotted line, you can edit the text. Clicking the dotted-line border changes it to a solid-line border. This means the entire object is selected, and you can change settings that affect everything within the shape.

Formatting Shapes

When a shape is selected, Word provides a contextual Format tab, which contains many tools you can use to add pizzazz to the shape, including shape Styles, Shadow Effects, and 3-D Effects. The Format tab also has its own Insert Shapes gallery containing the same shapes as the Shapes gallery located in the Illustrations group on the Insert tab. When multiple shapes are selected, you can format, resize, or move them simultaneously.

Add Text and Format Text and Shapes

In this exercise, you will add text to a shape and format the text, and then you will format the shape.

1. Save your file as **WD09-D02-Brochure-[FirstInitialLastName]**.

2. If necessary, select the rectangle shape at the top margin.

3. Tap [Caps Lock], type **ERGONOMIC OFFICE SOLUTIONS**, tap [Enter], and type **PRESENTS**. *Notice that the text was automatically centered in the shape.*

4. Click the border of the shape, taking care not to drag.

Selecting a shape by the border selects everything inside the shape. Thus, the text in the shape is selected, although it is not highlighted.

5. Choose **Home→Font→Font menu ▼,** and then choose **Tahoma**.

6. Keep the shape selected and apply **Bold 22 pt** font.

7. If your shape is not big enough for the larger text, drag a sizing handle to enlarge it. *Next, you will use the Shape Styles gallery to format the shape.*

8. Make sure the object is selected so the contextual Format tab is available.

9. Choose **Drawing Tools→Format→Shape Styles**.

10. Follow these steps to format the shape:

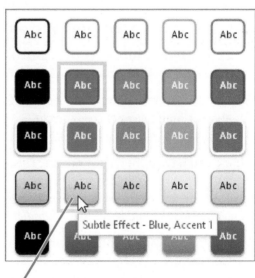

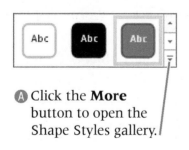

Ⓐ Click the **More** button to open the Shape Styles gallery.

Ⓑ Choose **Subtle Effect – Blue, Accent 1**.

11. Save your file.

Word 2013

Aligning Objects

Video Library   http://labyrinthelab.com/videos   Video Number: WD13-V0903

You can drag and drop objects to align them, but using the Align Objects feature on the contextual Format tab is more precise. You select the objects you want to align and then choose the desired alignment.

DEVELOP YOUR SKILLS WD09-D03
Align Objects

In this exercise, you will add a WordArt object and align it with a shape. You will insert a picture into a preexisting table, and format and move the table.

1. Save your file as **WD09-D03-Brochure-[FirstInitialLastName]**.
2. Click in the document below the rectangle.
3. Choose **Insert→Text→Insert WordArt** 🄰.
4. Choose **Fill – Blue, Accent 1, Outline – Background 1, Hard Shadow – Accent1**, and then type **The Ergonomically Challenged Office**.
5. Place the mouse pointer on the border of the WordArt object, and then drag to position it about 1 inch below the rectangle.

   Don't worry about centering it below the shape; you will align the objects in the next steps.

Align Objects

6. With the WordArt object still selected, hold down ⌷Shift⌷ and click **Round Rectangle**.

   Both objects should be selected—handles appear on both.

7. Choose **Drawing Tools→Format→Arrange→Align Objects** 🄴, and then choose **Align Center**.

   This center-aligns the objects with each other.

8. If necessary, drag the selected objects so they are centered between the margins.
9. Click in the document to deselect the objects.

Insert a Picture in the Brochure

10. Scroll down, and position the insertion point in the left cell of the table.

11. Choose **Insert→Illustrations→Pictures** .

12. Navigate to the **WD2013 Lesson 09** folder and double-click the **WD09-D03-Keyboard** file to insert it.

13. Using the left margin area, click to select the table row.

14. Position the mouse pointer on the line between the two cells and double-click to resize both columns to their best fit.

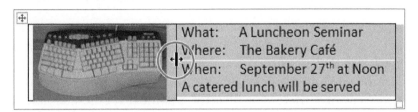

15. Position the mouse pointer on the table's **move handle** , and then drag to the right to center the table under the other objects.

16. If necessary, select the table again. Then, choose **Home→Paragraph→Borders** menu ▼.

17. Choose **No Border** to complete the page.

ERGONOMIC OFFICE SOLUTIONS

PRESENTS

The Ergonomically Challenged Office

What:	A Luncheon Seminar
Where:	The Bakery Café
When:	September 27th at Noon
A catered lunch will be served	

18. If gridlines appear in the table (although they won't print), follow these steps to remove them. Otherwise, go to the next step.

   ■ Make sure the table is selected.
   ■ Choose **Table Tools→Layout→Table→View Gridlines** ☒.

19. Save your file.

Working with Text Boxes

Video Library http://labyrinthelab.com/videos   Video Number: WD13-V0904

A text box is a special type of shape designed for you to insert text or graphics. You may wonder how inserting a text box is different from drawing a shape and adding text inside it. It's because of the formatting. For example, when you apply a theme to a document, the theme includes formatting such as fill and line colors for shapes. Text boxes do not contain those formatting characteristics; you type in it, there is no fill color, and the text entered is left-aligned, starting at the top of the box. You can format all of the text by selecting the text box itself, or format only a portion of the text by selecting the part you want to change.

Adding a Text Box

A text box tool appears in the Shapes gallery as shown in the following illustration.

As with other shapes, you either click to place a text box in the document or drag it to the desired size. You can also use the Text Box gallery in the Text group (Insert tab) to draw a text box or choose a preformatted one from the gallery. If you insert the text box by clicking in the document, the text box widens to the edge of the paper as you type and then begins to wrap the text. However, if you drag to draw the text box, it remains the same size. But you can resize with a sizing handle if needed.

Formatting a Text Box

You can format a text box just like any other object. You must select the text box before you can change the line surrounding it, change the fill color, resize it, or perform any other options available on the contextual Format tab.

QUICK REFERENCE	WORKING WITH TEXT BOXES
Task	**Procedure**
Insert a text box	Choose Insert→Illustrations→Shapes→Text Box, and then click in the document or drag to draw to the desired size; or, choose Insert→Text→Text Box and choose a preformatted text box or choose Draw Text Box.
Format a text box	Select the text box and choose the desired formatting commands from the Format tab.

Work with Text Boxes

In this exercise, you will insert a text box, reposition it, and format the text within it.

1. Save your file as **WD09-D04-Brochure-[FirstInitialLastName]**.

2. Choose **Insert→Illustrations→Shapes** ⬡, and then choose **Text Box** 🔤 from the Shapes gallery.

3. Position the mouse pointer below the WordArt object, and then drag to draw a text box about **2¾ inches wide** and **½ inch tall**.

4. Type the text shown here. If necessary, size the text box so the text wrapping is the same as that shown.

> Email EOS@Yahoo.com for an electronic
> registration form or call 712-555-1234.

5. If the email address appears as a hyperlink, click in the hyperlink, and then right-click it and choose **Remove Hyperlink**.

   Now you'll format the text box.

6. Make sure the text box is selected.

7. Choose **Drawing Tools→Format→Shape Styles→Shape Outline** 🖊 and choose **No Outline**.

8. Choose **Drawing Tools→Format→Shape Styles→Shape Fill** 🎨 and choose **Blue, Accent 1, Lighter 40%**.

9. With the text box still selected, hold down [Shift] and select the two objects above it.

10. Choose **Drawing Tools→Format→Arrange→Align Objects** 📐 and choose **Align Center**.

11. Click in the document to deselect the three objects.

12. Save your file.

Working with SmartArt

Video Library   http://labyrinthelab.com/videos   Video Number: WD13-V0905

It's often easier to grasp concepts if information is presented graphically rather than textually. Word provides a large variety of SmartArt graphics that you can add to documents. They make it easy to combine predesigned graphics with text to create sophisticated figures. The SmartArt Graphic dialog box contains a large array of graphic images.

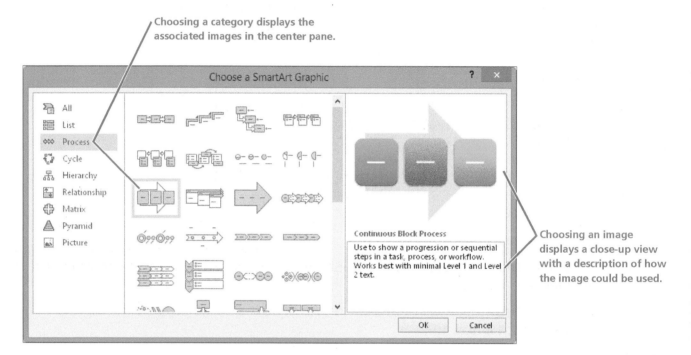

Choosing a category displays the associated images in the center pane.

Choosing an image displays a close-up view with a description of how the image could be used.

SmartArt Categories

SmartArt images are divided into the following categories:

Category	Purpose
List	Shows nonsequential data
Process	Shows steps in a process or progression
Cycle	Shows a continual process
Hierarchy	Creates a hierarchical structure or shows a decision tree
Relationship	Illustrates associations
Matrix	Shows how parts relate to a whole
Pyramid	Shows proportional relationships
Picture	Used when you want to convey your message with or without explanatory text, or when you want to use pictures to complement a list or process

Using the SmartArt Text Pane

You use a SmartArt text pane to add text to your image. When you insert the image, the text pane may or may not be open. If the pane is not open, click the tab that appears on the left side of the image. The same tab closes the text pane. The [Text] placeholders are replaced with the text you enter in the SmartArt text pane.

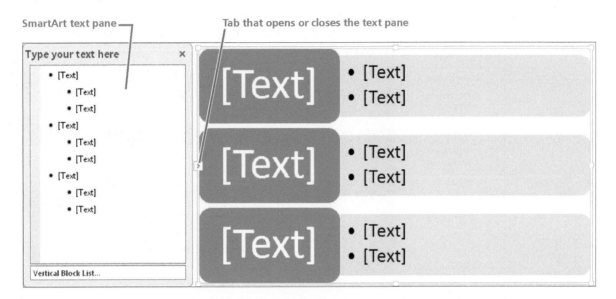

SmartArt text pane

Tab that opens or closes the text pane

You type in a bulleted list in the Type Your Text Here pane as shown in the preceding illustration. As you type, the text is added to the image. Word adjusts the font size based on the amount of information you type.

You can also type directly in the graphic, just like typing in a shape.

Modifying SmartArt

If you cannot find the exact image you want, you can modify, add, and delete shapes within the graphic. SmartArt objects are formatted in the same way as other graphic shapes.

As you enter and format text here, it appears in the graphic.

You can select objects within a graphic if you wish to format or resize them separately.

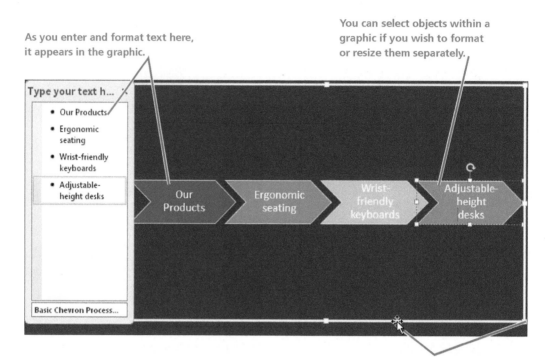

You can position the mouse pointer on the border to display the move handle, or you can drag a handle to resize.

QUICK REFERENCE	USING SMARTART
Task	**Procedure**
Insert a SmartArt image	Choose Insert→Illustrations→SmartArt, select the desired category, choose the desired object, and click OK.
Add text to a SmartArt object	If necessary, click the tab on the left side of the image, use the text pane to add text to the object, or type directly in the shape.
Apply a SmartArt Style	Choose SmartArt Tools→Design→SmartArt Styles and choose the desired style.

Insert SmartArt

In this exercise, you will use two SmartArt graphics: one to list the seminar topics and one to list the ergonomic products. You will customize and resize the graphics.

1. Save your file as **WD09-D05-Brochure-[FirstInitialLastName]**.

2. Press Ctrl + End to move the insertion point to the bottom of the document.

3. Press Ctrl + Enter to insert a page break.

4. Choose **Home→Paragraph→Center** ☰.
   Your image will be center-aligned when you insert it.

Insert SmartArt

5. Choose **Insert→Illustrations→SmartArt** 📊.

6. Follow these steps to insert a SmartArt object:

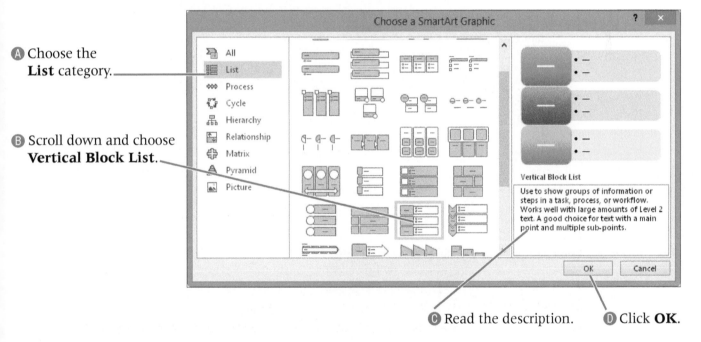

Ⓐ Choose the **List** category.

Ⓑ Scroll down and choose **Vertical Block List**.

Ⓒ Read the description.　Ⓓ Click **OK**.

7. If the text pane is not visible, click the tab.

Customize the Image

This image has three major text objects, but you will only use one.

8. Position the mouse pointer to the left of the first major bullet, and then drag down to select the first six bullets.

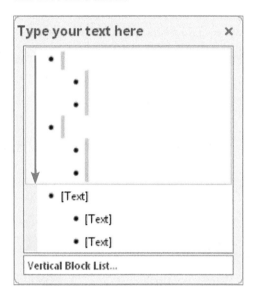

9. Tap ⬚Delete to remove the bullets.

10. Follow these steps to begin entering the seminar topics:

Ⓐ Position the insertion point to the right of the first bullet and type **Seminar Topics**.

Ⓑ Tap ↓ on the keyboard and type **Placement of equipment and furniture**.

Ⓒ Notice that the text appears in the graphic as you type.

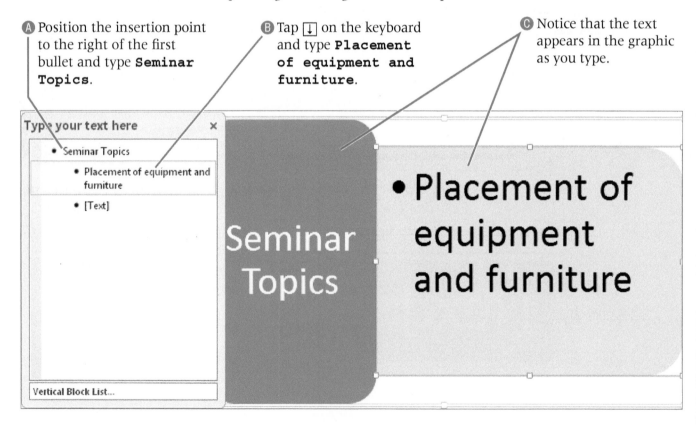

11. Tap ⬇ to go to the next line, and type **Office furnishings**.

12. Tap Enter to generate the next bullet, and then type **Lighting**.

13. Tap Enter as necessary, and then type the following items to complete the list:
    ■ **Power and phone lines**
    ■ **Questions and answers**

14. Click the **Close** × button in the upper-right corner of the Type Your Text Here pane.

15. Click the outside border frame to make sure the *entire* SmartArt image is selected.

    You will resize the SmartArt object next. If an object within *the main frame is selected, you could accidentally resize only a part of the SmartArt object. Clicking the outside border frame prevents that.*

16. Drag the bottom-center sizing handle up until the image is approximately half as tall as the original image.

17. Save your file.

Changing a SmartArt Style

Video Library   http://labyrinthelab.com/videos   Video Number: WD13-V0906

The SmartArt Styles gallery provides interesting variations of the original graphic. Live Preview lets you see the effect of the various styles without actually applying them.

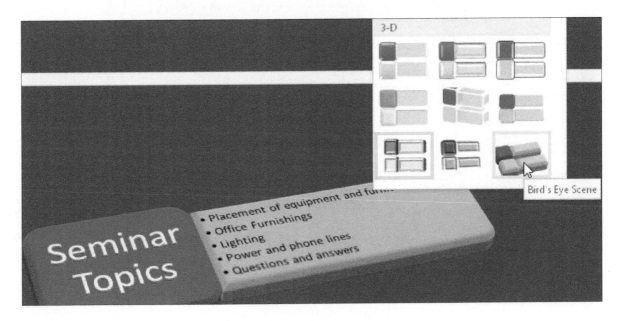

Apply a SmartArt Style

In this exercise, you will customize SmartArt graphics by applying colors and styles.

1. Save your file as **WD09-D06-Brochure-[FirstInitialLastName]**.

2. Make sure the SmartArt image is selected.

3. Choose **SmartArt Tools→Design→SmartArt Styles→Change Colors** .

4. In the Accent 1 category, choose **Gradient Loop – Accent 1**.

5. Choose **SmartArt Tools→Design→SmartArt Styles→More** ⊽ **button** to display the entire gallery.

6. In the 3-D category, choose **Metallic Scene**.
   Next you will add another SmartArt image.

7. Press ⌈Ctrl⌉+⌈End⌉ to move to the end of the document, and then tap ⌈Enter⌉ twice.

8. Choose **Insert→Illustrations→SmartArt** .

9. Follow these steps to insert the next image:

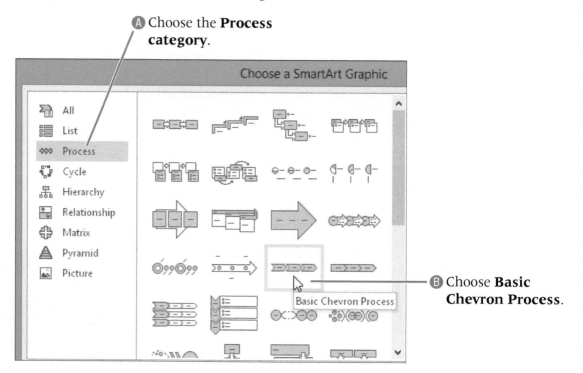

ⒶChoose the **Process category**.

ⒷChoose **Basic Chevron Process**.

10. Click **OK** to insert the image.

Type in the Graphic Image

11. Click the **[Text] placeholder** in the first arrow and type **Our products**.

    You can type directly in the image without opening the text pane.

12. Click in each arrow and enter the text shown in the following illustration.

13. With the image selected, follow these steps to add an arrow:

Ⓐ Click the tab to open the text pane.

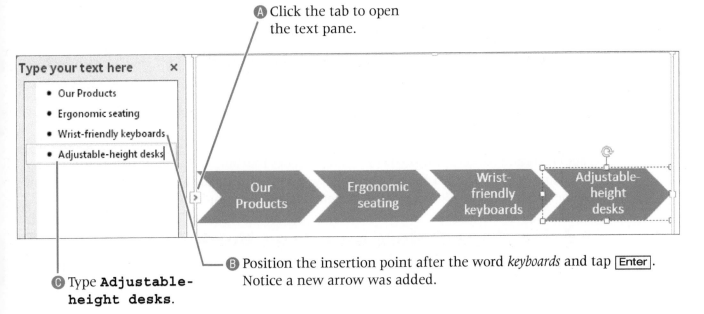

Ⓒ Type **Adjustable-height desks**.

Ⓑ Position the insertion point after the word *keyboards* and tap Enter. Notice a new arrow was added.

14. **Close** ⨯ the text pane.

Format the Image

15. With the shape selected, choose **SmartArt Tools→Design→SmartArt Styles→Change Colors**.

16. Choose the fourth item in the Accent 1 category, **Gradient Loop – Accent 1**.

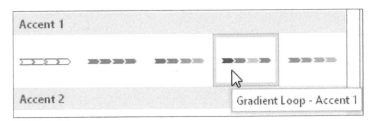

17. Click the **More** ⯆ button on the SmartArt Styles gallery. In the 3-D category, choose **Cartoon**.

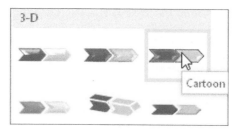

18. Click in the document to deselect the image.

19. Save the file.

Formatting the Page Background

Video Library   http://labyrinthelab.com/videos   Video Number: WD13-V0907

Word has great page background formats that add color and visual variety to your documents. Page colors and borders provide the finishing touches that add professional polish and pizzazz. For example, you can add colors from a gallery specifically designed to blend with a document's theme. Border theme colors are also designed to tastefully complement page colors.

Adding Page Colors and Page Borders

The Page Colors gallery is similar to other galleries you have worked with. The colors that appear in the Theme Colors section of the gallery, as the name implies, are based on the Theme currently in effect.

Page borders surround the outer edges of the entire page. You can adjust the color (again, based on the current Theme), line thickness, and other features of the border.

The Borders and Shading Dialog Box

This dialog box allows you to make settings similar to those you can set for paragraph borders.

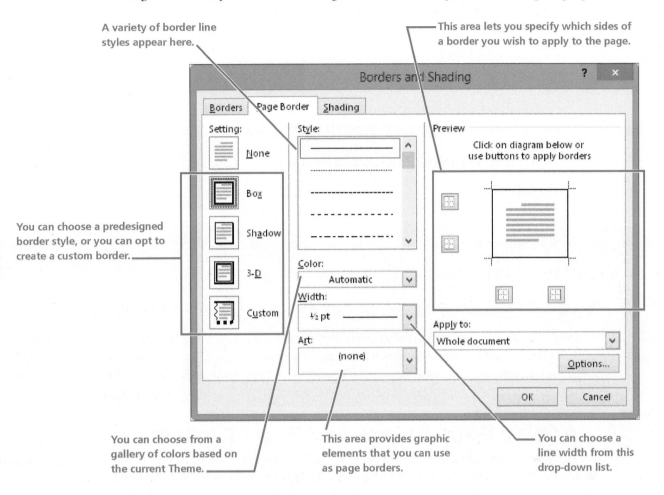

A variety of border line styles appear here.

This area lets you specify which sides of a border you wish to apply to the page.

You can choose a predesigned border style, or you can opt to create a custom border.

You can choose from a gallery of colors based on the current Theme.

This area provides graphic elements that you can use as page borders.

You can choose a line width from this drop-down list.

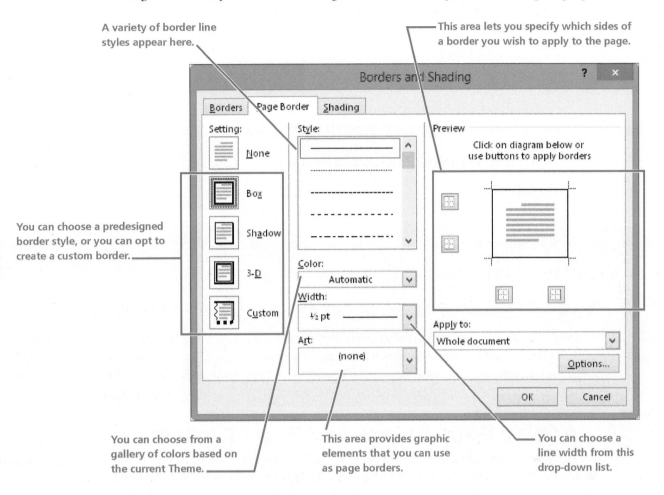

Borders and Shading

Borders   Page Border   Shading

Setting:

None

Box

Shadow

3-D

Custom

Style:

Color:
Automatic

Width:
½ pt

Art:
(none)

Preview

Click on diagram below or use buttons to apply borders

Apply to:
Whole document

Options...

OK   Cancel

Inserting a Watermark

A watermark is text or a graphic that is placed behind the text or other objects in a document; it is visible only in Page Layout or Read Mode view. Some common watermarks include a faint image of the word *Draft* or *Confidential* in the background.

This is an example of a watermark. Notice the word *Draft* in the background.

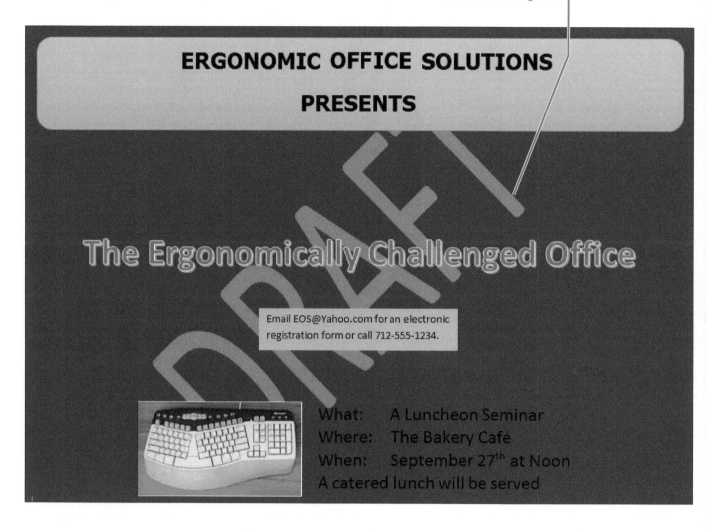

ERGONOMIC OFFICE SOLUTIONS

PRESENTS

The Ergonomically Challenged Office

Email EOS@Yahoo.com for an electronic registration form or call 712-555-1234.

What: A Luncheon Seminar
Where: The Bakery Café
When: September 27th at Noon
A catered lunch will be served

There are built-in text watermarks, or you can create your own custom text. A clip art image or picture can also be used as a watermark.

You can choose this option to insert a picture as a watermark.

You can customize a watermark with your own text.

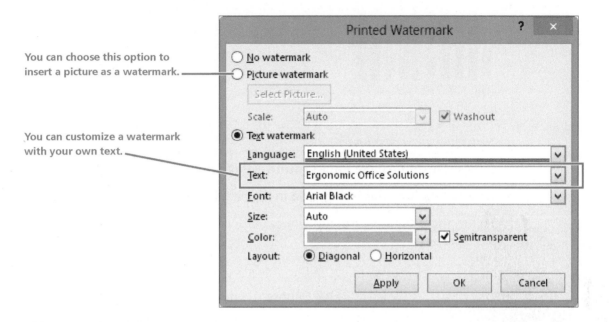

QUICK REFERENCE	FORMATTING PAGE BACKGROUNDS
Task	**Procedure**
Add a page color	■ Choose Design→Page Background→Page Color and choose the desired color.
Add a page border	■ Choose Design→Page Background→Page Borders and choose the desired style, color, width, and other options.
Add a watermark	■ Choose Design→Page Background→Watermark and choose the desired watermark or Custom Watermark.

DEVELOP YOUR SKILLS WD09-D07
Apply a Page Color, Page Border, and Watermark

In this exercise, you will add a background color to your brochure and a border surrounding the pages. Finally, you will add a Draft watermark to the document.

1. Save your file as **WD09-D07-Brochure-[FirstInitialLastName]**.

2. Choose **Design→Page Background→Page Color** .

3. Hover the mouse pointer over several colors in the Theme Colors area of the gallery, and Live Preview displays the effects of the different colors.

4. Choose the color in the fifth column, bottom row, **Blue**, **Accent 1**, **Darker 50%**.

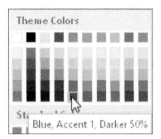

Now you'll add a page border.

5. Choose **Design→Page Background→Page Borders** .

6. Choose **Box** from the Setting area in the panel on the left.

7. Follow these steps to format the page border:

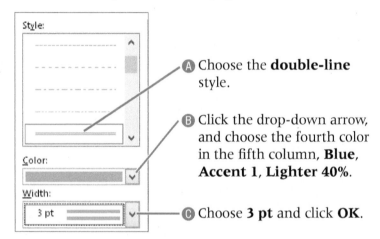

Ⓐ Choose the **double-line** style.

Ⓑ Click the drop-down arrow, and choose the fourth color in the fifth column, **Blue**, **Accent 1**, **Lighter 40%**.

Ⓒ Choose **3 pt** and click **OK**.

Now you will add a Draft watermark, and then finalize the document by removing it.

8. Choose **Design→Page Background→Watermark** , and then choose **Draft 1** from the gallery.

9. Scroll through the document to view the watermark, page border, and page color on both pages.

10. **Undo** to remove the watermark from the document.

11. Save and close your file.

Working with Forms

Video Library   http://labyrinthelab.com/videos   Video Number: WD13-V0908

Many organizations use forms to collect data. Forms contain both fields, where users enter information, and objects, such as checkboxes and drop-down lists, to assist users with data entry. With Word, you can easily set up forms to meet the needs of your organization and distribute them in any of the following formats:

- **Printed:** Printed forms are produced and filled out on paper.
- **Electronic:** Non-printed forms are distributed to Word users and filled out in Word. They are often available via a network or sent in an email.
- **Internet-Based:** These forms are posted to a website and filled out using a web browser. The data is stored in an electronic database. Word lets you set up forms and save them as web pages.

Setting Up Forms

You can set up forms using the same tools and techniques used to create any other type of document. However, tables are often used because they allow you to lay out forms with an orderly structure. Creating a form in a table is much easier than using tabs. Word also provides special form fields.

DEVELOP YOUR SKILLS WD09-D08
Set Up the Form

In this exercise, you will use a table as the basis for the form, and you'll add custom tab stops to align form fields. You will use the form to enroll prospective customers in The Ergonomically Challenged Office seminar.

1. Open **WD09-D08-Registration** from the **WD2013 Lesson 09** folder and save it as **WD09-D08-Registration-[FirstInitialLastName]**.

2. If necessary, click the **Show/Hide ¶** button to turn on formatting marks.

   The formatting marks make it easier for you to see exactly what you are doing in the form.

3. If necessary, choose **View→Show→Ruler** to display the ruler.

4. Check that Left Tab is active in the Tabs box. If not, click the **Tabs box** at the left end of the ruler until it displays a symbol that resembles an uppercase L.

   You will be setting left tabs in the form.

5. Click in the first table cell, and then follow these steps to begin adding text to the form:

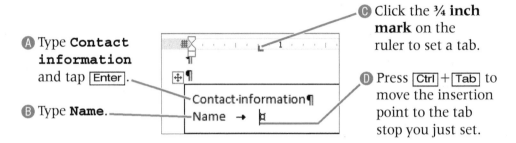

Ⓐ Type **Contact information** and tap ⌅Enter.

Ⓑ Type **Name**.

Ⓒ Click the **¾ inch mark** on the ruler to set a tab.

Ⓓ Press Ctrl + Tab to move the insertion point to the tab stop you just set.

You will insert a form field at this position in the next exercise.

Press Ctrl + Tab to move the insertion point *within* a cell; tap Tab to move the insertion point to the *next* cell.

6. Save your file.

Understanding Form Fields

Video Library http://labyrinthelab.com/videos Video Number: WD13-V0909

Fields in a form are made up of controls. There are three types of controls you can use in a form: content controls, legacy forms, and ActiveX controls. The type of document you are creating, and who will be using it, determine which control set to use in the form. See the following table for descriptions of each type of control.

FORM CONTROLS	
Type	**Description**
Content Controls	These controls were introduced in Word 2007. The group contains controls that did not exist in the legacy tools. These controls have limitations on data-restriction properties. For example, you can insert a Plain Text Content Control, but there is no option to limit the maximum length for the entry.
Legacy Forms	This older set of form fields is still available. This set does not include the newer controls, such as the Date Picker and Picture controls, but these fields can be used in any Word version and allow data restrictions to be set.
ActiveX Controls	This set of controls is reserved for documents used in a web page.

The Developer Tab

All three types of controls are found in the Developer tab, which does not appear on the Ribbon by default. You must activate it by placing a checkmark next to Developer in the Word Options dialog box, as shown in the following illustration. The three types of controls in the Developer tab appear on the right.

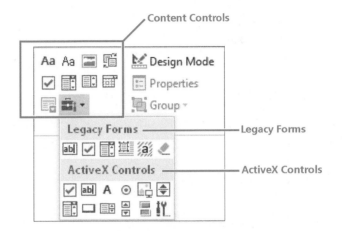

Content Controls

Legacy Forms

ActiveX Controls

QUICK REFERENCE	INSERTING FORM FIELDS
Task	Procedure
Insert a content control in a form	Choose Developer→Controls and choose the desired content control.
Insert a form field from the Legacy Tools	Choose Developer→Controls→Legacy Tools and choose the desired form field.

Using the Form

After you create the form, you must protect it in order to activate the form fields so users can enter data. You will protect the form later in the lesson.

DEVELOP YOUR SKILLS WD09-D09

Insert Form Fields

In this exercise, you will display the Developer tab. You will then use a combination of content controls and legacy forms controls to insert text fields, a date field, checkboxes, and drop-down fields in your document.

1. Save your file as **WD09-D09-Registration-[FirstInitialLastName]**.

2. Right-click the **Home** tab and choose **Customize the Ribbon**.

3. Place a checkmark in the **Developer** checkbox.

4. Click **OK** to display the Developer tab.

5. If necessary, click **Show/Hide** ¶ to turn on the formatting marks.

6. If necessary, position the insertion point at the ¾ **inch tab stop** in the second line of the first cell.

Insert Form Fields

All form fields in this form will come from the Legacy Forms controls, except the date field.

7. Choose **Developer→Controls**.

8. Follow these steps to insert a legacy Text Form Field:

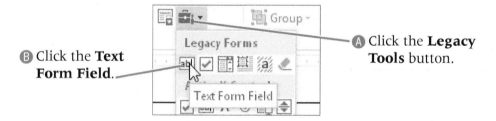

Ⓐ Click the **Legacy Tools** button.

Ⓑ Click the **Text Form Field**.

If formatting marks and shading are turned on, the form field displays small circles and shading.

9. If a shaded box is not visible, follow these steps; otherwise, go to the next step.
   - Choose **Developer→Controls→Legacy Tools** 🖹.
   - Choose **Form Field Shading** ⓐ.

10. Tap [Enter] and type **Phone**.

11. Press [Ctrl]+[Tab] and insert another **Text Form Field**.

12. Tap [Enter] and type **Email**.

13. Press [Ctrl]+[Tab] and insert another **Text Form Field**.

Insert a Content Control

14. Tap ⎣Tab⎦ to move to the next table cell.

15. Choose **Home→Paragraph→Align Right** ▤.

16. Choose **Developer→Controls→Date Picker Content Control** ⎚. (This is not a legacy tool.)

Your form should now look like the following illustration.

17. Save your file.

Using the Checkbox and Drop-Down List

Video Library   http://labyrinthelab.com/videos   Video Number: WD13-V0910

In addition to a Text Form Field, Word provides a Check Box Form Field and a Drop-Down Form Field. Drop-down fields allow you to enter specific choices to be displayed in a list, while checkboxes restrict answers to a yes/no type of response.

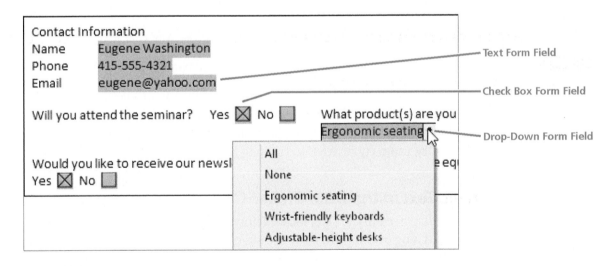

DEVELOP YOUR SKILLS WD09-D10
Add Checkboxes and Drop-Down Lists

In this exercise, you will continue adding form fields to the document, including checkboxes and drop-down lists.

1. Save your file as **WD09-D10-Registration-[FirstInitialLastName]**.

2. Position the insertion point in the first cell of the second row.

3. Type **Will you attend the seminar?**

4. Click the **2-inch mark** on the ruler to set a left tab and press Ctrl + Tab.

5. Type **Yes** and tap Spacebar twice.

6. Choose **Developer→Controls→Legacy Tools 🛠** and choose **Check Box Form Field ☑**.

7. Tap Spacebar twice, type **No**, and then tap Spacebar twice.

8. Insert another **Legacy Check Box Form Field ☑**.

9. Tap Tab to move to the next table cell.

10. Type **What product(s) are you most interested in?** and tap Enter.

11. Choose **Developer→Controls→Legacy Tools** then **Drop-Down Form Field 📋**.

12. Tap Tab to move to the next table cell.

13. Insert Legacy text and checkboxes in the last row as shown, tapping Enter and Spacebar as indicated.

Would·you·like·to·receive·our·newsletter?¶ Yes··☐··No··☐·¤	Would·you·like·a·free·equipment·consultation?¶ Yes··☐··No··☐·¤

14. Save your file.

Applying Field Properties

Video Library   http://labyrinthelab.com/videos   Video Number: WD13-V0911

Each field type has various form field properties associated with it. For example, you can restrict the type and set the maximum length for data entered in text fields. You can have Word automatically format a date to a particular format. Although you cannot prevent all errors during data entry, property restrictions help in that effort.

Modifying Text in the Date Picker Content Control and Legacy Fields

Default text is displayed in the Date Picker Content Control when you insert it. You can modify the default text by typing over it. When the form is used, the text in the control is replaced when the user selects the date from the calendar icon that appears when the user clicks the field's drop-down arrow.

Legacy fields use the form field options dialog boxes to modify properties. Options in the dialog boxes vary based on the field selected.

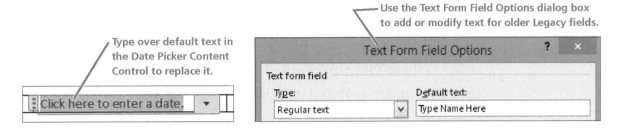

Type over default text in the Date Picker Content Control to replace it.

Use the Text Form Field Options dialog box to add or modify text for older Legacy fields.

Click here to enter a date.

QUICK REFERENCE	APPLYING FIELD PROPERTIES
Task	**Procedure**
Modify text in the Date Picker Content Control	■ Type over the text in the control.
Set field properties for legacy form fields	■ Select the field and choose Developer→Controls→Properties, or double-click the form field.
	■ Make the desired choices in the Form Field Options dialog box.

DEVELOP YOUR SKILLS WD09-D11
Set Field Properties

In this exercise, you will set field properties for the various field types and finish formatting the table.

1. Save your file as **WD09-D11-Registration-[FirstInitialLastName]**.

2. Follow these steps to add default instruction text to the Name field:

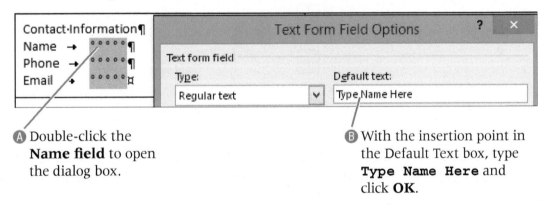

Ⓐ Double-click the **Name field** to open the dialog box.

Ⓑ With the insertion point in the Default Text box, type **Type Name Here** and click **OK**.

3. Use the same process to add text to the **Phone** and **Email** fields.
   ■ Phone: **Type Phone Number Here**
   ■ Email: **Type Email Address Here**

4. Select the default text in the date field at the top of the right-hand column and type **Click arrow; select today's date**.

Set List Properties

5. Double-click the field in the right-hand column of the second row.

6. Type **All** in the **Drop-Down Item box** and click **Add**.

7. Type **None** in the **Drop-Down Item box** and click **Add**.

8. Use the same process to add the remaining items to the list.

   - **Ergonomic seating**
   - **Wrist-friendly keyboards**
   - **Adjustable-height desks**

9. Click **OK**.

Finalize the Appearance of the Form

10. Select the table, choose **Home→Paragraph→Borders** 🔲 **menu ▼**, and choose **Borders and Shading**.

11. Follow these steps to format the borders:

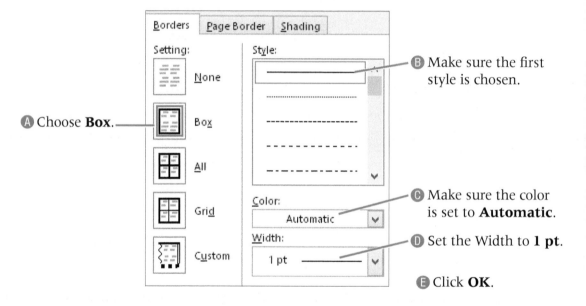

Ⓐ Choose **Box**.

Ⓑ Make sure the first style is chosen.

Ⓒ Make sure the color is set to **Automatic**.

Ⓓ Set the Width to **1 pt**.

Ⓔ Click **OK**.

12. If necessary, with the table selected, choose **Table Tools→Layout→Table→View Gridlines** to turn off gridlines.

13. If necessary, choose **Home→Paragraph→Show/Hide** ¶ to turn off formatting marks.

14. Choose **Developer→Controls→Legacy Tools→Form Field Shading** to turn off shading.

15. Save your file.

Protecting Forms

Video Library http://labyrinthelab.com/videos   Video Number: WD13-V0912

The Restrict Editing feature can prevent users from making changes other than in the form fields. Protecting forms also triggers the form fields to behave like form fields. For example, clicking a checkbox will insert or remove an X. You unprotect a form when designing or modifying it, and you protect it when you are ready to use it.

QUICK REFERENCE	PROTECTING FORMS
Task	**Procedure**
Protect a form	▪ Choose Developer→Protect→Restrict Editing.
	▪ In the Restrict Editing task pane, check the Allow Only This Type of Editing in the Document checkbox.
	▪ Choose Filling in Forms from the drop-down list and click Yes, Start Enforcing Protection.
	▪ Add and confirm a password, and click OK. Or, leave the password fields blank and click OK.
Stop protection	▪ Click the Stop Protection button in the Restrict Editing task pane, enter a password if prompted, and click OK.

Distributing and Using Forms

You can simply print and distribute paper forms to users. Electronic forms are typically distributed via email. Users can complete an electronic form in Word and return the completed form to the person responsible for collecting the data.

DEVELOP YOUR SKILLS WD09-D12
Protect and Use the Form

In this exercise, you will protect the form and enter data in the special form fields. You will also finalize the table formatting and turn off the Developer tab.

1. Save your file as **WD09-D12-Registration-[FirstInitialLastName]**.

2. Choose **Developer→Protect→Restrict Editing** 🔒.
   The Restrict Editing task pane opens.

3. Follow these steps to protect the form:

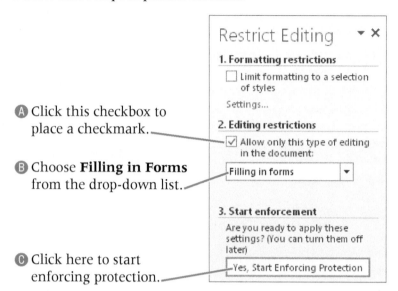

Ⓐ Click this checkbox to place a checkmark.

Ⓑ Choose **Filling in Forms** from the drop-down list.

Ⓒ Click here to start enforcing protection.

4. You won't set a password, so click **OK** to dismiss the password dialog box.

5. Tap ⌈Tab⌉ twice to move the insertion point from field to field.

You cannot tab out of a content-control field, such as the Date Picker Content Control; you must click or use the arrow keys.

6. Press ⌈Shift⌉+⌈Tab⌉ twice to move backwards to the **Name** field.

Fill Out the Form

7. Type **Eugene Washington** and tap ⌈Tab⌉.

8. Type **712-555-4321** and tap ⌈Tab⌉.

9. Type **eugene@yahoo.com** and tap ⌈Tab⌉.

10. Follow these steps to insert the date:

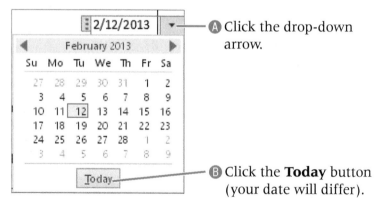

Ⓐ Click the drop-down arrow.

Ⓑ Click the **Today** button (your date will differ).

11. In the second table row, click **Yes**.

12. Follow these steps to make a choice from the drop-down field.

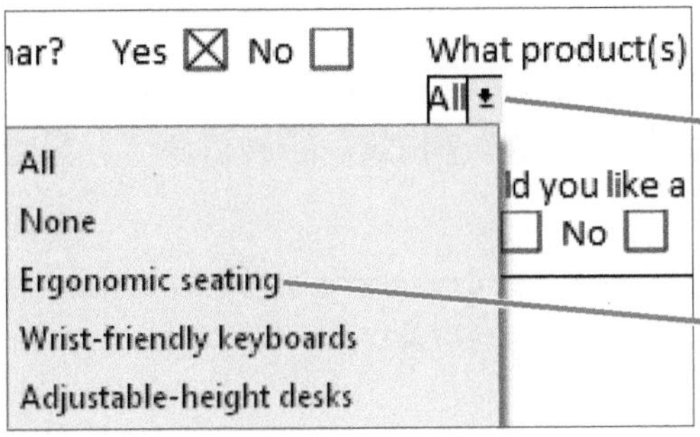

ar? Yes ☒ No ☐ What product(s)	Ⓐ Click the **What Product(s)** drop-down field.
All ±
All
None
Ergonomic seating
Wrist-friendly keyboards
Adjustable-height desks	Ⓑ Choose **Ergonomic seating**.

13. In the last row, click both **Yes** checkboxes.

Your form should now look like the following illustration. The date will vary.

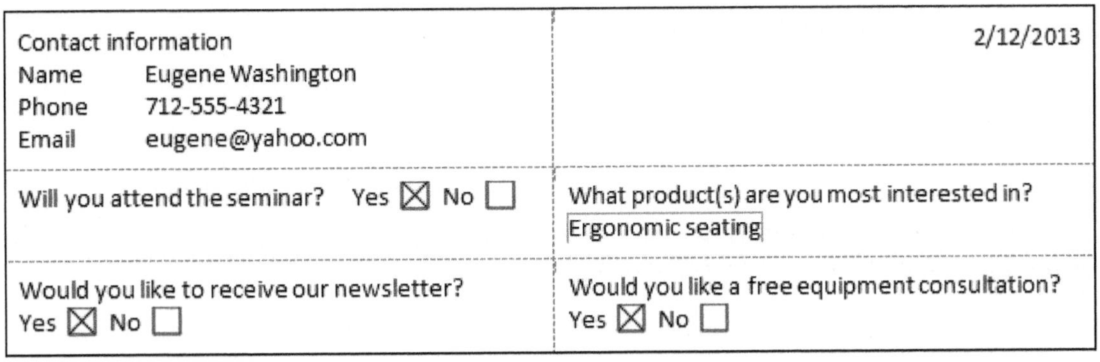

| Contact information
Name   Eugene Washington
Phone   712-555-4321
Email eugene@yahoo.com	2/12/2013
Will you attend the seminar? Yes ☒ No ☐	What product(s) are you most interested in?
Ergonomic seating
Would you like to receive our newsletter?
Yes ☒ No ☐	Would you like a free equipment consultation?
Yes ☒ No ☐

Stop Protection

14. Click the **Stop Protection** button in the Restrict Editing task pane, and then close it.

15. Right-click the **Home** tab and choose **Customize the Ribbon**.

16. Remove the checkmark from the **Developer** checkbox and click **OK**.

17. Save and close your file. Exit **Word**.

Concepts Review

To check your knowledge of the key concepts introduced in this lesson, complete the Concepts Review quiz by choosing the appropriate access option below.

If you are...	Then access the quiz by...
Using the Labyrinth Video Library	Going to http://labyrinthelab.com/videos
Using eLab	Logging in, choosing Content, and navigating to the Concepts Review quiz for this lesson
Not using the Labyrinth Video Library or eLab	Going to the student resource center for this book

Reinforce Your Skills

Use Shapes, SmartArt, and Add Page Color and a Border

In this exercise, you will create a certificate using graphic Shapes and SmartArt, and then you will format the certificate background with a page color and a page border.

Work with Shapes

1. Start **Word**. Create a new document based on the **Blank Document template** and save it in your **WD2013 Lesson 09** folder as `WD09-R01-Certificate-[FirstInitialLastName]`.

2. Choose **Page Layout→Page Setup→Orientation**, and then choose **Landscape**.

3. If necessary, choose **Home→Paragraph→Show/Hide** ¶ to display formatting marks.

4. Tap Enter fifteen times.
   It can be easier to work with graphics if some spacing is already set up.

5. Choose **Design→Document Formatting→Themes**, and then choose the **Slice** Theme.

6. If necessary, choose **View→Views→Ruler** to turn on the ruler.

7. Choose **Insert→Illustrations→Shapes**. In the Stars and Banners category, choose **Down Ribbon**.

8. Position the mouse pointer, which appears as a crosshair, next to the paragraph symbol at the top of the page.

9. Press and hold the mouse button, drag to the right until the image is about **6 inches wide**, and drag down until the image is approximately **2 inches high**.

10. Type **Outstanding Member** in the image.

11. Click the border of the image to select the entire image.

12. Choose **Home→Font**, choose **Comic Sans MS**, **28 pt**, and click **Bold** B.

13. Choose **Home→Font→Font Color ▼ menu button**, and choose **Red** in the Standard Colors section.

14. If necessary, drag the object to center it between the margins.

15. Click in the document to deselect the image.

Work with Text Boxes

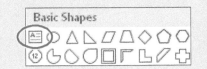

16. Choose **Insert→Illustration→Shapes** , and then choose **Text Box** from the Basic Shapes category.

17. Position the mouse pointer approximately one inch below the other graphic, and draw a text box that is approximately **5 inches wide and 1 inch tall**.

18. Enter the following text in the text box:

    ```
    Janisha Robinson
    Second Quarter: Most Volunteer Days
    ```

19. Select *Janisha Robinson* and change the font size to **28 pt**. Select the second line and change the font size to **18 pt**.

20. Click the text box border to select the entire object.

21. Choose **Home→Paragraph→Center** .

22. Choose **Drawing Tools→Format→Shape Styles→Shape Outline menu ▼** and choose **No Outline**.

23. Choose **Drawing Tools→Format→Shape Styles→Shape Fill menu ▼** and choose **White, Background 1, Darker 5%**.

24. If necessary, drag the text box by its border to center it between the margins.

25. Scroll down until the bottom of the page is visible.

26. Choose **Insert→Illustrations→Shapes** , and then choose **Text Box** .
    It should now appear in the Recently Used Shapes at the top of the gallery.

27. Draw a text box that is approximately **2 ½ inches wide and 1 inch high**, positioning it in the bottom-right corner, but within the 1-inch bottom and right-hand margins.

28. Type the following text:

    ```
    Presented by Kids for Change
    July 10, 2013
    ```

29. Click the border of the text box.

30. Choose **Drawing Tools→Format→Shape Styles→Shape Outline menu ▼** and choose **No Outline**.

31. Choose **Home→Font** and then choose **14 pt** from the Font Size drop-down list.

32. Resize the text box for the new font size.

33. With the text box selected, choose **Drawing Tools→Format→Shape Styles→Shape Fill menu ▼**, and then choose **White, Background 1, Darker 5%**.

Insert a SmartArt Object

34. Position the insertion point next to the last paragraph symbol.

35. Choose **Insert→Illustrations→SmartArt** , and then choose the **List** category in the left-hand pane.

36. Scroll down, choose **Vertical Chevron List**, and click **OK**.

Don't be concerned about the position of objects. You'll fix that shortly.

37. Click the tab on the left side of the graphic to open the **Type Your Text Here pane**.

The text pane may open on the right side of the image. You can resize the text pane like other objects by positioning the mouse pointer on the border and dragging when the mouse pointer appears as a double-headed arrow.

38. If necessary, resize the text pane until you can see all nine bullets.

39. Click and drag in the text pane to select the first six bullets, and then tap `Delete`.

40. Type this text:

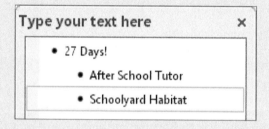

41. In the text pane, select the text for the first bullet.

42. Choose **Home→Font→Font Color** .

43. If the font color on the button face is red, click the button face. Otherwise, click the menu ▼ and choose **Red** in the Standard Colors section, and then close the **Type Your Text Here pane**.

44. Position the mouse pointer on the sizing handle in the bottom-right corner of the graphic. When the mouse pointer changes to a double-headed arrow, drag up and to the left until the image is approximately **3½ inches wide** and **1 inch tall**.

The graphic should pop up to the first page when you resize it. If necessary, continue resizing until it moves to the first page.

45. With the object selected, click the **Layout Options smart tag** next to it and choose **Top and Bottom** text wrapping.

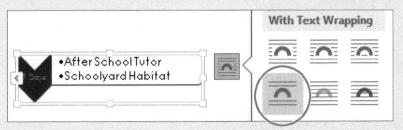

The smart tag can be a little shy at times. You may need to deselect and then reselect the image to encourage the smart tag to appear. Applying text wrapping allows you to freely position the SmartArt graphic on the page.

46. If necessary, drag both the SmartArt image and the bottom text box close to the bottom of the page.

47. Press Shift and click the bottom text box. (Both images should display handles.)

48. Choose **Drawing Tools→Format→Arrange→Align Objects**, and then choose **Align Top**.

49. Click in the document to deselect the images.

50. Click the **SmartArt image** and then click the border of the object with the bullets.
    Handles should appear on the bulleted object.

51. Choose **SmartArt Tools→Format→Shape Styles→Shape Fill ▼ menu**, and then choose **White, Background 1, Darker 5%**.

52. Click in the document to deselect the object.

Apply a Page Color and a Page Border

53. Choose **Design→Page Background→Page Color**, and then choose **White, Background 1, Darker 5%**.

54. Choose **Design→Page Background→Page Borders**.

55. In the Borders and Shading dialog box, click the drop-down arrow in the **Art** field, scroll down, and choose the first row of stars. Click **OK**.

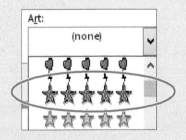

56. Make any sizing and positioning modifications you deem necessary.

57. If necessary, choose **Home→Paragraph→Show/Hide ¶** to turn off formatting marks.

58. Save and close the certificate; exit **Word**.

59. Submit your final file based on the guidelines provided by your instructor.
    To see examples of how your final file or files should look at the end of this exercise, go to the student resource center.

Create a Form

In this exercise, you will create a form that will be distributed to Kids for Change volunteers to make sure their information is current. You will use legacy form fields, including text-form fields, drop-down lists, and checkboxes, and you will use the Date Picker Content Control. You will use a Word table as the basis for the form.

Set Up the Form

1. Start **Word**. Open **WD09-R02-Volunteer** from your **WD2013 Lesson 09** folder and save it as **WD09-R02-Volunteer-[FirstInitialLastName]**.

2. Right-click the **Home** tab and choose **Customize the Ribbon**.

3. Place a checkmark in the **Developer** checkbox in the right-hand list and click **OK**.

4. If necessary, choose **Home→Paragraph→Show/Hide ¶** to display formatting marks.

5. If necessary, choose **View→Show→Ruler** to display the ruler.

6. Position the insertion point in the first table cell and type this text:

   > Contact·information¶
   > Name¤

7. Check the ruler to make sure a **Left Tab** is in effect. If not, click the **Tab** box until the tab symbol looks like an uppercase L.

8. Click the ruler to place a tab at the **1¼-inch mark**.

9. Make sure the insertion point is next to *Name* in the second line of the cell, and then press Ctrl + Tab to position the insertion point at the tab.

Insert Form Fields

10. Choose **Developer→Controls→Legacy Tools** 🛠. Choose **Text Form Field** 🔤 from the menu.

11. If the text field is not shaded, follow these steps. Otherwise, go to the next step.
    - Choose **Developer→Controls→Legacy Tools** 🛠.
    - Choose **Form Field Shading** 🄰.

12. Tap Enter, type **Primary phone**, and press Ctrl + Tab.

13. Insert another **Text Form Field** 🔤.

14. Tap Enter and type **Secondary phone**.

15. Press Ctrl + Tab to position the insertion point.

16. Insert another **Text Form Field** 🔤.

17. Set a tab on the ruler at the **2¼-inch mark** and then press Ctrl + Tab.

18. Type **Type** and then tap Spacebar twice.

19. Choose **Developer→Controls→Legacy Tools** 🧰.

20. Choose **Drop-Down Form Field** 🗒️.

21. Tap Enter and type `Preferred contact method`.

22. Press Ctrl + Tab and insert another **Drop-Down Form Field** 🗒️.

23. Tap Tab to position the insertion point in the next cell.

24. Choose **Home→Paragraph→Align Right** ≡.

25. Choose **Developer→Controls→Date Picker Content Control** 📅 (not a legacy tool).

26. Position the insertion point in the first cell of the second row, type `Availability`, and tap Enter.

27. Type `Preferred day` and set a tab on the ruler at the **1¼- inch mark**.

28. Press Ctrl + Tab to position the insertion point.

29. Insert a **Drop-Down Form Field** 🗒️.

Add Checkboxes and Complete the Form

30. Tap Enter, type `Preferred time`, and press Ctrl + Tab.

31. Type `Morning` and tap Spacebar twice.

32. Choose **Developer→Controls, Legacy Tools** 🧰.

33. Choose **Check Box Form Field** ☑.

34. Tap Spacebar twice and type `Afternoon`.

35. Tap Spacebar twice, and then insert another **Check Box Form Field** ☑.

36. Tap Tab to move to the next table cell.

37. Complete the form as shown and using these guidelines:
    - Set a tab at the **4¾-inch mark**.
    - The first two lines contain **Drop-Down Form Fields** 🗒️.
    - The last line contains **Check Box Form Fields** ☑.
    - Apply spacing as shown in the illustration.

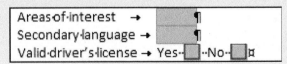

Apply Field Properties

38. Double-click the text field next to **Primary phone** in the first cell.

39. Change the Maximum Length field to **12** and click **OK**.
    This prevents users from typing too many characters for the phone number.

40. Double-click the text field next to **Secondary phone**, change the Maximum Length field to **12**, and click **OK**.

41. Double-click the drop-down field next to **Type**.

42. Type **Home** and click **Add** to place the first entry in the Items in the Drop-Down List field.

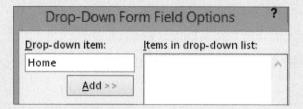

43. Follow the same process to add **Cell** and **Business** to the list; click **OK**.

44. Double-click the **Preferred contact** method drop-down field and add these items: **Email**, **Phone**. Click **OK**.

45. Tap Tab to position the insertion point in the next table cell.

46. Type **Click arrow; choose today's date**.

47. In the first cell of the second row, double-click the **Preferred day field** and add six days, **Monday** through **Saturday**, to the Items in Drop-Down List field.

48. Click **OK**.

49. In the second cell of the second row, double-click the **Areas of interest field** and add these items to the Items in Drop-Down List field:
   - **After School Tutor**
   - **Schoolyard Habitat**
   - **Recycling**
   - **Food Drive**

50. Click **OK**.

51. Double-click the **Secondary language field** and add these following items to the Items in Drop-Down List field:
   - **Spanish**
   - **Chinese**
   - **Vietnamese**
   - **Arabic**
   - **American Sign Language**

52. Click **OK**.

53. Choose **Home→Paragraph→Show/Hide ¶** to turn off formatting marks.

54. Choose **Developer→Controls→Legacy Tools**, and then choose **Form Field Shading**.

Protect and Use the Form

55. Choose **Developer→Protect→Restrict Editing** 🔒.

56. Make the choices shown at right in the Editing Restrictions area of the Restrict Editing task pane.

57. Click **Yes, Start Enforcing Protection**, and then click **OK** to bypass using passwords.

58. If the Name field is not highlighted, click to the right of the word Name at about 1 ¼″ on the Ruler to display the highlight.

59. Type **Stella Harris** in the Name field and tap `Tab`.

60. Type **712-555-1478** as the primary phone and tap `Tab` and type **712-555-9632** as the secondary phone.

61. Choose **Cell** from the Type drop-down list.

62. Choose **Phone** from the Preferred contact method drop-down list.

63. Tap `Tab` to position the insertion point in the next table cell.

64. Click the arrow, and then click **Today** to enter the current date.

65. Complete the second row as shown:

Availability		Areas of interest	Schoolyard Habitat
Preferred day	Saturday	Secondary language	Vietnamese
Preferred time	Morning ☐ Afternoon ☒	Valid driver's license	Yes ☒ No ☐

66. Click the **Stop Protection** button in the task pane then close it.

67. Right-click the **Home** tab and choose **Customize the Ribbon**.

68. Remove the checkmark from the Developer checkbox in the right-hand list and click **OK**.

69. Save and close your file; exit from **Word**.

70. Submit your final file based on guidelines provided by your instructor.

    To see examples of how your file or files should look at the end of this exercise, go to the student resource center.

Create a Flyer and a Form

In this exercise, you will create a flyer using graphic shapes and SmartArt. You will format and size the images, and add a page background color and a page border. You will also create, protect, and fill in a form.

Work with Shapes

Kids for Change is partnering with a local charity that collects clothing and household products for people with developmental disabilities. One of the members is creating a flyer to help in the collection process.

1. Start **Word**. Open **WD09-R03-Donations** from your **WD2013 Lesson 09** folder and save it as **WD09-R03-Donations-[FirstInitialLastName]**.

2. If necessary, choose **Home→Paragraph→Show/Hide ¶** to display formatting marks.

3. If necessary, choose **View→Show→Ruler** to display the ruler.

4. Check that the box at the left side of the ruler is displaying a **Left Tab**. If not, click the **Tab box** until the symbol looks like an uppercase L.

5. Choose **Insert→Illustrations→Shapes**, and then choose **Wave** in the Stars and Banners category.

6. Starting at the left margin, drag the crosshair mouse pointer to the right until the image is about **6 inches wide** and down until it is about **2 inches tall**.

7. Type this text on two separate lines:

   We need your gently used clothing, shoes, and household items!
   Donating is as easy as 1-2-3!

Format the Shape

8. Click the border of the object to select it.

9. Choose **Home→Font** and choose **16 pt** from the Font Size list.

10. If necessary, drag the shape until it is just below the clip art image and centered between the margins.

11. With the object selected, choose **Drawing Tools→Format→Shape Styles→Shape Fill menu ▼** and choose **Blue, Accent 1, Darker 25%**.

Insert a SmartArt Image

12. Position the insertion point on the second blank line below the Shape.

13. Choose **Insert→Illustration→SmartArt**, and then choose **List** in the left-hand pane.

14. Choose **Vertical Curved List** and click **OK**.

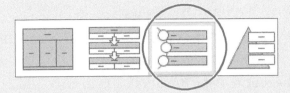

Don't be concerned about the position and size of the object. You'll fix that shortly.

15. Click the tab on the left side of the graphic to display the **Type Your Text Here** box.

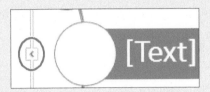

16. Enter this text, and then close the text pane.

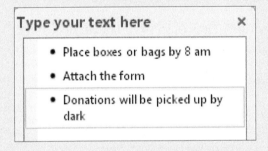

17. Place the mouse pointer in the bottom-center handle of the SmartArt object and drag up until the image is about **2 inches tall**.

18. Position the mouse pointer on the right-hand sizing handle and drag left until the right edge is close to the word *dark* in the last line.

19. With the object selected, click the **Layout Options smart tag** and choose **Top and Bottom** text wrapping.

Now you can move the image freely on the page.

20. Drag the **SmartArt image** close to the bottom of the Wave Shape and center it between the margins.

Apply a SmartArt Style

21. If necessary, select the image, and then click the border of the first rectangle.

Handles should appear around the rectangle.

22. Press Shift and click the other two rectangles.

Handles should now appear around all three rectangles.

23. Choose **SmartArt Tools→Format→Shape Styles→Shape Fill menu ▼,** and then choose **Blue, Accent 1, Darker 25%**.

Add a Page Color and a Page Border

24. Click in the document to deselect the **SmartArt image**.

25. Choose **Design→Page Background→Page Color** ⬙, and then choose **Blue, Accent, Lighter 60%**.

26. Choose **Design→Page Background, Page Borders** ⬜. In the **Art** field, choose the border shown.

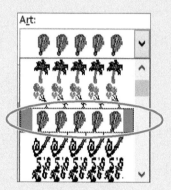

27. Click **OK**. Adjust the size and position of any objects you deem necessary.

Create a Form

28. Delete five paragraph symbols below the SmartArt image to place the table at the bottom of the first page.

29. Right-click the **Home** tab and choose **Customize the Ribbon**.

30. Place a checkmark in the **Developer** checkbox in the right-hand list and click **OK**.

31. Position the insertion point in the first table cell.

32. Place a tab on the ruler at the **1¼-inch mark**.

33. Type **Name** and press ⌈Ctrl⌉+⌈Tab⌉ to position the insertion point.

34. Choose **Developer→Controls→Legacy Tools→Text Form Field** ⌊abl⌋.

35. Tap ⌈Enter⌉ and then type **Street address**.

36. Press ⌈Ctrl⌉+⌈Tab⌉ to position the insertion point.

37. Insert another **Text Form Field** ⌊abl⌋.

38. Tap ⌈Tab⌉ to position the insertion point in the next table cell.

39. Place a tab on the ruler at the **2-inch mark** and type **What day do you prefer?**

40. Press ⌈Ctrl⌉+⌈Tab⌉ to position the insertion point.

41. Choose **Developer→Controls→Legacy Tools→Drop-Down Form Field** ⬛.

42. Tap ⌈Enter⌉ and type **What time do you prefer?**

    If tapping ⌈Enter⌉ placed part of the table on a second page, resize a graphic image until everything fits on one page.

43. Press ⌈Ctrl⌉+⌈Tab⌉ to position the insertion point, type **AM**, and tap ⌈Spacebar⌉ twice.

44. Choose **Developer→Controls→Legacy Tools→Checkbox Form Field** ☑.

45. Tap Spacebar twice, type **PM**, and tap Spacebar twice.

46. Choose **Developer→Controls→Legacy Tools→Checkbox Form Field** ☑.

Apply a Field Property

47. Double-click the field to the right of *What day do you prefer?* to open the **Drop-Down Form Fields dialog box**.

48. Type **Monday** in the Drop-Down Item field and click **Add** to place the item in the **Items in Drop-Down List field**.

49. Use the same process to add the days **Tuesday** through **Saturday** to the list; click **OK**.

50. Choose **Home→Paragraph→Show/Hide** ¶ to turn off formatting marks.

51. Choose **Developer→Controls→Legacy Tools→Form Field Shading** 🗛 to turn off the feature.

Protect and Use the Form

52. Choose **Developer→Protect→Restrict Editing** 🔒.

53. Make the choices shown at right in the Editing Restrictions area of the Restrict Editing task pane.

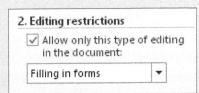

54. Click **Yes, Start Enforcing Protection**, and then click **OK** to bypass using a password.

55. If the *Name* field is not highlighted, click to the right of it to display the highlight.

56. Type **Janice Johnson** in the **Name** field.

57. Tap Tab and type **123 Cherry Blossom Lane**.

58. Tap Tab and choose **Wednesday** from the drop-down field.

59. Click the **AM** checkbox

60. Click the **Stop Protection** button in the task pane, and then close it.

61. Save and close your file; exit **Word**.

62. Submit your final file based on guidelines provided by your instructor.

Apply Your Skills

Create a Flyer

In this exercise, you will create a flyer, and add and format a shape and a SmartArt image. You will then add a page background color and a page border.

Insert and Format a Shape and Align Objects

1. Start **Word**. Open **WD09-A01-CarRental** from your **WD2013 Lesson 09** folder and save it as `WD09-A01-CarRental-[FirstInitialLastName]`.

2. If necessary, turn on formatting marks and the ruler.

3. Choose the **Double Wave** shape.

4. About a half-inch below the picture, draw the shape about **4½ inches wide** and **1 inch tall**.

5. Type `Book now!` in the shape. Change the font size to **36 pt** and adjust the shape size as necessary.

6. Change the **Shape Fill** color to **Tan, Background 2, Darker 50%**.

7. Select the WordArt heading, the picture, and the Double Wave Shape at the same time.

8. Use the contextual **Format** tab and the **Align Objects** ⬚ feature to center-align the objects.

Insert, Apply a Style to, and Format a SmartArt Image

9. Position the insertion point on the first blank line below the shape.

10. Insert the **Table List SmartArt graphic** (in the List category) shown here.

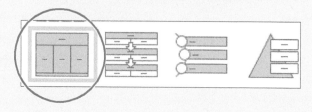

11. Open the **Type Your Text Here pane** and type the text shown. When finished, close the text pane.

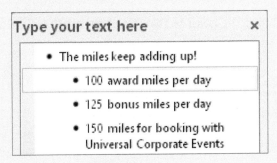

12. Using the SmartArt Styles gallery on the contextual Design tab, apply the 3-D **Inset** style.

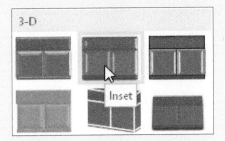

13. Select the individual objects within the SmartArt Graphic—the top row, the thin bottom row, and the three squares in between.

14. Change the **Shape Fill** color to **Tan, Background 2, Darker 50%**.

15. Use the bottom-center sizing handle to change the height of the image to about **2 inches**. It should now fit on the first page. If not, reduce the height until it does.

16. Use the **Layout Options smart tag** to change the text wrapping to **Top and Bottom**.

17. If necessary, drag the SmartArt image up to page 1 and center it between the margins.

18. Delete enough paragraph symbols at the bottom of the page to reduce the document to one page.

Add a Page Color and a Page Border

19. Change the **Page Color** to **Tan, Background 2, Darker 25%**.

20. Apply the border style shown here. The color is **Tan, Background 2, Darker 50%**.

21. Turn off formatting marks.

22. Save and close your file; exit **Word**.

23. Submit your final file based on guidelines provided by your instructor.

    To see examples of how your final file or files should look at the end of this exercise, go to the student resource center.

APPLY YOUR SKILLS WD09-A02

Create a Trip-Planning Form

In this exercise, you will create a form containing checkboxes, text fields, and a drop-down list. You will add field properties, and then you will protect the form and fill it in.

Set up a Form and Insert Form Fields

1. Start **Word**. Open **WD09-A02-CorpTravel** from your **WD2013 Lesson 09** folder and save it as **WD09-A02-CorpTravel-[FirstInitialLastName]**.

2. If necessary, display formatting marks, the ruler, and the Developer tab.

3. Position the insertion point in the first table cell.

4. Follow these guidelines to enter the information shown in the following illustration.

■ Apply spacing as shown in the illustration.

■ Use the **Legacy Tools Check Box Form Fields**.

■ Space twice after each checkbox and type the labels shown.

■ The checkboxes in the second column are aligned on left tabs set at **2½ inches**.

5. Position the insertion point in the second table row, below the word *Flight*.

6. Follow these guidelines to enter the data shown in the following illustration.

■ Apply spacing as shown.

■ In the first row of information, set left tabs at **2** and **4** inches; use **Legacy Tools' Check Box Form Fields**.

■ In the second row, use the tab set at **2** inches; use **Legacy Tools' Text Form Fields**.

■ In the third row, leave the tab at 2 inches in place; use **Legacy Tools' Text Form Fields**.

■ In the last row, insert a **Legacy Tools' Drop-Down Form Field**.

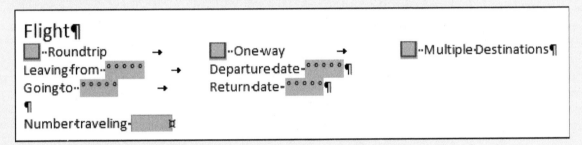

Apply Field Properties

7. Apply the field properties shown to the **Departure date** and **Return date** fields.

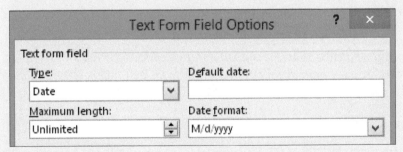

8. Add the numbers **1 - 9** to the **Drop-Down Form Field** at the bottom of the form.

Protect and Complete the Form

9. If necessary, turn off formatting marks and **Form Field Shading** ▨.

10. Apply the **Editing Restrictions** as shown.

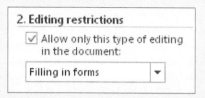

11. Start protecting the form; bypass using a password.

12. Fill in the form using the data and choices shown here.

☐ Flight   ☐ Flight + Hotel
☐ Hotel   ☐ Flight + Car
☐ Car   ☒ Flight + Hotel+ Car
☐ Cruise   ☐ Hotel+ Car

Flight
☐ Roundtrip   ☐ One way   ☒ Multiple Destinations
Leaving from New York City   Departure date 8/13/2013
Going to London   Return date 8/20/2013

Number traveling ⃞3

13. Stop protection and close the **Restrict Editing task pane**.

14. Save and close your file; exit **Word**.

15. Submit your final file based on guidelines provided by your instructor.

    To see examples of how your final file or files should look at the end of this exercise, go to the student resource center.

APPLY YOUR SKILLS WD09-A03

Create a Flyer and a Form

In this exercise, you will insert shapes and a SmartArt graphic. Then you will set up a form in a table and use text fields, checkboxes, a drop-down list, and the Date Picker Content Control. Finally, you will add a page color and a page border.

Work with Shapes

1. Start **Word**. Open **WD09-A03-Universal** from your **WD2013 Lesson 09** folder and save it as **WD09-A03-Universal-[FirstInitialLastName]**.

2. If necessary, display formatting marks and turn on the ruler.

3. Turn on **Form Field Shading** ▨.

4. Choose the **Horizontal Scroll** shape.

5. Draw the shape at the top of the document, sizing it at the width of the page but between the margins and about **1½ inches tall**.

6. Type **Universal Corporate Events** in the shape and change the font size to **26 pt**.

7. Insert a text box shape about a half-inch below the top shape, making it about **3½ inches wide** and ½ **inch tall**.

8. Type **Services We Offer** in the box and change the font size to **26 pt**.

9. Apply the **Text Effect** 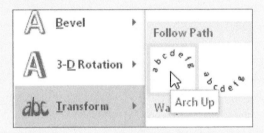 shown here.

10. Apply the Text Fill color in the fifth column, **Dark Red, Accent 1, Darker 25%**.

11. Use **Shape Outline** to remove the outline.

12. Apply the **Shape Fill** color in the first column, **White, Background 1, Darker 15%**.

13. Position the insertion point on the second blank line below the text box.

Insert and Format a SmartArt Graphic

14. Insert the **Vertical Box List** SmartArt graphic.

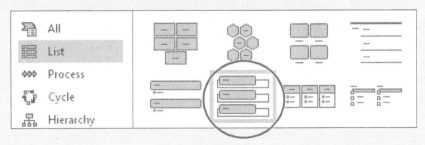

15. Open the **Type Your Text Here pane** and enter this text:

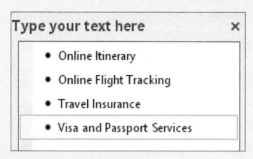

16. Close the text pane.

17. Select the four rounded rectangles within the SmartArt Shape and apply italics.

Apply a Page Color and a Page Border

18. Apply the third page color in the first column, **White, Background 1, Darker 15%**.

19. Apply the page border shown here. The color is **Dark Red, Accent 1, Darker 25%**.

Set Up a Form

20. Insert a **2x2 table** about a half-inch below the SmartArt image.

21. On the **Layout** tab, change the top and bottom cell margins to **0.08**.

22. Position the insertion point in the first table cell.

23. Set a left tab at the ¾-**inch mark** on the ruler and enter the information shown, inserting the **Legacy Tools' Text Form Fields** where indicated.

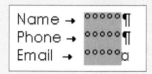

24. In the second cell of the first row, insert the **Date Picker Content Control**  right-aligned.

25. Enter the information shown in the following illustration in the first cell of the second row using these guidelines:

   - Apply spacing as shown.
   - Place a **left tab** at the **1½-inch mark** on the ruler.
   - Insert a **Drop-Down Form Field** below Destination.
   - Use **Check Box Form Fields** for the services.

26. Enter the information shown in the following illustration in the last table cell using these guidelines:

   - Apply spacing as shown.
   - Set a **left tab** at the **4¾-inch mark** on the ruler.
   - Use **Text Form Fields**.

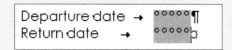

Resize and reposition graphic images and delete paragraph symbols as necessary to fit everything on one page.

Apply Field Properties

27. Click the **Date Picker Content Control** in the second cell of the first row and type **Click arrow; choose today's date**.

28. In the first cell of the second row, add these destinations to the Drop-Down Form Field: **Samoa, Fiji, Tahiti, Tonga**.

29. Apply these properties to the two text fields in the last cell.

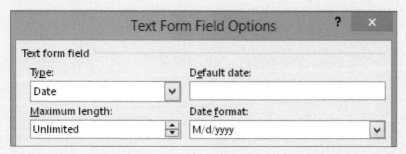

Protect and Use the Form

30. If necessary, turn off formatting marks and **Form Field Shading** 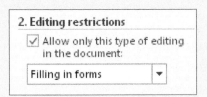.

31. Apply the Editing Restrictions as shown in the following illustration.

> 2. **Editing restrictions**
>
> ☑ Allow only this type of editing in the document:
>
> | Filling in forms | ▼ |

32. Fill in the form with the information shown, using the current date in the second cell of the first row. Bypass setting a password.

Name Ned Bennett Phone 712-555-4563 Email Ned@Yahoo.com	2/16/2013
Destination	Services	Departure date 10/10/2013 Return date 10/21/2013

Destination	Services	
Tonga	☒ Air	Departure date 10/10/2013
	☒ Hotel	Return date 10/21/2013
	☐ Car	

33. Stop protection and close the **Restrict Editing task pane**.

34. Save and close your file; exit **Word**.

35. Submit your final file based on guidelines provided by your instructor.

Extend Your Skills

In the course of working through the Extend Your Skills exercises, you will think critically as you use the skills taught in the lesson to complete the assigned projects. To evaluate your mastery and completion of the exercises, your instructor may use a rubric, with which more points are allotted according to performance characteristics. (The more you do, the more you earn!) Ask your instructor how your work will be evaluated.

WD09-E01 That's the Way I See It

As the owner of a small online business, you want to promote a new product you are carrying. Start a new Word document and save it in your **WD2013 Lesson 09** folder as `WD09-E01-NewProd-[FirstInitialLastName]`. Create a brochure using shapes and SmartArt graphics to announce the product. Add the formatting of your choice to the graphic images. Add a page background color and page border to the brochure. Add a second page that contains a discount voucher form. Include text fields where customers will enter their contact information, include a drop-down list where they can choose the type of credit card they will use, and include at least three checkboxes where customers can specify their preferred shipping method. Apply appropriate field properties. Protect the form, and then fill it in with data of your choice. Finally, unprotect the form.

You will be evaluated based on the inclusion of all elements specified, your ability to follow directions, your ability to apply newly learned skills to a real-world situation, your creativity, and the relevance of your topic and/or data choice(s). Submit your final file based on the guidelines provided by your instructor.

WD09-E02 Be Your Own Boss

As the owner of Blue Jean Landscaping, you're hoping to increase sales as your customers get ready to spruce up their gardens with spring plants. Start a new Word document and save it to your **WD2013 Lesson 09** folder as `WD09-E02-Spring-[FirstInitialLastName]`. Create a flyer using shapes and SmartArt graphics with upbeat verbiage about spring gardening. Size and format the graphics based on your personal preferences. Add a survey form at the bottom of the flyer that includes checkboxes so customers can indicate the products they are interested in, such as shrubs, flowers, potting soil, and so forth. Conduct an online search for eco-friendly fertilizers. Include a drop-down list of at least three different fertilizers so customers can indicate their preference. Include a text-form field where customers can comment about your company's service. Limit the amount of text they can type to 200 characters. Apply other form properties as appropriate. Protect the form and then fill it in with data of your choice. Finally, unprotect the form.

You will be evaluated based on the inclusion of all elements specified, your ability to follow directions, your ability to apply newly learned skills to a real-world situation, your creativity, and your demonstration of an entrepreneurial spirit. Submit your final file based on the guidelines provided by your instructor.

Transfer Your Skills

In the course of working through the Transfer Your Skills exercises, you will use critical-thinking and creativity skills to complete the assigned projects using skills taught in the lesson. To evaluate your mastery and completion of the exercises, your instructor may use a rubric, with which more points are allotted according to performance characteristics. (The more you do, the more you earn!) Ask your instructor how your work will be evaluated.

WD09-T01 Use the Web as a Learning Tool

Throughout this book, you will be provided with an opportunity to use the Internet as a learning tool by completing WebQuests. According to the original creators of WebQuests, as described on their website (WebQuest.org), a WebQuest is "an inquiry-oriented activity in which most or all of the information used by learners is drawn from the web." To complete the WebQuest projects in this book, navigate to the student resource center and choose the WebQuest for the lesson on which you are currently working. The subject of each WebQuest will be relevant to the material found in the lesson.

WebQuest Subject: Creating a well-designed brochure.

Submit your final file(s) based on the guidelines provided by your instructor.

WD09-T02 Demonstrate Proficiency

Stormy BBQ is expanding to include a catering department! You have been asked to create a brochure announcing this new venture. Start a new Word document and save it in your **WD2013 Lesson 09** folder as **WD09-T02-Catering-[FirstInitialLastName]**. Include shapes and SmartArt graphics promoting the services Stormy BBQ will offer. Add a second page containing a form that customers can use for placing catering orders. It should include contact information and a drop-down list where they can choose the type of event (e.g., birthday, wedding, corporate luncheon). Include two columns of checkboxes with at least three items per column so customers can choose BBQ items, such as brisket and ribs, in the first column, and side-dish items, such as baked beans and coleslaw, in the second column. Apply form properties as appropriate. Include a background color and page border. And, because this brochure will need approval before being sent out, include a watermark indicating the document is in Draft mode.

Submit your final file based on the guidelines provided by your instructor.

WORD 2013

Organizing Long Documents

LEARNING OBJECTIVES

After studying this lesson, you will be able to:

- Create a table of contents
- Add headers and footers
- Insert an index and cross-reference
- Keep text together
- View a Master Document

Word offers several great tools for organizing long documents. A table of contents and an index help readers locate specific topics in documents. Headers and footers are useful for displaying information, such as page numbers and chapter names, and cross-references inform the reader of related material dispersed through a long document. In this lesson, you will work with these tools to organize long documents.

Refining a Policies and Procedures Manual

Raritan Clinic East is a pediatric medical practice. The practice serves patients ranging in ages from newborn to 18 years. You recently accepted a position in the human resources department at Raritan Clinic. You have been tasked with reviewing the current policies and procedures manual, and you have identified numerous "finishing" features that need to be added to the manual to make it easier to use. By adding a table of contents, index, headers and footers, and cross-references, you believe the document will be more user-friendly.

Table of Contents

Index

Creating a Table of Contents

Video Library   http://labyrinthelab.com/videos   Video Number: WD13-V1001

Word's Table of Contents feature automatically builds a table of contents by gathering up the headings that are formatted with heading styles. Word organizes the headings in the order in which they appear in the document. In addition, it applies TOC styles that correspond to the heading levels. The styles then format the table entries. For example, Heading 2 entries are subordinate to Heading 1 entries. You can automatically update a table of contents created with Word's heading styles.

Table of Contents Links

A table of contents is inserted as a large field composed of the various table entries. Each entry within the table functions as a hyperlink. You can navigate to a page within the document by pressing Ctrl while clicking a table entry.

Table of Contents

MISSION STATEMENT ....

SCOPE OF SERVICES ....

PATIENT MANAGEMENT PROC   file:///c:\lesson
10\wd10-d09-raritanp&p-sstudent.docx
Ctrl+Click to follow link

ENTRY INTO SERVICES.................

PATIENT APPOINTMENTS AND BILLING................................

PATIENT RECORDS...

Using a Predesigned Table of Contents

You can apply a predesigned table of contents format from the Table of Contents gallery. Toward the bottom of the gallery is a manual table of contents design option that you can fill out independently of the document content.

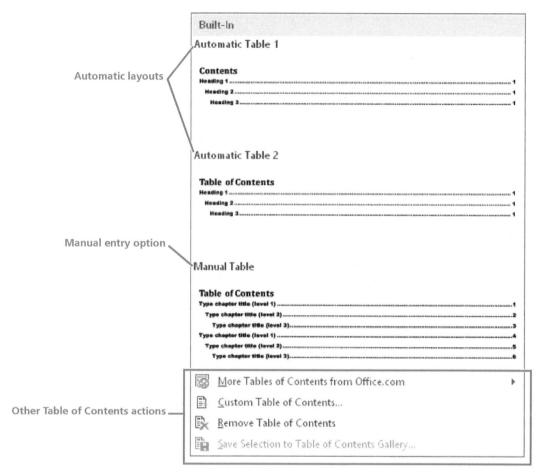

Automatic layouts

Manual entry option

Other Table of Contents actions

Table of Contents gallery

Creating a Page for the Table of Contents

In most documents, the table of contents appears at the beginning of the document—and just after the title page in documents containing a title page. Because the table of contents is often created after the document is complete, you may need to create a new page to hold the table.

When headers and footers or other page-level formatting such as page numbering appear in a document, it is better to create a page to hold the table of contents using a section break. This allows flexibility, such as numbering the table of contents page(s) with Roman numerals (i, ii, iii) and the rest of the document with Arabic numerals (1, 2, 3).

Insert a Table of Contents

In this exercise, you will open the Raritan Clinic East policies and procedures manual and review its heading styles. Then you will create a table of contents and navigate in the document using the links. Finally, you will remove the table of contents.

1. Open **WD10-D01-RaritanP&P** from your **WD2013 Lesson 10** folder and save it as `WD10-D01-RaritanP&P-[FirstInitialLastName]`.

   Replace the bracketed text with your first initial and last name. For example, if your name is Bethany Smith, your filename would look like this: WD10-D01-RaritanP&P-BSmith.

2. Choose **Home→Styles→dialog box launcher** ⬚ to open the Styles task pane.

3. Scroll to **page 2** and position the insertion point in the heading *Mission Statement*.

   Notice that a rectangle appears around Heading 1 in the Styles task pane, indicating that is the style used to format the heading.

4. Position the insertion point in several additional headings on page 2.

   You will notice that you have both Heading 1 and Heading 2 styles on the page.

5. **Close** ⬚ the Styles task pane.

6. Position the insertion point in front of the heading *Mission Statement*.

   Now you will insert a section break to create a blank page for the table of contents.

7. Choose **Page Layout→Page Setup→Breaks** ⬚, and then choose **Next Page**.

8. If necessary, choose **Home→Paragraph→Show/Hide** ¶ to display formatting marks.

9. Scroll up and position the insertion point to the right of the paragraph symbol, just in front of the section break, and tap Enter.

10. Choose **References→Table of Contents→Table of Contents** ⬚, and then choose **Automatic Table 2** from the gallery.

11. Scroll up and review the table of contents.

    You can see that the headings in the document are used as the table of contents entries.

Navigate Using Hyperlinks

12. Hover the mouse pointer over the *Initial Diagnostic Evaluation* entry in the table, and notice the pop-up message.

13. Press Ctrl and click the link.

    Word jumps to that heading in the document.

14. Scroll up to the table of contents and click the table to select it.

15. In the table of contents, click the **Table of Contents** ⬚ button in the upper-left corner.

16. Choose **Remove Table of Contents** at the bottom of the gallery.

17. Save your file and leave it open.

Using the Update Table Button

Video Library   http://labyrinthelab.com/videos   Video Number: WD13-V1002

When you make changes to headings or move text in a document, you need to update the table of contents. Word has an Update Table button that makes this task easy. Whenever the insertion point is anywhere in the table of contents, Word displays two buttons in the upper-left corner of the table. One button displays the Table of Contents gallery, which includes the command to remove the table of contents; the other button updates the table of contents.

FROM THE RIBBON

References→Table of Contents→Update Table

FROM THE KEYBOARD

F9 to update a table of contents

Displays the Table of Contents gallery ———— Update Table... ———— Updates the table of contents

Table of Contents

When you click the Update Table button, Word presents options for updating page numbers only or the entire table. Choose the page numbers options if you have been adding text but haven't changed any headings.

You can right-click a table of contents and choose Update Field from the menu.

Using the Table of Contents Dialog Box

The Table of Contents gallery probably provides the fastest method for creating a table of contents, but if you wish to have more control over the formatting of your table, you can use the Table of Contents dialog box. When you use the dialog box, you must also manually add the title that precedes the table. In addition, when a table of contents is generated from the dialog box, Word displays no Table of Contents or Update buttons at the top of the table as it does for a table generated from the Table of Contents gallery. To update a manual table of contents, you can use the F9 shortcut keystroke.

A preview of the styles that will be applied appears here.

Controls for page number alignment and tab leader design appear here.

Word offers various formats. You can also choose how many heading levels appear in the table of contents.

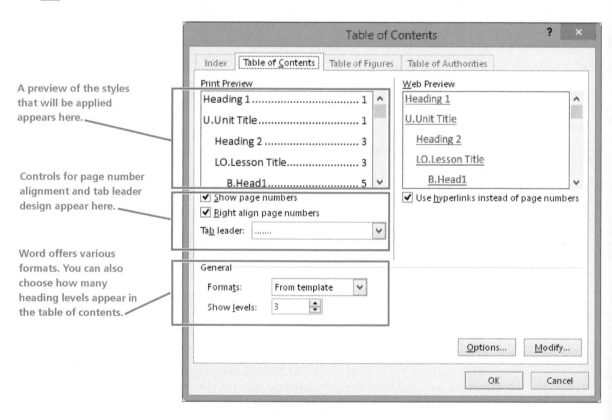

QUICK REFERENCE	CREATING AND UPDATING A TABLE OF CONTENTS
Task	**Procedure**
Create a table of contents from a predesigned format	▪ Format table of contents entries with heading styles. ▪ Choose References→Table of Contents→Table of Contents and choose a predesigned style.
Create a table of contents from the Table of Contents dialog box	▪ Choose References→Table of Contents→Table of Contents and choose the Custom Table of Contents option.
Update a table of contents	▪ If you used a predesigned table of contents, hover the mouse pointer over the table and click Update Table. ▪ If you used the Table of Contents dialog box, select the table of contents and tap F9; or, right-click the table of contents and choose Update Field.

DEVELOP YOUR SKILLS WD10-D02
Insert a Table of Contents Using the Dialog Box

In this exercise, you will insert a new table of contents using the Table of Contents dialog box. You will also edit a heading and then update the table of contents.

1. Save your file as **WD10-D02-RaritanP&P-[FirstInitialLastName]**.

2. If necessary, choose **Home→Paragraph→Show/Hide** ¶ to display formatting marks.

3. Position the insertion point just to the left of the section break at the top of **page 2**.

4. Tap Enter to create a new blank line.

   The blank line will hold the title. Next you will reformat its paragraph symbol with your desired title formatting.

5. Follow these steps to format and add the table title:

Ⓐ Select this paragraph symbol. Ⓑ Choose **Home→Font→Clear All Formatting.**

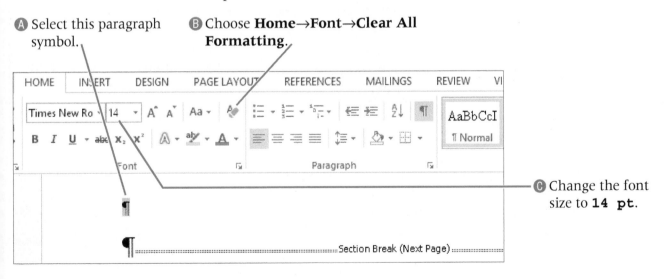

Ⓒ Change the font size to **14 pt.**

Ⓓ Type **Table of Contents** and tap Enter.

6. Choose **References→Table of Contents→Table of Contents**.

7. Choose **Custom Table of Contents** at the bottom of the gallery to open the Table of Contents dialog box.

8. Follow these steps to generate a table of contents:

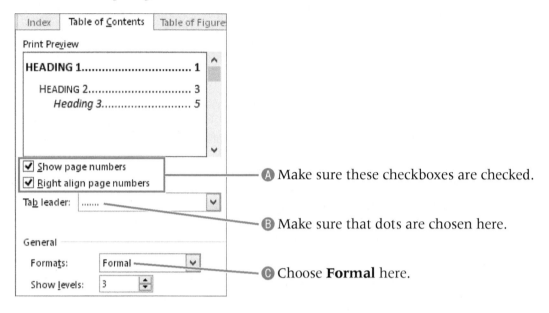

A Make sure these checkboxes are checked.

B Make sure that dots are chosen here.

C Choose **Formal** here.

9. Click **OK** to insert the table of contents.

10. Scroll to the bottom of the table and delete the extra paragraph symbol.

Edit a Heading and Update the Table of Contents

11. Search for the heading *Patient Attendance and Billing* and change *Attendance* to **Appointments**.

12. Scroll up to **page 2** and position the insertion point in the table of contents.
    Notice that there is no Update Table button in the upper-left corner of the table.

13. Tap F9 to begin the update.

14. When the Update Table of Contents dialog box appears, choose **Update Entire Table** and click **OK**.

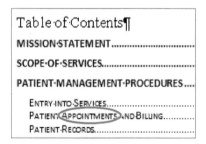

The word Attendance *changed to* Appointments.

15. Save your file.

Working with Multiple Headers and Footers

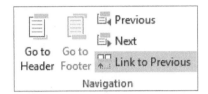 Video Library   http://labyrinthelab.com/videos   Video Number: WD13-V1003

Initially, Word uses the same header and footer content throughout a document, because the Link to Previous feature is turned on by default, as shown in the following illustration.

When a document contains multiple sections, you can break the link between sections, and thereby create a new header and footer for each document section if you wish. For example, suppose you want to number the front matter of a long document using small Roman numerals and the body of the document using Arabic numerals. Creating additional sections is the first important step before creating multiple headers and footers within a document.

Restarting and Formatting Page Numbers

When you have more than one section in a document, you may wish to control the starting page number within a section. Typically the body of a document starts page numbering with 1 rather than continuing the numbering from the front matter. You may also want to control the page number formats. The Page Number Format dialog box provides options to restart numbering and to modify the number format, such as changing from Roman numerals to Arabic numerals.

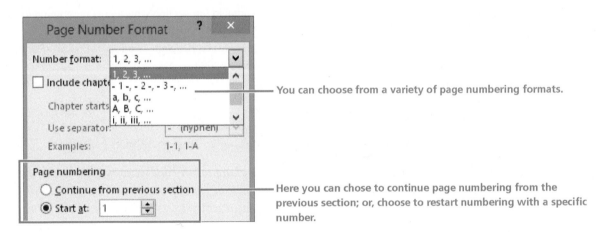

You can choose from a variety of page numbering formats.

Here you can chose to continue page numbering from the previous section; or, choose to restart numbering with a specific number.

Setting Up a Different First Page Header or Footer

There may be times when all you want to do is set up a different header or footer on the first page of a document. For example, suppose you want all pages of a document numbered in the footer area of each page except for the cover page. You can set a different first page header or footer simply by checking Different First Page, as shown in the following illustration.

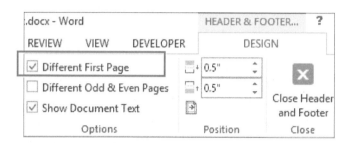

QUICK REFERENCE	SETTING HEADERS AND FOOTERS
Task	**Procedure**
Set up a different first page header/footer	■ With the insertion point in a header/footer, choose Header and Footer Tools→Design→Options→Different First Page.
Use multiple headers and footers	■ Segment the document with section breaks, and then position the insertion point in a header/footer.
	■ Choose Header and Footer Tools→Design→Navigation→Link to Previous to break the link between sections, and then insert different headers and footers in the document sections.
Restart and format page numbers	■ Position the insertion point in the section where new numbering/formatting begins.
	■ Choose Header & Footer Tools→Design→Header & Footer→Page Number→Format Page Number.

DEVELOP YOUR SKILLS WD10-D03
Work with Multiple Headers and Footers

In this exercise, you will insert header text that will appear in both sections of the document. Then you will break the connection between footers so you can have different footers in each section. You will change the starting page number on the second page of the document.

1. Save your file as **WD10-D03-RaritanP&P-[FirstInitialLastName]**.

2. If necessary, choose **Home→Paragraph→Show/Hide ¶** to display formatting marks.

3. Position the insertion point in **section 2**, which begins with *Mission Statement*.

4. Choose **Insert→Header & Footer→Header**, and then choose **Edit Header** at the bottom of the gallery.

5. Take a moment to observe the header area.

   You will recall that you inserted a section break when you created the page for the table of contents. Therefore, you have two sections in your document. The table of contents and title pages are section 1; the rest of the document is section 2.

   The Header -Section 2- *tab indicates that the insertion point is in the header area of section 2; the* Same as Previous *tab indicates that text you type in section 2 will carry over to the previous section. In other words, the sections are linked. You want the header sections to be linked because the word* DRAFT *should appear on all pages.*

6. Tap `Tab` to position the insertion point at the center of the header area and then type **DRAFT**.

7. Format the header text with **bold 14 pt.**

8. Double-click in the body of the document to close the header area.

9. Scroll up to the table of contents.

   Notice that the word DRAFT *appears in the header. That's because the headers in both sections are linked. Now you will add a footer that appears in only one section.*

10. Scroll down and position the insertion point in **section 2**.

11. Choose **Insert→Header & Footer→Footer** 📄, and then choose **Edit Footer**.

    Notice the Same as Previous tab in the footer area. You don't want the footer text to appear on the table of contents page, so you will break the link.

12. Choose **Header & Footer Tools→Design→Navigation**.

    The Link to Previous button is highlighted, meaning it is turned on and the footers in sections 1 and 2 are linked.

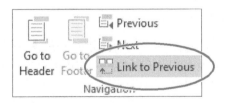

13. Click the **Link to Previous** 🔳 button to turn it off and break the link between the two sections.

    The Same as Previous tab at the right side of the footer area disappeared.

14. Choose **Header & Footer Tools→Design→Header & Footer→Footer** 📄, and then choose **Blank**.

15. Click **Type Here** and type **Policies & Procedures Manual**.

16. Tap ⊤ab to position the insertion point in the center of the footer area, and then type **Raritan Clinic East**.

17. Tap ⊤ab to position the insertion point at the right side of the footer.

18. Choose **Header & Footer Tools→Design→Header & Footer→Page Number** 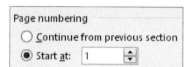.

19. Choose **Current Position** and then choose **Plain Number**.

Change the Starting Page Number
You want to start numbering with a 1 on the first page of the document body.

20. Choose **Header & Footer Tools→Design→Header & Footer→Page Number** 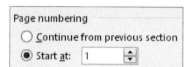.

21. Choose **Format Page Numbers** and then choose **Start At**.
    Word automatically chooses the number 1, but you could change it if you needed to.

Page numbering
○ Continue from previous section
● Start at: 1

22. Click **OK** to restart page numbering with a 1, and then double-click in the document body to close the header and footer areas.

23. Scroll up and notice that the footer does not appear on the table of contents page. Scroll down and observe the footer text in the rest of the document.
    Because page numbering changed, you need to update the table of contents again.

24. Scroll to **page 2** and position the insertion point in the table of contents.

25. Tap F9, choose **Update Entire Table**, and click **OK**.

26. Save your file.

Creating an Index

Video Library   http://labyrinthelab.com/videos   Video Number: WD13-V1004

Word offers two distinct procedures for creating an index:

- Manually marking items to include in the index
- Generating the index by creating a concordance of words to be included in the index

Regardless of which procedure you use, Word automatically generates the index using the words and phrases you identify. In addition, Word sorts the words and phrases alphabetically and groups the contents of the index according to the first letter of the word or phrase. Index styles format the main entries and subentries and apply other formats to the index.

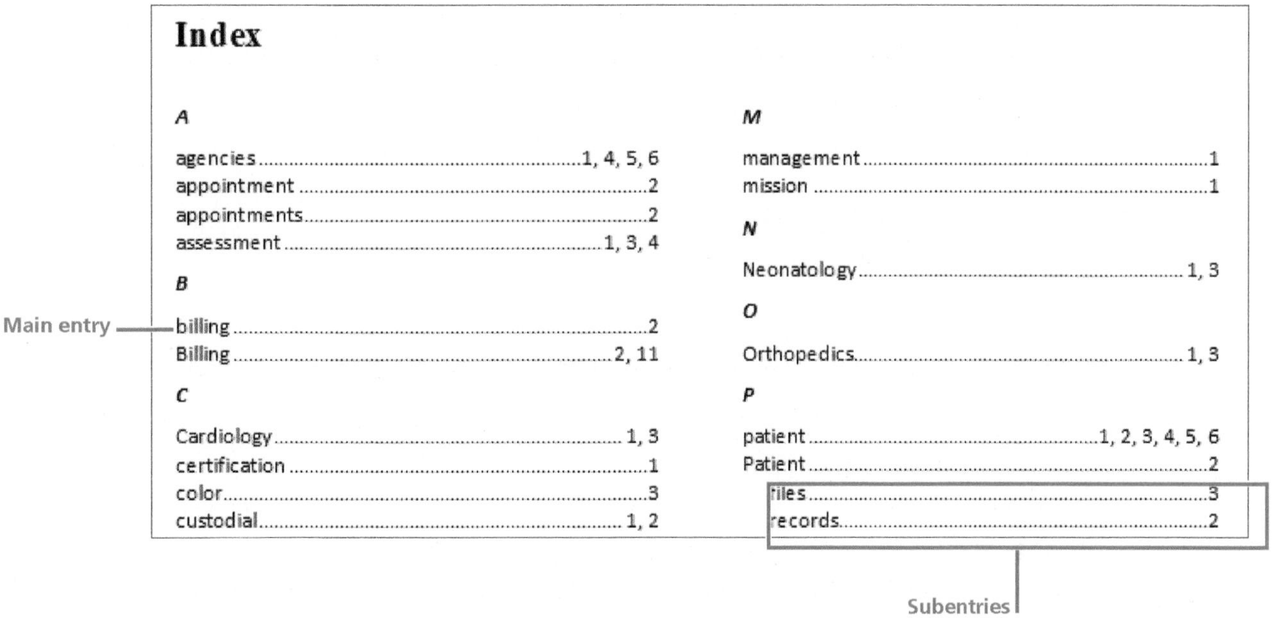

Index

Main entry

Subentries

Marking Index Entries

The first step in creating an index is to mark the main index entries and subentries. These are the words and phrases that will appear in the index. For example, a main entry might be *Patient*, and its subentries might be *files* and *records*.

Entries are marked using the Mark Index Entry dialog box. It's important to note that marking index entries is a case-sensitive action. If you mark all occurrences of a word such as *Billing* for inclusion in the index, Word will only mark those occurrences for the word where the *B* is capitalized. So, it's important to consider which occurrences you want marked before selecting Mark All.

Marking Index Subentries

Index subentries appear in the index indented below main entries. Entering subentries in the Mark Index Entry dialog box is a bit more tedious than marking main entries. As a result, many organizations create indices using only main entries. There are two primary ways to create subentries.

- Type text for the subentry as you mark text for main entries.
- Select the text for the subentry, which places it in the Main Entry field. Cut the text from the Main Entry field and paste it in the Subentry field. Type the Main Entry text.

TIP As you mark text for all index entries, you can keep the Mark Index Entry dialog box open for easy access.

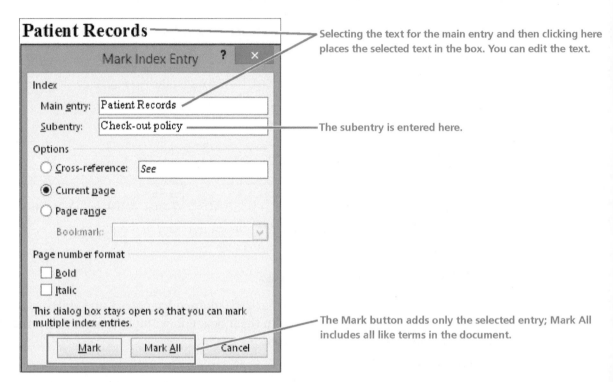

Selecting the text for the main entry and then clicking here places the selected text in the box. You can edit the text.

The subentry is entered here.

The Mark button adds only the selected entry; Mark All includes all like terms in the document.

QUICK REFERENCE	CREATING AN INDEX
Task	**Procedure**
Mark an index main entry	▪ Select the desired word or phrase in the document. ▪ Choose References→Index→Mark Entry; or, use [Alt]+[Shift]+[X] and click Mark.
Mark an index subentry	▪ In the document, select the main entry text, open the Mark Index Entry dialog box, enter the Subentry, and click Mark.
Insert an index	▪ Choose References→Index→Insert Index.
Change the text of an index entry	▪ Edit the text directly in the code created when the entry was originally marked. (You then need to update the index.)
Delete an index entry	▪ Delete the code created when the entry was marked. (You then need to update the index.)
Update the index	▪ Select the index and choose References→Index→Update Index.

Mark Index Entries

In this exercise, you will mark index entries and subentries in preparation for generating an index.

1. Save your file as **WD10-D04-RaritanP&P-[FirstInitialLastName]**.

2. Go to the first page of the body of the manual.

3. If necessary, choose **Home→Paragraph→Show/Hide ¶** to display the formatting marks.
   Displaying formatting marks allows you to see the index codes in your document.

4. Select the heading *Mission Statement*.

5. Choose **References→Index→Mark Entry** .
   Now you'll edit the main entry text.

6. Type **Goals** in the Main Entry box to replace the text that Word automatically inserted.
   The text that was in the box came from the words you selected in the document. You can always replace or edit the suggested entries in this manner.

7. Click **Mark** at the bottom of the dialog box.
   Now you'll examine an index code.

8. If necessary, drag the dialog box to the side, and notice that Word inserted a {XE"Goals"} code in the document.
   This code identifies Goals as a main index entry.

9. Select the word *specialties* at the end of the second line in the second paragraph under the *Mission Statement* heading.

10. Click the **Mark Index Entry** dialog box to activate it, and then click **Mark** to use the proposed text as the main entry.

11. Select *General Medicine* in the first line of the third paragraph below *Scope of Services*, click the dialog box, and click **Mark**.

12. Scroll down and select *Patient* in the heading *Patient Appointments and Billing*, click the dialog box, and click **Mark**.

Mark All Entries
Depending on the nature of the document you are marking, there may be text you want to mark every time it appears.

13. Select *Billing* in the heading *Patient Appointments and Billing*, and then click the dialog box.

14. Click **Mark All** to mark all occurrences of *Billing* for inclusion in the index.
    Remember, this only marks Billing if it begins with a capital letter.

15. Select *billing* toward the end of the first line of the third paragraph below *Patient Appointments and Billing*, click the dialog box, and click **Mark All**.

Mark Subentries

16. If necessary, scroll down to the *Patient Records* heading. Then, follow these steps to mark *records* as a subentry:

A Select *Patient* in the heading.

B Click the **Mark Index Entry** dialog box to make it active.

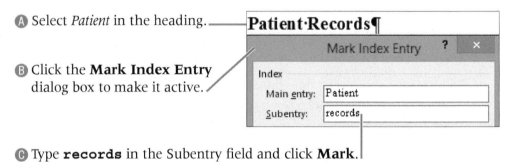

C Type **records** in the Subentry field and click **Mark**.

17. Navigate to the second paragraph below the *Patient Records* heading, select *files* in the first line, and click the dialog box to make it active.

18. Double-click *files* in the Main Entry field and then press Ctrl + X to cut it.

19. Click the **Subentry** field, and then press Ctrl + V to paste *files* into the field.

20. Type **Patient** in the Main Entry field, and then click **Mark**.

21. Close the **Mark Index Entry** dialog box.

22. Save your file.

Generating Index Entries Using a Concordance

Video Library   http://labyrinthelab.com/videos   Video Number: WD13-V1005

If a document is extremely long, marking index entries can be overwhelming. Word offers an automatic option for marking words and phrases to be included in an index. This option allows you to create a list of words and phrases you want to include and saves it as a separate file that acts as a concordance file.

When you use a concordance file to generate an index, it's important to know how Word reacts. These guidelines will provide you with some basic information.

■ The list of words and phrases to be included as main entries should be typed in one column straight down the left margin of the document or in the first column of a table.

■ The document should contain only the words and phrases to be marked.

■ To mark main entries with subentries, create the concordance using a table layout. In the first column, type the words you want to mark as the main entry. In the second column, type the main entry followed by a colon, followed by the text for the subentry, without spaces, as shown in the following illustration:

patient	patient:records

■ Entries can be listed in any order in the concordance—Word will sort them and group them alphabetically when you generate the index. However, sorting the words helps identify duplicate words in the concordance.

Mark Index Entries Using a Concordance

In this exercise, you will mark index entries using a concordance document.

1. Save your file as **WD10-D05-RaritanP&P-[FirstInitialLastName]**.

2. If necessary, choose **Home→Paragraph→Show/Hide** ¶ to display formatting marks.

3. Open **WD10-D05-P&PConcordance** from the **WD2013 Lesson 10** folder.

4. Scroll through the document, review its contents, and then close the document.

5. Position the insertion point at the top of the document.

6. Choose **References→Index→Insert Index** 📄.

7. Click **AutoMark** at the bottom of the dialog box to display the Open Index AutoMark File dialog box.

8. Navigate to the **WD2013 Lesson 10** folder and double-click **WD10-D05-P&PConcordance**.

   Although nothing appears to happen, Word compares the list of words and phrases in the concordance with the manual. When it finds a word on the concordance list, it automatically marks the entry in the manual.

9. Scroll through and review the document.

   Notice the numerous index marks Word added from the concordance in addition to the individually marked items from the previous exercise.

10. Turn off formatting marks.

    Because index codes can be quite lengthy, displaying them can cause text to roll onto other pages. Turning off formatting marks will allow you to ensure that page numbers are accurate.

11. Save the file.

Inserting an Index

Video Library   http://labyrinthelab.com/videos   Video Number: WD13-V1006

After all of the index entries are marked, you can generate the index using the Index dialog box. You can choose the overall format for the index and several other formatting options. The normal position for an index is at the end of a document on a new page or section.

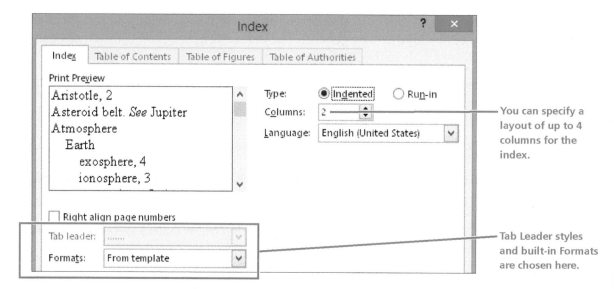

You can specify a layout of up to 4 columns for the index.

Tab Leader styles and built-in Formats are chosen here.

Modifying and Deleting Entries, and Updating the Index

There are several ways to modify an index once you create it.

FROM THE RIBBON
References→Index→
Update Index

- You can select the index and display the Index dialog box and then change various formatting options.

- You can also format the index directly; however, the format active in the Index dialog box will be reapplied if you update the index.

- You can change the text of an entry by replacing it directly in the code that was created when you originally marked it. Then update the index.

- You can delete an index entry by selecting the index code, deleting it, and then updating the index.

DEVELOP YOUR SKILLS WD10-D06
Insert and Modify the Index

In this exercise, you will generate an index from the entries you marked in the previous exercises. Then you will modify the format of the index.

1. Save your file as **WD10-D06-RaritanP&P-[FirstInitialLastName]**.

2. Press ⌈Ctrl⌉+⌈End⌉ to move to the end of the document.
   An index should begin on a blank page.

3. Type the heading **Index** and tap ⌈Enter⌉.

4. Select the heading, and format the text as **bold 16 pt**.

5. Position the insertion point on the blank line below the *Index* heading.

6. Choose **References→Index→Insert Index** 📄.

7. Choose **Formal** from the Formats list at the bottom of the dialog box, and then click **OK** to insert the index.

Modify the Index Format

8. Click anywhere in the index.

9. Choose **References→Index→Insert Index** 📄.

10. Choose **Modern** at the bottom of the dialog box, and then choose **Run In** at the top-right corner of the dialog box.

11. Click **OK**. Click **OK** when the message appears asking if you want to replace the selected index.

    The new index is inserted with the Run In number style. Notice how the Run In style affects the subentries.

12. Click **Undo** ↶ twice to reverse the change.

13. Save the file.

Adding Cross-References

Video Library   http://labyrinthelab.com/videos   Video Number: WD13-V1007

FROM THE RIBBON
Insert→Links→Cross-Reference

Cross-references point you to items such as headings and footnotes located in other parts of a document. The following illustration shows a cross-reference.

You can type descriptive text, such as *see Appendix I*, before inserting the cross-reference.

file folder. This form is attached inside the back of the file cover. A Correspondence Record (see

Policies and Procedures Manual   Raritan Clinic East   4

DRAFT

Appendix I on page 15) inside the back file cover should document when written reports are distributed, as well as any other written correspondence other than routine scheduling contacts.

This cross-reference refers to the heading Appendix I on page 15.

A cross-reference can be one of several types, such as a heading, bookmark, or footnote. The Insert Reference To options vary depending on the Reference type chosen. For example, a Heading can refer to a page number or another heading. Inserting a reference as a hyperlink allows the reader to electronically jump to the cross-reference target.

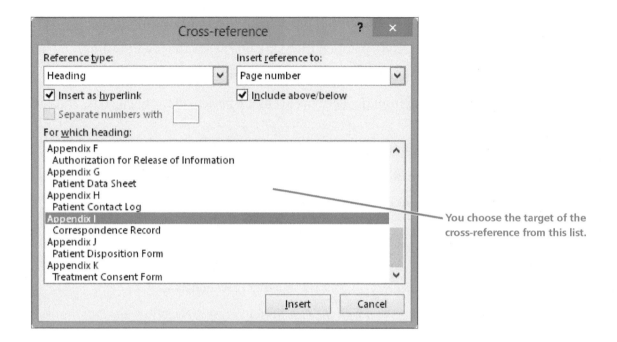

You choose the target of the cross-reference from this list.

Updating Cross-References

Cross-references need to be updated if the pagination of a document changes or if the text you refer to is modified. You can update individual cross-references and other fields by right-clicking the desired field and choosing Update Field from the pop-up menu. You can also use the F9 key to update selected fields.

QUICK REFERENCE	WORKING WITH CROSS-REFERENCES
Task	**Procedure**
Insert a cross-reference	■ Choose Insert→Links→Cross-Reference and make the desired choices in the dialog box.
Update a cross-reference	■ Right-click the Cross-Reference field and choose Update Field from the menu; or, click the Cross-Reference field and tap F9.

DEVELOP YOUR SKILLS WD10-D07

Insert a Cross-Reference

In this exercise, you will insert a cross-reference to a page number, and then follow the hyperlink to the specified page. You will also add a cover page to the manual.

1. Save your file as **WD10-D07-RaritanP&P-[FirstInitialLastName]**.

2. If necessary, choose **Home→Paragraph→Show/Hide ¶** to turn on formatting marks.

3. Navigate to the heading *Patient Contact*.

4. Position the insertion point between the two spaces after the text *Correspondence Record* in the paragraph below the heading.

Patient·Contact¶

→ Any·contact·that·is·made·with·patients·other·than·when·associated·with·an·evaluation[·XE·"evaluation".]·or·treatment[·XE·"treatment".]·session,·should·be·documented·on·the·Patient·Contact·Log·in·the·patient[·XE·"patient".]'s·permanent[·XE·"permanent".]·file·folder[·XE·"folder".]·This·form·is·attached·inside·the·back·of·the·file·cover.·A·Correspondence·Record|·(inside·the·back·file·cover)·should·document·when·written·reports·are·distributed,·as·well·as·any·

5. Type **(see Appendix I** followed by ⬚Spacebar. (You will type the closing parenthesis later.)

6. Turn off formatting marks so they don't affect page numbering.

7. Choose **References→Captions→Cross-Reference** 🔲.

8. Follow these steps to insert the cross-reference:

Ⓐ Choose **Heading** here.

Ⓑ Choose **Page Number** here.

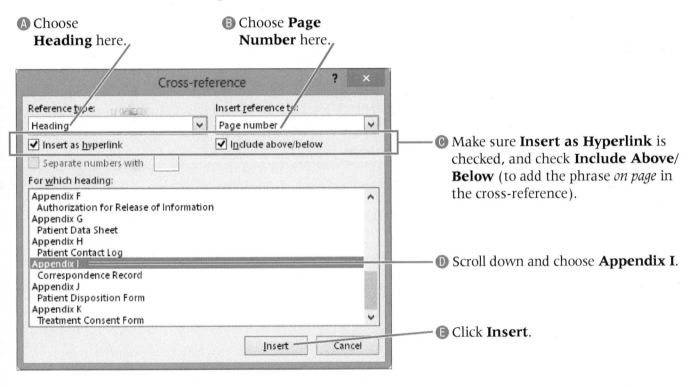

Ⓒ Make sure **Insert as Hyperlink** is checked, and check **Include Above/Below** (to add the phrase *on page* in the cross-reference).

Ⓓ Scroll down and choose **Appendix I**.

Ⓔ Click **Insert**.

9. Close the **Cross-Reference dialog box**.
   The insertion point should be just to the right of the cross-reference.

10. Type the closing parenthesis.

11. Remove the parentheses from the next phrase to avoid two parenthetical phrases next to each other.

12. Position the mouse pointer over *page 15* in the cross-reference you created.
    A tip appears explaining how to follow the link.

13. Press ⬚Ctrl and click the cross-reference.
    The insertion point jumps to the referenced heading.

Add a Cover Page

14. Choose **Insert→Pages→Cover Page** , and then choose **Slice (Light)** from the gallery.

15. Delete the *Document Subtitle* object below the title and the *School* and *Course Title* objects at the bottom of the cover page.

> **TIP** Delete the text box surrounding the *School* and *Course Title* objects, and all three objects are deleted at once.

16. Select the clinic graphic on page 2, click the **Layout Options smart tag**, and choose the **Top and Bottom** wrapping option.

17. Drag the graphic up to **page 1** and position it below the manual's title at the top of the page.

18. On page 2, delete the *Policies and Procedures* title and the page break that follows it. You may wish to turn on formatting marks to see the page break. If so, turn off formatting marks when you are finished.

19. Save your file.

Keeping Text Together

Video Library   http://labyrinthelab.com/videos   Video Number: WD13-V1008

If you're working on a long document that goes through multiple revision cycles, controlling pagination can be a challenge. Word offers several options in the Paragraph dialog box that can be helpful.

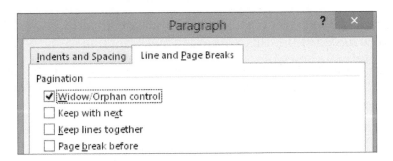

- **Widow/Orphan control:** This option, which is checked by default, places at least two lines of a paragraph at the top or bottom of a page.
- **Keep with next:** This option forces a paragraph to appear with the paragraph that follows it. This is often used to keep a heading with the following paragraph.
- **Keep lines together:** This option prevents a page break in the middle of a paragraph.
- **Page break before:** This option forces a page break before a specific paragraph.

DEVELOP YOUR SKILLS WD10-D08
Keep Text Together

In this exercise, you will use the Keep with Next option to ensure that specified segments of text stay together when Word automatically paginates the document. You will apply the option twice.

1. Save your file as **WD10-D08-RaritanP&P-[FirstInitialLastName]**.

2. On the first page of the document body, select the *Patient Management Procedures* heading and the *Entry into Services* subheading.

   A heading should not appear alone at the page bottom. Although that is not the case now, further editing may split a heading from the paragraph that follows.

3. Choose **Home→Paragraph→dialog box launcher** 🔲.

4. If necessary, click the **Line and Page Breaks tab**, check **Keep with Next**, and click **OK**.

   This ensures that the heading, the subheading, and the paragraph following the subheading will "stick together" during future edits and automatic pagination.

5. Scroll down to the next page and select the *Patient Appointments and Billing* heading.

6. Choose **Home→Paragraph→dialog box launcher** 🔲, check **Keep with Next**, and click **OK**.

7. Save and close your file.

Viewing Master Documents

Video Library   http://labyrinthelab.com/videos   Video Number: WD13-V1009

Sometimes documents you create will be much longer than Word can comfortably handle, such as a 1,000-page reference manual. Managing such documents can be tedious. You may find it easier to work with pieces of the document individually and then add them to a Master Document.

Master documents consist of a shell (the master layout) and individual smaller documents called *subdocuments*. This feature can make working with long documents easier and more efficient.

Master Document tools appear on the Outlining contextual tab, which is active when the Outline view is displayed.

FROM THE RIBBON

Outlining→Master Document→Expand Subdocuments

Outlining→Master Document→Collapse Subdocuments

Double-clicking this icon or pressing Ctrl and clicking a link opens the subdocument.

Master Document tools appear on the Outlining contextual tab.

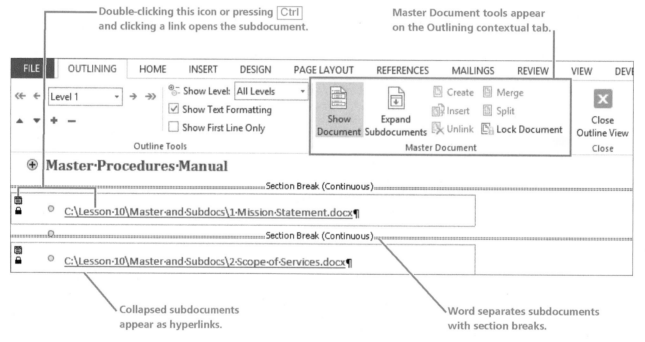

Collapsed subdocuments appear as hyperlinks.

Word separates subdocuments with section breaks.

 The Master Document file and all subdocuments must be stored in the same folder.

DEVELOP YOUR SKILLS WD10-D09
Display Master and Subdocuments

In this exercise, you will open a master document, expand and collapse subdocuments, and review the structure of a master document.

1. Open **WD10-D09-Master** from within the **Master and Subdocs** subfolder of your **WD2013 Lesson 10** folder.

2. Choose **View→Views→Outline** 📰.

3. Choose **Outlining→Master Document→Expand Subdocuments** 📄.
   Word displays the paragraphs contained in each subdocument.

4. Choose **Outlining→Master Document→Collapse Subdocuments** 📄.

5. Press ⌨Ctrl and click the second link in the list to open *Scope of Services*.
   You can open and edit any subdocument from within the master document.

6. Close the subdocument. Choose **Outlining→Close→Close Outline View** ⊠.

7. Close the file without saving changes. Exit **Word**.

Concepts Review

To check your knowledge of the key concepts introduced in this lesson, complete the Concepts Review quiz by choosing the appropriate access option below.

If you are...	Then access the quiz by...
Using the Labyrinth Video Library	Going to http://labyrinthelab.com/videos
Using eLab	Logging in, choosing Content, and navigating to the Concepts Review quiz for this lesson
Not using the Labyrinth Video Library or eLab	Going to the student resource center for this book

Reinforce Your Skills

Create a Table of Contents, and Use Multiple Headers and Footers

In this exercise, you will you will create a table of contents for a multi-page document. You will insert headers and footers in section 2 of the document, but not in section 1.

Insert a Table of Contents

1. Start **Word**. Open **WD10-R01-Organizations** from your **WD2013 Lesson 10** folder and save it as **WD10-R01-Organizations-[FirstInitialLastName]**.

2. If necessary, choose **Home→Paragraph→Show/Hide** ¶ to display formatting marks.

3. Choose **Home→Styles→dialog box launcher** ⌐ to display the **Styles task pane**.

4. Scroll through the document. Starting on **page 3**, position the insertion point in the headings and notice the heading styles in effect.

5. **Close** ✕ the Styles task pane.

6. On **page 2**, notice the section break at the top of the page. Position the insertion point on the blank line above the section break.

7. Choose **References→Table of Contents→Table of Contents** 📄, and then choose **Automatic Table 1** from the gallery.

Modify a Heading and Update the Table of Contents

8. Scroll to **page 3**. In the first subheading below the *Change for Kids* heading, select *Tutoring* and replace it with **Teaching**.

9. On **page 2**, position the insertion point in the table of contents.

10. Click the **Update Table** 📋 button at the top of the table of contents.

11. When the Update Table of Contents dialog box appears, choose **Update Entire Table** and click **OK**.

    The table of contents entry changed to One-on-One Literacy Teaching. *Since the document is quoting directly from the website, the content should not be changed.*

12. Click **Undo** ↺ enough times to return the table of contents and the title in the body of the document to its original state.

Use the Table of Contents Dialog Box

13. Scroll back to **page 2**, choose **References→Table of Contents→Table of Contents** 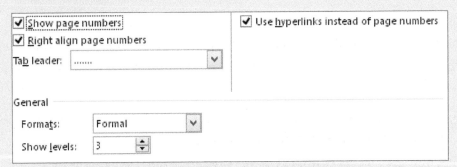, and choose **Custom Table of Contents**.

14. Make sure all three checkboxes are checked, and then choose **Formal** from the Formats drop-down list.

15. Click **OK**. When the message appears confirming the replacement, click **Yes**.

Work with Multiple Headers and Footers

16. Position the insertion point in **section 2** of the document, which begins with *Introduction*.

17. Choose **Insert→Header & Footer→Header** , and then choose **Edit Header**.

Notice the Same as Previous tab at the right side of the header area. You will now break the link between sections 1 and 2.

18. Choose **Header & Footer Tools→Design→Navigation→Link to Previous** .

Notice that the Same as Previous tab no longer appears at the right side of the header.

19. Tap Tab to position the insertion point in the center of the header, and then type **Kids for Change**.

20. Double-click the body of the document to close the header area.

21. Scroll up and notice that the header doesn't appear on pages 1 and 2. Scroll down and observe the header on pages 3 and 4.

22. If necessary, position the insertion point in the page starting with *Introduction*, which is section 2.

23. Choose **Insert→Header & Footer→Footer** , and then choose **Edit Footer**.

Notice the Same as Previous tab at the right side of the footer area.

24. Choose **Header & Footer Tools→Design→Navigation→Link to Previous** to turn it off and break the link between sections 1 and 2.

25. Choose **Header & Footer Tools→Design→Header & Footer→Footer** , and then choose **Austin**.

Notice that the footer Building Block placed a border around the page, and notice that page numbering starts at page 2. You will now change the numbering to start at page 1.

26. Choose **Header & Footer Tools→Design→Header & Footer→Page Number** , and then choose **Format Page Numbers**.

27. In the Page Number Format dialog box, choose **Start At**, at the bottom of the dialog box.
The number defaults to 1, which is what you want.

28. Click **OK**. Double-click in the body of the document to close the footer area.

29. Scroll down and notice the numbering on the third and fourth pages. Scroll up and notice that there are no footers on the first two pages.

30. Save and close the file; exit **Word**.

31. Submit your final file based on the guidelines provided by your instructor.
To see examples of how your file or files should look at the end of this exercise, go to the student resource center.

Create an Index and a Cross-Reference, and View a Master Document

In this exercise, you will create an index and a cross-reference. You will also examine a Master Document.

Mark Index Entries and Subentries

1. Start **Word**. Open **WD10-R02-Sustainability** from your **WD2013 Lesson 10** folder and save it as `WD10-R02-Sustainability-[FirstInitialLastName]`.

2. If necessary, choose **Home→Paragraph→Show/Hide ¶** to turn on formatting marks.

3. Select *wood products* in the first bullet point.

4. Choose **References→Index→Mark Entry** 📄.
That places wood products *in the Main Entry field.*

5. Type `salvaged` in the Subentry field and then click **Mark**.
Notice the colon between wood products *and* salvaged *in the index code. This indicates that* salvaged *is a subentry of* wood products.

6. Select *salvaged* in the Subentry field, type `recycled` in its place, and click **Mark**.
This adds another subentry for wood products.

7. Select *light bulbs* in the third bullet point and then click the dialog box to activate it.

8. Type `fluorescent` in the Subentry field and then click **Mark**.

9. Select *fluorescent* in the Subentry field, type `standard` in its place, and click **Mark**.
This adds another subentry for light bulbs.

10. Select *paper products* in the fifth bullet point, click the dialog box, and click **Mark**.

11. Select *recycle* in the second line of the sixth bullet point, and then click the dialog box.

12. Mark the following terms as subentries for *recycle*.

- **wood products**
- **paper products**
- **plastic containers**
- **cell phones**
- **electronics**

13. Close the dialog box.

Insert an Index

14. Press Ctrl + End to move to the end of the document, and then press Ctrl + Enter to insert a page break.

15. Type **Index** and tap Enter. Format the heading with **bold 16 pt**, and then position the insertion point on the blank line below the heading.

16. Turn off formatting marks.

Remember, displaying index codes can affect page numbering.

17. Choose **References→Index→Insert Index** 📄.

18. Follow these guidelines to complete the index:

- Choose **Classic** in the Formats drop-down list.
- Check the **Right Align Page Numbers** checkbox.
- Choose the dots from the Tab Leader drop-down field.

19. Click **OK**.

Modify an Entry and Update the Index

20. Scroll to the second to last bullet point and select *Computer Takeback Campaign*.

21. Choose **References→Index→Mark Entry** 📑.

This phrase will be a subentry under recycle, so you will cut the term and paste it into the Subentry field.

22. Press Ctrl + X, position the insertion point in the Subentry field, and press Ctrl + V.

23. Type **recycle** in the Main Entry field, and then click **Mark**.

24. Close the dialog box, and then scroll down to the index.

25. Turn off formatting marks.

Word turned on formatting marks when you marked the last entry.

26. Hover the mouse pointer over the index, right-click, and choose **Update Field**.

Add a Cross-Reference

Now you will set up the cross-reference target as a bookmark so the cross-reference will have something to link to.

27. Scroll up to **page 2** and then select *(1)* below the Sources heading.

28. Choose **Insert→Links→Bookmark** 🔖.

29. Type **GlobalLocal** (no spaces) as the bookmark name and click **Add**.

30. Scroll up to **page 1**, position the insertion point after the asterisk at the end of *Think Globally, Act Locally,* and tap [Spacebar].

31. Press [Ctrl] + [B] to turn off Bold.

32. Type **(see the footnote** and tap [Spacebar].

33. Choose **References→Captions→Cross-Reference** ⊞.

34. Follow these guidelines to complete the cross-reference:

    - Choose **Bookmark** from the Reference Type drop-down list.
    - Choose **Page Number** from the Insert Reference To drop-down list.
    - Check the **Include Above/Below** checkbox to make the phrase *on page* appear in the cross-reference.
    - Click **Insert**, and then close the dialog box.
    - Type a closing parenthesis.

    Now, you'll test the cross-reference.

35. Hover the mouse pointer over the page number, press [Ctrl], and click.

    The insertion point moves to the bookmarked item.

Keep Text Together

This document could go through some revisions, so you want to be sure the lines in the second to last bullet point don't split between pages if repagination takes place.

36. Scroll up and select the bullet point that begins with *Recycle old electronics....*

37. Choose **Home→Paragraph→dialog box launcher** ⌐.

38. If necessary, click the **Line and Page Breaks** tab, check **Keep Lines Together**, and click **OK**.

39. Save and close the file.

View a Master Document

Kids for Change plans to expand on some of the topics in the Sustainability document. The administrator created several documents and placed them in a master document so they can be worked on separately.

40. Open **WD10-R02-SustainMaster** from the **SustainMasterSubdocs** subfolder in your **WD2013 Lesson 10** folder.

41. Choose **View→Views→Outline** ▤.

42. Choose **Outlining→Master Document→Expand Subdocuments** ▤.

    Word displays the contents of the subdocuments.

43. Choose **Outlining→Master Document→Collapse Subdocuments** ▤.

44. Press ⌈Ctrl⌉ and click the third link to open the **Paper Products** document.

   At this point, you could make changes to the document and save and close it. The updated version would then be part of the master document.

45. Close the **Paper Products** document.

46. Choose **Outlining→Close→Close Outline View** ☒.

47. Close the master document file without saving changes. Exit **Word**.

48. Submit your final file based on the guidelines provided by your instructor.

   To see examples of how your final file or files should look at the end of this exercise, go to the student resource center.

REINFORCE YOUR SKILLS WD10-R03

Organize a Long Document

In this exercise, you will create a table of contents and headers and footers. You'll insert an index and a cross-reference, and then you will use a pagination option. Finally, you will view a master document.

Create a Table of Contents Page and a Table of Contents

1. Start **Word**. Open **WD10-R03-WikiSustain** from your **WD2013 Lesson 10** folder and save it as `WD10-R03-WikiSustain-[FirstInitialLastName]`.

2. If necessary, choose **Home→Paragraph→Show/Hide** ¶ to display formatting marks.

3. Scroll through the document and observe some of the heading styles.

4. On **page 2**, position the insertion point in front of *Introduction*.

5. Choose **Page Layout→Page Setup→Breaks** ⊟, and then choose **Next Page**.

6. Scroll up and position the insertion point in front of the section break (to the right of the paragraph symbol), and then tap ⌈Enter⌉.

7. Choose **References→Table of Contents→Table of Contents** 📄, and then choose **Automatic Table 2**.

Navigate Using Hyperlinks and Update the Table of Contents

8. Hover the mouse pointer over *Energy* in the table of contents, and then press ⌈Ctrl⌉ and click to jump to that heading in the document.

9. Position the insertion point at the end of the **Energy** heading, tap the ⌈Spacebar⌉, and then type **Consumption**.

10. Scroll up and position the insertion point in the table of contents.

11. Click the **Update Table** 🗋 button.

12. In the Update Table of Contents dialog box, choose **Update Entire Table** and click **OK**.

   Notice that the table of contents updated with the change.

Use the Table of Contents Dialog Box

13. Choose **References→Table of Contents→Table of Contents** 📄, and then choose **Custom Table of Contents**.

14. Choose **Formal** from the Formats drop-down list and click **OK**. When the message appears confirming the replacement, click **OK**.

Work with Multiple Headers and Footers

15. Scroll down and position the insertion point in **section 2**, which begins with *Introduction*.

16. Chooser **Insert→Headers & Footers→Header** 📄, and then choose **Edit Header**.
    Now you will break the link between sections 1 and 2.

17. Choose **Header & Footer Tools→Design→Navigation→Link to Previous** 📄 to break the link.

18. Tap `Tab` twice to position the insertion point at the right side of the header area, and then type `Sustainability in the Twenty-First Century`.

19. Double-click in the body of the document to close the header area.
    Notice that the header appears throughout section 2, but it does not appear in section 1.

20. Position the insertion point in **section 2**.

21. Choose **Insert→Header & Footer→Footer** 📄, and then choose **Edit Footer**.

22. Choose **Header & Footer Tools→Design→Navigation→Link to Previous** 📄 to break the link to section 1.

23. Choose **Header & Footer Tools→Design→Header & Footer→Footer** 📄, and then choose **Austin**.
    Now you will set the page numbering to start at 1 in section 2.

24. Choose **Header & Footer Tools→Design→Header & Footer→Page Number** 📄, and then choose **Format Page Numbers**.

25. Choose **Start At**, at the bottom of the dialog box, and the page number defaults to 1.

26. Click **OK**.

27. Double-click in the body of the document to close the footer area.

Create an Index

28. Select the *Atmosphere* heading toward the top of page 1.

29. Choose **References→Index→Mark Entry** 📄.

30. Type `global warming` in the Subentry field, and then click **Mark**.

31. Select the text in the **Subentry field**, type `carbon reduction` in its place, and click **Mark**.

32. Select the **Subentry text**, type `air pollution:nitrogen oxides` (no spaces surrounding the colon), and click **Mark**.
    Whether you're creating a concordance or marking entries in the Mark Index Entry dialog box, the word(s) to the right of the colon is a subentry of the word(s) on the left.

33. Now mark these items in the Subentry field:

```
air pollution:sulfur oxides
air pollution:photochemical smog
air pollution:acid rain
air pollution:sulfate aerosols
```

34. Click in the document, and scroll down and select *Management of human consumption* toward the bottom of page 2. Then, click the dialog box to activate it.

35. Type **Energy Consumption:increase in CO2** in the Subentry field and click **Mark**.

36. Mark these entries in the Subentry field:

```
Energy Consumption:fossil fuel emissions
Energy Consumption:climate change
harvesting rainwater
ethical consumerism
local food production
circular material flow
renewable sources
industrial ecology
```

37. Close the dialog box.

Insert an Index

38. Position the insertion point at the end of the document and press ⎡Ctrl⎤ + ⎡Enter⎤ to create a new page for the index.

39. Turn off formatting marks.
Remember, the index codes can cause a change in pagination.

40. Type **Index** and tap ⎡Enter⎤. Format the text with **bold 14 pt**, and then position the insertion point on the blank line below the text.

41. Choose **References→Index→Insert Index** 🗎.

42. Choose **Modern** in the Formats drop-down field, check **Right Align Page Numbers**, choose the dots in the Tab Leader drop-down field, and click **OK**.
Notice the subentries under air pollution *and* Energy Consumption. *Now you'll mark another entry and then update the index.*

43. Scroll to **page 1** and select the *Fresh Water and Oceans* heading.

44. Choose **References→Index→Mark Entry** 🗎 and click **Mark**.

45. Click in the document and select the *Land use* heading on **page 2**.

46. Click the dialog box and choose **Mark**. Close the dialog box.

47. Turn off formatting marks.
Word turned on formatting marks when you marked the new index entries.

48. Position the insertion point in the index and tap ⎡F9⎤.

Add a Cross-Reference

Your first step is to bookmark the target of the cross-reference.

49. At the bottom of **page 2**, select *Management* in the *Management of human consumption* heading.

50. Choose **Insert→Links→Bookmark** 🔖.

51. Type **MgmtConsumption** (no spaces) in the Bookmark Name field and click **Add**.

52. At the top of **page 1**, position the insertion point after *management* in the first line of the paragraph below the *Environmental management* heading.

53. Tap [Spacebar], type **(see Management of human consumption**, and tap [Spacebar].

54. Choose **References→Captions→Cross-Reference** 🔲. In the dialog box, make the choices shown here.

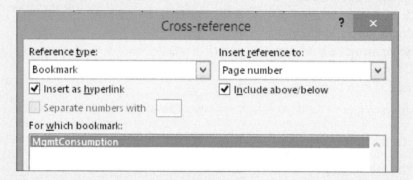

55. Click **Insert**, and then close the dialog box.

    The insertion point should be just to the right of the cross-reference.

56. Type a closing parenthesis.

    Now you will test the cross-reference.

57. Hover the mouse pointer over **page 2** and press [Ctrl] while you click the cross-reference.

    The insertion point jumps to the referenced bookmark.

Keep Text Together

If this document is revised, using some of Word's pagination features will simplify the process. In this example, you want the Management of human consumption *heading to always be at the top of a new page.*

58. Position the insertion point in front of *Management of human consumption*.

59. Choose **Home→Paragraph→dialog box launcher** 🔲. And if necessary, click the **Line and Page Breaks** tab.

    Some pagination options are already in place for this text.

60. Check the **Page Break Before** checkbox and click **OK**.

    This ensures that this heading will always start on a new page. Because pagination has changed, it's a good idea to update the table of contents and the index.

61. Position the insertion point in the table of contents and click **Update Table**.

62. In the Update Table of Contents dialog box, choose **Update Entire Table** and click **OK**.

63. Position the insertion point in the index and tap F9.

64. Save and close the document.

View a Master Document

65. Open **WD10-R03-WikiMaster** from the **WikiSustain** subfolder in your **WD2013 Lesson 10** folder.

66. Choose **View→Views→Outline** 🔲.

67. Choose **Outlining→Master Document→Expand Subdocuments** 🔲.
    Word displays the content of the subdocuments.

68. Choose **Outlining→Master Document→Collapse Subdocuments** 🔲.

69. Press Ctrl and click the first link to open the **Atmosphere** document; then close the document.

70. Choose **Outlining→Close→Close Outline View**.

71. Close the file without saving changes; exit **Word**.

72. Submit your final file based on the guidelines provided by your instructor.

Apply Your Skills

Create a Table of Contents, and Use Multiple Headers and Footers

In this exercise, you will insert a table of contents and headers and footers in a document.

Insert a Table of Contents and Add Headers and Footers

1. Start **Word**. Open **WD10-A01-Munich** from your **WD2013 Lesson 10** folder and save it as **WD10-A01-Munich-[FirstInitialLastName]**.

2. Open the **Styles task pane**, scroll through the document and observe some of the heading styles in use, and then close the task pane.

3. Position the insertion point in front of *Introduction* on the first page of the body and insert a **Next Page** section break.

4. If necessary, display formatting marks. Then, scroll up and position the insertion point in front of the section break and tap ⌷Enter⌷.

5. Insert an **Automatic Table 1** table of contents and use the **Parks** hyperlink to jump to that heading.

6. Position the insertion point at the end of the heading, tap ⌷Spacebar⌷, and type: **and Recreation**.

7. Update the table of contents to reflect the change.

8. Open the Table of Contents dialog box, apply the **Classic** style, choose the dots from the Tab Leader drop-down list, and click **OK**.

9. When the message box appears confirming the replacement, click **OK**.

10. Position the insertion point in **section 2**, which begins with *Introduction*, choose **Edit Header**, and break the link between sections 1 and 2.

11. Insert a header using the **Banded style** in the Header gallery; close the header area.

12. Choose **Edit Footer** and break the link between sections 1 and 2. Then, insert a **Banded** footer.

13. Format the page numbers to start at **1** in section 2; close the footer area.

14. Save and close the document; exit **Word**.

15. Submit your final file based on the guidelines provided by your instructor.

    To see examples of how your file or files should look at the end of this exercise, go to the student resource center.

Create an Index and a Cross-Reference, Use Keep Text Together, and View a Master Document

In this exercise, you will mark main entries and subentries and use a concordance to create an index. Then you will make additions to the index and update it. You will create and test a cross-reference, and finally, you will view a Master Document and open a subdocument.

Mark Index Entries and Use a Concordance

1. Start **Word**. Open **WD10-A02-Bangalore** from your **WD2013 Lesson 10** folder and save it as **WD10-A02-Bangalore-[FirstInitialLastName]**.

2. If necessary, display formatting marks so you can see index codes.

3. Select the three main headings on page 1, *Background*, *Weather*, and *Get in*, and mark them as main index entries.

4. Mark *By plane* as a subentry of *Get in*.

5. On **page 6**, mark *Landmarks* and *Temples* as main index entries.

6. Navigate to your **WD2013 Lesson 10** folder, open **WD10-A02-Concordance**, examine the file, and then close it.

7. Use the **AutoMark** button in the Index dialog box, together with **WD10-A02-Concordance**, to mark additional index entries.

8. Turn off formatting marks.
   Remember, displaying formatting marks can affect pagination.

Insert an Index and Add a Cross Reference

9. Scroll to the end of the document and insert a page break to create a blank page for your index.

10. Type **Index** at the top of the new blank page and tap [Enter].

11. Format Index with **bold 14 pt**. Then, position the insertion point on the blank line below the heading and insert an index using the **Formal format**.

12. Scroll up to **page 1** and select *Background*.

13. Choose **References→Index→Mark Entry** [icon]. Mark these terms as subentries of *Background:*
    - population
    - Garden City of India
    - IT industry

14. Turn off formatting marks and update the index.

15. On **page 1**, position the insertion point to the right of *Get in* and tap [Spacebar].

16. Type this text: (**see By car** and tap [Spacebar].

17. Insert a cross-reference using these guidelines:
    - Reference Type: **Heading**
    - Insert Reference to: **Page Number**
    - Make sure **Insert as Hyperlink** is checked
    - Check **Include Above/Below**
    - Choose *By car* from the list of headings

18. Click **Insert** and then close the dialog box.

19. Type a closing parenthesis.

20. Test the hyperlink in your cross-reference.

Keep Text Together and View a Master Document

21. On **page 1**, select the *Background* heading.

22. Open the **Paragraph dialog box** and check **Keep with Next** on the Line and Page Breaks tab.

23. Select the *Weather* heading and apply the **Keep with Next** option.

24. Select the *Get in* and *By plane* headings and apply the **Keep with Next** option.

25. Save and close the file.

26. Open **WD10-A02-BangaloreMaster** from the **Bangalore** subfolder in your **WD2013 Lesson 10** folder.

27. Switch to **Outline** view. In the Outlining tab, choose **Expand Subdocuments** .

28. Collapse the **subdocuments** , and then click the fourth hyperlink to open the **By car** document.

29. Close the **By car** document and then close **Outline view**.

30. Close the master document without saving changes; exit **Word**.

31. Submit your final file based on the guidelines provided by your instructor.

    To see examples of how your file or files should look at the end of this exercise, go to the student resource center.

Organize a Long Document

In this exercise, you will create a table of contents and an index, work with multiple headers and footers, and add a cross-reference. You will also set up a page break pagination option and view a Master Document.

Create a Table of Contents and Work with Headers and Footers

1. Start **Word**. Open **WD10-A03-Basque** from your **WD2013 Lesson 10** folder and save it as `WD10-A03-Basque-[FirstInitialLastName]`.

2. If necessary, display formatting marks.

3. Choose **Home→Styles→dialog box launcher** 🔲 to open the Styles task pane.

4. Scroll through the document and observe the heading styles, and then close the task pane.

5. Position the insertion point in front of the heading, *The Basque Country*, on page 2.

6. Insert a **Next Page section break** to create a new page for the table of contents.

7. Scroll up, position the insertion point in front of the section break, and tap Enter.

8. Insert a table of contents using the **Automatic Table 2** format.

9. Use the **Climate link** in the table of contents to jump to the *Climate* heading.

10. Type **Basque** Spacebar in front of *Climate*.

11. Update the table of contents to reflect the change.

12. Open the **Table of Contents** dialog box and apply the **Distinctive** format to the table of contents.

13. Position the insertion point in **section 2**, which begins with *The Basque Country* heading, choose **Edit Header**, and break the link between sections 1 and 2.

14. Insert a header using the **Blank style** from the gallery.

15. Type **The Basque Country** in the Type Here area; close the header area.

16. With the insertion point in **section 2**, choose **Edit Footer** and break the link between sections 1 and 2.

17. Insert a footer using the **Austin** style.

18. Format the starting page number to start at page **1**. Close the footer area.

Mark Entries and Create an Index

19. Mark index main entries and subentries using the headings indicated in this table.

Main Entry	Subentry
Features	■ Atlantic Basin
	■ Middle section
	■ Ebro Valley
Basque Climate	
Transport	■ Road
	■ Rail
	■ Airports
	■ Seaports

20. Turn off formatting marks. Then, position the insertion point at the end of the document and insert a page break.

21. Type **Index** and tap Enter. Format the text with **bold 14 pt**. Then, position the insertion point on the blank line below the heading and insert a **Formal** index.

22. Mark the *Cuisine* heading (page 4) as a main entry, turn off formatting marks, and then update the index.

Add a Cross-Reference

23. Create a bookmark for *The Ebro Valley* heading (page 2), naming it **Ebro**.

24. Position the insertion point after the *Features* heading (page 1) and tap Spacebar . Type **(see The Ebro Valley** and tap Spacebar .

25. Create a cross-reference using these options.

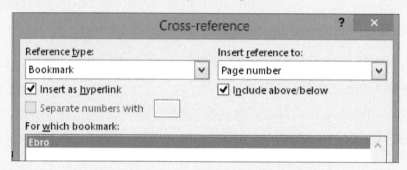

26. Type a closing parenthesis; then test your cross-reference.

Keep Text Together and View a Master Document

27. Position the insertion point in front of the *Transport* heading (page 2) and insert the **Page Break Before** pagination option.

28. Since you changed pagination, update the table of contents and the index. Then, save and close the file.

29. Open **WD10-A03-BasqueMaster** in the **Basque** subfolder in your **WD2013 Lesson 10** folder.

30. Switch to **Outline view**. In the Outlining tab, choose **Expand Documents** .
    Notice that the pictures in the subdocuments do not display in this view.

31. Collapse the **subdocuments** , and then use the first hyperlink to open the **Features** document.
    The pictures are visible again.

32. Close the **Features** document, and then close **Outline view**.

33. Close the master document without saving changes. Exit **Word**.

34. Submit your final file based on the guidelines provided by your instructor.

Extend Your Skills

In the course of working through the Extend Your Skills exercises, you will think critically as you use the skills taught in the lesson to complete the assigned projects. To evaluate your mastery and completion of the exercises, your instructor may use a rubric, with which more points are allotted according to performance characteristics. (The more you do, the more you earn!) Ask your instructor how your work will be evaluated.

WD10-E01 That's the Way I See It

As a small-business owner, you want to offer your customers a document that provides an in-depth, categorized overview of your products. If you were a bookstore owner, for example, you might categorize books by genre (e.g., history, biography, fiction). Start a new Word document and save it to your **WD2013 Lesson 10** folder as **WD10-E01-ProductDescriptions-[FirstInitialLastName]**.

Decide on the type and name of your business. Type an introduction (3–4 sentences) for each main product category, providing longer content for the subcategories. Format main categories with Heading 1 and give each at least three subcategories (in Heading 2). Your document should be at least seven pages including a cover page, a table of contents, one or more cross-references (with a Word heading or a bookmark that you create as the target), index (ten main entries and at least three subentries), multiple footers (page numbering starting at page 1 in section 2, no footers in section 1), and the Keep Text Together option (keep heading lines together with the paragraph following headings; apply this feature at least twice). You may copy content from the Internet, but cite your sources.

You will be evaluated based on the inclusion of all elements specified, your ability to follow directions, your ability to apply newly learned skills to a real-world situation, your creativity, and the relevance of your topic and/or data choice(s). Submit your final file based on the guidelines provided by your instructor.

WD10-E02 Be Your Own Boss

As the owner of Blue Jean Landscaping, you want to provide your customers with in-depth information for their spring gardens, focusing on fruits, vegetables, and legumes. Start a new Word document and save it to your **WD2013 Lesson 10** folder as **WD10-E02-SpringPlanting-[FirstInitialLastName]**.

Create an introduction (3–4 sentences). Do online research to create at least three subcategories for each category. Format the category headings with Heading 1 and the subcategories with Heading 2. Provide detailed information, such as the best growing conditions for a particular type of tomato. Your document should be at least seven pages, with a cover page, table of contents, and index. You may copy content from the Internet but cite your sources. Include two cross-references, with a Word heading and a bookmark as targets. Insert a Next Page section break between the table of contents and the document body. Use page numbers in the section 2 footer, starting at page 1; use no footer in section 1. Your index should include twenty main entries and at least five subentries.

You will be evaluated based on the inclusion of all elements specified, your ability to follow directions, your ability to apply newly learned skills to a real-world situation, your creativity, and your demonstration of an entrepreneurial spirit. Submit your file based on the guidelines provided by your instructor.

Transfer Your Skills

In the course of working through the Transfer Your Skills exercises, you will use critical-thinking and creativity skills to complete the assigned projects using skills taught in the lesson. To evaluate your mastery and completion of the exercises, your instructor may use a rubric, with which more points are allotted according to performance characteristics. (The more you do, the more you earn!) Ask your instructor how your work will be evaluated.

WD10-T01 Use the Web as a Learning Tool

Throughout this book, you will be provided with an opportunity to use the Internet as a learning tool by completing WebQuests. According to the original creators of WebQuests, as described on their website (WebQuest.org), a WebQuest is "an inquiry-oriented activity in which most or all of the information used by learners is drawn from the web." To complete the WebQuest projects in this book, navigate to the student resource center and choose the WebQuest for the lesson on which you are currently working. The subject of each WebQuest will be relevant to the material found in the lesson.

WebQuest Subject: Research a career in indexing.

Submit your final files based on the guidelines provided by your instructor.

WD10-T02 Demonstrate Proficiency

Stormy BBQ is planning to sell a book about BBQ cooking, and you have been asked to provide the research, which you will do online. You can feel free to copy content from online sources—just remember to cite your sources.

Start a new Word document and save it to your **WD2013 Lesson 10** folder as `WD10-T02-BBQBook-[FirstInitialLastName]`. The book will include three main categories: BBQ Grills and Tools, BBQ Tips and Techniques, and BBQ Recipes. Each category heading should be formatted with the Heading 1 style. Create a short introduction (3–4 sentences) for each main category. Based on your research, identify at least two subcategories for each category; format the subcategory headings with the Heading 2 style. Use a Next Page section break to designate a cover page and table of contents as section 1 and the rest of the document as section 2. Insert a header with the company name that only appears in section 2. Insert a page number footer that appears only in section 2 and that starts numbering at page 1. Create an index of at least fifteen terms of your choice, including main entries and at least five subentries.

Submit your final file based on the guidelines provided by your instructor.

WORD 2013

Collaborating in Word

LEARNING OBJECTIVES

After studying this lesson, you will be able to:

- Use the highlighter tool
- Work with Track Changes and comments
- Send Word emails
- Use AutoSave and AutoRecover
- Work with SkyDrive and Office Web Apps

The Internet makes it easy for project teams to collaborate on drafting documents. Team members can exchange documents across the country as easily as they can across the hall. In addition to the ability to insert comments in a document, Word has several features that make collaboration activities more efficient. For example, Word can track all of the changes made on a document by each team member and combine these changes into a single document for review. In this lesson, you will work with these collaboration tools.

Collaborating on a Manual

As a member of the human resources department, you have been working to finalize the Raritan Clinic East Policies & Procedures Manual. It's now ready for review by personnel in the human resources department. As others review the manual, they will use Word's collaboration tools to mark suggested changes. Some reviewers will insert comments to identify their recommendations, while others will use Word's Track Changes feature to mark suggested edits. Some will highlight text to identify wording that needs revising. Your task will be to review all suggested edits and comments and finalize the document for printing.

Raritan Clinic East

Pediatric Diagnostic Specialists

A Track Changes markup

Patient Management Procedures

It is important that standard management procedures be used to maintain the standards of treatment that each patient deserves. These procedures are described in the following pages.

Pediatric General Medicine, Cardiology, and Orthopedics, Pediatric Emergency Medicine, and Neonatology. The practice serves a patient community ranging in ages from newborn to 18 years.

Highlighted text

to provide a clinical and educational environment in d in the programs of pediatric diagnostic specialties undergraduate and graduate students observe and

Suzanne Student A few seconds ago
This phrase sounds awkward.¶

A comment added to the document

Using the Highlighter

Video Library   http://labyrinthelab.com/videos   Video Number: WD13-V1101

Word's highlighter pen works just like its real-life counterpart (except that you can easily erase the highlighting). The pen applies a transparent color to the background of the text. You apply a highlight by selecting a highlight color and dragging over text, or you can select the text and then click the Text Highlight Color button to apply the color to the selected text.

The Text Highlight Color pen offers a variety of highlighting colors, so you can color-code the highlights you use in a document if you wish. For example, you might highlight a note to yourself in yellow and a "waiting for information" reminder in green.

FROM THE RIBBON
Home→Font→Text
Highlight Color

FROM THE KEYBOARD
Tap Esc to turn off the
highlighter pen

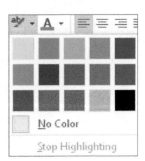

DEVELOP YOUR SKILLS WD11-D01
Highlight Text

In this exercise, you will highlight a note to yourself and a reminder that you are waiting for additional information.

1. Open **WD11-D01-PolicyManual** from your **WD2013 Lesson 11** folder and save it as **WD11-D01-PolicyManual-[FirstInitialLastName]**.

   Replace the bracketed text with your first initial and last name. For example, if your name is Bethany Smith, your filename would look like this: WD11-D01-PolicyManual-BSmith.

2. Make sure the insertion point is at the beginning of the document.

3. Search the document for *Pediatric General Medicine*, and position the insertion point at the beginning of the first line where the text appears on page 2.

4. Type this text: **Chin has more information about these specialties:** then tap Spacebar

5. Choose **Home→Font→Text Highlight Color** menu button ▼ and then choose **Bright Green** from the gallery.

   When the mouse pointer is in the body of the document, it looks like a highlighter pen.

6. Drag the pen across the text you just added to highlight it.

7. Choose **Home→Font→Text Highlight Color** to turn off the pen.

   Notice that the color on the button face reflects the most recently used color.

Tapping Esc also turns off the pen.

8. Press Ctrl + End to move to the end of the document.

9. Type this text: **Check with Finance to see if they have information to add.**

10. Select the sentence, choose **Home→Font→Text Highlight Color** menu button ▼, and then choose **Yellow**.

    This highlights the selected text and changes the button color to yellow.

11. Select the sentence again.

12. Choose **Home→Font→Text Highlight Color** ![aby] menu ▼.

13. Choose **No Color** to remove the highlight.

14. Click **Undo** ![undo] enough times to remove both added sentences.
    If you Undo too many times, you can always click Redo.

15. Save the file and leave it open.

Tracking Changes to Documents

Video Library   http://labyrinthelab.com/videos   Video Number: WD13-V1102

The Track Changes feature is one of Word's most useful collaboration tools. You can electronically distribute copies of a document to different team members, and with Track Changes, Word marks the changes they make. You can merge the changes from all copies into a single document, and you can then review each change and accept or reject it.

Reviewers can also use Word's Comment feature to leave messages in a document as a means of communicating and collaborating with the originator.

Steps in a Typical Editing and Reviewing Process

Following are the steps showing how a typical review process might progress in today's world of requests for instant feedback.

THE EDITING AND REVIEW PROCESS		
Step	**Description**	**Performed by**
1	You send an electronic copy of the document via email to all those who need to review it.	You
2	Each reviewer makes revisions to the copy of the document. Word's Track Changes feature marks the edits and identifies the date and person making the edit, as well as the type of revision made.	Reviewers
3	Reviewers return the edited document to you.	Reviewers
4	After receiving all copies of the document, you can review each document manually and accept or reject the edits, or you can combine all edited documents into one document so you have one document that contains all edits from all reviewers.	You

Viewing Tracked Changes

Word offers options for viewing edits made to documents using Track Changes.

- **Inline:** Edits are marked directly within sentences and paragraphs. Text that is deleted by the reviewer is colored and marked through with a line, and text that is added appears underlined and in a different color.

- **Balloons:** Comments and edits appear in balloons on the right side of the document text. Each balloon identifies the person who made the edit as well as the type of edit made—inserted text, deleted, and so forth.

Tracked changes shown in line with the text

Patient·Management·Procedures¶

→   It·is·important·that·standard·management·procedures·be·used·to·maintain·the·standards·of··· treatment·that·each·patient·deserves.·These·procedures·are·described·in·the·following·page.¶

for·each·patient·is·determined.·When·schedule/room·changes·occur,·the·supervisor·and·practicum· student·are·notified·via·the·Notice·of·Schedule/Room·Change·Form.·Children·must·be·	**Suzanne Student** Deleted: ·(see·Appendix·B)
accompanied·to·the·appointment·by·the·custodial·parent·or·legal·guardian.·If·unable·to·attend,·the· parent·or·legal·guardian·must·sign·a·Release·expressing·permission·for·the·services·to·be·	**Suzanne Student** Deleted: (see·Appendix·C)

Tracked changes shown as balloons in the Markup Area

The following table describes different ways you can display tracked changes and comments.

DISPLAY OPTIONS FOR TRACKED CHANGES AND COMMENTS

Show Markup Views	Description
Show all revisions inline	- Deleted text appears in the document body with a strikethrough font; added text is underlined in the document body.
	- Comments highlight the selected text, and you read the comment by hovering the mouse pointer over it.
	- Moved text uses a strikethrough font at the *moved from* area, and it appears underlined in the body of the document in the *moved to* area.
Show revisions in balloons	- Deleted text, comments, and formatting changes appear in balloons in the Markup Area to the right of the document being reviewed.
	- Added text is underlined in the body of the document.
	- Moved text appears in a balloon at the *moved from* area; it appears underlined in the body of the document in the *moved to* area.
Show only comments and formatting in balloons	- Comments and formatting changes appear in balloons; all other changes appear inline.

The descriptions in the preceding table relate to working in a view called All Markup. Variations occur when you make other viewing choices. You will learn about viewing choices later in this lesson.

✓	Show Revisions in **B**alloons
	Show All Re**v**isions Inline
	Show Only **C**omments and Formatting in Balloons

The Show Markup Balloons menu provides options for displaying marked changes.

NOTE

The balloons method is the primary method used in this lesson.

Setting the Username and Initials

Video Library   http://labyrinthelab.com/videos   Video Number: WD13-V1103

The Track Changes feature uses information set up in the Word Options dialog box to identify your username for edits you make to a document. As a result, whenever you collaborate on a document where Track Changes is used, it is important to make sure your username and initials are set correctly.

Setting Reviewer Ink Colors

Track Changes can use different colors to distinguish the edits of each reviewer who works on the document. Each reviewer can specify colors for his or her comments and tracked changes. This makes it easier to rapidly identify changes submitted by a specific reviewer. It also allows you to keep a consistent color for a reviewer you work with frequently, rather than settling on colors Word may assign automatically.

In the Formatting and Insertions examples (square with red on top and blue on the bottom), Word will automatically assign colors.

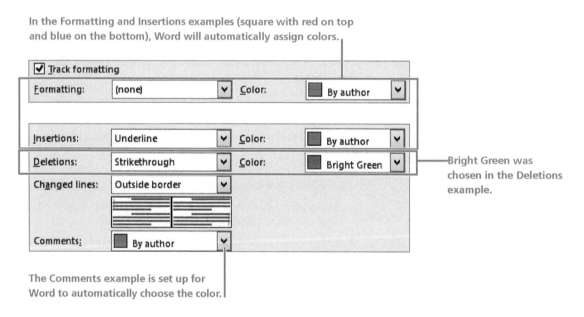

Bright Green was chosen in the Deletions example.

The Comments example is set up for Word to automatically choose the color.

QUICK REFERENCE	TRACKING CHANGES
Task	**Procedure**
Turn on Track Changes	Choose Review→Tracking→Track Changes.
Choose a method of tracking	Choose Review→Tracking→Show Markup, and then choose the desired options.
Associate your name and initials with changes	Choose Review→Tracking→dialog box launcher, click the Change User Name button, and enter your name and initials.
Set reviewer ink colors	Choose Review→Tracking→dialog box launcher, click the Advanced Options button, and then make the desired choices.

Change Tracking Colors, Username, and Initials

In this exercise, you will turn on Track Changes, change the tracking colors, and set the user's name and initials for the Revised Raritan Clinic East Procedures Manual.

You will not save a new copy of the file in this exercise, since no changes are made to the document.

1. Choose **Review→Tracking→dialog box launcher** 🔳, and then click the **Advanced Options** button.

2. Follow these steps to choose options for your reviewer ink color settings.

Ⓐ Set the color for Insertions to **Blue**.

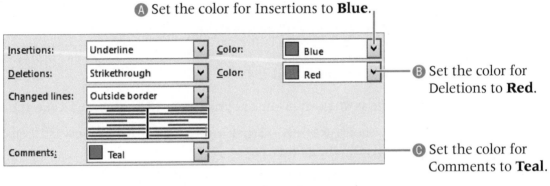

Ⓑ Set the color for Deletions to **Red**.

Ⓒ Set the color for Comments to **Teal**.

Ⓓ Click **OK** once.

3. Click the **Change User Name** button at the bottom of the Track Changes Options dialog box, enter your username and initials, and click **OK** twice.

Adding Comments to a Document

Video Library   http://labyrinthelab.com/videos   Video Number: WD13-V1104

Word's Comment feature is a great collaboration tool. It allows reviewers and originators to communicate about a document by posting comments to each other. A reviewer might want to point out the reason for a deletion, for example. You can place comments in the body of a document, in a balloon in the Markup Area to the right of the document, or in the Reviewing Pane, which you can position at the side or bottom of the Word window. Word displays the name of the comment's author and the date and time the comment was inserted.

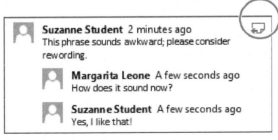

The reply button in the comments balloon allows threaded conversations between the originator and reviewers.

Word 2013

Task	Procedure
Insert a comment	Choose Review→Comments→New Comment.
Display comments inline or in a balloon in the Markup Area	Choose Review→Tracking→Show Markup→Balloons, and then choose the desired method from the menu.
Delete a comment	Whether the comment is inline or in a balloon, right-click the comment and choose Delete Comment; or, choose Review→Comments→Delete.

DEVELOP YOUR SKILLS WD11-D03
Work with Track Changes

In this exercise, you will choose the balloon display for tracking changes, and then you will insert a comment and make revisions in the document.

1. Save your file as **WD11-D03-PolicyManual-[FirstInitialLastName]**.

2. If necessary, choose **Review→Tracking→Display for Review** 🔛 then choose **All Markup** form the menu.

3. Choose **Review→Tracking→Track Changes** 📝.

4. If necessary, display formatting marks.

5. If necessary, choose **Review→Tracking→Show Markup→Balloons→Show Revisions in Balloons**.

   Deleted text, comments, and formatting changes will appear in balloons in the Markup Area. Added text will be underlined in the body.

6. Scroll to **page 2**. In the last paragraph on the page, select *Referral* at the beginning of the paragraph.

7. Choose **Review→Comments→New Comment** 🗨.

   Notice the Markup Area that appears to the right of the document. This is where comment balloons and editing balloons appear.

8. Type this text in the comment balloon: **Indent to match other paragraphs.**

9. Locate and select the text *(see Appendix A)* in the next line; delete it.

   Word places deleted text in a balloon in the Markup Area and places a gray change bar in the left margin to help reviewers locate changes, as shown in the following illustration.

10. Follow these guidelines to continue with deletions:
    - Search for the word *see* to locate each additional cross-reference to an appendix.
    - Delete the cross-references for **Appendices B–K**.
    - Delete extra spaces between words where appropriate.

11. Search for *Patient Management Procedures*, then position the insertion point at the end of the heading.

12. Follow these steps to insert introductory text for the heading:

Ⓐ Tap `Enter`. 　 Ⓑ Tap `Tab`, and then type the text shown here.

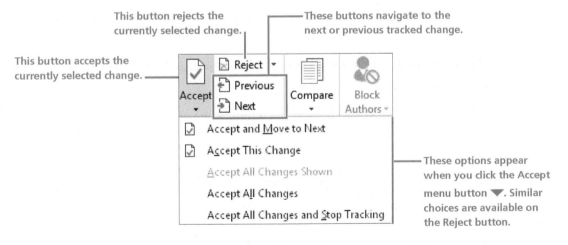

Patient·Management·Procedures¶

→ It is important that standard management procedures be used to maintain the standards of treatment that each patient deserves. These procedures are described in the following page.¶

Ⓒ Notice the gray change bar in the left margin that helps locate changes.

Notice the formatting balloons in the Markup Area. Although the font is the same for the other body text, the Word styles are different; therefore, Word notes the difference.

13. Save the file and leave it open.

Reviewing Tracked Changes

Video Library　http://labyrinthelab.com/videos　Video Number: WD13-V1105

Word makes it easy to find and review changes to a document. When you review changes, Word jumps from one change to the next, giving you the opportunity to accept or reject each change. You can also accept or reject all changes at once. After you accept or reject a change, Word removes the revision marks.

This button rejects the currently selected change.

These buttons navigate to the next or previous tracked change.

This button accepts the currently selected change.

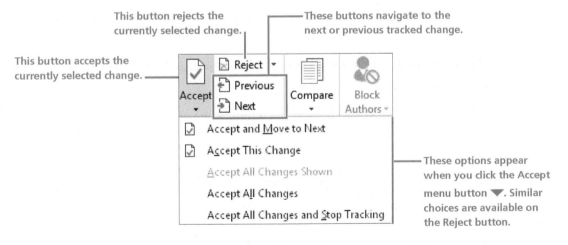

Accept 　Reject ▾ 　Previous 　Next 　Compare 　Block Authors ▾

☑ Accept and <u>M</u>ove to Next
☑ A<u>c</u>cept This Change
Accept All Changes Shown
Accept A<u>l</u>l Changes
Accept All Changes and <u>S</u>top Tracking

These options appear when you click the Accept menu button ▼. Similar choices are available on the Reject button.

You can also right-click a proposed change and choose an Accept or a Reject command from the pop-up menu.

Displaying Tracked Changes

Word allows you to display tracked changes in four distinctive views. Depending on the type of detail you want to focus on, each view offers specific advantages. For example, you may want to view how the document would look after the changes are incorporated. In this case, you would choose the No Markup option. If you want to see how the document looked before any changes were made, you would choose Original.

| All Markup | ▾ |
| Simple Markup |
| All Markup |
| No Markup |
| Original |

VIEWS FOR TRACKED CHANGES	
Markup	**Description**
Simple Markup	Shows where a change occurred with a red change bar in the margin. Clicking the change bar displays the markup details.
All Markup	Shows all markups.
No Markup	Hides all markups and displays a final document appearance with the proposed changes.
Original	Shows the original document appearance without the changes.

DEVELOP YOUR SKILLS WD11-D04
Review Tracked Changes

In this exercise, you will display the document using different markup views. Then you will review tracked changes to the document, accepting some changes and rejecting others.

1. Save your file as **WD11-D04-PolicyManual-[FirstInitialLastName]**.

2. Choose **Review→Tracking→Display for Review** 📑 **menu ▾**, choose **Original**, and scroll through the document.

   The document now appears as it did before you made changes.

3. Choose **Review→Tracking→Display for Review** 📑 **menu ▾**, choose **All Markup**, and scroll through the document.

   Notice the balloons in the Markup Area on the right. Deleted text, comments, and formatting changes appear in balloons, while inserted text is underlined in the body.

4. Choose **Review→Tracking→Display for Review** 📑 **menu ▾**, choose **Simple Markup**, and scroll through the document.

   Red change bars appear in the margin where changes occurred. Clicking the change bar displays the change in detail; clicking it again hides the detail. This is a good view for documents with lots of changes.

5. Choose **Review→Tracking→Display for Review** 📑 **menu ▾**, choose **No Markup**, and scroll through the document.

   This view helps you see what the final document will look like.

Accept and Reject Changes

6. Position the insertion point at the top of the document.

7. Choose **Review→Changes→Next** 📄.

   Word switches to All Markup view, and then jumps to and highlights the paragraph you added to the document. This is a good addition to the document, so you will accept it.

8. Choose **Review→Changes→Accept** ☑.

   Word removes the change marks from the new paragraph and moves to the next change—the formatting balloon associated with the change you just accepted.

9. Choose **Review→Changes→Accept** ☑.

10. Choose **Review→Changes→Accept** ☑.

11. Choose **Review→Changes→Next** ⊡ to skip the comment and move to the next change, the Deleted reference to Appendix A.

12. Choose **Review→Changes→Reject** ⊠.

    Word restores the deleted text and moves to the next tracked change.

13. Reject each deleted reference to an appendix.

    Word returns to your comment.

Delete a Comment

14. Choose **Review→Comments→Delete** ⬚.

15. Choose **Review→Tracking→Track Changes** ⬚ to turn off the feature.

16. Position the insertion point at the beginning of the paragraph starting with *Referral* (bottom of page 2) and tap ⎯Tab⎯ to indent the first line.

17. Save the file and keep it open.

Saving and Sending Files

Video Library   http://labyrinthelab.com/videos   Video Number: WD13-V1106

Before reviewers can do their job, you must decide how to get the document to them. You can use the Internet to share your document several ways, including the following:

- Email
- Microsoft SkyDrive
- Network drive

This lesson uses email as the method for sharing files.

Sharing Files via Email

Sharing files via email is a simple procedure, but as with any process, it has its strengths and weaknesses.

PROS AND CONS OF SHARING VIA EMAIL	
Strengths	**Weaknesses**
■ No Microsoft Account ID is required	■ Managing several versions of the same document can be time consuming
■ Most users are already familiar with using email	■ Large documents containing video, audio, or other linked files can be problematic to email
■ Attaching a document to an email is a simple process	■ Each reviewer must have Word installed to edit the document or insert comments
■ As reviewers must have Word, they can add comments directly to the document	

The Share tab of Backstage view contains an Email option that includes commands to attach the current document as a Word file, a PDF file, or an XPS document. When you choose one of these options, Word displays an email form with the file attached. You just need to address the email and type your message. You can also change the Subject line, which defaults to the name of the file you are sending.

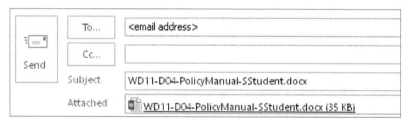

The Outlook message window (with document automatically attached) waiting to be addressed

Selecting an Email Program

When you use the send via email directly from Word feature, your email message is automatically created and the document automatically attached to the message. Word works with any email program or webmail service that you can select from the Windows Control Panel. If you want to change the default email service, you should make this selection before starting Word. Some email services (for example, most webmail services) don't support attaching the presentation automatically, so you must do so manually.

QUICK REFERENCE	SETTING THE DEFAULT EMAIL PROGRAM
Operating System	**Procedure**
Set the default email program (Windows 8)	▪ Tap the Windows key, if necessary, to display the Desktop. ▪ Press Windows + C. ▪ Click Settings. ▪ Click Control Panel. ▪ Click Programs. ▪ Click Set Your Default Programs. ▪ Select your preferred email program from the list at the left. ▪ Click Set This Program as Default in the right column.
Set the default email program (Windows 7)	▪ Choose Start→Control Panel. ▪ Click Programs. ▪ Click Set Your Default Programs. ▪ Select your preferred email program from the list at the left. ▪ Click Set This Program as Default in the right column.

Naming Reviewer Copies

Experience shows that it works best to name each copy of a document sent for review with the reviewer's name. Then, as the documents are returned from review, it's easy to track which reviewer sent each one.

TIP

Save all reviewer copies in a single folder to keep them together.

QUICK REFERENCE	SENDING A DOCUMENT FOR REVIEW VIA EMAIL
Task	**Procedure**
Send a document for review using a program that automatically attaches the document	▪ Open the document in Word. ▪ (Optional but recommended) Choose Review→Tracking→Track Changes. ▪ (Optional but recommended) Choose File→Save As, rename the document to include the reviewer's name, and click Save. ▪ Choose File→Share→Email→Send as Attachment. (This option formats the attachment as a Word document.) ▪ Enter the recipient's email address and, if desired, revise the Subject line. Click Send. ▪ Repeat the preceding steps for each reviewer.
Send a document for review by using another email program	▪ Open your email program and address a message for the first reviewer. ▪ Use your email program's procedure to attach the saved copy of the document and click Send.

Send a Document for Review

In this exercise, you will send an email with a copy of the policy manual document attached. For this example, you will send the attachment to your own email address.

1. Choose **Review→Tracking→Track Changes** .

   Turning on the feature helps ensure that the reviewers will use Track Changes.

2. Choose **File→Share→Email** and then choose **Send as Attachment**.

3. Follow these steps to complete the email form:

   If your user ID was not set up as a user with an Outlook account, you will see a message saying that no profiles have been created. If so, just dismiss the message, turn of Track Changes, and read through the rest of the exercise.

   Ⓐ Enter your actual email address here (don't type the text shown).

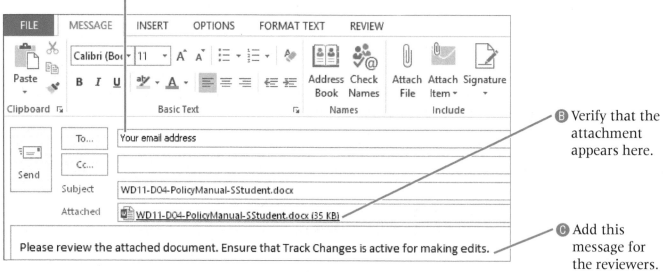

Ⓑ Verify that the attachment appears here.

Ⓒ Add this message for the reviewers.

4. Send the email.

5. Choose **Review→Tracking→Track Changes** to turn it off.

Reviewing Changes from Multiple Reviewers

Video Library   http://labyrinthelab.com/videos   Video Number: WD13-V1107

If you set up a document to track changes, you can send copies of the document for review by others. As these reviewers make revisions, Word tracks their changes. When the reviewers send you their edited copies, you can combine the tracked changes into a single document. Word marks each reviewer's changes in a different color, so you can recognize input from different reviewers. After the changes are merged, you can navigate through the combined document and accept and reject edits from all users at one time. In fact, by seeing the edits from all reviewers in one document, you will be able to identify the trouble spots in the document, because different reviewers may try to modify the same area of the document.

Reviewing a Summary of Proposed Changes

The Reviewing Pane summarizes reviewer changes in a window that you can scroll through to examine the proposed changes. When you click a change in the Reviewing Pane, the document scrolls to the location of the change so you can see it in context.

Brett Reynolds Inserted

. The receptionist will then notify the designated personnel of the patient's arrival.¶

forwarding payment. All patient contact records must contain complete, accurate information.¶

→ Patients using the Clinic for services must notify the receptionist of their arrival. The receptionist will then notify the designated personnel of the patient's arrival.¶

→ Supervisors will keep accurate attendance records and complete monthly billing sheets or

The Reviewing Pane on the left with the document scrolled to the selected change

Showing Source Documents

There are different views you can use to compare the original with reviewed documents. The view you choose is a matter of personal preference. You may find that you switch views depending on the type and extent of a reviewer's changes. It may be helpful, for example, to display the original and the marked documents side by side for comparison purposes, or hide the summary of changes list to get a larger view of the combined document.

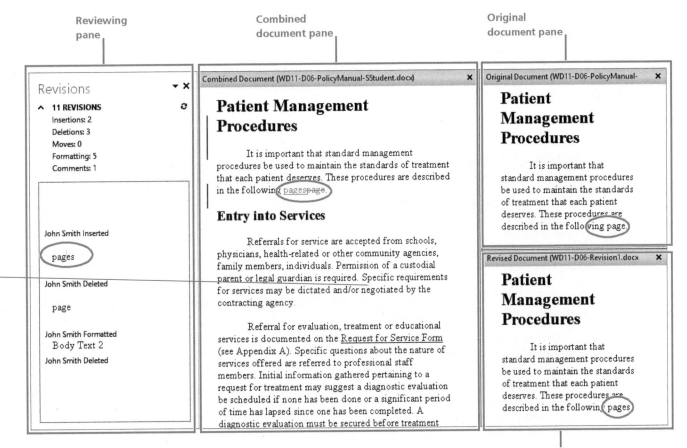

SOURCE DOCUMENT VIEWS	
Option	**Description**
Hide Source Documents	Displays the original document with the reviewer's changes embedded.
Show Original	Displays the original side-by-side with the marked document. The documents scroll simultaneously for easy comparison.
Show Revised	This view displays the original with the reviewer's changes embedded in the original next to the reviewer's tracked changes document.
Show Both	This view displays the unmarked original, the marked reviewer document, and the original with the reviewer's changes embedded.

Displaying Specific Markups

Word offers numerous options for displaying tracked changes for combined documents. For example, you may want to look at only the insertions and deletions suggested by reviewers. Word stores one set of formatting changes at a time. If you don't need to keep track of formatting changes, you may wish to turn off the Formatting option so Word won't prompt you to choose whether to keep the original formatting or the formatting from the reviewer's copy.

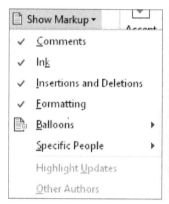

Displaying Specific Reviewers

If you combine two reviewer documents with the original, you can choose to see changes from both at once, or you may wish to focus on the proposed changes from just one reviewer, which you can do by removing the checkmark in front of the other reviewer's name.

QUICK REFERENCE	COMBINING DOCUMENTS AND VIEWING TRACKED CHANGES
Task	**Procedure**
Combine documents for review	■ Open the original document. ■ Choose Review→Compare→Compare→Combine. ■ In the Combine dialog box, choose the original and revised documents and click OK. ■ Repeat the process if you wish to work with additional reviewed documents at once.
Display the Reviewing Pane	■ Choose Review→Tracking→Reviewing Pane menu ▼ and choose the desired orientation.
Choose source documents to display	■ Choose Review→Compare→Compare→Show Source Documents and make the desired choice from the menu.
Display specific types of changes and choose which reviewers' change marks should appear	■ Choose Review→Tracking→Show Markup and make the desired menu choices.

Combine Tracked Changes from Two Reviewers

In this exercise, you will combine proposed changes from two reviewers with the original document. You will also explore additional features used for working with combined documents.

1. Save your file as **WD11-D06-PolicyManual-[FirstInitialLastName]**.

2. Choose **Review→Compare→Compare** and then choose **Combine**.

3. Follow these steps to begin combining documents:

Ⓐ Choose **WD11-D06-PolicyManual-[FirstInitialLastName]** here.

Ⓑ Click **Browse** and open **WD11-D06-Revision1** from your **WD2013 Lesson 11** folder.

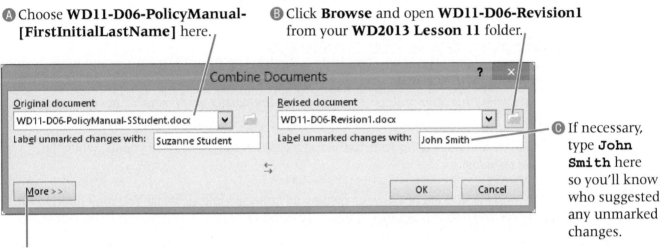

Ⓒ If necessary, type **John Smith** here so you'll know who suggested any unmarked changes.

Ⓓ Click **More** to expand the dialog box.

> **NOTE** If Track Changes is not turned on, the reviewer's name does not appear with the change. Normally changes are tracked, and the name does not need to be entered in the dialog box.

4. Follow these steps to control document display:

Ⓐ Ensure that **Word Level** is active.

Ⓑ Choose **Original Document**.

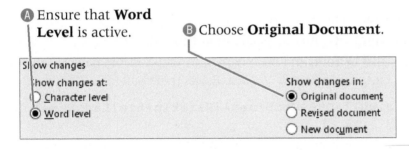

Ⓒ Click the **Less** button to collapse the dialog box; click **OK**.

The Word Level option causes Word to highlight the entire word, even if only one character or punctuation mark changes. This makes it easier to spot small edits. Now John Smith's proposed edits are embedded in the original document, ready for review.

Hide Source Documents

5. Choose **Review→Compare→Compare** [img], slide the mouse pointer to **Show Source Documents**, and then if necessary, choose **Hide Source Documents**.

   This provides more room on the screen.

6. Repeat the procedures outlined in steps 2–4 to combine the second reviewed document named **WD11-D06-Revision 2** with the original document.

7. Type **Brett Reynolds** in the **Label Unmarked Changes With** field.

   Brett Reynolds' edits are now displayed with the original and John Smith's edits.

8. Click **OK**.

Turn On the Reviewing Pane

9. If necessary, choose **Review→Tracking→Reviewing Pane** [img] **menu** ▼ and then choose **Reviewing Pane Vertical**.

   The Reviewing Pane (labeled Revisions *at the top) summarizes the proposed changes from both reviewers.*

10. Scroll down the Reviewing Pane to the suggested change by Brett Reynolds, where he deleted *attending*.

The Reviewing Pane does not always display all changes immediately. You may need to turn the feature off and then on again. Or, you may need to switch to Reviewing Pane Horizontal and back to Reviewing Pane Vertical.

11. Click *attending* in the Reviewing Pane and notice that Word scrolls the document to the location of the change.

    Notice the Deleted: attending *balloon in the Markup Area.*

12. Click **Close** [×] at the top of the Reviewing Pane.

13. Press Ctrl + Home to move to the top of the document.

14. Use techniques learned earlier in this lesson to review all changes to the document:

    ■ Delete all comments and accept all formatting changes.

    ■ Accept all edits by John and Brett with one exception: On page 3, John deleted a space between *(see Appendix B)* and *Children*. Reject that change.

15. Save the file as **WD11-D06-Combined-[FirstInitialLastName]**, and then close it.

Comparing Documents

Video Library   http://labyrinthelab.com/videos   Video Number: WD13-V1108

Sometimes documents that are sent for review are returned with no visible edits. Reviewers might turn off Track Changes so that the edits they make are not immediately evident. To determine whether edits have been made, you can use Word's Compare feature. It enables you to merge two documents into one file; then Word examines each document and automatically marks up the document using Track Changes so that you can locate edits.

Combining or Comparing Documents?

The basic procedures are the same for comparing and combining documents, but each command has a different use.

The Combine command allows you to combine the *tracked* changes from *one or multiple* reviewers in one document, and then you can go through the single document to accept or reject the changes.

The Compare command is designed for comparing two documents: *one* edited version of a document, where the reviewer *did not* use Track Changes, and the original. If you attempt to use the Compare feature to add a second reviewer's document, Word will advise you that it will automatically accept the first person's changes before comparing the second edited document. Thus, you won't have the option of accepting or rejecting changes from the first reviewer.

QUICK REFERENCE	COMPARING DOCUMENTS
Task	**Procedure**
Compare documents	■ Choose Review→Compare→Compare→Compare.
	■ Choose the original and revised documents, click More and change any defaults you desire, and click OK.

DEVELOP YOUR SKILLS WD11-D07

Compare Two Unmarked Documents

In this exercise, you will compare an original document with a document received from a reviewer that appears to have no changes in it.

1. Open **WD11-D06-PolicyManual-[FirstInitialLastName]** from the **WD2013 Lesson 11** folder and save it as `WD11-D07-PolicyManual-[FirstInitialLastName]`.

2. Choose **Review→Compare→Compare** 📄 and then choose **Compare** from the menu.

3. Follow these steps to compare this file with another document:

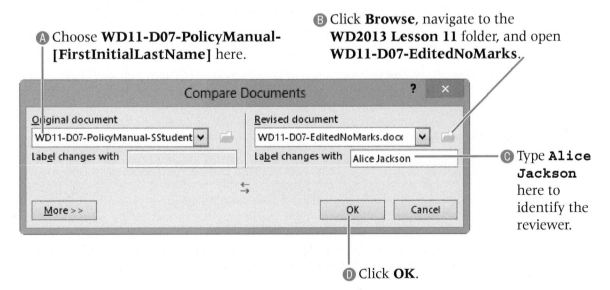

Ⓐ Choose **WD11-D07-PolicyManual-[FirstInitialLastName]** here.

Ⓑ Click **Browse**, navigate to the **WD2013 Lesson 11** folder, and open **WD11-D07-EditedNoMarks**.

Ⓒ Type **Alice Jackson** here to identify the reviewer.

Ⓓ Click **OK**.

Reviewing Changes from Multiple Reviewers **WD11.19**

4. If you are prompted to continue with the comparison, click **Yes**.

5. Scroll through the document and observe Alice's edits.

   You won't accept and reject changes in this example.

6. Save the file as **WD11-D07-AliceEdits-[FirstInitialLastName]** and then close it.

Using AutoSave and AutoRecover

Video Library   http://labyrinthelab.com/videos   Video Number: WD13-V1109

As you work, Word automatically saves your document every ten minutes by default. Whether you close a file without saving or something causes Word to close before you complete your work, the ability to retrieve the document is important. Word allows you to restore the last autosaved copy of the document the next time you open the file.

You choose this option in the Word Options
dialog box to work with Word's Save settings.

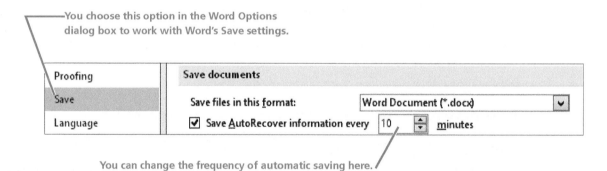

You can change the frequency of automatic saving here.

The automatically saved versions of your opened document appear in the Info screen in Backstage view. You can compare or restore a specific version.

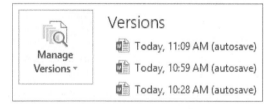   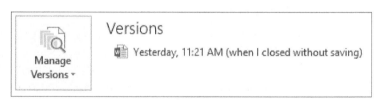

When you choose the version you want to open, Word displays an alert bar.

This option compares the selected autosaved version to the currently open
version. Word marks differences between the versions using Track Changes.

| ! | AUTOSAVED VERSION   A newer version is available. | Compare | Restore |

This command abandons the current version and opens the autosaved version.

If you close a document and specifically choose Don't Save, Word *does not* save the *latest* autosaved version of the document.

Recovering Unsaved Documents

You can also recover recent unsaved documents using the Recover feature. If you are creating or editing documents and you accidentally lose your connection to Word, you can still recover all edits made to the documents up through the last autosave. Here are some guidelines for recovering these files.

- If the document was one that had already been saved and named, Word displays the autosaved version in the Document Recovery task pane when you open the original file again. You can view the autosaved version to determine whether it is more recent than the original to help determine which version to keep.

- If the document is a new document that has not yet been saved, you can use the Recover Unsaved Documents command in the Info screen in Backstage view. Word displays a folder containing all unsaved files, and you can open each one to determine if it is the document you created and lost. An alert bar will prompt you to save a recovered document if you wish to keep it.

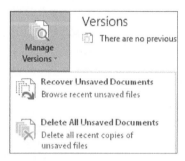

QUICK REFERENCE	MANAGING AUTOSAVE AND AUTORECOVER
Task	**Procedure**
Set AutoSave and AutoRecover options	■ Choose File→Options, click Save, and choose the number of minutes in the Save AutoRecover Information field. ■ Check the Keep the Last AutoSaved Version If I Close Without Saving checkbox.
Open an autosaved version of a document	■ Choose File→Info→Versions and double-click the version to restore.
Recover never-saved files	■ Choose File→Info and click Manage Versions. ■ Click Recover Unsaved Documents, open the autosaved file, click Save As at the top of the document window, and save the file.
Recover the autosaved version of a previously saved file	■ Choose File→Info→Versions→select the version labeled *(when I closed without saving)*. ■ Click Restore in the alert bar to overwrite any previously saved versions and replace them with the autosaved version. Or, when you open the original file after losing your connection to Word, use the Document Recovery task pane to determine whether to retain the original or autosaved version.
Compare an autosaved version to the original	■ With the original document open, choose File→Info→Versions; double-click the autosaved version of the document you want to compare to the original. ■ Accept and reject tracked changes using standard procedures.

Work with AutoSave Versions

In this exercise, you will ensure that the AutoSave and AutoRecover settings are active and work with versions of the Raritan Clinic East's policy manual.

1. Open **WD11-D07-PolicyManual-[FirstInitialLastName]** from your **WD2013 Lesson 11** folder and save it as `WD11-D08-PolicyManual-[FirstInitialLastName]`.

2. Choose **File→Options** to open the Word Options dialog box.

3. Choose the **Save** category in the left-hand pane.

4. Follow these steps to ensure options are set:

    Ⓐ Ensure that the **AutoRecover** option is checked.

    Ⓑ Set the minutes to **1**.

    Save documents

    Save files in this format: Word Document (*.docx)

    ☑ Save *A*utoRecover information every   1   minutes

    ☑ Keep the last autosaved version if I close without saving

    Ⓒ Ensure that this option is checked.

5. Click **OK**, change the word *AND* in the title to an ampersand (**&**), and wait for at least one minute.

6. Choose **File→Info→Versions** and review the information.
   Now you will reset the Autosave duration back to ten minutes.

7. Choose **File→Options**, and then choose **Save** in the left-hand pane.

8. Change the AutoRecover duration to ten minutes and click **OK**.

9. Save and close the file. Exit **Word**.

Introducing SkyDrive and Office Web Apps

Video Library   http://labyrinthelab.com/videos   Video Number: WD13-V1110

You may not always have access to your computer when you need to edit a file. For example, you may need to edit an important work document from home, but have no access to your work computer. With SkyDrive, you can store files online so they are available from any computer with an Internet connection.

Office Web Apps 2013 is the free version of Microsoft Office "in the cloud." The applications are not as robust as the desktop applications, but they may meet your needs. With Office Web Apps, you can edit files on SkyDrive even if you don't have the actual Microsoft Office programs installed on your computer.

Signing In with a Microsoft Account ID

SkyDrive and Office Web Apps 2013 require a Microsoft Account ID (formerly Windows Live ID) to sign in before you can use the service. The Microsoft Account ID is a free account that you use to sign into services such as SkyDrive, Outlook.com, Messenger, or Windows phone. If you already use one of those services, you already have a Microsoft Account ID.

QUICK REFERENCE	CREATING A MICROSOFT ACCOUNT ID AND USING SKYDRIVE
Task	**Procedure**
Create a Microsoft Account ID	■ Start your web browser and navigate to http://www.live.com. ■ Click Sign Up Now and fill out the form to create a free Microsoft Account ID.
Save a document to SkyDrive	■ Open the document in Word, and then choose File→Save As→SkyDrive. ■ Click Sign In and sign in with your Microsoft Account ID. ■ Select the SkyDrive folder in which you'd like to save the document; click Save As. ■ Name the file, click Save, and wait as the document is uploaded.
Access a file stored on SkyDrive	■ Start your web browser and navigate to http://www.skydrive.com. ■ Sign in with your Microsoft Account ID, and then click the folder containing the desired file. ■ Click a file to view it, or point to the file you want to access and click an action, such as Edit in Browser, Share, or More.

DEVELOP YOUR SKILLS WD11-D09
Save a Document to SkyDrive

WebSim   WD13-W1109

In this exercise, you will save a document to SkyDrive.

1. Type the URL for the student resource center into the address bar of your web browser and tap ⎙Enter⎙.

   The student resource center URL is printed on the inside front cover of your book.

2. From the left navigation bar, click **Lessons 10–14** and then **WD11**; then, click **DYS WD13-W1109 Save a Document to SkyDrive**.

   The WebSim loads. The Revised Raritan Clinic East Procedures Manual is open in Word.

3. Work your way through the onscreen exercise instructions.

4. Click the **Back to Course** link.

Editing Files with Office Web Apps 2013

Video Library   http://labyrinthelab.com/videos   Video Number: WD13-V1111

Files that have been saved to SkyDrive can be edited online using Office Web Apps 2013, which run directly in your browser instead of on your computer. Web Apps have limited functionality, but they work for most simple business documents. The apps use the Ribbon interface, so when you open a document in the app, the environment seems familiar.

Edit a Document with Office Web Apps 2013

`WebSim` WD13-W1110

In this exercise, you will edit a document with Office Web Apps 2013.

1. From the left navigation bar, click **Lessons 10–14** and then **WD11**; then, click **DYS WD13-W1110 Edit a Document with Office Web Apps 2013**.

   The WebSim loads and the SkyDrive start page appears. The computer represented in the WebSim does not have Word installed. You will edit the document using Office Web Apps 2013.

2. Work your way through the onscreen exercise instructions.

3. Click the **Back to Course** link.

Sharing Files with SkyDrive

`Video Library` http://labyrinthelab.com/videos Video Number: WD13-V1112

In addition to editing files stored on SkyDrive, you can share files and allow others to edit or comment on them. Alternatively, you can share files and allow others to only view or comment on them, but not edit.

When you share a file on SkyDrive, you actually share the SkyDrive folder containing the file. Therefore, all files stored in the folder are shared. To easily manage permissions, you could create one folder that stores files you allow others to edit and a different folder containing files that can only be viewed.

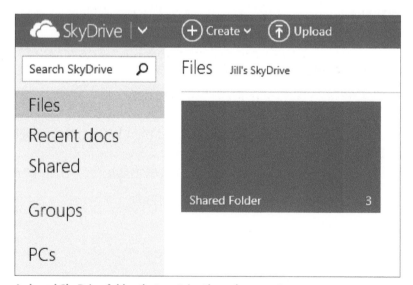

A shared SkyDrive folder that contains three documents

QUICK REFERENCE	WORKING WITH SKYDRIVE FOLDERS
Task	**Procedure**
Create a folder	■ Use your web browser to login to http://www.skydrive.com. ■ Choose Create→Folder from the menu bar above the folder icons, and type a folder name. ■ Drag and drop documents from your computer into the folder; set share permissions as necessary.
Share a folder	■ Use your web browser to login to http://www.skydrive.com, and then right-click the folder and choose Sharing. ■ Enter the email address of the person with whom you will share the folder, type a message if desired, and click Share. ■ If asked, click the link to complete the security check, and click Share again. ■ Click Done.
Access a shared file	■ Click the "x files" link in the message to see all files in the folder, then double-click a file to open it, or click the document link in the message to directly open the document. ■ Click the Edit Document button in the menu bar, and choose to edit in Word or in Word Web Apps.

DEVELOP YOUR SKILLS WD11-D11
Create a SkyDrive Folder

WebSim   WD13-W1111

In this exercise, you will create a SkyDrive folder to store shared documents.

1. From the left navigation bar, click **Lessons 10–14** and then **WD11**; then, click **DYS WD13-W1111 Create a SkyDrive Folder**.

   The WebSim loads and the SkyDrive start page appears. You are already logged in as DrJacksonRaritan@outlook.com.

2. Work your way through the onscreen exercise instructions.

3. Click the **Back to Course** link.

Moving Files in SkyDrive

Video Library http://labyrinthelab.com/videos Video Number: WD13-V1113

Since permissions are set on folders and not individual files, you may find it necessary to move files from one SkyDrive folder to another.

DEVELOP YOUR SKILLS WD11-D12
Move Files

WebSim WD13-W1112

In this exercise, you will move a file from one SkyDrive folder to another.

1. From the left navigation bar, click **Lessons 10–14** and then **WD11**; then, click **DYS WD13-W1112 Move Files**.

   The WebSim loads and the SkyDrive start page appears. You are already logged in as DrJacksonRaritan@outlook.com.

2. Work your way through the onscreen exercise instructions.

3. Click the **Back to Course** link.

Setting Folder Permissions

Video Library http://labyrinthelab.com/videos Video Number: WD13-V1114

After a folder is created, you can set its permissions, allowing others to view or edit the files inside. You can specify groups or individuals by the email address. Any files stored in the folder will inherit the folder's permissions.

DEVELOP YOUR SKILLS WD11-D13
Share a Folder

WebSim WD13-W1113

In this exercise, you will share a SkyDrive folder and all the files within.

1. From the left navigation bar, click **Lessons 10–14** and then **WD11**; then, click **DYS WD13-W1113 Share a Folder**.

   The WebSim loads and the SkyDrive page appears, displaying the contents of the For Review folder. You are already logged in as DrJacksonRaritan@outlook.com.

2. Work your way through the onscreen exercise instructions.

3. Click the **Back to Course** link.

Accessing Shared Files

Video Library   http://labyrinthelab.com/videos   Video Number: WD13-V1115

Once a file has been shared with you, accessing it is simple. You can click the "x files" link to go to the folder, or click a file name link to go to a specific document. Login with your Microsoft Account ID if prompted, and view or edit the file. You may wish to save the invitation email, as the links provide an easy way to access the files.

Clicking this link displays the shared folder.

Clicking one of these links opens a shared file.

Jill has 3 files to share with you on SkyDrive. To view them, click the links below.

Meeting Agenda.docx

Client Proposal.docx

Quarterly Report.docx

Publishing a Blog Post

Video Library   http://labyrinthelab.com/videos   Video Number: WD13-V1116

In addition to posting files to folders on SkyDrive, Word 2013 contains additional tools that enable you to post documents as blogs. To use the feature, you must have a blog account to which to post the file. The first time you use the feature, you will be prompted to register for the blog.

You can create a blog with the Blog Post template or any Word document. Using the template allows you to control the process using the Blog Post tab on the Ribbon. If you use a regular Word document, you can publish the document by choosing the Post to Blog command in the Share tab in Backstage view.

Concepts Review

To check your knowledge of the key concepts introduced in this lesson, complete the Concepts Review quiz by choosing the appropriate access option below.

If you are...	Then access the quiz by...
Using the Labyrinth Video Library	Going to http://labyrinthelab.com/videos
Using eLab	Logging in, choosing Content, and navigating to the Concepts Review quiz for this lesson
Not using the Labyrinth Video Library or eLab	Going to the student resource center for this book

Reinforce Your Skills

Use the Highlighter and Track Changes, and Email from Word

In this exercise, you will use the highlighter to place reminders in your document, add comments, and track and review changes. You will also email your document as an attachment.

In this exercise, you will use an article from the Internet. Normally you would not modify the content of a cited work; however, since you are not representing this as your own work, you can make the changes for the sake of the exercise.

Use the Highlighter

1. Start **Word**. Open **WD11-R01-CompanionPlant** from your **WD2013 Lesson 11** folder and save it as **WD11-R01-CompanionPlant-[FirstInitialLastName]**.

2. If necessary, display formatting marks.

3. Position the insertion point at the end of the first paragraph and tap Enter.

4. Type this text: **Make copies on 3-hole punched paper**.

5. Choose **Home→Font→Text Highlight Color** [aby] **menu ▼** and then choose **Turquoise**.

6. Drag the mouse pointer, which now appears as a highlighter pen, across the sentence you just typed.

7. Choose **Home→Font→Text Highlight Color** [aby] to turn off the highlighter.

8. Press Ctrl + End to move to the bottom of the document.

9. Type this text: **Reminder: Check with Ilsa to see if lupin and savory attract lady bugs**.

10. Select the sentence and choose **Home→Font→Text Highlight Color** [aby] **menu ▼→ Bright Green**.

Change Tracking Colors and User Name and Initials

11. Choose **Review→Tracking→dialog box launcher** [⤢] and then click **Change User Name**.

12. If necessary, enter your username and initials and click **OK** once. Click **Advanced Options**.

13. Choose the following colors:
    - Insertions: **Pink**
    - Deletions: **Dark Blue**
    - Comments: **Violet**

14. Click **OK** twice.

Work with Comments and Track Changes

15. Select the word *March* in the third line of the first paragraph.

16. Choose **Review→Comments→New Comment** ⬚ and type this text: `Do we have a specific date yet?`

17. Scroll down to the *Tomatoes and cabbage* combination and select the last word, *leaves*.

18. Choose **Review→Comments→New Comment** ⬚ and type this text: `Did Ilsa verify that this combination really works?`

    Now you'll turn on Track Changes and make some editing changes.

19. Choose **Review→Tracking→Track Changes** 📝.

20. In the first sentence below the *Companion Planting* heading on page 1, select *makes for* and type **produces** in its place.

21. In the last line of the same paragraph, select *mate* and type **pair** in its place.

22. In the first line of the *Radishes and spinach* section on page 2, select *yor* and type **your** in its place.

23. Scroll down to the *Collards and catnip* section and position the insertion point at the end of the sentence.

24. Tap [Spacebar] and type this text: `And it will make your cat very happy!`

25. Position the insertion point at the end of the *Marigolds and Melons* section and tap [Enter].

26. Type this text: `Asparagus and basil: Seems to encourage lady bugs.`

27. Select *Asparagus and basil:* and choose **Home→Font→Bold** B.

Review Tracked Changes

28. Choose **Review→Tracking→Display for Review** 🖼 menu ▼→**Original** and scroll through the document.

    The document now appears as it was before making changes.

29. Use the same process as in step 28 to experiment with **Simple Markup**, **No Markup**, and **All Markup**. Then leave **All Markup** as the active view.

    Now you'll respond to comments and accept and reject the changes.

30. Position the insertion point at the top of the document.

31. Choose **Review→Changes→Next** 🔁.

    The insertion point moves to the first comment. For the moment, pretend that you are a reviewer and not the originator of the comment.

32. Click **Reply** 🖵 in the upper-right corner of the comment balloon and type this text: `I'll check with Ilsa.`

33. Choose **Review→Changes→Next** 🔁.

    The insertion point moves to the makes for *deletion.*

34. Choose **Review→Changes→Accept** ✅.

    The focus moves to the added word produces.

35. Choose **Review→Changes→Accept** ✅.

36. **Accept** the deletion of *mate* and the addition of *pair*.

   The insertion point moves to the next comment. Again pretend you are a reviewer and not the originator.

37. Click the reply button in the comment balloon, and then type this text: `I'll check with her.`

38. Choose **Review→Changes→Next** 📄 and accept the deletion of *yor* and the addition of **your**.

39. Accept the *"happy cat"* addition.

40. Reject the *Asparagus and basil* addition.

Send a Document for Review

41. Make sure **Track Changes** is still on.

   Remember, you want to ensure that reviewers use Track Changes.

42. Choose **File→Share→Email** 📧 and then choose **Send as Attachment**.

   If your user ID was not set up as a user with an Outlook account, you will see a message saying that no profiles have been created. If so, just dismiss the message, turn off Track Changes, and read through the rest of this exercise.

43. In the email form, enter your email address in the **To** field, and change the **Subject** to `Policy Manual attached`.

   Notice that Word has attached the document.

44. Type this text: `Please be sure Track Changes is turned on when you review the document.`

45. Click **Send**.

46. Choose **Review→Tracking→Track Changes** 📝 to turn it off.

47. Save and close the file; exit from **Word**.

48. Submit your final file based on the guidelines provided by your instructor.

   To see examples of how your file or files should look at the end of this exercise, go to the student resource center.

REINFORCE YOUR SKILLS WD11-R02

Combine and Compare Tracked Changes; Use AutoSave and AutoRecover

In this exercise, you will examine edits to a document that were made by two different reviewers and accept and reject changes. Then you will open a document that was edited without Track Changes and use the Compare feature to determine what changes were made. Finally, you will work with AutoSave and AutoRecover.

NOTE In this exercise, you will use articles from the Internet. Normally you would not modify the content of a cited work; however, since you are not representing this as your own work, you can make the changes for the sake of the exercise.

Combine Reviewed Documents

1. Start **Word**. Open **WD11-R02-CleanCoast** from your **WD2013 Lesson 11** folder and save it as **WD11-R02-CleanCoast-[FirstInitialLastName]**.

2. If necessary, choose **Review→Tracking→Display for Review** 📝→**All Markup**.

3. Choose **Review→Tracking→Show Markup** 📄, slide the mouse pointer to **Balloons**, and choose **Show Only Comments and Formatting in Balloons**.

4. Choose **Review→Compare→Compare** 📑 and then choose **Combine**.

5. Choose **WD11-R02-CleanCoast-[FirstInitialLastName]** from the Original Document drop-down list.

6. Click **Browse** on the right side of the dialog box and open **WD11-R02-CleanCoastElla** from your **WD2013 Lesson 11** folder.

7. Click **More** to expand the dialog box and make sure **Word Level** and **Original Document** are chosen.

8. Click **Less** to collapse the dialog box; click **OK**.

9. Choose **Review→Compare→Compare** 📑, slide the mouse pointer down to **Show Source Documents**, and if necessary, choose **Hide Source Documents**.

10. Combine the second document, named **WD11-R02-CleanCoastNed**, with the original document.

11. Save the document.

12. Choose **Review→Tracking→Reviewing Pane** 📋 menu ▼→**Reviewing Pane Vertical**.

13. Scroll down the Reviewing Pane to Ella's comment about getting schools involved.

 The Reviewing Pane does not always display all changes immediately. You may need to turn the feature off and then on again. Or, you may need to switch to Reviewing Pane Horizontal and back to Reviewing Pane Vertical.

14. Click Ella's comment in the Reviewing Pane and notice that Word scrolls to that location in the document.

15. Click **Close** ⊠ at the top of the Reviewing Pane.

16. Position the insertion point at the top of the document and follow these guidelines to review the changes:
    - Accept all additions and deletions made by Ella and Ned.
    - Accept all formatting changes.
    - Reply to Ned's first comment with: `I'll check.`
    - Reply to Ella's comment with: `I'll contact one of the Park School teachers.`
    - Reply to Ned's second comment with: `I'll check the website and get back to you.`

17. Save the file as **WD11-R02-CoastEllaNed-[FirstInitialLastName]** and then close it.

Compare Documents

18. Open **WD11-R02-Pups** from the **WD2013 Lesson 11** folder and save it as `WD11-R02-Pups-[FirstInitialLastName]`.

19. Choose **Review→Compare→Compare** 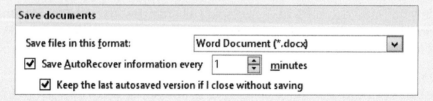→**Compare**.

20. Choose **WD11-R02-Pups-[FirstInitialLastName]** in the Original Document drop-down list.

21. Click **Browse** on the right side of the dialog box and open **WD11-R02-PupsArthur** from the **WD2013 Lesson 11** folder.

22. If necessary, type **Arthur Menendez** in the Label Changes With field on the right and click **OK**. If you are prompted to continue with the comparison, click **Yes**.

23. Make sure the insertion point is at the top of the document.

24. Choose **Review→Changes→Next** .

25. Reject the *Raising Volunteers* addition and the *Raisers* deletion.

26. Accept all remaining changes.

27. Click **OK** when the message appears indicating there are no more changes.

28. Save the file as `WD11-R02-PupsCompare-[FirstInitialLastName]` and then close it.

Use AutoSave

29. Open **WD11-R02-AutoSave** from the **WD2013 Lesson 11** folder and save it as `WD11-R02-AutoSave-[FirstInitialLastName]`.

30. Choose **File→Options**, and then choose **Save** in the left-hand pane.

31. Make the choices shown, and then click **OK**.

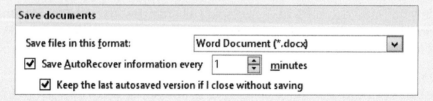

Save documents

Save files in this format: Word Document (*.docx)

☑ Save AutoRecover information every 1 ⬍ minutes

   ☑ Keep the last autosaved version if I close without saving

32. Delete the words *by default* at the end of the first sentence, and then wait for at least one minute.

33. Choose **File→Info→Versions** to view the autosaved version of your document.

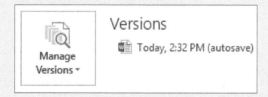

Versions

  Today, 2:32 PM (autosave)

Manage Versions ▾

Now you will change the AutoSave duration back to ten minutes.

34. Choose **File→Options**, and then choose **Save** in the left-hand pane.

35. Change the AutoRecover duration to ten minutes; click **OK**.

36. Save and close the file; exit **Word**.

37. Submit your final files based on the guidelines provided by your instructor.

    To see examples of how your file or files should look at the end of this exercise, go to the student resource center.

Use SkyDrive and Office Web Apps

WebSim <u>WD13-WR1102</u>

38. If necessary, type the URL for the student resource center into the address bar of your web browser and tap [Enter].

    The student resource center URL is printed on the inside front cover of your book.

39. From the left navigation bar, click **Lessons 10–14** and then **WD11**; then, click **RYS WD13-WR1102 Use SkyDrive and Office Web Apps**.

40. Work your way through the onscreen exercise instructions.

41. Click the **Back to Course** link.

Collaborate in Word

In this exercise, you will collaborate in Word using the highlighter and track changes. You will set a reviewer's name and initials and ink colors, and you will share a file using Word's email capability. You will combine tracked changes from two reviewers, and you will compare documents with a reviewer who didn't use Track Changes. Finally, you will work with the AutoSave and AutoRecover features.

NOTE In this exercise, you will use articles from the Internet. Normally you would not modify the content of a cited work; however, since you are not representing this as your own work, you can make the changes for the sake of the exercise.

Use the Highlighter

1. Open **WD11-R03-Global** from your **WD2013 Lesson 11** folder and save it as `WD11-R03-Global-[FirstInitialLastName]`.

2. Scroll down to the first **CATHERINE MANN** paragraph on page 1 and position the insertion point at the end of the paragraph.

3. Tap [Spacebar], and then type this text: `Jennifer has some information on costs.`

4. Choose **Home→Font→Text Highlighter Color** aby menu ▼ and then choose **Red**.

5. Drag the mouse pointer across the sentence you just typed.

6. Choose **Home→Font→Text Highlighter Color** aby to turn off the highlighter.

7. Click the insertion point at the end of the next paragraph, tap [Spacebar], and type this text: `See Heather about outsourcing.`

8. Select the sentence and choose **Home→Font→Text Highlight Color** aby.

    The sentence is highlighted because you selected it first.

Set Username and Initials and Tracking Colors

9. Choose **Review→Tracking→dialog box launcher** ⬚ and then click **Change User Name**.

10. If necessary, enter your username and initials and click **OK** once. Click **Advanced Options**.

11. Set the following colors:
    - Insertions: **Bright Green**
    - Deletions: **Dark Red**
    - Comments: **Red**

12. Click **OK** twice.

Work with Track Changes

13. Choose **Review→Tracking→Track Changes** ⬚.

14. Scroll to page 2 and the first **MANN** paragraph. In the first line, replace the capitalized *What* with a lowercase *what*.

15. In the next line, delete the word *ever*.

16. In the first line of the next **MANN** paragraph, delete the second occurrence of *by*.

17. In the last sentence of the same paragraph, select *make the choice* and replace it with **choose**.

18. Scroll to the top of page 3 and the **BAUMOL** paragraph.

19. In the second line, right-click the incorrectly spelled word (red underline) and choose the correct spelling from the menu.

Review Tracked Changes

20. Choose **Review→Tracking→Show Markup** ⬚, slide the mouse pointer down to **Balloons**, and choose **Show Revisions in Balloons**.

    Deleted text, comments, and formatting changes will appear in balloons in the Markup Area. Added text will appear underlined in the body of the document.

21. If necessary, choose **Review→Tracking→Display for Review** ⬚ and then choose **All Markup**.

22. Position the insertion point at the top of the document.

23. Choose **Review→Changes→Next** ⬚.

24. Choose **Review→Changes→Accept** ⬚ to accept the deletion of *What*.

    Word jumps to the insertion of what *in the body.*

25. Choose **Review→Changes→Accept** ⬚ to accept the insertion of *what*.

26. In the Markup Area, right-click the next balloon, the one indicating the deletion of *ever*.

27. Choose **Accept Deletion**.

28. Use the Ribbon commands to find and accept the rest of the changes. Click **OK** when the message appears indicating that there are no more changes.

    You no longer need the highlighted information, so you'll delete those items next.

29. Scroll up to page 1, and delete both sentences highlighted in red.

30. Right-click both deletion balloons and choose **Accept Deletion**.

Share a File via Email

Next you will ask your colleagues, Gretchen and Charles, to review the document.

31. Check to make sure **Track Changes** is still turned on.

    Remember, you want to ensure that the reviewers use Track Changes.

32. Choose **File→Share→Email** and then choose **Send as Attachment**.

    In this example, you will send the email to yourself. If your user ID was not set up as a user with an Outlook account, you will see a message saying that no profiles have been created. If so, just dismiss the message, turn off track changes, and read through the rest of the email portion of the exercise.

33. In the email form, enter your email address in the **To** field and change the **Subject** to **Global research attached**.

    Notice that Word has attached the document.

34. Type this text: **Please review and propose any changes you would like.**

35. Click **Send**.

Combine Tracked Changes from Two Reviewers

36. Choose **Review→Compare→Compare →Combine** to open the Combine Documents dialog box.

37. In the Original Document field, choose **WD11-R03-Global-[FirstInitialLastName]** from the drop-down list.

38. On the right side of the dialog box, click **Browse**, and open **WD11-R03-GlobalGretchen** from your **WD2013 Lesson 11** folder.

39. Click **OK**.

40. If a message appears regarding formatting changes, make sure your document is chosen and click **Continue with Merge**.

41. Choose **Review→Compare→Compare →Combine**.

42. Follow the procedure outlined in steps 38–41 to combine the second reviewed document, **WD11-R03-GlobalCharles**, with the original.

43. Choose **Review→Tracking→Reviewing Pane menu ▼→Reviewing Pane Vertical**.

    The Reviewing Pane (labeled Revisions at the top) summarizes the changes from both Gretchen and Charles.

44. Scroll down the Reviewing Pane to the **Charles Aiken** revisions where he inserted *increasing*.

The Reviewing Pane does not always display all changes immediately. You may need to turn the feature off and then on again. Or, you may need to switch to Reviewing Pane Horizontal and back to Reviewing Pane Vertical.

45. Click the item in the **Reviewing Pane** and notice that the document scrolls to that position.

46. **Close** ☒ the Reviewing Pane.

47. Save the file as **WD11-R03-GlobalCombined-[FirstInitialLastName]**.

48. Position the insertion point at the top of the document.

49. Use **Next** ⮐ and **Accept** ☑ to accept all proposed changes.

50. Click the **Charles Aiken** comment balloon, and then click the reply button in the upper-right corner of the balloon.

51. Type this text: **Yes, I have the information.**

52. Click the **Gretchen Harris** comment, click the reply button, and type this text: **Could you please email that to me?**

53. Save and then close the file.

Compare Documents

54. Open **WD11-R03-Obesity** from the **WD2013 Lesson 11** folder and save it as **WD11-R03-Obesity-[FirstInitialLastName]**.

55. Choose **Review→Compare→Compare** 🗒 **→Compare**.

56. In the Original Document field, choose **WD11-R03-Obesity-[FirstInitialLastName]** from the drop-down list.

57. Click **Browse** on the right side of the dialog box and open **WD11-R03-ObesityMargo** from the **WD2013 Lesson 11** folder.

58. If necessary, type **Margo Meyers** in the Label Changes With field; click **OK**. If you are prompted to continue with the comparison, click **Yes**.

59. Scroll through the document and observe Margo's edits.

You won't accept and reject changes in this example.

60. Save the file as **WD11-R03-MargoEdits-[FirstInitialLastName]**, and then close it.

Use AutoSave and AutoRecover

61. Open **WD11-R03-Recover** from the **WD2013 Lesson 11** folder and save it as **WD11-R03-Recover-[FirstInitialLastName]**.

Now you will change the AutoSave duration to one minute.

62. Choose **File→Options** to open the Word Options dialog box.

63. Choose **Save** in the left-hand pane.

64. Make the choices shown and then click **OK**.

Save documents		
Save files in this _format:_	Word Document (*.docx)	▾
☑ Save _A_utoRecover information every	1 ⬍	minutes
☑ Keep the last autosaved version if I close without saving		

65. Delete the words *you can* in the first line and then wait for at least one minute.

66. Choose **File→Info** and then click the **Manage Versions** button.

    The button displays the command you can use to review any documents that were not saved; to the right of the button, you see the AutoSaved version of your document.

    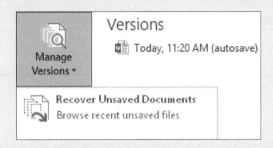

    Now you will change the AutoSave duration back to ten minutes.

67. Choose **Options** on the left of the screen and then choose **Save** in the left-hand pane.

68. Change the AutoRecover duration to **ten minutes** and then click **OK**.

69. Save and close the file; exit **Word**.

70. Submit your final files based on the guidelines provided by your instructor.

Use SkyDrive and Office Web Apps 2013

WebSim   WD13-WR1103

71. If necessary, type the URL for the student resource center into the address bar of your web browser and tap Enter.

    The student resource center URL is printed on the inside front cover of your book.

72. From the left navigation bar, click **Lessons 10–14** and then **WD11**; then, click **RYS WD13-WR1103 Use SkyDrive and Web Apps 2013**.

73. Work your way through the onscreen exercise instructions.

74. Click the **Back to Course** link.

Apply Your Skills

Highlight Text, Track Changes, and Email from Word

In this exercise, you will use the highlighter and set the username, initials, and ink color. You will add comments and edit the document, and you will review the changes. Finally, you will email the file from within Word.

In this exercise, you will use an article from the Internet. Normally you would not modify the content of a cited work; however, since you are not representing this as your own work, you can make the changes for the sake of the exercise.

Use the Highlighter

1. Start **Word**. Open **WD11-A01-Crete** from your **WD2013 Lesson 11** folder and save it as **WD11-A01-Crete-[FirstInitialLastName]**.

2. Use the **Text Highlighter Color** ⟨aᵇ⟩ button to highlight the last sentence of the first paragraph in pink.

3. Position the insertion point at the end of the first paragraph below the *Crete* heading.

4. Tap ⟨Spacebar⟩ and then type this text: **The Roman and Turkish remnants are worth adding to the tour.**

5. Highlight the sentence you just typed with pink.

Set the Username and Ink Colors; Track Changes and Add Comments

6. Open the **Track Changes Options** dialog box and click **Change User Name**. If necessary, enter your username and initials.

7. Click the **Advanced Options** button in the same dialog box and choose these colors:
   - Insertions: **Green**
   - Deletions: **Red**
   - Comments: **Turquoise**

8. Select the city name, *Heraklion*, in the first bullet point.

9. Use the **New Comment** ⟨📝⟩ button to insert this comment: **A quick stop in Heraklion to see Knossos would be nice.**

10. Select the city name, *Elounda,* at the beginning of the fifth bullet point and insert this comment: **A good spot for celebrity watching.**

11. Turn on **Track Changes** ⟨📝⟩.

12. In the fourth line of the paragraph below the *Crete* heading, replace *was* with **were**.

13. In the next line, replace *place* with **island**.

14. In the second line of the second bullet point, replace *Brits* with `British`.

15. Scroll to page 2 and the third from the last bullet point about the city of Rethymno.

16. Position the insertion point after the space at the end of the paragraph and type this text:
    `There is a daily ferry from Athens.`

Review Tracked Changes and Email the File

17. Ensure that **All Markup** is active in the **Display for Review** 🔳 field.

18. Position the insertion point at the top of the document.

19. Use **Next** 🔁 and **Accept** ☑ to find and accept all editing changes.

20. Send your file as an email attachment using these guidelines:
    - Use Word's Email and Send as Attachment features.
    - Insert your email address in the To field.
      If your user ID was not set up as a user with an Outlook account, you will see a message saying that no profiles have been created. If so, just dismiss the message, turn off track changes, and read through the rest of this exercise.
    - Change the subject to `Crete Review`.
    - Add this message: `I hope my comments are helpful.`

21. Save and close the file; exit **Word**.

22. Submit your final file based on guidelines provided by your instructor.
    To see examples of how your final file or files should look at the end of this exercise, go to the student resource center.

APPLY YOUR SKILLS WD11-A02

Combine and Compare Documents, and Use AutoRecover

In this exercise, you will combine the documents from two reviewers into your original document, and you will compare your original document with a revised document where the reviewer did not use Track Changes. Finally, you will close a document without saving it and use AutoRecover to save the document.

In this exercise, you will use articles from the Internet. Normally you would not modify the content of a cited work; however, since you are not representing this as your own work, you can make the changes for the sake of the exercise.

Combine Changes from Two Reviewers and Compare Documents

1. Start **Word**. Open **WD11-A02-Whistler** from your **WD2013 Lesson 11** folder and save it as `WD11-A02-Whistler-[FirstInitialLastName]`.

2. Ensure that the **Display for Review** 🔳 feature in the Tracking group is set to **All Markup**.

3. Choose **Show Markup** 📄 and the **Balloons** option. If necessary, choose **Show Revisions in Balloons**.

4. Combine your original document, **WD11-A02-Whistler-[FirstInitialLastName]**, with the revised document, **WD11-A02-WhistlerColleen**.

5. Combine your original document, **WD11-A02-Whistler-[FirstInitialLastName]**, with the revised document, **WD11-A02-WhistlerAnthony**.

6. Choose **Compare→Compare**, slide the mouse pointer to **Show Source Documents**, and choose **Show Both**.

   Notice the combined document in the middle pane and the revised documents on the right.

7. Scroll down in the combined document and notice that the revised documents scroll simultaneously.

8. Scroll to the top of the combined document, and then scroll to the bottom of the **Review Pane** (labeled Revisions at the top) on the left.

9. Click the last item in the list and notice that the documents scroll to the position of that revision.

10. Choose **Compare→Compare**, slide the mouse pointer to **Show Source Documents**, and choose **Hide Source Documents**.

11. **Close** ⊠ the Reviewing Pane.

12. Position the insertion point at the top of the document.

13. Accept all changes made by Colleen and Anthony except the change in the first paragraph of the article where Colleen changed kilometers to miles. Reject both the deletion and the addition.

14. Save the file as **WD11-A02-Whistler_CC_AN-[FirstInitialLastName]** and then close it.

15. Open **WD11-A02-SanDiego** from the **WD2013 Lesson 11** folder and save it as **WD11-A02-SanDiego-[FirstInitialLastName]**.

16. Compare **WD11-A02-SanDiego-[FirstInitialLastName]** in the Original Document field with **WD11-A02-SanDiegoMel** located in the **WD2013 Lesson 11** folder. If you are prompted to continue with the comparison, click **Yes**.

17. Scroll through the document and observe the changes.

    All the changes look good, so you'll accept them all at once.

18. Choose **Review→Changes→Accept** ☑ **menu ▼→Accept All Changes**.

19. Save the file as **WD11-A02-SDCompared-[FirstInitialLastName]** and then close it.

Use AutoRecover

Now you will start a document, and then close it without saving. Then you will use the AutoRecover feature to locate and save the file.

20. Start a new blank document and type **Universal Corporate Events**.

21. Close the document. When prompted to save, choose **Don't Save**.

22. Start a new blank document.

23. Choose **File→Info** to open Backstage view, click **Manage Versions**, and choose **Recover Unsaved Documents**.

24. Double-click the file with the current date that shows *Universal Corporate Events*.

25. Click the **Save As** button at the top of the screen and save the file as **WD11-A02-AutoRec-[FirstInitialLastName]** in your **WD2013 Lesson 11** folder.

26. Close the recovery screen; exit **Word**.

27. Submit your final files based on the guidelines provided by your instructor.
    To see examples of how your final file or files should look at the end of this exercise, go to the student resource center.

Use SkyDrive and Office Web Apps

WebSim WD13-WA1102

28. If necessary, type the URL for the student resource center into the address bar of your web browser and tap Enter.
    The student resource center URL is printed on the inside front cover of your book.

29. From the left navigation bar, click **Lessons 10–14** and then **WD11**; then, click **AYS WD13-WA1102 Use SkyDrive and Web Apps**.

30. Work your way through the onscreen exercise instructions.

31. Click the **Back to Course** link.

APPLY YOUR SKILLS WD11-A03

Collaborate on a Document

In this exercise, you will use Tracked Changes and combine and compare documents, and you will set tracking options. You will use Word's email feature to send a document as an attachment, and you will use the AutoSave and AutoRecover features.

In this exercise, you will use articles from the Internet. Normally you would not modify the content of a cited work; however, since you are not representing this as your own work, you can make the changes for the sake of the exercise.

Use the Highlighter

1. Start **Word**. Open **WD11-A03-Cabo** from your **WD2013 Lesson 11** folder and save it as **WD11-A03-Cabo-[FirstInitialLastName]**.

2. Highlight the last sentence in the first paragraph with blue.
   That color makes it difficult to read the text.

3. Change the highlight color to turquoise.

Track Changes and Add Comments

4. Use the **Show Markup** 📄 feature and the **Balloons** option to ensure that **Show Revisions in Balloons** is chosen.

5. Choose **Review→Tracking→dialog box launcher** 🗔 and make sure your username and initials appear in the Word Options dialog box.

6. Change the colors in the Advanced Track Changes Options dialog box as follows:
   - Insertions: **Bright Green**
   - Deletions: **Turquoise**
   - Comments: **Dark Red**

7. Turn on **Track Changes** 🗒.

8. Replace the last word in the first paragraph below the *See* heading, *abundant*, with `plentiful`.

9. In the fourth line of the first bullet point, replace *allows for* with `provides`.

10. In the second line of the next bullet point, enter a `comma` after *old* and delete the word *and*.

11. Position the insertion point at the top of the document.

12. Use the **Next** 🗒 button to locate the first change, and reject the *abundant* deletion and the *plentiful* addition.

13. Accept the rest of the changes.

14. Turn off **Track Changes** 🗒.

15. Select *Submarine* in the second bullet point below the Scuba Diving & Watersports heading.

16. Add this comment: `This looks like a fun activity. Let's check it out.`

17. Scroll to the bottom of page 2, select the *Cruises* heading, and add this comment: `Are these cruise companies still in business?`

Check Tracked Changes Options and Email Files

18. Check that **Display for Review** 🗒 is set to **All Markup**.

19. Use the **Email** 🗒 feature and the **Send as Attachment** option to send an email as shown.
   If your user ID was not set up as a user with an Outlook account, you will see a message saying that no profiles have been created. If so, just dismiss the message and go to the next step.

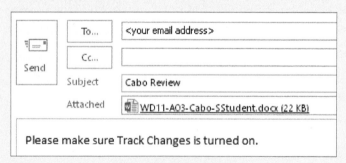

Combine Tracked Changes and Compare Documents

20. Use the **Combine** feature to combine the following documents:
   - The original document is **WD11-A03-Cabo-[FirstInitialLastName]**.
   - The first revised document is **WD11-A03-CaboAudrey**.
   - The second revised document is **WD11-A03-CaboJose**.

21. Use the **Compare** 📄 feature to show both source documents.

22. Scroll down the **Reviewing Pane** (labeled Revisions at the top), click one of the revisions, and notice that the documents scroll to the position of the change.

23. Close the **Reviewing Pane** and then use the **Compare** feature to hide source documents.

24. Accept all changes.

25. Click the reply button in the first comment and type this text: `I'll give them a call.`

26. Click the reply button in the second comment and type this text: `I'll find out.`

27. Save the file as `WD11-A03-CaboCombo-[FirstInitialLastName]` and then close it.

28. Open **WD11-A03-Singapore** from the **WD2013 Lesson 11** folder and save it as `WD11-A03-Singapore-[FirstInitialLastName]`.

29. Compare this file with **WD11-A03-SingEllen**. If you are prompted to continue with the comparison, click **Yes**.

30. Accept all changes and save the file as `WD11-A03-SingComp-[FirstInitialLastName]`. Close the file.

Use AutoSave and AutoRecover

31. Start a new blank document.

32. Use the **Word Options** dialog box **Save** category to ensure that the **AutoRecover** duration is 10 minutes.

33. Type the following: `This is an AutoRecover test`.

34. Close the file without saving it.

35. Start a new blank document.

36. Choose **File→Info**, click **Manage Versions**, and choose **Recover Unsaved Documents**.

37. Open the **This is an AutoRecover test** file and save it as `WD11-A03-AutoRecTest-[FirstInitialLastName]`. Close the **AutoRecover window**. Exit **Word**.

38. Submit your final files based on guidelines provided by your instructor.

Use SkyDrive and Office Web Apps 2013

WebSim   WD13-WA1103

39. If necessary, type the URL for the student resource center into the address bar of your web browser and tap Enter.
The student resource center URL is printed on the inside front cover of your book.

40. From the left navigation bar, click **Lessons 10–14** and then **WD11**; then, click **AYS WD13-WA1103 Use SkyDrive and Web Apps 2013**.

41. Work your way through the onscreen exercise instructions.

42. Click the **Back to Course** link.

Extend Your Skills

In the course of working through the Extend Your Skills exercises, you will think critically as you use the skills taught in the lesson to complete the assigned projects. To evaluate your mastery and completion of the exercises, your instructor may use a rubric, with which more points are allotted according to performance characteristics. (The more you do, the more you earn!) Ask your instructor how your work will be evaluated.

WD11-E01 That's the Way I See It

You are a college senior, and your professor has asked you to prepare a report on the best business opportunities for the coming year. To begin, choose a business that appeals to you. Then, create a short introduction (4–5 sentences) summarizing your reasons for choosing the business. Copy content of one to two pages on business prospects, citing your sources. Save the file as **WD11-E01-Biz-[FirstInitialLastName]** in the **WD2013 Lesson 11** folder.

Create two copies of the file (**WD11-E01-BizJohn** and **WD11-E01-BizJorge**) and save them in the **WD2013 Lesson 11** folder. For the "John" document, enter **John Swales** as the username in the Track Changes Options dialog box. Turn on Track Changes and revise the document using your own ideas and judgment. Do the same for the "Jorge" document, using **Jorge Martinez** as the username and different revisions than you did for John. Combine the revised files with your original file, accepting and rejecting revisions as you see fit, and then save and close the file.

You will be evaluated based on the inclusion of all elements specified, your ability to follow directions, your ability to apply newly learned skills to a real-world situation, your creativity, and the relevance of your topic and/or data choice(s). Submit your final files based on the guidelines provided by your instructor.

WD11-E02 Be Your Own Boss

As the owner of Blue Jean Landscaping, you decide to research recent articles on business opportunities in landscaping to determine future growth potential. Create a report of one or two pages using content you find online (citing your sources). Provide a short introductory paragraph (4–5 sentences) summarizing the outlook for the landscaping business. Name your file **WD11-E02-Landscape-[FirstInitialLastName]**. Make a copy of the document, naming it **WD11-E02-Landscape-Art-[FirstInitialLastName]**.

Begin to share the document with Art via email from within Word. Fill out the email form. Make up Art's email address and a subject. When complete, tap [PrtScn] and paste the screenshot into a new Word document named **WD11-E02-Email-[FirstInitialLastName]**. Close the email form without sending. For the "Art" document, use the Track Changes Options dialog box and enter **Art Reese** as the username. Revise the document without Track Changes. Insert at least one comment, and then save the document. Save both files in your **WD2013 Lesson 11** folder. Compare your original with the "Art" file. Display the Reviewing Pane in a vertical alignment, and then tap [PrtScn]. Add the screenshot to your Email document. Accept and reject revisions as you see fit, and include a reply to Art's comment. Save the file.

You will be evaluated based on the inclusion of all elements specified, your ability to follow directions, your ability to apply newly learned skills to a real-world situation, your creativity, and your demonstration of an entrepreneurial spirit. Submit your final files based on the guidelines provided by your instructor.

Transfer Your Skills

In the course of working through the Transfer Your Skills exercises, you will use critical-thinking and creativity skills to complete the assigned projects using skills taught in the lesson. To evaluate your mastery and completion of the exercises, your instructor may use a rubric, with which more points are allotted according to performance characteristics. (The more you do, the more you earn!) Ask your instructor how your work will be evaluated.

WD11-T01 Use the Web as a Learning Tool

Throughout this book, you will be provided with an opportunity to use the Internet as a learning tool by completing WebQuests. According to the original creators of WebQuests, as described on their website (WebQuest.org), a WebQuest is "an inquiry-oriented activity in which most or all of the information used by learners is drawn from the web." To complete the WebQuest projects in this book, navigate to the student resource center and choose the WebQuest for the lesson on which you are currently working. The subject of each WebQuest will be relevant to the material found in the lesson.

WebQuest Subject: Research different editing processes.

Submit your final files based on the guidelines provided by your instructor.

WD11-T02 Demonstrate Proficiency

As an employee of Stormy BBQ, you have been asked to research the advantages of grass-fed beef. Using content from online articles, create a report of one or two pages (be sure to cite your sources). Provide an introductory paragraph of four or five sentences summarizing the benefits of grass-fed beef. Name the report **WD11-T02-Beef-[FirstInitialLastName]** and save it in the **WD2013 Lesson 11** folder. Make a copy of the file, naming it **WD11-T02-BeefCarla** and save it in the **WD2013 Lesson 11** folder as well. In the Track Changes Options dialog box, enter **Carla Agosto** as the username.

Change the reviewer ink settings for insertions, deletions, and comments to Red. Tap ⌨PrtScn, and then paste the screenshot of the Advanced Track Changes Options dialog box in a new Word document named **WD11-T02-Ink-[FirstInitialLastName]**.

Make revisions to the "Carla" file, including at least one comment; save it. Combine the "Carla" file with your original file, accepting and rejecting changes as you see fit and inserting a reply to the comment. Highlight one sentence with bright green, and then save the file.

Submit your final files based on the guidelines provided by your instructor.

WORD 2013

Sharing and Securing Content in Backstage View

In this lesson, you will work in Backstage view to control document access. Online storage, such as SkyDrive, allows people to store and retrieve documents from any computer with Internet access, and virtual collaboration means that your documents are often in others' hands. Word 2013 provides features that help you control document content and security, and guard your personal information.

LESSON OUTLINE

Preparing Documents for Sharing
Controlling Document Access
Attaching Digital Signatures to Documents
Concepts Review
Reinforce Your Skills
Apply Your Skills
Extend Your Skills
Transfer Your Skills

LEARNING OBJECTIVES

After studying this lesson, you will be able to:

- Use Word's file compatibility features
- Check documents with the Document Inspector
- Restrict formatting and editing in a document
- Mark a document as final
- Secure documents with passwords and digital signatures

Securing Confidential Information

Raritan Clinic East

Pediatric Diagnostic Specialists

At Raritan Clinic East, privacy and security of patient records are vitally important. As an employee of Raritan, you want to explore Word's features that ensure that documents sent outside the clinic remain confidential and contain no information that could enable those receiving the documents to learn more about the clinic than they need to know. You will use Backstage view and identify some of the security features you can use.

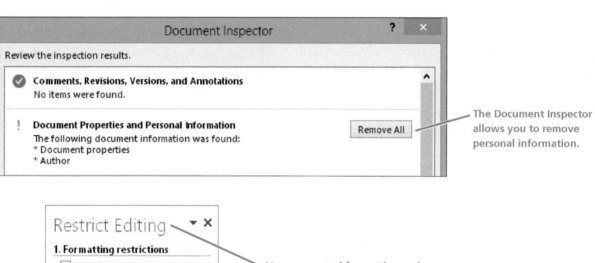

The Document Inspector allows you to remove personal information.

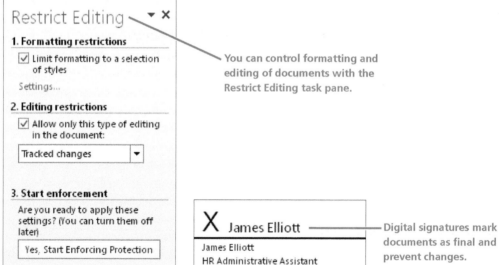

You can control formatting and editing of documents with the Restrict Editing task pane.

Digital signatures mark documents as final and prevent changes.

Preparing Documents for Sharing

Video Library   http://labyrinthelab.com/videos   Video Number: WD13-V1201

There are a number of things to think about when sharing documents with colleagues or clients. Compatibility issues between Word 2013 and earlier versions of Word should be considered. Additionally, Word documents can contain hidden or personal information about your organization or about a document that you do not want to share publicly. The Document Inspector can help you deal with these items.

Considering Compatibility Issues

Word 2013 uses the file format *.docx, which was introduced in Word 2007. Versions of Word prior to 2007 used a *.doc file format. The benefits of the later format include smaller file size, improved damaged-file recovery, and more control of personal information. It is important to understand how Word 2013 behaves with documents created in earlier versions. Likewise, you need to make sure your Word 2013 documents can be read by people using Word 97–2003. There are several things to think about in dealing with compatibility issues.

- Opening documents in Word 2013 that were created in earlier versions
- Converting documents to Word 2013 that were created in earlier versions
- Creating documents in Word 2013 that are compatible with earlier versions
- Using the Compatibility Pack with documents created in earlier versions

Opening Documents in Compatibility Mode

If you open a document in Word 2013 that was created in a version prior to Word 2013, it opens in *Compatibility Mode*. Older Word documents do not understand the new features in Word 2013; therefore, those features are limited or disabled so people using earlier versions still have full editing capability. The words Compatibility Mode appear in the title bar at the top of the screen, as shown in the following illustration.

WD12-D01-2003ProcMan.doc [Compatibility Mode] - Word

Limitations of Compatibility Mode

When creating documents in Word 2013, you can save them in the Word 97–2003 (*.doc) format, but some features of Word 2013 either won't be available or they will be modified in a manner more compatible with older versions.

Open a Document in Compatibility Mode

In this exercise, you will open a Word 2003 document in Word 2013 Compatibility Mode. You will then try to insert a Word 2013 SmartArt graphic in the 2003 document and see how Word deals with the feature.

1. Open **WD12-D01-2003ProcMan** from your **WD2013 Lesson 12** folder and save it as **WD12-D01-2003ProcMan-[FirstInitialLastName]**.

   Replace the bracketed text with your first initial and last name. For example, if your name is Bethany Smith, your filename would look like this: WD12-D01-2003ProcMan-BSmith.

   Notice the term Compatibility Mode *in Word's title bar at the top of the screen.*

   WD12-D01-2003ProcMan-SStudent.doc [Compatibility Mode] - Word

   Now you will attempt to add a Word 2013 SmartArt graphic to the Word 2003 Compatibility Mode document.

2. If necessary, display formatting marks.

3. Position the insertion point in front of the paragraph mark at the top of page 2.

4. Choose **Insert→Illustrations→SmartArt** 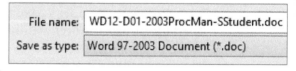.

   Note that Word opens the Word 2003 Diagram Gallery, rather than the Word 2013 SmartArt gallery, because the Compatibility Mode document is not capable of working with Word 2013's SmartArt feature.

5. Click **Cancel** to close the Diagram Gallery.

   Next you will observe how Word saves the compatibility mode document.

6. Choose **File→Save As** and navigate to your **WD2013 Lesson 12** folder.

File name:	WD12-D01-2003ProcMan-SStudent.doc
Save as type:	Word 97-2003 Document (*.doc)

   *Notice that Word 2013 defaults to the Word 97-2003 Save As Type option. Word 2013 defaults to the older format unless you purposely convert the document to a *.docx format or save it as a Word document (*.docx) via the Save As Type drop-down list.*

7. Click **Cancel**, and then click **Back** ⬅ in the upper-left corner to return to the document. Leave the file open.

To Convert or Not to Convert

Video Library   http://labyrinthelab.com/videos   Video Number: WD13-V1202

If most of the people you share documents with are using pre-2007 versions of Word, it's a good idea to keep their documents in Compatibility Mode. This ensures that documents will look the same in Word 2013 as they do in the older version. It also ensures that the features available in Word 2013 will be limited to, or similar to, the features available in older versions.

Choosing a Conversion Method

If you are working with a Compatibility Mode document that would benefit from the full functionality of Word 2013 features that are currently disabled or limited, you have a candidate for conversion. When you convert the document, Word 2013 turns on the new and enhanced features.

There are two ways to convert an older version (*.doc) document to a Word 2007-2013 (*.docx) document:

- Use the Convert command on the Info tab in Backstage view.
- Use the Save As command to save a *copy* of the document in the new format.

Using the Convert Command

The Convert command appears on the Info tab in Backstage view when a document is open in Compatibility Mode. Using the command performs a conversion that overwrites the original document. As a result, the older version document is no longer available.

Using the Save As Command

When you resave and rename a document using the Save As command, you are actually making a *copy* of the document. When you perform a Save As with a Compatibility Mode document, you still have the original *.doc file, and you create a new second document, a *.docx file.

Considering the User

Always keep the person who sent you the document or the person to whom you are sending a document in mind before converting. If you are editing a document that needs to be returned to someone who is using an earlier version of Word, leave the document in its original format rather than converting it.

DEVELOP YOUR SKILLS WD12-D02

Convert a Word 2003 Document to the 2013 Format

*In this exercise, you will convert a Word 2003 document to the *.docx format and then add a Word 2013 feature to the document.*

1. Save your file as **WD12-D02-2003ProcMan-[FirstInitialLastName]**.

2. Choose **File→Info→Convert**.

   A message appears indicating that conversion may cause some minor layout changes. For example, in this document, the pagination is altered slightly when converted.

3. Click **OK** to acknowledge the message.

   Notice that the words Compatibility Mode *have disappeared from the title bar.*

4. Position the insertion point on page 2 at the beginning of the third paragraph, just below the *Scope of Services* heading. Be sure the insertion point is to the left of the tab that begins that paragraph.

5. Tap ⌨Enter, and then position the insertion point next to the paragraph mark for the blank line you just created.

6. Choose **Insert→Illustrations→SmartArt** 📰.

   Since you converted the document, the SmartArt gallery is now available.

7. Follow these steps to insert a SmartArt graphic:

Ⓐ Choose **All** from the category options.

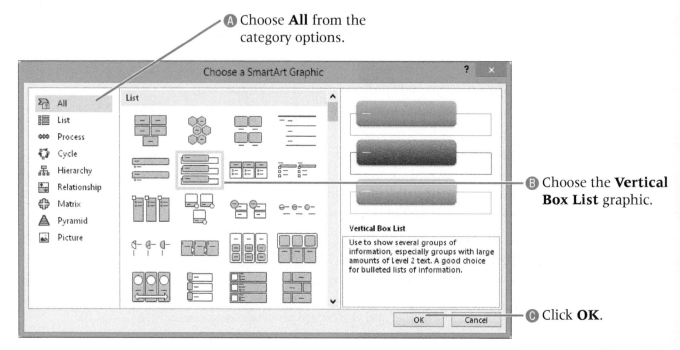

Ⓑ Choose the **Vertical Box List** graphic.

Ⓒ Click **OK**.

8. If necessary, click the tab at the left side of the graphic to open the Type Your Text Here pane.

9. Type the text shown.

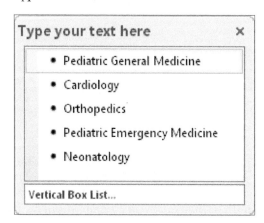

10. **Close** ⊠ the Type Your Text Here pane.

11. Save the document and leave it open.

Preparing Backward-Compatible Documents in Word 2013

Video Library   http://labyrinthelab.com/videos   Video Number: WD13-V1203

If you know that you'll be working with people who have older versions of Word, and if it's important that all features are compatible among the versions, you might start your new document by saving it as a Word 97–2003 document. That way, you avoid using features unavailable in older versions.

Using the Compatibility Checker

If you save a Word 2013 document down to an older Word version, the Compatibility Checker notifies you if the document contains features unique to newer versions of Word. You can also manually run the Compatibility Checker before saving the document in older versions of Word.

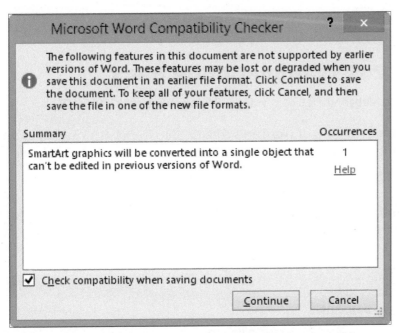

The Compatibility Checker alerts you to how Word 2013 features will be handled if you save a document to an earlier version of Word.

Round-Tripping Documents

Round-tripping is a term that you may hear as you work with documents created in various versions of Word. Round-tripping refers to the practice of converting a document to a different format and then saving it back to the original format. For example, you may open a Word *.doc file, convert it to a *.docx, and then decide to save your changes back to *.doc format. Round-tripping can create issues with the document that corrupt it so that it acts strangely or is damaged beyond repair. Avoid round-tripping your documents to prevent unwanted loss of time and data.

Save a Word 2013 Document to the 97–2003 Format

In this exercise, you will begin the process to save a Word 2013 document to Word 97–2003 format version for people who have not yet upgraded to Word 2007.

1. Choose **File→Save As**, and then navigate to your file storage location.

2. Click the **Save as Type** drop-down field and choose **Word 97–2003 Document**.

3. Click **Save**.

   Word displays the compatibility checker with a message indicating that you will not be able to edit the SmartArt graphic.

4. Click **Cancel**.

   You will not complete the conversion.

The Office 2013 Compatibility Pack

Video Library   http://labyrinthelab.com/videos   Video Number: WD13-V1204

People who have earlier versions of Word and who need to work with Word 2013 documents can download a Compatibility Pack from the Microsoft website to open, edit, and save Word 2013 documents. However, some features will still not be available.

Do a search in your favorite search engine for "office 2013 compatibility pack" for the latest information on this free software.

QUICK REFERENCE	USING WORD'S COMPATIBILITY FEATURES
Task	**Description**
Open a document in Compatibility Mode	■ In Word 2013, open a document created in Word 97–2003. (Word 2013 automatically displays the document in Compatibility Mode.)
Convert a Word 97-2003 document to a Word 2013 document	■ Open an earlier version document in Word 2013 and choose File→Info→Convert. Or, open the desired document in Word 2013, choose Office→Save As, and choose Word Document (*.docx) from the Save as Type list (retains the *.doc document and creates a new *.docx version).
Prepare a backward-compatible document	■ Create a document in Word 2013, choose File→Save As, and choose Word 97-2003 Document (*.doc) from the Save as Type list. If the Compatibility Checker appears, click Continue.
Install the Compatibility Pack	■ Download the Compatibility Pack from the Microsoft website and follow the prompts to install it.

Working with the Document Inspector

If you intend to share a document with colleagues or clients, you may want to use the Document Inspector to ensure that your document contains no hidden or personal information in the document or in the document properties. For example, a document could contain comments and tracked changes that are hidden from view. Document properties could contain information such as the author's name and the company name.

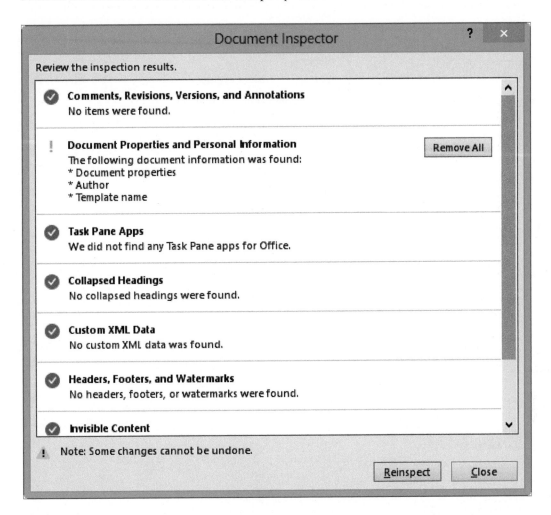

The Document Inspector will display a list of issues found in a document. The only option for removing data for a category is to remove all data within that category. Sometimes you may want to manually review information before deciding which data to remove.

Before you use the automatic Remove All option for a category, make a copy of the document, run the Document Inspector on the copy, and remove all issues to see the effect. This will help prevent unwanted data loss.

Examining Document Properties

Valuable information about a document appears in the Properties panel in Backstage view. Among the data Word stores within a document are the author's name, dates for file creation and editing, and the file storage location. Sending this data along with a document can inadvertently reveal to recipients some data that you would rather protect.

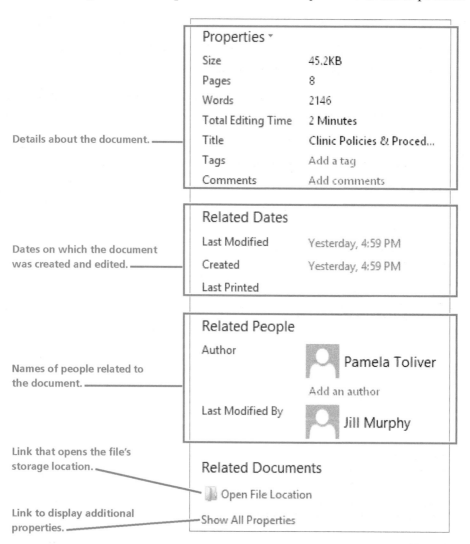

Details about the document.

Dates on which the document was created and edited.

Names of people related to the document.

Link that opens the file's storage location.

Link to display additional properties.

Inspect a Document

In this exercise, you will view document properties and run the Document Inspector. You will remove all personal data from the document.

1. Save your file as **WD12-D04-2003ProcMan-[FirstInitialLastName]**.

2. Choose **File→Info** and review the Properties listed in the panel on the right.
   Notice that names appear in the Related People area.

3. In the Info window, click **Check for Issues** and then choose **Inspect Document**.
   At this point you can remove the checkmark from any items you don't want inspected. In this example, you will leave all checkboxes checked.

4. Click **Inspect** at the bottom of the dialog box. Review the results.

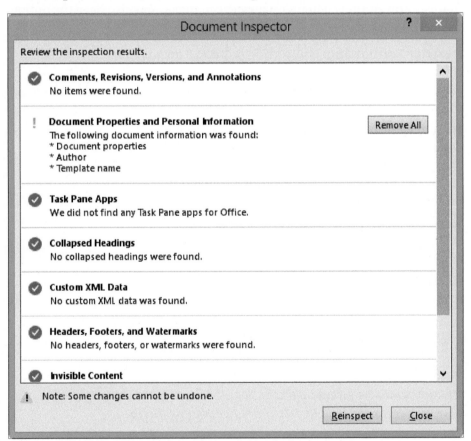

The inspector found document properties and personal information. You will remove the properties and personal information.

5. Click **Remove All** to the right of *Document Properties and Personal Information* and then click **Close**.

6. In the Properties panel, notice that names have been removed.

7. Click **Back** ⊕ in the upper-left corner of the Info window.

8. Save the file and leave it open.

Controlling Document Access

When you share documents with colleagues and clients, it can be helpful to control the changes that others can make. Word provides several features to assist you with protecting documents. For example, you can restrict the kinds of formatting and editing changes a reviewer can make. You can add a password to a document, and you can mark a document as final, thereby preventing any changes to it.

Restricting Formatting and Editing

When you share a document with multiple reviewers, it is easy to imagine a jumble of formats and edits if there are no restrictions. The Restrict Editing task pane enables you to limit the formatting and editing changes reviewers can make. You also have the option to further limit access with a password.

- **Restrict Formatting:** This setting protects a document from the use of any styles not approved and prevents reviewers from modifying any styles. This helps to enforce consistent formatting.

- **Restrict for Tracked Changes:** This setting protects a document from having Track Changes disabled. Every change to the document will be noted. In addition, no one can accept or reject changes while the document is protected.

- **Restrict for Comments:** This setting permits reviewers to insert and edit comments in the document, but not to edit the document itself.

- **Restrict for Filling in Forms:** This setting permits users to only insert data in unrestricted areas of a form.

Word's Restrict Editing task pane allows you to set various restrictions on the formatting and editing of a document.

DEVELOP YOUR SKILLS WD12-D05

Restrict Editing

In this exercise, you will set editing restrictions to allow tracked changes. You will also assign a password to the document to prevent unauthorized users from editing the file.

1. Save your file as **WD12-D05-2003ProcMan-[FirstInitialLastName]**.

2. Choose **File→Info→Protect Document→Restrict Editing**.

3. Follow these steps to turn on document protection for tracked changes:

Ⓐ Ensure this checkbox is checked.

Ⓑ Ensure **Tracked Changes** is chosen here.

Ⓒ Click **Yes, Start Enforcing Protection**.

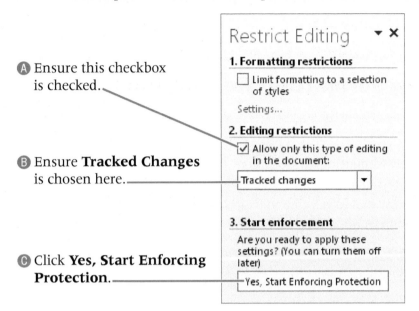

Word displays the Start Enforcing Protection dialog box. At this point, you can either click OK to restrict editing without a password or enter the desired password.

4. Follow these steps to add a password:

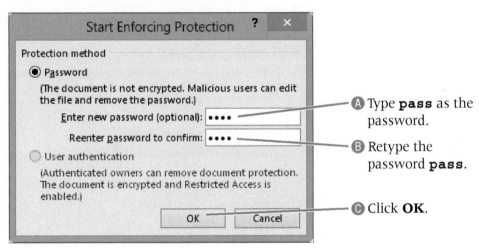

Ⓐ Type **pass** as the password.

Ⓑ Retype the password **pass**.

Ⓒ Click **OK**.

5. On page 2, delete *of Services* in the *Scope of Services* heading.
   Word marks the change with Track Changes. No one can alter the document without changes being marked.

6. Click **Stop Protection** at the bottom of the Restrict Editing task pane.
   Word prompts you to enter the password in order to switch off editing restrictions.

7. Type **pass** and then click **OK**.

8. Click **Close** ⊠ in the upper-right corner of the Restrict Editing task pane.

9. Choose **Review→Changes→Next** ⭻.

10. **Accept** 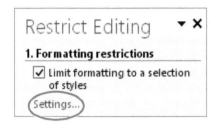 the change. Click **OK** when the message box appears.

11. Save the file and leave it open.

Applying Formatting Restrictions

Video Library http://labyrinthelab.com/videos Video Number: WD13-V1206

Formatting is restricted to a list of specified Word styles, thus preventing anyone from indiscriminately formatting the document. The *Settings* link, shown in the following illustration, opens the Formatting Restrictions dialog box.

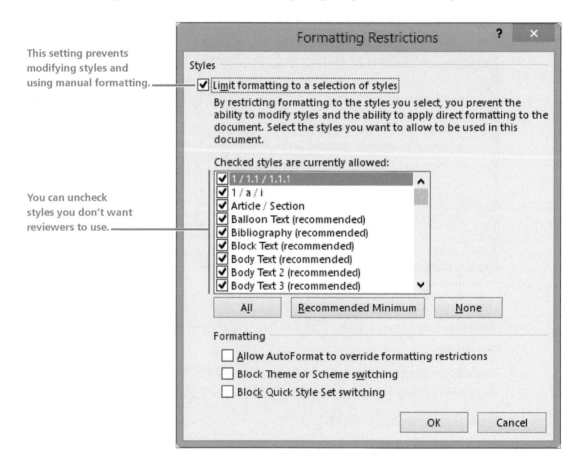

The Formatting Restrictions dialog box lets you specify which Word styles a reviewer can use.

Set Formatting Restrictions

In this exercise, you will use the Restrict Editing task pane to apply formatting restrictions.

1. Save your file as **WD12-D06-2003ProcMan-[FirstInitialLastName]**.

2. Choose **File→Info→Protect Document→Restrict Editing**.

3. Follow these steps to open the Formatting Restrictions dialog box:

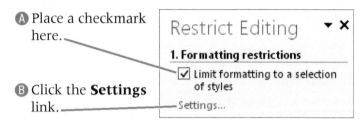

Ⓐ Place a checkmark here.

Ⓑ Click the **Settings** link.

Word displays the Formatting Restrictions dialog box.

4. Follow these steps to set specific restrictions:

Ⓐ Click **None** to uncheck all of the checkboxes at once.

Ⓑ Scroll down and place checkmarks in the **Heading 1** and **Heading 2** checkboxes.

The only formatting change a reviewer can make is to add Heading 1 or Heading 2 formatting.

5. Click **OK**.

6. When Word displays a message asking if you want to remove other styles, click **No**.
   Removing other styles from the document would reformat the entire document, possibly with unexpected results.

7. Click **Yes, Start Enforcing Protection** in the Restrict Editing task pane.
   In this example, you will not add a password.

8. Click **OK** to dismiss the password dialog box.

   Notice that the task pane now contains a link to Available Styles.

9. Click the **Available Styles** link to display the Styles task pane.

   In addition to the Normal style, the only styles available are Heading 1 and Heading 2.

10. Scroll to the top of page 2 and apply the **Heading 1** style to *Our Mission*.

11. **Close** ☒ the Styles task pane.

12. Display the **Home** tab.

    Notice that all of the Font and Paragraph formats are grayed out in the Ribbon, because formatting is restricted to two heading styles.

13. Click **Stop Protection** at the bottom of the Restrict Editing task pane.

    Notice that the Font and Paragraph formats are restored.

14. Choose **Review→Changes→Next** ⬧.

15. Choose **Review→Changes→Accept** ⬧ to accept your formatting change.

16. Click **OK** when the message box appears.

17. Save the file and leave it open.

Applying Editing Exceptions

Video Library   http://labyrinthelab.com/videos   Video Number: WD13-V1207

If you choose *Comments* or *No Changes (Read Only)* in the Editing Restrictions list, the Exceptions option appears where you can specify certain areas of a document that a person can edit freely. For example, if a document is in its final version except for one section, you can exempt the incomplete section of the document so that it can be edited.

If you want people to be able to edit a part of the document, you select the text to be edited, and then choose the people you want to allow to edit. You can choose *Everyone*, or you can use the More Users link to add specific users.

QUICK REFERENCE	SETTING FORMATTING AND EDITING RESTRICTIONS
Task	**Description**
Set formatting restrictions	■ Choose File→Info→Protect Document→Restrict Editing, or choose Review→Protect→Restrict Editing to display the Restrict Editing task pane.
	■ Place a checkmark in the Formatting Restrictions area, click the Settings link, and check the styles you want available to reviewers.
Set editing restrictions	■ Choose File→Info→Protect Document→Restrict Editing, or choose Review→Protect→Restrict Editing to display the Restrict Editing task pane.
	■ Place a checkmark in the Editing Restrictions section of the task pane and choose the type of editing permitted.
Apply exceptions to editing restrictions	■ Choose Comments or No Changes (Read Only) in the Editing Restrictions area, and then select the text that will be an exception to the restrictions.
	■ Under Exceptions, click Everyone, or click the More Users link and add users.

DEVELOP YOUR SKILLS WD12-D07
Apply Editing Exceptions

In this exercise, you will specify the document as read-only; however, you will apply an exception to three paragraphs so the reviewer can make changes to them.

1. Save your file as **WD12-D07-2003ProcMan-[FirstInitialLastName]**.

2. Follow these steps to restrict editing:

Ⓐ Make sure a checkmark appears here.

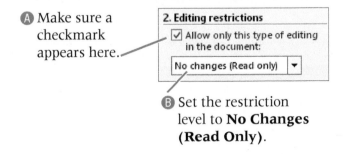

Ⓑ Set the restriction level to **No Changes (Read Only)**.

3. Scroll to page 3 and select the three paragraphs below the heading *Entry into Services*.

4. Place a checkmark in the **Everyone** checkbox under Exceptions (Optional), as shown at right.

   This specifies that all reviewers will be able to edit these paragraphs.

Exceptions (optional)
Select parts of the document and choose users who are allowed to freely edit them.
Groups:
☑ Everyone

5. Click **Yes, Start Enforcing Protection** at the bottom of the task pane.

6. Click **OK** to bypass setting a password.

7. Click to deselect the paragraphs.

   Notice that the editable paragraphs are shaded to make them readily visible to reviewers.

Attempt to Edit in a Restricted Area

8. Select a word anywhere there is no shading and tap ⎡Delete⎤.

   Nothing happens because you are restricted to editing only the shaded paragraphs.

9. Delete the third paragraph in the highlighted area.

   The deletion is allowed, because it is in the area that was specified as an exception.

10. Click **Stop Protection** at the bottom of the task pane.

11. Select the two remaining highlighted paragraphs and then remove the checkmark from the **Everyone** checkbox in the task pane.

12. Click in the document and notice the shading has been removed.

13. **Close** ⎡×⎤ the Restrict Editing task pane and then save the file.

Setting Document Passwords

Video Library   http://labyrinthelab.com/videos   Video Number: WD13-V1208

By using commands on the Backstage view Info tab, you can set two passwords for a document. If you use both passwords, the reviewer would need a password to open the document as well as another password to edit the document.

Encrypting Documents

Adding a document password also encrypts the document. Encryption means Word alters information using a code or mathematical algorithm so the information is inaccessible to unauthorized readers. When you encrypt a document, Word prompts you for a password. After you enter the password, Word presents a second prompt so you can enter the password again. This ensures that you have typed the password correctly without any typos.

The first dialog box prompts you for a password.

The second dialog box prompts you to confirm the password.

Note that passwords are case-sensitive.

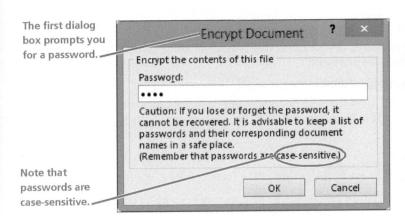

Opening an Encrypted Document

If you try to open a document that is encrypted with a password and enter an incorrect password, Word displays a message advising you that Word cannot open the document.

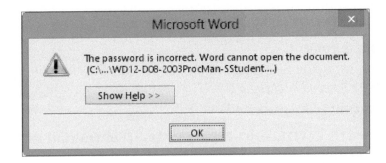

Removing Passwords

After a document has been reviewed and returned to you, you can remove the password. You simply delete the password from the Encrypt with Password dialog box to remove the protection from the document.

Reviewing Protect Settings

When you assign a password, Word displays the security setting on the Info screen in Backstage view.

QUICK REFERENCE	SETTING AND REMOVING DOCUMENT PASSWORDS
Task	**Description**
Set a document password	■ Choose File→Info→Protect Document→Encrypt with Password, and then type and confirm the password.
Remove a document password	■ Open the document using the password.
	■ Choose File→Info→Protect Document→Encrypt with Password. Delete the password in the dialog box and click OK.

DEVELOP YOUR SKILLS WD12-D08
Set and Remove a Document Password

In this exercise, you will set a document password, and then you will remove it.

1. Choose **File→Info→Protect Document→Encrypt with Password**.

2. Type **pass** in the Encrypt Document dialog box and click **OK**.

3. Type **pass** in the Confirm Password dialog box and click **OK**.

4. Click **Back** in the upper-left corner to return to the document.

5. Save and then close the document.

   Depending on the security settings on your computer, you may receive a message asking if you would like to increase the security. Respond by clicking No.

   Now you'll open the document with a password.

6. Choose **File→Open** and click **WD12-D07-2003ProcMan-[FirstInitialLastName]** at the top of the Recent Documents list.

   In some classrooms, the Recent Documents list may be cleared upon rebooting the computer. If so, navigate to your file storage location to open the document.

7. Type **pass** in the password box and click **OK**.

   Now you will remove the password.

8. Choose **File→Info→Protect Document→Encrypt with Password**.

9. Select the characters in the password field, tap Delete , and click **OK**.

10. Click **Back** in the upper-left corner to return to the document.

Marking a Document as Final

Video Library   http://labyrinthelab.com/videos   Video Number: WD13-V1209

Another way to control edits and access to the content is to mark the document as "final." Using the Mark as Final command makes a document *read-only.* As a result, readers and reviewers will know that this document appears as it did when it went to a client, was filed electronically, or was in some other way beyond the point where edits would be useful. Marking as final also prevents accidental altering of the document.

When a document is marked as final, the following message appears in the Info tab in Backstage view.

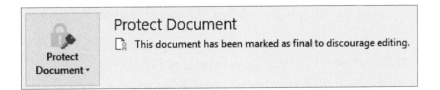

Editing Documents Marked as Final

When the Marked as Final feature is turned on, a yellow bar appears at the top of the document. The message in the bar lets you know that the document has been marked as final to discourage editing, and the Ribbon is hidden. Note that this feature only *discourages* editing. It is not secure, as a password would be. The button in the message bar enables you to edit the document anyway.

The Marked as Final icon appears on Word's status bar when you open a document that is marked as final.

Reversing Marked as Final Status

If you want to re-enable editing for a document marked as final, you choose the Mark as Final command again. This turns off the feature and removes the Marked as Final bar at the top of the screen and the Marked as Final icon on the status bar.

QUICK REFERENCE	
Task	**Description**
Mark a document as final	▪ Choose File→Info→Protect Document→Mark as Final.
Enable the document for editing	▪ Choose File→Info→Protect Document→Mark as Final to turn the feature off; or, click Edit Anyway on the bar at the top of the screen.

Mark a Document as Final

In this exercise, you will mark a document as final, and then you will remove the designation in order to re-enable editing.

1. Choose **File→Info→Protect Document→Mark as Final**.

   Word displays a message that the document will be marked as final and saved.

2. Click **OK**.

   Word displays additional information about this setting.

3. Take a moment to read the information and then click **OK**.

4. Click **Back**  in the upper-left corner to return to the document.

   Notice the Marked as Final bar at the top of the screen and the Marked as Final icon on the left side of the status bar.

   PAGE 1 OF 7   2032 WORDS

5. Select the heading *Our Mission* on page 2.

6. Tap [Delete] and the text is not deleted.

   Notice the message on the status bar at the bottom of the screen.

   This modification is not allowed because the selection is locked.

The message disappears after a few seconds. Tap [Delete] again to redisplay the message if you missed it.

   Remember, the Edit Anyway button at the top of the screen allows you to edit the document despite the author's marking it as final. Next, you will enable editing in Backstage view.

7. Choose **File→Info→Protect Document→Mark as Final** to turn off the feature.

8. Click **Back**  in the upper-left corner of the screen.

   The Marked as Final bar at the top of the screen and the Marked as Final status bar icon no longer appear.

Attaching Digital Signatures to Documents

Video Library   http://labyrinthelab.com/videos   Video Number: WD13-V1210

With the capability to rapidly pass documents globally, security concerns may arise. For example, how can a client know for certain that a critical document originated at your office? A digital signature is a secure means of stamping a document as authentic and originating only from you. Other people cannot modify a signed document without removing the digital signature or marking it as invalid.

You may use a digital signature when passing documents to others as an email attachment, as a downloadable file on your organization's intranet, from a website, or on a disk. You add a digital signature to a file by first attaching a digital certificate.

Creating a Digital Certificate

Purchase a Certificate from a Third-Party Vendor: Digital certificates may be obtained from third-party vendors, who check identification before issuing a certificate. If you post documents on an intranet or the Internet, your network administrator will usually provide you with an authentic digital certificate.

Choosing this option from the Add a Signature Line menu links to a Microsoft website where you can choose a third-party vendor.

Use a Self-Created Certificate: You may create your own digital certificate, although its use is limited. It is not verified by any outside agency; therefore, it is not necessarily a reliable measure, but it is the most convenient.

DEVELOP YOUR SKILLS WD12-D10
Create a Digital Certificate

In this exercise, you will create a temporary digital certificate on your local computer. You will start by locating the SELFCERT application on your computer, which is installed as part of the Microsoft Office 2013 package.

1. Open **File Explorer** and navigate to the **SELFCERT** application through a path such as C:\Program Files\Microsoft Office\Office 15.

You may need to consult with your instructor to determine the correct file path for this application. You may not have user permission to create a digital certificate on your classroom computer.

2. Scroll to locate the **SELFCERT** application. SELFCERT.EXE

3. Double-click the file. When the Create Digital Certification dialog box opens, type **James Elliott** in the **Your Certificate's Name** field.

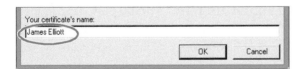

4. Click **OK**. When a message appears indicating that a certificate was successfully created for James Elliott, click **OK**.

   You have now created a digital certificate *that can be used to apply a digital* signature *to your files.*

5. Close the **File Explorer** window.

Adding a Digital Signature

Video Library   http://labyrinthelab.com/videos   Video Number: WD13-V1211

There are two ways to add a digital signature to a document.

- You can add a *visible signature line* to a document, and then capture the digital signature when the document is signed.
- If a visible signature line is not necessary, you can add an *invisible digital signature*. A signature button appears on the status bar at the bottom of the screen, so the recipient can verify that the document has a digital signature.

QUICK REFERENCE	ADDING AND REMOVING DIGITAL SIGNATURES
Task	**Procedure**
Add a signature line to a document	■ Choose Insert→Text→Add a Signature Line and then complete the Signature Setup dialog box.
Add a signature to a signature line	■ Right-click the signature line and choose Sign.
	■ Type your name, or click Select Image to select a signature image file.
Remove a signature and signature line from a document	■ Click This Document Contains Signatures on the status bar, right-click the signature, and choose Remove Signature.
	■ Select the signature line and tap Delete.
Add an invisible digital signature	■ Choose File→Info→Protect Document→Add a Digital Signature, add any desired information, and click Sign.
Remove an invisible signature	■ Click This Document Contains Signatures on the status bar, right-click the signature, and choose Remove Signature.

DEVELOP YOUR SKILLS WD12-D11
Add a Digital Signature to a Document

In this exercise, you will add a signature line to a document, and then you will add a digital signature. You will then attempt to modify the signed document. Finally, you will remove the visible signature and add an invisible digital signature.

1. Save your file as **WD12-D11-2003ProcMan-[FirstInitialLastName]**.

2. Press Ctrl + End to move to the end of the document and then tap Enter twice.

3. Choose **Insert→Text→Add a Signature Line** ⬚ to display the Signature Setup dialog box.

4. Complete the information as shown.

The Instructions to the Signer *text is provided by default. You can modify it, if necessary. In this exercise, you'll leave the text as it is.*

5. Click **OK** to complete the signature setup.

A signature line appears with the signer's name and title below. Now you'll sign the document.

6. Right-click the signature line and choose **Sign**.

7. Follow these steps to sign the document:

Ⓐ Type **James Elliott** here.

Ⓑ If the Signing As name isn't the one you want, click **Change**, choose **James Elliott**, and click **OK**. Click **Yes** when the message appears to use the certificate.

Ⓒ Click **Sign**.

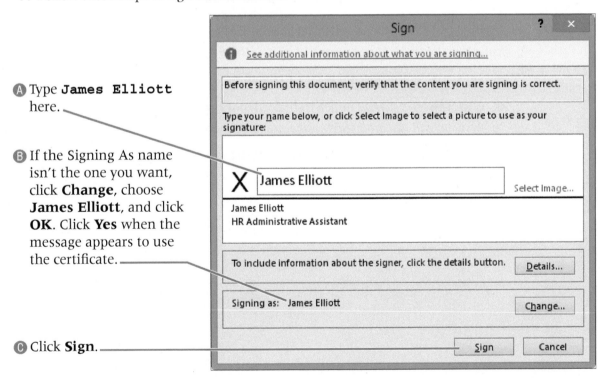

If you didn't change the Signing As name, a message appears indicating the certificate cannot be verified and asking if you want to use this certificate. Remember, a self-created certificate is not verified by a third-party agency.

Attaching Digital Signatures to Documents **WD12.25**

8. If necessary, click **Yes** to use the certificate.

9. When a message appears indicating your signature has been saved, click **OK**.

   A yellow bar appears at the top of the document indicating that the document is marked as final, and a signature button appears on the status bar indicating that there is a signature in the document.

   PAGE 7 OF 7   2032 WORDS

10. Attempt to delete a word in the paragraph above the signature line.

    Notice a message that appears on the status bar when you try to make a change.

    This modification is not allowed because the selection is locked.

    Now you will remove the signature so you can add an invisible signature. Remember, you can use an invisible signature when a visible signature is not required; however, a signature button will still appear on the status bar.

11. Click the signature button on the status bar to display the Signatures task pane.

    You may notice the term Recoverable Error at the top of the task pane. This is because you are using a self-created certificate.

12. Right-click the **James Elliott** signature in the task pane and choose **Remove Signature**.

    A message appears verifying that you want to remove the signature.

13. Click **Yes** to remove the signature.

    A message appears indicating that the signature was removed.

14. Click **OK** to dismiss the message.

Remove the Signature Line and Add an Invisible Digital Signature

15. Select the signature line and tap Delete to remove it.

16. Click **Close** × in the upper-right corner of the Signatures task pane.

    Now you will add an invisible signature, which you do in Backstage view.

17. Choose **File→Info→Protect Document→Add a Digital Signature**.

18. Follow these steps to add the signature:

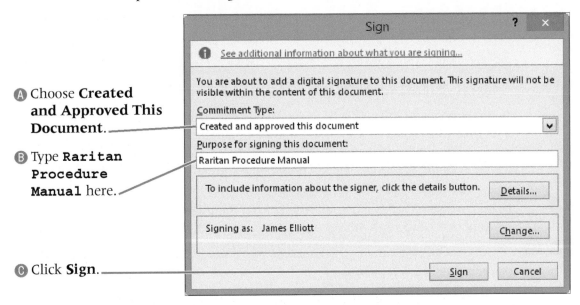

Ⓐ Choose **Created and Approved This Document**.

Ⓑ Type **Raritan Procedure Manual** here.

Ⓒ Click **Sign**.

A message appears indicating the certificate cannot be verified. Again, a self-created certificate is not verified by a third-party agency.

19. Click **Yes** to use the certificate.

A message appears indicating the signature has been saved with the document.

20. Click **OK**.

Notice the Marked as Final note in the yellow bar at the top of the screen and the signature button on the status bar.

Since you cannot edit a document once a signature is attached, there is no option to save the document. When you close the document, the signature will still be attached.

21. Close the file. Exit **Word**.

Concepts Review

To check your knowledge of the key concepts introduced in this lesson, complete the Concepts Review quiz by choosing the appropriate access option below.

If you are...	Then access the quiz by...
Using the Labyrinth Video Library	Going to http://labyrinthelab.com/videos
Using eLab	Logging in, choosing Content, and navigating to the Concepts Review quiz for this lesson
Not using the Labyrinth Video Library or eLab	Going to the student resource center for this book

Reinforce Your Skills

Work with Compatibility Issues

In this exercise, you will open a Word 2003 document in Compatibility Mode and attempt to insert a Word 2013 SmartArt graphic. Then you will convert the document to Word 2013 format and insert a SmartArt graphic. You will consider what's involved in creating a backward-compatible document, as well as work with the Document Inspector and document properties.

In this exercise, you will use an article from the Internet. Normally you would not modify the content of a cited work; however, since you are not representing this as your own work, you can make changes for the sake of the exercise.

Open a Document in Compatibility Mode

1. Start **Word**. Open **WD12-R01-Trout** from your **WD2013 Lesson 12** folder and save it as **WD12-R01-Trout-[FirstInitialLastName]**.

   Observe the words Compatibility Mode *in the title bar. Now you will attempt to add a SmartArt graphic to the document.*

2. Press Ctrl + End to position the insertion point at the end of the document.

3. Choose **Insert→Illustrations→SmartArt** .

   Word opens the Word 2003 Diagram Gallery, because a Word 2003 document is not compatible with the SmartArt feature in Word 2013.

4. Click **Cancel** to close the Diagram Gallery.

   Next, you will observe the Save As dialog box when saving a Word 2003 document.

5. Choose **File→Save As** and navigate to your **WD2013 Lesson 12** folder.

   Notice that Word defaults to the Word 97–2003 document format in the Save As Type field.

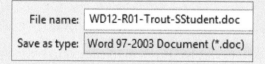

File name:	WD12-R01-Trout-SStudent.doc
Save as type:	Word 97-2003 Document (*.doc)

6. Click **Cancel**.

Convert the Document Using the Convert Command

7. Click **Info** on the left and then click **Convert**.

8. Click **OK** when the conversion message appears.

   Notice that Compatibility Mode no longer appears in the title bar; the document is now in the Word 2013 format.

9. If necessary, press Ctrl + End to position the insertion point at the end of the document.

   Now you will insert a Word 2013 SmartArt graphic.

10. Choose **Insert→Illustrations→SmartArt** 📧.

11. Choose the **Process** category on the left, and then choose **Continuous Block Process** and click **OK**.

12. Click the tab on the left side of the graphic to display the Type Your Text Here pane.

13. Type **Hatch** at the first bullet and **Release** at the second bullet. Close the text pane.

14. Click the third text box in the graphic image to select it and tap [Delete].

15. Position the insertion point on the upper-right corner sizing handle, and then drag down diagonally toward the center of the image until it is about half its original size.

Prepare a Backward-Compatible Document

Now you will see what is involved in formatting a Word 2013 document to be compatible with earlier versions.

16. Choose **File→Save As** and navigate to your **WD2013 Lesson 12** folder.

17. Click the **Save as Type** drop-down list, choose **Word 97–2003 Document (*.doc)**, and click **Save**.

    The Compatibility Checker opens indicating that SmartArt graphics are not supported in earlier versions of Word. You will cancel the conversion so the SmartArt graphic will work as intended.

18. Click **Cancel**.

Work with the Document Inspector and Document Properties

19. Choose **File→Info** and observe the Properties panel on the right.
    Names appear in the Related People area.

20. In the Info window, choose **Check for Issues→Inspect Document**.
    A message appears indicating that you should save your changes since the Document Inspector may remove data that can't be restored.

21. Click **Yes** to save the file.
    In this example, you will leave all checkboxes checked.

22. Click **Inspect**.
    The inspector found properties and personal info, which you will remove.

23. Click **Remove All** in the Document Inspector. Close the dialog box.

24. Choose **File→Info** and notice that the names were removed from the Related People area in the Properties panel.

25. Click **Back** ⊙ to return to the document.

26. Save and close the file; exit from **Word**.

27. Submit your final file based on the guidelines provided by your instructor.
    To see examples of how your file or files should look at the end of this exercise, go to the student resource center.

Control Document Access

In this exercise, you will control document access by applying editing restrictions, setting a document password, and marking a document as final. Then you will create a digital certificate and add a digital signature to a document.

 In this exercise, you will use an article from the Internet. Normally you would not modify the content of a cited work; however, since you are not representing this as your own work, you can make changes for the sake of the exercise.

Restrict Formatting and Editing

1. Start **Word**. Open **WD12-R02-Bees** from your **WD2013 Lesson 12** folder and save it as `WD12-R02-Bees-[FirstInitialLastName]`.

2. Choose **File→Info→Protect Document→Restrict Editing**.

3. Place a checkmark in the checkbox below the **Editing Restrictions** heading.

4. Choose **Tracked Changes** from the drop-down list, and then click **Yes, Start Enforcing Protection**.

5. When the Start Enforcing Protection dialog box opens, enter **pass** in both password fields and click **OK**.

6. Select *method* in the first line of the first paragraph below the *Counting the Vanishing Bees* heading, and type **technique** in its place.
   Word marks the change, because no one can modify the document without changes being tracked.

7. Click **Stop Protection** at the bottom of the task pane.

8. When the Unprotect Document box appears, type **pass** in the Password field and click **OK**.
   Now you will accept the changes you made.

9. Choose **Review→Changes→Next** 🔁.

10. **Accept** ☑ the changes. Click **OK** when the message box appears.

Apply Formatting Restrictions

11. Place a checkmark in the checkbox below the **Formatting Restrictions** heading, and then click the **Settings** link.

12. Click **None**, and then scroll down and place checkmarks in the checkboxes for the **Heading 1**, **Heading 2**, and **Title** styles. Click **OK**.
    Word displays a message asking if you want to remove other styles. This could reformat the document, and you do not want to do that.

13. Click **No**.

14. Click **Yes, Start Enforcing Protection** in the task pane.

15. Click **OK** to close the password dialog box without setting a password.

16. Click the **Available Styles** link in the task pane to open the Styles task pane.

    Notice that the only special styles available are the Heading 1, Heading 2, and Title styles.

17. At the top of page 1, click in the *Counting the Vanishing Bees* heading and apply the **Title** style.

18. Close the **Styles** task pane, and then click the **Home** tab and notice that the Font and Paragraph groups are grayed out.

    Formatting restrictions prevent direct formatting.

19. Click **Stop Protection** and notice that the Font and Paragraph groups are now available for formatting.

    Now you will review and accept your formatting changes.

20. Choose **Review→Changes→Next** ⬄.

21. Choose **Review→Changes→Accept** ☑ and click **OK** when the message box appears.

Apply Editing Exceptions

Now you will apply editing exceptions and specify only certain parts of the document that can be edited. You will, however, allow reviewers to add comments anywhere in the document.

22. Choose **Comments** from the drop-down list in the Editing Restrictions section of the task pane.

23. Select the first three paragraphs in the main article.

24. Place a checkmark in the **Everyone** checkbox below the Exceptions (Optional) heading in the task pane.

25. Click **Yes, Start Enforcing Protection**.

26. Click **OK** to close the dialog box without setting a password.

27. Click to deselect the paragraphs, and notice that the unprotected area is highlighted, making it easy for reviewers to locate.

28. Select a word outside the highlighted section and attempt to delete it.

    The deletion doesn't work, because only the highlighted area can be edited.

29. In the first line of the third highlighted paragraph, select *decline in*, and replace it with `waning`.

    The change is allowed because it is in the area specified as an exception. Now you will add a comment since comments were specifically permitted in the Restrict Editing task pane.

30. In the fifth paragraph of the article, select *$200 billion*.

31. Choose **Review→Comments→New Comment** 🗋.

    Comments are allowed, not only in the exceptions area, but anywhere in the document.

32. Type this text: `Can anyone verify this dollar amount?`

33. Click **Stop Protection**.

34. Select the highlighted paragraphs, and then remove the checkmark from the **Everyone** checkbox in the task pane. Close the **Restrict Editing** task pane.

35. Right-click the comment in the markup area and choose **Delete Comment**.

Set and Remove a Document Password

36. Choose **File→Info→Protect Document→Encrypt with Password**.

37. Type **pass** in the Encrypt Document dialog box and click **OK.**

38. Type **pass** in the Confirm Password dialog box and click **OK**; save and close the document.

Depending on the security setting on your computer, you may receive a message asking if you would like to increase the security. Respond by clicking No.

39. Choose **File→Open** and click **WD12-R02-Bees-[FirstInitialLastName]** at the top of the Recent Documents list.

40. Type **pass** in the password box and click **OK**.

41. Choose **File→Info→Protect Document→Encrypt with Password**.

42. Select the characters in the password field, tap Delete , and click **OK**.

Mark a Document as Final and Reverse it

43. In the Info window, choose **Protect Document** again and choose **Mark as Final**. When the message appears, click **OK**.

    Word displays additional information about this setting.

44. Click **OK**.

45. Click **Back**  to return to the document.

    Notice the Marked as Final bar at the top of the screen and the Marked as Final icon on the status bar.

46. Select the first paragraph in the main article and tap Delete .

    The text is not deleted since the document is marked as final.

47. Choose **File→Info→Protect Document→Mark as Final** to turn off the feature.

48. Click **Back** to return to the document.

    The Marked as Final bar at the top of the document and the Marked as Final icon on the status bar no longer appear.

Create a Digital Certificate

Now you will generate a self-created digital certificate so you can apply a digital signature to your document. Remember, a self-created certificate is not verified by an outside agency.

49. Open **File Explorer** and navigate to the **SELFCERT** application through a path such as C:\Program Files\Microsoft Office\Office 15.

You may need to consult with your instructor to determine the correct file path for this application. You may not have user permission to create a digital certificate on your classroom computer.

50. Scroll to locate the **SELFCERT** application.   ▣ SELFCERT.EXE

51. Double-click the file. When the Create Digital Certificate dialog box appears, type **Charles Eng** in the field at the bottom of the dialog box.

52. When the message appears indicating the certificate was successfully created, click **OK**.

53. Close the **File Explorer** window.

Add Digital Signatures to a Document

54. Press ⌈Ctrl⌉+⌈End⌉ to move to the end of the document.

55. Choose **Insert→Text→Add a Signature Line** 🖉.

56. Follow these guidelines to complete the information in the dialog box:
    - Suggested Signer: **Charles Eng**
    - Suggested Signer's Title: **Project Manager**
    - Suggested Signer's E-mail Address: **CharlesEng@Kids.com**

57. Click **OK** to complete the setup.

58. Right-click the signature line and choose **Sign**.

59. Type **Charles Eng** next to the X in the Signature dialog box.

60. If the *Signing As* name at the bottom of the dialog box *is not* the one you want, follow these steps:
    - Click the **Change** button, choose **Charles Eng**, and click **OK** to close the Windows Security dialog box.
      A message appears indicting the certificate cannot be verified, because a self-created certificate is not verified by an outside agency.
    - Click **Yes** to use the certificate.
    - Click the **Sign** button to close the Sign dialog box.

61. If the *Signing As* name at the bottom of the dialog box *is* the one you want, follow these steps:
    - Click the **Sign** button to close the Sign dialog box.
      A message appears indicting the certificate cannot be verified, because a self-created certificate is not verified by an outside agency.
    - Click **Yes** to use the certificate.

62. Click **OK** when the message appears indicating the signature has been saved.

63. Attempt to delete a word in the document.
    The deletion does not work, because you cannot edit a signed document. Now you will remove the signature so you can add an invisible signature.

64. Click the signature button on the status bar to display the Signatures task pane.
    You may notice the term Recoverable Error *at the top of the task pane. This is because you are using a self-created certificate.*

65. Right-click the signature in the task pane and choose **Remove Signature**.

66. When the message box appears, click **Yes** to remove the signature.

67. When the message appears indicating the signature was removed, click **OK**.

68. Click the signature line and tap ⌈Delete⌉.

69. **Close** ⌈×⌉ the Signatures task pane.

Next you will add an invisible digital signature to a document.

70. Choose **File→Info→Protect Document→Add a Digital Signature**.

71. In the Sign dialog box, choose **Approved This Document** from the Commitment Type drop-down list.

72. In the Purpose for Signing This Document field, type **Counting Bees Project** and click **Sign**.

A message appears indicating the certificate cannot be verified. Because this is a self-created certificate, it is not verified by an outside agency.

73. Click **Yes** to use the certificate.

74. When the message appears indicating the signature has been saved, click **OK**.

Notice the Marked as Final bar at the top of the screen and the signature button on the status bar. Since you cannot edit a signed document, there is no option to save the document; however, the signature is still attached to the document.

75. Close the file; exit from **Word**.

76. Submit your final file based on the guidelines provided by your instructor.

To see examples of how your file or files should look at the end of this exercise, go to the student resource center.

REINFORCE YOUR SKILLS WD12-R03

Prepare a Document for Sharing

In this exercise, you will prepare a document for sharing by considering compatibility issues and controlling access to the document. Finally, you will apply a digital signature to the document.

 In this exercise, you will use an article from the Internet. Normally you would not modify the content of a cited work; however, since you are not representing this as your own work, you can make changes for the sake of the exercise.

Open a Document in Compatibility Mode

1. Start **Word**. Open **WD12-R03-4H** from your **WD2013 Lesson 12** folder and save it as **WD12-R03-4H-[FirstInitialLastName]**.

Notice the term Compatibility Mode *in the title bar, indicating that this document was created in an earlier version of Word. You will attempt to add a Word 2013 WordArt graphic to the compatibility mode document.*

2. If necessary, display formatting marks.

3. Position the insertion point on the second blank line following the *Project Manager* title at the top of page 1.

4. Choose **Insert→Text→WordArt** ⍱.

   Notice that Word opens the Word 2003 WordArt gallery rather than the Word 2013 WordArt gallery.

5. Click in the document to close the gallery.

   Next you will observe how Word saves the compatibility mode document.

6. Choose **File→Save As** and navigate to your **WD2013 Lesson 12** folder.

   Notice that Word 2013 defaults to Word 97–2003 in the Save as Type drop-down list at the bottom of the dialog box.

7. Click **Cancel**.

Convert the Word 2003 Document to Word 2013

8. Click the **Info** option on the left and then click **Convert**.

9. When the message appears indicating that the conversion may cause changes, click **OK**.

   Notice that the term Compatibility Mode *no longer appears in the title bar.*

10. If necessary, position the insertion point in the second blank line following *Project Manager* at the top of the document.

11. Choose **Insert→Text→WordArt** ⍱.

    This time Word opens the Word 2013 WordArt gallery.

12. Choose the second option in the first row, **Fill – Blue, Accent 1, Shadow**.

13. Click the border of the WordArt object to select the entire object.

14. Choose **Home→Font**, and then choose **20 pt.** from the Font Size drop-down list.

15. Select the default text and type `Get Involved`.

16. Turn off formatting marks. If necessary, position the object so it is well aligned on the page.

Save a Word 2013 Document to the 97–2003 Format

17. Choose **File→Save As** and navigate to the **WD2013 Lesson 12** folder.

18. Click the **Save as Type** drop-down list, choose **Word 97–2003 Document (*.doc)**, and click **Save**.

    Word displays the Compatibility Checker indicating that features may change.

19. Click **Cancel** to prevent the conversion.

Work with the Document Inspector

20. Choose **File→Info** and review the Properties listed in the panel on the right.

    Names appear in the Related People area.

21. In the Info window, choose **Check for Issues→Inspect Document**.

22. When the message to save changes appears, click **Yes**.

23. If the Save As dialog box appears, click **Save**. Click **OK** to replace.

24. When the Document Inspector opens, leave all checkboxes checked.

25. Click **Inspect** at the bottom of the dialog box and review the inspection results.
    Word found properties and personal information in the document.

26. Click **Remove All**, and then close the Document Inspector.

27. Choose **File→Info** and notice that the names have been removed in the Related People area of the Properties panel.

Restrict Formatting and Editing

28. In the Backstage Info view, choose **Protect Document→Restrict Editing**.

29. If necessary, check the checkbox below the **Editing Restrictions** heading and choose **Tracked Changes** from the drop-down list.

30. Click **Yes, Start Enforcing Protection**.

31. Click **OK** to close the dialog box without setting a password.

32. In the first paragraph below the *About 4-H* heading, position the insertion point in front of *universities*, type **colleges and**, and tap ⎡Spacebar⎤.
    Word marks the change since Tracked Changes was chosen in the Restrict Editing task pane.

33. Click **Stop Protection** at the bottom of the task pane.

34. Right-click the tracked change and choose **Accept Insertion**.
    Now you will apply formatting restrictions.

35. Place a checkmark in the checkbox below the **Formatting Restrictions** heading at the top of the task pane, and then click the **Settings** link.

36. In the Formatting Restrictions dialog box, click **None** to remove all checkmarks.

37. Check **Heading 1**, **Heading 2**, and **Heading 3**, and then click **OK**.

38. Click **No** when prompted to remove styles.

39. Click **Yes, Start Enforcing Protection**. Click **OK** to close the dialog box without setting a password.

40. Click the **Available Styles** link in the task pane to open the Styles task pane.
    Headings 1–3 are the only special styles available to reviewers.

41. Position the insertion point in the *About 4-H* heading, and then click **Heading 2** in the Styles task pane.

42. Position the insertion point in the *Cooperative Extension System* heading and apply the **Heading 3** style.

43. Apply the **Heading 3** style to the three remaining headings in the document.

44. Click **Stop Protection** in the Restrict Editing task pane.

45. **Close** ⎡×⎤ the Styles task pane.
    Because you set editing restrictions for Tracked Changes, the formatting changes are marked.

46. Position the insertion point at the top of the document.

47. Choose **Review→Changes→Next** ⎡↷⎤.

48. Choose **Review→Changes→Accept** ☑.

49. Continue to accept all changes. When the message appears indicating there are no more comments or tracked changes, click **OK.**

Apply Editing Exceptions

50. Choose **No Changes (Read only)** from the drop-down list in the Editing Restrictions section of the task pane.

51. Select the two paragraphs below the *Cooperative Extension System* heading on page 1, and then check the **Everyone** checkbox in the task pane.

52. Click **Yes, Start Enforcing Protection**, and click **OK** to bypass setting a password.

53. Click in the document to deselect the text, and notice that the exceptions text is highlighted.

54. If necessary, display formatting marks.

55. Position the insertion point next to the paragraph symbol at the end of the third line in the second paragraph.

56. Tap ⌐Delete⌐ to combine the paragraphs, and then tap ⌐Spacebar⌐.

57. Click **Stop Protection** at the bottom of the task pane.

58. Select the two highlighted paragraphs, and then remove the checkmark from the **Everyone** checkbox.

59. Click in the document and notice that the highlighting has been removed.

60. Close the **Restrict Editing** task pane.

Set and Remove a Document Password

61. Choose **File→Info→Protect Document→Encrypt with Password**.

62. Type **pass** in the Encrypt Document dialog box and click **OK**. Type **pass** in the Confirm Password dialog box and click **OK**.

63. Save and then close the document.

Depending on the security settings on your computer, you may receive a message asking if you would like to increase the security. Respond by clicking No.

Now you'll open the document with a password.

64. Choose **File→Open** and click **WD12-R03-4H-[FirstInitialLastName]** at the top of the Recent Documents list.

65. Type **pass** in the password box and click **OK**.
    Now you will remove the password.

66. Choose **File→Info→Protect Document→Encrypt with Password**.

67. Select the characters in the password field, tap ⌐Delete⌐, and click **OK**.

Mark a Document as Final and Reverse the Final Status

68. Choose **Protect Document→Mark as Final**.

69. When Word displays a message indicating that the document will be marked as final and saved, click **OK**.

70. Word displays additional information about this setting; click **OK**.

71. Click **Back** to return to the document.

    Notice the Marked as Final bar at the top of the screen and the Marked as Final icon on the left side of the status bar.

72. Choose **File→Info→Protect Document→Mark as Final** to turn off the feature.

73. Click **Back** to return to the document.

    The Marked as Final bar at the top of the screen and the Marked as Final status bar icon no longer appear.

Create a Digital Certificate

Now you will generate a self-created digital certificate so you can apply a digital signature to your document. Remember, a self-created certificate is not verified by an outside agency.

74. Open **File Explorer** and navigate to the **SELFCERT** application through a path such as C:\Program Files\Microsoft Office\Office 15.

You may need to consult with your instructor to determine the correct file path for this application. You may not have user permission to create a digital certificate on your classroom computer.

75. Scroll to locate the **SELFCERT** application.   `SELFCERT.EXE`

76. Double-click the file. When the **Create Digital Certificate** dialog box appears, type **Julio Martinez** in the field at the bottom of the dialog box.

77. Click **OK**. When the message appears indicating the certificate was successfully created, click **OK**. Close the **File Explorer** window.

Add a Digital Signature

78. Press `Ctrl` + `End` to move to the end of the document.

79. Choose **Insert→Text→Add a Signature Line** to display the Signature Setup dialog box.

80. Complete the information as shown.

81. Click **OK** to complete the setup.

82. Right-click the signature line and choose **Sign**.

83. Type **Julio Martinez** next to the X in the Sign dialog box.

84. If the *Signing As* name at the bottom of the dialog box *is not* the one you want, follow these steps:

   ■ Click the **Change** button, choose **Julio Martinez**, and click **OK** to close the Windows Security dialog box.

   A message appears indicting the certificate cannot be verified, because a self-created certificate is not verified by an outside agency.

   ■ Click **Yes** to use the certificate.

   ■ Click the **Sign** button to close the Sign dialog box.

85. If the *Signing As* name at the bottom of the dialog box is the one you want, follow these steps:

   ■ Click the **Sign** button to close the Sign dialog box.

   A message appears indicting the certificate cannot be verified, because a self-created certificate is not verified by an outside agency.

   ■ Click **Yes** to use the certificate.

86. Click **OK** when the message appears indicating the signature has been saved.

87. Close the file; exit **Word**.

88. Submit your final file based on guidelines provided by your instructor.

Apply Your Skills

Work with Compatibility Issues

In this exercise, you will work with compatibility issues and convert a Word 2003 document to the Word 2013 format. You will examine issues that arise when converting a Word 2013 document to an earlier version. Finally, you will work with the Document Inspector and document properties.

In this exercise, you will use an article from the Internet. Normally you would not modify the content of a cited work; however, since you are not representing this as your own work, you can make changes for the sake of the exercise.

Work with Compatibility Issues and the Convert Command

1. Start **Word**. Open **WD12-A01-MexCity** from your **WD2013 Lesson 12** folder and save it as **WD12-A01-MexCity-[FirstInitialLastName]**.

   The term Compatibility Mode *appears in the title bar. You will attempt to add a Word 2013 SmartArt graphic.*

2. Position the insertion point at the end of the document.

3. Attempt to insert a Word 2013 SmartArt graphic and notice that Word opens the Word 2003 Diagram Gallery.

4. Close the gallery.

5. Use the **Convert** command in Backstage view to convert the Word 2003 document to a Word 2013 format.

   Notice that Compatibility Mode no longer appears in the title bar.

6. If necessary, position the insertion point at the end of the document.

7. Open the **Choose a SmartArt Graphic** dialog box and choose **List**. Then choose the second graphic in the second row, **Vertical Box List**.

8. Open the **Type Your Text Here** pane and add this text at the bullet points:
   - History
   - Economy
   - Climate

9. Close the text pane, and then resize the graphic to about half its original size.

10. Use the **Save As** command and navigate to your **WD2013 Lesson 12** folder.

11. Choose **Word 97–2003 Document (*.doc)** from the Save as Type list and click **Save**.

12. If a message appears to replace the file, click **Yes**.

   When the Compatibility Checker opens, notice that the SmartArt graphic will be converted to an object that can't be edited. You may want to edit the object in the future so you will prevent the conversion.

13. Click **Cancel**.

Use the Document Inspector and Document Properties

14. Choose **Info** in Backstage view and notice the names in the Related People area in the Properties panel on the right.

15. Use the **Document Inspector** to inspect all categories listed in the dialog box.

16. Remove all document properties and personal information; close the dialog box.

17. Go to **Backstage view** and notice that no names appear in the **Related People** area of the Properties panel.

18. Save and close the file; exit **Word**.

19. Submit your final file based on the guidelines provided by your instructor.

   To see examples of how your file or files should look at the end of this exercise, go to the student resource center.

Control Document Access

In this exercise, you will restrict editing and formatting, and work with a document password. You will mark the document as final and then reverse the final status. Finally, you will create a digital certificate and add a digital signature.

In this exercise, you will use an article from the Internet. Normally you would not modify the content of a cited work; however, since you are not representing this as your own work, you can make changes for the sake of the exercise.

Restrict Formatting and Editing, and Apply Editing Exceptions

1. Start **Word**. Open **WD12-A02-SanFran** from your **WD2013 Lesson 12** folder and save it as **WD12-A02-SanFran-[FirstInitialLastName]**.

2. Open the **Restrict Editing** task pane and restrict editing to **Tracked Changes**.

3. Enforce protection and enter **pass** as the password.
   Notice the message in the task pane indicating that all changes will be tracked.

4. In the fourth line of the first paragraph of the main article, delete *road*.

5. Replace *Within* at the beginning of the second paragraph with **In**.

6. In the second line of the same paragraph, delete the comment in parentheses.

7. Stop protection, enter your password, and accept the changes you made.
   Now you will use formatting restrictions.

8. Apply formatting restrictions that limit formatting to the use of the **Heading 1** style. Do not allow Word to remove other formatting or styles.

9. Start enforcing protection and bypass using a password.

10. Display the available styles; apply the **Heading 1** style to the *Landmarks* and *Neighborhoods* headings.

11. Stop protection, and then accept the formatting changes.
    Now you will apply an editing exception.

12. Restrict editing to **Comment**, and then select the *Chinatown* paragraph at the top of page 2.

13. Check the **Everyone** checkbox to make the paragraph editable by all reviewers.

14. Start enforcing protection; do not use a password.

15. In the first line of the *Chinatown* paragraph, delete the words *part tourist trap, part.*

16. Select the *Landmarks* heading at the top of page 1 and type this comment: **A trip to Muir Woods to see giant redwoods is a great side trip.**

17. Stop protection. Select the *Chinatown* paragraph and remove the checkmark from the **Everyone** checkbox.

Work with a Document Password and Mark a Document as Final

18. Use the **Info** option in Backstage view to protect the document with an encrypted password. Use **pass** as the password.

19. Save and close the file, and then re-open the file using your password.

20. Delete the document password.

21. Use the **Info tab** in Backstage view to mark the document as final.

22. Display the document and observe the Marked as Final bar at the top of the document and the Marked as Final icon on the status bar.

23. Return to **Backstage view** and turn off the **Mark as Final** feature.

24. Return to the document and notice that the Marked as Final elements no longer appear.

Create a Digital Certificate and Add Visible and Invisible Signatures

25. Open **File Explorer** and navigate to the **SELFCERT** application.

> **NOTE** You may need to consult with your instructor to determine the correct file path for this application. You may not have user permission to create a digital certificate on your classroom computer.

26. Scroll to the **SELFCERT** application and double-click it.

27. Type **Ella Mae Chang** in the field at the bottom of the Create Digital Certificate dialog box.

28. Close the **File Explorer** window.
    Now you will add the signature line.

29. Position the insertion point at the end of the document and tap $\boxed{\text{Enter}}$ twice.

30. Use the **Add a Signature Line** ✐ command on the Ribbon to open the Signature Setup dialog box.

31. Follow these guidelines to enter the information in the dialog box:
    - Suggested Signer: **Ella Mae Chang**
    - Suggested Signer's Title: **Project Manager**
    - Suggested Signer's E-mail Address: **EllaMae@uce.com**

32. Add **Ella Mae Chang** to the signature line.

    Remember, you may need to change the Signing As name, and a self-created digital certificate is not verified by an outside agency.

33. Attempt to delete a word in the document.

    Word does not permit the deletion since a signed document cannot be modified.

34. Open the **Signature** task pane and remove the signature.

35. Delete the signature line in the document.

    Now you will add an invisible signature.

36. Use the **Info** tab in Backstage view to add a digital signature.

37. In the Sign dialog box, choose **Created This Document** from the Commitment Type list.

38. In the **Purpose for Signing This Document** field, type **San Francisco Itinerary**.

39. Click **Yes** to use the certificate. When the message appears indicating the signature has been saved, click **OK**.

40. Save and close the file; exit **Word**.

41. Submit your final file based on the guidelines provided by your instructor.

    To see examples of how your file or files should look at the end of this exercise, go to the student resource center.

Prepare a Document for Sharing

In this exercise, you will prepare a document to share with your colleagues. You will consider compatibility issues and work with the Document Inspector and document properties. You will apply editing and formatting restrictions to the document, and you will mark the document as final. You will also create a digital certificate and add a digital signature line.

In this exercise, you will use an article from the Internet. Normally you would not modify the content of a cited work; however, since you are not representing this as your own work, you can make changes for the sake of the exercise.

Open and Convert a Word 2003 Document

1. Start **Word**. Open **WD12-A03-CapeTown** from your **WD2013 Lesson 12** folder and save it as **WD12-A03-CapeTown-[FirstInitialLastName]**.

   Notice that the document is in Compatibility Mode.

2. Choose **Design→Document Formatting→Themes** and notice that the feature is not available in a Word 2003 document.

   Now you will convert the document to the Word 2013 format.

3. Use the **Convert** command on the **Info tab** in Backstage view to convert the document to the Word 2013 format.

   Compatibility Mode *disappears from the title bar.*

4. Choose **Design→Document Formatting** and notice that the Themes feature is now available.

Create a Backward-Compatible Document and Use the Document Inspector

5. Use the **Save As** command and navigate to your **WD2013 Lesson 12** folder.

   Notice that Word Document (*.docx) appears in the Save as Type field. This is a result of the conversion.

6. Click the **Save as Type** drop-down list and observe the Word 97–2003 format.

   You would choose that option if you wanted to create a backward-compatible document. In this example, since you will apply a Word 2013 theme to the document, you will not complete the backward conversion.

7. Cancel out of the Save As dialog box and return to the document.

8. Apply the **Slice** theme to the document.

   The theme change will become apparent later when a Word style is applied to the document.

9. Go to **Backstage view** and notice that people's names appear in the Related People area of the Properties panel.

10. Use the **Document Inspector** to remove **Document Properties and Personal Information** from the document.

Apply Editing and Formatting Restrictions and Exceptions

11. Apply the editing restriction that forces **Tracked Changes** but don't apply a password.

12. In the first line of the first paragraph in the main article, replace *neighborhood* with `community`.

13. At the end of the same line, replace *inhabited* with `occupied`.

14. Stop protection, and then accept the editing changes.

15. Apply formatting restrictions that limit formatting to the **Heading 1** and **Title** styles. Do not allow Word to remove any other formatting or styles.

16. Enforce protection, but don't set a password.

17. Display the available styles; apply the **Heading 1** style to the *What to See in Cape Town* heading.

18. Stop protection and accept the formatting change you made.

    Now you will apply editing exceptions to specify an area of the document where reviewers can freely edit.

19. Restrict editing to **Comments**, select the *Kirstenbosch Botanical Gardens* paragraph at the bottom of page 1, and then check the **Everyone** checkbox in the task pane.

20. Enforce protection and set `pass` as the password.

21. In the second line of the paragraph, right-click *diverse*, slide the mouse pointer to **Synonyms** in the menu, and choose **varied**.

22. Select *Bo-Kaap* at the beginning of the first paragraph of the Cape Town article and type this comment: **I think we should definitely include this in the tour.**

23. Stop protection.

24. Select the exceptions paragraph, and then remove the checkmark from the **Everyone** checkbox. Close the task pane.

Set and Remove a Document Password

25. Set `pass` as a document password in Backstage view; save and close the document.

26. Open the document again, entering `pass` as the password.

27. Choose the **Encrypt with Password** command again, and delete the password.

Mark the Document as Final, and Reverse the Final Status

28. Mark the document as final, and notice the elements in the document that indicate the document is final.

29. Attempt to make an editing change and note that Word does not allow it.

30. Turn off the **Mark as Final** feature.

Create a Digital Certificate and Work with Digital Signatures

31. Open the **File Explorer** and navigate to the **SELFCERT** application.

NOTE You may need to consult with your instructor to determine the correct file path for this application. You may not have user permission to create a digital certificate on your classroom computer.

32. Double-click the SELFCERT file and enter **Marty Zane** at the bottom of the Create Digital Certificate dialog box. Close the **File Explorer** window.

33. Position the insertion point at the end of the document.

34. Use the **Add a Signature Line** command to set up the signature line with the following information:
    - Suggested Signer: **Marty Zane**
    - Suggested Signer's Title: **Project Manager**
    - Suggested Singer's E-mail Address: **MartyZane@uce.com**

35. Sign the signature line by entering **Marty Zane** next to the X in the Sign dialog box.

36. If necessary change the **Signing As** name.
    Next you will remove the visible signature and add an invisible signature.

37. Use the signature button on the status bar to open the Signatures task pane.
    If you notice the term Recoverable Error at the top of the task pane, it is because you are using a self-created certificate.

38. Right-click the signature in the task pane, remove the signature, and delete the signature box from the document.

39. Use the **Add a Digital Signature** command in Backstage view to add an invisible signature, following these guidelines:
    - Commitment Type: **Approved This Document**
    - Purpose for Signing This Document: **Cape Town Tour**

40. Save and close the file; exit **Word**.

41. Submit your final file based on the guidelines provided by your instructor.

Extend Your Skills

In the course of working through the Extend Your Skills exercises, you will think critically as you use the skills taught in the lesson to complete the assigned projects. To evaluate your mastery and completion of the exercises, your instructor may use a rubric, with which more points are allotted according to performance characteristics. (The more you do, the more you earn!) Ask your instructor how your work will be evaluated.

WD12-E01 That's the Way I See It

As the owner of a small business, you are considering adding a new product to your product line. Decide on the type of business you are in, as well as what the new product will be. Conduct online research of the product you will be adding.

Once you're ready, create a short introduction (3–5 sentences) describing why you think the new product will enhance your line. Copy content of one to two pages about the product, citing your sources. Include at least two headings. Save the file in the Word 97–2003 Document (*.doc) format as **WD12-E01-NewProd-[FirstInitialLastName]** in the **WD2013 Lesson 12** folder.

Attempt to insert a Word 2013 graphic. Since that won't work, use the Convert command in Backstage view to convert the file to the Word 2013 format. Insert a SmartArt graphic from the List category and list three benefits of your new product. Restrict formatting to Word's Heading 1 and Heading 2 styles, and then apply heading styles to all of the headings. Restrict editing to Comments. Select one paragraph and make it exception text that all reviewers may freely edit. Add a Comment to a location that is not part of the exception text.

You will be evaluated based on the inclusion of all elements specified, your ability to follow directions, your ability to apply newly learned skills to a real-world situation, your creativity, and the relevance of your topic and/or data choice(s). Submit your final files based on the guidelines provided by your instructor.

WD12-E02 Be Your Own Boss

As a member of the marketing team at Blue Jean Landscaping, you decide to conduct online research of marketing articles specifically targeted to the landscaping business. After researching several articles, decide which marketing approach you will use, and then write a short introduction (5–6 sentences) describing the benefits of your chosen approach.

Copy the article as the basis for your research document, citing your source. Save the document as **WD12-E02-Market-[FirstInitialLastName]** in your **WD2013 Lesson 12** folder. Examine the document properties to determine if your name is visible in the Properties panel. Use the Document Inspector to remove all personal information from the document. Set a document password, **pass**, for the document. Create a digital certificate in your name and apply a visible digital signature to the end of the document.

You will be evaluated based on the inclusion of all elements specified, your ability to follow directions, your ability to apply newly learned skills to a real-world situation, your creativity, and your demonstration of an entrepreneurial spirit. Submit your final files based on the guidelines provided by your instructor.

Transfer Your Skills

In the course of working through the Transfer Your Skills exercises, you will use critical-thinking and creativity skills to complete the assigned projects using skills taught in the lesson. To evaluate your mastery and completion of the exercises, your instructor may use a rubric, with which more points are allotted according to performance characteristics. (The more you do, the more you earn!) Ask your instructor how your work will be evaluated.

WD12-T01 Use the Web as a Learning Tool

Throughout this book, you will be provided with an opportunity to use the Internet as a learning tool by completing WebQuests. According to the original creators of WebQuests, as described on their website (WebQuest.org), a WebQuest is "an inquiry-oriented activity in which most or all of the information used by learners is drawn from the web." To complete the WebQuest projects in this book, navigate to the student resource center and choose the WebQuest for the lesson on which you are currently working. The subject of each WebQuest will be relevant to the material found in the lesson.

WebQuest Subject: Research the purpose of digital signatures and what industries typically use digital signatures and why.

Submit your final files based on the guidelines provided by your instructor.

WD12-T02 Demonstrate Proficiency

The owner of Stormy BBQ is considering expanding the business to include a BBQ food truck. Conduct online research regarding how to start a food truck business. Create a one- to two-page report, copying information from the Internet and citing your sources. Write a short introduction (4–5 sentences) summarizing why you think a food truck is a good or bad addition to the business. Save the document as **WD12-T02-FoodTruck-[FirstInitialLastName]** in your **WD2013 Lesson 12** folder.

Examine your document's properties in Backstage view, and then use the Document Inspector to remove all personal information. Apply editing restrictions to your document, making it a read-only document. Enforce protection, and assign the password, **pass**, to the document. Select a paragraph in the document and apply the exception that makes the paragraph available to all reviewers to edit. Finally, create a digital certificate in your name and apply an invisible digital signature to the document.

Submit your final file based on the guidelines provided by your instructor.

Personalizing Word

LEARNING OBJECTIVES

After studying this lesson, you will be able to:

- Customize Word options
- Modify document properties
- Create and run macros
- Edit macros

Word offers a number of options for personalizing the application. You can customize Word options and modify document properties to meet your needs. You can automate repetitive tasks by creating macros and then assign the macros to buttons or shortcut keys for quick access! Each of these features helps increase efficiency. In this lesson, you will work with Word options, document properties, and macros to learn how you might set up Word to enhance the way you work.

Setting Up Word for the Way You Work

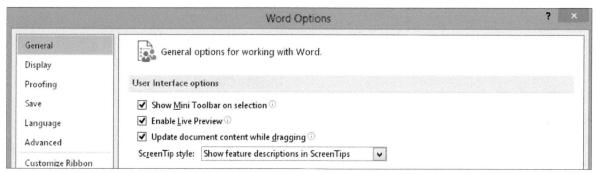

Raritan Clinic East

Pediatric Diagnostic Specialists

You have been working with Raritan Clinic East, a pediatric diagnostic clinic, for several months. By examining the types of documents you have created during this time, you have some ideas for setting up Word to make it more efficient. You have learned that most documents are saved in folders in a specific location, and you want to set the default directory to access your main folder. You plan to pin documents you use all the time to the Recent Documents list so they are always at the top of the list, and you have discovered that using document properties can be helpful in searching for files located in a large group of files. Finally, you have identified several tasks that you perform repeatedly, and you want to automate the tasks so that they are easier to perform. As you work through the tasks to personalize your Word environment, you will use the following tools.

Word Options enable you to customize Word defaults.

Word properties provide details about documents, and you can create your own custom properties.

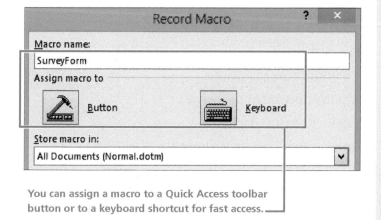

You can assign a macro to a Quick Access toolbar button or to a keyboard shortcut for fast access.

Customizing Word Options

Video Library   http://labyrinthelab.com/videos   Video Number: WD13-V1301

The Word Options dialog box contains numerous categories of options that enable you to control the way Word acts. You have worked with some of these options earlier in this course.

In the Save category, you can change the AutoRecover time interval and identify the default folder you want to use to store files. You can use the Advanced category to set the number of documents that appear in the Recent Documents list.

General
Display
Proofing
Save
Language
Advanced
Customize Ribbon
Quick Access Toolbar
Add-Ins
Trust Center

Option categories that appear in the Word Options dialog box.

Changing the AutoRecover Time Interval

If you are concerned about power failures or you're working on an important document, you may wish to reduce the amount of time between automatic saves. Word saves your documents every ten minutes by default.

Changing the Default File Location

When Word and other Office programs are installed on a computer, default file locations are set up. Word sets up a general folder for storing documents created on the computer. By changing the default file location, you can reduce the time it takes to navigate to that location.

You may not have user permissions to change the AutoRecover interval or the Default File Location on a classroom computer.

Task	**Procedure**
Change the AutoRecover time interval	▪ Choose File→Options→Save category→Save Documents options. ▪ In the Save AutoRecover Information Every *x* Minutes option, set the desired time interval.
Modify the default file location	▪ Choose File→Options→Save category→Save Documents options. ▪ In the Default Local File Location option, use the Browse button to navigate to the desired folder.

DEVELOP YOUR SKILLS WD13-D01

Change AutoRecover Time and the Default File Location

In this exercise, you will use the Word Options dialog box to set the AutoRecover time interval to five minutes. Then you will change the default file location where Word saves files.

Before You Begin: Verify with your instructor, staff, or class notes whether you have user permissions to change the AutoRecover interval or default file location on a classroom computer. If you do have user permissions, verify the procedure for restoring the original AutoRecover interval or default file location.

If you are unable to make the changed described, read the steps to familiarize yourself with the process.

1. Start **Word**. Create a new document using the **Blank Document** template.

2. Choose **File**→**Options** to display the Word Options dialog box.

3. Choose the **Save** category on the left.

4. Follow these steps to change the AutoRecover interval:

Ⓐ Locate the **Save Documents** area at the top of the dialog box.

Ⓑ Write down the current **AutoRecover** duration so you can reset it later.

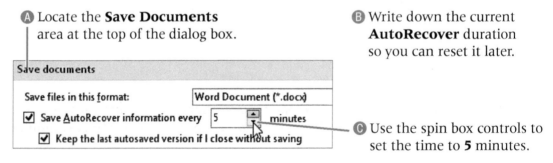

Ⓒ Use the spin box controls to set the time to **5** minutes.

Word will now save your documents every five minutes.

5. Follow these steps to change the default file storage location:

Ⓐ In the Save Documents area, locate **Default Local File Location**.

Ⓑ Write down the current default file location so you can reset it later.

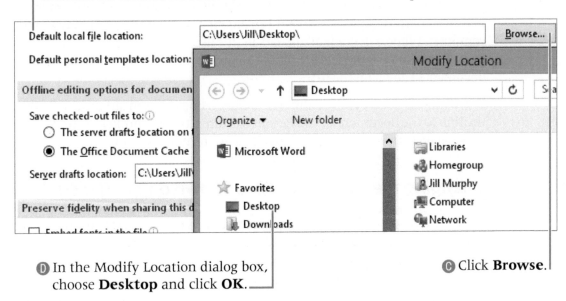

Ⓓ In the Modify Location dialog box, choose **Desktop** and click **OK**.

Ⓒ Click **Browse**.

6. Click **OK** to close the Word Options dialog box.

   Next, you will display the Save As window in Backstage view and observe the default Desktop file location.

7. Choose **File→Save As**, click **Computer** 🖳 in the Save As panel, and click **Browse** at the bottom of the Computer panel on the right.

   Notice that the path at the top of the Save As dialog box leads to the Desktop. Your path may differ, but Desktop should be the last item in the path.

   If you save a file in a location other than the location you set as the default, the Browse button will take you to the location where the file was originally stored for subsequent saves of that particular file.

8. Click **Cancel** at the bottom of the Save As dialog box.

9. Click **Back** ⊕ in the upper-left corner of Backstage view.

   If you made the changes in this exercise, you will reset them to their original state later in this lesson.

Modifying the Recent Documents List

Video Library   http://labyrinthelab.com/videos   Video Number: WD13-V1302

Backstage view displays a list of recent documents accessed on the computer when you choose File→Open. By default, the Recent Documents list shows the last 25 documents opened on the computer. When a document appears in this list, you can open it by clicking the document name. You can turn the feature off so that no documents are listed or change the number of documents shown on the list.

If you move a document to a different folder using an application such as Windows Explorer, the link to the document in the Recent Documents list is broken. After moving a document to a new folder, you would need to re-navigate to the new location to open the file.

Changing the Number of Files Shown on the Recent Documents List

When you work with only a few documents in Word, the documents you need will always appear on the Recent Documents list. If you find that you primarily work with the last few documents before moving on to new documents, you may want to change the number of documents shown on the list to reduce the number of documents you have to select from. Setting the number of documents to show on the Recent Documents list is controlled by settings in the Word Options dialog box. Settings range from zero to fifty.

The Recent Documents list options appear in the Advanced category.

The Display area shows the Recent Documents options.

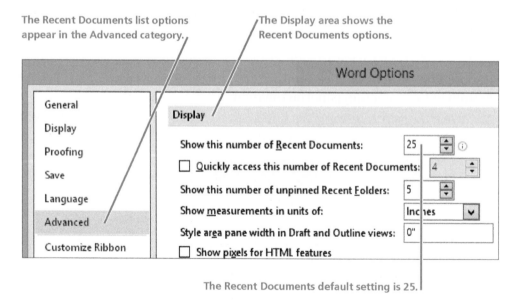

The Recent Documents default setting is 25.

Pinning a File to the Recent Documents List

Periodically, you may find yourself modifying a document over an extended period of time. To ensure that the document always appears in the Recent Documents list, you can pin it to the list. Pinned documents appear at the top of the list and remain in the list regardless of how many additional documents you access. You can use the pop-up menu or the pushpin icon to pin or unpin a document.

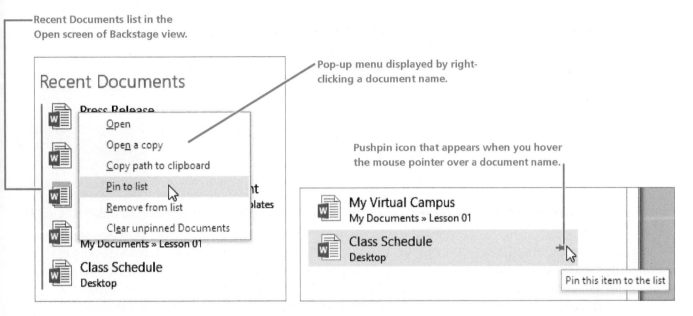

Recent Documents list in the Open screen of Backstage view.

Pop-up menu displayed by right-clicking a document name.

Pushpin icon that appears when you hover the mouse pointer over a document name.

When a document is pinned to the Recent Documents list, Word moves the document name to the top of the list and shows it as pinned. A line separates pinned items from other documents on the list.

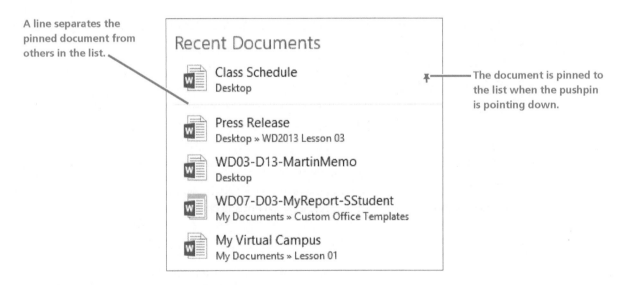

A line separates the pinned document from others in the list.

The document is pinned to the list when the pushpin is pointing down.

Clearing the List of Recently Used Files

Workers who perform tasks associated with specific projects might enjoy the ability to clear all unpinned items from the Recent Documents list, thus displaying only the document you purposely pinned. In addition, if you are using a computer you share with others, you may want to clear the list so that others will be unable to identify the documents you used.

Setting the number of recent files to zero clears the list. To turn the feature back on, set the number to something other than zero, and then files must be opened again before they will appear on the list. You can also right-click any file in the Recent Documents list and choose Clear Unpinned Documents.

Adding a Quick Access List to the Backstage Navigation Bar

In addition to the Recent Documents list, you can also add a Quick Access list to the bottom of the Backstage navigation bar. Documents that appear in this list are the most recent documents you have accessed. You set the number of documents you want listed (1–25) when you turn on the feature.

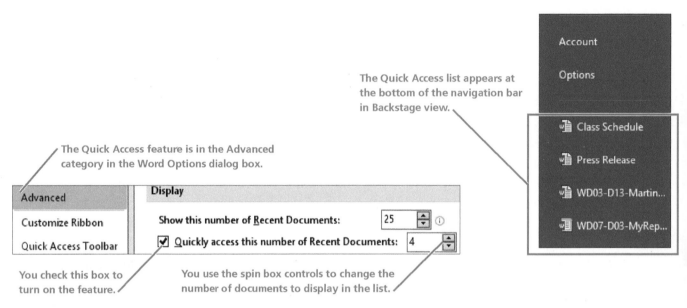

The Quick Access list appears at the bottom of the navigation bar in Backstage view.

The Quick Access feature is in the Advanced category in the Word Options dialog box.

You check this box to turn on the feature.

You use the spin box controls to change the number of documents to display in the list.

You may not have user permissions to change the Recent Documents list on a classroom computer.

QUICK REFERENCE	MODIFYING THE RECENT DOCUMENTS LIST
Task	**Procedure**
Change the number of documents in the Recent Documents list	■ Choose File→Options→Advanced→Display. ■ Change the number in the Show This Number of Recent Documents option as desired.
Clear a single document from the Recent Documents list	■ Right-click the document and choose Remove from List.
Clear all unpinned documents from the Recent Documents list	■ Choose File→Options→Advanced→Display and change the Show This Number of Recent Documents option to zero. Or, right-click any document in the Recent Documents list and choose Clear Unpinned Documents.
Pin or unpin a file to the Recent Documents list	■ **Pin:** Right-click the file and select Pin to List or click the pushpin icon. ■ **Unpin:** Right-click the file and choose Unpin from List or click the pushpin icon.
Add a Quick Access List to the Backstage Navigation Bar	■ Choose File→Options→Advanced→Display, check the checkbox for Quickly Access This Number of Recent Documents, and choose the desired number of files.

Customize the Recent Documents List

In this exercise, you will work with the Recent Documents list to customize it using both the Word Options dialog box, the pop-up menu, and the pushpin icon. You will also add a Quick Access list to the navigation bar in Backstage view.

Before You Begin: Verify with your instructor, staff, or class notes whether you have user permissions to change the Recent Document list. If you do have user permissions, verify the procedure for restoring the original Recent Document settings.

If you are unable to make the changed described, read the steps to familiarize yourself with the process.

1. Choose **File→Options** to open the Word Options dialog box.

2. Follow these steps to change the number of documents shown on the Recent Documents list:

Ⓐ Click **Advanced**.   Ⓑ Scroll down to the **Display** options.

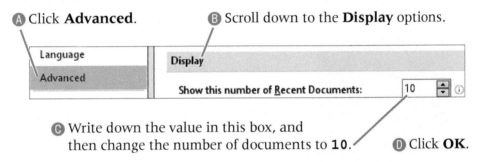

Ⓒ Write down the value in this box, and then change the number of documents to **10**.   Ⓓ Click **OK**.

3. Choose **File→Open** and note that a maximum of ten documents appear in the Recent Documents list. (Your list may have fewer than ten documents.)

4. Right-click any document in the Recent Documents list and notice (but don't click) the Clear Unpinned Documents command.
   Clicking this option would clear all unpinned documents from the list.

5. Tap ⎋Esc to close the menu.
   Now you will pin, and then unpin, a document in the list.

6. Right-click any document in the list and choose **Pin to List**.
   Word moves the document to the top of the list and the pushpin icon is pointing down, indicating that the document is pinned.

7. Click the pushpin icon of the document you just pinned to unpin it.
   Now you will create a Quick Access list.

8. Choose **Options** in the panel on the left.

9. Follow these steps to turn on the Quick Access list:

Ⓐ Choose the **Advanced** category.

Ⓑ Scroll down to the **Display** options.

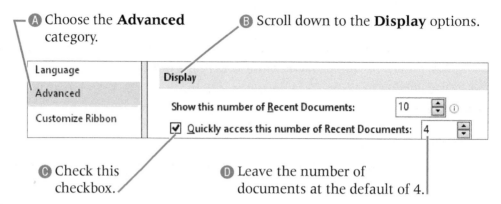

Ⓒ Check this checkbox.

Ⓓ Leave the number of documents at the default of 4.

10. Click **OK**.

11. Click the **File** tab and observe the Quick Access list at the bottom of the Navigation bar. (Your filenames will differ from those shown.)

12. Click the **Back** ⊖ button to return to the document.

If you made the changes in this exercise, you will reset them to their original state in the next exercise.

Restoring Default Settings

Video Library http://labyrinthelab.com/videos Video Number: WD13-V1303

Setting custom options for the way you work is a great practice for a computer that is assigned to you. However, when you are working on a computer you share with others, it is generally a good idea to restore the default settings you have changed.

Restore Default Settings

In this exercise, you will restore default settings in the Word Options dialog box. By restoring the options to their original state, you also will review the features just covered.

Before You Begin: Retrieve the list of default settings you wrote down as you modified the Word options earlier in this lesson.

1. Choose **File→Options**.

2. Follow these steps to restore your AutoRecover setting and your default file storage location:

   Ⓐ Choose the **Save** category.   Ⓑ Reset the AutoRecover duration to **10** or enter the setting you wrote down when you made the change in this field.

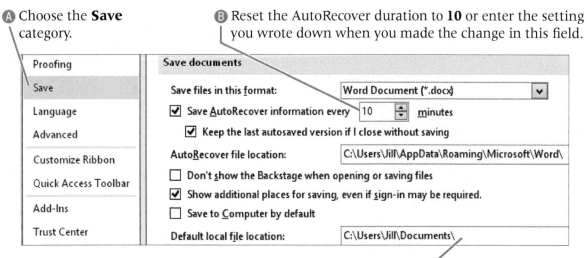

   Ⓒ Enter the file location path you wrote down earlier.

3. Leave the Word Options dialog box open, and follow these steps to restore your Recent Documents and Quick Access list settings:

   Ⓐ Choose the **Advanced** category.   Ⓑ Reset the number of recent documents to **25**, or enter the original setting you wrote down when you made the change in this field.

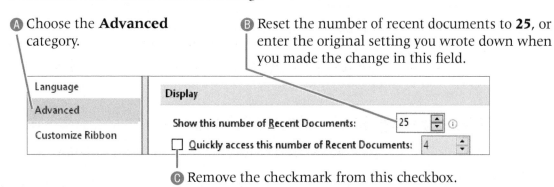

   Ⓒ Remove the checkmark from this checkbox.

4. Click **OK**.

Using Document Properties

Video Library   http://labyrinthelab.com/videos   Video Number: WD13-V1304

Each time you create a new document, Word pulls properties information from options set on your computer as well as information it detects about the document, and you can also add your own custom properties. Properties information appears in the Properties Panel of the Info screen in Backstage view. Information includes such items as the size of the file, the date on which it was created, and the author name. You can also use properties information to search for documents.

Identifying Document Properties Tools

As you have most likely discovered, Microsoft often creates multiple tools or techniques for completing the same task. The procedure you choose depends on the way you work. There are three options you can use to add your own document properties. Entering information in one tool replicates the information in the other tools when the same fields are available.

■ The Properties Panel on the Info screen in Backstage view

■ The Document Panel

■ The Advanced Properties dialog box

The following illustration of the Properties Panel in Backstage view shows some areas where you can add properties.

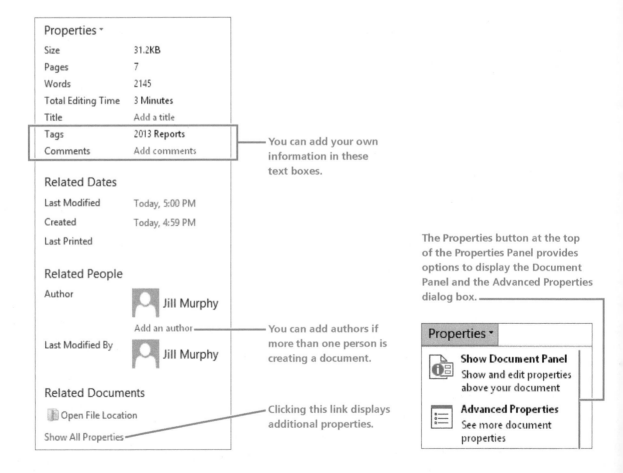

The following illustration is the Document Panel, which appears at the top of the document when activated.

Entering the *2013 Reports* tag in the Properties Panel fills in keywords in the Document Panel.

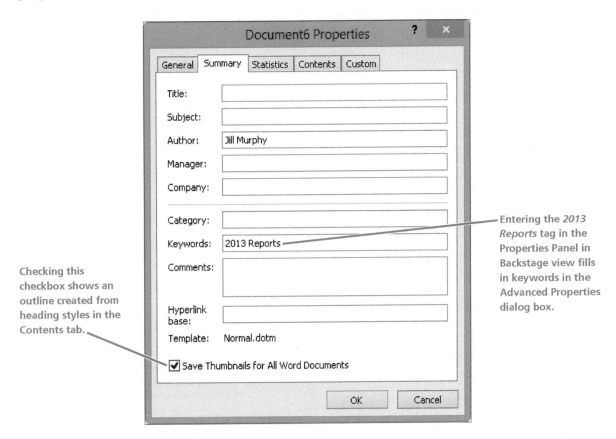

Document Properties ▼			Location:	C:\Users\Jill\Documents\Policies and Procedures
Author:	Title:	Subject:	Keywords:	Category:
Jill Murphy			2013 Reports	
Comments:				

The Advanced Properties dialog box in the following illustration contains the widest array of properties.

Checking this checkbox shows an outline created from heading styles in the Contents tab.

Entering the *2013 Reports* tag in the Properties Panel in Backstage view fills in keywords in the Advanced Properties dialog box.

Following are descriptions of the tabs in the Advanced Properties dialog box.

- **General:** Contains some of the same information as the Properties Panel in Backstage view, plus additional information, including location and file attributes such as Read Only.
- **Summary:** Contains the same text boxes as the Properties Panel and the Document Panel, including Title, Keywords (Tags), and Comments. Checking the Save Thumbnails for All Word Documents checkbox fills in the Contents tab with headings (Heading 1 through Heading 3 styles) that appear in the document.
- **Statistics:** Contains many of the same statistics as the Properties Panel in Backstage view and the Document Panel, plus additional fields, such as Paragraphs, Lines, and Characters.

- **Contents:** Contains the document headings (Heading 1 through Heading 3 styles) when the Save Thumbnails for All Word Documents checkbox is checked on the Summary tab.
- **Custom:** This tab allows you to define additional fields, which can be useful when searching for a document in a large group of documents.

DEVELOP YOUR SKILLS WD13-D04
Add Keywords (Tags) and Comments to Properties

In this exercise, you will use all three tools to add comments and keywords (tags) to the procedures manual.

1. Open **WD13-D04-DraftProc** from your **WD2013 Lesson 13** folder and save it as **WD13-D04-DraftProc-[FirstInitialLastName]**.

2. Choose **File→Info** and review the document properties in the **Properties Panel** on the right side of the screen.

3. Follow these steps to add a comment in the Properties Panel:

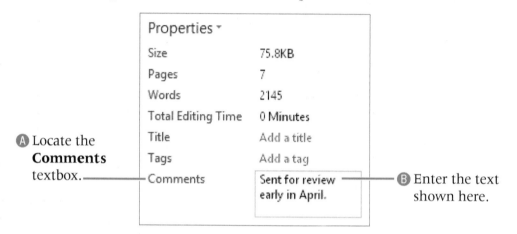

Ⓐ Locate the **Comments** textbox.

Ⓑ Enter the text shown here.

4. Follow these steps to display the Document Panel:

Ⓐ Click the **Properties** button at the top of the Properties Panel.

Ⓑ Choose **Show Document Panel**.

The Document Panel appears at the top of the document.

5. Follow these steps to enter document properties:

Ⓐ Type your name in the **Author** field.

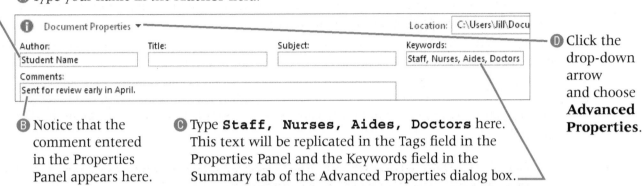

Ⓑ Notice that the comment entered in the Properties Panel appears here.

Ⓒ Type **Staff, Nurses, Aides, Doctors** here. This text will be replicated in the Tags field in the Properties Panel and the Keywords field in the Summary tab of the Advanced Properties dialog box.

Ⓓ Click the drop-down arrow and choose **Advanced Properties**.

6. Follow these steps to add another property:

Ⓐ Ensure the **Summary** tab is in the foreground.

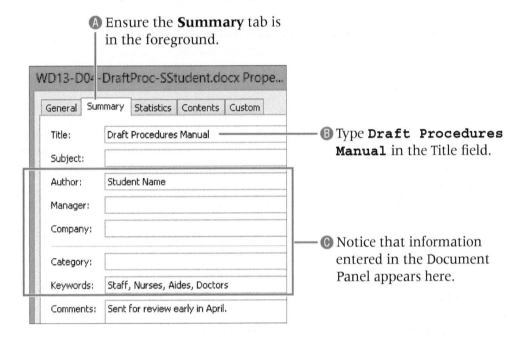

Ⓑ Type **Draft Procedures Manual** in the Title field.

Ⓒ Notice that information entered in the Document Panel appears here.

7. Click **OK**, and then click **Close** × in the upper-right corner of the Document Panel.

8. Save the changes and leave the document open.

Creating a Custom Property

Video Library   http://labyrinthelab.com/videos   Video Number: WD13-V1305

Though the properties available for Word are sufficient for most documents, there may be times when you want to store additional properties. When there is no existing property to meet your needs, you can create a custom property and define the type of data you plan to place in the field including Text, Date, Number, and Yes or No. Word provides a list of suggested names for custom fields, but you can also define your own property names. For example, if you want to include a due date for a document, you can create a new Due Date property and assign Date as the data type.

QUICK REFERENCE	DISPLAYING AND MODIFYING PROPERTIES
Task	**Procedure**
Display the Document Panel	■ Choose File→Info, click the Properties button, and choose Show Document Panel.
Display the Advanced Properties dialog box	■ Choose File→Info, click Properties, and choose Advanced Properties. Or, display the Document Panel, click Document Properties, and choose Advanced Properties.
Add keywords (tags)	■ Display the Properties Panel in Backstage view, the Document Panel, or the Advanced Properties dialog box.
	■ Click the Tags (Properties Panel) or Keywords field (Document Panel or Advanced Properties dialog box) and type the appropriate terms.
Add comments	■ Display the Properties Panel in Backstage view, the Document Panel, or the Advanced Properties dialog box.
	■ Click the Comments field and type the appropriate text.
Create a custom property	■ Display the Advanced Properties dialog box, click the Custom tab, and type a name for the custom field or choose one from the list.
	■ Select a data type from the Type list and type the value to assign to the property.

DEVELOP YOUR SKILLS WD13-D05
Create a Custom Property

In this exercise, you will create a custom property for the procedures manual to hold the due date for the final version of the document.

1. Choose **File→Info**.

2. Click **Properties** at the top of the Properties Panel, and then select **Advanced Properties**.

3. Follow these steps to create a new custom property:

Ⓐ Click the **Custom** tab.

Ⓑ Type **Due Date** in the Name field.

Ⓒ Select **Date** from the Type list.

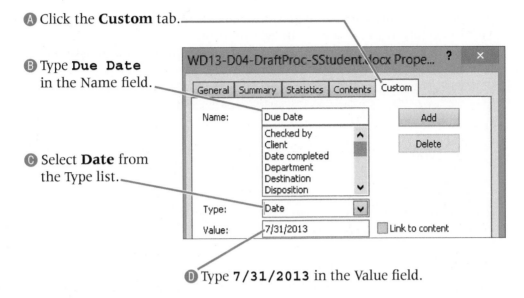

Ⓓ Type **7/31/2013** in the Value field.

4. Click **OK**.

5. Save and then close the document.

Automating Word Tasks Using Macros

Video Library   http://labyrinthelab.com/videos   Video Number: WD13-V1306

Macros are useful for automating routine tasks, especially those that involve many steps. You can record a series of steps using Word's macro recorder, and then play them back automatically when needed. For example, you may need to switch to a color printer frequently. You can record the steps of the process in a macro, and when it's time to switch printers, the macro can quickly perform the steps. Whenever you find yourself doing the same thing over and over, you have a candidate for a macro.

The Developer Tab

Basic macro tools appear on the View tab. In addition, a full set of macro tools appears on the Developer tab. This tab must be added to the Ribbon using the Word Options dialog box. As you become more familiar with macros and their benefits, you may want to explore the Developer tab.

Assigning Macros to a Toolbar Button or Keyboard Shortcut

If you intend to use a macro frequently, you can assign it to a keyboard shortcut or a button on the Quick Access toolbar for easy access. This is not required, though. You can always run a macro directly from the Macros dialog box.

Storing Macros

Macros can be stored in documents or templates, including the Normal.dotm template, which is Word's default. The *m* in the .dotm file extension indicates the template is capable of containing macros. Macros stored there are available to all documents on the system.

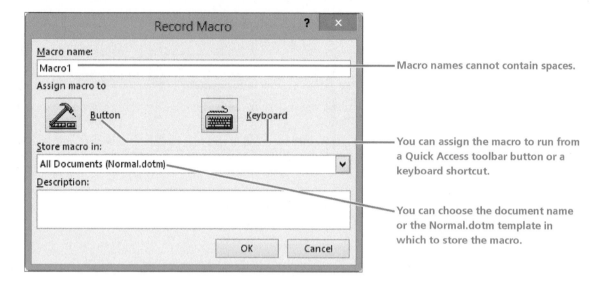

Macro names cannot contain spaces.

You can assign the macro to run from a Quick Access toolbar button or a keyboard shortcut.

You can choose the document name or the Normal.dotm template in which to store the macro.

Recording Limitations

Certain mouse motions such as scrolling, selecting options from drop-down lists, and resizing windows cannot be recorded in macros. You may also find that certain commands are grayed out on the Ribbon or in drop-down lists during macro recording. You can overcome these limitations by choosing alternative techniques. For example, if selecting an item from a drop-down list doesn't record in a macro, display the dialog box containing the feature and make the selection there. Instead of scrolling in a document, use arrow keys to position the insertion point (keystrokes are recorded). Likewise, when selecting text with the mouse fails to record, try Shift plus arrow keys or other keyboard shortcuts.

When you record a macro and change settings in a dialog box using arrow keys, the change normally sticks until you exit Word; therefore, the dialog box doesn't reset to its default state until you exit Word. As a result, running the macro again in the same session may change the setting to the *next* option in the dialog box.

Reset the dialog box to the default state as part of the macro when necessary.

QUICK REFERENCE	RECORDING, RUNNING, AND EDITING MACROS
Task	**Procedure**
Record a macro	■ Choose View→Macros→Macros menu ▼→Record Macro, name the macro (no spaces), and click OK.
	■ Execute the steps to record and then choose View→Macros→Macros menu ▼→Stop Recording.
Run a macro	■ Choose View→Macros→Macros menu ▼→View Macros.
	■ Choose the macro and click Run; or, use the Quick Access toolbar macro button or keyboard shortcut if assigned.
Edit	■ Choose View→Macros→Macros menu ▼→View Macros, choose the macro, and click Edit.
	■ Make the editing changes and then choose File→Close and Return to Microsoft Word.

DEVELOP YOUR SKILLS WD13-D06

Record and Run a Macro

In this exercise, you will record a macro that sets up the orientation, margins, and page size for a survey form. The macro also will insert and format text.

1. If necessary, create a new blank document.

2. Choose **View→Macros→Macros** 📄 **menu** ▼ and then choose **Record Macro**.

3. Follow these steps to name the macro and begin the recording process:

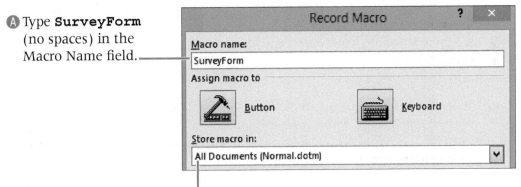

Ⓐ Type **SurveyForm** (no spaces) in the Macro Name field.

Ⓑ Ensure that the storage location is the **Normal.dotm** template, which makes the macro available to all documents on your computer.

4. Click **OK** and then click **Yes** if prompted to replace the macro.

The mouse pointer now has a cassette tape attached to it, indicating that Word is recording your steps. Now you will perform the steps you wish to record.

5. Choose **Home→Styles** and click the **No Spacing** style in the Quick Styles gallery.

This sets line spacing at 1.0 and removes the after-paragraph spacing.

6. Choose **Home→Font→Bold B**.

7. Type **Raritan Clinic East Pediatric Diagnostic Specialties**.

8. Choose **Page Layout→Page Setup→Orientation** and then choose **Landscape**.

9. Choose **Page Layout→Page Setup→Margins** and then choose **Custom Margins** at the bottom of the gallery.

10. Set the top and bottom margins to **0.4"** and the left and right margins to **0.5"**.

11. Click the **Paper** tab at the top of the dialog box and set the width to **7"** and the height to **5"**.

12. Click **OK** to apply the settings.

Stop Recording and Run the Macro

13. Choose **View→Macros→Macros→** menu ▼**→Stop Recording**.
The macro is now ready for playback.

14. Close the document without saving it, and then create a new blank document.

15. Choose **View→Macros→Macros→** menu ▼**→View Macros**.

16. Follow these steps to run the macro:

Ⓐ If necessary, choose **All Active Templates and Documents** here.

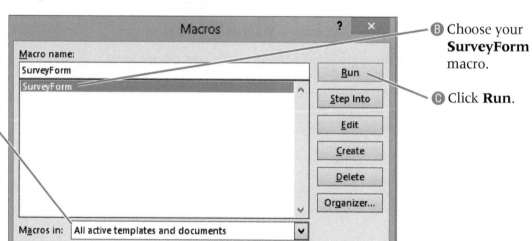

Ⓑ Choose your **SurveyForm** macro.

Ⓒ Click **Run**.

Your macro should create a copy of your survey form. The heading line is selected. You can click to deselect. If you made an error in the macro, you could delete the incorrect macro and record it again. Later in the lesson you will learn to make minor edits in the VBA Editor.

17. Close the document without saving it. Create a new blank document.

Using the VBA Editor to Edit Macros

Video Library http://labyrinthelab.com/videos Video Number: WD13-V1307

Visual Basic for Applications (VBA) is a macro programming language that runs in Office 2013 applications. When you record a macro, you are creating a Visual Basic module containing program instructions that execute when you run the macro. This topic provides a brief introduction to Visual Basic, but a complete discussion is beyond the scope of this course.

You can edit a macro by displaying the Visual Basic module and modifying the code. The editor has its own menus, toolbars, and commands which allow you to develop, edit, and test Visual Basic applications. The following illustration shows the programming code from the SurveyForm macro that you just recorded.

Visual Basic for Applications editor menu bar and toolbar.

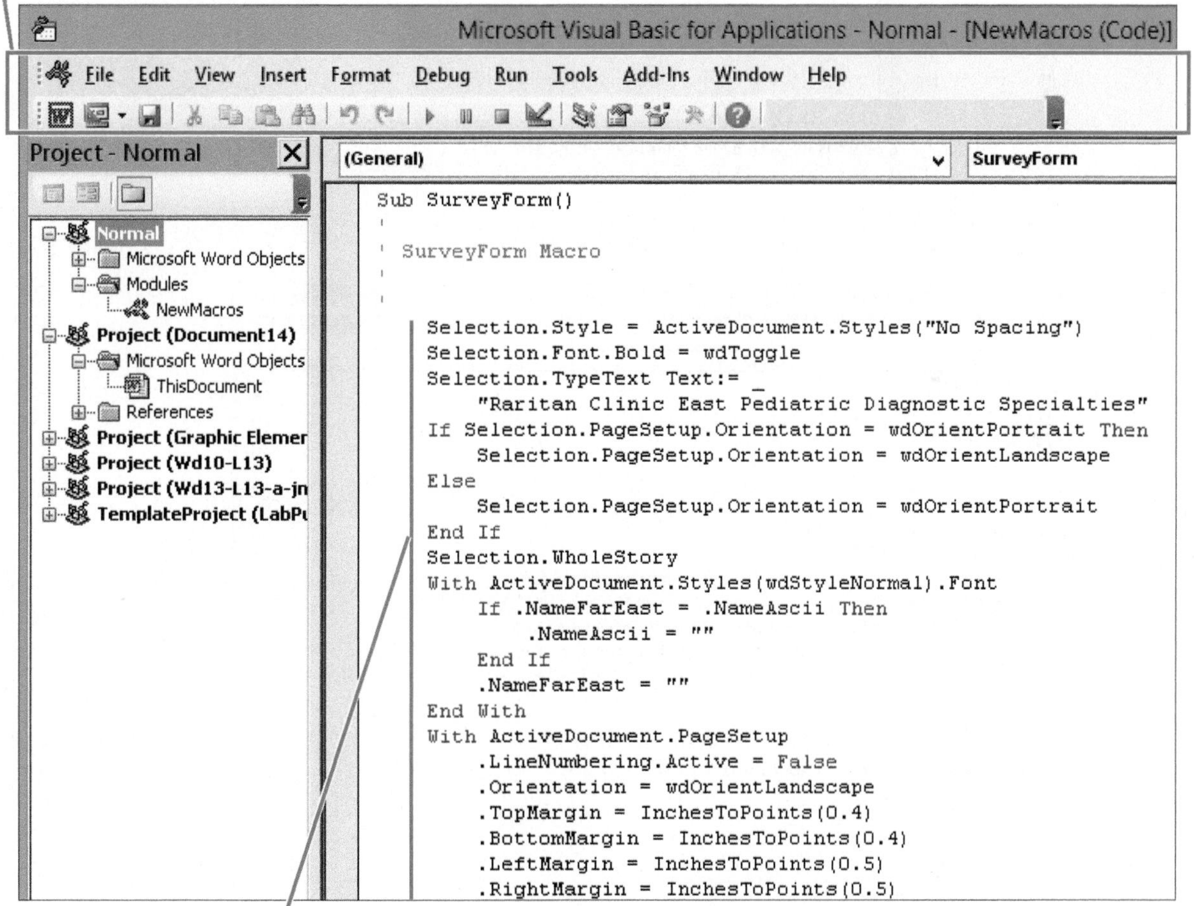
Microsoft Visual Basic for Applications - Normal - [NewMacros (Code)]
File Edit View Insert Format Debug Run Tools Add-Ins Window Help
Project - Normal
Normal
Microsoft Word Objects
Modules
NewMacros
Project (Document14)
Microsoft Word Objects
ThisDocument
References
Project (Graphic Elemer
Project (Wd10-L13)
Project (Wd13-L13-a-jn
TemplateProject (LabPu
(General)
SurveyForm
Sub SurveyForm()
'
' SurveyForm Macro
'
'
Selection.Style = ActiveDocument.Styles("No Spacing")
Selection.Font.Bold = wdToggle
Selection.TypeText Text:= _
"Raritan Clinic East Pediatric Diagnostic Specialties"
If Selection.PageSetup.Orientation = wdOrientPortrait Then
Selection.PageSetup.Orientation = wdOrientLandscape
Else
Selection.PageSetup.Orientation = wdOrientPortrait
End If
Selection.WholeStory
With ActiveDocument.Styles(wdStyleNormal).Font
If .NameFarEast = .NameAscii Then
.NameAscii = ""
End If
.NameFarEast = ""
End With
With ActiveDocument.PageSetup
.LineNumbering.Active = False
.Orientation = wdOrientLandscape
.TopMargin = InchesToPoints(0.4)
.BottomMargin = InchesToPoints(0.4)
.LeftMargin = InchesToPoints(0.5)
.RightMargin = InchesToPoints(0.5)

Code that compiled as you recorded the macro.

Open the Editor and Modify the Code

In this exercise, you will open the Visual Basic editor and revise your macro. Then you will run the modified macro.

1. Choose **View→Macros→Macros→▢ menu ▼→View Macros**.

2. Follow these steps to begin the editing process:

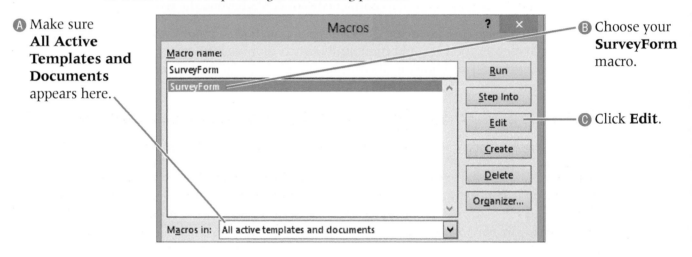

Ⓐ Make sure **All Active Templates and Documents** appears here.

Ⓑ Choose your **SurveyForm** macro.

Ⓒ Click **Edit**.

3. Follow these steps to modify the code:

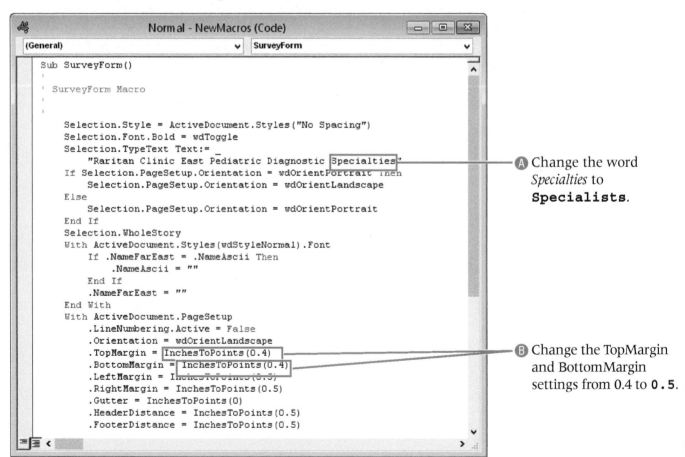

Ⓐ Change the word *Specialties* to **Specialists**.

Ⓑ Change the TopMargin and BottomMargin settings from 0.4 to **0.5**.

4. Choose **File→Close and Return to Microsoft Word**.

   The changes are saved automatically. Now you will run the edited macro.

5. Choose **View→Macros→Macros→🖳 menu ▼→View Macros**.

6. Choose **SurveyForm** in the Macro Name list and then click **Run**.

   Notice that the word Specialties *was changed to* Specialists.

7. Choose **Page Layout→Page Setup→Margins ▢** and then choose **Custom Margins**.

   Notice that the top and bottom margins are now set to 0.5".

8. Close the dialog box.

9. Close the document without saving; create a new blank document.

Running Macros from the Quick Access Toolbar

Video Library   http://labyrinthelab.com/videos   Video Number: WD13-V1308

When you create a macro to automate repetitive tasks, you are trying to increase efficiency. To make running macros more efficient, you can assign them to a button on the Quick Access toolbar or to shortcut keystrokes. By taking advantage of these time-saving tools, you alleviate the tedium of displaying the Macros dialog box and selecting the macro each time you want to run it.

You can assign a toolbar button or keyboard shortcut to a macro as you record it. In addition, you can assign a toolbar button to an existing macro using the Quick Access toolbar commands in the Word Options dialog box. Word offers numerous button images that you can choose to help keep your macro buttons straight. The following illustration shows how you can add a Quick Access toolbar button to an existing macro.

The Quick Access toolbar category contains tools for customizing the toolbar.

Choosing Macros displays a list of macros.

The SurveyForm macro button will appear on the Quick Access Toolbar.

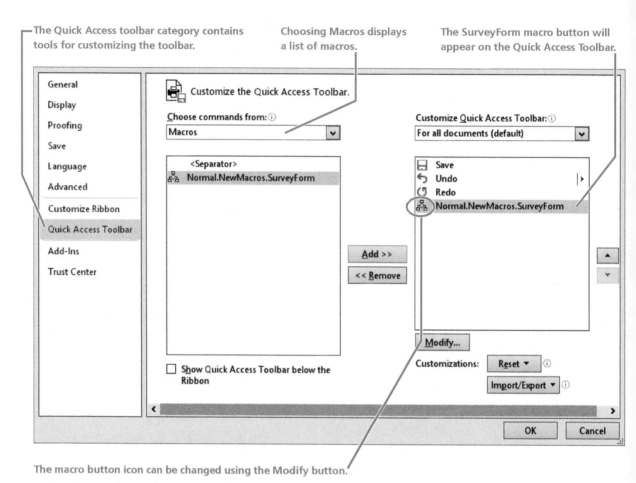

The macro button icon can be changed using the Modify button.

QUICK REFERENCE	ASSIGNING A MACRO TO A TOOLBAR BUTTON OR A KEYBOARD SHORTCUT
Task	**Procedure**
Record a macro and assign it to a Quick Access toolbar button	■ Choose View→Macros→Macros menu ▼→Record Macro. ■ Name the macro and click the Button icon in the Assign Macro To area. ■ Click the macro in the left column then click Add. ■ To change the button image, click Modify, choose an icon, modify the Display Name if desired, and click OK twice. ■ Execute the steps to record and then choose View→Macros→Macros menu ▼→Stop Recording.
Record a macro and assign it to a keyboard shortcut	■ Choose View→Macros→Macros menu ▼→Record Macro. ■ Name the macro and then click the Keyboard icon in the Assign Macro To area. ■ In the Commands box, click the macro name and, in the Press New Shortcut Key box, type the desired shortcut keystrokes. ■ Click Assign, and then Close. ■ Execute the steps to record and then choose View→Macros→Macros menu ▼→Stop Recording.
Assign a Quick Access toolbar macro button to an existing macro	■ Choose Word→Options→Quick Access Toolbar and then choose Macros from the Choose Commands From list. ■ Choose the desired macro and click Add. ■ To change the ToolTip text and/or the button icon, click Modify and make the desired changes.

Place a Macro Button on the Quick Access Toolbar

In this exercise, you will assign the SurveyForm macro to a Quick Access Toolbar button and modify the icon for the macro.

1. Choose **File→Options** and then click the **Quick Access Toolbar** category.

2. Follow these steps to assign a macro button to the Quick Access toolbar:

Ⓐ Select **Macros** here.   Ⓑ Ensure that **For All Documents (Default)** appears here.

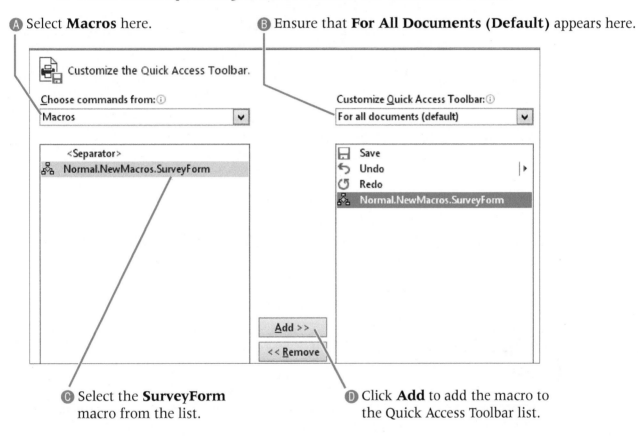

Ⓒ Select the **SurveyForm** macro from the list.   Ⓓ Click **Add** to add the macro to the Quick Access Toolbar list.

3. Click the **Modify** button at the bottom of the dialog box.

4. Follow these steps to assign a button icon:

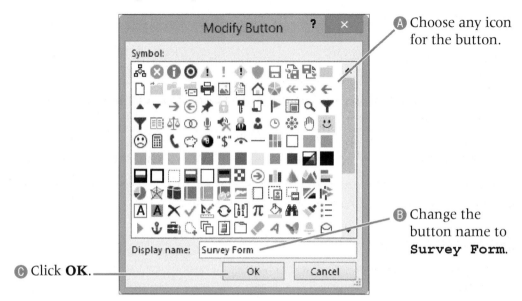

Ⓐ Choose any icon for the button.

Ⓑ Change the button name to **Survey Form**.

Ⓒ Click **OK**.

5. Click **OK** again to close the Word Options dialog box.

   Notice that your button appears on the Quick Access toolbar.

6. Hover the mouse pointer over the button to see the button name in a ToolTip; click the button to execute the macro.

7. Leave the document open.

Using Macro Security

Video Library   http://labyrinthelab.com/videos   Video Number: WD13-V1309

Macro attacks were more prevalent in earlier versions of Microsoft Office. Added security features in recent versions have caused virus creators to pursue other avenues; however, it's always better to be safe than sorry. The Trust Center in the Word Options dialog box contains security settings.

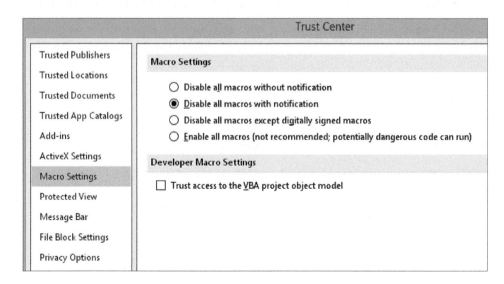

Following are the Macro Settings options:

- **Disable all macros without notification:** Word disables all macros and does not notify users.

- **Disable all macros with notification:** This is the default setting. It gives the user the option to enable or disable a macro.

- **Disable all macros except digitally signed macros:** Allows users to enable or disable only digitally signed macros.

- **Enable all macros (not recommended; potentially dangerous code can run):** This option significantly reduces security and could potentially cause serious damage.

If you work in an environment that requires high security, you may wish to consider other Trust Center options listed on the left side of the Trust Center window.

Deleting Macros

You may create a macro for use in a special project, and when the project is complete, you no longer need the macro. Deleting a macro when it's no longer required helps keep the list of macros from becoming unwieldy.

QUICK REFERENCE	SETTING MACRO SECURITY AND DELETING A MACRO
Task	**Procedure**
Setting macro security	■ Choose File→Options→Trust Center, click Trust Center Settings, and make the desired choice.
Deleting a macro	■ Choose View→Macros→Macros menu ▼→View Macros. ■ Choose the macro to be deleted and click Delete.

DEVELOP YOUR SKILLS WD13-D09
Observe Security Options and Delete a Macro

In this exercise, you will observe security settings, and then you will delete the macro you created in the previous exercise. Finally, you will remove the macro button from the Quick Access toolbar.

1. Choose **File→Options** and then choose the **Trust Center** category on the left.

2. Click the **Trust Center Settings** button, and observe the Macro Settings options at the top of the dialog box. Also notice the additional Trust Center categories on the left.

   You will not make any changes to security settings.

3. Click **Cancel** twice to close the dialog box.

   Now you will delete your macro.

4. Choose **View→Macros→Macros** 🖳 **menu ▼→View Macros**.

5. If necessary, choose **All Active Templates and Documents** from the Macros In drop-down list.

6. Choose the **SurveyForm** macro in the Macro Name list and click **Delete**.

7. Click **Yes** to verify the deletion; close the dialog box.

   Now you will remove the macro button from the Quick Access toolbar.

8. Right-click the macro button and choose **Remove from Quick Access Toolbar**.

9. Exit **Word** without saving the document.

Concepts Review

To check your knowledge of the key concepts introduced in this lesson, complete the Concepts Review quiz by choosing the appropriate access option below.

If you are...	Then access the quiz by...
Using the Labyrinth Video Library	Going to http://labyrinthelab.com/videos
Using eLab	Logging in, choosing Content, and navigating to the Concepts Review quiz for this lesson
Not using the Labyrinth Video Library or eLab	Going to the student resource center for this book

Reinforce Your Skills

Customize Word Options and Properties

In this exercise, you will use Word Options. Then you will work with document properties using the Properties Panel in Backstage view, the Document Panel, and the Advanced Properties dialog box.

Before You Begin: If necessary, verify whether you have user permissions to change the AutoRecover interval, default file location, and Recent Documents list on a classroom computer. If you do, verify the procedure for restoring the settings. In some instances, the computer lab may use software that automatically resets default settings upon rebooting.

If you are unable to make the changed described, read the steps to familiarize yourself with the process.

Change the AutoRecover Time Interval and the Default File Location

1. Start **Word**. Open **WD13-R01-WordOptions** from your **WD2013 Lesson 13** folder and save it as **WD13-R01-WordOptions-[FirstInitialLastName]**.

2. Choose **File→Options** and then choose the **Save** category on the left.
   The option for the AutoRecover interval appears in the Save Documents area at the top of the dialog box.

3. Make a note of the current AutoRecover setting so you can reset it later, if necessary.

4. Change the interval to **15** minutes.

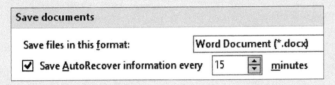

5. Leave the Word Options dialog box open.

6. Locate the **Default Local File Location field** in the Save Documents area.

7. Make a note of the current default file location so you can reset it later, if necessary.

8. Click the **Browse** button to the right of the field.

9. In the Modify Location dialog box, navigate to the **Desktop** and click **OK**.
   Now you will take a screenshot of the Word Option dialog box and paste it into your Word Options document.

10. Press [Alt] + [PrtScn] to take a screenshot of the **Word Options** dialog box.
    You need to close the Word Options dialog box before you can paste the screenshot.

11. Click **OK** to close the Word Options dialog box.

12. Position the insertion point at the end of the document, and press [Ctrl] + [V] to paste the screenshot.

13. Resize the screenshot to about a third of the original size.

    Now you will start a new document and observe the default file location in Backstage view. Remember, when a file has already been saved in a location other than the default location, the Browse button will take you to the location where the file was originally saved.

14. Create a new blank document.

15. Choose **File→Save As**, click **Computer** 🖳 in the Save As panel, and click **Browse** at the bottom of the Computer panel on the right.

    Notice that the path at the top of the dialog box leads to the Desktop.

16. Click **Cancel** to close the Save As dialog box.

17. In Backstage view, click the **Close** option on the left to close the blank document without saving.

Customize the Recent Documents List

18. Choose **File→Options** and choose the **Advanced** category on the left.

19. Scroll down to the **Display** options and make a note of the Recent Documents setting so you can reset it later.

20. Change the number of recent documents to **8**.

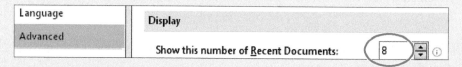

21. Press ⎡Alt⎤ + ⎡PrtScn⎤ to take a screenshot of the **Word Options** dialog box.

22. Click **OK** to close the Word Options dialog box.

23. Move to the end of the document and then tap ⎡Enter⎤ to generate a blank line.

24. Paste the screenshot into your document and then resize the screenshot to about a third of the original size.

25. If necessary, resize both screenshots until they both fit on the first page of the document.

26. Choose **File→Open** and notice that a maximum of eight documents appear in the Recent Documents list.

    Now you will pin a document to the Recent Documents list; pinned documents always appear at the top of the list.

27. Hover the mouse pointer over a filename to display the pushpin icon 📌.

28. Click the icon to pin the document to the list.

    The document moves to the top of the list, and the pushpin is pointing down, indicating that the document is pinned. The document will remain in the list until it is unpinned.

29. Right-click the document you just pinned and choose **Unpin from List**.

    You can clear all documents, except pinned documents, from the list using a pop-up menu.

30. Right-click any document in the **Recent Documents** list and notice (but don't click) the Clear Unpinned Documents command.

    Choosing this option would clear all unpinned documents from the list.

31. Tap Esc to close the menu.

Add a Quick Access List to the Backstage Navigation Bar

32. Choose **Options** on the left, and then choose the **Advanced** category.

33. Scroll down to the **Display** area and check the **Quickly access...** checkbox, leaving the default number of documents at 4.

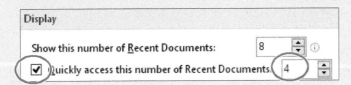

34. Press Alt + PrtScn to take a screenshot of the **Word Options** dialog box; close the dialog box.

35. Position the insertion point at the bottom of the document and tap Enter enough times to create a new page.

36. Paste your screenshot onto the new page and resize it to about a third of its original size.

37. Click the **File** tab and observe the Quick Access list at the bottom of the Navigation bar on the left. Remain in Backstage view.

Restore Default Settings

38. Retrieve the list of default settings that you wrote down earlier in this exercise.

39. Choose **Options** on the left, and then choose the **Save** category.

40. In the Save Documents area at the top of the dialog box, reset the **AutoRecover** interval to the number you noted earlier. Also reset the default file location to the one you noted earlier.

41. Click the **Advanced** category on the left and scroll down to the **Display** area.

42. Reset the number of recent documents to the number you noted earlier, and remove the checkmark from the Quickly access... checkbox.

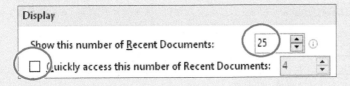

43. Click **OK** to close the Word Options dialog box.

Use the Document Properties Tools

44. Choose **File→Info**, and then click the **Properties** button at the top of the Properties Panel on the right.

45. Choose **Show Document Panel**.

46. Enter your name in the **Author** field at the left end of the Document Panel.

47. Tap PrtScn to take a screenshot of the **Document Panel**.

48. Click in your document and position the insertion point at the end of the document.

49. Tap Enter to generate a blank line, and then paste the screenshot into the document.

50. Resize the images so two screenshots fit on the second page.

51. **Close** × the Document Panel.

52. Choose **File→Info** and notice your name in the **Author** field of the Properties Panel.

Create a Custom Property

53. Click the **Properties** button at the top of the Properties Panel and choose **Advanced Properties**.

54. Click the **Custom** tab, choose **Checked By** from the Name list, leave the data type at **Text**, and type **My Instructor** in the Value field.

55. Click **Add** to add the custom property to the Properties list, and then click **OK**.

    The custom property can be used when searching for this document.

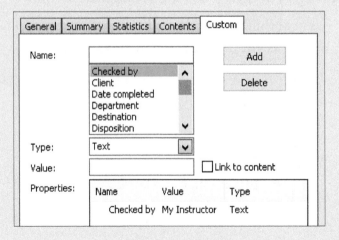

56. Click **Back** ⬅ to return to the document.

57. Save and close the file; exit **Word**.

58. Submit your final file based on the guidelines provided by your instructor.

    To see examples of how your file or files should look at the end of this exercise, go to the student resource center.

REINFORCE YOUR SKILLS WD13-R02

Record, Run, and Edit a Macro

In this exercise, you will automate a Word task using a macro, and then you will modify your macro using the VBA editor. You will create a Quick Access toolbar button to run your macro, and then you will review macro security settings, and delete your macro.

Record and Run a Macro

1. Start **Word** and create a new blank document.

    Now you will create a header macro that Kids for Change can use when creating documents.

2. Choose **View→Macros→Macros** 🔲 menu ▼→**Record Macro**.

3. Name the macro **Header** and verify that the **Normal** template is chosen in the Store Macro In field.

4. Click **OK** to start recording; choose **Yes** if prompted to replace the macro.

    The mouse pointer now has a cassette tape attached to it indicating that Word is recording your steps.

5. Choose **Insert→Header** 🔲 and then choose **Edit Header** at the bottom of the gallery.

6. Tap Tab to position the insertion point in the center of the header and type **Kids for Change**.

7. Choose **Header & Footer Tools→Design→Close→Close Header and Footer** ☒.

8. Choose **View→Macros→Macros** 🔲 menu ▼→**Stop Recording**.

9. Close the document without saving; start a new blank document.

    Now you will run the macro.

10. Choose **View→Macros→Macros** 🔲 menu ▼→**View Macros**.

11. Make sure the **Header** macro is chosen and then click **Run** and observe the header.

12. Close the document without saving; start a new blank document.

Use the VBA Editor to Edit the Macro

13. Choose **View→Macros→Macros** 🔲 menu ▼→**View Macros**.

14. Verify that the **Header** macro is chosen, and then click **Edit** to open the VBA Editor.

15. Locate the *Kids for Change* text.

```
Sub Header()
'
'  Header Macro
'
'
    If ActiveWindow.View.SplitSpecial <> wdPaneNone Then
        ActiveWindow.Panes(2).Close
    End If
    If ActiveWindow.ActivePane.View.Type = wdNormalView Or ActiveWindow. _
        ActivePane.View.Type = wdOutlineView Then
        ActiveWindow.ActivePane.View.Type = wdPrintView
    End If
    ActiveWindow.ActivePane.View.SeekView = wdSeekCurrentPageHeader
    Selection.TypeText Text:=vbTab & "Kids for Change"
    ActiveWindow.ActivePane.View.SeekView = wdSeekMainDocument
End Sub
```

16. Position the insertion point to the right of the word *Change*, tap `Spacebar`, and type **Carbon Footprint Project**.

17. Choose **File→Close and Return to Microsoft Word**.

    Now you will assign the macro to a Quick Access toolbar button and run the macro to see your editing changes.

Run a Macro from the Quick Access Toolbar

18. Choose **File→Options** and then choose **Quick Access Toolbar** on the left.

19. Click the **Choose Commands From** drop-down list and choose **Macros**.

20. Choose the **Header macro** in the list on the left and click **Add**.

    The macro now appears in the list on the right. Next you will modify the macro icon and the macro name.

21. Click **Modify** to display the Modify Button dialog box.

22. Choose an icon of your choice from the gallery.

23. Change the Display Name to **Header** and click **OK**. Click **OK** again to close the Word Options dialog box.

    Your new blank document is still open on the screen.

24. Click the macro button on the Quick Access toolbar and notice the change in the header.

25. Save the file in your **WD2013 Lesson 13** folder as **WD13-R02-HeaderMacro-[FirstInitialLastName]**.

Review Macro Security and Delete a Macro

26. Choose **File→Options** and then choose the **Trust Center** category on the left.

27. Click the **Trust Center Settings** button and observe Macro Settings at the top of the dialog box.

    You will not change any security settings.

28. Click **Cancel** twice to close the dialog box.

29. Choose **View→Macros→Macros** 📋 **menu ▼→View Macros**.

30. Verify that the **Header** macro is chosen and click **Delete**.

31. When the message appears, click **Yes** to confirm. Close the **Macros** dialog box.

    Now you will remove the macro button from the Quick Access toolbar.

32. Right-click the macro button and choose **Remove from Quick Access Toolbar**.

33. Close the file; exit **Word**.

34. Submit your final file based on the guidelines provided by your instructor.

    To see examples of how your file or files should look at the end of this exercise, go to the student resource center.

REINFORCE YOUR SKILLS WD13-R03

Customize Word Options, Properties, and Create a Macro

In this exercise, you will work with Word options, including AutoRecover, the default file storage location, and the Recent Documents list. You will add a Quick Access list to Backstage view and work with document properties. Finally, you will record and edit a macro, and create a Quick Access toolbar button for running it.

Before You Begin: If necessary, verify whether you have user permissions to change the AutoRecover duration, the default file storage location, and the Recent Document list. If you do, verify the procedure for restoring the settings. In some instances, the computer lab may use software that automatically resets default settings upon rebooting.

If you are unable to make the changed described, read the steps to familiarize yourself with the process.

Change the AutoRecover Time Interval and Default File Location

1. Start **Word**. Open **WD13-R03-Tutoring** from your **WD2013 Lesson 13** folder and save it as **WD13-R03-Tutoring-[FirstInitialLastName]**.

2. Choose **File→Options** and then choose the **Save** category on the left.

3. Locate the **AutoRecover** option in the Save Documents area at the top of the dialog box.

4. Write down the current **AutoRecover** interval so you can reset it later, and then change the time to **5** minutes.

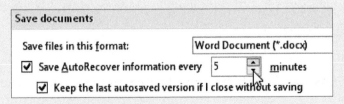

5. Locate the **Default Local File Location** option, also in the Save Documents area.

6. Write down the default location so you can reset it later.

7. Click the **Browse** button to the right of the field.

8. In the Modify Location dialog box, choose **Desktop** and click **OK**. Click **OK** to close the Word Options dialog box.

   Next you will observe the change to the default file location.

9. Start a new blank document.

   Remember, you saved your Tutoring file outside of Word's default location. Therefore, if you click Browse, you will access the original storage location. So, you will use a new blank document to test the default file storage location you just set.

10. Choose **File→Save As**, click **Computer** 🖥 in the Save As panel, and click **Browse** at the bottom of the Computer panel.

    Notice that the path at the top of the Save As dialog box leads to the Desktop.

11. Click **Cancel** to close the Save As dialog box.

12. Choose **Close** on the left to close the blank document without saving it.

Customize the Recent Documents List

13. Choose **File→Options** and then choose the **Advanced** category on the left.

14. Scroll down to the **Display** area and notice the Recent Documents option at the top of the Display area.

15. Make a note of the value in this box so you can reset it to its original state later.

16. Change the value to **7** and click **OK**.

17. Choose **File→Open** and observe that a maximum of seven documents appears in the Recent Documents list.

    Now you will pin a document to the Recent Documents list; pinned documents always appear at the top of the list.

18. Right-click any file in the list and choose **Pin to List**.

    The filename now appears at the top of the list, and the pushpin icon is pointing down, indicating that the file is pinned.

19. Right-click the pinned document and choose **Remove from List**.

20. Right-click any document in the Recent Documents list and observe (but don't click) the Clear Unpinned Documents command.

    Choosing this option would clear all documents from the list except pinned documents.

21. Tap ⎋Esc to close the menu. Stay in Backstage view.

Add a Quick Access List to Backstage View

22. Choose **Options** on the left and then choose **Advanced** on the left of the Word Options dialog box.

23. Scroll down to the **Display** area and check the **Quickly access...** checkbox; leave the number of documents at 4.

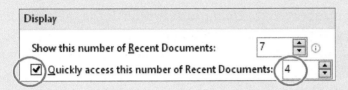

24. Click **OK**.

25. Click the **File** tab and observe the list of documents at the bottom of the Navigation bar on the left. Remain in Backstage view.

Restore Default Settings

26. Retrieve the default settings that you noted earlier in this exercise.

27. Choose **Options** on the left and then choose the **Save** category.

28. In the Save Documents area at the top of the dialog box, change the **AutoRecover** interval to the setting you noted earlier.

29. In the Save Documents area, reset the **Default Local File Location** to that which you noted earlier.

30. Choose the **Advanced** category on the left, and then scroll down to the **Display** area.

31. At the top of the Display area, enter the number of recent documents you noted earlier.

32. Remove the checkmark from the **Quickly access...** option and click **OK**.

Use the Document Properties Tools

33. Choose **File→Info** and observe the Properties Panel on the right.

34. Type **Weekly Tutoring Schedule** in the Title text box, and type **Send out every Monday** in the Comments text box.

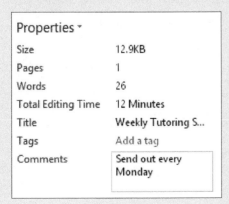

35. Click the **Properties** button at the top of the Properties Panel and choose **Show Document Panel**.

The panel appears at the top of the document.

36. Notice the title and comment that carried over.

37. Type **Tutoring** in the Keywords field in the Document Panel.

38. Click the drop-down arrow next to **Document Properties** in the upper-left corner of the Document Panel and choose **Advanced Properties**.

This opens the Advanced Properties dialog box.

39. If necessary, click the **Summary** tab and note the entries that you made in the Properties Panel and the Document Panel.

Create a Custom Property

40. Click the **Custom** tab.

41. Choose **Project** from the Name list. Leave the data Type at **Text**, type **Tutoring** in the Value field, and click **Add** to save the information in the Properties list.

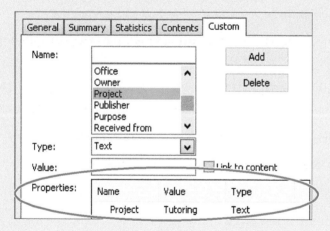

42. Click **OK** to save the changes.

43. **Close** ⊠ the Document Panel.

Record and Run a Macro

Now you will create a table macro that Kids for Change can use each week to set up the tutoring schedule.

44. Position the insertion point at the end of the document.

45. Choose **View→Macros→Macros** 📋 menu ▼→**Record Macro**.

46. Name the macro **TutorTable** and verify that the **Normal** template is chosen in the Store Macros In field.

47. Click **OK** to begin recording; click **Yes** if prompted to replace the macro.

48. Choose **Insert→Tables→Table** ⊞ and drag in the grid to create a **5x7** table.

The insertion point should be in the first table cell. Macro recording limitations do not allow you to drag the mouse pointer to select cells, so you will need to use keyboard commands instead.

49. Press ⎡Shift⎤ and tap →̲ five times to select the first row.

50. Choose **Table Tools→Layout→Merge→Merge Cells** ⊟.

51. Choose **Table Tools→Layout→Alignment→Align Center** ☰ and type **Weekly Tutoring Schedule**.

52. Enter the remaining text shown, using arrow keys to position the insertion point.

Remember, macro recording limitations don't allow you to position the insertion point with the mouse pointer.

Weekly Tutoring Schedule				
	Max	Allison	Manuel	Margarita
Monday				
Tuesday				
Wednesday				
Thursday				
Friday				

53. Choose **View→Macros→Macros** 🗔 menu ▼→**Stop Recording**.

Now you will remove the table so you can edit the macro and run it again.

54. Select the table. Choose **Table Tools→Layout→Rows & Columns→Delete** ⊞ and choose **Delete Table**.

Use the VBA Editor to Edit the Macro

Allison will not be able to participate in the tutoring program, so you will enter Nelly in her place.

55. Choose **View→Macros→Macros** 🗔 menu ▼→**View Macros**.

56. Make sure your **TutorTable macro** is chosen and click **Edit**.

57. Locate Allison's name.

```
End With
Selection.MoveRight Unit:=wdCharacter, Count:=5, Extend:=wdExtend
Selection.Cells.Merge
Selection.SelectCell
Selection.ParagraphFormat.Alignment = wdAlignParagraphCenter
Selection.Cells.VerticalAlignment = wdCellAlignVerticalCenter
Selection.TypeText Text:="Weekly Tutoring Schedule"
Selection.MoveRight Unit:=wdCell
Selection.MoveRight Unit:=wdCell
Selection.TypeText Text:="Max"
Selection.MoveRight Unit:=wdCell
Selection.TypeText Text:="Allison"
Selection.MoveRight Unit:=wdCell
```

58. Double-click *Allison* to select it and type **Nelly**.

59. Choose **File→Close and Return to Microsoft Word**.

    Now you will run the macro to see your editing changes.

60. Choose **View→Macros→Macros** 🖻 **menu ▼→View Macros**.

61. Make sure your macro is chosen, and then click **Run**.

    Notice Nelly's name in the table. Now you will remove the table and assign a Quick Access toolbar button to the macro.

62. Select the table.

63. Choose **Table Tools→Layout→Rows & Columns→Delete** 🖾 and choose **Delete Table**.

Run the Macro from the Quick Access Toolbar

64. Choose **File→Options** and then choose **Quick Access Toolbar** on the left.

65. Click the **Choose Command From** field and choose **Macros**.

66. Choose your macro in the list on the left, and then click **Add**.

67. Click **Modify** and choose an icon from the gallery.

68. Change the Display Name to `Tutor Table` and click **OK**. Click **OK** to close the Word Options dialog box.

69. Make sure the insertion point is at the end of the document, and then click the macro button on the Quick Access toolbar.

Delete the Macro and the Toolbar Button

70. Choose **View→Macros→Macros** 🖻 **menu ▼→View Macros**.

71. With your macro chosen, click **Delete**.

72. When the message appears, click **Yes** to confirm the deletion. Close the **Macros** dialog box.

73. Right-click the macro button on the Quick Access toolbar and choose **Remove from Quick Access Toolbar**.

74. Save and close the file; exit **Word**.

75. Submit your final file based on the guidelines provided by your instructor.

Apply Your Skills

Modify Word Options and Document Properties

In this exercise, you will modify Word options, including the AutoRecover interval, the default file location, and the Recent Documents list. You will also add a Quick Access list to the Backstage Navigation bar. Finally, you will modify document properties and create your own custom property.

Before You Begin: If necessary, verify whether you have user permissions to change the AutoRecover interval, default file location, and Recent Documents list on a classroom computer. If you do, verify the procedure for restoring the settings. In some instances, the computer lab may use software that automatically resets default settings upon rebooting.

If you are unable to make the changed described, read the steps to familiarize yourself with the process.

Change the AutoRecover Time and the Default File Location

1. Start **Word**. Open **WD13-A01-Efficiency** from your **WD2013 Lesson 13** folder and save it as **WD13-A01-Efficiency-[FirstInitialLastName]**.

2. Open the **Word Options** dialog box. In the **Save** category, make a note of the current AutoRecover setting.

3. Change the interval to **30** minutes.

4. With the Word Options dialog box still open, locate the **Default Local File Location** field and make a note of the current location.

5. Use the **Browse** button to set the path to the **Desktop**. Take a screenshot of the **Word Options** dialog box.

6. Paste the screenshot at the end of your document. Then, resize the screenshot to about a third of its original size.

7. Create a new blank document. Choose **File→Save As** and the **Computer** 🖳 option.

8. Click the **Browse** button to test your default file locations, and then close the blank document.

Work with the Recent Documents List and Add a Quick Access List

9. Use the **Word Options** dialog box, the **Advanced** category, and the **Display** area to set the number of Recent Documents to **6**.

10. Check the **Quickly Access This Number of Recent Documents** checkbox but don't change the number of documents.

11. Take a screenshot of the **Word Options** dialog box.

12. Position the insertion point at the end of your document, generate a blank line, and paste the screenshot.

13. Resize the screenshot to about a third of its original size; if necessary, resize both screenshots so they fit on the first page.

14. Use the **Open** option in Backstage view to verify that the number of **Recent Documents** is a maximum of six.

15. Pin one of the documents to the Recent Documents list using the pushpin icon.

16. Use the pushpin icon to unpin the document.

17. Right-click one of the recent documents and observe (but don't click) the **Clear Unpinned Documents** command. Close the menu.

Restore Default Settings

18. Retrieve your list of default settings you wrote down earlier.

19. Open the **Word Options** dialog box.

20. In the **Save** category, reset the **AutoRecover** interval and the default file location to the settings you noted earlier.

21. In the **Advanced** category, reset the number of recent documents to the setting you noted earlier, and uncheck the **Quick Access** checkbox.

Use Document Properties and Create a Custom Property

22. In the **Properties Panel** of Backstage view, type `Efficiency` in the Tags field.

23. Use the **Properties** button at the top of the Properties Panel to open the **Document Panel**.

24. Type `Follow up with staff next Monday` in the **Comments** field.

25. Use the **Document Properties** button in the Document Panel to open the **Advanced Properties** dialog box.

26. Follow these guidelines to add a custom property:
    - Property Name: **Client**
    - Property Type: **Text**
    - Property Value: `Rogers and Co.`
    - Click the **Add** button

27. Take a screenshot of the **Custom** tab.

28. Position the insertion point at the end of the document, generate a blank line, and paste the screenshot.

29. **Close** ⌧ the Document Panel.

30. Save and close the file; exit from **Word**.

31. Submit your final file based on the guidelines provided by your instructor.

    To see examples of how your file or files should look at the end of this exercise, go to the student resource center.

Create, Run, and Edit a Macro

*In this exercise, you will record a macro with airport instructions for one of Universal Corporate Events'
clients. Since this paragraph will be inserted in a number of letters, it makes sense to record it as a macro.
Then you will make an editing change to the macro and assign a Quick Access toolbar button to run your
macro.*

Record and Run a Macro

1. Start **Word**. Open **WD13-A02-LasVegasMacro** from your **WD2013 Lesson 13** folder
   and save it as `WD13-A02-LasVegasMacro-[FirstInitialLastName]`.

2. Start a new blank document. Then, access the **Record Macro** command and name the
   macro **LasVegas**.

3. Verify that the **Normal** template is chosen in the Store Macro In field.

4. Record this text:

   `Upon arrival at the airport, pick up your bags in the luggage area,`
   `then look for a limousine driver with a Silicon Tech Group sign. The`
   `driver will take you to the MGM Grand where you will be staying`
   `during your visit.`

5. Stop the macro recorder, and then test your macro to ensure it runs as expected.

Edit a Macro and Create a Quick Access Toolbar Macro Button

6. Open the macro editor and locate the word *airport* in the VBA code.

7. Position the insertion point in front of *airport*, type **Las Vegas**, then tap ⎡Spacebar⎤.

8. Close the macro editor and then open the **Word Options** dialog box.

9. Access the **Quick Access Toolbar** category and choose **Macros** from the commands list.

10. Add your macro to the list on the right, choose a new icon, and change the Display Name to
    Las Vegas.

11. Run the macro from the Quick Access toolbar and verify your editing change.

12. Take a screenshot of the document you used to run your macro, and then switch to **WD13-
    A02-LasVegasMacro-[FirstInitialLastName]**.

13. Position the insertion point at the bottom of the document, and then paste the screenshot.

14. Delete the macro, and remove the macro button from the Quick Access toolbar.

15. Save and close the file; exit **Word** and don't save the document you used to run your macro.

16. Submit your final file based on the guidelines provided by your instructor.
    *To see examples of how your file or files should look at the end of this exercise, go to the student
    resource center.*

Customize Word Options, Properties, and Record a Macro

In this exercise, you will modify Word options and properties, and then you will create, run, and edit a macro. You will also add a macro button to the Quick Access toolbar. Finally, you will delete the macro and remove the macro button from the toolbar.

Before You Begin: If necessary, verify whether you have user permissions to change the AutoRecover interval, default file location, and Recent Documents list on a classroom computer. If you do, verify the procedure for restoring the settings. In some instances, the computer lab may use software that automatically resets default settings upon rebooting.

If you are unable to make the changed described, read the steps to familiarize yourself with the process.

Change the AutoRecover Interval and Default File Storage Location

1. Start **Word**. Open **WD13-A03-BrownBag** from your **WD2013 Lesson 13** folder and save it as **WD13-A03-BrownBag-[FirstInitialLastName]**.

2. Open the **Word Options** dialog box. In the **Save** category, make a note of the current AutoRecover setting.

3. Change the interval to **20** minutes.

4. Write down the path for the **Default Local File Location** so you can reset it later.

5. Use the **Browse** button to change the location to the **Desktop**.

6. Take a screenshot of the **Word Options** dialog box.

7. Position the insertion point at the end of your document and paste the screenshot.

8. Resize the screenshot to about a third of its original size.

   Now you will create a new document so you can test your default file location in Backstage view.

9. Create a new blank document.

10. Choose **File→Save As**, click **Computer** 🖵, and click **Browse**.

    Notice that the path at the top of the Save As dialog box leads to the Desktop.

11. Click **Cancel** to close the Save As dialog box. Close the blank document without saving.

Work with the Recent Documents List and the Quick Access List

12. Open the **Word Options** dialog box and choose the **Advanced** category.

13. Scroll to the **Display** area and make a note of the number of recent documents.

14. Change the number of recent documents to **5**.

15. Check the **Quick Access** checkbox and make a note of the number of Quick Access documents.

16. Set the number of documents at **5**.

17. Take a screenshot of the **Word Options** dialog box.

18. Position the insertion point at the bottom of your document, generate a blank line, and paste the screenshot.

19. Resize the screenshots as necessary so they both fit on the first page.

20. Choose **File→Open** and check that the maximum number of documents in the Recent Documents list is five.

21. In the Quick Access list at the bottom of the navigation bar, ensure there are five documents listed.

    Now you will pin a file to the Recent Documents list.

22. Right-click any document in the list and choose **Pin to List**.

23. Use the **pushpin** 📌 icon to unpin the document.

Restore Default Settings

24. Retrieve the default settings that you noted earlier in this exercise.

25. Open the **Word Options** dialog box and restore the following settings to the values you noted earlier.

    - Reset the **AutoRecover** interval to its original setting.
    - Reset the **Default Local File Location** to that which you noted earlier.
    - Reset the number of **Recent Documents** to the original setting.
    - Reset the number of **Quick Access** documents to the setting you noted earlier, and uncheck the checkbox.

Modify Document Properties and Create a Custom Property

26. Choose **File→Info** and type **Brown Bag Lunch** in the Title text box in the Properties Panel on the right.

27. Use the **Properties** button at the top of the Properties Panel to open the **Document Panel**.

28. Enter **Training** in the **Keywords** field in the Document Panel.

29. Use the **Document Properties** menu in the upper-left corner of the Document Panel to open the **Advanced Properties** dialog box.

30. Display the **Summary** tab and notice that the properties you entered in the Properties Panel and the Document Panel appear here.

31. Switch to the **Custom** tab and create a custom property using these guidelines:
    - Choose **Office** from the Name list.
    - Leave the data Type at **Text**.
    - Enter **San Diego** as the Value.
    - Click **Add**.

32. Take a screenshot of the **Custom** tab, and then click **OK** to close the dialog box.

33. **Close** ⊠ the Document Panel.

34. Position the insertion point at the end of your document and tap Enter enough times to generate a new page.

35. Paste your screenshot on the second page and resize it to about half its original size.

Create, Run, and Edit a Macro

Now you will create a macro that you will use in client letters for those members of the tour who will visit the Van Gogh Museum. Because this information will be used in many letters, it is a good candidate for a macro.

36. Position the insertion point at the end of your document and generate a blank line.

37. Turn on the macro recorder, name the macro **VanGogh**, and ensure the **Normal** template appears in the Store Macro In field.

38. Record the following text:

    `The Van Gogh Museum is open daily from 9 am to 5 pm. It is located at Amstel 51, Amsterdam, and you can get there by boat shuttle or the Hop on, Hop off Bus.`

39. Turn off the macro recorder and tap Enter to generate a blank line.

40. Open the **Macros** dialog box and **Run** the macro to test it.

    Now you will enter additional information in the macro.

41. Open the macro editor and locate the word *Bus* at the end of the macro text.

42. Position the insertion point after the period following the word *Bus* and tap Spacebar.

43. Add the following text, and then close the macro editor:

    `Be sure to see The Potato Eaters and Starry Night.`

Create a Macro Button; Delete a Macro and a Macro Button

44. Open the **Word Options** dialog box and choose the **Quick Access Toolbar** category.

45. Choose **Macros** in the commands list and add your macro to the list on the right.

46. Modify the button icon and enter **Van Gogh** as the **Display Name**.

47. Position the insertion point at the end of your document and generate a blank line.

48. Run the macro from the macro button on the Quick Access toolbar and observe the change you made in the macro editor.

49. Delete the macro and remove the macro button from the Quick Access toolbar.

50. Save and close your file; exit **Word**.

51. Submit your final file based on the guidelines provided by your instructor.

Extend Your Skills

In the course of working through the Extend Your Skills exercises, you will think critically as you use the skills taught in the lesson to complete the assigned projects. To evaluate your mastery and completion of the exercises, your instructor may use a rubric, with which more points are allotted according to performance characteristics. (The more you do, the more you earn!) Ask your instructor how your work will be evaluated.

WD13-E01 That's the Way I See It

As the owner of a small business, you realize it's important for your staff to operate as efficiently as possible. You're a whiz with Word, and you want to show your employees some features that can help them effectively organize the Word environment. Write a one- to two-page document explaining how the following might help them:

- When it would be beneficial to change the AutoRecover time interval
- Under what circumstances would changing the default file location be helpful
- What the benefit is of pinning documents to the Recent Documents list
- How the Quick Access list can help users
- How using custom properties can help organize a large collection of files

Add two or three screenshots to help make your concepts come alive. Add your own Title and Comment to the Properties panel in Backstage view for the document you create. Save your file as **WD13-E01-WordIdeas-[FirstInitialLastName]** in the **WD2013 Lesson 13** folder.

You will be evaluated based on the inclusion of all elements specified, your ability to follow directions, your ability to apply newly learned skills to a real-world situation, your creativity, and the relevance of your topic and/or data choice(s). Submit your final files based on the guidelines provided by your instructor.

WD13-E02 Be Your Own Boss

As an administrator at Blue Jean Landscaping, you realize that macros can greatly increase efficiency. You want to create a macro that will rapidly create a letterhead, with the added benefit of avoiding printing costs. Create a new Word document, saved as a Word Macro-Enabled Document (*.docm) file and named **WD13-E02-BJLetterhead-[FirstInitialLastName]** in your **WD2013 Lesson 13** folder. Record the macro, naming it **Letterhead**, and store it in the current document—not the Normal.dotm template. (Note: This type of macro would ordinarily be saved in the Normal.dotm template so it would be available for any new letter. But for this exercise, you're saving it in the document in which it is created.)

Type **Blue Jean Landscaping** as the company name and make up the rest of the letterhead content; stop the recorder. Delete the text you used to create the macro, and then test the macro. Delete the letterhead text, and then edit the macro to add a comma, Spacebar, and **Inc.** at the end of the company name. Test the macro again. If it runs as intended, save the document.

You will be evaluated based on the inclusion of all elements specified, your ability to follow directions, your ability to apply newly learned skills to a real-world situation, your creativity, and your demonstration of an entrepreneurial spirit. Submit your final files based on the guidelines provided by your instructor.

Transfer Your Skills

In the course of working through the Transfer Your Skills exercises, you will use critical-thinking and creativity skills to complete the assigned projects using skills taught in the lesson. To evaluate your mastery and completion of the exercises, your instructor may use a rubric, with which more points are allotted according to performance characteristics. (The more you do, the more you earn!) Ask your instructor how your work will be evaluated.

WD13-T01 Use the Web as a Learning Tool

Throughout this book, you will be provided with an opportunity to use the Internet as a learning tool by completing WebQuests. According to the original creators of WebQuests, as described on their website (WebQuest.org), a WebQuest is "an inquiry-oriented activity in which most or all of the information used by learners is drawn from the web." To complete the WebQuest projects in this book, navigate to the student resource center and choose the WebQuest for the lesson on which you are currently working. The subject of each WebQuest will be relevant to the material found in the lesson.

WebQuest Subject: How can macros help you in your work?

Submit your final file based on the guidelines provided by your instructor.

WD13-T02 Demonstrate Proficiency

The owner of Stormy BBQ just attended a Microsoft Word class at the local community college and it opened his eyes to some of the beneficial features that he had not been aware of before. Knowing that you are a very experienced Word user, he has asked you to record some ideas about how Word options and macros can benefit the business. Write a one- to two-page paper explaining what Word options (at least three) you would modify and why. Also, think of three different types of Word documents you use at Stormy BBQ and suggest at least one macro for each document type that would make creating the document more efficient. Don't forget to explain why! Use the Document Panel to add a Title, Subject, and Keyword.

Save your file as **WD13-T02-OptsMacros-[FirstInitialLastName]** in the **WD2013 Lesson 13** folder. Submit your final file based on the guidelines provided by your instructor.

Integrating Word with Excel, PowerPoint, and the Web

LEARNING OBJECTIVES

After studying this lesson, you will be able to:

- Embed and link Excel objects in Word
- Use an Excel worksheet as a Mail Merge data file
- Create Word outlines from PowerPoint presentations
- Create PowerPoint presentations from Word outlines
- Convert Word documents to web pages

One advantage to using a suite of applications is that they are designed to share data and information and to work together seamlessly. This advantage enables you to save time by using data that was created in one application in other documents or files. As a result, you can display data originally stored in an Excel worksheet in a Word document or use Excel data as the source document in Mail Merge. You can send a Word outline to PowerPoint to create a new presentation, or you can insert a PowerPoint presentation in a Word document. In addition, you can use Word to format data for posting on the web so that it can be viewed using a web browser. In this lesson, you will explore the features that allow Word to interact with other Office programs.

Multitasking Using Word, Excel, and PowerPoint

Pediatric Diagnostic Specialists

You are an administrative assistant at Raritan Clinic East. A clinic advisory committee meets quarterly to review the budget and clinic activities. In preparation for an upcoming meeting, you will help create the quarterly expense report. The data is in an Excel worksheet, so you will use the Excel data in the report that you will prepare in Word. You will add the chart contained in the Excel file to the report and prepare a PowerPoint presentation using an outline of headings from the clinic's Annual Report. You will generate a letter to all committee members and use the Excel name and address file to address the letters. Finally, you will format the report for posting to the clinic website for others to review.

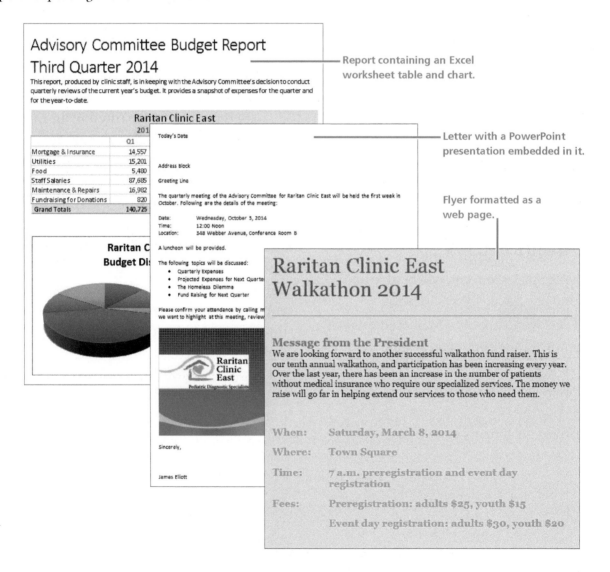

Report containing an Excel worksheet table and chart.

Letter with a PowerPoint presentation embedded in it.

Flyer formatted as a web page.

Embedding and Linking Excel Objects

Video Library http://labyrinthelab.com/videos Video Number: WD13-V1401

You can share data and objects among the programs in the Office 2013 suite. *Object* is a term for an element that you share between files. For example, you can place data and chart objects from an Excel file in a Word document. You would choose to *embed* an object if you don't want it to change when the original source file is updated. On the other hand, if you want the Word document to stay current with any changes in the source file, you would *link* the object to its original file, so your document will be updated when the source file is modified.

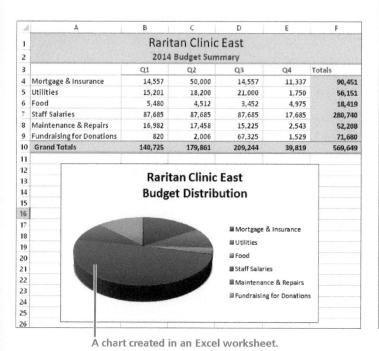

A chart created in an Excel worksheet.

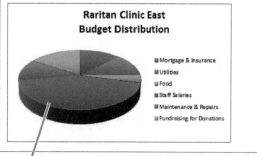

Advisory Committee Budget Report
Third Quarter 2014

This report, produced by clinic staff, is in keeping with the Advisory Committee's decision to conduct quarterly reviews of the current year's budget. It provides a snapshot of expenses for the quarter and for the year-to-date.

The same chart placed in a Word document.

Linking or Embedding Data

Whether you are embedding or linking to files, Word offers two techniques for inserting data from other files.

- **Copy/Paste:** Using this procedure, you open the source document, such as an Excel file, select the data you want to include in the Word document, and copy the data to the Clipboard. You can then paste it directly into the Word document using the Paste Special command, and you can choose to link the data or not at the time that you paste it. This procedure is useful when you want to include only a portion of a file in a document.

- **Insert Object:** You can insert a file, such as an Excel workbook, from within Word, and you can choose to link the data or not at the time you insert it. This procedure is useful when you want to include an entire file in a document.

Embed an Excel Object in a Word Document

In this exercise, you will embed an Excel worksheet in a Word document and test its static nature.

1. Start **Word**. Create a new document using the **Blank Document** template.

2. Save the file in your **WD2013 Lesson 14** folder as **WD14-D01-BudgetRpt-[FirstInitialLastName]**.

   Replace the bracketed text with your first initial and last name. For example, if your name is Bethany Smith, your filename would look like this: WD14-D01-BudgetRpt-BSmith.

3. Type the following heading lines:

   Advisory Committee Budget Report

   Third Quarter 2014

4. Tap [Enter] and then select both heading lines.

5. Choose **Home→Styles→More** ⊽ on the Quick Styles gallery, and choose the **Title** style.

6. Position the insertion point in the blank line below the heading lines and type this introductory paragraph:

   This report, produced by clinic staff, is in keeping with the Advisory Committee's decision to conduct quarterly reviews of the current year's budget. It provides a snapshot of expenses for the quarter and for the year-to-date.

7. Tap [Enter].

Embed an Excel Object

8. Choose **Insert→Text→Object** ▭.

9. Follow these steps to identify the Excel file from which to embed the data:

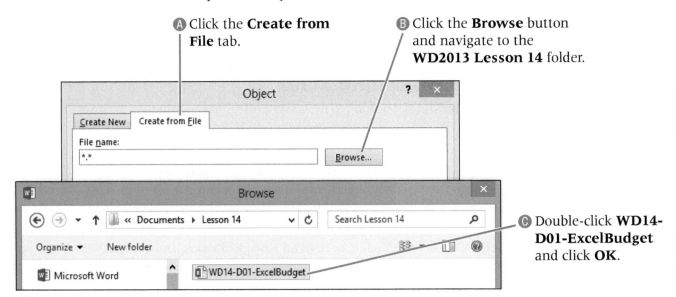

Ⓐ Click the **Create from File** tab.

Ⓑ Click the **Browse** button and navigate to the **WD2013 Lesson 14** folder.

Ⓒ Double-click **WD14-D01-ExcelBudget** and click **OK**.

Modify the Source File

10. Start **Excel**. Open **WD14-D01-ExcelBudget** from your **WD2013 Lesson 14** folder and save it as **WD14-D01-ExcelBudget-[FirstInitialLastName]**.

11. Follow these steps to edit a value in the source file:

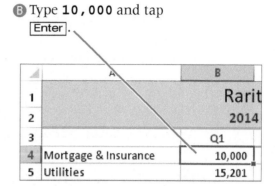

Ⓐ Click the cell for **14,557** (Q1, Mortgage & Insurance) and tap Delete.

Ⓑ Type **10,000** and tap Enter.

12. Switch to **Word** and verify that the value for Q1 Mortgage & Insurance remains **14,557**.

    Because the table is embedded (not linked) in the document, the data in Word is not affected by changes made to the file in Excel.

13. Switch back to **Excel** and click **Undo** 🔄 to return the value for Q1 to its original amount.

Delete the Embedded Data

Because you actually want the report to reflect the most recent data in the worksheet, you will delete the embedded object, and then you will link to the data in the next exercise.

14. Switch back to **Word**, click the embedded worksheet to select it, and tap Delete.

15. Save the **Word** file; leave all files open.

Linking Objects

Video Library   http://labyrinthelab.com/videos   Video Number: WD13-V1402

When you *link* data from another application, such as Excel or PowerPoint to a Word document, the original information resides in Excel or PowerPoint. This is known as the *source* file because it is the source of the data. When you place the information (object) in a Word document, the Word document becomes the destination file. By linking source files with Word documents, you create a dynamic tie between the two files.

For example, you might start working on a quarterly report before the end of the quarter, and if there is a linked chart in the report, it updates with the current information as the numbers change in Excel. That way, updates are centralized, and you don't have to keep track of making changes in two places.

Word offers three ways to link information added to Word documents:

■ Choose Insert→Object→Create from File, and check Link to File.

■ Use the Paste Special command, and click the Paste Link option button.

■ Use the Paste Options Smart Tag, and choose a linking option.

Inserting a Linked Object

You can link an entire file to a Word document from within Word. The Link to File option appears in the Object dialog box, as shown in the following illustration.

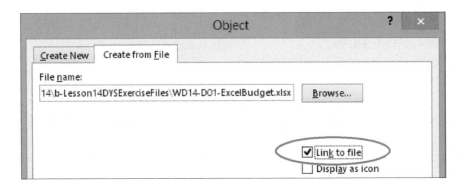

Linking Objects with Paste Special

If you want to link a range of cells or a chart rather than the entire file, you copy the cells or chart to the Clipboard. Then you use the Paste Special command, which opens the Paste Special dialog box, where you can choose the Paste Link option, as shown in the following illustration.

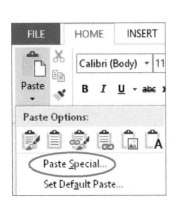
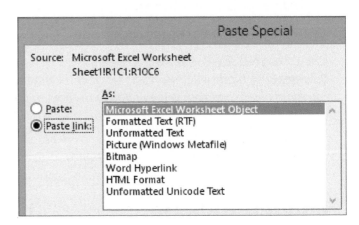

Linking Objects Using the Paste Options Smart Tag

The Paste Options smart tag contains options for linking objects to their original documents. The following smart tag appears when you are pasting Excel data in a Word document. The buttons displaying chain links identify the linking options. When you paste an Excel chart, slightly different buttons are displayed.

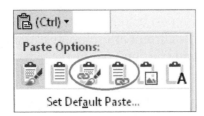

 Buttons that appear in the Paste Options smart tag vary depending on the source file. Use ToolTips to determine which button to choose.

Regardless of what you are pasting, Word displays the data or object in the document as you point to each Paste Options button. This enables you to preview the data as it would appear if you click that button.

QUICK REFERENCE	INSERTING AND PASTING OBJECTS
Task	**Procedure**
Insert an embedded object	▪ In Word, choose Insert→Text→Object, click the Create from File tab, and click Browse. ▪ Navigate to the desired file and double-click its filename.
Insert a linked object	▪ In Word, choose Insert→Text→Object, click the Create from File tab, and click Browse. ▪ Navigate to the desired file, double-click the filename, and check the Link to File checkbox.
Link an object using Paste Special	▪ In the source document, select and copy the data/object to be linked. ▪ Switch to the destination document and choose Home→Clipboard→ Paste menu ▼→Paste Special. ▪ Choose Paste Link and then choose the appropriate object type from the As list.
Link Excel data or a chart in Word using the Paste Options smart tag	▪ In the source document, select and copy the data/chart to be linked. ▪ Switch to the destination document, paste the object, click the smart tag, and choose the appropriate linking button.

DEVELOP YOUR SKILLS WD14-D02
Link Excel Data to a Word Document

In this exercise, you will link Excel data to a Word document using Paste Special. You will then modify the Excel worksheet and observe how the changes update the Word document. Then you will link an Excel chart to the document using the Paste Options smart tag.

1. Save your file as **WD14-D02-BudgetRpt-[FirstInitialLastName]**.

2. Switch to **Excel** and follow these steps to select and copy the Excel data:

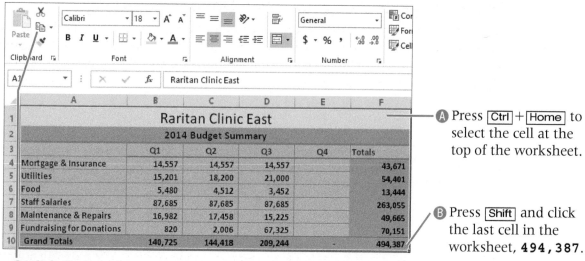

Ⓐ Press Ctrl + Home to select the cell at the top of the worksheet.

Ⓑ Press Shift and click the last cell in the worksheet, **494,387**.

Ⓒ Click **Copy**.

3. Switch to **Word** and position the insertion point at the end of the document.

4. Choose **Home→Clipboard→Paste** 📋 **menu ▼→Paste Special**.
   The Paste Special dialog box appears.

5. Follow these steps to paste the object:

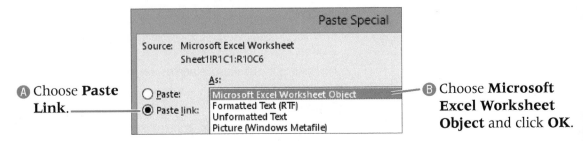

Ⓐ Choose **Paste Link**.

Ⓑ Choose **Microsoft Excel Worksheet Object** and click **OK**.

Now you will edit the worksheet and observe the change to the linked object in Word.

6. Switch to **Excel** and tap ⎋Esc to remove the marquee (animated dashed line) surrounding the table.
   The marquee in Excel identifies the cells copied.

7. Click **cell E4**, which is for the Q4 cell for Mortgage & Insurance.

8. Type the Q4 projections shown, tapping ⏎Enter after typing each number.
   The formulas in the Totals cells automatically update as you enter the data.

Q4
11,337
1,750
4,975
17,685
2,543
1,529

9. Switch to **Word**.
   The linked table updated with the additions you made in the Q4 column. If the Excel table failed to update on your computer, right-click the Excel object, and select Update Link.

10. Position the insertion point on the blank line below the worksheet data and tap ⏎Enter twice.

Link an Excel Chart in Word

Now you will use the Paste Options smart tag to link a chart to Word.

11. Switch to **Excel**, click the **Sheet2** tab at the bottom of the Excel window, and click the pie chart border once to select it.

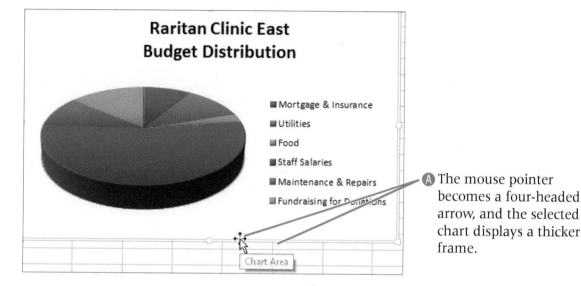

Ⓐ The mouse pointer becomes a four-headed arrow, and the selected chart displays a thicker frame.

12. Choose **Home→Clipboard→Copy** 📋 and then switch back to **Word**.

13. Choose **Home→Clipboard→Paste** 📋.

14. Follow these steps to paste a link for the chart object:

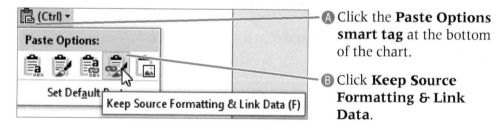

Ⓐ Click the **Paste Options smart tag** at the bottom of the chart.

Ⓑ Click **Keep Source Formatting & Link Data**.

15. Save the **Word** file.

16. Exit **Excel**, saving changes when prompted.

Opening Excel and Chart Tools from Word

Video Library   http://labyrinthelab.com/videos   Video Number: WD13-V1403

When data or objects from other sources are linked to Word documents, you can open source program tools directly from the Word document and use these tools to edit the object. There are several ways to activate these tools. These procedures assume that an Excel object and chart are linked to a document.

- Double-click either the worksheet data object or the chart to launch or switch to Excel for making edits.
- Right-click the chart and choose Edit Data to launch or switch to Excel for editing data in Excel.
- Click the chart to display the Excel Chart Tools on the Word Ribbon, shown in the following illustration. This allows you to make formatting changes to the chart directly in Word without modifying the look of the chart in Excel.

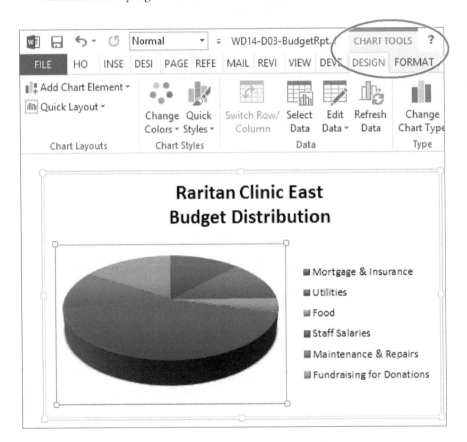

DEVELOP YOUR SKILLS WD14-D03

Launch Excel and Display Chart Tools from Within Word

In this exercise, you will launch Excel from within Word and edit data in the worksheet. Then you will use Live Preview with the Excel Chart Tools on the Word Ribbon to view potential formatting changes.

1. Save your file as **WD14-D03-BudgetRpt-[FirstInitialLastName]**.

2. Double-click anywhere in the **Excel worksheet table object** to open the Excel file.

   At this stage, you can make editing changes that will be reflected in the Word document.

3. In Excel, click in the Q1 cell for Staff Salaries (**cell B7**), type **1,000**, and tap Enter.

4. Switch to **Word** and ensure that the data and chart both updated.

   If your table failed to update, right-click the Excel worksheet table and choose Update Link from the menu. It's possible the worksheet table will update but not the chart. If your chart failed to update, click the chart border and choose Chart Tools→Design→Data→Refresh Data.

5. Switch to **Excel** and click **Undo** ⟲ on the Quick Access toolbar.

6. Switch to **Word**.

   The chart and the worksheet data update to their original values. If your table failed to update, right-click the Excel worksheet table and choose Update Link from the menu. It's possible that the worksheet table will update but not the chart. If your chart failed to update, click the chart border and choose Chart Tools→Design→Data→Refresh Data.

7. If you did not use Chart Tools in the previous step, click the chart border to select the chart background and display the Chart Tools on the Ribbon.

8. Choose **Chart Tools→Format→Shape Styles→Shape Fill** ⬚ **menu ▼**.

9. Hover the mouse pointer over several different colors to see Live Preview display the effects as they impact the chart area background color.

10. Tap ⎋Esc to close the gallery. Then tap ⎋Esc again to deselect the chart.
    The Chart Tools tabs disappear from the Ribbon.

11. Save and then close the **Word** file. Leave the **Excel** file open.

Updating and Breaking Links

Video Library   http://labyrinthelab.com/videos   Video Number: WD13-V1404

Linked objects in Word automatically update if Word is open at the time the source document changes. Naturally, Word is not always open when you modify an Excel spreadsheet; however, Word will prompt you to update links when you open a document containing links.

You can break the link between a linked object and its source document. Once the final figures for a period are in, you may want to break the link between Word and Excel so that the linked object is converted to an embedded object. Then, the Word report always reflects the closing numbers for that period.

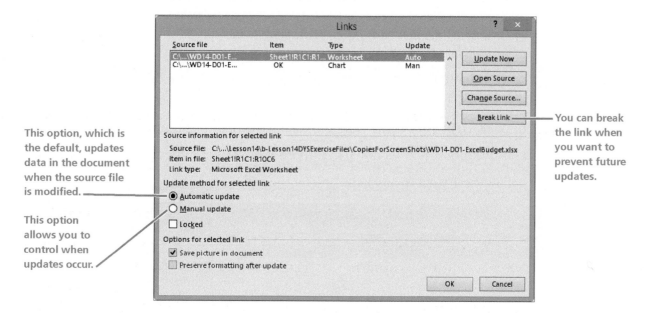

This option, which is the default, updates data in the document when the source file is modified.

This option allows you to control when updates occur.

You can break the link when you want to prevent future updates.

DEVELOP YOUR SKILLS WD14-D04

Update Links by Opening a Document and Break a Link

In this exercise, you will modify the linked Excel file and observe the prompt to update links when you open the Word document. Then you will break the link to the worksheet data, and then test to see that the links are broken.

1. In Excel, click **cell C4** (Mortgage & Insurance for Q2), type **50,000**, and tap Enter.

   You're typing an overly large number so that changes in the associated worksheet table and chart will be easy to see.

2. Open **WD14-D03-BudgetRpt-[FirstInitialLastName]**, which contains the linked objects.

3. When the message appears prompting you to update links, click **Yes**.

   Observe the change in the worksheet data and in the chart. If your table failed to update, right-click the Excel worksheet table and choose Update Link from the menu. It's possible the worksheet table will update but not the chart. If your chart failed to update, click the chart border and choose Chart Tools→Design→Data→Refresh Data.

4. Save the Word file as **WD14-D04-BudgetRpt-[FirstInitialLastName]**.

   Now you will break the link between the objects in Word and the Excel file.

5. In Word, right-click in the worksheet data to display a pop-up menu.

6. Slide the mouse pointer down to **Linked Worksheet Object** and choose **Links**.

7. Follow these steps to break the link for the table:

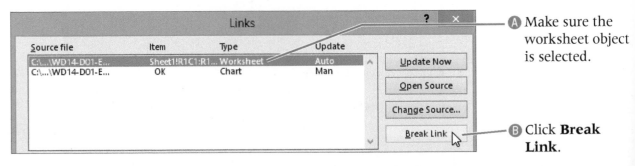

Ⓐ Make sure the worksheet object is selected.

Ⓑ Click **Break Link**.

8. When the message appears asking if you want to break the link, click **Yes**.

   The link disappears from the Links dialog box. The remaining link is already highlighted.

9. Click the **Break Link** button to break the link between Excel and the chart.

10. When the message box appears, click **Yes**.

    The Source File now displays the term NULL, indicating there is no source file attached.

11. Click **OK** to close the Links dialog box.

    Now you will test to see if the links are broken.

12. Right-click the worksheet object, review the menu options, and note that the Update Links option is gone.

13. Click the chart border to select the chart.

14. Choose **Chart Tools→Design→Data**, and notice that the **Refresh Data** button is grayed out indicating that the link is broken.

15. Save and close the **Word** and **Excel** files, but leave the program windows open.

Using Excel as a Mail Merge Data Source

Video Library   http://labyrinthelab.com/videos   Video Number: WD13-V1405

You may recall that Word's Mail Merge feature is most often used for generating personalized form letters. Word can use a variety of file types as data sources, including Excel files. Whether you type a new data-source list from within Word or you create your data source in Excel, the rules for effective data sources apply.

The more data is split into small segments, the more flexibility you have in the merge. A rule to remember is that you cannot merge part of a field. If the name field, for example, contains the title, first name, and last name, you will not be able to use those elements separately. For instance, in the greeting line, you will not be able to drop the first name and use *Dear Title Last Name*.

In Excel, the columns are treated as separate fields in a mail merge. Therefore, in a name and address list, it is a good idea to place the title, first name, and last name in separate columns, as shown in the following illustration.

	A	B	C	D	E	F	G
1	Title	First Name	Last Name	Address	City	State	Zip
2	Ms.	Sally	Redding	756 Locust Street	Los Angeles	CA	91025
3	Mr.	Jose	Lopez	7812 Olive Road	Los Angeles	CA	91357
4	Mr.	Charles	Douglas	91 Sycamore Ave.	Los Angeles	CA	91642
5	Mr.	Gregor	Alexandre	38 Alder Street	Los Angeles	CA	92564
6	Ms.	Ellen	Rosario	1748 Oak Street	San Francisco	CA	90256
7	Ms.	Grace	Melrose	852 Willow Way	San Francisco	CA	94612
8	Ms.	Olivia	Morales	9577 Chestnut Street	San Francisco	CA	94621
9	Mr.	James	Washington	2453 Dogwood Lane	San Francisco	CA	94652

When an Excel file is used as a merge data source file, the first row of the worksheet must contain the field names. In addition, all columns and rows must be adjacent to each other in order for Mail Merge to identify all entries as part of the same data source. You cannot have blank rows and columns within the Excel worksheet data.

QUICK REFERENCE	USING EXCEL AS A MAIL MERGE DATA SOURCE
Task	**Procedure**
Designate the main document	■ Choose Mailings→Start Mail Merge→Start Mail Merge and choose the type of main document.
Connect to the data source	■ Choose Mailings→Start Mail Merge→Select Recipients, choose Use an Existing List, open the Excel file, and choose the desired Excel worksheet.
	■ Choose Mailings→Write & Insert Fields and insert the merge fields in the main document.
Conduct the merge	■ Choose Mailings→Finish→Finish & Merge, choose Edit Individual Documents, make the desired choices in the Merge to New Document dialog box, and click OK.

DEVELOP YOUR SKILLS WD14-D05
Use an Excel Worksheet with Mail Merge

In this exercise, you will begin by examining the Excel worksheet that you will use as the data source. Next you will open a letter and designate it as the main document. Then you will connect the Excel data source to it and conduct the merge.

1. Open **WD14-D05-CommAddress** (an Excel file) from the **WD2013 Lesson 14** folder.

   Each column represents a mail merge field; Title is a field, First Name is a field, and so on.

2. Look at the bottom of the Excel worksheet and notice the tab labeled Sheet 1.

   This is the name of the page in the Excel workbook that contains the address list. You will see Sheet 1 again later in this exercise.

3. Close the file and exit **Excel**.

4. In **Word**, open **WD14-D05-CommLtr** from the **WD2013 Lesson 14** folder and save it as **WD14-D05-CommLtr-[FirstInitialLastName]**.

5. Choose **Mailings→Start Mail Merge→Start Mail Merge** and then choose **Letters**.

   This designates the letter as the main document.

6. If necessary, display formatting marks.

   Being able to see the formatting marks will be helpful later in this exercise. Now you will connect to the Excel data source.

7. Choose **Mailings→Start Mail Merge→Select Recipients** and then choose **Use an Existing List**.

8. Navigate to the **WD2013 Lesson 14** folder and open **WD14-D05-CommAddress**.

9. When the Select Table dialog box appears, notice that Sheet 1 is highlighted.

   Earlier you observed Sheet 1 as the name of the page in the Excel workbook that contains the address list.

10. Click **OK**.

11. In the letter, select the **Today's Date** text; delete it, but don't delete the paragraph symbol at the end of the line.

    Deleting the paragraph symbol would throw off proper business letter spacing.

12. Type the current date in its place.

Insert the Merge Codes

13. Select and delete the **Address Block** text, but don't delete the paragraph symbol at the end of the line.

14. Choose **Mailings→Write & Insert Fields→Address Block** 📄.

15. When the Insert Address Block dialog box appears, click **OK** to accept the default settings for the inside address.

16. Delete the **Greeting Line** text, but not the paragraph symbol at the end of the line.

17. Choose **Mailings→Write & Insert Fields→Greeting Line** 📄.

18. When the Insert Greeting Line dialog box appears, change the Greeting Line Format from a comma to a colon and click **OK**.

Conduct the Merge

19. Choose **Mailings→Finish→Finish & Merge** 📄 and then choose **Edit Individual Documents**.

20. When the Merge to New Document dialog box opens, click **OK** to merge all of the records from the Excel file.

21. Turn off formatting marks.

22. Scroll through the letters to see the results of the merge and then close the merge document without saving it.

23. Save and close **WD14-D05-CommLtr-[FirstInitialLastName]**.

Integrating Word with PowerPoint

Video Library   http://labyrinthelab.com/videos   Video Number: WD13-V1406

PowerPoint is another program that Word can share files with. Word outlines can be used to create PowerPoint presentations. This structure uses Heading 1 topics as the slide's title and headings such as Heading 2, Heading 3, and so forth as the bullet and sub-bullet entries in the slide.

Using Word Outline View

The following illustration is an example of an outline created specifically for generating a PowerPoint presentation. Clicking entries in the outline displays the Word heading level in the Outlining tab on the Ribbon.

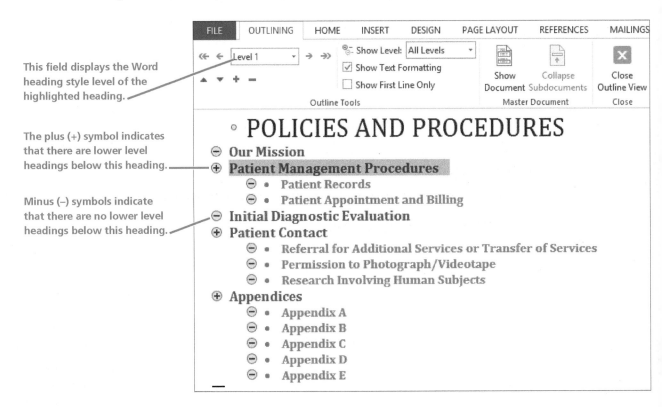

Although you can use an existing document that contains Word headings to create a PowerPoint presentation, PowerPoint cannot extract just the headings from a document, so if you use an existing document with body text in addition to the headings, you will have to edit the PowerPoint presentation accordingly.

The procedures used to launch PowerPoint are the same as those used to launch Word. No special knowledge of PowerPoint is required to complete the following exercise.

DEVELOP YOUR SKILLS WD14-D06
Create a PowerPoint Presentation from a Word Outline

In this exercise, you will use a Word outline to create a PowerPoint presentation. Then you will observe how the different heading levels are displayed in a presentation.

1. Open **WD14-D06-ProcOutline** from the **WD2013 Lesson 14** folder.

2. Choose **View→Views→Outline** 🔲.

3. Click several different entries in the outline and notice the Word heading level indicated on the Ribbon.

4. Close the document.

5. Start **PowerPoint**. Click the **Blank Presentation** template on the PowerPoint Start screen to open the PowerPoint window.

6. Choose **File→Open** and navigate to your **WD2013 Lesson 14** folder.

7. In the bottom-right corner of the **Open** dialog box, click the file type drop-down list and choose **All Files (*.*)**.

8. Double-click **WD14-D06-ProcOutline** to open it.

9. Follow these steps to display a slide containing a title and bullet points:

Ⓐ Click the third slide in the panel on the left.

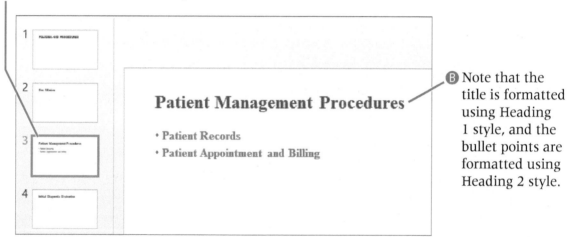

Ⓑ Note that the title is formatted using Heading 1 style, and the bullet points are formatted using Heading 2 style.

10. Exit **PowerPoint** without saving the file.

Adding a PowerPoint Presentation to a Word Document

Video Library   http://labyrinthelab.com/videos   Video Number: WD13-V1407

When you create a document that will be distributed electronically, it could be useful to include a PowerPoint presentation within the document. For example, suppose you want to distribute a presentation and include a letter with it. You can create the letter and place the presentation in the body of the letter.

When you insert a presentation into a Word document, only the first slide appears in the document. Double-clicking the slide image plays the slide show automatically.

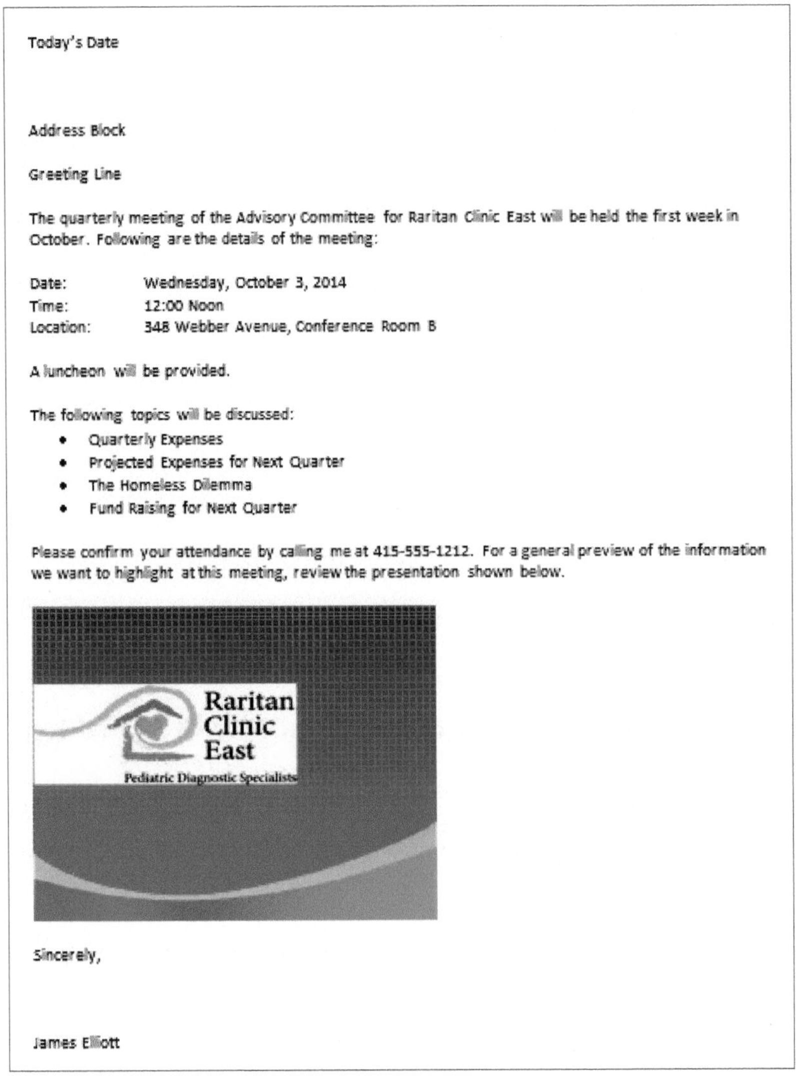

Today's Date

Address Block

Greeting Line

The quarterly meeting of the Advisory Committee for Raritan Clinic East will be held the first week in October. Following are the details of the meeting:

Date: Wednesday, October 3, 2014
Time: 12:00 Noon
Location: 348 Webber Avenue, Conference Room B

A luncheon will be provided.

The following topics will be discussed:
- Quarterly Expenses
- Projected Expenses for Next Quarter
- The Homeless Dilemma
- Fund Raising for Next Quarter

Please confirm your attendance by calling me at 415-555-1212. For a general preview of the information we want to highlight at this meeting, review the presentation shown below.

Raritan Clinic East
Pediatric Diagnostic Specialists

Sincerely,

James Elliott

QUICK REFERENCE	INTEGRATING WORD AND POWERPOINT
Task	**Procedure**
Create a PowerPoint presentation from a Word outline	■ Create a new PowerPoint presentation.
	■ Choose File→Open, choose All Files from the File Type list, and navigate to the folder containing the outline.
	■ Double-click the outline to open it in PowerPoint.
Add a PowerPoint presentation to Word and view the slide show	■ Position the insertion point in the document, choose Insert→Text→Object, and click Create from File.
	■ Click Browse, navigate to the folder containing the presentation, and double-click the filename.
	■ Click OK to insert a picture of the first slide in the document.
	■ Double-click the slide to start the slide show.

Add a PowerPoint Presentation to a Word Document

In this exercise, you will insert a PowerPoint presentation into the letter being sent to board members.

1. Open **WD14-D07-AdvisoryLtr** from your **WD2013 Lesson 14** folder and save it as **WD14-D07-AdvisoryLtr-[FirstInitialLastName]**.

2. Turn on formatting marks.

3. Position the insertion point on the middle paragraph symbol just before the complimentary close for the letter.

4. Choose **Insert→Text→Object** and click the **Create from File** tab.

5. Click **Browse** and navigate to the **WD2013 Lesson 14** folder.

6. Double-click **WD14-D07-IntroToRCE** (a PowerPoint file) and then click **OK** to close the dialog box.

   Word adds a picture of the first slide in the letter. Notice that the image is large and makes the letter extend to two pages. Next you will size the image so that the letter fits on one page.

7. Click the slide image to display the sizing handles.

8. Drag the lower-right sizing handle diagonally up toward the center of the image until the letter fits on one page.

9. Double-click the slide image in the letter to start the slide show.

10. Click the mouse pointer anywhere on the screen to advance the slides.

11. When the black screen appears at the end of the show, click one more time to close it.

12. Save and close the file.

Word 2013

Creating Web Pages from Word Documents

Video Library   http://labyrinthelab.com/videos   Video Number: WD13-V1408

Word 2013 allows you to create web pages from Word documents. As you might imagine, this saves you the need to learn a more specialized web design or coding program. Another advantage is that Word can display a document in Web Layout view so that you can make edits before posting the file on the web.

Formatting Web Pages

Web pages are often set up in tables to help align text in multiple columns, and Word's Table feature works well for this purpose.

The blank column helps align the document text toward the center of the screen.

Raritan Clinic East Walkathon 2014

Message from the President

We are looking forward to another successful walkathon fund raiser. This is our tenth annual walkathon, and participation has been increasing every year. Over the last year, there has been an increase in the number of patients without medical insurance who require our specialized services. The money we raise will go far in helping extend our services to those who need them.

Gridlines will be hidden when the page is viewed in a web browser.

When:	Saturday, March 1, 2014
Where:	Town Square
Time:	7 a.m. preregistration and event day registration
Fees:	Preregistration: adults $25, youth $15
	Event day registration: adults $30, youth $20

When you save a document as a web page, Word converts it to the HTML (hypertext markup language) authoring language for web pages. When you convert a document to HTML, some formatting features may be lost. However, most of your documents should translate cleanly into attractive web pages.

QUICK REFERENCE	SAVING AND DISPLAYING A WORD DOCUMENT AS A WEB PAGE
Task	**Procedure**
Save a Word document as a web page	▪ Choose File→Save As and then choose Web Page (*.htm; *.html) from the Save as Type list. ▪ (Optional) Click Change Title and type a new title to appear in the title bar or a web browser tab, and click OK. ▪ Click Save.
Open a web page in Internet Explorer	▪ Launch your browser and choose File→Open. ▪ In the Open dialog box, click Browse, navigate to the web page location, and open the file.

DEVELOP YOUR SKILLS WD14-D08

Save a Document as a Web Page

In this exercise, you will examine the format of a document to be saved as a web page and then save the document.

1. Open **WD14-D08-RCEWalk** from the **WD2013 Lesson 14** folder and save it as **WD14-D08-RCEWalk-[FirstInitialLastName]**.

    The document is set up in a table. The gridlines are visible so you can see the column with no content on the left side of the table. Web pages may appear too far to the left in a browser window, so the blank column is acting as a spacer to position the content farther to the right.

If no gridlines appear, choose Table Tools→Layout→Table→View Gridlines.

2. Choose **File→Save As** and navigate to your **WD2013 Lesson 14** folder.

3. Follow these steps to set the format and title of the web page document:

Ⓐ Choose **Web Page** from the Save as Type drop-down list.

Ⓑ Click the **Change Title** button to open the Enter Text dialog box.

Ⓒ Type **RCE Walkathon** in the Page Title field.

Ⓓ Click **OK**.

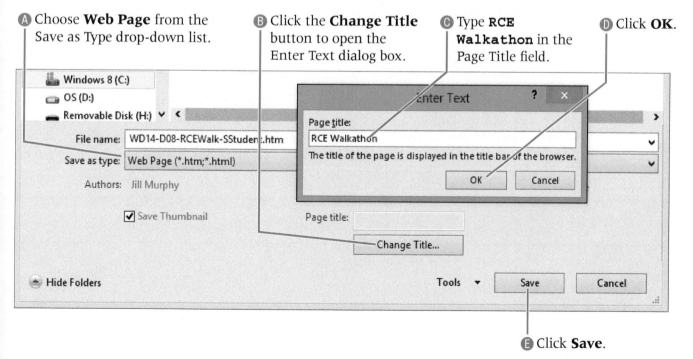

Ⓔ Click **Save**.

The page title appears in the web browser title bar or a tab when the file is open in a browser. After you click Save, Word automatically switches to Web Layout view so you can see how the document will appear in a browser window. Now you will open the document in a web browser.

4. Launch **Internet Explorer** or your default browser.

   Steps for opening the file in your default browser may vary slightly. Consult your instructor if you need assistance.

5. Press Ctrl + O and navigate to your **WD2013 Lesson 14** folder.

6. Double-click the file and click **OK**.

   If you do not see the .htm file extension, look closely, and you will see that the web page file has a slightly different icon from a Word file icon.

7. Review the document layout and notice that the gridlines do not appear.

8. Close the browser and the Word web page file.

Editing Web Pages in Word

Video Library   http://labyrinthelab.com/videos   Video Number: WD13-V1409

When you create a web page in Word, you can use Word to edit the page as well. You open the *.htm page from within Word, make the necessary changes, and then resave the file. When you open it in the browser again, you will see the editing changes that you made in Word.

DEVELOP YOUR SKILLS WD14-D09
Edit a Web Page in Word

In this exercise, you will open the web page you created in the previous exercise and edit it. Then you will reopen the page in your browser and observe the change.

1. Open **WD14-D08-RCEWalk.htm** from the **WD2013 Lesson 14** folder.

   If Windows is not set up to display the .htm file extension, look very carefully and notice that the web page version of the file has a slightly different icon than a Word file.

2. Change the walkathon date from March 1 to March **8**.

3. Save and close the file.

4. Restart your browser.

   Steps for opening the file in your default browser may vary slightly. Consult your instructor if you need assistance.

5. Press Ctrl + O and navigate to your **WD2013 Lesson 14** folder.

6. Double-click **WD14-D08-RCEWalk.htm** and click **OK**.

7. Observe the date change you made in the web page.

8. Close your browser. Exit **Word**.

Concepts Review

To check your knowledge of the key concepts introduced in this lesson, complete the Concepts Review quiz by choosing the appropriate access option below.

If you are...	Then access the quiz by...
Using the Labyrinth Video Library	Going to http://labyrinthelab.com/videos
Using eLab	Logging in, choosing Content, and navigating to the Concepts Review quiz for this lesson
Not using the Labyrinth Video Library or eLab	Going to the student resource center for this book

Reinforce Your Skills

Embed and Link Excel Objects in Word

In this exercise, you will produce a sales report for the Kid for Change's fund-raising consignment shop, Collectibles & Curiosities. You will insert and embed a worksheet table in Word, and then copy and link the worksheet table and its related chart in Word. You will update links when opening a Word document, and finally, you will break the links between Word and Excel.

Embed an Excel Object in a Word Document

1. Start **Word**. Open **WD14-R01-Q1SalesRpt** from your **WD2013 Lesson 14** folder and save it as **WD14-R01-Q1SalesRpt-[FirstInitialLastName]**.
   You may have to switch to Print Layout view.

2. Turn on formatting marks.

3. Position the insertion point on the first blank line below the main paragraph.

4. Choose **Insert→Text→Object** □.

5. Click the **Create from File** tab, click **Browse**, and navigate to your **WD2013 Lesson 14** folder.

6. Double-click **WD14-R01-Collectibles**.
   Since you are embedding (not linking) the data in Word, you won't check the Link to File checkbox.

7. Click **OK** to close the dialog box.
   Having distributed this report to the board members, you will now link this worksheet table in the Word document so you can begin collecting year-to-date data.

8. Click the embedded worksheet table once to select it and tap ⌷Delete⌷.

Link Excel Data to a Word Document

9. Start **Excel**. Click the **Open Other Workbooks** link at the bottom of the Recent list on the left of the Start screen and navigate to your **WD2013 Lesson 14** folder.

10. Open **WD14-R01-Collectibles** and save it as **WD14-R01-Collectibles-[FirstInitialLastName]**.

11. Press ⌷Ctrl⌷+⌷Home⌷ to select the first cell in the worksheet, and then press ⌷Shift⌷ and click the last cell in the table (value of $1,464.00).

12. Choose **Home→Clipboard→Copy** 🖹.

13. Switch to **Word** and position the insertion point in the first blank line below the main paragraph.

14. Choose **Home→Clipboard→Paste** 📋 menu ▼→**Paste Special**.

15. Click the **Paste Link** option button and **Microsoft Excel Worksheet Object**.

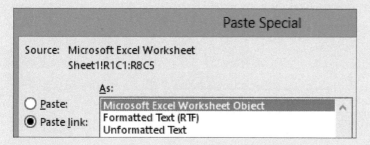

16. Click **OK**.

    Now you will edit the worksheet in Excel and observe the change in the linked table.

17. Switch to **Excel** and tap ⌑Esc⌑ to remove the marquee surrounding the table.

18. Click the cell at the top of the worksheet to select it.

19. Double-click the cell to position the insertion point in the cell, and then click and drag to select **Quarter 1**.

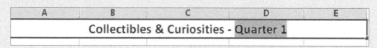

20. Type **Year-to-Date** and tap ⌑Enter⌑.

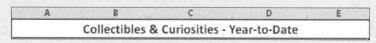

21. Switch to **Word**.

    Notice that the linked table updated with the change you made. If the table failed to update, right-click it and choose Update Link.

22. Position the insertion point on the blank line below the table.

    Now you will link an Excel chart in Word using the Paste Options smart tag.

23. Switch to **Excel**. Click the **Sheet 2** tab at the bottom of the workbook, and then click the chart border to select it.

24. Choose **Home→Clipboard→Copy** 📋 and then switch back to **Word**.

25. Choose **Home→Clipboard→Paste** 📋.

26. Click the **Paste Options smart tag** at the bottom of the chart.

27. Click the **Keep Source Formatting & Link Data** button.

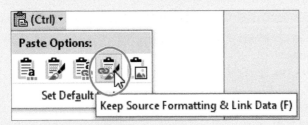

28. Switch to **Excel**. Exit **Excel**, saving changes when prompted.

Open Excel and Display Chart Tools from Within Word

29. Double-click in the worksheet table in Word to open the Excel file.

    You realize that there is an error in the March sales figure for Glass & Crystal, so you will make that change in the worksheet.

30. Click **cell B7** and tap Delete.

	Glass & Crystal
January	2,350.00
February	1,502.00
March	2,000.00
Total Sales	$5,852.00

31. Type **1,500.00**, and tap Enter.

32. Switch to **Word** and ensure that the table and chart both updated.

    If your table failed to update, right-click the Excel worksheet table and choose Update Link from the menu. It's possible the worksheet table will update but not the chart. If your chart failed to update, click the chart border and choose Chart Tools→Design→Data→Refresh Data.

33. Save the document; exit **Word**.

Update Links, and Break the Links Between Word and Excel

34. In **Excel**, click to select **cell D5**, the January sales figure for Vintage Jewelry.

Vintage Jewelry
546.00
976.00
1,126.00
$2,648.00

35. Tap Delete, type **600**, and tap Enter.

36. Open **WD14-R01-Q1SalesRpt-[FirstInitialLastName]**. When the message appears prompting you to update links, click **Yes**.

    If your table failed to update, right-click the Excel worksheet table and choose Update Link from the menu. It's possible the worksheet table will update but not the chart. If your chart failed to update, click the chart border and choose Chart Tools→Design→Data→Refresh Data.

37. In **Word**, right-click the worksheet table to display the pop-up menu.

38. Slide the mouse pointer down to **Choose Linked Worksheet Object** and choose **Links**.

39. With **Worksheet Type** selected, click **Break Link**.

40. When the message appears verifying the break, click **Yes**.
The remaining chart link is already highlighted.

41. Click the **Break Link** button to break the link between Excel and the chart in Word.

42. When the message appears, click **Yes**.
The Source File now displays the term NULL, indicating there is no source file attached.

43. Click **OK** to close the Links dialog box.
Now you will test to ensure that the link is broken.

44. Right-click the worksheet table in Word and notice that Update Links does not appear in the menu.

45. Click the border of the chart to select it.

46. Choose **Chart Tools→Design→Data→Refresh Data** .
The Refresh Data button should be grayed out, indicating the link is broken.

47. Save and close the files; exit **Word** and **Excel**.

48. Submit your final files based on the guidelines provided by your instructor.
To see examples of how your file or files should look at the end of this exercise, go to the student resource center.

REINFORCE YOUR SKILLS WD14-R02

Incorporate Word with Excel, PowerPoint, and the Web

In this exercise, you will use an Excel file as the data source in a mail merge. You will create a PowerPoint presentation from a Word document, and you'll insert PowerPoint slides in a Word document. Finally, you will create a web page from a Word document.

The Kids for Change project manager will use the letters to invite members to a meeting, where they will view a PowerPoint presentation regarding a project where kids will help seniors with their autumn garden cleanup.

Use Excel as a Mail Merge Data Source

1. Start **Word**. Open **WD14-R02-GardenLtr** from your **WD2013 Lesson 14** folder and save it as **WD14-R02-GardenLtr-[FirstInitialLastName]**.

2. Choose **Mailings→Start Mail Merge→Start Mail Merge** and then choose **Letters**.
Word will now recognize your letter as the main document.

3. If necessary, turn on formatting marks.
Now you will connect to an Excel file as the data source.

4. Choose **Mailings→Start Mail Merge→Select Recipients** and then choose **Use an Existing List**.

5. Navigate to your **WD2013 Lesson 14** folder and open **WD14-R02-AddressLst** (an Excel file).

6. When the Select Table dialog box appears, make sure **Sheet 1**, which contains the address list, is selected. Click **OK**.

   Now you will insert the merge codes in your letter.

7. In the letter, delete the **Address Block** text but not the paragraph symbol at the end of the line.

8. Choose **Mailings→Write & Insert Fields→Address Block** 📄.

9. When the Insert Address Block dialog box appears, click **OK** to accept the default formats for the inside address.

10. Delete the **Greeting Line** text but not the paragraph symbol at the end of the line.

11. Choose **Mailings→Write & Insert Fields→Greeting Line** 📄.

12. When the Insert Greeting Line dialog box appears, choose **Joshua** from the drop-down list.

13. Click **OK** to insert the Greeting Line code.

    Now you will conduct the merge.

14. Choose **Mailings→Finish→Finish & Merge** 📄 and then choose **Edit Individual Documents**.

15. When the Merge to New Document dialog box opens, click **OK**.

16. Turn off formatting marks.

17. Scroll through the document to see the results of the merge and then close the document without saving it.

18. Save and close **WD14-R02-GardenLtr-[FirstInitialLastName]**.

Create a PowerPoint Presentation from a Word Outline

Now you will create the PowerPoint presentation that Kids for Change will use during the meeting to remind team members of the various gardening tasks that must be completed during their cleanup project. You will generate the presentation from a Word outline.

19. Open **WD14-R02-GardenTasks** from your **WD2013 Lesson 14** folder.

20. Choose **View→Views→Outline** 📄.

21. Click several different entries and notice the heading levels indicated on the Ribbon.

    Level 1 entries will provide slide titles, and level 2 entries will provide bullet points.

22. Close the outline document.

23. Start **PowerPoint**. Click the **Open Other Presentations** link at the bottom of the Recent list on the left of the Start screen.

24. Navigate to your **WD2013 Lesson 14** folder.

25. In the bottom-right corner of the **Open** dialog box, click the drop-down list and choose **All Files (*.*)**.

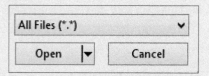

26. Double-click **WD14-R02-GardenTasks**.

27. Click several slide icons in the left panel. Notice that the titles are formed from the level 1 outline entries and the bullet points come from the level 2 outline entries.

28. Exit **PowerPoint** without saving.

Add a PowerPoint Presentation to a Word Document

29. Open **WD14-R02-PPTLetter** from your **WD2013 Lesson 14** folder and save it as `WD14-R02-PPTLetter-[FirstInitialLastName]`.

30. Position the insertion point at the end of the document.

31. Choose **Insert→Text→Object** ▭ and then click the **Create from File** tab.

32. Click **Browse** and navigate to the **WD2013 Lesson 14** folder.

33. Double-click **WD14-R02-GardenPPT** and then click **OK** to close the dialog box.
    Word adds a picture of the first slide to the letter.

34. Double-click the slide image to start the slide show, and then click the mouse pointer anywhere on the screen to advance the slides.

35. When the black screen appears at the end of the show, click one more time to end the show.

36. Save and close the file.

Save a Document as a Web Page
In planning for the Kids for Change garden cleanup project, the project manager needs to determine what gardening supplies members can contribute to use during the project.

37. Open **WD14-R02-GardenSupplies** from your **WD2013 Lesson 14** folder and save it as `WD14-R02-GardenSupplies-[FirstInitialLastName]`.
    The document is set up in a table, which is common when organizing web pages. Also, notice the blank column on the left, which acts as a spacer to help center the document in a browser. If you cannot see the table gridlines, go to the next step. If gridlines are visible, skip to step 39.

38. Choose **Table Tools→Layout→Table→View Gridlines** ▦.
    Now you will save the document as a web page.

39. Choose **File→Save As** and navigate to your **WD2013 Lesson 14** folder.

40. Choose **Web Page** from the Save as Type list.

41. Click the **Change Title** button, type `Gardening Supplies` in the Enter Text dialog box, and click **OK**.

    This text will appear in the title bar or a tab in your default browser.

42. Click **Save** in the Save As dialog box.

    Word automatically switches to Web Layout view. Now you will open the document in your web browser. Steps for opening the file in your default browser may vary slightly. Consult your instructor if you need assistance.

43. Launch your default web browser, press Ctrl+O, and navigate to your **WD2013 Lesson 14** folder.

44. Double-click the **Garden Supplies** file you just saved as a web page.

    If you do not see the .htm file extension, look closely, and you will see that the web page file has a slightly different icon from a Word file icon.

45. Click **OK**, review the web page layout, and close the browser.

Edit the Web Page in Word
The Word web page document should still be open.

46. Position the insertion point after the word *mowers* and type a comma, Spacebar, and `edgers`.

47. Save and close the file.

    Steps for opening the file in your default browser may vary slightly. Consult your instructor if you need assistance.

48. Restart your browser, press Ctrl+O, and click **Browse**.

49. Navigate to your **WD2013 Lesson 14** folder, double-click **WD14-R02-Garden Supplies-[FirstInitialLastName].htm**, and click **OK**. If necessary, use the file icon to identify the web page file.

50. Observe the change you made to the web page, and then close your browser. Exit all programs.

51. Submit your final files based on the guidelines provided by your instructor.

    To see examples of how your file or files should look at the end of this exercise, go to the student resource center.

REINFORCE YOUR SKILLS WD14-R03

Integrate Word with Excel, PowerPoint, and the Web

In this exercise, you will link an Excel file in Word and use an Excel file as the data source in a mail merge. Then you will create a PowerPoint presentation from a Word outline and add a PowerPoint presentation to a Word document. Finally, you will create a web page from a Word document.

Embed and Link an Excel File in Word

Kids for Change has a monthly used book sale to raise funds for their many projects. You are in charge of tracking and reporting sales.

1. Start **Word**. Open **WD14-R03-BookSalesLtr** from your **WD2013 Lesson 14** folder and save it as `WD14-R03-BookSalesLtr-[FirstInitialLastName]`.

   You may have to switch to Print Layout view.

2. Position the insertion point at the end of the document.

3. Choose **Insert→Text→Object** and then click the **Create from File** tab.

4. Click the **Browse** button, navigate to your **WD2013 Lesson 14** folder, and double-click **WD14-R03-UsedBookSales**.

   Because you are embedding (not linking) the data in Word, you won't check the Link to File checkbox.

5. Click **OK** to close the dialog box.

   Since it is the end of the first quarter, you will now link the file in Word, so you can start adding the book sales data for the second quarter.

6. Click the embedded worksheet table once and tap [Delete].

Link Excel Data to a Word Document

7. Start **Excel**. Click **Open Other Workbooks** at the bottom of the Recent list on the left side of the Start screen.

8. Navigate to your **WD2013 Lesson 14** folder, open **WD14-R03-UsedBookSales**, and save it as `WD14-R03-UsedBookSales-[FirstInitialLastName]`.

9. Press [Ctrl]+[Home] to select the first cell in the worksheet, press [Shift], and then click the last cell in the table that contains the value of **$1,424.00**.

10. Press [Ctrl]+[C] and then switch to **Word**.

11. If necessary, display formatting marks.

12. Position the insertion point on the second blank line below the letter closing.

13. Choose **Home→Clipboard→Paste** menu ▼→**Paste Special**.

14. Click the **Paste Link** option button and the **Microsoft Excel Worksheet Object**.

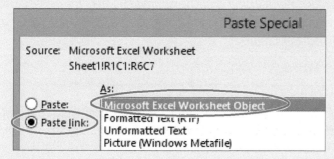

15. Click **OK**.

    Now you will edit the worksheet in Excel, and then observe the change in the linked object in Word.

16. Switch to **Excel** and tap $\boxed{\text{Esc}}$ to remove the marquee.

17. Click **cell G5** (for March, Science Fiction).

18. Tap $\boxed{\text{Delete}}$, and then type **$587.00** and tap $\boxed{\text{Enter}}$.

19. Switch to **Word**.

    Notice the change in the linked table. If the table failed to update, right-click the table and choose Update Link.

20. Position the insertion point at the end of the document.

    Now you will link an Excel chart in Word using the Paste Options smart tag.

21. Switch to **Excel**. Click the **Sheet 2 tab** at the bottom of the workbook, and then click the chart border to select it.

22. Press $\boxed{\text{Ctrl}}+\boxed{\text{C}}$ and switch to **Word**.

23. Press $\boxed{\text{Ctrl}}+\boxed{\text{V}}$ to paste the chart at the bottom of the document, and then click the **Paste Options smart tag** at the bottom of the chart.

24. Click **Keep Source Formatting & Link Data**.

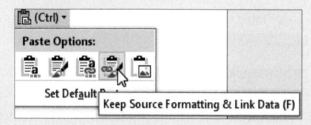

25. Switch to **Excel**. Save the file and exit **Excel**.

Open Excel and Display Chart Tools from Within Word

26. Double-click the worksheet table in Word to open the Excel file.

    You need to correct the January sales figure for Historical Fiction.

27. Click **cell C3** (the January, Historical Fiction cell).

28. Type **$385.00** and tap $\boxed{\text{Enter}}$.

29. Switch to **Word** and verify that the worksheet table and chart both updated.

    If your table failed to update, right-click it and choose Update Link. It's possible the worksheet table will update but not the chart. If your chart failed to update, click the chart border and choose Chart Tools→Design→Data→Refresh Data.

30. Save the file and close **Word**.

Update and Break Links

Now you will make another change in the Excel file, and when you open Word, you will see that you will be prompted to update links.

31. In **Excel**, select **cell B3** (the January sales cell for Autobiography).

32. Type **$600.00** and tap $\boxed{\text{Enter}}$.

33. Open **WD14-R03-BookSalesLtr-[FirstInitialLastName]**. When the message appears prompting you to update links, click **Yes**.

    If your table failed to update, right-click it and choose Update Link. It's possible the worksheet table will update but not the chart. If your chart failed to update, click the chart border and choose Chart Tools→Design→Data→Refresh Data.

    Now you will break the link between Word and Excel.

34. In **Word**, right-click the worksheet table to display the pop-up menu. Slide the mouse pointer to **Linked Worksheet Object** and choose **Links**.

35. Make sure **Worksheet** is selected in the Type column, and then click **Break Link**.

36. When the message appears verifying the break, click **Yes**.

    The remaining chart link is highlighted.

37. Click the **Break Link** button to break the link between Excel and the chart in Word.

38. When the message appears, click **Yes**. Click **OK** to close the dialog box.

    Now you will test to verify that the link is broken.

39. Right-click the worksheet table in Word and notice that Update Links does not appear in the menu.

40. Save and close the **Word** file.

41. Save the **Excel** file; exit **Excel**.

Use Excel as a Mail Merge Data Source and Conduct a Merge

Now you will use an Excel name and address list to merge with a letter to all board members. The letter announces a meeting where you will discuss the second quarter projects that you intend to fund with used book sales. First, you will open the letter and designate it as the main document.

42. Open **WD14-R03-BoardLetter** from your **WD2013 Lesson 14** folder and save it as `WD14-R03-BoardLetter-[FirstInitialLastName]`.

43. Choose **Mailings→Start Mail Merge→Start Mail Merge** 📄, and then choose **Letters**.

44. If necessary, turn on formatting marks.

    Now you will connect an Excel file as the data source.

45. Choose **Mailings→Start Mail Merge→Select Recipients** 📇 and then choose **Use an Existing List**.

46. Navigate to your **WD2013 Lesson 14** folder and open **WD14-R03-BoardList**.

    When the Select Table dialog box appears, Sheet 1, which contains the board members' addresses, is selected.

47. Click **OK**.

    Next you will insert merge codes in the main document.

48. Delete the **Address Block** text but not the paragraph symbol at the end of the line.

49. Choose **Mailings→Write & Insert Fields→Address Block** 📄.

50. When the Insert Address Block dialog box appears, click **OK** to accept the default formats for the inside address.

51. Delete the **Greeting Line** text but not the paragraph symbol at the end of the line.

52. Choose **Mailings→Write & Insert Fields→Greeting Line** 📄.

53. When the Greeting Line dialog box appears, click **OK** to insert the greeting line.

54. Choose **Mailings→Finish→Finish & Merge** 📄 and then choose **Edit Individual Documents**.

55. When the Merge to New Document dialog box opens, click **OK**.

56. Turn off formatting marks.

57. Scroll through and observe the letters; close the merged document without saving.

58. Save and close **WD14-R03-BoardLetter-[FirstInitialLastName]**.

Create a PowerPoint Presentation from a Word Outline

You will create a PowerPoint presentation to use in the board members' meeting to guide the discussion regarding the projects for second quarter. You will use a Word outline to create the presentation.

59. Open **WD14-R03-BrdMtgOutline** from your **WD2013 Lesson 14** folder.

60. Choose **View→Views→Outline** 📄.

61. Click several different entries, and notice the heading levels on the Outlining tab.
    The level 1 entries will become slide titles, and the level 2 entries will provide bulleted lists in the slides.

62. Close the outline document.

63. Start **PowerPoint**. Click **Open Other Presentations** at the bottom of the Recent list on the left side of the Start screen.

64. Navigate to your **WD2013 Lesson 14** folder. In the bottom-right corner of the dialog box, choose **All Files (*.*)** from the drop-down list.

65. Double-click **WD14-R03-BrdMtgOutline** to open it in PowerPoint.

66. Click the different slide icons on the left, and notice that the titles come from the level 1 entries in the outline, and the bullet points come from the level 2 entries in the outline.

67. Exit **PowerPoint** without saving the file.

Add a PowerPoint Presentation to a Word Document

Now you will send an email attachment containing a copy of the presentation to the board members so they can review the topics that will be covered in the meeting.

68. Open **WD14-R03-BoardMtgPPT** from your **WD2013 Lesson 14** folder and save it as `WD14-R03-BoardMtgPPT-[FirstInitialLastName]`.

69. Position the insertion point at the end of the document.

70. Choose **Insert→Text→Object** 📄 and click the **Create from File** tab.

71. Click **Browse** and navigate to your **WD2013 Lesson 14** folder.

72. Double-click **WD14-R03-ProjectsPPTLtr** to open it and click **OK**.

73. Double-click the slide image to start the presentation, and then click the mouse pointer on the screen to advance the slides.

74. When the black screen appears, click again to close the presentation.

75. Save and close the file.

Create a Web Page from a Word Document

You've created a flyer announcing the Foster Home Fair for Golden Retriever Rescue, which will take place at the Community Center. You will save it as a web page so it can be posted on the Community Center website.

76. Open **WD14-R03-FosterHomeFair** from your **WD2013 Lesson 14** folder and save it as **WD14-R03-FosterHomeFair-[FirstInitialLastName]**.

    The document is set up as a table, which is a technique often used for organizing web pages. Notice the blank spacer column on the left to help center the document in a browser. If you cannot see the table's gridlines, choose Table Tools→Layout→Table→View Gridlines.

77. Choose **File→Save As** and navigate to your **WD2013 Lesson 14** folder.

78. Choose **Web Page** from the Save as Type list.

79. Click **Change Title**, type **Foster Home Fair** in the dialog box, and click **OK**.

    This text will appear in the title bar or a tab in your browser.

80. Click **Save** in the Save As dialog box.

    Word opens the document in Web Layout View. Now you will open the document in your browser. Steps for opening the file in your default browser may vary slightly. Consult your instructor if you need assistance.

81. Start your default web browser, press [Ctrl]+[O], navigate to your **WD2013 Lesson 14** folder, and double-click the **Foster Home Fair** file you just saved as a web page.

    If you do not see the .htm file extension, look closely, and you will see that the web page file has a slightly different icon from a Word document.

82. Click **OK** and review the web page. Close the browser.

Edit the Web Page in Word

The Word web page document should still be open.

83. Position the insertion point at the end of the last bullet point and tap [Enter].

84. Type **Fire Department BBQ Cook-off**.

85. Save and close the file.

    Steps for opening the file in your default browser may vary slightly. Consult your instructor if you need assistance.

86. Restart your browser, press [Ctrl]+[O], navigate to your **WD2013 Lesson 14** folder, double-click **WD14-R03-FosterHomeFair-[FirstInitialLastName].htm**, and click **OK**.

87. Observe the change you made to the web page; close the browser. Exit **Word**.

88. Submit your final files based on the guidelines provided by your instructor.

Apply Your Skills

Embed and Link Excel Objects in Word

In this exercise, you will produce a report for the Universal Corporate Events management team comparing the sales of four tours over three months. You will first embed an Excel worksheet table in a Word document, and then you will link an Excel worksheet table and chart in the document. You will update links when changes are made in Excel, and finally you will break the link between Word and Excel.

Embed and Link Excel Objects in Word

1. Start **Word**. Open **WD14-A01-MgmtLtr** from your **WD2013 Lesson 14** folder and save it as `WD14-A01-MgmtLtr-[FirstInitialLastName]`.
   You will now embed an Excel worksheet table in Word.

2. If necessary, display formatting marks. Then position the insertion point on the second blank line below the letter.

3. Choose **Insert→Text→Object** ⬚ and use the **Create from File** tab to embed **WD14-A01-1stQSales** in your letter.

4. Delete the embedded worksheet table so you can link the worksheet table and start collecting data for second quarter.

5. Start **Excel**. Open **WD14-A01-1stQSales** from your **WD2013 Lesson 14** folder and save it as `WD14-A01-1stQSales-[FirstInitialLastName]`.

6. Press Ctrl + Home to select the cell at the top of the table, press Shift, and click the last cell in the table that displays the value of **$150,000**.

7. Copy the table. Then switch to **Word** and make sure the insertion point is on the second blank line below the letter.

8. Click **Paste** 📋 **menu ▼→Paste Special**. Link the Microsoft Excel Worksheet Object in Word.
   Now you will make a change to the Excel table and observe the change in the linked table in Word.

9. Switch to **Excel** and turn off the marquee.

10. Click **cell C3** and enter **45,000** to replace the current number.

11. Switch to **Word** and notice the change you made.
    If your worksheet table failed to update, use the Update Link command. Now you will link an Excel chart from the same file in the document.

12. Position the insertion point at the end of the document.

13. In **Excel**, click the **Sheet 2** tab and then click the chart border.

14. Copy the chart. Then switch to **Word** and paste the chart.

15. Use the **Paste Options smart tag** and the **Keep Source Formatting & Link Data** button to link the chart in Word.

16. Switch to **Excel** and save your changes; exit **Excel**.

Open Excel from Word and Edit the Worksheet

17. Double-click the worksheet table to open **Excel**. Change the data in **cell B5** (Bahamas Cruise, March) to **39,000**.

18. Switch to **Word** and observe the change. If necessary, use **Update Link** to update the worksheet table and **Refresh Data** to update the chart.

19. Save and close the file; exit **Word**.

Update and Break Links
Now you'll make a change in Excel and update links when you re-open the Word document.

20. In **Excel**, replace the data in **cell D4** (Florida Spa, February) with **28,000**.

21. Open **WD14-A01-MgmtLtr-[FirstInitialLastName]** from your **WD2013 Lesson 14** folder and update links.

22. If necessary, use **Update Link** to update the worksheet table and **Refresh Data** to update the chart.
    Now you will break the link between Word and Excel.

23. In the **Links** dialog box, break the link for both the worksheet and the chart.

24. Right-click the worksheet table and ensure that the **Update Links** command is not available.

25. Click the chart border to select it.

26. Choose **Chart Tools→Design→Data** and observe that the **Refresh Data** button is grayed out because the chart is not linked to the Excel file.

27. Save and close all files; exit **Word** and **Excel**.

28. Submit your final files based on the guidelines provided by your instructor.
    To see examples of how your file or files should look at the end of this exercise, go to the student resource center.

Incorporate Word with Excel, PowerPoint, and the Web

In this exercise, you will use an Excel name and address list as the data source in a mail merge. Then you will create a PowerPoint presentation from a Word outline and insert a PowerPoint presentation in a Word document. Finally, you will create a web page from a Word document.

Use Excel as a Mail Merge Data Source and Conduct the Merge

1. Start **Word**. Open **WD14-A02-TourLtr** from your **WD2013 Lesson 14** folder and save it as **WD14-A02-TourLtr-[FirstInitialLastName]**.

2. Designate the letter as the main document for your merge.

3. Use an existing list, **WD14-A02-TourAddrLst**, as the data source for your merge; Sheet 1 of the Excel file contains the name and address list.

4. If necessary, turn on formatting marks.

5. In the letter, insert the **Address Block field** in place of the Address Block placeholder text in the letter. Accept the default formats for the inside address.

6. Insert the **Greeting Line field** in place of the Greeting Line placeholder text in the letter. Accept the defaults in the Insert Greeting Line dialog box.

7. Finish the merge using the **Edit Individual Documents** option; merge all records.

8. Review the merged letters, and then close the document without saving.

9. Save and close **WD14-A02-TourLtr-[FirstInitialLastName]**.

Create a PowerPoint Presentation from a Word Outline, and Add a PowerPoint Presentation to a Word Document

Now you will create a PowerPoint presentation to guide the discussion in the meeting with employees who will be attending the tour of Turkey. You will begin building your presentation with a Word outline.

10. Open **WD14-A02-TurkeyOutline** and switch to **Outline** ▦ view.

11. Observe the different heading levels indicated in the Outlining tab, which will become the title and bullet-point entries in the PowerPoint slides.

12. Close the outline document.

13. Start **PowerPoint** and click **Open Other Presentations** at the bottom of the Recent list.

14. Navigate to your **WD2013 Lesson 14** folder.

15. In the bottom of the **Open** dialog box, choose **All Files (*.*)** from the drop-down list.

16. Double-click **WD14-A02-TurkeyOutline** to open it.

17. Click through the slides in the left-hand panel and observe the effect of the different heading levels in the outline.

18. Exit **PowerPoint** without saving.

    Now you will add a PowerPoint presentation to a letter you're sending as an email attachment to the tour members.

19. Open **WD14-A02-TurkeyPPTLtr** from your **WD2013 Lesson 14** folder and save it as `WD14-A02-TurkeyPPTLtr-[FirstInitialLastName]`.

20. Position the insertion point at the end of the document, and then insert **WD14-A02-TurkeyPPT**.

21. View the presentation, and then save and close the file.

Create and Edit a Web Page in Word

You have been asked to create a web page for the Universal Corporate Events website showing the side tours offered for the tour of Turkey.

22. Open **WD14-A02-TurkeyWebPage** and save it as `WD14-A02-TurkeyWebPage-[FirstInitialLastName]`.

    Notice the table structure used in the page and the blank spacer column on the left that helps center the page in a browser. Now you will save the document as a web page.

23. In the Save As dialog box, choose **Web Page** from the Save as Type drop-down list.

24. Change the title to `Side Trips in Turkey`.

25. Open the web page in your browser; close the browser.

    Now you will add a side-tour destination to the web page. The web page document should still be open.

26. Position the insertion point after *Turkish Bath*, tap Enter, and type `Istanbul`.

27. Save and close the file.

28. Open the file in your browser again and observe the change you made to the page; close your browser.

29. Exit from **Word**.

30. Submit your final files based on the guidelines provided by your instructor.

    To see examples of how your file or files should look at the end of this exercise, go to the student resource center.

APPLY YOUR SKILLS WD14-A03

Integrate Word with Excel, PowerPoint, and the Web

In this exercise, you will embed and link an Excel file and chart in Word, and you will use an Excel file as the data source in a mail merge. Then you will create a PowerPoint presentation from a Word outline, and insert a PowerPoint presentation in a Word file. Finally, you will convert a Word file to a web page.

Embed and Link an Excel File in Word

The sales manager for Universal Corporate Events likes his reps to submit their monthly sales figures in an Excel worksheet format. As a Universal Corporate Events sales rep, Mavis Wentworth has completed her figures for the third quarter, and she will submit the Excel data in a Word document.

1. Start **Word**. Open **WD14-A03-MavisLtr** from your **WD2013 Lesson 14** folder and save it as `WD14-A03-MavisLtr-[FirstInitialLastName]`.

2. Position the insertion point at the end of the document and embed **WD14-A03-3rdQSales**.

    Mavis submitted her third-quarter sales numbers to her sales manager, so now she will link the data in Word so she can start collecting fourth-quarter sales data.

3. Delete the embedded worksheet table.

4. Start **Excel**. Open **WD14-A03-3rdQSales** from the **WD2013 Lesson 14** folder and save it as `WD14-A03-3rdQSales-[FirstInitialLastName]`.

5. Press $\boxed{\text{Ctrl}}$ + $\boxed{\text{Home}}$ to select the first cell in the worksheet, press $\boxed{\text{Shift}}$, and click the last cell in the table (contains a value of 12,430).

6. Copy the worksheet table and then switch to **Word**.

7. If necessary, display formatting marks, and then position the insertion point on the first blank line below the letter.

8. Use the **Paste Special** command to paste and link the worksheet object in the letter.
   Now you will switch to Excel and edit the worksheet, and then observe the change in the linked worksheet table.

9. Switch to **Excel** and remove the marquee.

10. Replace the contents in **cell C4** (Best Storage, August) with **1,500**.

11. Switch to **Word** and notice the change in the linked worksheet table.
    If the table failed to update, use the Update Link command to update the figure. Now you will link the chart that is associated with the sales data in Word.

12. Switch to **Excel**. Click the **Sheet 2** tab and then click the chart border to select it.

13. Copy the chart and then switch to **Word**.

14. Position the insertion point at the end of the document, and use the **Paste Options smart tag** and the **Keep Source Formatting & Link Data** button to paste and link the chart in Word.

15. Switch to **Excel** and save the file; exit **Excel**.
    Now you will open the Excel file from within Word and make an editing change.

16. Double-click the worksheet table to open **Excel**. Change the sales figure in **cell D3** (Advanced Devices, July) to **3,580**.

17. Switch to **Word** and verify that both the worksheet table and chart updated.
    If your table and chart failed to update, update them now.

18. Save and close **Word**.
    Now you will make a change to the Excel file, and then you will observe the prompt to update links when you re-open the Word file.

19. In **Excel**, change the figure in **cell E4** (Bales Construction, August) to **2,575**.

20. Switch to Word and open **WD14-A03-MavisLtr-[FirstInitialLastName]**. When the message appears prompting you to update links, click **Yes**.
    If your table and chart failed to update, update them now. Next you will break the link between Word and Excel.

21. In **Word**, use the **Links** dialog box to break the link to the worksheet table and the chart.

22. Verify that the link is broken in both the worksheet table and the chart.

23. Save and close the **Word** file.

24. Save the **Excel** file; exit **Excel**.

Use an Excel Name and Address List as a Mail Merge Data Source

Mavis sold an Australian Tour to Rogers Ltd., and she will send a letter to the tour winners inviting them to an orientation meeting in preparation for the tour.

25. Open **WD14-A03-AustraliaLtr** from your **WD2013 Lesson 14** folder and save it as **WD14-A03-AustraliaLtr-[FirstInitialLastName]**.

26. Designate the letter as the main document in a mail merge.
    Now you will connect an Excel name and address list as the data source for the merge.

27. Designate Sheet 1 of the **WD14-A03-AustraliaN&A** Excel file as the recipient list.
    Now you will insert merge codes in the main document.

28. Replace the **Address Block** placeholder text with the Address Block code, accepting the default formats for the inside address.

29. Replace the **Greeting Line** placeholder text with the Greeting Line code, accepting the default formats for the greeting line.

30. Finish the merge, choosing Edit Individual Documents, and merge all records.

31. Review the merged letters, and then close the merged file without saving.

32. Save and close **WD14-A03-AustraliaLtr-[FirstInitialLastName]**.

Create a PowerPoint Presentation from a Word Outline

Mavis will create a PowerPoint presentation to guide the discussion during her meeting with the Rogers Ltd. employees. She will begin creating the presentation with a Word outline.

33. Open **WD14-A03-AussieOutline** from your **WD2013 Lesson 14** folder.

34. Observe the document in **Outline view** and note the different heading levels that will be used in the PowerPoint presentation.

35. Close the outline and then start **PowerPoint**.

36. Open **WD14-A03-AussieOutline** and click the slide icons on the left to view all of the slides. Exit **PowerPoint** without saving.

Insert a PowerPoint Presentation in a Word Document

Mavis will send a copy of her PowerPoint slides as an email attachment to the Australia Tour members following the presentation so they can review the topics covered in the meeting.

37. Open **WD14-A03-OrientLtr** from your **WD2013 Lesson 14** folder and save it as **WD14-A03-OrientLtr-[FirstInitialLastName]**.

38. Position the insertion point at the end of the document. Then, insert **WD14-A03-AussiePPT** and view the presentation.

39. Save and close the file.

Create and Edit a Web Page in Word

A member of the Rogers Ltd. IT department has requested some web pages about Australia that they can display on their website. Mavis created the document in Word, and now she will convert it to a web page.

40. Open **WD14-A03-AussieWebPage** from your **WD2013 Lesson 14** folder and save it as `WD14-A03-AussieWebPage-[FirstInitialLastName]`.

41. Save the file as a **Web Page**, changing the title to `Australia Overview`.

42. Review the web page file in your browser; close the browser.

    Now you will edit the web page in Word. The web page file should still be open.

43. Position the insertion point after the word *Territories*, tap `Enter`, and type `History`. Save and close the web page file.

44. View the web page in your browser, observe the editing change you made, and then close the browser.

45. Exit from **Word**.

46. Submit your final files based on the guidelines provided by your instructor.

Extend Your Skills

In the course of working through the Extend Your Skills exercises, you will think critically as you use the skills taught in the lesson to complete the assigned projects. To evaluate your mastery and completion of the exercises, your instructor may use a rubric, with which more points are allotted according to performance characteristics. (The more you do, the more you earn!) Ask your instructor how your work will be evaluated.

WD14-E01 That's the Way I See It

As a sales rep for a small business, you track your quarterly sales in Excel. It's the end of the third quarter, and you will submit the end-of-quarter figures and the associated chart to your boss in a Word document. Create a one-paragraph Word file indicating that you are submitting your third quarter sales summary. Name it **WD14-E01-MyLetter-[FirstInitialLastName]** and save it in your **WD2013 Lesson 14** folder. Link the worksheet table and chart from **WD14-E01-3rdQSales** (**WD2013 Lesson 14** folder). The product names are generic. Decide what products your company sells and change the product names in the Excel file accordingly; update the linked objects in your Word document, too.

Your boss has asked you to use Mail Merge to send a mailing to customers announcing a new product. Decide on the new product, and then write a letter (1–2 paragraphs) describing it. Save it in your **WD2013 Lesson 14** folder as **WD14-E01-MyMergeLtr-[FirstInitialLastName]**. Designate the letter as the main document and **WD14-E01-Addresses** (**WD2013 Lesson 14** folder) as the recipient list. Add the Address Block and Greeting Line merge codes; conduct the merge. Save the merged file as **WD14-E01-Merged-[FirstInitialLastName]**.

You will be evaluated based on the inclusion of all elements specified, your ability to follow directions, your ability to apply newly learned skills to a real-world situation, your creativity, and the relevance of your topic and/or data choice(s). Submit your final files based on the guidelines provided by your instructor.

WD14-E02 Be Your Own Boss

As the owner of Blue Jean Landscaping, you plan to hold a seminar to discuss your products and services. You want a PowerPoint presentation to guide your seminar. Use the Word outline **WD14-E02-BJLGardens** (**WD2013 Lesson 14** folder) to create the slides and save the presentation as **WD14-E02-BJL_PPT-[FirstInitialLastName]**. Note that the process for saving a PowerPoint file is the same as saving a Word file. After the seminar, you will email a Word document with the presentation inserted to attendees. Create a letter (1–2 paragraphs) thanking customers for attending the seminar. Note that the presentation is included, and add instructions on how to play the slide show. Save the Word document as **WD14-E02-BJLLetter-[FirstInitialLastName]** in your **WD2013 Lesson 14** folder. Save the document as a web page and test it in your default browser. (You cannot play the slide show from your browser when it's embedded in a Word document.)

You will be evaluated based on the inclusion of all elements specified, your ability to follow directions, your ability to apply newly learned skills to a real-world situation, your creativity, and your demonstration of an entrepreneurial spirit. Submit your final files based on the guidelines provided by your instructor.

Transfer Your Skills

In the course of working through the Transfer Your Skills exercises, you will use critical-thinking and creativity skills to complete the assigned projects using skills taught in the lesson. To evaluate your mastery and completion of the exercises, your instructor may use a rubric, with which more points are allotted according to performance characteristics. (The more you do, the more you earn!) Ask your instructor how your work will be evaluated.

WD14-T01 Use the Web as a Learning Tool

Throughout this book, you will be provided with an opportunity to use the Internet as a learning tool by completing WebQuests. According to the original creators of WebQuests, as described on their website (WebQuest.org), a WebQuest is "an inquiry-oriented activity in which most or all of the information used by learners is drawn from the web." To complete the WebQuest projects in this book, navigate to the student resource center and choose the WebQuest for the lesson on which you are currently working. The subject of each WebQuest will be relevant to the material found in the lesson.

WebQuest Subject: Explore the benefits of integrating Word with Excel and PowerPoint.

Submit your files based on the guidelines provided by your instructor.

WD14-T02 Demonstrate Proficiency

Stormy BBQ sponsors an annual rodeo. To encourage a big turnout, you've been asked to prepare a PowerPoint presentation to use as an email attachment for Stormy's customers. To begin, open **WD14-T02-RodeoOutline** from your WD2013 **Lesson 14** folder in PowerPoint. Save the presentation as **WD14-T02-RodeoPres-[FirstInitialLastName]**. Then, create a two- or three-paragraph Word document describing the rodeo and why people should attend. Save it in your **WD2013 Lesson 14** folder as **WD14-T02-RodeoWordDoc-[FirstInitialLastName]**. Insert a PowerPoint presentation, **WD14-T02-RodeoPPT**, in the document. Remember to include instructions on how to run the slide show.

There will be a Rodeo Raffle, and you've been asked to create a web page to put on Stormy's website listing the prizes. Convert **WD14-T02-RodeoWebPage** to a web page named **WD14-T02-RodeoWebPage-[FirstInitialLastName]**. Test it in your browser. Add a prize, a $50 Starbuck's gift card, to the bottom of the list or prizes in the web document, and then test it again in your browser.

Submit your final files based on the guidelines provided by your instructor.

Index

Notes

Notes

Notes

Notes

Notes

Notes

Notes

Notes